musique 89.2

THE**GREEN**GUIDE
France

General Manager   Cynthia Clayton Ochterbeck

THEGREENGUIDE **FRANCE**

Editor	Alison Coupe
Contributing Writers	Paul Shawcross, Glenn Harper
Production Manager	Natasha G. George
Cartography	Alain Baldet, Michèle Cana, Peter Wrenn
Photo Editor	Yoshimi Kanazawa
Proofreader	Eleanor O'Byrne
Interior Design	Chris Bell
Layout	Michelin Apa Publications Ltd.
Cover Design	Chris Bell, Christelle Le Déan
Cover Layout	Michelin Apa Publications Ltd.

Contact Us

The Green Guide
Michelin Maps and Guides
One Parkway South
Greenville, SC 29615
USA
www.michelintravel.com

Michelin Maps and Guides
Hannay House
39 Clarendon Road
Watford, Herts WD17 1JA
UK
℘01923 205240
www.ViaMichelin.com
travelpubsales@uk.michelin.com

Special Sales

For information regarding bulk sales,
customized editions and premium sales,
please contact our Customer Service
Departments:
USA   1-800-432-6277
UK   01923 205240
Canada 1-800-361-8236

HOW TO USE THIS GUIDE

PLANNING YOUR TRIP

The blue-tabbed PLANNING YOUR TRIP section at the front of the guide gives you **ideas for your trip** and **practical information** to organise it. You'll find tours, practical information, a host of outdoor activities, a calendar of events, information on shopping, sightseeing, children's activities and more.

INTRODUCTION

The orange-tabbed INTRODUCTION section explores France's **Nature**, geography and geology. The **History** section spans Megalithic culture through the Middle Ages to the present day. The **Art and Culture** section covers architecture, art, literature and music, while **France Today** delves into modern French lifestyle, people and cuisine.

DISCOVERING

The green-tabbed DISCOVERING section features Principal Sights by region, featuring the most interesting local **Sights**, **Walking Tours**, nearby **Excursions**, and detailed **Driving Tours**. Admission prices shown are normally for a single adult.

ADDRESSES

We've selected the best hotels, restaurants, cafés, shops, nightlife and entertainment to fit all budgets. See the Legend on the cover flap for an explanation of the price categories. See the back of the guide for an index of where to find hotels and restaurants.

Sidebars

Throughout the guide you will find blue, orange and green-coloured text boxes with lively anecdotes, detailed history and background information.

😊 A Bit of Advice 😊

Green advice boxes found in this guide contain practical tips and handy information relevant to the sight in the Discovering section.

STAR RATINGS★★★

Michelin has given star ratings for more than 100 years. If you're pressed for time, we recommend you visit the ★★★, or ★★ sights first:

★★★	**Highly recommended**
★★	**Recommended**
★	**Interesting**

MAPS

- 🗺 Country map
- 🗺 Principal Sights map
- 🗺 Region maps
- 🗺 Maps for major cities and villages
- 🗺 Local tour maps

All maps in this guide are oriented north, unless otherwise indicated by a directional arrow. The term "Local Map" refers to a map within the chapter or Tourism Region. A complete list of the maps found in the guide appears at the back of this book.

PLANNING YOUR TRIP

INTRODUCTION TO FRANCE

DISCOVERING FRANCE

CONTENTS

Welcome to France

France is a large and extremely varied country, which ranges from the flat plains of the Pas de Calais in the north to the majestic Alps and Pyrénées in the south and the vast Alsace Plain in the east to the long sandy beaches of the Côte d'Argent in the west. In the northwest, the rugged peninsula of Brittany contrasts sharply with the rural nature of much of the centre. The twelve regions selected for this Guide exemplify this diversity and enable the visitor to appreciate *la Belle France* to the full.

ALSACE LORRAINE CHAMPAGNE *(pp94–135)*

Alsace has a very Germanic character and many of its towns and villages reflect this. To the west of the Vosges mountains is Lorraine, which, despite being part of Germany for a while, is more French. Further west is Champagne, well known for its sparkling wine, and to the north, the heavily wooded Ardenne region.

ATLANTIC COAST *(pp136–165)*

The Atlantic Coast region extends from the River Loire in the north to the mighty Pyrénées in the south. It includes most of Aquitaine and Poitou-Charentes – once the territory of the Dukes of Aquitaine – which, for many years, was held by the English.

AUVERGNE RHÔNE VALLEY *(pp166–191)*

The unique volcanic landscape of the Massif Central is at the centre of the Auvergne region and the mountains vary from classic volcanic cones to more eroded rugged shapes. To the east, the land slopes down to the Rhône Valley, where the rivers Rhône and Saône converge on their journey south towards the great city of Lyon and eventually the Mediterranean sea.

BRITTANY *(pp192–217)*

This rugged Celtic peninsula in the north west, with its indented coastline and islands battered by the Atlantic, narrow inlets and sandy bays, has a mysterious past, which is reflected in the many prehistoric remains scattered around the region, such as the menhirs at Carnac. The separate identity and culture of the Bretons make this a fascinating part of France.

BURGUNDY JURA *(pp218–241)*

Formerly a great dukedom, Burgundy is placed on the great trade route linking the north with the Mediterranean. Coupled with the proceeds of its viticulture, this led to great wealth which resulted in amazing buildings like the Hôtel-Dieu at Beaune. The Jura in the Franche-Comté Region to the east consists of forested uplands and pasture which produces such culinary delights as Vacherin and Comté cheeses.

CHÂTEAUX OF THE LOIRE *(pp242–265)*

Renowned for its magnificent Renaissance Châteaux such as Chambord and Chenonceau, the Loire Valley in the Centre Region is also referred to as the "Garden of France" due to the cultivation of vines, flowers and horticultural crops. The many châteaux actually sit on the banks of the River Loire's tributaries, the Indre and the Cher and date from the 16C onwards.

CORSICA *(pp266–273)*

Referred to by the ancient Greeks as "Kallisté", meaning "most beautiful", and by the French as *L'Île de Beauté*, this mountainous island certainly lives up to its name. Totally unspoilt, it has both Italian and French influences. From the gulfs and ruggedness of the west coast to the promontory of the Cap Corse and the cliffs of Bonifacio, this is a truly exceptional place.

DORDOGNE BERRY LIMOUSIN
(pp274-299)

The Dordogne, or the Périgord, is very well known to visitors due to its agreeable climate, its impressive castles and cave systems, not to mention the meandering Dordogne River itself. The Berry and the Limousin to the north, on the other hand, are relatively undiscovered, and provide a great deal of interest, especially at Bourges (in Berry) and Limoges (in Limousin)

FRENCH ALPS *(pp300-317)*

In the south east of France, stretching from the Mediterranean to Lac de Genève (Lake Geneva), the Alps provide a great variety of scenery from bare rock to snow-covered peaks and from green valleys to gushing torrents and lakes. There are National and Regional Parks, which reflect the richness of this environment and allow access to these amazing landscapes.

FRENCH RIVIERA *(pp318–339)*

The Côte d'Azur – or French Riviera – iruns along the Mediterranean coastline of south-east France from Menton to Cassis. What started as a popular winter health resort in the late 18C continues to draw thousands of tourists each year. Resort towns here include Cannes, Beaulieu-sur-Mer ad St-Tropez among many others. You can't beat its 300 days of sunshine per year and true holiday-feel atmosphere.

LANGUEDOC ROUSSILLON TARN GORGES *(pp340–379)*

Stretching in an arc from the Rhône Delta to the Pyrénées and characterised by vineyards and

Street in Cannes

D. Pazery/MICHELIN

popular beaches, the Languedoc Roussillon is steeped in history from the Roman era to the medieval. The Gorges du Tarn (Tarn Gorges) to the north are cut into the Grand Causses, from which there are amazing views from the corniche roads.

NORTHERN FRANCE & THE PARIS REGION *(pp380–479)*

Paris, at the centre of the Île de France, has been the capital since medieval times, and ever since this lively metropolis has played a dominant role in the country's political and cultural life. To the north, Amiens, the cradle of Gothic architecture, and Flanders, with its distinctive Flemish architecture, have much to interest the visitor.

PROVENCE *(pp480–511)*

Centred around the impressive Rhône Delta in the south, this ancient region, blessed with sunshine and occupied successively by Celts, Romans and Franks, retained its independence from the French crown until the 15C. Fascinating cities such as Nîmes, Marseille, Aix-en-Provence and Arles and the astonishingly well-preserved Roman remains, such as those at St-Rémy-de-Provence, ensure the ongoing popularity of this region.

Principal Sights

TOULOUSE	★★★	Highly recommended
Autun	★★	Recommended
<u>Giverny</u>	★	Interesting
Montélimar		Other sights described in this guide

Seaside resorts ☺, spas ✚ and winter resorts ✦ are classified according to the quality and range of facilities offered.

Shown on this map are the towns and sights in the Discovering France section of the guide, with the additional sights attached to them, as well as principal resorts.

A number of other places, monuments, historical events and natural sites appear in this guide and may be found in the index.

0   100 km

REGIONS

1	Alsace Lorraine, Champagne	**8**	Dordogne, Berry, Limousin
2	Auvergne, Rhône Valley	**9**	French Alps
3	Atlantic Coast	**10**	French Riviera
4	Brittany	**11**	Languedoc Roussillon, Midi-Pyrénées
5	Burgundy, Jura	**12**	Normandy
6	Châteaux of the Loire	**13**	Northern France and the Paris Region
7	Corsica	**14**	Provence

Cassis, Provence
G. Magnin/MICHELIN

257 172

3

Three-Star Sights★★★

Sights in the *Discovering France* section of the guide are star rated and can be found easily on the Principal Sights map (&see pp8–15). The following sights are those Michelin recommends most highly, with three stars:

CHÂTEAUX AND ABBEYS

- & **CHÂTEAU D'AZAY-LE-RIDEAU** – *p 247*
- & **CHÂTEAU DE CHAMBORD** – *p 250*
- & **CHÂTEAU DE CHANTILLY** – *p 414*
- & **CHÂTEAU DE CHENONCEAU** – *p 251*
- & **CHÂTEAU DE CHEVERNY** – *p 252*
- & **CHÂTEAU DE PEYREPERTUSE** – *p 352*
- & **CHÂTEAU DE VAUX-LE-VICOMTE** – *p 470*
- & **CHÂTEAU DE VERSAILLES** – *p 475*
- & **JARDINS ET CHÂTEAU DE VILLANDRY** – *p 265*
- & **FONTAINEBLEAU** – *p 425*
- & **ABBAYE DE FONTENAY** – *p 233*
- & **ABBAYE DE JUMIÈGES** – *p 396*

CITIES AND TOWNS

- & **ALBI** – *p 355*
- & **ANGERS** – *p 244*
- & **ANNECY** – *p 301*
- & **GROTTE DE L'AVEN ARMAND** – *p 379*
- & **AVIGNON** – *p 491*
- & **LA BAULE** – *p 193*
- & **LES BAUX-DE-PROVENCE** – *p 495*
- & **AIGUILLES DE BAVELLA** – *p 268*
- & **BELLE-ÎLE** – *p 194*
- & **BIARRITZ** – *p 140*
- & **BONIFACIO** – *p 269*
- & **BORDEAUX** – *p 144*
- & **BOURGES** – *p 275*
- & **CAEN** – *p 384*
- & **CANNES** – *p 319*
- & **CARCASSONNE** – *p 342*
- & **CHARTRES** – *p 415*
- & **COLMAR** – *p 99*

- & **COMPIÈGNE** – *p 418*
- & **CONQUES** – *p 360*
- & **CORDES-SUR-CIEL** – *p 361 (Excursion)*
- & **DEAUVILLE** – *p 389*
- & **DIJON** – *p 229*
- & **DINARD** – *p 200*
- & **LOURDES** – *p 363*
- & **LYON** – *p 173*
- & **MARSEILLE** – *p 500*
- & **METZ** – *p 127*
- & **PRINCIPAUTÉ DE MONACO** – *p 323*
- & **NANCY** – *p 130*
- & **NANTES** – *p 204*
- & **NICE** – *p 327*
- & **NÎMES** – *p 504*
- & **AVEN D'ORGNAC** – *p 508*
- & **PARIS** – *p 435*
- & **REIMS** – *p 118*
- & **RIQUEWIHR** – *p 105*
- & **ROCAMADOUR** – *p 299*
- & **LA ROCHELLE** – *p 159*
- & **ROUEN** – *p 400*
- & **ST-MALO** – *p 210*
- & **SARLAT-LA-CANÉDA** – *p 286*
- & **STRASBOURG** – *p 109*
- & **TOULOUSE** – *p 373*
- & **LE TOUQUET** – *p 473*
- & **TROYES** – *p 123*
- & **VÉZELAY** – *p 235*
- & **VICHY** – *p 190*

NATURAL SITES

- & **CAP CORSE** – *p 270*
- & **CAP FRÉHEL** – *p 201*
- & **CASCADE DU HÉRISSON** – *p 233*
- & **CHAMONIX-MONT-BLANC** – *p 304*
- & **CIRQUE DE GAVARNIE** – *p 363*
- & **CIRQUE DE NAVACELLES** – *p 350*
- & **LES PLAGES DU DÉBARQUEMENT** – *p 389*
- & **SAUT DU DOUBS** – *p 239*
- & **GORGES DE L'ARDÈCHE** – *p 486*
- & **GORGES DU TARN** – *p 378*

When and Where to Go

SEASONS

Depending on the purpose of your visit, **spring**, **summer** and **autumn** are generally the best seasons to visit France, each with its own appeal, and there is a region for every season. For **winter** sports, the season runs from December to April.

For relaxing out of doors, high summer can be beautiful but resorts and sightseeing areas are much more crowded. A better time to travel is May, June or September when French children are at school. Many visitors may prefer the more moderate warmth of these early and late summer months to the higher temperatures of Jul and August, especially in the southern half of the country.

CLIMATE

For an overview of the weather in a specific region of the country, see the **Michelin Green Guide** series, which covers 24 regions of France. In general the French climate is a moderate one; extremes of either heat or cold are rare for the most part, so that outdoor activity of some kind is almost always possible.

Inland the winters are chilly and darkness comes early, especially in the northern latitudes. As spring turns to summer, the days become long and warm and by June the sun lingers well into the evening. Spring and autumn provide opportunities to explore the outdoors and enjoy the lovely countryside and coastal areas of France. In winter, snowfall throughout much of the interior of the country, as well as in the mountainous regions near Italy, permits a wide array of winter sports, including downhill skiing and snowboarding at many world-famous Alpine resorts. However, grey skies in this period are not unusual for much of the rest of the country, especially in Paris.

WEATHER FORECAST

National forecast: ℰ 32 50. Information about the weather is also available online at www.meteofrance. com. *See Temperature Chart p51.*

What to See and Do

France offers a wide selection of leisure activities, from spa treatments and wine tours to a variety of outdoor sports and cruises. Below are suggestions of ways to enhance your visit.

LEISURE ACTIVITIES

Information and brochures for all sporting, special interest and outdoor facilities may be obtained from the French Government Tourist Office or from the local tourist information centres shown within the *Discovering France* section of this guide.

WINE TOURS

In most wine-making regions, wine tours taking in the main vineyards and wineries, or *caves*, are signposted. There are also many local guided tours in wine regions. For information apply to the local Tourist Information Centre. Buying your own wine directly from the grower can be an adventurous and satisfying holiday occupation. Signs announce farm-gate sales (*vins-vente directe*) or wine tasting and sales (*dégustation vente*).

CRAFTS

Many arts-and-crafts studios (weaving, wrought iron, cooking, painting, pottery) on the coast and inland give vacation courses in summer. Apply to the Tourist Information Centre.

CYCLING HOLIDAYS

Many UK tour operators organise cycle touring holidays in France, for example Susi Madron's Cycling for Softies (www.cycling-for-softies.co.uk) and Headwater (www.headwater. com). In France, the cyclists' touring association, **Fédération Française de Cyclotourisme**, organises cycle tours, provides itineraries detailing distances, difficulty of the routes, and sights to visit. 12 r. Louis Bertrand 94207 Ivry-sur-Seine Cedex. ℘01 56 20 88 88. www.ffct.org
Lists of local cycle hire shops are available from the Tourist Information Centres. The main railway stations also hire out cycles which can be returned at a different station.

HIKING

Short-, medium- and long-distance footpaths network the whole country. For the nationwide system of long-distance paths, Topo-Guides are published by the **Fédération Française de la Randonnée pédestre** – Comité National des Sentiers

Sancerre and its vineyards

de Grande Randonnée. These give detailed maps of the paths and offer valuable information to the hiker, and are on sale at the Information Centre: 64 r. du Dessous des Berges, 75013 Paris; ℘01 44 89 93 90; www.ffrandonnee.fr.

FISHING

Current brochures: folding map *Fishing in France* (*Pêche en France*) published and distributed by the Conseil Supérieur de la Pêche (134 av. de Malakoff, 75016 Paris; ℘01 45 02 20 20); also available from the departmental fishing organisations.

For information about regulations contact the Tourist Information Centres or the offices of the Water and Forest Authority (Eaux et Forêts).

RIVER AND CANAL CRUISING

The extensive network of navigable waterways in France can be explored at leisure (maximum speed 6km/h/3.7mph). Many tour operators offer touring vacations with motor cruisers. Information on boat hire companies is available from the **Féderation des Industries Nautiques** (℘33 01 44 37 04 00; www.france-nautic.com). Charges usually include boat hire, insurance, technical assistance. Some charter companies offer bicycles which enable visitors to go shopping and for rides or excursions along the towpath or to neighbouring villages. Visitors usually operate the locks on small canals by themselves; otherwise, it is customary to give a hand to the lock-keeper.

Two publishers produce collections of guides to cruising on French canals. Both series include numerous maps and useful information and are provided with English translations. The publishers are: Grafocarte (125 r. J.-J. Rousseau BP 40, 92132, Issy-les-Moulineaux; ℘01 41 09 19 00; www.grafocarte.fr) and Guides Vagnon, Les Éditions du Plaisancier (100 av. du Général-Leclerc, 69641 Caluire Cedex; ℘04 78 23 31 14).

SAILING

Many resorts have sailing clubs offering courses. In season it is possible to hire boats with or without crew; apply to the **Fédération Française de Voile**: 17 r. Henri Bocquillon, 75015 Paris; ℘01 40 60 37 00; www.ffvoile.net.

CANOEING

Apply to **Fédération Française de Canoe-Kayak** (87 quai de la Marne, 94344 Joinville-le-Pont; ℘01 45 11 08 50; www.ffck.org). A guide is published annually indicating schools and places where canoeing may be practised.

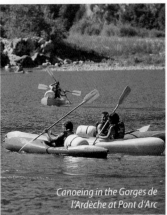

Canoeing in the Gorges de l'Ardèche at Pont d'Arc

J.Damase/MICHELIN

MOTOR BOATING AND WATER-SKIING

Enquire at local Tourist Information Centres or at resorts waterfronts. Anyone who intends to drive a powered boat (6hp – 50hp) within five nautical miles of a French harbour must qualify for a sea certificate (*carte mer*). Beyond the five nautical mile limit an additional sea permit (*permis mer*) is required. Yachts and boats with engines of less than 6hp are exempt.

WINDSURFING

The sport, subject to certain regulations, is permitted on lakes, seafronts and in sports and leisure centres. *See Sailing.*

Val Thorens – one of the great resorts in the Alps

S. Sauvignier/MICHELIN

SCUBA-DIVING

Apply to the **Fédération Française d'Études et de Sports Sous-Marins** (24 quai de Rive Neuve, 13284 Marseille Cedex 07; ℘04 91 33 99 31; www.ffessm.fr). The federation publishes *Subaqua*, a bimestrial journal on diving in France.

RIDING AND PONY TREKKING

Apply to the **Comité Nationale du Tourisme Équestre, Parc équestre** (41 600 Lamotte; ℘02 54 94 46 80; www.ffe.com), which publishes an annual handbook covering the whole of France.

GOLF

For location, addresses and telephone numbers of golf courses in France, consult the map *Golfs, les Parcours français,* published by Edition Plein Sud based on **Michelin maps**. You can also contact the **Fédération Française de Golf** (68 r. Anatole France, 92 300 Levallois-Perret; ℘01 41 49 77 00; www.ffgolf.org).

SKIING

The French Alps is one of the world's major ski and winter sports areas. There is also good skiing in the French Pyrenees. For all enquiries contact the **Club Alpin Français**, a national federation of 174 local moutain sports associations, based at 24 av. de Laumière, 75019 Paris; ℘01 53 72 87 00; www.ffcam.fr.

CLIMBING

Excursions with qualified instructors are organised by sections of the Club Alpin Français *(see Skiing for address information on regional sections)* or by local guides. For information apply to the Tourist Information Centres or to the **Fédération Française de la Montagne et de l'Escalade** (8–10, quai de la Marne, 75019 Paris; ℘01 40 18 75 50; www.ffme.fr).

SPELEOLOGY

Apply to the Speleology sections of the Club Alpin Français *(see Skiing)*.

GLIDING

Apply to the **Fédération Française de Vol à Voile** (29 r. de Sèvres, 75006 Paris; ℘01 45 44 04 78; www.ffvv.org).

SPA AND WELL-BEING

Spas have long been part of French life. They are gradually become less medical, more pampering. Numerous coastal and mountain resorts offer treatments.

ACTIVITIES FOR CHILDREN

In this guide, sights of particular interest to children are indicated with a KIDS symbol (👫). Some attractions may offer discount fees for children.

MAIN TOURIST RESORTS

Most of the resort areas listed below have a wide range of accommodation and leisure facilities and are therefore characterised only in terms of their setting or other special features.

Aix-en-Provence ★★– Spa – Casino – 18C spa complex built next to site of Roman baths.

Aix-les-Bains ★★– Spa – Palais de Savoie Casino and Nouveau Casino – prestigious "Season" – Parks – Lakeside esplanade★ – Dr Faure Museum★.

Ajaccio★★ – Sandy beach – Casino – Place Maréchal-Foch – other beaches around Ajaccio Bay.

L'Alpe-d'Huez★ – Mountain resort (1 860–3 350m/6 100–10 990ft) with winter sports– Lac Blanc Summit★★★ (by cableway and cable-car): view of Écrins Massif and Mont Blanc – Lake Besson★ (6.5km/4mi).

Amélie-les-Bains★ – Spa – Casino – Restored Roman baths – Montdony Gorges.

Annecy ★★★– Swimming in lake – Lakeside★★★ – Riverside walk.

Arcachon★★ – Sandy beach – Casino – Seafront with views over Arcachon Bay.

Argelès-Gazost – Spa – Panorama of the Pyrenees.

Argelès-Plage – Casino – Sandy beach at northern end of Côte Vermeille★★.

Avoriaz★★ – Mountain resort (winter sports).

Ax-les-Thermes★ – Spa – Mountain resort with winter sports (1 400–2 400m/4 590–7 870ft) – Ladres Valley – Bonascre Plateau★ (View★★ of Ariège heights and Andorra mountains).

Bagnères-de-Bigorre★★ – Spa – Casino – Salut spa complex and park★.

Bagnoles-de-l'Orne ★★– Spa – Casino – Lake★ – Park★ – Roc-au-Chien Walk★ (in Tessé-la-Madeleine).

Bandol★ – Sandy beach – Casino – Jean-Moulin avenue★.

Barèges – Spa – Mountain resort with winter sports (1 250-2 350m/4 100-7 710ft) – Lienz Plateau – Font d'Ayré funicular.

La Baule★★★ – Sandy beach – Thalassotherapy centre – Casino – Seafront★★ – Dryades Park★ – La-Baule-les-Pins★★.

Beaulieu-sur-Mer ★★– Sandy beach – Casino – Villa Kerylosa (setting★) – Fourmis Bay★.

Belle-Ile★★ – Thalassotherapy centre.

Bénodet★ – Sandy beach – Casino – Pyramide lighthouse (panorama★ over Cornouaille coast and Glénan islands).

Biarritz★★★ – ⚲See Index
Sandy beach with rocks – Thalassotherapy centre – Casino – La Perspective viewpoint★★ – St-Martin Point (view★) – Vierge Rock★ – Museum of the Sea★.

Le Boulou – Spa – Casino – Setting at foot of Albères Mountains.

La Bourboule★★ – Spa – Fenestre Park★ – Charlannes Plateau.

Cabourg★★ – Sandy beach – Casino – Marcel-Proust Promenade.

Canet-Plage – Sandy beach – Casino – Active sports centre.

Cannes ★★★– Sandy beach – Fleurs Casino, Palm Beach Casino, Casino Municipal) – Boulevard de la Croisette★★ – La Croisette Point★ – Super-Cannes Observatory (panorama★★★) – La Castre Museum★.

Cap-d'Antibes ★★– Sandy beach with rocks – Round tour★★ – La Garoupe Plateau (panorama★★) – Thuret Gardens★.

Capvern-les-Bains★ – Spa – View of Pyrenees.

Carnac – Thalassotherapy centre.

Cauterets★ – Spa – Mountain resort with winter sports (930– 2 340m/3 050–7 680ft) – Casino Esplanade – Espagne Bridge★★ – Lutour Valley★ and Falls★★; Jeret Valley★★.

Chamonix★★★ – Mountain resort with winter sports (1 035–3 842m/3 400–12 604ft) – Setting at foot of Aiguille du Midi with view of Mont-Blanc.

Châtelguyon★★ – Spa – Casino – Prades Valley★ – Enval Gorge★.

Chaudes-Aigues – Spa – Source of the River Par – Neighbourhood saints in niches.

Combloux★ – Mountain resort with winter sports (1 000– 1 853m/3 280–6 080ft) – View★ of Mont-Blanc.

Contrexéville★ – Spa – Casino – La Folie Lake.

Courchevel★★ – Mountain resort with winter sports (1 300– 2 700m/4 260–8 860ft) – Panorama★ – La Saulire *(cableway and cable-car)*: panorama★★.

Dax★ – Spa – Casino – Warm springs – *9km/5.6mi NE:* Buglose (birthplace of St Vincent de Paul).

Deauville★★★ – Sandy beach – Summer and Winter Casinos – Boardwalk★ (Promenade des Planches).

Les Deux-Alpes★ – Twin mountain resorts (L'Alpe-du-Mont-de-Lans and L'Alpe-de-Venosc) with winter sports (1 650–3 560m/5 410– 11 680ft) – From L'Alpe-de-Venosc: La Croix viewpoint★ and Cimes viewpoint★ *(by cableway)*.

Dieppe★★ – Pebble beach – Casino – Boulevard de la Mer (view★) – Boulevard du Maréchal-Foch.

Dinard ★★★– Sandy beach with rocks – Thalassotherapy centre – Casino – Moulinet Point (view★★) – Grande Plage beach★ – Clair de Lune Promenade★.

Divonne★ – Spa – Casino – Park.

Douarnenez★ – Thalassotherapy centre.

Enghien ★– Spa – Casino – Lake★.

Évian ★★★– Spa – Casino – English Garden.

Font-Romeu★★ – Mountain resort with winter sports (1 850–2 204m/6 070–7 230ft) – Casino – Hermitage★ (Camaril★★) – Calvary (panorama★★ over the Cerdagne).

Gérardmer★★ – Spa – Mountain/ forest setting – Winter sports (870–1 130m/2 850–3 710ft) – Lake★.

La Grande-Motte★★★ – Sandy beach – Casino – Modern resort architecture.

Hossegor★ – Sandy beach – Casino – Lakeside Promenade★.

Juan-les-Pins★★ – Sandy beach – Casino: Eden Beach – Fine coastal setting.

Luchon ★★– Spa – Mountain setting with winter sports at Super-Bagnères (1 420–2 260m/4 660–7 420ft) – d'Étigny avenues.

Megève ★★★ – Alpine setting with winter sports (1 067–2 350/3 510–7 710ft) – Casino – Mont d'Arbois *(by cable-car)*: panorama★★★ over Aravis mountains and Mont-Blanc.

Menton★★ – Pebble beach – Casino du Soleil – Promenade du Soleil★★ – Carnolès Palace Museum★.

Les Menuires★★ – Mountain resort with winter sports (1 067–2 350m/3 500–7 710ft) – Mont de la Chambre★★

Le Mont-Dore★★ – Spa – Mountain resort with winter sports (1 350–1 850m/4 430–6 070ft) – Casino – Promenade des Artistes★ – Salon du Capucin (funicular).

Monte-Carlo★★★ – Sandy beach with rocks – Grand Casino, Casino du Sporting Club, Casino Loews – Museum of Dolls and Automata★.

Morzine★★ – Mountain setting with winter sports (1 000–2 460m/3 280–8 070ft) – Meeting point of six valleys – Le Pléney *(cable-car)*: panorama.

Nice★★★ – Pebble beach – Casino-club.

Perros-Guirec★ – Sandy beach – Thalassotherapy centre – Casino – Le Château Point (view★) – Viewing table (view★) – Douaniers Path★★.

Plombières★ – Spa – Casino – Park designed by Haussmann.

Pornichet★ – Sandy beach – Casino – Boulevard des Océanides.

Propriano★ – Sandy beach – Valinco Bay★.

Quiberon – Sandy beach with rocks – Thalassotherapy centre – Casino – Côte Sauvage★★.

La Rochelle★★★ – Sandy beach – Casino.

Roscoff★ – Thalassotherapy centre – Sandy beaches with some pebbles – Aquarium★ – Notre-Dame-de-Kroaz-Betz Church★ (Belfry★, alabaster statues★).

Royan★★ – Sandy beach – Casino (at Pontaillac) – Seafront★ – Notre-Dame Church★.

Royat★★ – Spa – Casino – Set among foothills of Monts Dômes – Spa Park and Bargoin Park

Les Sables-d'Olonne★★ – Sandy beach – Casino de la Plage – Casino des Sports – Remblai promenade★ – Fishermen's quarter.

St-Cast-le-Guildo★★ – Sandy beach – St-Cast Point (view★★) – La Garde Point (view★★).

St-Gervais ★★– Spa – Mountain resort with winter sports (850–2 350m/2 790–7 710ft) – Bettex scenic route★★★ – Eagle's Nest and Bionassay glacier★★ (Mont-Blanc mountain railway).

St-Jean-de-Luz★★ – Sandy beach – Casino.

St-Malo★★★ – Sandy beach – Thalassotherapy centre – Casino.

St-Nectaire★★ – Spa.

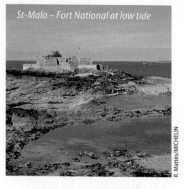
St-Malo – Fort National at low tide

R. Mattès/MICHELIN

St-Raphaël★ – Sandy beach – Casino – Sheltered setting at foot of Esterel Massif – Seafront.

St-Trojan – Sandy beach – Pinetum.

St-Tropez★★ – Sandy beach – Harboura and quaysides – L'Annonciade Museum★★ – View★ from harbour wall – View★ from citadel.

Ste-Maxime★ – Sandy beach – Casino – Panorama★ from semaphore.

Serre-Chevalier★ – Winter sports.

Super-Lioran★ – Mountain resort with winter sports (1 160– 1 830m/3 810–6 000ft) – Plomb du Cantal★ (cable-car): panorama★★.

Talloires★★ – Bathing in the lake – Lakeside setting★★★ (Petit Lac d'Annecy).

Thonon★★ – Spa.

Le Touquet-Paris-Plage★★★ – Sandy beach – La Forêt and Quatre Saisons Casinos – Seafront promenade – Woodland – Lighthouse (view★★).

Trégastel★★ – Sandy beach – Rocky coastline of the Breton Corniche★ – White Shore (La Grève blanche) footpath★.

Trouville★★ – Sandy beach – Casino – Corniche road★ – Boardwalk (Promenade des Planches).

Le Val-André★★ – Sandy beach – Casino – Pléneuf Pointa (View★★) – Promenade de la Guette★.

Val-d'Isère★★★ – Mountain resort with winter sports (1 850– 3 450m/6 070–11 320ft) – Rocher de Bellevarde (cable-car): panorama★★★ – Tête du Solaise (cable-car): panorama★★.

Val-Thorens★★ – Mountain resort with winter sports (1 067– 3 200m/7 546–10 499ft) – Cime de Carona★ (cable-car).

Vichy ★★★ – Spa – Élysée Palace Casino, Grand Casino – Sources Park★ – Allier Park★.

Villard-de-Lans★ – Mountain resort with winter sports (1 050– 2 170m/3 450–7 120ft) – Vercors Regional Park setting – Bourne Gorge★★★.

Vittel ★★★ – Spa – Casino – Landscape park★.

THE ISLANDS OF FRANCE

&See **Michelin Green Guides** to: *Normandy, Brittany, French Atlantic Coast, Provence, French Riviera, and Corse (in French).*

France has an extensive coastline (2 700km/1 678mi) along which are dotted idyllic islands, some as small as a field and others very large – Corsica is three times the size of a small country such as Luxembourg. The islands are perfect destinations for a change of scenery and pace; their isolation as well as an air of mystery and charm add to the fascination of a way of life shaped by the sea. The list overleaf includes the principal islands ranging from north to south and west to east.

ÎLES DU PONANT

(English Channel-Atlantic Ocean)

- **Îles Chausey★:** *65sq km/0.25sq mi* at high tide attached to **Granville.**

- **Île de Bréhat★:** *318sq km/1.2sq mi; 10min* crossing from **Arcouest** near **Paimpol.**

- **Île de Batz:** *357sq km/1.4sq mi; 15min* crossing from **Roscoff.**

- **Île d'Ouessant★★:** the westernmost island off the Atlantic coast. *1 558sq km6sq mi, highest point 60m/197ft; 2hr 30min* crossing from **Brest** or *1hr 30min* from **Conquet.**

- **Île de Molène:** *100sq km/0.38sq mi; 30min* crossing from **Pointe St-Matthieu.**

- **Île de Sein:** *50sq km/0.19sq mi, highest point 6m/20ft; 1hr* crossing from **Audierne.**

- **Îles de Glénan:** a group of 10 islets, mostly uninhabited, attached to **Fouesnant.**

- **Île de Groix★:** *1 770sq km/7sq mi, highest point 49m/160ft; 45min* crossing from **Lorient.**

- **Îles du Golfe de Morbihan★★:** Among the string of islets in the bay, the most noteworthy are Île-aux-Moines★, *310sq km/1.2sq mi,* and **Île d'Arz**, *324ha/1.25sq mi.*

- **Belle-Île-en-Mer★★:** *8 400sq km/48sq mi; 1hr* crossing from **Quiberon.**

- **Île d'Houat:** *288sq km/1sq mi; 1hr* crossing from **Quiberon.**

- **Île d'Hoedic:** *209sq km/0.8sq mi; 1hr 30min* crossing from **Quiberon** via **Houat.**

- **Île d'Yeu★★:** *2 300sq km/ 9sq mi;* this island is the furthest from the mainland; *1hr15min* crossing from **Fromentine.**

- **Île d'Aix★:** *129sq km/0.5sq mi; 20min* crossing from **Fouras.**

- **Île de Noirmoutier,** Île de Ré★ and Île d'Oléron★: These are linked to the mainland by a road bridge.

ÎLES DU LEVANT

(Mediterranean Sea)

- **Archipel du Frioul: Île de Pomègues** and **Île Ratonneau** linked by Frioul harbour, **Îlot d'If★★:** *1hr30min* excursion from **Marseille.**

- **Îles des Calanques: Maire, Jarre, Calseraigne, Riou** are great spots for underwater fishing.

- **Île de Bendor★:** *7min* from **Bandol.**

- **Îles d'Hyères★★★: Porquerolles★★★,** *1 254sq km/5sq mi, 20min crossing from Giens;* Port-Cros★★, *640sq km/ 2.5sq mi, 45min* crossing from **Port-de-Miramar;** Île du Levant, *996sq km/3.8sq mi, 35min* crossing from **Le Lavandou.**

- **Îles de Lérins★★: St-Honorat★★,** *60sq km/0.2sq mi;* **Ste-Marguerite★★,** *210sq km/0.8sq mi, 30min* crossing from **Cannes** or **Juan-les-Pins.**

- **Îles Sanguinaires★★:** *60min* crossing from **Ajaccio.**

- **Îles Lavezzia:** *30min* crossing from **Bonifacio.**

SHOPPING
OPENING HOURS

Ordinary shop hours in towns and villages are typically open Tue–Sat 9am–noon or 12.30pm, 3–7pm. The lunch break is often longer in the South. Food shops may open earlier in the morning, but later in the afternoon, and some, especially bakeries (*pâtisseries*) and grocery stores, open on Sunday morning. In resorts, shops may keep longer hours and stay open all day, all week. Department stores are open Mon–Sat 9am–6.30pm (often with one or more later evenings per week). Hypermarkets are usually open Mon–Sat 9am–10pm.

MARKETS

When travelling around France make sure you have a look around the different local markets, an important domestic institution, or the various agricultural fairs which are held regularly throughout the year.

VALUE ADDED TAX

In France a sales tax (*TVA* or VAT) is added to all purchases. For non-EU residents on holiday this tax can be refunded as long as you have bought more than 175€ worth of goods at the same time and in the same shop, and have completed the appropriate *Bordereau* form at the shop. The amount permitted may vary, so it is advisable to check first with the VAT-refund counter (*service de détaxe*). Present the *Bordereau* forms to Customs officials on leaving France for processing. Customs Information Centre: ℘08 20 02 44 44 or www.douane.gouv.fr.

WHAT YOU CAN TAKE HOME

There are no limits on the value of goods EU residents may take home from France, provided everything is for personal use. However, in the UK, HM Revenue and Customs attempt to limit the amount of alcohol and tobacco considered reasonable for personal use. These are: 3 200 cigarettes, 200 cigars, 400 cigarillos, 3kg/6.6lb tobacco, 110l/29gal beer, 90l/19.7gal wine, 10l/2/2gal spirits and 20l/4/4gal fortified wine. More information is available at **www.hmrc.gov.uk**.

Americans are allowed to take home, tax-free, up to US$800 worth of goods, Canadians up to CND$750, Australians up to AUS$900 and New Zealanders up to NZ$700.

BOOKS
POLITICS AND HISTORY

France in the New Century: Portrait of a Changing Society by John Ardagh (*Penguin 2001*)
    An acclaimed overview of the political landscape, by one of the most respected commentators on French life.

The French by T Zeldin (*Kodansha Globe 1996*)
    A perceptive and entertaining look at the character of this enigmatic nation.

Market in Brive-la-Gaillarde, Limousin

S. Sauvignier/MICHELIN

Searching for the New France by
J Hollifield and G Ross *(Routledge 1998)*
   Why France is so anxious about its
   identity, its role and its future.
*Betrayal: France, the Arabs and
the Jews* by David Pryce-Jones
(Encounter Books 2008)
   How France's relations with the
   Arab world have led it into trouble.
Horrible Histories: France by Terry
Deary (Author), Martin Brown (Illustrator) *(Scholastic Hippo 2002)*
   A comical cartoon summary of
   French history.

CULTURE

The Lost World of the Impressionists
by A Bellony-Rewald (Bulfinch
   Press 1988). Beautiful art
   collection evocatively recapturing
   the past.

TOURING

Exploring Rural France by Andrew
   Sanger (Passport Books 1994).
   Itineraries for off-the-beaten-track
   tourists.
*The Wines and Winelands of France –
Geological Journeys* by C Pomerol
(McCarta Publishing 1990)
   What lies behind the extraordinary
   diversity of the French wine list.
*Green Guide to the Wine Regions
of France* by Michelin *(2008)*
   All you need to explore, visit, and
   taste your way around the country.
1000 Charming Hotels and Guesthouses
by Michelin (2005)
   An appealing selection of places
   to stay.

FILMS

La Route Napoléon (1953)
   Villagers in the Provence back-
   country play along when a hotel
   claims the Emperor stopped there.
La Grande Illusion (1937)
   Prisoners of war strike up an
   unlikely friendship as they try to
   escape over the mountains.
Les Vacances de Monsieur Hulot (1953)
   Tati's gentle and comic view of
   the conventions of a respectable
   seaside resort in Brittany.

Au Revoir les Enfants (1987)
   True story of a Catholic school
   which hides a Jewish boy from the
   Nazis.
La Règle du Jeu (1939)
   Renoir's classic on bourgeois
   France, set in a French château.
Les Misérables (1998)
   Based on Victor Hugo's novel
   about a convict's struggle to
   redeem himself.
Germinal (1993)
   The miners in a 19C northern town
   go on strike.
*To Catch a Thief (1955) ; Pierrot le Fou
(1965); Et Dieu... créa la femme (1956)*
   Three great classic films set on the
   Riviera.
French Kiss (1995)
   Comic romance as a Canadian out
   to save her marriage plans and a
   petty crook who is using her travel
   to Cannes together.
Les Parapluies de Cherbourg (1964)
   Director J. Demy's remarkable love
   triangle set in this French port, in
   which every word is sung!
La Haine (1995)
   Violence and racism as three
   youths, one black, one a Jew, one
   an Arab, get involved in riots in the
   Paris suburbs.
*Le Fabuleux destin d'Amélie Poulain
(2001)*
   Touching and lighthearted adven-
   tures of the naive Amélie as she
   looks for love in Paris.
*Jean de Florette and Manon des
Sources (1986)*
   Two peasants in rural Provence
   outwit the new owner of the
   neighbouring property. In the
   second movie, his death is aven-
   ged by his daughter Manon.
Le Retour de Martin Guerre (1982)
   No one is sure of his identity when
   long-lost Martin returns to the
   village – not even his 'wife'.
Les Petites Vacances (2006)
   Grandmother kidnaps the children
   and takes them on a crazy 'holiday' in the Alps.

Calendar of Events

This list includes a selection of festivals and events likely to be of interest to visitors.

RELIGIOUS AND CIVIC FESTIVALS

FEBRUARY

Nice ✆0892 70 74 07
Carnival

Chalon-sur-Saône ✆03 85 48 08 39
Carnival, Winter Fur and Pelt Fair

Menton ✆04 92 41 76 76
Lemon Festival

Paris Paris International Agricultural Show. www.salon-agriculture.com

Le Touquet ✆03 21 06 72 00
Motorbike Race along the beach

MAUNDY THURSDAY

Le Puy-en-Velay ✆04 71 09 79 77,
White Penitents Procession

Saugues ✆04 71 77 71 30
White Penitents Procession (at nightfall)

GOOD FRIDAY

Arles-sur-Tech ✆04 68 39 11 99
Black Penitents Procession

Burzet ✆04 75 94 43 99
The Passion re-enacted

Collioure ✆04 68 82 15 47
Penitents Procession

Black Penitents Procession, Perpignan

M.-H. Carcanague/MICHELIN

Perpignan ✆04 68 66 30 30
Black Penitents Procession

Roquebrune-Cap-Martin
✆04 93 35 62 87
Procession of the Entombment of Christ

Sartène ✆04 95 77 15 40
U Catenacciu Procession

EASTER SUNDAY

St-Benoit-sur-Loire
✆02 38 35 79 00
Easter Service

EASTER MONDAY

Cassel ✆03 28 40 52 55
Carnival of the Giants Reuze-Papa and Reuze-Maman

APRIL

Chartres ✆02 37 21 51 91
Students' Pilgrimage

Gérardmer ✆03 29 27 27 27
Flower Festival

EARLY MAY

Orléans ✆02 38 24 05 05
Joan of Arc Festival

MID-MAY

St-Tropez ✆0892 68 48 28
Procession in honour of St-Tropez (Bravade)

Tréguier ✆02 96 92 22 33
Pardon of St-Ives

Mont-St-Michel ✆02 33 60 14 30
Feast of St Michael in Spring

LATE MAY

Rouen ✆02 35 08 32 40,
Joan of Arc Festival

Les Saintes-Maries-de-la-Mer
✆04 90 97 82 55
Gypsy Pilgrimage

WHITSUN (PENTECOTE)

Honfleur ✆02 31 89 23 30
Seamen's Festival

EARLY JUNE

La Rochelle ✆05 46 41 14 68
International Regatta

Utah Beach-Omaha Beach
📞02 33 41 31 18
Commemoration of the D-Day
Landings (American sector)

Gold-Juno-Sword
📞02 31 86 53 30
Commemoration of the D-Day
Landings (Anglo-Canadian sector).
*The two events are combined every
five years.*

MID-JUNE
Chambord 📞01 41 40 32 32
Game Fair
Le Mans 📞03 43 40 24 24
24-hour car race
Amboise 📞02 47 57 14 47
"At The Court of King François"
(until late Aug)

MID-JULY
Douai 📞03 27 88 26 79, Carnival of
the Giant Gayant and his family
Carcassonne 📞04 68 10 24 30,
Illumination of the City

LATE JULY
Ste-Anne-d'Auray 📞02 97 57 69 16,
Great Pardon of Ste-Anne

EARLY AUGUST
Bayonne 📞0820 42 64 64,
Corrida and Street Festival
Colmar 📞03 89 20 68 92,
Alsatian Wine Festival

MID-AUGUST
Béziers 📞04 67 76 13 45, Bullfighting
Festival
Chamonix 📞04 50 53 00 88,
Mountain Guides Festival
Pomarez 📞05 58 89 30 28,
Running of the Cows
St-Palais 📞05 46 23 22 58,
Basque Festival
Concarneau 📞02 98 97 09 09,
Festival of the Blue Nets

AUGUST
Boulogne-sur-Mer 📞03 21 30 22 70,
Pilgrimage to Notre-Dame-de-
Boulogne
Monteux 📞04 90 66 97 52
Fireworks Festival

EARLY SEPTEMBER
Dinan 📞02 96 39 75 40
Ramparts Festival (biennial – next
in 2010)
Lille 📞03 20 30 81 00
Grand jumble sale
Le Mas Soubeyran 📞04 66 85 02 72
National Protestant Assembly

LATE SEPTEMBER
Mont-St-Michel 📞02 33 60 14 30
Feast of the Archangel St Michael

MID-NOVEMBER
Beaune 📞03 80 24 47 00
Auction sale of the wines of the
Hospices de Beaune

EARLY DECEMBER
Marseille 📞04 91 54 91 11
Santons Fair
Mont-Ste-Odile 📞03 88 95 80 53
Pilgrimage (the most important
in Alsace)
Strasbourg 📞03 88 52 28 28
Christmas Market

25 DECEMBER
Les-Baux-de-Provence 📞04 90 97
34 39, Shepherds' Midnight Mass
Son et Lumière in the Loire Valley

Azay-le-Rideau 📞02 47 45 44 40
"The Imaginary World of the
Château d'Azay-le-Rideau"

Blois 📞02 54 78 72 76
"The Story of Blois"

Fêtes de Bayonne

E. Lamibere/MICHELIN

Chenonceau 📞02 47 23 94 45
"The Ladies of Chenonceau"

Cheverny 📞02 54 42 69 03
"The River Loire down the ages"

Loches 📞02 47 59 07 98
"The Strange Story of Bélisane"

Le Lude 📞02 43 94 62 20
"Spectacular Historical Events"

Valençay 📞02 54 00 04 42
"Esclarmonde"

CULTURAL FESTIVALS

Some of the more important annual festivals around the country. Book accommodation well in advance at festival times, even out of season:

JULY
Aix-en-Provence 📞0820 922 923
International Music Festival

MID-JULY/EARLY AUGUST
Albi 📞05 63 49 48 80
Classical Music

2ND WEEK JULY/MID-SEPTEMBER
Arles 📞04 90 96 76 06
International Photo Festival

JULY
Avignon 📞04 90 27 66 50
Theatre Festival

LATE NOV/EARLY DECEMBER
Belfort 📞03 84 22 94 44
Cinema

LATE JUNE/EARLY JULY
Bellac 📞05 55 60 87 61
Drama, music

SEPTEMBER
Besançon 📞03 81 25 05 85
Classical music–Young Conductors Competition

MID-JULY
Béziers 📞04 67 36 82 30
Classical music

LATE APRIL
Bourges 📞02 48 27 28 29
Music Festival

MAY
Cannes 📞01 53 59 61 00
International Film Festival

JULY
Carcassonne 📞04 68 11 59 15
Theatre, music and dance

2ND-HALF JUL
Carpentras 📞04 90 60 46 00
Music and dance

LATE AUG
La Chaise-Dieu 📞04 71 09 48 28
Religious music

2ND WEEK IN APRIL
Chartres 📞02 22 06 87 87
Music festival

APRIL-OCTOBER
Chaumont-sur-Loire 📞02 54 20 99 22
International Garden Festival

1ST-HALF SEPTEMBER
Deauville 📞02 31 14 14 14
American film Festival

LATE AUG/EARLY SEPTEMBER
Divonne 📞04 50 90 17 70
Chamber music

2ND-HALF AUGUST
Entrecasteaux 📞04 94 72 91 62
Chamber music

LATE-MAY
Évian 📞04 50 26 85 00
Classical music

2ND-HALF JULY
Gannat 📞04 70 90 12 67
International folk music

MID JULY
Juan-les-Pins 📞04 97 23 11 10
World Jazz Festival

OCTOBER
Lannion ☎02 96 35 14 14
Organ and choral music

MID-MARCH/MID-JULY
Lille ☎03 28 52 30 00
Music, art and theatre

LATE JULY/EARLY AUGUST
Lorient ☎02 97 21 24 29
Celtic festival

2ND-HALF SEPTEMBER
Lyon☎04 72 77 69 69
even years: dance; odd years:
music and modern art

LATE MAY
Montauban ☎05 63 63 66 77
Music festival

LATE AUGUST
Montesquieu-Volvestre
☎05 61 90 65 74
British Film Festival

EARLY JULY
Nantes ☎02 40 47 04 51
International Flower Show

MID-MAY
Orange ☎02 40 14 58 60
Music and opera

MID-JUNE/MID JULY
Pau ☎05 59 27 27 08
Theatre, music and dance

LATE JULY/MID-AUGUST
Prades ☎04 68 96 33 07
Chamber music
(Festival Pablo Casals)

MID-SEPTEMBER
Le Puy-en-Velay ☎04 71 09 38 41
Bird King Renaissance Festival

2ND-HALF JULY
Quimper ☎02 98 55 53 53
Cornouaille Festival

EARLY JULY
Rennes ☎02 99 67 11 11
Theatre, music, dance and poetry

LATE JULY/MID-AUGUST
St-Céré ☎05 34 50 40 10
Opera

MID-AUGUST
St-Donat-sur-l'Herbasse
☎04 75 45 10 29
Bach Festival

LATE JUNE/JULY
St-Guilhem-le-Désert
☎04 67 57 44 33
Baroque music

LATE OCTOBER
St-Malo ☎02 99 40 39 63
Comics Festival

MID-JULY/MID-SEPTEMBER
St-Rémy-de-Provence
☎04 90 92 05 22
Organ music

LATE JULY/EARLY AUGUST
Salon-de-Provence ☎04 90 56 27 60
Music Festival

MID-JULY
Sarlat ☎05 53 31 10 83
Theatre

MID-JULY/MID-SEPTEMBER
Sceaux ☎01 46 60 07 79
Classical music

LATE JUN/LATE AUGUST
Toulouse ☎05 62 27 60 60
Classical, jazz and rock music

JULY AND AUGUST
Vaison-la-Romaine ☎04 90 36 02 11
Theatre and dance-Folklore

MID-AUGUST
Vannes ☎0825 13 56 10
Arvor Festival (folk music)

LATE-MARCH/LATE OCTOBER EVERY
WEEKEND AND BANK HOLIDAY
Versailles ☎01 30 83 78 98
Fountain display with musical
performances (*Les Grandes Eaux
Musicales*)

Know Before You Go

USEFUL WEBSITES

**www.ambafrance-us.org,
www.ambafrance-uk.org**
The French Embassy has a website in the US and UK providing basic information (geography, demographics, history), a news digest and business-related information. It offers special pages for children, pages devoted to culture, language study and travel, and links to other selected French sites (regions, cities, ministries).

www.franceguide.com
The French Government Tourist Office/ Maison de la France site is packed with practical information, advice and tips for those travelling to France, including choosing package tours and even buying a property.

www.francekeys.com
This site has plenty of practical information for visiting France. It covers all the regions, with links to tourist offices and related sites. Very useful for planning all the details of your tour in France!

www.franceway.com
This is an online magazine that focuses on culture and heritage. For each region, there are also suggestions for activities and practical information on where to stay and how to get there.

www.ViaMichelin.com
This site has maps, tourist information, travel features, suggestions on hotels and restaurants, and a route planner for numerous locations in Europe. In addition, you can look up weather forecasts, traffic reports and service station location, particularly useful if you will be driving in France.

www.holidayfrance.org.uk
The website of the Association of British Travel Organisers to France features a holiday-finder, with a big selection of inclusive package deals.

TOURIST OFFICES

- **Australia & New Zealand**
  Level 13, 25 Bligh Street, 2000 NSW, Sydney, Australia
  61 (0)2 9231 5244
  Fax 61 (0)2 9221 8682
  http://au.franceguide.com

- **Canada**
  1800 av. McGill College, Suite 1010, Montreal, Quebec H3A 3J6
  ℰ(514) 288-2026
  Fax (514) 845-4868
  http://ca-en.franceguide.com

- **Republic of Ireland**
  ℰ(1) 560 235 235
  http://ie.franceguide.com

- **United Kingdom**
  Lincoln House, 300 High Holborn, London WC1V 7JH.
  ℰ09068 244 123 (60p/min)
  http://uk.franceguide.com

- **United States**
  Three offices are available, but the quickest way to have a response to any question or request is by phone.

  New York
  825 Third Avenue, 29th Floor, New York NY 10022

  Los Angeles
  9454 Wilshire Bld – Suite 210, Beverly Hills 90212 CA

  Chicago
  205 N.Michigan Ave, Suite 3770, Chicago 60601, IL
  ℰ514 288 1904
  http://us.franceguide.com

NATIONAL TOURIST OFFICES

France has a national network of regional and local tourist offices able to provide information useful in planning your trip and answering your questions.

- **Fédération Nationale des Comités Régionaux de Tourisme**
  17 av. de l'Opéra,
  75001 Paris
  ✆01 47 03 03 10
  Fax 01 47 03 05 10
  www.fncrt.com

- **Fédération Nationale des Comités Départementaux du Tourisme**
  74–76 r. de Bercy, 75012 Paris
  ✆(01) 44 11 10 20
  Fax (01) 45 55 96 66.
  www.fncdt.net

- **Fédération Nationale des Offices de Tourisme et Syndicats d'Initiative**
  11 r. du Faubourg Poissonnière,
  75009 Paris
  www.tourisme.fr

REGIONAL TOURIST OFFICES

Alsace Lorraine Champagne

- *Alsace*
  20a r. Berthe-Molly, BP 50247,
  ✆03 89 24 73 50
  www.tourisme-alsace.com
- *Lorraine*
  Abbaye des Prémontrés, BP 97,
  54704 Pont-à-Mousson
  ✆03 83 80 01 80
  www.tourisme-lorraine.fr
- *Champagne-Ardenne*
  50 av. du Général Patton, 51000
  Châlons-en-Champagne
  ✆03 26 21 85 80. www.tourisme-champagne-ardenne.com

Atlantic Coast

- *Aquitaine*
  Cité Mondiale, 23 parvis des Chartrons, 33074 Bordeaux Cedex
  ✆05 56 01 70 00
  www.tourisme-aquitaine.fr

Presqu'île de Crozon, Brittany
R. Mattès/MICHELIN

- *Poitou-Charentes*
  8 r. Riffault, BP 56,
  F-86002 Poitiers Cedex
  ✆05 49 50 10 50
  www.visit-poitou-charentes.com

Auvergne – Rhone Valley

- *Auvergne*
  Parc Technologique Clermont-Ferrand La Pardieu, 7 allée Pierre de Fermat, CS 50502, 63178 Aubière Cedex
  ✆0810 827 828
  www.auvergne-tourisme.info
- *Rhône-Alpes*
  104 rte de Paris,
  69260 Charbonnières-les-Bains
  ✆04 72 59 21 59.
  www.rhonealpes-tourisme.com

Brittany

- *Bretagne*
  1 r. Raoul-Ponchon,
  35069 Rennes Cedex
  ✆02 99 28 44 30
  www.brittanytourism.com

Burgundy Jura

- *Bourgogne*
  5 av. Garibaldi,
  21006 Dijon Cedex
  ✆03 80 28 02 80
  www.bourgogne-tourisme.com
- *Franche-Comté*
  La City,
  25044 Besançon Cedex
  ✆03 81 25 08 08
  www.franche-comte.org

Chateaux of the Loire
- *Centre-Val de Loire*
  37 av. de Paris, 45000 Orléans
  ℘02 38 79 95 00
  www.visaloire.com
- *Pays de la Loire*
  1 pl. de la Galarne,
  44202 Nantes Cedex 2
  ℘02 40 48 24 20
  www.enpaysdelaloire.com

Corsica
- *Corse*
  ATC, 17 bd du Roi-Jérôme,
  BP 19, 20181 Ajaccio
  ℘04 95 51 00 00
  www.visit-corsica.com

Dordogne Berry Limousin
- *Limousin*
  30 cours Gay-Lussac , C.S. 500 95,
  87003 Limoges Cedex 1
  ℘05 55 11 05 90
  www.tourismelimousin.com

French Alps
- *Rhone-Alpes*
  104 rte de Paris,
  69260 Charbonnières- les-bains
  ℘04 72 59 21 59
  www.rhonealpes-tourisme.com
- *Provence-Alpes*
  10 pl. de la Joliette,
  13567 Marseille Cedex 02
  ℘04 91 56 47 00
  www.decouverte-paca.fr

French Riviera
- *Riviera-Côte d'Azur*
  400, Promenade des Anglais,
  BP 3126, 06203 Nice Cedex 3
  ℘04 93 37 78 78.
  www.guideriviera.com

Languedoc Roussillon Midi-Pyrénées
- *Languedoc-Roussillon*
  954 av. Jean Mermoz,
  34960 Montpellier Cedex 2
  ℘04 67 200 220
  www.sunfrance.com

- *Midi-Pyrénées*
  54 bd de l'Embouchure, BP 52
  166, 31022 Toulouse Cedex 2
  ℘05 61 13 55 48
  www.tourism.midi-pyrenees.co.uk

Normandy
- *Normandie*
  14 r. Charles Corbeau, 27000
  Evreux ℘02 32 33 79 00
  www.normandie-tourisme.fr

Northern France and the Paris Region
- *Île-de-France*
  11 r. du Faubourg Poissonnière
  75009 Paris
  ℘01 73 00 77 00.
  www.new-paris-ile-de-france.co.uk
- *Nord-Pas-de-Calais*
  6 Place Mendès-France, BP 99,
  59028 Lille Cedex
  ℘03 20 14 57 57.
  www.tourisme-nordpasde calais.fr
- *Paris*
  There are eight city tourist offices
  in Paris, including:
  Paris Convention and Visitors Bureau,
  25 r. des Pyramides,
  75001 Paris
  ℘0892 683 000 (0.34€/min)
  http://en.parisinfo.com
- *Picardie*
  11, Mail Albert 1er, B.P. 2616,
  80026, Amiens Cedex 1
  ℘03 22 97 37 37
  www.cr-picardie.fr

INTERNATIONAL VISITORS
EMBASSIES AND CONSULATES
Australia Embassy
  4 r. Jean-Rey, 75015 Paris
  ℘01 40 59 33 00;
  Fax 01 40 59 33 10

Canada Embassy
  35, avenue Montaigne, 75008 Paris
  ℘01 44 43 29 00;
  Fax 01 44 43 29 99
  www.international.gc.ca/canada-europa/france

Ireland Embassy
2 av. Foch, 75116 Paris
℘01 44 17 67 00;
Fax 01 44 17 67 50
www.embassyofirelandparis.com

New Zealand Embassy
7ter r. Léonard-de-Vinci,
75016 Paris
℘01 45 00 24 11;
Fax 01 45 01 26 39
www.nzembassy.com/france

UK Embassy
35 r. du Faubourg-St-Honoré,
75383 Paris Cedex 08
℘01 44 51 31 00;
Fax 01 44 51 32 34
www.ukinfrance.fco.gov.uk/en

UK Consulate
18bis r. d'Anjou, 75008 Paris
℘01 44 51 31 00;
Fax 01 44 51 31 27
There are also UK Consulates in
Bordeaux, Lille, Lyon and Marseille.

USA Embassy
2 av. Gabriel, 75008 Paris
℘01 43 12 22 22
Fax 01 42 66 97 83
http://france.usembassy.gov

USA Consulate
2 r. St-Florentin, 75001 Paris
℘01 43 12 22 22
There are **American Presence
Posts** in Bordeaux, Lyon, Rennes
and Toulouse, and a Virtual Presence Post in Lille.

ENTRY REQUIREMENTS

Passport – EU citizens entering
France from a Schengen Agreement
EU country do not need any documents. Those coming from all other
countries (including the UK) must
be in possession of a valid national
passport or recognised identity document. In case of loss or theft, report
to the embassy or consulate and the
local police.

Visa – Not required by EU, US,
Canadian, Australia and New Zealand
citizens for a stay in France of up to
90 days. Citizens of other countries
should check with a French consulate
or travel agent. US citizens are advised
to consult www.travel.state.gov for
entry requirements, security and other
information including contact numbers of US embassies and consulates.
In an emergency call the **Overseas
Citizens Services** ℘1-888-407-4747
(℘1-202-501-4444 from overseas).

CUSTOMS REGULATIONS

In the UK, **HM Revenue and Customs**
(www.hmrc.gov.uk) publishes *A Guide
for Travellers* on customs regulations
and duty-free allowances. **US citizens**
should view *Tips for Traveling Abroad*
online *(travel.state.gov/travel/tips/bro-
chures/brochures_1225.html)* for general information on visa requirements,
customs regulations, medical care, etc.
There are no customs formalities when
bringing caravans, pleasure-boats and
outboard motors into France for a stay
of less than six months, but a boat's
registration certificate should be kept
on board.

HEALTH

It is advisable to take out comprehensive travel insurance cover, as tourists
receiving medical treatment in French
hospitals or clinics have to pay for it
themselves. **Nationals of non-EU
countries** should check with their
insurance companies about policy
limitations. Remember to keep all
receipts.

British and Irish citizens, if they are
not already in possession of an **EHIC**
(European Health Insurance Card),
should apply for one before travelling.
The card entitles UK residents to red-
uced-cost medical treatment. Apply
at UK post offices, call ℘0845 606
2030, or visit www.ehic.org.uk. Details
of the healthcare available in France
and how to claim reimbursement are
published in the leaflet *Health Advice
for Travellers*, available from post
offices. All prescription drugs taken

into France should be clearly labelled; it is recommended to carry a copy of prescriptions.

ACCESSIBILITY

The sights described in this guide most easily accessible to people of reduced mobility are indicated in the Admission times and charges by the symbol &.

On French TGV and Corail trains there are wheelchair spaces in 1st class carriages available to holders of 2nd-class tickets. On Eurostar and Thalys special rates are available for accompanying adults. All airports are equipped to receive physically disabled passengers. Disabled drivers may use the EU blue card for parking entitlements. Information about accessibility is available from French disability organizations such as **Association des Paralysés de France** (17 bd. Auguste Blanqui, 75013 Paris; &01 40 78 69 00; www.apf.asso.fr), who also maintain a nationwide network of branches throughout the country.

The guide **Michelin Camping France** indicates camp sites with facilities suitable for the physically handicapped.

Getting There

BY PLANE

Numerous airlines, from national carriers to budget operators, fly into **Paris** several times each day.

The principal airports are Roissy-Charles de Gaulle, north of the city, and the smaller Orly, south of the city. Both airports have excellent transport links into the city.

Many airlines, especially on shorter-haul journeys, also operate services to **Nice**, **Lyon** and **Marseille**, as well as other provincial cities, including **Bordeaux**, **Mulhouse**, **Nantes**, **Toulouse**, **Montpellier**, **Perpignan** and **Nîmes**.

Most North American airlines fly to Paris only, but France's regional airports are well connected to both the Parisian airports and to each other.

Many have several flights a day to Paris. Many visitors from other European countries arrive on inclusive package-tour flights with a rail or coach link-up, as well as Fly-Drive schemes. Information, brochures and timetables are available from airlines, tour operators and travel agents.

CROSSING THE CHANNEL

Drivers travelling from the British Isles to France have a wide choice of **cross-Channel services**. For bookings and information, visit the operators' websites, contact them on the UK numbers given below, or ask any travel agent.

Brittany Ferries
From Cork (Ireland), Plymouth, Poole and Portsmouth to Roscoff, Cherbourg, St Malo and Caen.
&0871 244 0744
www.brittany-ferries.com

♦ **Irish Ferries**
Between Rosslare (Ireland) and Cherbourg or Roscoff.
&08717 300 400
www.irishferries.com

♦ **Norfolk Line**
Low cost Dover-Dunkerque car ferries. &0844 847 5042.
www.norfolkline-ferries.co.uk

♦ **P&O Ferries**
Car ferries between Dover and Calais. &08716 645 645.
www.poferries.com

♦ **SeaFrance**
Car ferries between Dover and Calais.
&0871 423 7119
www.seafrance.com

To choose the most suitable route between one of the ports along the north coast of France and your destination, use the **Michelin France Tourist and Motoring Atlas, Michelin map 726** (which gives travel times and mileages) or **Michelin Local Maps** (with yellow covers).

Eurotunnel
The fastest way across the English Channel – and you don't see the water. Drive straight onto a rail shuttle that travels through the Channel Tunnel between the M20 near Folkestone (junction 11A) and the A16 near Calais (junction 42). ℘08705 35 35 35 www.eurotunnel.com

BY COACH/BUS
Eurolines, together with National Express, operate regular services between all parts of the UK and towns throughout France. The main UK terminus is Victoria Coach Station, in central London.
℘08717 818 181 (in the UK) www.eurolines.com

BY CAR
France has an excellent network of major and minor roads covering long distances, including *autoroutes* – motorways or major highways, often with a toll to pay. Note that when entering the country at a land border, you may already be driving on an *autoroute*. After a short free section, a toll may be payable.

BY TRAIN
High-speed **Eurostar** trains run many times daily from London (St Pancras International) to **Paris** (Gare du Nord) via the Channel Tunnel. Some stop at Ebbsfleet (Kent), **Frethun** (near Calais) and **Lille**. The journey from London to Paris takes an average 2hrs15min. Fast onward rail services connect with Eurostar at Lille, or can be reached in Paris by transferring to other stations. Eurostar also operate services from London to **Disneyland Paris** and summer-only services to **Avignon**,

Gare du Nord, Paris
©Eurostar/Lydia Shalet

in Provence. In winter, Eurostar **ski trains** run from London direct to the French Alps. Eurostar can book onward rail services, hotels and car hire if required.
Railways within France are run by state-owned **SNCF**, who offer a range of rail passes for seniors, families, young people, and friends travelling together, as well as InterRail passes for Europe-wide travel. SNCF's subsidiary outside France is **Rail Europe**.

♦ **Eurostar**
℘08705 186 186
℘+44 1233 617 575
(from outside the UK)
www.eurostar.com

♦ **Rail Europe In the UK**
Rail Europe Travel Centre,
1 Lower Regent Street,
London SW1Y 4XT
℘08448 484 064.
www.raileurope.co.uk

♦ **In the US**
℘1-877 257 2887

♦ **SNCF** – Information and bookings in English by phone and on the internet. Or buy rail tickets at any SNCF train station in France.
℘08 90 36 10 10 (in France)
℘+33 892 35 35 35 (from outside France) www.sncf.com

Getting Around

BY TRAIN

Rail travel is a pleasure in France, where trains are comfortable, punctual and inexpensive. A comprehensive rail network, provided by the state's rail operator SNCF, covers almost the entire country. Their sleek, fast TGV trains operate between main towns, with door-to-door journey times that easily rival air travel, especially Paris-Lyon (2 hours) and Paris-Marseille (3 hours). TGVs must always be booked in advance, and all seats are reserved. However, it is often possible to reserve a TGV seat up to just a few minutes before the train departs. Apart from TGVs, the main city-to-city lines are also served by other comfortable modern trains which do not require advance booking. Away from these major lines, SNCF operates a reliable stopping service within each region, including a variety of smaller trains that reach into rural areas, sometimes supplemented by SNCF's bus services.

Before booking rail tickets, be sure to enquire at the station whether you are entitled to obtain one of the many rail **discount passes**. For example, groups of friends travelling together, or families with a young child, may be eligible. When first starting any journey by train, remember that rail tickets **must be validated** (composter)

☺ Speed Limits ☺

- **Toll motorways** (péage) 130kph/80mph (110kph/68mph when raining)
- **Dual carriage roads** and motorways without tolls 110kph/68mph (100kph/62mph when raining)
- **other roads** 90kph/56mph (80kph/50mph when raining) and in towns 50kph/31mph
- **outside lane** on motorways during daylight, on level ground and with good visibility
- **min speed limit** of 80kph/50mph

Petrol/Gasoline

In France the main types of fuel are:
sans plomb 95 – unleaded 95 octane
sans plomb 98 – unleaded 98 octane
diesel/gazole – diesel
The French Tourist Office issues a map showing the location of cheaper petrol stations within a mile or so of motorway exits, usually in a hyper-market complex.

by using the orange automatic date-stamping machines at the platform entrance.

BY CAR

Driving in France should not present much difficulty. For British drivers unaccustomed to driving on the right, extra care will be needed at first, but the rules of the road are otherwise similar to those in other Western countries. Road signs generally use easy-to-understand international visual symbols instead of words. When driving a motor vehicle in France, nationals of EU countries must be in possession of their own valid **national driving licence**. Nationals of non-EU countries should obtain an **international driving permit** (IDP). In the US, the State Department has authorised the American Automobile Association (www.aaa.com) and the National Automobile Club (www.thenac.com) to provide the international permit. To apply for an international driving permit, you must at least 18 years old, and you will need to present two passport-size photographs and your valid US licence. The international driving permit costs $15. The international permit does not replace your own driving licence but is simply an approved translation and should be used in conjunction with your licence – both should be carried. All drivers must also have with them the vehicle's registration papers and a current insurance certificate. The originals of all documents are required. Copies are not acceptable.

ENFORCEMENT

Police have wide powers to check documents at any time and to impose heavy on-the-spot fines for almost all driving offences. In the case of more serious offences, especially if alcohol is involved, they may at their own discretion confiscate the vehicle. If paying an on-the-spot fine, you should be given a copy of the officer's report form, a receipt for any money paid, and information on how to proceed if you wish to plead not guilty. In addition to carrying the correct documentation, the driver of a vehicle registered outside France is expected to display a nationality plate of approved size close to the registration plate on the back of the vehicle, unless this already forms part of the registration plate.

INSURANCE

Insurance cover is compulsory and although an International Motor Insurance Certificate (known in the UK as a green card) is no longer a legal requirement in France for vehicles registered in the UK, it is still the most effective proof of insurance cover and is internationally recognised by the police and other authorities. If you have comprehensive insurance, you may want to check that your insurance cover is unaffected by driving abroad. Some insurers wish to be informed if you intend to take your vehicle abroad. Most British insurance policies give only the minimum third-party cover required while in France – but this amounts to less than it would in the UK. Therefore check with your insurance company before leaving to ensure you are fully covered in the event of an accident.

Ensure you have adequate breakdown cover before arriving in France. UK motoring organisations, for example the **AA** and the **RAC**, offer accident insurance and breakdown service programmes, either on a yearly basis or for temporary periods, for both members and non-members. These offer an emergency phone number in the UK, and a reliable standard of service and workmanship provided locally but approved by the organisation.

Members of the **American Automobile Association** should obtain the free brochure *Offices To Serve You Abroad*. The affiliated organisation for France is the **Automobile Club National** (5 r. Auber, 75009 Paris; ℰ01 44 51 53 99).

HIGHWAY CODE

See **www.legifrance.gouv.fr.**

Age limits
Minimum driving age in France is 18.

Priorité à Droite
On all two-way roads, traffic drives on the right. The rule of *priorité à droite* also means that priority must be given – in other words, you must give way – to **all vehicles coming from the right, even from minor roads (but not private property), unless signs indicate otherwise.** The principal sign indicating that you have priority over all other roads, even those on the right, is a yellow diamond. In practice, the yellow diamond normally gives priority to traffic on all main roads outside built-up areas.

Traffic within a roundabout (traffic circle) has priority over vehicles entering the roundabout, unless signs indicate otherwise.

Traffic Signals
Vehicles must always stop when the lights turn red at road junctions. They may filter to the right **only where indicated by a flashing amber arrow**.

Seat belts/Safety belts
It is compulsory for the front-seat and back-seat passengers to wear **seat belts** where they are fitted. Children under the age of ten should not travel in the front of the car.

Lights

Full or dipped headlights must be switched on in rain, poor visibility and at night; use sidelights only when the vehicle is stationary. Headlight beams should be adjusted for driving on the right. It is illegal to drive with faulty lights in France, so it is advisable to take a spare set of bulbs with you.

Breakdown

In the case of a **breakdown**, a red warning triangle or hazard warning lights are obligatory.

Alcohol

The regulations on **drinking and driving** are strictly enforced. The maximum permissible blood alcohol content is currently 0.50g/l.

PARKING REGULATIONS

In most town centres parking is either prohibited or metered; tickets should be obtained from the ticket machines (*horodateurs* – small change necessary) and displayed inside the windscreen on the driver's side; failure to display may result in a heavy fine (and, in extreme cases, removal of the offending vehicle!). A common arrangement is that parking is permitted on one side of the street only. In most large towns there are "blue" parking zones (**zone bleue**), marked by a blue line on the pavement, blue lines around parking spaces, or a blue signpost with a P and a small square underneath. In this particular case motorists should display a "parking disc" which can be adjusted to display their time of arrival and which allows a stay of up to 1hr 30min (2hr30min over lunchtime) free. These discs are on sale in supermarkets, petrol stations or local kiosks (ask for a *disque de stationnement*).

ROUTE PLANNING

The road network is excellent and includes many motorways. The roads are very busy during the holiday period (particularly weekends in Jul and August), and to avoid traffic congestion it is advisable to follow the recommended secondary routes (signposted as *itinéraires bis*). The motorway network includes rest areas (*aires*) every 10–15km/6–10mi and service areas, with fuel, restaurant and shopping, about every 40km/25mi. For 24hr motorway information dial ✆01 47 05 90 01. For general information on traffic and *itinéraires bis*, contact Bison Futé; ✆0800 100 200; www.bison-fute.equipement.gouv.fr

TOLLS

In France, most motorway sections are subject to a toll (*péage*). Tolls can be paid in cash or with a credit card (Visa, Mastercard).

CAR RENTAL

There are car hire desks at airports, railway stations and in all large towns throughout France. The cars usually have manual transmission. Those wishing to rent a car with automatic transmission must book it in advance. The minimum age for car rental is generally 20 years, and there may be a premium payable for drivers under 25. It is relatively expensive to rent a car in France; Americans in particular will notice the difference and should consider booking a car from home before leaving, or taking advantage of Fly-Drive schemes. Those who rent a car before leaving home should make sure that they inform the car rental company that they intend to take the car to France, so that their rental contract includes insurance while abroad.

Reservation Numbers in France

♦ **Avis**
   ✆08 20 05 05 05
   www.avis.com
♦ **Europcar**
   ✆08 25 35 83 58
   www.europcar.com
♦ **Budget**
   ✆08 25 00 35 64
   www.budget.com
♦ **Hertz**
   ✆01 41 91 95 25
   www.hertz.com

Where to Stay and Eat

Hotel and restaurant listings fall within the *Discovering France* **section** of the guide; they can be found in the **Addresses** sections of the Principal Sights. To enhance your stay, hotel selections have been chosen for their location, comfort, value for the money, and in many cases, their charm. Prices indicate the cost of a standard room for two people in peak season.

French cuisine is as varied as it is delicious. We have highlighted an array of eating places primarily for their atmosphere, location and regional delicacies. Prices indicate the average cost of a starter, main dish and dessert for one person. The Legend on the cover flap explains the symbols and abbreviations used in the Addresses sections.

WHERE TO STAY
FINDING A HOTEL

The **Addresses** in this guide describe a number of lodgings arranged by price category. They appear in many of the cities and towns described in the guide. For an even greater selection, use the **Michelin Guide France**, with its famously reliable star-rating system and hundreds of establishments throughout France. The **Michelin Charming Places to Stay** guide contains a selection of 1 000 hotels and guest houses at reasonable prices. Be sure to book ahead to ensure that you get the accommodation you want, not only in the tourist season but year round, as many towns fill up during trade fairs, arts festivals etc. Some places require an advance deposit or a reconfirmation. Reconfirming is especially important if you plan to arrive after 6pm.

For further assistance, **Loisirs Accueil** is a booking service that has offices in some French départements: *280 bd St-Germain, 75007 Paris.* ☎01 44 11 10 44. www.loisirs-accueil.fr.

The handbook of a respected federation of good-value, family-run hotels (most with restaurants), **Logis et Auberges de France**, is available from the French Tourist Office, as are lists of other kinds of accommodation such as hotel-châteaux, bed-and-breakfasts, etc. Another resource, which publishes a catalogue for each French *département*, for vacation villas, apartments or chalets is the **Fédération Nationale des Locations de France Clévacances** (54 bd de l'Embouchure, BP 52166, 31022 Toulouse Cedex 2; ☎05 61 13 55 66; www.clevacances.com). **Relais & Châteaux** provides information on booking in luxury hotels with character (15 r. Galvani, 75017 Paris; ☎0825 32 32 32; www.relaischateux.com).

ECONOMY CHAIN HOTELS

If you need a place to stop en route, these lodgings can be useful, as they are inexpensive (around 35–45€ for a double room) and generally located near the main road. While a simple breakfast is available, there may not be a restaurant; rooms are small and functional, with a television and bathroom. All can be booked online.

For reservations

- **Akena**
  ☎01 69 84 85 17
  www.hotels-akena.com
- **Accor Hotels**
  ☎0825 88 00 00
  www.accorhotels.com/fr
- **Villages Hôtel**
  ☎03 80 60 92 70
  www.villages-hotel.com

The hotels listed below are expensive (from 45€), but offer more amenities.

For reservations

- **Campanile, Climat de France, Kyriad**
  ☎01 64 62 59 70
  www.campanile.com
- **Etap**
  ☎0892 688 900
  www.etaphotel.com
- **Ibis**
  ☎0892 686 686
  www.ibishotel.com

RENTING A COTTAGE, BED AND BREAKFAST

The **Maison des Gîtes de France** is an information service on self-catering accommodation in France. Gîtes usually take the form of a cottage or apartment decorated in the local style where visitors can make themselves at home, or bed and breakfast accommodation (chambres d'hôtes) which consists of a room and breakfast at a reasonable price. Contact the **Gîtes de France** office in Paris (56 r. St-Lazare, 75439 Paris Cedex 09; &01 49 70 75 75; www. gites-de-france.fr), which has a good English version. From the site, you can choose and book a gîte, or order catalogues for different regions illustrated with photographs of the properties, as well as specialised catalogues (bed and breakfasts, farm stays, etc.).

Regional sites also have information about cottages in their area, for example www.loire-valley-holidays. com, on which you can view and book cottages in the Loire Valley chateaux country and contact the local tourist offices which may have lists of more properties and local bed and breakfast establishments.

HOSTELS, CAMPING

The international youth hostels movement, International Youth Hostel Federation or Hostelling International, has dozens of hostels in France. There is an online booking service on www.hihostels.com, which you may use to reserve rooms as far as six months in advance. To stay in hostels, you may need a membership card. To obtain an IYHF or HI card (there is no age requirement) contact the IYHF or HI in your own country for information and membership applications (in the UK &01629 592700. In the US, there are many HI centres; check the website to find your nearest). There are two main youth hostel associations

(auberges de jeunesse) in France, the **Ligue Française pour les Auberges de la Jeunesse** (67 r. Vergniaud, 75013 Paris, &01 44 16 78 78; www. auberges-de-jeunesse.com) and the **Fédération Unie des Auberges de Jeunesse** (27 r. Pajol, 75018 Paris, &01 44 89 87 27, Fax 01 44 89 87 10). There are thousands of officially graded **campsites** with varying standards of facilities throughout the country. The **Michelin Camping France** guide lists a selection of camp sites. It is wise to reserve in advance.

WHERE TO EAT
FINDING A RESTAURANT

Turn to the Addresses within the *Discovering France* section for descriptions and prices of selected places to eat in the different locations covered in this guide. The Legend on the cover flap explains the symbols and abbreviations used in these Addresses. Use the red-cover **Michelin Guide France**, with its respected star-rating system and hundreds of establishments all over France, for an even greater choice. If you would like to experience a meal in a highly rated restaurant from the **red-cover Michelin Guide**, be sure to book ahead. Restaurants usually serve lunch between noon–2pm and dinner between 7.30–10pm. It is not always easy to find something to eat at other times, except for a simple baguette sandwich in a café, or an ordinary hot dish in a brasserie.

In French restaurants and cafés, the service charge and all taxes are included in the price, so tipping is not necessary. However, it is usual to leave any small change from the bill on the table when leaving.

For a glossary of gastronomic terms and for information on local specialities, ⌕see the section entitled Food and Drink in the Introduction.

Useful Words and Phrases

Sights

	Translation
Abbey	Abbaye
Belfry	Beffroi
Bridge	Pont
Castle	Château
Cemetery	Cimetière
Chapel	Chapelle
Church	Église
Cloisters	Cloître
Convent	Couvent
Courtyard	Cour
Fountain	Fontaine
Garden	Jardin
Gateway	Porte
Hall	Halle
House	Maison
Lock (Canal)	Écluse
Market	Marché
Monastery	Monastère
Museum	Musée
Park	Parc
Port/harbour	Port
Quay	Quai
Ramparts	Remparts
Square	Place
Street	Rue
Statue	Statue
Tower	Tour
Town Hall	Mairie
Windmill	Moulin

Natural Sites

	Translation
Abyss	Abîme
Swallow-hole	Aven
Dam	Barrage
Viewpoint	Belvédère
Waterfall	Cascade
Pass	Col
Ledge	Corniche
Coast, Hillside	Côte
Forest	Forêt
Cave	Grotte

Lake	Lac
Beach	Plage
River	Rivière
Stream	Ruisseau
Beacon	Signal
Spring	Source
Valley	Vallée

On the Road

	Translation
Car Park	Parking
Driving Licence	Permis de conduire
East	Est
Garage (For Repairs)	Garage
Left	Gauche
Motorway/highway	Autoroute
North	Nord
Parking Meter	Horodateur
Petrol/gas	Essence
Petrol/gas Station	Station essence
Right	Droite
South	Sud
Toll	Péage
Traffic Lights	Feu tricolore
Tyre	Pneu
West	Ouest
Wheel Clamp	Sabot
Zebra Crossing	Passage clouté

Time

	Translation
Today	Aujourd'hui
Tomorrow	Demain
Yesterday	Hier
Winter	Hiver
Spring	Printemps
Summer	Été
Autumn/fall	Automne
Week	Semaine
Monday	Lundi
Tuesday	Mardi
Wednesday	Mercredi
Thursday	Jeudi
Friday	Vendredi
Saturday	Samedi
Sunday	Dimanche

Numbers

	Translation
0	zéro
1	un
2	deux
3	trois
4	quatre
5	cinq
6	six
7	sept
8	huit
9	neuf
10	dix
11	onze
12	douze
13	treize
14	quatorze
15	quinze
16	seize
17	dix-sept
18	dix-huit
19	dix-neuf
20	vingt
30	trente
40	quarante
50	cinquante
60	soixante
70	soixante-dix
80	quatre-vingt
90	quatre-vingt-dix
100	cent
1000	mille

Shopping

	Translation
Bank	Banque
Baker's	Boulangerie
Big	Grand
Butcher's	Boucherie
Chemist's	Pharmacie
Closed	Fermé
Cough Mixture	Sirop pour la toux
Cough Sweets	Cachets pour la gorge
Entrance	Entrée
Exit	Sortie
Fishmonger's	Poissonnerie
Grocer's	Épicerie
Newsagent, Bookshop	Librairie
Open	Ouvert
Post Office	Poste
Push	Pousser
Pull	Tirer
Shop	Magasin
Small	Petit
Stamps	Timbres

Food and Drink

	Translation
Beef	Bœuf
Beer	Bière
Butter	Beurre
Bread	Pain
Breakfast	Petit-déjeuner
Cheese	Fromage
Dessert	Dessert
Dinner	Dîner
Fish	Poisson
Fork	Fourchette
Fruit	Fruits
Glass	Verre
Chicken	Poulet
Ice Cream	Glace
Ice Cubes	Glaçons
Ham	Jambon
Knife	Couteau
Lamb	Agneau
Lunch	Déjeuner
Lettuce Salad	Salade
Meat	Viande
Mineral Water	Eau minérale
Mixed Salad	Salade composée
Orange Juice	Jus d'orange
Plate	Assiette

Fromage - Brie de Meaux

S. Sauvignier/MICHELIN

Pork	Porc
Restaurant	Restaurant
Red Wine	Vin rouge
Salt	Sel
Spoon	Cuillère
Sugar	Sucre
Vegetables	Légumes
Water	De L'eau
White/red wine	Vin blanc/rouge
Yoghurt	Yaourt

Travel

Travel	Voyager
Airport	Aéroport
Credit Card	Carte de crédit
Customs	Douane
Passport	Passeport
Platform	Voie
Railway Station	Gare
Shuttle	Navette
Suitcase	Valise
Train Ticket	Billet de train
Plane Ticket	Billet d'avion
Wallet	Portefeuille

Clothing

	Translation
Coat	Manteau
Jumper	Pull
Raincoat	Imperméable
Shirt	Chemise
Shoes	Chaussures
Socks	Chaussettes
Stockings	Bas
Suit	Costume
Tights	Collants
Trousers	Pantalon

Common Words

	Translation
Goodbye	Au revoir
Hello/good Morning	Bonjour
How	Comment
Excuse Me	Excusez-moi
Thank You	Merci
Yes/no	Oui/non
I Am Sorry	Pardon
Why	Pourquoi

When	Quand
Please	S'il vous plaît

USEFUL PHRASES

Do you speak English?
Parlez-vous anglais?
I don't understand
Je ne comprends pas
Talk slowly
Parlez lentement
Where's...?.
Où est...?
When does the ... leave?
A quelle heure part...?
When does the ... arrive?
A quelle heure arrive...?
When does the museum open?
A quelle heure ouvre le musée?
When is the show?
A quelle heure est la
représentation?
When is breakfast served?
A quelle heure sert-on le
petit-déjeuner?
What does it cost?
Combien cela coûte?
Where can I buy a newspaper in English?
Où puis-je acheter un journal
en anglais?
Where is the nearest petrol/ gas station?
Où se trouve la station essence
la plus proche?
Where can I change traveller's cheques?
Où puis-je changer un traveller's
chèque
Where are the toilets?
Où sont les toilettes?
Do you accept credit cards?..
Acceptez-vous les cartes de crédit?

GASTRONOMIC TERMS

*See Food and Drink in the
Introduction section.*

Basic Information

BUSINESS HOURS

Offices and other businesses are open Mon–Fri, 9am–noon, 2–6pm. Many also open Saturday mornings. Town and village shops are generally open Tue–Fri; there are local variations. Midday breaks may be much longer in the South. However, in cities, tourist centres or resorts, businesses may keep longer hours or stay open all day, seven days a week, especially if they primarily serve the tourist market.

ELECTRICITY

The electric current is 220 volts/50 Hz. Circular two-pin plugs are the rule. Adapters should be bought before you leave home; they are on sale in most airports.

EMERGENCIES

See Emergency Numbers box.
First aid, medical advice and chemists' night-service rotas are available from chemists/drugstores (*pharmacie,* identified by a green cross sign). American Express offers its cardholders a service, "Global Assist", for any medical, legal or personal emergency: 01 47 77 70 00.

EMERGENCY NUMBERS	
Police (Gendarme):	17
Fire (Pompiers):	18
Ambulance (SAMU):	15

MAIL/POST

Look for the bright yellow *La Poste* signs. Main post offices are generally open Mon–Fri 9am–7pm, Sat 9am–noon. Smaller branches generally open 9am–noon, 2–4pm weekdays. There are often automatic tellers (*guichets automatiques*) inside which allow you to weigh packages and buy postage and avoid a queue. You may also find that you can use a Minitel, change money, make copies, send faxes and make phone calls in a post office. To mail a letter from the street look for the bright yellow post boxes. Stamps are also sold in newsagents and cafés that sell cigarettes (*tabac*). Stamp collectors should ask for *timbres de collection* in any post office (there is often a *philatélie* counter). France uses a five-digit postal code that precedes the name of the city or town on the last line of the address. The first two digits indicate the *département* and the last three digits identify the *commune* or local neighbourhood. www.laposte.fr.

✉ POSTAGE VIA AIR MAIL		
UK	Letter	(20g) 0.65€
North America	Letter	(20g) 0.85€
	Postcard	0.85€
Australia	Letter	(20g) 0.85€
	Postcard	0.85€
New Zealand	Letter	(20g) 0.85€
	Postcard	0.85€

MONEY
CURRENCY

There are no restrictions on the amount of currency visitors can take into France. Visitors wishing to export currency in foreign banknotes in excess of the given allocation from France should complete a currency declaration form on arrival.

Coins and notes – The unit of currency in France is the **euro** (€). One euro is divided into 100 cents or *centimes d'euro*. Old franc notes can still be exchanged by the Banque de France until early 2012.

BANKS AND CURRENCY EXCHANGE

Banks are generally open between Mon–Fri 9am–5.30pm. Some branches are open for limited transactions on Saturday. Banks limit opening hours on the day before a bank holiday. A passport or other ID may be necessary when cashing cheques (travellers' or ordinary) in banks.

Commission charges vary and hotels usually charge considerably more than banks for cashing cheques, especially for non-residents.

By far the most convenient way of obtaining French currency is the **24hr cash dispenser** or **ATM** (*distributeur automatique de billets* in French), found outside many banks and post offices and easily recognisable by the CB (Carte Bleue) logo. Most accept international credit cards (don't forget your PIN) and almost all also give instructions in English. Note that American Express cards can be used only in dispensers operated by the Crédit Lyonnais bank or by American Express. Foreign currency can also be exchanged in major banks, post offices, hotels or private exchange offices found in main cities and near popular tourist attractions.

CREDIT CARDS

Major credit cards (Visa, Mastercard, Eurocard) are widely accepted in shops, hotels, restaurants and petrol stations. However, pay-at-the-pump automatic petrol stations normally only accept cards issued by French banks – foreign cards cannot be used. If your card is lost or stolen call the appropriate 24hr hotlines:

American Express ✆ (01) 4777 72 00
Visa ✆ (08) 36 69 08 80
Mastercard ✆ 0800 90 13 87

You should also report any loss or theft to the local police who will issue you with a certificate (useful proof to show the credit card company).

PUBLIC HOLIDAYS

There are 11 public holidays in France. In addition, there are other religious and national festivals days, and a number of local saints' days, etc. On all these days, museums and other monuments may be closed or may vary their hours of admission.

SCHOOL HOLIDAYS

French schools close for holidays five times a year. In these periods, all tourist sites and attractions, hotels, restaurants,

PUBLIC HOLIDAYS	
1 January	New Years Day (*Jour de l'An*)
13 April	Easter Monday (*Pâques*)
1 May	Labour Day
8 May	VE Day
Thurs 40 days after Easter	Ascension Day (*Ascension catholique*)
1 June	Whit Monday (*Pentecôte*)
14 July	*Fête* National France's National Day (or Bastille Day)
15 August	Assumption (*Assomption*)
1 November	All Saints Day (*Toussaint*)
11 November	Armistice Day
25 December	Christmas Day (*Noël*)

and roads are busier than usual. These school holidays are one week at the end of October, two weeks at Christmas, two weeks in February, two weeks in spring, and the whole of Jul and August.

SMOKING REGULATIONS

In February 2007, France banned smoking in public places such as offices, universities and railway stations. The law became effective for restaurants, cafés, bars, nightclubs and casinos in January 2008.

TELEPHONES

The telephone system in France is still operated largely by the former state monopoly France Télécom. They offer an English-language enquiries service on ✆ 0800 364 775 (within France) or ✆ 00 33 1 55 78 60 56 (outside France). The French **ringing tone** is a series of long tones; the engaged (busy) tone is a series of short beeps.

To use a **public phone** you need to buy a prepaid phone card (*télécartes*). Some telephone booths accept credit cards (Visa, Mastercard/Eurocard). *Télécartes* (50 or 120 units) can be bought in post offices, cafés that sell cigarettes (*tabac*) and newsagents, and can be used to make calls in France and abroad. Calls can be received at phone boxes where the blue bell sign is shown.

MOBILE/CELL PHONES

While in France, all visitors from other European countries should be able to use their cell phone just as normal. Visitors from some other countries notably the US, need to ensure before departure that their phone and service contract are compatible with the European system (GSM).

All the charges are given in the 'welcome' message you will receive on using your phone for the first time in France. The three main mobile phone operators in France are SFR, Orange and Bouygues. If you do not have your cell phone with you, or you discovered it would not be compatible with the European system, depending on the length of your visit and on how often you plan on using the phone, it may be wise to consider buying or renting one with a coverage plan that fits your needs. There are a variety of options you can choose from making it less expensive than you might imagine.

Orange www.orange.fr
Bouygues www.bouyguestelecom.fr
SFR www.sfr.fr

NATIONAL CALLS

French telephone numbers have 10 digits. Numbers begin with 01 in Paris and the Paris region; 02 in northwest France; 03 in northeast France; 04 in southeast France and Corsica; 05 in southwest France. However, all 10 numbers must be dialled even with the local region.

INFORMATION
International Information **UK** ℰ 00 33 12 44
International Information **USA/Canada** ℰ 00 33 12 11
International Operator ℰ 00 33 12 + country code
Local Directory Assistance ℰ 12

INTERNATIONAL DIALLING CODES	
Australia	61
Eire	353
United Kingdom	44
Canada	1
New Zealand	64
United States	1

INTERNATIONAL CALLS

To call France from abroad, dial the country code 33, omit the initial zero of the French number, and dial the remaining 9-digit number. When calling abroad from France dial 00, followed by the country code (see below), followed by the local area code (usually without any initial zero), and the number of your correspondent.

To use the personal calling card of a telephone company, follow the instructions on the card, dialling the access code for the country you are in, e.g.:

AT&T ℰ 0800 99-0011
BT ℰ 0800 99-0244
MCI/Verizon ℰ 0800 99-0019
Sprint ℰ 0800 99-0087
Canada Direct ℰ 0800 99-0016

Cheap rates with 50% extra time are available from private telephones to the UK on weekdays 9.30pm–8am, from 2pm on Saturdays and all day on Sundays and holidays. Cheap rates to the USA and Canada are from 2am–noon all week, and to Australia Mon–Sat 9.30pm–8am and all day Sunday.

Toll-free numbers in France (also known as Numéro Verte) begin with 0800.

For more information about using phones in France, visit
www.orange.fr

TIME

France is in the Central European time zone. During the winter months, from 2am on the last Sunday of October to 2am on the last Sunday of March, France is one hour ahead of GMT. From

TEMPERATURE CHART THROUGHOUT FRANCE

	Jan	Feb	Mar	Apr	May	Jun	Jul	Aug	Sep	Oct	Nov	Dec
	9	10	15	17	20	23	25	25	23	18	12	8
Bordeaux	1	2	4	9	12	13	13	13	12	8	4	2
	8	9	11	13	15	18	19	20	18	15	11	9
Brest	4	3	4	7	8	11	12	13	11	8	6	4
	7	8	13	16	19	23	25	25	22	16	11	7
Clermont	-1	-1	2	5	7	11	13	12	10	6	3	0
	5	8	13	16	20	23	26	26	23	16	10	6
Grenoble	-3	-2	2	5	8	12	14	13	11	6	3	-1
	5	6	10	13	17	20	22	22	19	14	9	6
Lille	0	0	2	4	7	10	12	12	10	7	3	1
	12	13	14	17	20	23	26	26	24	20	16	13
Nice	4	4	5	9	12	16	18	16	12	8	5	
	7	7	12	15	19	22	24	24	21	15	10	6
Paris	1	1	3	6	9	12	14	14	11	8	4	2
	12	13	16	18	21	25	28	28	25	20	15	12
Perpignan	3	4	7	9	12	16	19	18	16	12	8	5
	3	5	11	15	19	23	24	25	20	14	8	4
Strasbourg	-2	-1	1	4	6	11	13	13	10	5	2	-1

Maximum temperatures in red; minimum temperatures in black.

WHEN IT IS **NOON IN FRANCE,** IT IS	
11am	in London
7pm	in Perth
11am	in Dublin
9pm	in Sydney
6am	in New York
11pm	in Auckland
3am	in Los Angeles

2am on the last Sunday of March to 2am on the last Sunday of October, it adopts daylight saving time and is two hours ahead of GMT.

Because the UK changes its clocks to British Summer Time (i.e. daylight saving time) at the same times and on the same dates, France always remains one hour ahead of the UK.

In France the 24-hour clock is widely applied.

TIPPING

Under French law, any service charge (as well as any taxes) is automatically included in the prices displayed for meals and accommodation. Any additional tipping in restaurants and hotels is therefore unnecessary and is entirely at the discretion of the visitor. However, in bars and cafés it is not unusual to leave any small change that remains after paying the bill, but this generally should not be more than 5 per cent. Taxi drivers do not have to be tipped, but again is usual to give a small amount, not more than 10%. Attendants at public toilets should be given a few cents. Hairdressers are usually tipped 10–15 per cent. Tour guides and tour drivers should be tipped according to the amount of service given: from 2 to 5 euros would not be unusual.

Pont Alexandre III at dusk, Paris
©Paul Reid/Dreamstime.com

France Today

21ST CENTURY

France still retains a strong rural tradition and, even though there are fewer people employed in agriculture than previously, many French people still have close ties with the land.

Nevertheless, France has a very advanced industrial economy although many believe that restrictive practices are holding back progress. The election of Nicolas Sarkozy as President in 2007 seemed to signal a new direction and his declared intention to free up the labour market, cut taxes and red tape and take a less protectionist stance, will make for an interesting period in French social and political life.

LIFESTYLE

For many the concept of the French lifestyle conjures up images of good living with an emphasis on strong family values and traditions. While this remains true for many, there has been a tendency in recent years for busy families to spend less time together and eat less well. This has led some social commentators to take the view that all is not well with french society.

POPULATION

The total population of France on Jan 1 2008 was 63,753,000, an increase of 361,000 over the previous year. Fewer babies were born in 2007, yet France remains one of the most fertile countries in Europe. The average age at marriage was 31.3 for men and 29.3 for women, although the rate of marriage is falling with many preferring to cohabit. France continues to have the longest-living citizens in Europe – for men life expectancy is 77.5 years while for women it is 84.4.

RELIGION

Freedom of religion is guaranteed by the Constitution and there is a strict separation of church and state.

However, France has traditionally been a Catholic country and approximately 80% of the population are thought to be Catholic although the numbers attending church have fallen considerably in recent years.

SPORT

The most watched sport in France is Football and the the success of 'Les Bleus', especially in 1998 and 2000, reinforced this. Both Rugby codes are also very popular as are Tennis and Cycling which are also mass participatory sports. Petanque or Boules are played anywhere there is a small patch of level ground and is taken very seriously indeed!

MEDIA

Newspapers, both national and local, and magazines are readily available at the many *maisons de la presse* (newsagents) which are to be found in all towns. English language newspapers such as the Guardian Weekly and International Herald Tribune are usually only available in larger centres. The internet is now widely available in hotels, fast-food outlets, internet cafés and even the local bar.

ECONOMY AND GOVERNMENT

France has both an entrenched bureaucracy and a vibrant democracy, with a parliament of 577 *députés* elected every five years and a president also elected every five years. The president has extensive personal powers. At the same time, France is divided into 22 regions with a high degree of autonomy, and within each region is a multitude of communes where there is a good deal of local self-determination under powerful mayors. Within the nation is a profound division between a disciplinarian right wing tendency and an equally authoritarian Socialist tradition. This authoritarianism goes hand in hand with an unruly streak that brings frequent strikes, demonstrations and even riots. In deference to the danger of unrest, the government frequently backs down in the face of popular protest, giving in to demands.

Economically, France has followed its own path, favouring extensive employee rights, state monopolies, state intervention, heavy subsidies and protectionism. In 2008 France was ranked the eight largest economy in the world just behind the UK.

FOOD AND DRINK

France is the land of good food and good living and it has a host of regional specialities. In addition to the **Michelin Guide France**, which describes hundreds of hotels and restaurants throughout the country, here are examples of traditional fare.

FRENCH CUISINE

Soups and Consommés

The best-known are cream of asparagus (*velouté d'asperges*), leek and potato (*soupe de poireaux-pommes de terre*), onion (*soupe à l'oignon or gratinée*), lobster (*bisque de homard*), *garbure* (a thick soup with cabbage popular in southwestern France), and *cotriade* (Breton fish soup), all of which are served at the start of a meal.

Hors d'œuvres

There are countless ways to begin a meal and French chefs have boundless imagination in this respect. The following, though, deserve a special mention: *salade niçoise* (tomatoes, anchovies, onions, olives), *salade lyonnaise* (using of Honfleur in Normandy, and of the bass grilled with fennel (*loup grillé au fenouil*) or baked over a fire of vine shoots (*au sarment de vigne*), a dish that is popular in Provence and on the Riviera. There are so many regional dishes that only a glimpse can be provided of the delights in store.

The best-known local meat dishes include Strasbourg sauerkraut (*choucroute* - cabbage, potatoes, pork, sausages and ham), Toulouse or Castelnaudary *cassoulet* (bean stew with pieces of goose or duck and pork-meat products), Caen-style tripe (*tripes à la mode de Caen*), Rouen pressed duck (*canard au sang*), Burgundy *meurette* (wine sauce) that is as good an accompaniment for poached eggs as for brains or beef – cooked Burgundy-style, of course! Also well worth a

mention are Auvergne *potée* (cabb... piece of pork, bacon and turnips) or ... cousin from Franche-Comté (cabbage, Morteau or Montbéliard sausage), *aligot* (a creamy blend of fresh tomme cheese and mashed potato seasoned with garlic) from Chaudes-Aigues, *tripoux* from Aurillac, Basque-style chicken (*poulet basquaise* with tomatoes and pimentoes), rabbit (*lapin*) *chasseur* and rabbit *forestier* (with mushrooms and diced bacon).

Cheese

There is such a wide range of cheeses that it is difficult to know them all, so it is worth defining the main "families":

I – Soft cheeses
   a) Cheese with surface mould (Brie de Meaux, Camembert, Chaource, etc)
   b) Cheese with washed rind (Livarot, Reblochon, Munster, Vacherin, etc)
   c) Cheese with natural rind (Tomme de Romans, Cendres de Bourgogne, Brie de Melun, etc.)

II – Hard pressed non-boiled cheeses
   (Cantal, Fourme de Laguiole, Gapron d'Auvergne, etc)

III – Hard pressed boiled cheeses
   (Emmental de Savoie, Comté de Franche-Comté, Beaufort de Savoie, and Beaufort de Dauphiné, etc)

IV – Blue cheeses
   a) Blue cheeses with natural crust (Bleu de Bresse, Bleu de Corse, Fourme de Montbrison, etc)
   b) Scraped blue cheeses (Roquefort, Bleu d'Auvergne, Bleu des Causses, etc).

V – Processed Cheeses
   Such as Crème de Gruyère, spreads with grapes or walnuts, and a whole range of cheese spreads.

ANCE TODAY

Galette de sarrasin with ham and egg

S. Sauvignier/MICHELIN

Fruit and Desserts

There are innumerable **desserts** to round off a meal. Apart from the baskets of fruit, strawberries and cream or strawberries in red wine, fruit salads and macedoines using all the orchard fruits, there are apple, pear, and peach compotes, and all sorts of cakes, such as *tarte Tatin* (a caramelised tart cooked with the filling underneath), Grenoble walnut cake (*gâteau aux noix*), Breton *far* (a baked custard dessert), gingerbread (*pain d'épices*) in the Gâtinais region, *clafoutis* (a blend of milk and eggs mixed with fruit and baked in the oven), and *kougelhopf* from Alsace baked in the form of a ring and served as a dessert or as an afternoon snack. Not to mention all the crème caramels, baked cream desserts, and soft meringues with custard sauce (*île flottante*) that are found in nearly every region of France.

Côtes du Rhône wines

J. Damase/MICHELIN

THE WINES OF FRANCE

The wines of France encompass every variety of taste from the sweetest whites to the driest, from rich, full-bodied reds to light easy-drinking roses, from unpretentious, drinkable tables wines to the greatest names in the world, including of course, the very symbol of celebration and delight, champagne.

For wine lovers, the **Michelin Guide The Wine Regions of France** offers a comprehensive introduction to French wine-making and features driving itineraries for the 14 main wine regions of the country: Alsace, Beaujolais, Le Bordelais (Bordeaux wines), Burgundy, Champagne, Cognac, Corse (Corsican wines), Jura, Languedoc-Roussillon, Loire Valley, Provence, Rhone Valley, Savoie-Bugey and the Southwest. Descriptions of over 500 restaurants, hotels and guest houses are included in this guide to enhance your journey through these regions.

See also the French regional **Michelin Green Guides** for the specific region in which you are interested, for example the *Green Guide Provence* describes Provençal wines.

The official French wine website, www.wines-france.com, features information about grapes, wine labels, France's wine regions and more.

FOOD GLOSSARY

Aïoli - Garlic mayonnaise
Andouille - Large chitterling sausage
Andouillettes - Chitterling sausages
Anis - Aniseed confectionery
Asperges - Asparagus
Bergamotes - Orange-flavoured sweets
Berlingots - Humbugs
Bêtises - Hard mints
Beurre blanc - White butter sauce
Bouillabaisse - Seafood stew
Bourride - Fish soup
Brandade - Creamed salt-cod
Cagouilles - Snails
Calissons - Almond and crystallised fruit sweetmeats
Canard au sang - Pressed duck
Cassoulet Stew with haricot beans and pork rinds

Cedrats confits - Crystallised citrus fruit
Cèpes - Cèpe mushrooms
Charcuterie - Smoked, cured or dried meats
Chipirones - Small cuttlefish, often stuffed
Choucroute - Sauerkraut
Confiseries - Confectionery
Confits - Goose preserved in fat
Crêpes dentelles - Thin pancakes
Dragées - Sugared almonds
Escargots - Snails
Esturgeons - Sturgeon
Far - Flan with prunes
Ficelles picardes - Ham pancakes with mushroom sauce
Foie gras - Goose liver
Fouace - Dough cakes
Fraises - Strawberries
Fruits confits - Crystallised fruit
Galettes - Thick pancakes or waffles
Gâteau d'amandes - Almond cake
Garbure - Meat and vegetable stew
Gratins - Dishes with a crusty topping
Jambon - Ham
Jambon cru des Ardennes - Ardennes cured ham
Kouign-Amam - Cake
Kougelhopf - Plain yeast cake
Lamproies - Lampreys
Macarons - Macaroons
Madeleines - Small sponge cakes
Magrets - Breast of duck
Marrons glacés - Crystallised chestnuts
Massepains - Marzipan cakes
Matelote - Eel stew
Meurette - Wine sauce
Mouclade - Mussel stew
Moutarde - Mustard
Mouton de pré-salé - Salt-pasture lamb
Noix - Nuts
Nougat - Sugar, honey and nut sweetmeat
Nougatine - Caramel syrup and almond sweetmeat
Ortolans - Buntings
Oursins - Sea urchins
Pain d'épice - Spiced honey cake
Pâté d'alouette - Lark paté

Espelette peppers and Basque charcuterie

B. Kaufmann/MICHELIN

Pâté de merle - Blackbird paté
Pauchouse - Fish stew with wine
Pieds de cochon   Pigs' trotters
Piperade Sweet pepper and tomato omelette
Poulardes - Chickens
Pralines - Caramelised almond confectionery
Pruneaux Prunes
Quenelles - Poached meat or fish dumplings
Quenelles de brochet - Poached Pike dumplings
Quiche (Lorraine) - Egg, cream andbacon flan
Rillettes - Potted pork
Rillons - Potted chopped pork
Saupiquet - Spiced wine sauce
Saucisse de Morteau - Morteau sausage
Saucisson - Dried sausage
Soupe au pistou - Vegetable soup with basil
Touron - Soft almond confectionery
Tourteau fromager - Goats' cheese gateau
Tripes - Tripe
Tripoux - Stuffed tripe
Truffes - Truffles
Volailles - Poultry

History

The great sweep of prehistory has left abundant traces in France, and it is to Frenchmen that much of our knowledge of prehistoric times is due. 👆*See Les EYZIES-DE-TAYAC: Prehistory.*

TIME LINE
ANCIENT TIMES

BC 5000	Megalithic culture flourishes in Brittany (Carnac), then in Corsica, lasting for over 2 500 years.
8C	Celtic tribes from central Europe arrive in Gaul where they build the fortified settlements known as oppidums.
600	Greek traders found a number of cities, including Marseille, Glanum (👆*see ST-RÉMY-DE-PROVENCE)* and Aléria in Corsica.
2C	Celtic culture, which had spread as far as Brittany, gives way to both Germanic and Roman influences. The port of Fréjus, on the Mediterranean coast, is founded in 154 by the Romans as a link on the sea-route to their possessions in Spain. By the year 122 they have established themselves at Aix, and four years later at Narbonne.
58–52	Julius Caesar's Gallic Wars. He defeats the Veneti in 56 BC (👆*see VANVES)*, then himself suffers defeat at the hands of Vercingetorix (👆*see CLERMONT-FERRAND)* in 52 BC, though the latter's surrender comes only a few months later.
AD 1C	During the reign of Augustus Roman rule in Gaul is consolidated and expanded (👆*see NÎMES)*. Fréjus is converted into a naval base and fortified.

5C	The monasteries set up by St Martin at Ligugé and by St Honorat at Lérins reinforce Christian beliefs and mark the beginning of a wave of such foundations (by St Victor at Marseille, by St Loup at Troyes, by St Maxime at Riez).

THE MEROVINGIANS (418–751)

451	Merovius, king of the Salian Franks (from the Tournai area in present-day Belgium), defeats Attila the Hun (👆*see CHÂLONS-EN-CHAMPAGNE).* It is to him that the dynasty owes its name.
476	Fall of the Roman Empire in the West; Gaul occupied by barbarian tribes.
496	Clovis, grandson of Merovius and King of the Franks, is baptised in Reims.
507	Defeat of the Visigoths under Alaric II at Vouillé (👆*see POITIERS)* by Clovis.
6C	Accompanied by Christian missionaries, settlers from Britain arrive in the Breton peninsulas, displacing the original Celtic inhabitants. But they too are overcome, first by the Franks (in the 9C), then by the Angevins (11C).
732	The Arab armies invading France are defeated at Moussais-la-Bataille (👆*see POITIERS)* by Charles Martel.

THE CAROLINGIANS (751–986)

751	Pepin the Short has himself elected king by an assembly of magnates and bishops at Soissons, sending the powerless Childeric, last of the Merovingians, to a monastery.
800	Charlemagne is crowned Emperor of the West in Rome.

THE GROWTH OF FRANCE

ARTOIS 1191

FLANDRES 1305

PICARDIE 1185-1214

NORMANDIE 1204

CHAMPAGNE 1314

LORRAINE 1766

PARIS

ALSACE 1648

PERCHE 1525

BRETAGNE 1532

MAINE 1204

ORLÉANAIS 1498

BOURGOGNE 1361

FRANCHE-COMTÉ 1678

ANJOU 1204

TOURAINE 1204

NIVERNAIS 1789

BERRY 1100

BRESSE 1601

POITOU 1204

BOURBONNAIS 1269

BUGEY

AUNIS 1224

ANGOUMOIS 1308

MARCHE 1269

LYONNAIS 1312

SAVOIE 1860

SAINTONGE 1224

LIMOSIN 1224

AUVERGNE 1269

DAUPHINÉ 1349

1947

PÉRIGORD 1224

GUYENNE-GASCOGNE 1591

COMTAT VENAISSIN 1791

COMTÉ DE NICE 1860

1947

COMTÉ DE TOULOUSE 1271

HAUT-LANGUEDOC 1271

PROVENCE 1486

BÉARN 1591

COMTÉ DE FOIX 1591

BAS-LANGUEDOC 1226

ROUSSILLON 1642

CORSE 1769

The original "France" of the Merovingians and Carolingians.

Aquisitions under the Direct Capetians.

Expansion under the Valois.

Expansion under the Bourbons.

Territorial gains during the French Revolution, under the Second Empire and under the Republics.

842	The Strasbourg Oaths.
843	By the Treaty of Verdun, the Carolingian Empire is divided between the sons of Louis I, Charles the Bald receiving the territories to the west, roughly corresponding to modern France.
850	Nominoé (◖ see VANNES) wrests eastern Brittany and the Rais country south of the Loire from its Frankish rulers.
910	Foundation of the great abbey at Cluny.
911	By the Treaty of St-Clair-sur-Epte, Charles the Simple and the Viking chief Rollo create the Duchy of Normandy.

THE CAPETIANS (987–1789)

The Direct Capetians (987–1328)

987	A descendant of Robert the Strong, Hugh Capet, Duke of "France", ousts Charles of Lorraine and has himself elected. By having his son crowned during his own lifetime, he consolidated his family's rule, which nevertheless does not become truly hereditary until the accession of Philippe Auguste in 1180.
1066	**William Duke of Normandy** (◖ see BAYEUX and CAEN) sets out for the English coast from Dives. His victory over Harold at the Battle of Hastings leads to his coronation as King of England, though technically speaking he is still a vassal of the French king.
1095	The First Crusade is preached at Clermont-Ferrand.

7 Louis VII weds Eleanor of Aquitaine (*see BORDEAUX*); the annulment of their marriage 15 years later is a disaster for the dynasty.
Foundation of the School of Medicine at Montpellier.

1204 Gaillard Castle falls to Philippe Auguste, who goes on to conquer Normandy, Maine, Touraine and Anjou.

1209 Start of the Albigensian Crusade.

1214 Victory at the Battle of Bouvines (*see LILLE*); for the first time, a genuinely French patriotism appears.

1244 Cathars burnt at the funeral pyre at Montségur.

1270 St Louis (Louis IX) dies aboard ship off Tunis on his way to the Eighth Crusade.

THE HOUSE OF VALOIS (1328-1589)

The Hundred Years' War – 1337–1475

Extending over six reigns, the war was both a political and dynastic struggle between Plantagenets and Capetians over who should rule in France. Accompanied by plague (including the Black Death of 1348) and religious confusion, it was a time of tribulation for the people of France, harassed as they were by bands of outlaws as well as by the English soldiery.

In 1337, Philippe VI of Valois resisted the claims to his throne made by Edward III of England, who was the grandson, on his mother's side of Philippe le Bel (the Fair). This marked the beginning of the war. Three years after the French defeat at Crécy, Philippe VI purchased the Dauphiné, up to then a territory of the Empire, from its ruler, Humbert II, thereby extending French rule far to the east of the Rhône.

In 1356 King John the Good was defeated by the Black Prince at the Battle of Poitiers (*see POITIERS*).

Under Charles V, Du Guesclin succeeded in restoring internal order. But at this point in their conflict, both adversaries were beset by problems of their own caused in England by the minority of Richard II. In France, Charles VI, too, was under age and later affected by madness. The War between Armagnacs and Burgundians began and the Church was torn by the Great Schism (*see AVIGNON*). Following the English victory at Agincourt (*see ST-OMER*) and the assassination of John the Fearless of Burgundy at Montereau (*see DIJON*), the Treaty of Troyes, promising the French crown to the English king, seemed to extinguish any hope of the future Charles VII succeeding.

In 1429, however, after having picked out the king from among the courtiers assembled at Chinon, Joan of Arc recaptured Orléans thereby preventing Salisbury's army from crossing the Loire and meeting up with the English troops who had been stationed in central and southwestern France following the Treaty of Brétigny in 1360. On 17 July Charles VII was crowned in Reims cathedral; in 1436 Paris was freed, followed by Normandy and Guyenne. In 1453 the French victory at Castillon-la-Bataille was the last important clash of arms in the war, which was formally brought to an end by the Treaty of Picquigny.

1515 Accession of François I; Battle of Marignano and the signing of peace in perpetuity with Switzerland.

1520 Meeting of François I and Henry VIII of England at the Field of the Cloth of Gold at Guînes.

1539 The Ordinance of **Villers-Cotterêts**, one of the bases of French law, is promulgated by François I. Among its 192 articles are ones decreeing the keeping of parish registers of births and deaths, as well as law reform outlawing the founding of guilds and instituting secret criminal investigation and

The Wars of Religion – 1562-1598

This is the name given to the 36-year-long crisis marked by complex political as well as religious conflict. During the latter half of the 16C, the French monarchy was in poor shape to withstand the looming hegemony of Spain, with political life in chaos and debt reaching incredible dimensions. The firm stand taken on religion by Spain and Italy on the one hand and by the Protestant countries on the other was missing in the France of Catherine de' Medici's regency, where both parties jostled for favour and a policy of appeasement applied.

The nobility took advantage of the situation, seeking to bolster their power base in the provinces and, under cover of religion, to grasp the reins of government. The Catholic League was formed by the Guise and Montmorency families, supported by Spain and opposed by the Bourbon, Condé and Coligny factions, Huguenots all, with English backing.

Though historians distinguish eight wars separated by periods of peace or relative tranquillity, the troubles were continuous: in the country, endless assassinations, persecutions and general lawlessness; at court, intrigues, volte-faces and pursuit of particular interests. Actual warfare, threatened ever since the Amboise Conspiracy, began at Wassy in 1562, following a massacre of Protestants. The names of Dreux, Nîmes, Chartres, Longjumeau, Jarnac, Montcontour, St-Lô, Valognes, Coutras, Arques, Ivry follow in bloody succession. The Peace of St-Germain in 1570 demonstrated a general desire for reconciliation, but only two years later came the St Bartholomew's Day Massacre in which some 20 000 Huguenots died.

The States General were convened at Blois at the request of the supporters of the League who were opposed to the centralisation of power into royal hands. Fearful of the power enjoyed by Duke Henri of Guise, head of the Catholic League and the kingdom's best military commander, King Henri III had him assassinated in the château at Blois one cold morning in December 1588, only to be cut down himself by a fanatical monk the following year.

This left the succession open for the Huguenot Henry of Navarre, the future Henri IV. By formally adopting the Catholic faith in 1593 and by promulgating the Edict of Nantes in 1598, this able ruler succeeded in rallying all loyal Frenchmen to his standard, putting at least a temporary end to the long-drawn-out crisis.

the compulsory use of French instead of Latin in legal matters. By this time provincialism was on the way out supplanted by a truly national consciousness, the outcome of three centuries of shared ordeals and triumphs.

1541 Calvin's "Institutes of the Christian Religion" is published. In it this native Frenchman, born at Noyon, attempts to stem the fissiparous tendencies of the Reformation and to proclaim its universality. Style, structure and significance combine in this work to make it the first great classic of French literature.

1559 Treaty of Le Cateau-Cambrésis is signed.

1560 The Amboise Conspiracy, harbinger of the looming political and religious crisis.

THE BOURBONS (1589–1789)

Henri IV – 1589–1610

Though his political manœuvrings and his personal conduct did not endear him to everybody, Henri IV put France's affairs on a firm footing once more, attaching the provinces of Bresse and Bugey to the kingdom and setting great architects like Du Cerceau and

Métezeau to work on projects in Paris such as the Place des Vosges and the Louvre Gallery, and in La Rochelle and Charleville in the provinces. Important economic reforms were undertaken, and the king's old Huguenot friend, Maximilien de Béthune, Duke of Sully, set the nation's finances in order, dug canals and laid out new roads and port facilities.

In 1600, the landowner Olivier de Serres published his great work on progressive farming technique "The Theatre of Agriculture and Field Husbandry", supporting Sully in his contention that "tilling and stock-keeping are the two breasts from which France feeds". The king's concern with his people's well-being found expression in his famous statement "a chicken in the pot every Sunday".

1610 Louis XIII becomes King. The country's trade flourishes with the development of inland ports and there are fine planned expansions to a number of towns (Orléans, La Rochelle, Montargis, Langres). The reign is marked by an aristocratic rebellion, as well as by the pioneering work of St Vincent de Paul in social welfare (hospitals, Sisters of Mercy). In the field of ideas, Descartes publishes his "Discourse on Method" (1637), with its reasoning based on systematic questioning ("Cogito, ergo sum"), a starting point for the intellectual revolution which, among other achievements, led to the invention of analytical geometry.

1624 The King's First Minister, Richelieu (1585–1642), is successful in his attempts to reduce the power of a Protestantism overinclined to seek foreign aid (La Rochelle) or to resist the unification of the kingdom (Montauban, Privas). A few exemplary executions serve to humble the nobility (Montmorency, Cinq-Mars), a process carried further by the demolition of castles. He strengthens France's role in Europe (Thirty Years' War) and, in 1635, founds the Academy (Académie française).

Louis XIV – 1643–1715

The 72 years of the Sun King's reign marked both France and Europe with the force of his personality (see PARIS and VERSAILLES). At the time of his accession, the king was only five years old and Anne of Austria confirmed Mazarin in his role as first minister. Five days later, the French victory at Rocroi (1643) signalled the end of Spanish dominance of Europe's affairs. In 1648, the Peace of Westphalia ended the Thirty Years War, confirmed France's claim to Alsace (apart from Strasbourg and Mulhouse) and established French as the language of diplomacy.

In 1657, while the king looked on, the two-month siege of Montmédy was brought to a triumphant conclusion by La Ferté and Vauban, thereby putting an end to Spanish rule in the Low Countries. In 1662, the king's first year of personal rule was crowned by the purchase of the port of Dunkirk, a result of the statesman Lionne's diplomacy; the place became a base for smugglers and for privateers like Jean Bart operating in the service of the king.

Anglo-French rivalry for control of the seas (see BELLE-ILE) now became the main theme of international politics. In 1678, the Treaty of Nijmegen marked the end of the war with Holland, the giving-up of the Franche-Comté and of 12 strongholds in Flanders by Spain, and the reconquest of Alsace. This was a high point in Louis' reign and in French expansion, insured by Vauban's work in fortifying the country's new frontiers. The politics of religion were not always straightforward; for 20 years, the king was in conflict with the Pope in what was known as the Affair of the Régale; in 1685 came the Revocation of the Edict of Nantes with all its dire consequences, and in 1702 the suppression of the camisard revolt. The monarch's later years were clouded by the country's economic exhaustion, though the Battle of Denain in 1712 saved France from invasion by the Austro-Dutch armies and led to the end of the War of the Spanish Succession.

Oriental Ventures

In 1664, a century after the voyages of Jean Ango and Jacques Cartier, the French East India Company was revived by Colbert, Louis XIV's great minister of finance. Two years later he authorised it to set up bases both at **Port-Louis** and on waste ground on the far side of the confluence of the Scorff and Blavet rivers. In 1671 the first great merchantman was fitted out for its journey to the East, and the new port was given the name of L'Orient in 1671 (**Lorient** in 1830). Anglo-French naval rivalry now began in earnest. Over a period of 47 years the Company put a total of 76 ships into use, which, in the course of their long and often dangerous voyages, would bring back cargoes of spices and porcelain (France alone importing over 12 million items of the latter). The initially fabulous profits eventually declined when the Company became a kind of state enterprise under the control of the bank run by the Scots financier Law. In the end, Lorient moved from a commercial role to a naval one.

1715   Louis XV succeeds to the crown at the age of five; the Duke of Orleans is Regent. The reign is marked by indecision, frivolity and corruption; many of France's colonies (Senegal, Québec, the Antilles, possessions in India) are lost. Internally, however, the country prospers, benefiting from a wise economic policy; the standard of living improves and a long period of stability favours agricultural development (introduction of the potato, artificial extension of grazing lands). Lorraine is absorbed into France in 1766, as was Corsica in 1769.

1774   Louis XVI becomes King. Lafayette takes part in the American War of Independence, brought to an end by the **Treaty of Versailles** in 1783.

The spirit of scientific enquiry leads to rapid technological progress, the growth of industry (textiles, porcelain, steam power) and to endeavours such as Lalande's astronomical experiments and the Montgolfier brothers' balloon flights at Annonay in 1783.

THE FRENCH REVOLUTION (1789–1799)

1789   French Revolution begins in Paris.

The Revolution, opening up the continent of Europe to democracy, was the outcome of the long crisis affecting the Ancien Régime.

The Vendée

This is the name given to the Royalist-led but popular uprising in western France in 1793 in reaction to the excesses of the Convention. The bocage countryside of much of the area favoured the guerrilla warfare waged by the "Whites" (Catholic royalists) against "Blues" (Republicans), who brought in the Alsatian general Kléber. In the winter of 1794 thousands of Whites were executed at Nantes, Angers, Fontenay... while the countryside was ravaged by mobile columns of vengeful soldiery (known as the infernal columns of General Turreau). Still resistance continued, until finally put to an end by the more conciliatory policies of Hoche.

Attack on the Bastille in 1789 (1845) by unknown artist

©ImageState/Tips Images

Hastened along by the teachings of the thinkers of the Enlightenment as much as by the inability of a still essentially feudal system to adapt itself to new social realities, the Revolution broke out following disastrous financial mismanagement and the emptying of the coffers of the state. The main events unfolded in Paris but their repercussions were felt in the provincial cities (Lyon, Nantes…) as well as in the countryside. The year 1789 heralded a number of major historical events for France. The Estates General were renamed the National Assembly, the Bastille was stormed, privileges were abolished (night of 4 July) and the Rights of Man were proclaimed. Two years later, in 1791, the king, fleeing with his family, was arrested in Varennes (22 June) and brought back to Paris, where he was suspended from office on 30 September.

The following year the Convention (1792–95) was signed, while in Valmy (20 September) Kellermann and Dumouriez saved France from invasion by forcing the Prussians to retreat; on 22 September France is proclaimed a one and indivisible Republic.

The major landmarks of 1793 were the execution of Louis XVI (21 January), the Vendée revolt, the crushing of the Lyon uprising and the siege of Toulon (July–December). In 1795 France adopted the metric system.

1799 Napoleon overthrows Revolutionary government, puts new constitution in place.

In 1799 Napoleon overthrew the **Directory** (*9 November*) and declared himself First Consul of the Republic. Finally, in 1801, the Code Napoléon was promulgated throughout the country

THE EMPIRE (1804–1815)

1804 On 2 December, Napoleon is crowned Emperor of the French in Notre-Dame by Pope Pius VII. The territorial acquisitions made in the course of the French Revolution now have to be defended against a whole series of coalitions formed by the country's numerous enemies.

1805 Napoleon gives up his plans for invasion of England, abandoning the great camp set up at Boulogne for that purpose. The Royal Navy's victory at Trafalgar gives Britain control of the seas, but France's armies win the

Battles of Ulm and Austerlitz (Slavkov).

1806 Intended to bring about England's economic ruin, the Continental Blockade pushes France into further territorial acquisitions.

1808 Some of the best French forces bogged down in the Peninsular War.

1812 Napoleon invades Russia. The Retreat from Moscow.

1813 The Battle of Leipzig. The whole of Europe lines up against France. Not even Napoleon's military genius can prevent the fall of Paris and the Emperor's farewell at Fontainebleau (20 April 1814). Napoleon is exiled to the island of Elba.

THE RESTORATION (1815–1830)

1814 Louis XVIII returns from exile in England.

1815 Battle of Waterloo. Napoleon is defeated.

1815 proved a decisive year for France. Following the Hundred Days (20 March–22 June) – Napoleon's triumphalist journey back to Paris from his exile in Elba – his attempt to re-establish the Empire ended with the victory of the Allies (principally England and Prussia, under the leadership of England's Duke of Wellington) at Waterloo on 18 June. Louis XVIII was once more on the throne and France was now forced to withdraw into the frontiers of 1792.

Talleyrand's efforts at the Congress of Vienna helped bring France back into the community of European nations. Marshal Ney was executed.

THE JULY MONARCHY (1830–1848)

1830 Charles X's "Four Ordinances of St-Cloud" violate the Constitution and lead to the outbreak of revolution. There follow the "Three Glorious Days" (27, 28 and 29 July) and the flight of the Bourbons. Louis-Philippe becomes King.

1837 France's first passenger-carrying railway is opened between Paris and St-Germain-en-Laye.

SECOND REPUBLIC AND SECOND EMPIRE (1848–1870)

1848 On 10 December, Louis Napoléon is elected President of the Republic by universal suffrage.

1851 On 2 December, Louis Napoléon dissolves the Legislative Assembly and declares himself President for a 10-year term.

1852 A plebiscite leads to the proclamation of the Second Empire (Napoleon III).

1855 The World Fair is held in Paris.

1860 Savoy and the county of Nice elect to become part of France.

1869 Freedom of the Press is guaranteed.

1870 War declared on Prussia on 19 July. On 2 September, defeat at Sedan spells the end of the Second Empire. Two days later Paris rises and the Republic is proclaimed. But the way to the capital lies open, and soon Paris is under siege.

THE REPUBLIC (1870–THE PRESENT DAY)

1870 Following the disaster at Sedan, the Third Republic is proclaimed on 4 September.

1871 The Paris Commune (21–28 May). By the Treaty of Frankfurt France gives up all of Alsace (with the exception of Belfort) and part of Lorraine.

1881 Jules Ferry secularises primary education, making it free and, later, compulsory.

1884 Trade unions gain formal recognition.

1885 Vaccination in the treatment of rabies (Pasteur). Inauguration of the Eiffel Tower (World Fair).

1894 The Dreyfus Affair divides the country. Forged evidence results in this Jewish General Staff captain being unfairly imprisoned for spying.

1897 Clément Ader's heavier-than-air machine takes to the air at Toulouse.

1904 Entente Cordiale.

1905 Separation of Church and State.

1914 Outbreak of World War I. On 3 August the German armies attack through neutral Belgium but are thrown back in the Battle of the Marne. Four years of trench warfare follow, a bloody climax being reached in 1916–17 around the fortress city of Verdun, where the German offensive is held, at immense cost in lives on both sides.

In 1919 the signing of the Treaty of Versailles brings World War I to an end.

1934 France is deeply divided; on 6 February, the National Assembly is attacked by right-wing demonstrators. Two years later, Léon Blum forms his Popular Front government.

1939 Outbreak of the Second World War.

1940 France invaded and concedes defeat.

In June 1940 France was overrun by the German army and Marshal Pétain's government requested an armistice. Much of the country was occupied (the north and the whole of the Atlantic seaboard), but the German puppet "French State" with its slogan of "Work, Family, Fatherland" is established at Vichy and collaborates closely with the Nazis. Almost all French Jews were rounded up by the French authorities and deported for extermination. France's honour was saved by General de Gaulle's Free French forces, active in many theatres of the war, and by the courage of the men and women of the Resistance.

1942 Whole country is occupied, and the French fleet scuttles itself at Toulon.

1944 In June the British and American Allies land in Normandy, and in the South of France in August. Paris is liberated.

1945 German surrender signed at Reims on 7 May 1945.

This major conflict (1939–1945), which inflamed all continents, is detailed in this guide under the places which it affected most in France.

1947 The Fourth Republic established. Its governments last an average of six months.

1954 Dien Bien Phu falls to the Vietminh. France abandons Indo-China and grants Morocco and Tunisia their independence (1956).

1958 The Algerian crisis leads to the downfall of the Fourth and the establishment of

Charles de Gaulle, 1967

© Hulton-Deutsch Collection/CORBIS

the Fifth Republic under De Gaulle. Civil war is narrowly averted. Nearly all its French population leaves Algeria, which becomes independent in 1962.

1958 The Fifth Republic established. The European Economic Community (EEC) comes into effect. The new constitution inspired by General de Gaulle is voted by referendum.

1962 Referendum establishing that the future President of the Republic be elected by universal suffrage.

1967 Franco-British agreement to manufacture Airbus.

1968 The "events of May"; workers join students in mass protests, roughly put down by riot police. The Gaullists triumph in national elections, but it is a hollow victory and De Gaulle, defeated in the referendum of April 1969, retires.

1969 Georges Pompidou is elected President (16 June).

1974 Valéry Giscard d'Estaing is elected President (19 May).

1981 François Mitterrand is elected President (10 May). Inauguration of the TGV line between Paris and Lyon (2hr40min); Paris-Marseille (1981); and Paris-Bordeaux (1990).

1994 Inauguration of the Channel Tunnel (6 May).

1995 Jacques Chirac is elected President (7 May).

1999 1 Jan, dubbed "€ Day," marks the beginning of circulation for Euro notes and coins.

2002 French Franc withdrawn from circulation.

2003 11,000 die in heatwave.

2005 Proposed European Constitution rejected in referendum of French electorate (May). Ethnic minorities rioting in several cities (summer).

2007 Nicolas Sarkozy elected President of France (6 May).

2009 (Jan) Storm Klaus hits SW France killing 8 and damaging large areas of forest.

CONTEMPORARY FRANCE

Although France is ranked among the industrialised nations and one of leading countries in the world in terms of international trade, it remains at the same time a nation with a strong **rural tradition**. Even if the number of people actually employed in farming is on the decline, the French continue to have close ties to the land. Many, wherever they live, maintain close contacts with their family's native region, either by acquiring a cottage in the country or by inheriting a family property.

For most French people the qualities associated with this ancestral land are encapsulated in the traditional **village** – the village where one was born, where one has chosen to live or where one spends one's holidays.

Leaving aside the differences attributed to climatic conditions and building materials, all villages feature common characteristics: the **main street** (Grand'rue) lined with small shops, the **marketplace**, where local cattle fairs used to be held, and of course, the **church**, whose chimes continue to herald the fortunes and misfortunes of the community.

Although they see a surge of activity during municipal and trade fairs, French villages are quiet, and peaceful most of the year. Only the traditional **café** and the **boules playing ground** echo the conversations of the locals idly debating the meaning of life.

This strong regionalism has led to frequent conflict with, and hostility to, the central government in Paris. To resolve this long-standing problem, a series of decentralisation reforms was implemented in 1982, creating regional governments with considerable autonomy.

Regional capitals were established – in all cases a former historic seat of local power – to strike a balance between the capital and the countryside. Despite their long history and local tradition, these regional urban centres, well subsidised by Paris, tend to be resolutely turned towards the future and illustrate the thriving character of the French regions. In 2003, extensive further powers were devolved to the regions.

However, **Paris**, with her nine-and-a-half million inhabitants, remains the administrative core of the country and a focal point for the whole nation. The seat of political power, and an important centre for world trade , "the city of lights" is also an exceptional destination for visitors. In the country which attracts more tourists each year than any other, the capital is the main attraction, thanks to its wealth of architectural marvels, its extraordinary collection of world-class museums, and its high cultural standards.

This brief description would not be complete without mentioning the **French** themselves. Frequently misunderstood by foreign visitors, often condemned as brusque and unhelpful, they are nonetheless always ready to protect and safeguard their age-old traditions and support a cause in defence of the interests of France and the French way of life. To those who make the effort of going towards them, and who cherish that way of life as they do, the French will always extend a warm, genuine welcome.

Art and Culture

A SURVEY OF FRENCH ART
FROM PREHISTORY TO THE GALLO-ROMAN ERA

Prehistory

While stone and bone tools appeared in the Lower Paleolithic period, prehistoric art did not make its entrance until the Upper Paleolithic, (350–100C BC), and reached its peak in the Magdalenian Period (*see Les EYZIES DE-TAYAC for the chronology of prehistoric eras*). The art of engraved wood and ivory objects together with votive statuettes developed alongside the art of wall decoration, which is well illustrated in France by caves in the Dordogne, the Pyrenees, the Ardèche and the Gard. Early artists used pigments with a mineral base for their cave paintings and sometimes took advantage of the natural shape of the rock itself to execute their work in low relief.

The Neolithic revolution (6500 BC), during which populations began to settle, brought with it the advent of pottery as well as a different use of land and a change in burial practices – some megaliths (dolmens and covered passageways) are ancient burial chambers. Menhirs, a type of megalith found in great numbers in Brittany (Carnac and Locmariaquer), are as yet of unknown origin. The discovery of metal brought prehistoric civilisation into the Bronze Age (2300–1800 BC) and then into the Iron Age (750–450 BC). Celtic art showed perfect mastery of metalwork as in the tombs of Gorge-Meillet, Mailly-le-Camp, Bibracte and Vix in which the treasures consist of gold torques (necklaces) and other items of jewellery, various coins and bronzeware.

ROMANESQUE PERIOD (11–12C)

In the early 11C, after the disturbances of the year 1000 (decadence of the Carolingian dynasty and struggles between feudal barons), the spiritual influence and power of the Church gave rise to the birth of Romanesque architecture.

Romanesque Architecture

Early Romanesque edifices were characterised by the widespread use of stone vaulting which replaced timber roofs, the use of buttresses and a return to architectural decoration (as in the churches of St-Martin-du-Canigou, and St-Bénigne in Dijon). The darkness of the nave was explained by the fact that for

The Gallo-Roman Era and the Early Middle Ages

When the Romans conquered Gaul (2–1C BC), they introduced the technique of building with stone. In cities, the Empire's administrative centres, the centralised power of Rome favoured a style of architecture that reflected its strength and prestige and imposed its culture. Theatres (Orange and Vienne), temples (the Square House or Maison Carrée in Nîmes), baths, basilicas and triumphal arches were constructed, while the local aristocracy took to building Roman villas with frescoes and mosaics (Vaison-la-Romaine and Grand). The presence of the Romans has had a lasting effect on the shape of France in terms of town-planning, roads, bridges and aqueducts (Pont du Gard). Towards the end of the late Empire, official recognition of the Christian church in the year 380 prompted the first examples of Christian architecture, among them the baptisteries of Fréjus, Riez, and Poitiers.

During the great barbarian invasions of the 5C, figurative art, unknown to Germanic peoples, gave place to abstract (intertwining, circular shapes) and animal motifs. The technique of *cloisonné* gold and silverware (Childeric's treasure) became widespread.

Merovingian art (6–8C), a synthesis of styles, included elements of antique, barbarian and Christian art (the Dunes hypogeum near Poitiers and the crypt in **Jouarre** (◔ see *Illustration overleaf*), out of which evolved medieval art.

The **Carolingian Renaissance** (9C) was marked by a great flowering of illuminated manuscripts and ivory-carving (the Dagulf psalter in the Louvre) and by a deliberate return to imperial, antique art forms (Aix-la-Chapelle and the oratory of Germigny-des-Prés).

The altar in churches of the period is sometimes raised above a vaulted area of the chancel known as the crypt which was originally on the same level as the nave (St-Germain of Auxerre and St-Philibert-de-Grand-Lieu).

structural reasons wide openings could not be cut into the walls supporting the vaulting.

The basilica plan with nave and side aisles, sometimes preceded by a porch, predominated in France although some churches were built to a central plan (the church of Neuvy-St-Sépulcre). Depending on the church, the east end might have been flat or have had apsidal chapels; it was often semicircular with axial chapels (as in the church of Anzy-le-Duc) or may have featured radiating chapels. More complex designs combined an ambulatory with radiating chapels (the churches of Conques and Cluny).

The first attempts at embellishment led to a revival of sculptural decoration of which the lintel of St-Genis-les-Fontaines Church is one of the earliest examples. Tympana, archivolts, arch shafts and piers were covered with carvings of a religious or profane nature (as in the illustration of the *Romance of Renart* in the church of St-Ursin in Bourges). Interior decoration consisted mainly of frescoes (the churches of St-Savin-sur-Gartempe and Berzé-la-Ville) and carved capitals with the occasional complex theme (as in the chancel capitals in Cluny). The Romanesque decorative style drew largely upon three main models, the Oriental (griffins and imaginary animals) which was spread by the Crusades, the Byzantine (illustrations of Christ in Majesty and a particular style for folds) and the Islamic (stylised foliage and pseudo-Kufic script).

Regional Characteristics

The Romanesque style spread throughout France affecting some areas earlier than others and developing special stylistic features according to the region. It first appeared in the south and

Detail on the tympanum of the Ste-Foy church doorway in Conques

S. Sauvignier/MICHELIN

in Burgundy, reaching the east of France at a much later date.

Romanesque architecture in the **Languedoc** owes much to Toulouse's St-Sernin Basilica, whose tall lantern tower pierced by ornamental arcading served as a model for many local bell-towers. The sculptures on the Miégeville doorway, completed in 1118, have a distinctive style, with highly expressive folds and a lengthening of the figures which is repeated in **Moissac** (&see Illustration p72) and, to a lesser extent, in St-Gilles-du-Gard.

Ecclesiastical architecture   **JOUARRE – Crypte St-Paul (7C)**

The crypts of Jouarre Abbey built in the Carollingian period are among the earliest examples of funerary religious architecture popular in the Middle Ages.

Groined vault

Ovolo moulding: egg and dart moulding

Abacus

Capitals generally with Classical orders: Corinthian style capitals enhanced by grooves, ovolo, beads

Recumbent figure

Cenotaph: funerary monument which does not contain remains

Fluting

Shell motif, symbol of immortality

Stone **sarcophagus**

Porphyry **shaft**

Torus: raised moulding

R.Corbel/MICHELIN

Ecclesiastical architecture

CLERMONT FERRAND (Puy-de-Dôme) – Ground plan of Basilique Notre-Dame-du-Port (11C-12C)

Latin-cross plan, the transverse aisle forming the **transept**

Narthex: vestibule: in Auvergne it is an integral part of the main structure and has one storey.

Arm of the transept

Side aisle

Radiating or **apsidal chapel**

Porch

Nave

Transept crossing **Chancel**

Ambulatory

Transept crossing

Bay: Transverse section of the nave between two sets of pillars

South doorway

Transept chapel

Apse: extension of the nave generally rounded at the end of the chancel. The exterior of the east end is known as the chevet in French.

R.Corbel/MICHELIN

In **Saintonge-Poitou**, the originality of the edifices derives from the great height of the aisles which serve to reinforce the walls of the nave and thus lend balance to the barrel vaulting.

The gabled façades, flanked by lantern towers, are covered in ornamental arcading with statue niches and low relief (as in the church of Notre-Dame-la-Grande in Poitiers).

In **Auvergne**, the transept crossing is often covered by a dome, buttressed by high, quadripartite vaulting and supported on diaphragm arches.

This constitutes an oblong mass which juts out above the roof beneath the bell-tower. The use of lava, a particularly difficult stone to carve, explains the limited sculptural decoration (as in the churches of St-Nectaire, Notre-Dame-du-Port in **Clermont-Ferrand** and that of **Orcival**, &see Illustrations above and p73). The tympana lintels are gable-shaped.

The development of the Romanesque in **Burgundy** was strongly influenced by the Abbey of Cluny (now destroyed) with its great chancel with radiating chapels, a double transept and the hint of direct lighting in the nave through slender openings at the base of the barrel vaulting. The churches of Paray-le-Monial and Notre-Dame in La Charité-sur-Loire were built on the Cluniac model.

The basilica of Sainte-Madeleine in Vézelay in the north of the Morvan, with its harmonious, simplified church body and its covering of groined vaults, was also to influence churches in the region.

In the **Rhine** and **Meuse** regions, architectural characteristics from the Carolingian era, with an Ottonian influence, tend to prevail. This is borne out by double chancels and transepts (as in Verdun) and a central plan and interior elevation like that of the Palatine Chapel in Aachen (as in Ottmarsheim).

Lastly, until a relatively late date the churches in **Normandy** faithfully retained the custom of a timber roof (as in Jumièges and Bayeux). As stone vaulting was introduced decorative ribs gradually came into use (as in St-Étienne in Caen). The monumental size of the edifices and their harmoniously proportioned façades with two towers, are also typical of the Anglo-Norman Romanesque style.

Apart from these regional features some buildings owe their individuality to their function. The **pilgrimage churches**, for instance, had an ambulatory around the chancel, transept aisles and two aisles on either side of the nave to give pilgrims easy access to the relics they wished to venerate. The main churches of this kind on the way to Santiago de Compostela were St Faith in Conques, St-Sernin in Toulouse, St-Martial in Limoges and St-

Martin in Tours (the two latter have since been destroyed).

Romanesque Religious Art

Liturgical items at the time consisted of church plate, manuscripts, precious fabrics and reliquaries. Church treasure would often include a Virgin in Majesty made of polychrome wood or embossed metal decorated with precious stones. The blossoming of **Limousin enamelware** marked a great milestone in the history of the decorative arts during the Romanesque period when it was exported throughout Europe.

The *champlevé* method consisted of pouring the enamel into a grooved metal surface of gilded copper.

Enamel was used in a number of ways to decorate items ranging from small objects such as crosses, ciboria and reliquaries to monumental works like altars (high altar of **Grandmont** abbey church and items in the Cluny Museum, Paris).

GOTHIC PERIOD (12–15C)

Architecture Transitional Gothic

In about 1140, important architectural innovations in St-Denis Cathedral, such as intersecting ribbed vaulting and pointed arches in the narthex and chancel, heralded the dawn of the Gothic style.

In the late 12C, there were further innovations common to a group of buildings in Île-de-France and in the north of France. They included ogives and mouldings which extended down from the vaulting into bundles of engaged slender columns around the pillars of great arches. Capitals were simplified, became smaller with time and gradually diminished in importance. New concepts of sculptural decorating, including the appearance of statue-columns, affected building façades. In Sens Cathedral, the rectangular layout of the bays called for sexpartite vaulting with alternating major and minor pillars to support large arches.

The major pillars supported three ribs while the minor ones supported a single intermediary rib. Apart from sexpartite vaulting with alternating supports, this early Gothic architecture typical of Sens, Noyon and Laon was also characterised by a four-storeyed elevation, great arches, tribunes, a triforium and tall bays.

In the years 1180–1200, in Notre-Dame Cathedral in Paris, raised vaults were reinforced by the addition of flying buttresses on the outside of the edifice while inside, alternating supports disappeared. These new measures gave rise to the emergence of a transitional style which led to Lanceolate Gothic.

Ecclesiastical architecture

MOISSAC – South doorway of the 12C abbey church

Torus: a large convex moulding separating the covings

Historiated tympanum (decorated with narrative scenes and figures, here Christ in Majesty)

Lintel

Embrasure: arch shafts, splaying sometimes adorned with statues or columns

Scallop motif

Coving: concave moulding

Archivolt: series of mouldings curving round an arch

Medallion

Pier adorned with interlaced lions

Engaged piers supporting the arched mouldings

R.Corbel/MICHELIN

Ecclesiastical architecture   **ORCIVAL – Notre-Dame Basilica (12C)**

Most of the Romanesque churches of the Auvergne belong to a school which developed in the 11C-12C and is considered one of the most unusual in the history of art in the Western world.

Relieving arch: relieves the weight of the wall above an opening.

Two-storeyed **octagonal bell-tower:** its thrusts are but tressed by the chevet, nave and the arms of the transept.

Twin windows

Transept

Semicircular window

Gable-wall

Window

Modillions: scroll shaped projecting mouldings supporting the cornice.

String-course with billet moulding: ornamental frieze consisting of bands of raised short cylindrical or square blocks placed at regular intervals.

Radiating or **apsidal chapel**

Buttress: external support for a wall, built against it.

Cornice adorned with chequered motif.

Chevet: the east end is the most beautiful and most characteristic of the Auvergne churches owing to the original layout of the various levels.

R.Corbel/MICHELIN

Ecclesiastical architecture

CHARTRES – West front of Cathédrale Notre-Dame (12C-13C)

Spire

Crockets

Pinnacle: small turret-like termination crowning a buttress, usually ornamented

Gargoyle: projecting water spout designed to drain rainwater

Gemel windows (grouped in pairs, the two openings separated by a central column)

Window adorned with tracery: the flame-design gave rise to the term Flamboyant describing the late Gothic style

Gallery of Kings: upper gallery adorned with statues of Kings, a feature of some cathedrals

Gable-wall: triangular upper portion of a wall to carry a pitched roof

Mullion: a vertical post dividing a window into two or more lights

Great rose window

Bell-tower with polygonal spire

Gable: decorative triangular feature above doors and windows

Projecting cornice

Pointed window

Blind arcading

Buttress

String-course: a projecting horizontal band or moulding set in a vertical surface

Central doorway

Triplet: three portals or windows often grouped under a relieving arch

R.Corbel/MICHELIN

Lanceolate Gothic

The Gothic style was at its peak during the reigns of Philippe Auguste (1180–1223) and St Louis (1226–70). The rebuilding of **Chartres Cathedral** (1210–30) gave rise to a model for what is known as the Chartres family of cathedrals (Reims, Amiens and Beauvais) which included oblong plan vaulting, a three-storeyed elevation (without tribunes) and flying buttresses. The chancel with its double ambulatory and the transept arms with side aisles made for a grandiose interior. The upper windows in the nave were divided into two lancets surmounted by a round opening.

The façades were subdivided into three horizontal registers, as in the cathedrals of Laon and Amiens. The doorways were set in deep porches with gables while above them was an openwork rose window with stained glass. A gallery of arches ran beneath the bell-towers.

There are a number of variations of Lanceolate Gothic in France. An example is Notre-Dame Church in Dijon where the ancient section of the sexpartite vaulting has been preserved.

Development of the Gothic Style to the 15C

The improvement in vaulting from a technical point of view, in particular the use of relieving arches, meant that the supporting function of walls was reduced and more space could be given over to windows and stone tracery as in St-Urbain's Basilica in Troyes and the

Flamboyant Gothic doorway, Basilique Notre-Dame, Avioth, Lorraine

Sainte-Chapelle in Paris (1248). This gave rise to the **High Gothic** style in the north of France from the end of the 13C to the late 14C. (Examples include the chancel in Beauvais Cathedral, Évreux Cathedral and the north transept of **Rouen Cathedral**, ⚲*see Illustration below*).

Gothic architecture in the centre and southwest of France developed along unusual lines in the late 13C. Jean Deschamps, master mason of Narbonne Cathedral, designed a massively proportioned building in which the vertical upsweep of the lines was interrupted by wide galleries

Ecclesiastical architecture

Attic or roof space

Pinnacle

Semicircular vault

Flying buttress

Clerestory windows

Pier of a flying buttress

ROUEN – Cross-section of Cathédrale Notre-Dame (12C-15C)

Capital

Buttress supporting the base of the wall

Nave

Side chapel

Side aisle

Ecclesiastical architecture

SENLIS – Cathédrale Notre-Dame (12C-13C)

Intersecting ribs

Lunette: surface of ribbed vault which does not extend to the keystone

Hanging keystone

Transverse arch: supporting rib, often separating one bay of a vault from the next

Tierceron: secondary rib

Quarter or **cell:** segment of vault between ribs

Tracery: ornamental store open work in the upper part of a window

Clerestory window

Tierce-point arch: pointed equilateral arch

Tribune: gallery

Open-work balustrade or **parapet**

Composite pillar: clustered columns

Large **pointed arch**

R.Corbel/MICHELIN

above the aisles. St Cecilia's Cathedral in Albi diverged completely from Gothic models in the north of France through the use of brick and a buttress system inherited from the Romanesque period. Throughout the 14C, church interiors were filled with sculptural decoration in the form of rood screens, choir screens and **stalls** (*see Illustration p77*), monumental altarpieces and devotional statues.

From the late 14C, development of the main principles of Gothic architecture came to a halt but decorative devices grew apace giving rise to the elaborate **Flamboyant Gothic** style with its gables, lancet arches, pinnacles and exuberant foliage. This ornamentation, occasionally referred to as Baroque Gothic, also played a part in **civil architecture** (*see Illustrations pp82–3) in section*). An example is the Great Hall in the Law Courts at Poitiers, carved by Guy de Dammartin in the last 10 years of the 14C. Riom's Sainte-Chapelle, built for the Duke Jean de Berry, is another early example. Flamboyant Gothic in

France left its mark on a good number of public and religious edifices (Palais Jacques Cœur in Bourges and the façade of St-Maclou Church in Rouen) as well as on liturgical furnishings (the choir screen and rood screen in **Ste-Cécile's Cathedral in Albi**, *see Illustration p77*).

Throughout the Gothic period castle architecture remained faithful to feudal models (Angers Castle, the walled city of Cordes and the mountain fortress of Merle Towers) and did not develop further until the beginning of the Renaissance.

Sculpture, Decorative Arts and Painting Gothic Sculpture

Progress towards naturalism and realism, the humanism of the Gothic style, can be seen in the statuary and sculptural decoration of the time. Statue-columns of doorways in the 12C tended still to be rigidly hieratic but in the 13C took on greater freedom of expression as may be seen in Amiens and Reims (the Smiling Angel). New themes emerged including

Ecclesiastical architecture

THANN – Choir stalls in Collégiale St-Thiébaut (14C-early 16C)

High-backed choir stalls

Open-work canopy

Arm rest

Choir stalls

Parclose: wooden partition between stalls. The woodwork on the different parts of the stalls is often decorated with humourously carved figures.

Misericord (or Miserere): a bracket on the underside of a hinged choir stall which can be turned up to give support to the occupant standing during long services (from the Latin "per misericordiam" in corn passion).

Cheek: a vertical panel at the end of a row of stalls

R.Corbel/MICHELIN

Ecclesiastical architecture

ALBI – Rood screen in Cathédrale Ste-Cécile (16C)

The **rood screen** was designed to separate the chancel (reserved for the clergy) from the nave (where the congregation gathered) and carry the Crucifix (rood). This example in Albi is typical of the Flamboyant Gothic style.

Flamboyant style **gallery** (flowing tracery evokes flames)

Pedestal: originally supported a statue

Mater Dolorosa

Adam

Crucifix (monumental in this case)

St John the Evangelist

Ogee arch, formed from an S and a reversed S-shaped curves

Eve

Niche

Side doorway, leading into the ambulatory

Entrance to the chancel

Pendant keystone

Gable decorated with foliated crockets

R.Corbel/MICHELIN

12-13C stained glass
Cathédral de Chartres

S. Sauvignier/MICHELIN

the Coronation of the Virgin, which first appeared in 1191, and thereafter became a popular subject.

Stained Glass

The four main areas producing stained glass in France in the 12C were St-Denis, Champagne, the west (Le Mans, Vendôme and Poitiers) and a group of workshops in the Rhine area in eastern France. Master glassworkers developed an intense blue-coloured glass known as Chartres blue which was to become famous. The invention of silver yellow in 1300–10 led to a more translucent enamelled glass with a subtler range of colour.

The combination of stained glass and Gothic architecture gave rise to larger bays – formerly opaque wall space could be opened up and filled with glass, thanks to new support systems. The fragility of stained glass explains the fact that there are very few original medieval windows intact today; many have been replaced by copies or later works. The windows of Chartres, Évreux and the Sainte-Chapelle are precious testimonies to the art.

Illumination and Painting

The art of illumination reached its peak in the 14C when artists freed from University supervision produced sumptuous manuscripts, including Books of Hours, for private use. Among them were Jean Pucelle *(Les Heures de Jeanne d'Évreux)* and the Limbourg brothers *(Les Très Riches Heures du Duc de Berry,* dating from the early 15C).

Easel painting first made its appearance n 1350 (the portrait of John the Good, now in the Louvre, is an example). Italian and more particularly Flemish influences, evident as much in depiction of landscape as in attention to detail, may be seen in works by great 15C artists like **Jean Fouquet, Enguerrand Quarton** and the **Master of Moulins**.

THE RENAISSANCE

Gothic art persisted in many parts of France until the middle of the 16C. In the Loire region, however, there were signs of a break with medieval traditions as early as the beginning of the century.

Italian Style and Early Renaissance

Renaissance aesthetics in Lombardy, familiar in France since the military campaigns of Charles VIII and Louis XII at the end of the 15C, at first affected only architectural decoration, through the introduction of motifs from Antiquity such as pilasters, foliage and scallops (as in the tomb of Solesmes, Château de Gaillon). Little by little, however, feudal, **military and defensive architecture** (*see Illustrations overleaf*) gave way to a more comfortable style of seigniorial residence. The Château de Chenonceau (begun before 1515) and that of Azay-le-Rideau (1518–27) are examples of this development, particularly in their regular layout, the symmetry of the façades and the beginnings of a new type of architectural decoration. However, it was the great royal undertakings of the time that brought about the blossoming of the Renaissance style.

Architecture Under François I (1515–1547)

The Façade des Loges (1520–24) in the **Château de Blois** (begun in 1515, *see Illustration p79*) is a free replica of the Vatican loggia in Rome. While the

Civil architecture

BLOIS – Château, François-1ᵉʳ staircase (16C)

The spiral stairway is built inside an octagonal staircase half set into the façade. It opens onto the main courtyard in a series of balconies which form loggias. The king and his court would view all sorts of entertainment from here: the arrival of dignitaries, jousting, hunting or military displays.

Candelabrum: an ornamental torch-shaped spike on top of a tower, chimney etc

Chimney stack

Ornate gable over dormer window

Cornice of shell motifs, very common ornamentation under François I

Sculpted stone **corbels**

Stone **canopy: baldaquin** decorated with any arches and pinnacles, designed to protect statues standing against the building

Field: plain background to decorative motif

Plain surface left bare of ornamentation

Medallion: sculpted portrait or other subject in a circular frame

Gargoyle: drain in the shape of an imaginary and often grotesque animal, through whose mouth rainwater would be projected away from the castle walls

Balustrade

Sculpted **parapet** (filled in protective wall)

Rampant arch: arch with ends springing from different levels

Sculpted **bracket** (projecting support, smaller than a corbel)

Crowned salamander: decorative motif of François I, sculpted in low relief

R.Corbel/MICHELIN

castle's irregular fenestration recalls the old medieval style, its great novelty is the preoccupation with Italianate ornamentation. During the reign of François I, the **Château de Chambord** (1519–47) which combines French architectural traditions (corner towers, irregular roofs and dormer windows) with innovative elements (symmetrical façades, refined decoration and a monumental internal staircase) served as a model for a good many of the Loire castles including Chaumont, Le Lude and Ussé.

After his defeat at the Battle of Pavia in 1525, François I left his residences in the Loire valley to turn his attention to those in Île-de-France. In 1527 building began on the Château de Fontainebleau under the supervision of Gilles Le Breton. The interior decoration by artists from the **First School of Fontainebleau** was to have a profound influence on the development of French art.

The Italian artist **Rosso** (1494–1540) introduced a new system of decoration to France that combined stuccowork, wood panelling and allegorical frescoes which drew upon humanistic, philosophical and literary references and were painted in acid colours.

The Mannerist style, characterised by the influence of antique statuary, a lengthening of lines and overabundant ornamentation, became more pronounced after **Primaticcio** (1504–70) arrived at the court in 1532.

The influence of this art could be felt until the end of the century in works by sculptors such as **Pierre Bontemps, Jean Goujon** (reliefs on the Fountain of the Innocents in Paris) and **Germain Pilon** (monument for the heart of Henri II in the Louvre) and painters like Jean Cousin the Elder. Court portraitists, on the other hand (**Jean and François Clouet** and **Corneille de Lyon**), were more influenced by Flemish traditions.

Château de Chambord

MICHELIN

Henri IV and Pre-Classicism

After the Wars of Religion (1560–98) new artistic trends revived the arts and heralded the dawn of Classicism. Royal interest in town-planning gave rise to the regular, symmetrical layout of squares (Place des Vosges and Place Dauphine in Paris) and to the harmonisation of the buildings that surrounded them (ground-level arcades and brick and stone façades). These were copied in the provinces (Charleville and Montauban) foreshadowing the royal squares of the 17C, France's *Grand Siècle*.

The Fontainebleau style of adornment continued to develop under the auspices of the **Second School of Fontainebleau**. This was made up of all the court

Military architecture

CARCASSONNE – East gateway of the Château Comtal (12C)

Twin towers framing the gate

Ridge crest (metal ornament)

Mounted hoarding: covered timber platforms projecting from the top of a tower or curtain wall

"Visigothic" tower: narrow construction with a curved external and flat internal wall

Merlon: solid part between the indentations (embrasures or crenels) in a battlement

Polygonal roof

Putlog-hole for support timber for hoardings

Horseshoe tower

Embrasure

Loophole

Battered wall: foot of the outside of the wall is flared to make sapping difficult and deflect attackers projectiles

Arrow-slit: loophole for archers

Dry moat: ditch intended to protect the curtain wall and castle towers

Curtain wall: stretch of fortified wall linking two towers

Fixed bridge

Broad arch

R.Corbel/MICHELIN

Military architecture

Château de BONAGUIL (13C – early 16C)

Bonaguil Castle, rebuilt from 1483 to 1510 by Béranger de Roquefeuil, is a good example of the improvements made to a defensive stronghold to take account of the development of firearms.

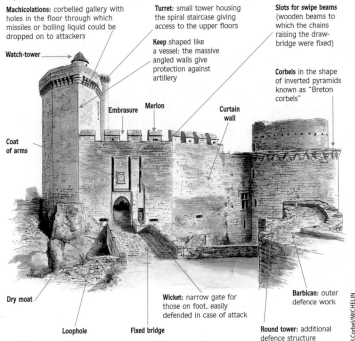

Machicolations: corbelled gallery with holes in the floor through which missiles or boiling liquid could be dropped on to attackers

Turret: small tower housing the spiral staircase giving access to the upper floors

Slots for swipe beams (wooden beams to which the chains raising the drawbridge were fixed)

Watch-tower

Keep shaped like a vessel: the massive angled walls give protection against artillery

Corbels in the shape of inverted pyramids known as "Breton corbels"

Embrasure **Merlon** **Curtain wall**

Coat of arms

Dry moat

Wicket: narrow gate for those on foot, easily defended in case of attack

Barbican: outer defence work

Loophole **Fixed bridge**

Round tower: additional defence structure

R.Corbel/MICHELIN

painters working during the reign of Henri IV and the regency of Marie de' Medici. The style was further shaped by decoration in other royal palaces including the Tuileries, the Louvre and Château-Neuf in St-Germain-en-Laye. **Toussaint Dubreuil** (1561–1602), **Ambroise Dubois** (1542–1614) and **Martin Fréminet** (1567–1619) continued the Mannerism of Fontainebleau (light effects, half-length figures and a lengthening of perspectives) in their works and at the same time sought greater classicism as well as a revival of themes from contemporary literature (*La Franciade* by Ronsard).

In the late 16C, castle architecture took on a new form with a single main building centred on a projecting section flanked by corner pavilions (Rosny-sur-Seine, and the Château de Gros-Bois). Right-angled wings were done away with and façades were given a brick facing with stone courses.

During the regency period, the architect Salomon de Brosse (Palais de Justice in Rennes, Palais du Luxembourg in Paris) designed sober, impressive monuments with a clarity of form which contained some of the characteristics of Classical architecture.

16C Decorative Arts

The 16C was a productive period for jewellery-making, in particular for small brooches fastened in the hair or hat and pendants which were used as articles of dress or simply as collectors' items. **Étienne Delaune** (1518–83) was one of the great goldsmiths of the time.

There was rich regional variety in ceramics. Beauvaisis produced famous blue-tinged stoneware. Following the example of Italy, Lyon and Nevers manufactured majolica (glazed and historiated earthenware).

The decorative arts in Saintonge were dominated by **Bernard Palissy** (c. 1510–

Military architecture

NEUF-BRISACH (1698-1703)

The polygonal stronghold was developed in the early 16C as firearms became more common in warfare: the cannon mounted on one structure covered the "blind spot" of the neighbouring position. This stronghold was built by Vauban, opposite the formidable Breisach, handed back to the Hapsburgs under the Treaty of Ryswick (1697).

Redan: a small ravelin

Glacis: forward slope of a fortification

Ditch

Gateway

Garrison church

Parade ground

Barracks

Ravelin (or **demi-lune**): a projecting outwork forming a salient angle

Tenaille: low work constructed in front of the curtain wall, the angle pointing inwards

Curtain wall: a wall between two bastions

Bastion: a polygonal defense work projecting from the outer wall of a fortification

Civil architecture

SERRANT – Château (16C-17C)

Imperial dome (pointed dome, vertical section of which is an ogee)

Balustrade: low protective wall composed of balusters

Corner tower

Dormer window surmounted by a broken pediment

Œil-de-bœuf window: small and circular ("bull's eye")

Triangular **pediment**

Main building, or *corps-de-logis*

Attic: small extra upper storey

Lantern

Cornice

Pilaster: flat engaged pillar, that is, projecting only slightly from the wall behind it

Avant-corps: part of a building projecting from the rest of the façade for the entire height of the building, roof included

Toothing: every other large-hewn stone is left projecting from the stone-work framing the windows for a more solid and more decorative bond with the adjoining schist walls

R.Corbel/MICHELIN

Civil architecture

BORDEAUX – Palais de la Bourse (18C)

Flaming urn: a characteristic feature in Classical architecture

Triangular pediment with allegorical carving

Œil-de-bœuf: a small, circular window ("bull's-eye")

Trophy: decorative carving of arms grouped around a breast plate or helmet

Dentils: a frieze of small, rectangular blocks

Architrave: the lowest part of the entablature resting directly upon the columns

Ionic capital: capital with a spiral volute

Mullioned window

Cartouche: a panel ornately framed and usually bearing an inscription

Column offset from the wall

Fanlight: upper section of a door or window

Mascaron: ornamental sculpture on keystone or voussoir

Colossal order spanning several storeys

Rusticated stonework: the massive blocks are dressed to a flat surface with chamfered edges

Groove marking the join between dressed stone blocks

R.Corbel/MICHELIN

c. 1590) who, apart from making a great many plates covered in reptiles, fish and seaweed, all modelled from nature, also decorated the grotto at the Château d'Écouen and that of the Tuileries. Some of his ceramics (nymphs in a country setting) were influenced by engravings from the Fontainebleau School.

The technique for painted enamel on copper with permanent colours was developed in Limoges in the 15C during the reign of Louis XI. J C Pénicaud and especially **Léonard Limosin** (1501–75) excelled in the technique, which was favoured in portrait painting by the French court.

FRENCH CLASSICISM IN THE EARLY 17TH CENTURY

Architecture

Three famous architects, **Jacques Lemercier** (c. 1585–1654), **François Mansart** (1598–1666) and **Louis le Vau** (1612–70), played an essential part in drawing up the standards for the French Classical architectural style. J Lemercier, who built the Château de Rueil, the town of Richelieu and the Église de la Sorbonne in Paris, supported the Italian style which was particularly evident in religious architecture: two-storeyed façades and projecting central sections with columns and triangular pediments. F Mansart was even more inventive (**Château de Balleroy**, **Château de Maisons-Laffitte** and the Gaston of Orléans Wing in the Château de Blois). From his time on, castle plans with a central pavilion and projecting section, architectural decoration that accentuated horizontal and vertical lines, and the use of orders (Doric, Ionic and Corinthian), remained constant features of Classical architecture. Le Vau, who began his career before the reign of Louis XIV by designing town houses

Detail of the Adoration of the Shepherds (c. 1644) by Georges de la Tour, Musée du Louvre

©World Illustrated/Photoshot

(Hôtel Lambert in Paris) for the nobility and the upper middle classes, favoured a grandiose style of architecture characteristic of Louis XIV Classicism (Château de Vaux-le-Vicomte).

Painting

The French school of painting blossomed as a result of Simon Vouet's (1590–1649) return to France in 1627 after a long stay in Rome and the foundation of the Royal Academy of Painting and Sculpture in 1648. References to Italian painting, in particular Venetian (richness of colour) and Roman (dynamism of composition), albeit tempered by a concern for order and clarity, are evident in the work of Vouet and that of his pupil **Eustache le Sueur** (1616–55). Painters such as **Poussin** (1595–1665) and **Philippe de Champaigne** (1602–74) produced highly intellectual works that drew upon philosophical, historical and theological themes – all emblematic of French Classicism. Other trends in French painting flourished in the first half of the century. The realism of the Italian painter Caravaggio influenced the Toulouse school of which the major artist was **Nicolas Tournier** (1590–post 1660). In Lorraine, **Georges de la Tour** (1593–1652) was deeply affected by Caravaggio's style, notably in the use of light and shade and the portrayal

of people from humble blackgrounds. The **Le Nain** brothers, Antoine (c. 1588–1648), Louis (c. 1593–1648) and Mathieu (c. 1607–77), who painted first in Laon and then in Paris, belonged to a trend known as "painters of reality" that favoured genre scenes, drawing more upon the world of the landed upper-middle classes than that of peasant farmers. Their work bore the stamp of Flemish craftsmanship.

Sculpture

Sculpture in the early 17C was influenced by contemporary Italian models. **Jacques Sarrazin** (1588–1660), who studied in Rome, worked in a moderate, Classic mode that derived from Antiquity and also drew upon paintings by Poussin (decoration in the Château de Maisons-Laffitte and the tomb of Henri of Bourbon in the Château de Chantilly). François Anguier (Montmorency Mausoleum in the Lycée chapel in Moulins) and his brother Michel (sculptural decoration on the St-Denis gateway in Paris) showed a more Baroque tendency in their treatment of dynamism and the dramatic stances of their sculptures.

VERSAILLES CLASSICISM

During the reign of Louis XIV (1643–1715) the centralisation of authority and the all-powerful Royal Academy gave rise to an official art that reflected the taste and wishes of the sovereign. The Louis XIV style evolved in Versailles and spread throughout France where it was imitated to a lesser degree by the aristocracy in the late 17C.

The style was characterised by references to Antiquity and a concern for order and grandeur, whether in architecture, painting or sculpture. French resistance to Baroque, which had but a superficial effect on French architecture, was symbolised by the rejection of Bernini's projects for the Louvre. One of the rare examples of the style is Le Vau's College of Four Nations (today's Institute of France) which consists of a former chapel with a cupola and semicircular flanking buildings.

In Versailles **Louis le Vau** and later **Jules Hardouin-Mansart** (1646–1708) favoured a majestic type of architecture: rectangular buildings set off by projecting central sections with twin pillars, flat roofs and sculptural decoration inspired by Antiquity. **Charles le Brun** (1619–90), the leading King's Painter, supervised all the interior decoration (paintings, tapestries, furniture and *objets d'art*), giving the palace remarkable homogeneity. There were dark fabrics and panelling, gilded stuccowork, painted coffered ceilings, and copies of Greco-Roman statues. The decoration became less abundant towards the end of the century.

In 1662, the founding of the **Gobelins**, the "Royal Manufactory for Crown Furniture", stimulated the decorative arts. A team of painters, sculptors, goldsmiths, warp-weavers, marble-cutters, and cabinet-makers worked under Charles le Brun, achieving a high degree of technical perfection. Carpets were made at the Savonnerie factory in Chaillot.

The massive furniture of the period was often carved and sometimes gilded. Boulle marquetry, a combination of brass, tortoiseshell and gilded bronze, was one of the most sumptuous of the decorative arts produced at the time.

Versailles park, laid out by **Le Nôtre** (1613–1700), fulfilled all the requirements of French landscape gardening with its emphasis on rigour and clarity. Its geometrically tailored greenery, long axial perspectives, fountains, carefully designed spinneys and allegorical sculptures reflect the ideal of perfect order and control over nature.

Sculptures were placed throughout the gardens. Many of the works were by the two major sculptors of the time, **François Girardon** (1628–1715) and **Antoine Coysevox** (1640–1720) who drew upon mythology from Antiquity. The work of **Pierre Puget** (1620–94), another important sculptor, was far more tortured and Baroque – an unusual style for the late 17C.

Orangery, Versailles

© Timehacker/Dreamstime.com

FRENCH ROCAILLE (1715–1750)

The 18C style in France grew from a reaction against the austerity and grandeur of the Louis XIV style, which was considered ill-adapted to the luxurious life and pleasures of the aristocracy and the upper-middle classes during the regency of Philippe of Orléans (1715–23) and the reign of Louis XV (1723–74). Rocaille was an 18C Rococo style or ornamentation based on rock and shell motifs.

Architecture

Rocaille architecture, at least on the outside, remained faithful to some of the principles of Classical composition – plain buildings with symmetrical façades and projecting central sections crowned by a triangular pediment – but the use of Classical orders became less rigid and systematic. The most representative examples of this new type of architecture were town houses such as the Hôtel de Soubise by **Delamair** and Hôtel Matignon by **Courtonne**, both in Paris.

The majestic formal apartments of the previous century gave way to smaller, more intimate rooms such as boudoirs and studies. Inside, woodwork, often white and gold, covered the walls from top to bottom (Hôtel de Lassay in Paris and the Clock Room or Cabinet de la Pendule in Versailles). The repertoire of ornamentation included intertwining plant motifs, curved lines, shells and other natural objects. Paintings of landscapes and country scenes were inserted in the woodwork above doors or in the corners of ceilings. **Verberckt**, who worked in Versailles for Louis XV, was an exceptionally skilled interior decorator.

Painting

The generation of painters working at the turn of the century was influenced by Flemish art. Artists such as **Desportes** (1661–1743), **Largillière** (1656–1746) and **Rigaud** (1659–1743) painted sumptuously decorative still lifes and formal portraits. Secular themes including scenes of gallantry (*fêtes galantes*), and

fashionable society life became popular. **Watteau** (1684–1721), **Boucher** (1703–70), **Natoire** (1700–77) and **Fragonard** (1732–1806) reflected the taste of the day in their elegant genre scenes, some with mythological overtones, of pastoral life and the game of love.

Religious painting was not neglected in spite of these trends. Charles de la Fosse (1636–1716), one of Le Brun's pupils, Antoine Coypel (1661–1722) and especially **Restout** (1692–1768) adapted it to the less stoical ideals of the 18C by stripping it of too strong a dogmatism. There was a revival in portraiture during the 18C. **Nattier** (1685–1766), official painter of Louis XV's daughters, produced likenesses in mythological guise or half-length portraits which were far less pompous than the usual court picture. The pastellist **Quentin de la Tour** (1704–88) excelled in portraying his subjects' individual temperament and psychology rather than their social rank by concentrating more on faces than dress and accessories.

The lesser genres (still-lifes and landscapes), scorned by the Academy but favoured by the middle classes for the decoration of their homes, blossomed considerably at the time. **Chardin** (1699–1779) painted simple still lifes in muted tones and Flemish-inspired scenes of everyday life, giving them a realistic, picturesque quality.

Sculpture

Baroque influence swept through sculpture in the first half of the century. The **Adam** brothers (Neptune Basin at Versailles), **Coustou** (1677–1746) (Horses of Marly), and **Slodtz** (1705–64) introduced the style's expressiveness into their work to lend movement and feeling. The main characteristics of Baroque art were flowing garments, attention to detail and figures shown in action.

In contrast, the contemporary work of **Bouchardon** (1698–1762) who trained in Rome and was therefore influenced by Antique sculpture, tended to be more Classical (Fountain in the Rue de Grenelle in Paris).

Decorative Arts

The rise of fashionable society brought with it a great need for luxury furniture that matched the style of woodwork inside elegant homes. New types of furniture were created: after commodes (chests of drawers) came writing-desks – upright or inclined, escritoires, chiffoniers and countless small tables. For the comforts of conversation there were wing-chairs and deep easy chairs. There were also *voyeuses* or conversation chairs (special seats in gaming houses placed behind players to allow spectators to watch) and all manner of sofas and seats on which to recline (couches, lounging-chairs, divans and settees). Curved lines were favoured, as were rare and precious materials like exotic woods and lacquered panelling often set off by floral marquetry and finely chased gilded bronze. Among the great rocaille cabinet-makers were Cressent, Joubert and Migeon, while the principal seat carpenters of the time were Foliot, Sené and Cresson.

The **Vincennes Porcelain Factory** moved to **Sèvres** in 1756 and produced luxury items of which some were decorated in deep blue known as Sèvres blue. Gilt ornamentation was theoretically used only for royal services. Rocaille gold and silver plate was adorned with reed motifs, crested waves, scroll-work and shells often arranged in asymmetrical patterns. **Thomas Germain** (1673–1748), one of the most prestigious names in the trade, supplied the princely tables of the time.

NEOCLASSICAL REACTION

The middle of the century brought a reaction against rocaille on moral and aesthetic grounds. The style was considered to be too florid and frivolous, the result of decadence in both morals and the arts. Classical models from Antiquity and the 17C were then deemed the only recourse to revive proper artistic creation.

Architecture

The new style of architecture that emerged was more austere and tended towards the monumental. Sculptural decoration on façades grew more restrained and the Doric order became widespread (Église St-Philippe-du-Roule by J F Chardin in Paris). Some buildings, like the Église Ste-Geneviève (the present-day Panthéon) in Paris by **G Soufflot** (1713–80), were direct copies of Antique models. Louis XVI commissioned men like **Victor Louis** (1731–1802) who designed the Bordeaux theatre, **A T Brongniart** (1739–1813) and **J F Bélanger** (1744–1818) for most of the great architectural undertakings of the time. The philosophical influence of the Enlightenment led to a keen interest in the architecture of functional, public buildings such as the Royal Salt-works in Arc-et-Senans by **Claude-Nicolas Ledoux** (1736–1806).

Sculpture

Sculptors distanced themselves from rocaille extravagance by striving towards a natural portrayal of anatomy.

E M Falconet (1716–91), P Julien (1731–1804) and G C Allegrain (1710–95) drew upon Greco-Roman models for their greatly admired sculptures of female bathers. **J A Houdon** (1741–1828), one of the greatest sculptors of the late 18C, made busts of his French and foreign contemporaries (Voltaire, Buffon and Madame Adélaïde for the first, and Benjamin Franklin and George Washington for the second) which constituted a veritable portrait gallery. The busts, executed in an extremely realistic manner, many without wigs or articles of dress to detract from the faces, were the culmination of modelled portraiture in France. Houdon also sculpted tombs and mythological statues. **J B Pigalle** (1714–85) maintained the style of sculpture predominant at the beginning of the century that the Neoclassical reaction had not managed to stifle entirely (mausoleum of the Marshal de Saxe in the Église St-Thomas in Strasbourg).

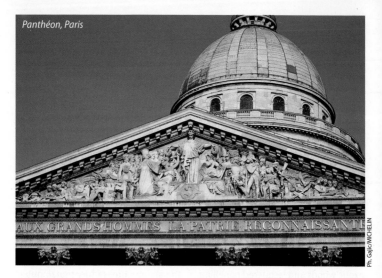

Panthéon, Paris

AUX GRANDS HOMMES LA PATRIE RECONNAISSANTE

Ph. Gajic/MICHELIN

Painting

In the 1760s, attempts by the Royal Academy to restore a style of painting known as the grand manner encouraged the emergence of new themes such as antique history, civic heroism and 17C tragedies. These were adopted by painters like **J L David** (1748–1825), **J B M Pierre** (1714–89) and **J F P Peyron** (1744–1814). The style drew upon low-reliefs and statuary from Antiquity and followed the principles of composition used by painters like Poussin and other 17C masters.

Works by **J M Vien** (1716–1809) and **J B Greuze** (1725–1805) showed a less austere approach to painting, with more room for sensibility and emotion, that heralded the romanticism that was to blossom after the Revolution.

Decorative Arts

Louis XVI furniture kept some of the characteristics inherited from the beginning of the century such as the use of precious materials and chased gilt bronze ornamentation, but curves and sinuous shapes gave way to straight lines. As far as decoration was concerned, while the floral motifs and ribbons of the past were maintained, ovoli friezes, Greek fretwork and fasces were willingly introduced. **René Dubois** (1738–99) and **Louis Delanois** (1731–92)

initiated the Greek style derived from Antique furniture seen in friezes at Herculaneum and Pompeii. Prestigious artists of the genre included Oeben and Riesener while Carlin followed by Beneman and Levasseur specialised in furniture adorned with plaques of painted porcelain.

At the end of the century new decorative motifs including lyres, ears of corn, wickerwork baskets and hot-air balloons were imported from England.

The technique of hard-paste porcelain that was introduced into France at the beginning of the 1770s took the lead over soft-paste porcelain in the factory at Sèvres. Figurines of **biscuit** porcelain (white, fired, unglazed pottery) shaped on models by Fragonard, Boucher and other artists, became very popular.

The iconoclasm that prevailed during the **Revolution** marked a break in the history of French art. The Louvre opened in 1793 paving the way for many more museums in France.

19TH CENTURY

Art During the First Empire

After his investiture in 1804, Napoleon favoured the emergence of an official style of art by commissioning palace decoration (Tuileries, destroyed in 1870, and Fontainebleau) and paintings that related the great events of the Empire.

The artists to benefit from the Emperor's patronage were men like J L David and his pupils **A J Gros** (1771–1835) and **A L Girodet-Trioson** (1767–1824).

Paintings of the time took on new themes derived from the romanticism in contemporary literature, orientalism and an interest in the medieval. National historic anecdotes were painted by artists who, like the troubadours, praised heroic deeds and fine sentiment.

Artistic development in the realm of architecture was less innovative. Napoleon commissioned large edifices commemorating the glory of the *Grande Armée* including the Carrousel Arch, the column in Place Vendôme and the Temple de la Madeleine (now a church). The official architects **Percier** (1764–1838) and **Fontaine** (1762–1853) were responsible for the overall supervision of the undertakings, setting models not only for buildings but also for decoration at official ceremonies and guidelines for the decorative arts.

Ambitious town-planning projects like the reconstruction of Lyon were also completed under the Empire.

Former royal palaces were refurnished. The style of First Empire furniture derived from the Neoclassical with massive, quadrangular, commodes and jewel-cases made of mahogany with gilt bronze plating and Antique decorative motifs. **Desmalter** (1770–1841) was the main cabinet-maker of the imperial court. The sculptors **Chaudet** (1763–1810) and **Cartellier** (1757–1831) supplied models for furniture ornamentation in the Neoclassical style which also inspired their statues. After the Egyptian Campaign motifs like sphinxes and lotuses began to appear in the decorative arts.

Restoration and the July Monarchy

Two major trends affected French art between 1815 and 1848. The first was the gradual disappearance of the Neoclassical style which, however, still influenced church building (Notre-Dame-de-Lorette and St-Vincent-de-Paul in Paris); and the second was the birth of historicism, a style that fostered regard for the architecture of the past, particularly of the medieval period (Église Notre-Dame in Boulogne-sur-Mer and Marseille Cathedral by Léon Vaudoyer). The trend was furthered by the founding of the *Monuments Historiques* (a body set up for the classification and preservation of the national heritage) in 1830 and the enthusiasm of **Viollet-le-Duc (1814–79)**.

The Second Empire

On the accession of Napoleon III the arts in general were affected by a spirit of **eclecticism**. The Louvre, completed by Percier's disciple Visconti (1791–1853) and **H Lefuel** (1810–80), and the Paris Opera by **Garnier** (1825–98) were among the greatest undertakings of the century. References to architectural styles of the past (16C, 17C and 18C) were present everywhere. Nevertheless, the introduction of new materials like glass and cast iron (the Gare du Nord by Hittorff and the Église St-Augustin by V Baltard) showed the influence of technological progress and a new rational approach to building.

Baron Haussmann (1809–91), Prefect of the *département* of the Seine, laid down the principles for a public works programme that was to modernise the

The Valpinçon Bather (1808) by Jean Auguste Dominique Ingres, Musée du Louvre

©World Illustrated/Photoshot

capital. Prefect C M Vaïsse carried out a similar plan in Lyon.

Academicism reigned over the **painting** of the time. **Cabanel** (1823–83), **Bouguereau** (1825–1905) and the portraitist **Winterhalter** (1805–73) drew their inspiration just as easily from Antique statuary as from works by 16C Venetian masters or Rococo ornamentation. However, **Courbet** (1819–77), **Daumier** (1808–79) and **Millet** (1814–75) formed an avant-garde group that fostered realism in painting with subjects from town and country life.

Ingres (1780–1867) who represented the Classical trend, and **Delacroix** (1798–1863), the great romantic painter of the century, were both at the height of their powers. Great architectural projects stimulated the production of **sculpture. Carpeaux** (1827–75), responsible for the high-relief of Dance on the façade of the Paris Opera, transcended the eclecticism of his time by developing a very personal style that was reminiscent of, and not simply a copy of, Flemish, Renaissance and 18C art. Dubois (1829–1905), Frémiet (1824–1910) and Guillaume (1822–1905) were more academic in their approach.

A taste for pastiche prevailed in the decorative arts. The shapes and ornamental motifs of the Renaissance, the 16C and 18C were reproduced on furniture and *objets d'art*. The advent of **industrialisation** affected certain fields. The goldsmith Christofle (1805–63) and the bronze-founder Barbedienne (1810–92) made luxury items for the imperial court as well as mass-produced articles for new clients among the rich upper-middle classes.

Late 19C Artistic trends

Architecture during the Third Republic was mainly marked by edifices built for Universal Exhibitions held in Paris (the former Palais du Trocadéro, the Eiffel Tower, the Grand-Palais and the Pont Alexandre-III). The pompous style of the buildings with their exotic ornamentation derived from the trend for eclecticism.

In the 1890s **Art Nouveau** architects, influenced by trends in England and Belgium, distanced themselves from the official style of the day. They harmonised decoration on façades with that inside their buildings and designed their creations as a whole – stained glass, tiles, furniture and wall-paper. Decoration

La Gare Saint-Lazare (1877) by Claude Monet, Musée d'Orsay

included plant motifs, stylised flowers, Japanese influences and asymmetrical patterns. **Guimard** (1867–1942) was the main proponent of the style in France (Castel Béranger in Paris and entrances to the capital's metro stations).

The decorative arts followed the Art Nouveau movement with works by the cabinet-maker **Majorelle** (1859–1929) and the glass and ceramics artist **Gallé** (1846–1904) in Nancy.

In the field of painting, the **Impressionists** began exhibiting their work outside official salons in 1874. **Monet** (1840–1926), **Renoir** (1841–1919) and **Pissarro** (1830–1903) breathed new life into the technique and themes of landscape painting by working out of doors, studying the play of light in nature and introducing new subjects drawn from contemporary life. **Manet** (1832–83) and **Degas** (1834–1917) joined the group temporarily.

Between 1885 and 1890, Neo-Impressionists like **G Seurat** (1859–91) and **Signac** (1863–1935) brought the Pointillist (painting with small dots) technique known as divisionism to a climax. The Dutch painter **Van Gogh** (1853–90) settled in France in 1886. His technique of using pure and expressionist colours with broad swirling brushstrokes coupled with his belief that expression of emotional experience should override impressions of the external world were to have a great influence on early 20C painters. **Cézanne** (1839–1906) and **Gauguin** (1848–1903), who were influenced by primitive and Japanese art, partly dispensed with Impressionism to give more importance to volume. In 1886, seeking new inspiration, Gauguin moved to Pont-Aven, a small town east of Concarneau in Brittany that had often been visited by the painter Corot in the 1860s. Fellow artists **Émile Bernard** and **Paul Sérusier** formed the Pont-Aven School that favoured synthesist theories and symbolic subjects which paved the way for the **Nabis**.

Among the Nabis were artists like **Denis** (1870–1943), **Bonnard** (1867–1947) and **Vuillard** (1868–1940) who advocated the importance of colour over shape and meaning. Sculpture at the end of the century was dominated by the genius of **Rodin** (1840–1917). His expressionistic, tormented, symbolic work stood free from formal academic conventions and was not always understood in his time.

20TH CENTURY

Avant-Garde Movements

At the beginning of the 20C, proponents of the avant-garde reacted against the many trends of the 19C including the restrictions laid down by official art, academicism in painting and Art Nouveau in architecture.

The **Stijl** movement was characterised in architecture by simple, geometric buildings adorned with sober low-reliefs. One of its most magnificent examples was the Théâtre des Champs-Élysées by the Perret brothers with sculptural decoration by **Bourdelle** (1861–1929). In the field of sculpture, the artists **Maillol** (1861–1944), **Bartholomé** (1848–1928) and J **Bernard** (1866–1931) opposed Rodin's aesthetic concepts and produced a very different type of art by simplifying their figures, in some cases to the point of schematic representation.

Fauvism was the great novelty at the Autumn Salon of painting in 1905. A Derain (1880–1964), **A Marquet** (1875–1947) and **M de Vlaminck** (1876–1958) broke up their subject-matter through the vivid and arbitrary use of colour, a technique which was to pave the way for non-figurative painting. After an early period with the fauvist movement, **Matisse** (1869–1904) went his own way developing a personal style based on the exploration of colour.

A further major avant-garde movement in painting followed on from **Cézanne**'s (1839–1906) structural analysis in which he broke up his subject matter into specific shapes. The trend was taken up by artists like **Braque** (1882–1963) and **Picasso** (1881–1973) whose exploration led to **Cubism**, a new perception of reality based not on what the eye saw but on an analytical approach to objects, depicting them as a series of planes, usually in a restricted colour range.

The style dominated their work from 1907 to 1914.

Members of the *Section d'Or* (golden section) Cubist group like **A Gleizes**, **J Metzinger** and **F Léger** (his early works) were less revolutionary and more figurative. The main contribution to French cubism in the field of sculpture came from **Henri Laurens**, who was influenced by Braque.

Surrealism breathed new life into the art world in the 1920s and 1930s. It was a subversive art form that created an irrational, dreamlike, fantasy universe. For the first time chance and promptings from the subconscious were integrated into the creative process. **Duchamp** (1887–1968), **Masson** (1896–1997), **Picabia** (1879–1953) and **Magritte** (1898–1967) all formed part of the movement.

Artistic Creation Since 1945

Abstract art began to affect the field of painting after World War II. **Herbin** defined it as the triumph of mind over matter. In 1949 he published Non-figurative, Non-objective Art (L'Art non figuratif non objectif) and greatly influenced young artists of the **geometric abstract** art movement. All his works from the 1950s onwards have been one-dimensional patterns of letters and simple geometric shapes painted in pure colours.

The **lyrical abstract** artists focused on the study of colour and texture. **Riopelle** applied his paint with a knife while **Mathieu** applied it directly from the tube. **Soulages**, who was influenced by art from the Far East, produced meditative, expressive work in shades of black. **Nicolas de Stael**'s art constituted a link between abstract and figurative in that his abstract compositions were the result of observations of real objects which could sometimes be distinguished in the final work.

There was an important revival in architecture with **Le Corbusier** (1897–1965) whose buildings fulfilled functional requirements with great clarity of form (Cité Radieuse in Marseille and Ronchamp Chapel).

In the 1960s, **New Realism** *(Nouveau Réalisme)*, a form of pop art, with **Pierre Restany** as its leading theoretician, attempted to express the reality of daily life. Industrial items, the symbols of modern society, were broken up (by the artist **Arman**) and assembled (by **César**) or trapped in glass.

Yves Klein (1928–62) took his adherence to New Realism a step further in his Monochromes by trying to capture the universal essence of objects. He worked in pure colours and created I B K, or International Klein Blue. He rejected formal and traditional values as did **Dubuffet** (1901–85) who, in 1968, wrote a pamphlet entitled Asphyxiating Culture (Asphyxiante culture) which made a stand for permanent revolution. Dubuffet's later art consisted of puzzles of coloured or black and white units.

Since the 1960s, the problems posed by town-planning have led to a re-evaluation of the relationship between architecture and sculpture and an attempt to reconcile the two arts. Architects and sculptors often work together as in the case of the project by Ricardo Bofill and D Karavan in Cergy-Pontoise northwest of Paris. Artists are increasingly being asked to modify townscapes.

The **Support-Surface** movement (**Claude Viallet**, **Pagès** and **Daniel Dezeuze**) of the 1970s reduced painting to its pure material state by focusing on the way the paint was applied. Paintings were removed from their stretchers and cut up, suspended and folded.

The 1980s saw the return of Figuration in manifold ways. References to tradition are evident in the work of artists like **Gérard Garouste** and **Jean-Charles Blais**. The great vitality of contemporary art can be seen in the extremely wide variety of styles and trends favoured by artists today.

Nature

TOPOGRAPHY

France has a fortunate location in the European continent – not detached from it like the British Isles, nor projecting away like Iberia or Greece, nor set deep in its interior like the countries of Central Europe, yet in touch with the resources and the life of the whole of Western Europe and the seas around it, Atlantic, Channel, Mediterranean and North Sea. These seas together with the other natural frontiers, the Alps and Pyrenees and the River Rhine, define the compact shape of the French "hexagon".

There are four main river systems: in the east is the Valley of the Rhone, (813km/505mi), which together with its tributary the Saône, (480km/298mi,) links the Paris basin with the Mediterranean; in the north, the Seine (776km/482mi) drains into the English Channel; in the west, the longest of all, the Loire (1010km/630mi) rises in central France and flows into the Atlantic as does its southern cousin the Garonne (575km/357mi) which rises in the Pyrénées and drains into the Gironde estuary. Within this unified and robust framework there flourishes a geographical identity which is unmistakably French yet of an unrivalled local richness and variety. Less a paradox than a wonderful synthesis, this coexistence of unity and diversity is the work of both Nature and Man.

"La France est diversité"
(France is diversity)
Fernand Braudel. French historian and educator (1902-1985)

GEOLOGICAL HISTORY

It has been said that the whole of Earth's history – the building of the planet – can be traced within the confines of France. The country's complex geological history starts in the Primary Era (600 million years ago), when the Hercynian folding was responsible for the raising up of the great mountain ranges which were the ancestors of today's Massif Central, Armorican Peninsula, Vosges and Ardennes.

In Secondary Era times (beginning 200 million years ago), the Paris region, Aquitaine, the Rhône and Loire valleys and the southern part of the Massif Central all lay under the sea which gradually filled them with sedimentary deposits.

New mountain ranges reared up in the Tertiary Era (beginning 60 million years ago): the Alps, Pyrenees, the Jura and Corsica. The shock-waves of this violent mountain-building were felt far afield, particularly in the Massif Central where great volcanoes erupted.

The Quaternary age (2 million years ago) saw an alternation of warm and cold periods; glaciers advanced and retreated and rivers swelled and shrank, sculpting much of the land surface into its present forms.

CLIMATE AND RELIEF

In climatic terms too, France gathers into herself each of the contrasting patterns of the continent as a whole; Atlantic, Continental and Mediterranean influences are all present (in northern and western France, central and eastern parts of the country, and the south), contributing decisively to the formation of soils and their mantle of vegetation as well as to the processes which have shaped the geological foundation into the patterns of today's relief.

The north of the country is largely composed of great sedimentary basins, scarp *(côtes)* and vale country, drained by slow-flowing rivers like the Seine and the Loire. At the extremities of these lowlands are rugged areas formed of Primary rocks, the much-eroded granites of Brittany and the gneisses and schists of the Ardennes, and the higher massifs of the Vosges and the centre. Beyond lie the fertile plains of Aquitaine and Languedoc while the corridor carved by the Rhône and Saône links the north and south of the country. Finally come the "young" mountains of the Jura, Alps and Pyrenees; their high peaks and ranges, while forming fine natural frontiers, are by no means impermeable to political, commercial and cultural currents.

Château de Chaumont
B. Kaufmann/MICHELIN

ALSACE LORRAINE CHAMPAGNE

Alsace forms France's window onto Central Europe. Its capital, Strasbourg, was part of the Holy Roman Empire. Together with the other towns and villages along this left bank of the Rhine, it has a picturesqueness of decidedly Germanic character. **Lorraine** owes its name to ancient Lotharingia, central of the three kingdoms into which Charlemagne's inheritance was divided. The presence of coal, iron-ore and salt led to the development of heavy industry. The **Champagne** region to the west is renowned for its sparkling wine, and the **Ardennes** to the north is one of Europe's most extensive areas of forest, with fine stands of oak, beech and conifers.

Highlights

1 Grünewald's masterpiece, The Issenheim Altarpiece, **Colmar** (p100)

2 La Petite France, **Strasbourg** (p112)

3 Gothic Cathédrale Notre-Dame, **Reims** (p118)

4 Old timber-framed houses, Vieux Troyes at **Troyes** (p123)

5 Place Stanislas, **Nancy** (p131)

Geography – The Rhine forms a frontier between Alsace and Germany, flowing through a broad rift valley defined by the Black Forest and the Vosges uplands. Further west in Lorraine, a series of limestone escarpments are pierced by major rivers flowing northwest. Around Reims, steep slopes carry vineyards, and beyond stretches one of France's most productive agricultural regions. To the north, the Ardennes stretch into Belgium and merge with the German Eifel.

History – Alsace and Lorraine have long been fought over by France and Germany. Part of the Germanic Holy Roman Empire until 1648, the territory has changed hands four times since 1871. Champagne has been part of France since the 14C and the Ardennes has seen many battles, from the Franco-Prussian War to World War II.

Economy – Alsace produces many varieties of wine. Together with Lorraine it is also one of the most important industrial areas of France. Lorraine depends heavily on timber production and dairy produce, while retaining an important metal sector. Champagne's economy is mainly agriculture, while the Ardennes depends heavily on timber, tourism and its agricultural industries.

Ecomusée d'
Alsace★★

Alsace

An open-air museum founded in 1984 to preserve local heritage comprises some 60 old buildings dotted over an area of 15ha/37 acres. The old buildings dating from the 15–19C, which were saved from demolition and carefully dismantled and re-erected to create a village setting, are fine examples of rural habitat from the various regions of Alsace. The museum, which is constantly evolving, also includes industrial structures; next door to the museum are the restored buildings of a potassium mine which was worked from 1911–1930.

ᴤ VISIT

ⓢ *Call for opening times and prices.*
☏ *03 89 62 43 00.*
www.ecomusee-alsace.fr.

Walk around the half-timbered buildings grouped by region (Sundgau, Reid, Kochersberg, Bas-Rhin) and complete with courtyards and gardens, to appreciate the development of building techniques and the varied architecture of farm buildings according to the regions and periods.

Specific buildings such as a fortified structure, a chapel, a school and a washhouse evoke community life in a traditional Alsatian village. Old plant varieties are grown in a typical field which also serves for farming demonstrations.

An area devoted to funfairs includes a rare merry-go-round (1909). Many local people act as volunteers and help with various entertainment features which really bring the trades of yesteryear to life. Visitors will discover the age-old crafts of carpenters, blacksmiths, clog makers, potters, coopers, coalmen and masons as well as the evolution of living conditions, from the reconstructed interiors complete with kitchens, alcoves and "stube", the living area with its terracotta stove.

Due to the efforts of its many voluntary workers and the gifting of numerous historical items, the Ecomusée d'Alsace has over the years become one of the largest in Europe with its 100ha/247 acres of village, fields and forests.

> ▸ **Population:** 1 815 493 (Alsace *département*)
> ⚙ **Michelin Map:** 315 H 9
> ▤ **Info:** L'Écomusée d'Alsace. 68190 Ungersheim. ☏03 89 62 43 00. www.ecomusee-alsace.fr.
> ◖ **Location:** The Ecomusée is about 16km/10mi NW of Mulhouse.
> ᴤ **Kids:** Kids will love exploring the Ecomusée.

One of the timber-framed Alsatian houses, Écomusée d'Alsace

R. Mattès/MICHELIN

Alsatian Dwellings

Potter's house in Outre-Forêt

Fisherman's house in the Reid

Farmstead in Kochersberg

House in the vineyards of Alsace

Farmhouse in the Sundgau

R. Corbel/MICHELIN – Source: Écomusée d'Alsace

Colmar★★★

Alsace

The capital of Upper Alsace is situated at the point where the Munster valley widens out into the broad plain of the Rhine. Since the 13C the town has prospered on the proceeds of the wine trade and boasts fine monuments. More recently, industries have spread along the Logelbach Canal.

A BIT OF HISTORY

In 1834 **Frédéric Bartholdi** was born here, the patriotic sculptor responsible for many striking works, including New York's Statue of Liberty.

Between 1871–1918 Alsace and Lorraine were part of Germany. A particular irritant to authority was the Colmar writer and caricaturist Jean-Jacques Waltz (1872–1951), known as "Hansi", who was imprisoned at the outbreak of war in 1914, but escaped to enlist in the French army.

In early February 1945, the French army under General de Lattre de Tassigny launched an attack on Colmar to eliminate German resistance. On 1 February the German lines north of Colmar were overrun by American troops, who stood aside to let the French 5th armoured division of General Schlesser enter Colmar.

▶ **Population:** 65 136
⚲ **Michelin Map:** 315 I 8
▯ **Info:** 4 r. des Hunterlinden. ℘03 89 20 68 92. www.ot-colmar.fr.
◗ **Location:** Locate the center of the Old Town at the Place de l'Ancienne Douane. The museum lies to your N, while S along the rue des Tanneurs you'll find picturesque flower-decked houses lining the canal of "Little Venice".
◉ **Don't Miss:** The **Retable d'Issenheim**, the 16C masterpiece of **Matthias Grünewald** on display at the Musée Unterlinden; **Colmar by Night** – The town's most beautiful buildings are lit up at night; a **Boat Trip** – ◖*See Little Venice.*
👥 **Kids:** Musée Animé du Jouet et des Petits Trains.

Guided Tours

Tours *(1hr15min)* of the old town are organised. *Run from Jul–Sept.* ℘03 89 20 68. ⬤4€.

Quiet canal in old Colmar

R.Mattes/MICHELIN

Detail on the Maison des Têtes

R. Mattes/MICHELIN

SIGHTS

Musée Unterlinden★★★

1 r. d'Unterlinden. ○*Open May–Oct daily 9am–6pm; Nov–Apr Wed–Mon 9am–noon, 2–5pm.* ○*Closed 1 Jan, 1 May, 1 Nov, 25 Dec.* ⬤*7€.* ✆*03 89 20 15 50. www.musee-unterlinden.com.*

The museum, situated on place d'Unterlinded through which flows the Logelbach canal, is housed in a former 13C monastery. The ground floor is devoted to religious art and presents rich collections of paintings and sculpture dating from the late Middle Ages and the Renaissance.

⛟ Musée Animé du Jouet et des Petits Trains

40 r. Vauban. ○*Open Sept daily 10am–noon, 2–6pm; Oct–Jun Wed–Mon 10am–noon, 2–6pm; Jul–Aug daily 10am–7pm; Dec daily 10am–6pm.* ⬤*4.50€, child 3.50€.* ✆*03 89 41 93 10. www.museejouet.com.*

Housed in a former cinema, collections include numerous railway engines, trains, and dolls in many different materials.

Retable d'Issenheim★★★

In the chapel.

In 1512 **Matthias Grünewald** was called to Issenheim 22km/14mi south of Colmar to paint the **Issenheim altarpiece** for the chapel of the Antonite convent. This extraordinary work should be seen, not as a collection of separate masterpieces, but as an integrated whole, conceived

and executed as a programme whose logic, while still puzzling to the specialist of today, probably lies in the convent superior's particular vision of the meaning of suffering. Everything contributes to the overall effect, not only the choice of themes and their relationship to one another, but also the pose and expression of the figures, the symbolic meaning of the various themes, animals and monsters, and even the use of colour. Note for example the figure of Mary Magdalene at the foot of the cross; her pose conveys both the attraction exercised over her by the figure of Christ as well as the revulsion she feels in the face of His agony. Note too the way contrast is handled, with the generally gloomy tone of the paintings shot through with flashes of light.

Grünewald's stature as one of the truly great masters of Western religious painting is fully revealed in the central panel of the altarpiece, the harrowing Crucifixion.

Ville Ancienne★★

The heart of the old town comprises the Place de l'Ancienne Douane, Rue des Marchands and Rue Mercière (Haberdasher Street). There are many picturesque old houses, with corner turrets, oriel windows and half-timbering, and balconies adorned with flowers. Particularly striking are the **Maison Pfister★★**, with frescoes and medallions and a pyramidal roof, and the Old Customs House, **Ancienne Douane★** of 1480 with a timber gallery and canted staircase tower.

ADDITIONAL SIGHTS

Église des Dominicains *(pl. des Dominicains)* – **stained glass★** and **Virgin in the Rose Bower★★**
Ancien Corps de Garde★ *(pl. de la Cathédrale)*
"Little Venice"★
Maison des Têtes★ *(19 r. des Têtes)*
Église St-Matthieu *(Grand r.;* ☏*call in advance for guided tour;* ✆*03 89 41 44 96)* – **Crucifixion window★**.

ADDRESSES

🛏 STAY

Chambre d'hôte Les Framboises – *128 r. des Trois-Épis, 68230 Katzenthal, 5km/3mi NW of Colmar, Kaysersberg direction then D10. ✆03 89 27 48 85. 4 rooms.* Leave Colmar behind and head for the open countryside and this village among the vines. The proprietor distils his own *marc* (grape brandy) from Gewürztraminer and provides accommodation in wood-panelled attic rooms. Don't miss the puppet show in the mornings!

Colbert – *2 r. des Trois-Épis. ✆03 89 41 31 05. 50 rooms. ▱6€.* This functional hotel near the station provides a comfortable place to stay for those travelling by train. The rooms are well equipped with new bedding, effective soundproofing and air conditioning, and some have a balcony. Bar and disco for those in search of nightlife.

Hôtel Au Moulin – *Rte d'Herrlisheim – 68127 Ste-Croix-en-Plaine, 10km/6.2mi S of Colmar on A35 and D1. ✆03 89 49 31 20. www.aumoulin. net. Closed 5 Nov–31 Mar. 14 rooms. ▱9€.* This old mill deep in the country is perfect for those seeking peace and quiet. Its spacious rooms are all the same but nicely arranged. A small museum of old local objects has been created in a neighbouring building.

Hôtel Turenne – *10 rte de Bâle. ✆03 89 41 12 26. www.turenne.com. Closed until Apr 2009. 83 rooms. ▱8.50€.* On the edge of the old town, this hotel occupies a large, pleasing building with a pink and yellow façade. Its rooms have been nicely renovated and are well soundproofed. A few small but neat and reasonably priced single rooms are available.

Hôtel Le Colombier – *7 r. de Turenne. ✆03 89 23 96 00. www. hotel-le-colombier.fr. 24 rooms. ▱12€.* This lovely 15C house in old Colmar combines old stone and contemporary décor by retaining elements from its past, such as the superb Renaissance staircase. Contemporary furniture, modern paintings and carefully arranged rooms.

🍽 EAT

Le Caveau St-Pierre – *24 r. de la Herse (Little Venice). ✆03 89 41 99 33. Closed Mon and Jan. Booking advisable.* A pretty wooden footbridge across the Lauch leads to this 17C house, which offers a little slice of paradise with its rustic, local-style décor and a terrace stretching out over the water. Local cuisine.

La Maison Rouge – *9 r. des Écoles. ✆03 89 23 53 22.* The somewhat ordinary façade hides a delightful rustic interior. Regional and homemade cooking take pride of place.

Schwendi Bier-U-Wistub – *23–25 Grand'Rue. ✆03 89 23 66 26.* You will instantly warm to this charming winstub with its ideal location in the heart of old Colmar. The principally wooden décor and the cooking, which is good quality and served in generous portions, are a tribute to Alsace. Huge terrace to be enjoyed in summer.

Winstub La Krutenau – *1 r. de la Poissonnerie. ✆03 89 41 18 80. Closed Christmas–end Jan, Sun and Mon out of season .* At this winstub beside the River Lauch you can go boating in Little Venice and eat a *flammekueche* on the flower-decked terrace beside the canal in summer. A fun way, with no obligations, to learn about this lovely part of Colmar – recommended.

Caveau Chez Bacchus – *2 Grand'Rue, Katzenthal, 5km/3mi NW of Colmar, Kaysersberg direction, then D10. ✆03 89 27 32 25. Closed at varying times; call in advance.* There's a lovely friendly atmosphere in this wine bar dating from 1789 in a winemaking village. Massive exposed beams and helpings of Alsatian cuisine to match – guaranteed to satisfy the healthiest of appetites. Automated puppets will entertain the children with a lively show.

Winstub Brenner – *1 r. de Turenne. ✆03 89 41 42 33. Closed at varying times; call in advance.* The terrace by the Lauch in Little Venice is very popular on fine days. Not surprising, as the setting is ideal and the food, though simple, is served in generous portions.

🎭 NIGHTLIFE

Théâtre de la Manufacture –
6, rte d'Ingersheim. 📞*03 89 24 31 78.*
Performances Mon–Wed and Fri 8.30pm,
Thu 7pm, Sat 6pm. www.atelierdurhin.
com. Contemporary theatre, music,
dance.

Alsation Folk Evenings – *pl. de*
l'Ancienne Douane. Mid-May–mid-Sept
Tue 8.30pm.

Théâtre Municipal – *3 r. Unterlinden.*
📞*03 89 20 29 01/02.* Classic plays,
comedy and opera.

🛒 SHOPPING

Domaine viticole de la Ville de
Colmar. *2 r. Stauffen.* 📞*03 89 79 11*
87. www.domaineviticolecolmar.com.
Founded in 1895, this estate grows
seven *cépages* and boasts a host of
grands crus in addition to sparkling
wines. Wide range of wines, brandies
and liquors on sale.

Caveau Robert-Karcher – *11 r. de l'Ours.*
📞*03 89 41 14 42. www.vins-karcher.com.*
The vineyards of this family business
are north-west of Colmar, but the cellar,
dating from 1602, is in the town centre.
Taste the whole range of Alsace wines
and be shown around the cellar.

Fortwenger – *32 r. des Marchands.*
📞*03 89 41 06 93. www.fortwenger.fr.*
It was in Gertwiller in 1768 that Charles
Fortwenger founded his gingerbread
factory, but this Colmar shop sells a
wide range of delicious sweet products.

Maison des Vins d'Alsace – *Civa, 12 ave*
de la Foire-aux-Vins, BP1217. 📞*03 89 20 16*
20. www.vinsalsace.com.
Five local organisations concerned with
Alsace wines are based in this centre.
Visitors can study a map showing all the
winemaking villages and *grands crus*, as
well as learn about winemaking from
hands-on models and a film.

Château du Haut-Kœnigsbourg ★★

Alsace

This vast mock-medieval edifice
in pink sandstone overlooks the
Alsace plain from its lofty rock rising
through the treetops of the Vosges
forest.

🚗 **Michelin Map:** 315 I 7

🔵 **Location:** The castle is
roughly 21km/13mi N of
Colmar. It is reached on
a steep winding access
road in the hills between
Sélestat and Ribeauvillé.

👁 **Don't Miss:** A superb
panorama★★ from the tall
bastion.

VISIT

♿🕐*Open Jan, Feb, Nov, Dec 9.30am–*
noon, 1–4.30pm; Mar, Oct 9.30am–5pm;
Apr, May, Sept until 5.15pm; Jun–Aug
until 6pm; closes 45min after ticket office
in eve. 🕐*Closed 1 Jan, 1 May, 25 Dec.*
💶*7.50€, no charge 1st Sun in the*
month (Nov–Mar). 📞*03 88 82 50 60.*
www.haut-kœnigsbourg.fr.
The castle, which was first mentioned
in 1147, was built by the Hohenstaufens
on a promontory overlooking the Alsace
plain, at an altitude of 700m/2297ft.
In 1479 it passed to the Hapsburgs who
had it rebuilt with a modern system of

defence. Sadly this did not prevent the
Swedes taking and sacking the castle
150 years later.
For the next 200 years it was an imposing ruin until in 1899 it was offered for
sale by the town of Sélestat.
The present building is the outcome
of an almost complete reconstruction
in neo-feudal style carried out on the
orders of Emperor William II between
1900 and 1908 during the period when
Alsace and Lorraine had been reincor-
porated into Germany.

Hunspach★★

Alsace

Carefully preserved and free from incongruous modern additions, Hunspach is one of Alsace's most charming villages. Flowers fill the streets of timber-framed houses with their projecting roofs and bull's-eye windows (a Baroque feature). Many of the buildings are in fact old farmhouses, with yards opening off the street; orchards, vines and long-handled pumps complete the picturesque scene.

EXCURSION
Seebach★
5km/3mi NE by D 249.
This is a wonderful example of the flower-decked Alsatian village with its

▶ **Population:** 615
Michelin Map: 315 I 3
▶ **Location:** Hunspach is in the extreme NE of the country, close to the River Rhine and the border with Germany.

half-timbered houses adorned with awnings and gardens.

Typical of the Wissembourg region, the buildings are clustered round the pink sandstone church tower. The curved windows of the houses with their colourful pelargoniums make it impossible for curious visitors to peer inside the houses!

Kaysersberg★★

Alsace

A typically pretty Alsace village, its flower-bedecked streets have many old houses, several dating from the 16C, and behind the pretty little town rise the serried ranks of vines on the slopes of the Vosges hills.

A BIT OF HISTORY
Kaysersberg was a Roman town known as *Caesaris Mons*, (the Emperor's Mountain), due to its strategic position along one of the most important routes linking ancient Gaul with the Rhine Valley.

In the Middle Ages it was one of the confederation of ten free cities known as the *Decapolis*, set up to resist feudal demands on their burgeoning urban culture. Tokay Vine plants brought back from Hungary during the 16C by Lazurus von Schwendi, the bailiff of the Holy Roman Emperor, later contributed to make Kaysersberg one of the finest wine growing areas of Alsace.

The great doctor, theologian and pioneer of Third World aid, Albert

▶ **Population:** 2 720
Michelin Map: 315 H 8
Info: 39 r. Gén de Gaulle. ℰ03 89 78 11 11. www.ville-kaysersberg.fr.
▶ **Location:** Kaysersberg is 12km/7.4mi NW of Colmar.
Parking: The village is completely pedestrianised, with car parks on its south, west and east approaches.

Schweitzer (1875–1965), was born, at 126, Rue du Général de Gaulle (next to the **Musée Albert-Schweitzer**; ◷*open May–Oct daily 9am–noon, 2–6pm;* ⊜*2€*) which contains memorabilia.

ADDITIONAL SIGHTS
Église de Sainte-Croix★ – **altarpiece★★**
Hôtel de Ville★
Vieilles maisons★ (old houses)
Pont fortifié★ (bridge)
Maison Faller-Brief★

Mulhouse★★

Alsace

Mulhouse became a free Imperial city as early as the end of the 13C, and in the 16C formed part of the *Decapolis,* the league of ten towns of Alsace.

A BIT OF HISTORY

A historic manufacturing and trading centre, the city's independent spirit led it into an association with the cantons of Switzerland. In 1524, the Republic's government adopted the principles of the Reformation and a little later on adhered to Calvinism. Theatrical performances were banned and inns had to close by 10pm. However, the spirit of the new religion spurred on industrial development and prompted social and cultural initiatives. It joined France voluntarily in 1798. Mulhouse was already long established as a textile centre, when, in 1746, three of its citizens, J-J Schmaltzer, the painter J-H Dollfus and the merchant S Koechlin together founded the first mill producing calico cotton fabrics. Production advanced by leaps and bounds. In 1812 the Dollfus and Mieg mill was the first to install steam power.

SIGHTS

▲▲ Hôtel de Ville★★

Since 1558, the City Hall has symbolised Mulhouse's civic and political liberties. It is a unique example in France of a building of the Rhineland Renaissance by a Basle architect; the exterior is decorated solely by artists from Konstanz. It was remodelled in 1698. It is this later decoration which has been restored to its former glory. The coats of arms of the Swiss cantons painted on the main façade on either side of the covered double flight of steps recall the historical link with Switzerland.

Musée de l'Automobile – Collection Schlumpf ★★★

192 ave de Colmar. &⃞⏰*Open 1–4 Jan, 7 Feb–3 Apr and 5 Nov–31 Dec daily 10am–5pm; 5 Jan–6 Feb Mon–Fri 1–5pm, Sat and Sun 10am–5pm;*

▶ **Population:** Alsace 112 260
⏱ **Michelin Map:** 315 i 10
▯ **Info:** 9 ave Foch. ℘03 89 35 48 48. www.mulhouse.fr.
◗ **Location:** This large city lies at the meeting point of France, Germany and Switzerland.
✎ **Don't Miss:** Find time for the fascinating textile museum, where beautiful fabrics with historic designs are on sale.
▲▲ **Kids:** Those who love cars – old and new – will enjoy the Musée de l'Automobile Collection Schlumpf. Also entertain kids at Cité du Train amd Électropolis.

4 Apr–4 Nov 10am–6pm. ◷*Closed 25 Dec.* ⊙*10.50€; child 8.10€.* ℘*03 89 33 23 21. www.collection-schlumpf.com.*
The splendid, definitive collection of 500 vehicles was lovingly built up by the mill-owning Schlumpf brothers. The collection vividly evokes the history of the motor car from the steam-powered Jacquot (1878) to the latest models. Most are in working order; several had famous owners – Charlie Chaplin's Rolls-Royce is here.

ADDITIONAL SIGHTS

▲▲ **Cité du Train –Musée français du Chemin de Fer** ★★★ *(2 r. Alfred de Glehn)*– history of railways.
Musée de l'Impression sur Étoffes (Textile Museum) ★ *(14 r. Jean-Jacques Henner)* – history of the printing of patterned cloths.
Musée Historique★★
▲▲ **Électropolis**★ *(55 r. du Pâturage)* – history of electric power.
Parc Zoologique et Botanique★★ *(51 r. jardin zoologique)*
Musée du Papier-peint★ *(La Commanderie, 28 r. Zuber, Rixheim, 6km/3.7mi east of Mulhouse)* – all about wallpaper.

Obernai★★

Alsace

Sited where the lower, vine-covered slopes of Mont Ste-Odile meet the plain, its ruined walls eloquent of its ancient independence and its narrow, winding streets lined with high-gabled houses, the little town of Obernai seems to represent the very essence of Alsace.

▸ **Population:** 9 610
◔ **Michelin Map:** 315 I 6
▤ **Info:** Place du Beffroi. ℘03 88 95 64 13. www.obernai.fr.
◖ **Location:** Obernai is north of Colmar on the main highway to Strasbourg.

SIGHTS

Place du Marché★★

With its cheerfully coloured timber-framed buildings, the picturesque market-place is Obernai's centrepiece, graced by a fountain with a statue of St Odile. Its Town Hall (**Hôtel de Ville**★, 15–16C) has a fine oriel window, a 16C Corn Hall (**Ancienne Halle aux blés**★) with a stork's nest above its doorway, and the Chapel Tower (**Tour de la Chapelle**★), a 13C bell-tower.

Maisons anciennes★ (Old houses)

There are many old houses in the streets around place du Marché. In rue des Pèlerins, note the three-storey stone house dating from the 13C.

Riquewihr★★★

Alsace

Situated along the Route des Vins (◖*see map following*), the tiny, beautiful village of Riquewihr is surrounded by medieval walls. prides itself on its fine Riesling; the vintners' houses in its picturesque streets were designed with the production of wine in mind. The town looks the same today as it did in the 16C

▸ **Population:** 1 212
◔ **Michelin Map:** 315 H 8
▤ **Info:** 2 r. de la 1re Armée. ℘03 20 36 09 22. www.ribeauville-riquewihr. com or http://riquewihr. reseaudescommunes. fr/communes.
◖ **Location:** Riquewihr is on the River Rhine border with Germany, in eastern France, nuzzled in the Vosges mountains. Rue du Général-de-Gaulle is the main road running east–west, from which the museum and the old houses are easily accessed.
▣ **Parking:** Use the parking facilities on the outside of the town: place des Charpentiers; rue de la Piscine; rocade Nord; près de la Poste.
◔ **Timing:** Allow 2hr and time to try a glass of the region's famous Riesling.

VISIT

Brick, red sandstone, timber or paint enliven the façades of the houses, adorned with balconies filled with flowers. Some of the dwellings (like the De Hugel house of 1494) go back to the end of the 15C, others to Renaissance times (like the Cour de Strasbourg house of 1597); most of them, however, are of 17C date, but they are all ornamented in the Rhineland Renaissance style which persisted longer in Alsace than elsewhere. Other notable houses are Maisons Liebrich (1535), Kiener (1574), Dissler (1610) and Preiss-Zimmer (1686).

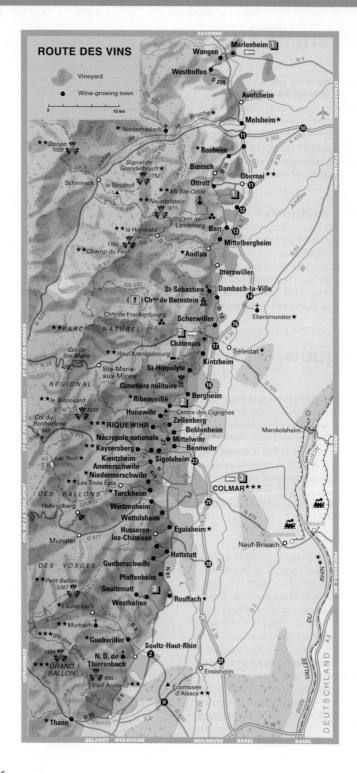

ROUTE DES VINS

Vineyard

● Wine-growing town

0　　　　　10 km

Riquewihr

R.Mattès/MICHELIN

ADDITIONAL SIGHTS
Musée du Dolder★ *(rue Principal, as you exit the town to the west)* – local history museum.
Former Church of Notre-Dame *(16 pl. des Trois-Eglise)*

Former chapel of Saint Erard
Stagecoach Museum *(5 r. des Écuries)*
Hansi Museum *(16 r. du Général de Gaulle)*

ADDRESSES

STAY
Chambre d'hôte Gérard Schmitt *3, chemin des Vignes.* ℘*03 89 47 89 72. Closed Jan–Mar. 2 rooms.*
A house with a garden in the higher part of the village, on the edge of a vineyard. The wood-panelled rooms have sloping ceilings. High standard of cleanliness and reasonable prices.

Hotel Riquewihr – *rte Ribeauvillé.* ℘*03 89 86 03 30. Closed Christmas, Jan–mid-Feb. 50 rms.* ⌷*10€.*
A large, neo-Alsatian style building on a road winding through the vineyards. Rooms are comfortable and well-kept. Mini fitness centre.

Hôtel L'Oriel – *3 r. des Écuries-Seigneuriales.* ℘*03 89 49 03 13. www.hotel-oriel.com. 22 rooms.* ⌷*11.50€.* This 16C hotel is easily recognised by its wrought-iron sign. The lack of straight lines in the building, combined with

simple décor and old Alsatian furniture and exposed beams, creates a romantic atmosphere. Three of the rooms, nestled in the annexe, are smarter and more modern.

EAT
Auberge St-Alexis – *68240 St-Alexis 6km/4mi W of Riquewihr on minor road and path.* ℘*03 89 73 90 38. Closed Fri.*
It's worth venturing into the forest along a dirt track to this former 17C hermitage. You will be rewarded with simple dishes, as authentic as the site, made from local farm produce.

Le Sarment d'Or – *4 r. du Cerf.* ℘*03 89 86 02 86. www.riquewihr-sarment-dor.com. Closed 5 Jan–11 Feb, 28 Jun–6 Jul, Sun eve, Tue lunch and Mon.*
Pale wood panelling, copper light-fittings, fireplace and huge beams create a lovely warm atmosphere in this restaurant. The cooking is traditional and uses seasonal ingredients. Also offers plush, comfortable rooms.

Route des Crêtes★★★

Alsace

In World War I, the French and German armies confronted each other along the old frontier between the two countries formed by the crest-line of the Vosges. Hugging the ridge is the strategic north–south road planned by French military engineers to serve the front; today it forms a fine scenic route, the Vosges Scenic Road, running for 63km/39mi from the Bonhomme Pass (Col du Bonhomme) in the north to Thann in the south. It offers the visitor a splendid introduction to the varied landscapes of these uplands, which include the sweeping pasturelands of the summits, an array of lakes, and the broad valleys of the Fisch and the Thur.

EXCURSIONS

Col du Bonhomme

949m/3 114ft high, this is the pass linking the provinces of Alsace and Lorraine.

Col de la Schlucht

1 139m/3 737ft. This is the steepest, but also one of the busiest of the routes through the Vosges. The eastern slopes are subject to intense erosion because of the gradient of the torrential rivers; at a distance of only 9km/5.6mi from

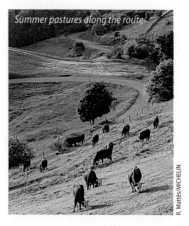
Summer pastures along the route

R. Mattes/MICHELIN

- 🚗 **Michelin Map:** 315 G 8, F 8, F 9 and G 9
- ▶ **Location:** The route starts 30km/18.6mi W of Colmar and heads S to Thann.
- 👁 **Don't Miss:** The panoramas between Le Hohneck and the Grand Ballon.

the pass, the town of **Munster**★ lies 877m/2 877ft below, while Colmar, 26km/16mi away is 1 065m/3 494ft lower.

Hohneck★★★

1 362m/4 469ft.
Rising near the central point of the range, this is one of the most visited of the Vosges summits. From the top there are superb **views**★★★; to the east, the **Munster Valley**★★ plunges steeply down towards the broad expanses of the Alsace plain, while to the west is the Lorraine plateau, cut into by the valley of the Vologne.

Grand Ballon★★★

1 424m/4 672ft. The Grand Ballon forms the highest point of the Vosges.
From the top *(30min round-trip on foot)* the magnificent **panorama**★★★ extends over the southern part of the range, whose physiognomy can be fully appreciated. The eastern and western slopes are quite unlike each other; the drop to the Alsace plain is abrupt, while to the west the land falls away gently to the Lorraine plateau. Glacial action in the Quaternary era is responsible for many features like the massive rounded humps of the summits *(ballons)*, and the morainic lakes in the blocked valleys. Above the tree-line, the forest clothing the hillsides gives way to the short grass of the wide upland grazing grounds known as the Hautes-Chaumes.

Vieil-Armand★★

The war memorial (monument national) marks one of the most bitterly contested battlefields of World War I.

Strasbourg★★★

Alsace

This important modern city, with a busy river port and renowned university, is not just the lively capital of Alsace. It is also where the Council of Europe and European Parliament are located.
At the same time, the historic centre around the cathedral, has been listed as a UNESCO World Heritage Site since 1988.

A BIT OF HISTORY

Strasbourg's name comes from the German meaning "city of the roads", and the place is indeed a meeting point for the highways, railways and waterways linking the Mediterranean with the Rhineland, Central Europe, the North Sea and the Baltic via the Belfort Gap and the Swabian Basin.

On 14 February 842, the **Strasbourg Oaths** were sworn by two of the sons of Louis the Pious (son of Charlemagne). Brothers Charles and Louis undertook to be loyal to one another in their attempt to frustrate the ambitions of their elder brother Lothair. Protocol demanded that each declare the oath in a language comprehensible to his brother's entourage; thus it was that the text read out by Louis the German is considered to be the oldest such document in a Romance language, the first written example of the language which has evolved into modern French. The same can be said for the German text.

Strasbourg remained a **free city** within the Holy Roman Empire even after the virtual incorporation of the rest of Alsace into France by the Peace of Westphalia in 1648, but eventually submitted to annexation by Louis XIV in 1681.

▶ **Population:** 427 245
Michelin Map: 315 K 5
Info: 17 pl. de la Cathédrale. ℘03 88 52 28 28; pl. de la Gare. ℘03 88 32 51 49; Pont de l'Europe. ℘03 88 61 39 23. www.strasbourg.com.
Location: On the banks of the river Ill, Strasbourg was built around its famous cathedral whose exterior can be enjoyed best from r. Mercière. If you follow the r. des Grandes Arcades you will come across Place Kléber, the most famous square in the city.
Don't Miss: Notre-Dame Cathedral and the Musée de l'Œuvre Notre-Dame.
Timing: Allow a whole day to see the old town. A choice of different passes (*Unipass, Strasbourg Pass, etc.*) is available from the tourist office.
Parking: Eight parking areas along the outskirts of Strasbourg allow you to leave your car and travel into the town centre by tram.

On 24 April 1792, Frédéric de Dietrich, Strasbourg's first constitutional mayor, threw a farewell celebration for the volunteers of the Army of the Rhine. The conversation turned to the need for a marching song to match the troops' enthusiasm.
Rouget de Lisle was asked to compose "something worth singing"; by morning he had finished, and sang his "marching

Strasbourg Pass

This pass is valid for 3 days. 11.40€ adult, 5.70€ child. Among other benefits, you get a free audio-guided tour of the old town, discounted entry to museums and some discounts in shops. For more information, contact the tourist office. *17 pl. de la Cathédrale. ℘03 88 52 28 28. www.otstrasbourg.fr. Open daily 9am–7pm.*

GUIDED TOURS

WALKING TOURS: A 90min audio-guided tour enables visitors to discover the cathedral, the old town and the Petite France at their own speed. Audio devices available in the tourist office for 6€ (30€ deposit).

TRAIN TOURS: *Run by CTS.* ℘*03 88 777 070. www.cs-strasbourg.* A 50min mini-tram tour takes you round place du Château, la Petite France district and the cathedral.

BOAT TOURS: Boat Trips on the Ill – Enjoy a 70min boat tour along the River Ill *(departure from the Palais Rohan pier)* taking in the Petite France, past Barrage Vauban, then the Faux Rempart moat as far as Palais de l'Europe. ◐*Departures Apr–Oct: every half-hour 9.30am–9pm; Nov–Dec and Jan–Mar: 4 departures a day 10.30am, 1pm, 2.30pm and 4.30pm.*

Boat Trips on the Rhine and tour of the harbour – ♿*Departure from the Promenade Dauphine pier.* ◐*Departures Jul–Aug; guided trip (2hr 15min) at 2.30pm.* ℘*03 88 84 13 13. www.strasbourgport.fr.* Contact: *Service Touristique du Port Autonome de Strasbourg. 15 r. de Nantes.* ℘*03 88 84 13 13. www.batorama.fr.*

song for the Army of the Rhine". Not long after, it was adopted by the Federates of Marseille, and ever since has been known as the **Marseillaise**.

In 1870, Strasbourg was seized by Germany after a long siege. It continued to grow, under the influence of Prussian culture. It became French at the 1918 Armistice, but was again taken by Germany from 1940 to 1944.

Detail on the western façade of Cathédrale Notre-Dame

©Fred Goldstein/Fotolia.com

SIGHTS

Cathédrale Notre-Dame★★★

1 r. Rohan. ◐*Open daily 7am–11.20am, 12.35pm–7pm; no visits during services.* ℘*03 88 21 43 34. www.cathedrale-strasbourg.fr.*

In 1176, the cathedral was rebuilt in red Vosges sandstone on a site above flood-level but nevertheless using bundles of oak piles as a foundation (these were recently reinforced with concrete).

Externally, this is still a Romanesque building as far as choir, transept and lantern-tower are concerned. The famous Gothic **spire**★★★ (👁3€) is an architectural masterpiece, its verticality emphasised by its forward position immediately over the west front. An unmistakable landmark, visible over much of the Alsace plain, it rises to a height of 142m/466ft. The openwork octagon supporting it was erected between 1399 and 1419 by a Swabian architect and given an extra 7m/23ft in height during the course of construction for reasons of prestige. Its final stage was designed and built between 1420 and 1439 by a Cologne architect, using techniques from the previous century; it is particularly notable for the projecting structures carrying the external staircases.

The High Gothic west front (**façade**★★★) was the work of Erwin von Steinbach. It is decorated with a wealth of sculpture (statues and low-reliefs of many different periods), especially in the central portal **(portail central)** with its double gable and delicate lancets masking part of the rose window. The three lower levels of the tympanum have particularly fine 13C work, including depictions of the Entry into Jerusalem, scenes of the Passion and Resurrection, and the Death of Judas; in the arching can be seen the Creation, the story of Abraham, the Apostles, the Evangelists and the Martyrs.

In the south doorway **(portail Sud)** is a famous portrayal of the Seducer about to succeed in tempting the most daring of the Foolish Virgins (she is undoing her dress). The statues of the Church and Synagogue (copies) on the south side of the cathedral are equally celebrated.

Inside, the nave elevation is a straightforward example of the High Gothic style of the 14C, with an openwork triforium and wide aisles lit by elegant window-openings.

In the south transept is the 13C Angel pillar **(pilier des Anges★★)** or Last Judgement **(du Jugement dernier)**; its delicate statuary, on three levels, raises Gothic art to a peak of perfection.

Stained-glass windows★★★ from the 12C, 13C, and 14C are remarkable. The **astronomical clock★** (clock chimes at 12.30pm) nearby, dating from 1838, continues to draw crowds with its automata ringing out the quarter-hours (the figure of Death has the privilege of sounding the hours) and the crowd of figures brought out to mark midday (12.30pm).

Musée de l'Œuvre Notre-Dame★★

3 pl. du Château. Open Tue–Fri noon–6pm, Sat–Sun 10am–6pm. Closed 1 Jan, Good Fri, 1 May, 1 and 11 Nov, 25 Dec. *5€ (no charge 1st Sun in the month).* 03 88 52 50 00. *www.musees-strasbourg.org/.*

Housed in a number of old dwellings just to the south, this museum greatly enhances the visitor's appreciation of the cathedral. Its great treasure is the famous Head of Christ **(Tête de Christ★★)** from Wissembourg in northern Alsace. In

addition, there is the oldest stained glass in existence and above all, many of the cathedral's original statues, including the Church and the Synagogue, the Wise and Foolish Virgins. The architect's drawings of the west front and the spire are here too.

Palais Rohan★

2 pl. du Château. 03 88 88 50 68/03 88 52 50. *www.musees-strasbourg.org.* Residence of the Prince-Bishops of Strasbourg, the palace was built between 1732 and 1742, a fine building in the Classical manner, with a curving entrance colonnade ornamented with statues and trophies, a main courtyard defined by balustraded galleries, a façade with dressings of pale limestone, a fine entablature, and mansard roofs lit by bull's-eye windows. The Prince-Bishops' state rooms are considered to be among the finest French interiors of the 18C. The building's most elegant façade is the one overlooking the River Ill; it has tall Corinthian columns, a dome and a balustraded terrace.

The palace also houses several **museums★★** (open Wed–Mon 10am–6pm; closed 1 Jan, Good Fri, 1 May, 1 and 11 Nov, 25 Dec. *4€, no charge 1st Sun in the month):*

Musée des Arts Décoratifs★★

Includes the State Apartments **(Grands Appartements)** and tells the story of the city's crafts and craftsmen. It has one of the finest **ceramic collections★★** in France, particularly rich in Strasbourg and Niderwiller faience and porcelain.

Musée des Beaux-Arts★

Known for its Italian paintings (Primitives and Renaissance), its Spanish works (Zurbaran, Murillo and Goya) and 15–17C Netherlandish Old Masters. Don't miss Nicolas de Largillière's 1703 portrait of *La Belle Strasbourgeoise,* the elegant, black-robed beauty.

Musée Archéologique★★

Covers the period between the Quaternary era and the end of the first millennium AD. There are displays on

La Petite France

R. Mattès/MICHELIN

prehistory, extinct animals, ceramics, and on Roman and Merovingian times.

The Old City (La Cité Ancienne)★★★

Two parts of the old city evoke the delightful spectacle of a bygone Alsace of timber-framed houses with the whole array of traditional features, wooden galleries, loggias on brackets, windows with tiny panes of coloured glass, as well as the overhanging upper storeys which continued to be built here after 1681 even though they had been banned in France proper.

Each house can be enjoyed for its own sake; together, they compose the most ravishing of townscapes.

Quartier de la Cathédrale★★★

In the cathedral quarter, two especially attractive buildings give onto the **Place de la Cathédrale**★; at the corner with the Rue Mercière there is the Pharmarcie du Cerf of 1268, supposedly the oldest pharmacy in France, and on the north corner is the Kammerzell House (**Maison Kammerzell**★) of the same date with frescoes and wooden sculptures.

Other streets and squares, like the Place du Marché-aux-cochons-de-lait (Sucking-Pig Market Square), Rue Mercière and Rue des Cordiers, complete the pleasures of a stroll.

La Petite France★★

This is the city's well-preserved historic core. It owes its name to a former French hospital and was once the abode of fishermen, tanners and millers. The arms of the Ill were provided with locks giving shipping from the Rhine access to the back door of virtually every shop. With its gabled Renaissance houses reflected in the green waters of the river, it forms a charming urban scene, notably in the **Rue du Bain-aux-Plantes**★★.

Place Kléber

This is the city's most famous square, named after Jean Kléber (1753–1800), the hero of the battles of Mainz (1793), Fleurus and Maastricht, who was assassinated in the course of Napoleon's campaign in Egypt.

Place Kléber

R.Mattès/MICHELIN

ADDITIONAL SIGHTS
Cour du Corbeau★
Covered Bridges★
View from the Barrage Vauban★★
Musée d'Art Moderne et contemporain★★ *(1 pl. Hans Jean Arp)*
Musée historique *(2 r. du Vieux Marché au Poissons)*
Église St-Thomas *(in the old town)* – mausoleum of Marshal de Saxe★★
Orangerie★
Palais de l'Europe★ *(SE of the Exhibition grounds)*

EXCURSION
Wine Villages
Some of the most picturesque villages in Alsace are a short drive from the city.
Saverne★
The town at the entrance to the Vosges uplands has **old house**s★ and a splendid red sandstone **château**★ with a monumental Louis XVI **façade**★★ giving onto the park.
Église de Marmoutier★★
This 12C former abbey church has a fine **west front**★★ in the red sandstone of the region, in Romanesque style incor porating Carolingian and Rhineland influences.

ADDRESSES

¶/ EAT
⊜ **Aux Fines Gourmandises** – *5 pl. Corbeau.* ℘*03 88 36 09 92. Booking advisable in summer.* Internet enthusiasts will love this spacious restaurant-tea room with its internet café. Wide choice of dishes including tartes flambées and choucroute and a delicious selection of pastries.

⊜ **Flam's** – *29 r. des Frères.* ℘*03 88 36 36 90. www.flams.fr. Booking advisable at weekends.* This half-timbered house very close to the cathedral houses a restaurant specialising in flammekueches. The three dining rooms and two cellars have been redecorated in lovely bright colours. Note the superb 15C painted ceiling.

⊜ **Au Hanneton** – *5 r. Ste-Madeleine.* ℘*03 88 36 93 76. Closed Tue lunch and Mon. Booking advisable.* This tiny winstub faithfully follows Alsace tradition with its warm, intimate country décor, its friendly atmosphere and regional specialities such as fish choucroute and Munster cordon bleu. Lovely terrace for sunny days.

⊜ **Pommes de Terre et Cie** – *4 r. de l'Écurie.* ℘*03 88 22 36. www.pommes-de-terre-cie.com. Booking advisable.* If you want a change from choucroute, this friendly restaurant mainly serves dishes with jacket potatoes and meat, fish or cheese.

⊜ **Zuem Strissel** – *5 pl. de la Grande-Boucherie.* ℘*03 88 32 14 73. www.strissel.fr.* An authentic wine bar, run by the same family since 1920. The much-loved décor consists of wood panelling, decorative wrought iron, stained-glass windows depicting Bacchus and a 14C wine press. Regional cooking accompanied by Alsace wines, including the famous kaefferkopf d'Ammerschwihr.

⊜⊜ **Caveau Gurtlerhoft** – *13 pl. de la Cathédrale.* ℘*03 88 75 00 75. www.gurtlerhoft.com.* Sample regional and traditional cooking in the lovely cellars of this 14C canonical building near the cathedral, with their splendid vaulting and massive pillars. Mouth-watering menus and fixed-price lunch. Unhurried service.

⊜⊜ **La Choucrouterie** – *20 r. St-Louis.* ℘*03 88 36 52 87. www.choucrouterie.com. Closed Aug, lunch both Sat and Sun.* This 18C coaching inn was the last place in Strasbourg to make pickled cabbage. Feast and have fun in a slightly chaotic setting, with music, cabaret or theatre dinners, as you like. Alsace cuisine served with local white wine.

⊜⊜ **La Coccinelle** – *22 r. Ste-Madeleine.* ℘*03 88 36 19 27. Closed mid-Jul–mid-Aug, Sat lunch and Sun. Booking advisable.* Wood panelling, beams, copperware, stained-glass windows and old photos lend this winstub (in the family since 1976) its typical Alsace feel. Regional cooking with choucroute, quenelles de foie (liver quenelles), jambonneau rôti (roast knuckle of ham) and bœuf gros sel (beef).

😋😋 **Petit Ours** – *3 r. de l'Écurie (quartier des Tonneliers).* *℘03 88 32 13 2. www. resto-petitours.com. Booking advisable.* Great little Tinsel, little wood figurines, twinkling stars and coloured baubles: you name it, they have it!

😋😋 **Le Pigeon** – *23 r. des Tonneliers.* *℘03 88 32 31 30. Closed 3 weeks in Jan and 18 Jul–12 Aug.* This typical winstub, which takes its name from the two pigeons sculpted on the façade, is situated in one of the oldest residences in Strasbourg (take a minute to look at the listed wooden staircase). Décor and cuisine in keeping with Alsace tradition.

😋😋 **Pont St-Martin** – *13–15 r. des Moulins.* *℘03 88 32 45 13. www.pont-martin.com. Booking advisable.* This ever-popular restaurant in a venerable half-timbered building is in the heart of the picturesque Petite France district, just above the water. Typical Alsace interior of panelling, wainscoting and checked tablecloths. Regional cooking.

😋😋 **La Taverne du Sommelier** – *Ruelle de la Bruche (Krutenau distict).* *℘03 88 24 24 10. Closed school hols, Christmas and New Year's Day. Booking essential.* The type of little restaurant it's always a pleasure to discover. The décor of

yellow walls and lithographs is perfect to set off the intimate atmosphere. The cooking follows the seasons, while the wine list features wines from the Languedoc region and the Rhône Valley.

🛒 SHOPPING

Au Paradis des Pains d'Epices – *14 r. des Dentelles, Petite France.* *℘03 88 32 33 34 32. www.paindesoleil.com. Closed Mon morning.* Scents of orange, honey, cinnamon and cardamom greet you as you enter this tiny shop located in a timber-framed house dating from 1643. Heaven on earth for gingerbread fans: soft or crunchy, sweet or savoury, even iced varieties to tempt you.

CALENDAR

Folklore shows – *Mid-Jul–early Aug, Square Louise-Weiss.* Local, national and international dancing. *℘03 88 60 97 14.*
European Fair – *Early Sept, Parc des Expositions du Wacken.* Over 1 000 exhibitors representing a wide range of activities. *℘03 88 37 21 21.*
Strasbourg, Christmas Capital – Countless events and shows all over town: Christmas market (Christkindelsmärik), illuminations, giant Christmas tree, exhibitions, nativity scene and concerts. *Programme available from tourist office.*

Bar-le-Duc★
Champagne-Ardenne

This old capital of the Duchy of Bar is divided into two sections. The historic Ville Haut rests on a plateau, while the industrial Ville Basse is laid out along the River Ornain and the Rhine-Marne canal.

▶ **Population:** 16 950
⌚ **Michelin Map:** 307 B6, E 5
ℹ **Info:** 7 r. Jeanne-d'Arc. *℘03 29 79 11 13.* www.barleduc.fr.
▶ **Location:** The town sits halfway between Strasbourg and Paris.

SIGHT
Ville haute★ (Upper Town)
Wonderfully aristocratic and grand, this Renaissance quarter is a beautiful ensemble of 16–18C houses, especially notable in the triangular Place St-Pierre. Église St-Étienne has a curious late 18C belfry-porch in the medieval

style; within are two works by the 16C master Ligier Richier, including the famous **Transi**★★ which owes much to advances in dissection technique and is far removed from the serene recumbent figures of the Middle Ages.

Châlons-en-Champagne★★
Champagne-Ardenne

Its centre traversed by the River Marne and two canals, the Mau and the Nau, Châlons, formerly known as Châlons-sur-Marne, is a dignified and attractive commercial town with some fine buildings.

▶ **Population:** 47 340
⌖ **Michelin Map:** 306 i 9
▣ **Info:** 3 quai des Arts.
  ℘03 26 65 17 89. www.chalons-tourisme.com.
◗ **Location:** Eastern Champagne, close to the A 26 and A 4 autoroutes.

A BIT OF HISTORY

The valley of the Aube to the southwest of the town was the setting in 451 for the series of battles known as the Catalaunian Fields (**Champs catalauniques**).

Having given up his intention of sacking Paris, then known as Lutetia, because of the intervention of St Genevieve, Attila the Hun was engaged here by the Roman army under Aetius; after fierce fighting, he quit the battlefield and fled eastwards.

During the Wars of Religion, the town remained loyal to the King who declared it to be the "main town of the Champagne region" and in 1589 it became the seat of an annexe of the Paris Parliament. Châlons was the birthplace in 1749 of Nicolas Appert, a pioneer of the food industry and the inventor of a system of preserving food by sterilisation.

SIGHTS

Cathédrale St-Étienne★★

℘05 61 03 03 03. ◷Open Feb–Dec. ⌨Admission charge.

The present building was begun around 1235 in the Lanceolate Gothic style invented 40 years previously at Chartres, though there is little evidence of stylistic development having taken place.

The cathedral is famous for its stained glass (**vitraux**), Renaissance as well as medieval. The 13C glass includes the tall windows in the choir, the north transept (with the wonderful hues of green characteristic of the region), and the first bay on the north side (the Tanners' window – note the hanging skins). The finest windows however are those of Renaissance date, in the side chapels

Stained-glass window of Église Notre-Dame-en-Vaux

of the south aisle, showing scenes from the Creation, the earthly Paradise, the Passion, the Life of Christ and the Lives of the Saints.

Église Notre-Dame-en-Vaux★

◷Open Jun–mid-Sept daily 10am–noon, 2–6pm, Sun 2.30–6pm; mid-Sept–Jun Mon–Sat 10am–noon, 2–6pm. ℘03 26 65 63 17.

A UNESCO World Heritage site, this typical early Gothic church with a characteristic four-tier elevation has a particularly noteworthy ambulatory, inspired by the one at St-Rémi in Reims, together with the stained glass in the windows of the north aisle, again showing superb skill in the use of green.

To the left of the church, the **Musée du Cloître de Notre-Dame-en-Vaux★★** (◷opening hours vary; call to verify; ◷closed 1 Jan, 1 May, 1 and 11 Nov, 25 Dec; ⌨4.60€, no charge 1st Sun in the month; ℘03 26 64 03 87) houses **sculptures★★** from the old Romanesque cloisters.

Monthermé★

Champagne-Ardenne

Monthermé has a spectacular site★ just downstream from the meeting-point of the Semoy with the Meuse, and makes a good starting point for walks or cycle rides into the Ardennes.

EXCURSION

La Meuse Ardennaise★★ (The Meuse Gorge Through The Ardennes)

72km/45mi.

One of Europe's great rivers,950km/ 590mi in length, the Meuse rises on the Langres uplands.

It flows between the escarpment of the Côte des Bars and the dip-slope of the Côte de la Meuse, before penetrating the schists of the high plateau of the Ardennes in a deep gorge. Its meanders here mark the course it traced out in Tertiary times; since then the plateau has been uplifted, but the river has succeeded in entrenching itself in the schists, a process known as superimposition.

From Charleville-Mézières to Givet there is a succession of single meanders (Monthermé, Fumay, Chooz), double (Revin) and even triple ones (Charleville). The valley has long formed a corridor of human activity, with its water, rail and

▶ **Population:** 2 790
Michelin Map: 306 K 3
Info: pl. J.-B. Clément.
℘03 24 54 46 73.
www.montherme.fr.
Location: The little town is close to Charleville-Mézières. The old and new parts of town are separated by the River Meuse

road communications, and with a skilled workforce producing engineering products and domestic appliances. At the beginning of the century, Monthermé was a centre of trade union activity, with considerable conflict between workers and employers.

Downstream from Monthermé the most interesting sites are: the **Roches de Laifour**★ and the **Dames de Meuse**★ opposite one another; Revin, where the old town and the industrial area each occupy their own peninsula; Fumay, with its old quarter, once famous for its quarries producing violet slate; Chooz, with its nuclear power stations; Givet, sited at the exit from a side valley originally fortified by Charles V and strengthened by Vauban. The composer Mehul (1763–1817) was born here, best known for his *Chant du Départ*, a patriotic song of the French Revolution.

Monthermé

©David Hughes/Bigstockphoto.com

Provins★★
Champagne-Ardenne

The ancient fortified city of Provins sits atop a ridge overlooking the Seine valley and the Champagne chalklands, roughly equidistant from both Paris and Troyes.
The town has a famous outline (once painted by Turner), dominated by a tower (Tour de César) and the dome of Église St-Quiriace. Provins' role as an important centre of commerce was confirmed in the 12C when it became one of the two capitals of the County of Champagne. Its annual fairs were renowned, part of a round of such events which also took place at Lagny, Bar-sur-Aube and Troyes. For a number of years in the 13C, Edmund of Lancaster was lord of Provins, at a time when the place was known for its roses, in those days a rare flower.
He incorporated a red rose into his emblem; a century-and-a-half later it was this flower which triumphed over the white rose of York in the Wars of the Roses.

VISIT
Ville Haute★★
Still protected to north and west by its 12C and 13C walls★★, its most splendid feature is the **Tour de César★★**, a massive 12C keep with an additional rampart built by the English in the Hundred Years' War as an artillery emplacement. There is also a 13C tithe barn (Grange aux Dîmes), which belonged to the canons of St-Quiriace. Also of note is the group of statues★★ at the Église St-Ayoul.

EXCURSION
Église de St-Loup-de-Naud★
11km/6mi SW.
The church belonged to a Benedictine priory of the Archbishopric of Sens, and was one of the first in the area to be vaulted in stone.
Erected in the 11C and 12C, it demonstrates the gradual evolution of the Romanesque into Early Gothic. The choir dates from the 11C, as does the

▶ **Population:** 11 670
◐ **Michelin Map:** 312 I 4
▤ **Info:** Maison du visiteur, Chemin de Villecran. ℘0 64 60 26 26. www.provins.net.
◖ **Location:** Provins is in the Ile de France region, SE of Paris. It can be easily reached by road or rail from the capital. On arrival, head for the Ville Haute. The tourist office offers a choice of guided tours on summer weekends.

early Romanesque cradle-vault next to it. The dome over the crossing, the barely projecting transepts and the first two bays of the nave were built at the beginning of the 12C.
Finally, around 1160, the last two bays of the nave were completed; they are square in plan and have alternating pillars and twin columns on the model of Sens cathedral. The well-preserved doorway **(portail★★)**, under the main porch, shows similarities with the Royal Doorway (Portail royal) of Chartres Cathedral; Christ in Majesty surrounded by symbols of the Evangelists on the tympanum, apostles in arched niches on the lintel, statue-columns in the splays, figures in between the arch mouldings.

Tour de César

S.Sauvignier/MICHELIN

Reims★★★

Champagne-Ardenne

The ancient university town on the banks of the river Vesle is famous for its magnificent and important cathedral, where French kings were traditionally crowned. It has a wealth of other architectural masterpieces. Reims is also (along with Epernay) the capital of champagne's wine industry. Most of the great champagne houses' cellars are open to the public.

▶ **Population:** 215 581
◔ **Michelin Map:** 306 G 7
▤ **Info:** 2 r. Guillaume de Machault. ℘03 26 77 45 00. www.reims-tourisme.com.
▶ **Location:** Reims is 143km/89mi NE of Paris on the A 4 autoroute, and 275km /171mi from Calais on the A 26, which skirts the town. Take any turning for Centre Ville.

A BIT OF HISTORY

Under the Romans, Reims was the capital of the province which was to become Belgium. It was at Reims, in 496, that Clovis, King of the Franks, was baptised by St Remigius (St Rémi). This was a political event of some significance, since it made the ambitious 35-year-old warrior the only Christian ruler in the chaotic times following the collapse of the Roman Empire. It was he who halted the advance of the Visigoths at Poitiers, subsequently pushing them back, first to Toulouse, then all the way into Spain. With him, the source of political authority in Gaul passed from Provence to the north.

At the time of the Carolingians, a feeling for beauty became evident at Reims; ancient texts were carefully copied, manuscripts illuminated, ivory carved and masterpieces of the goldsmith's art created. The period produced Charlemagne's Talisman (now in the Bishops' Palace) as well as the Épernay Gospel. In 816, Louis I the Pious had himself crowned here, as Charlemagne had done at Rome 16 years before. It was from this point that the dynasty acquired a sort of religious character, though it was not until the crowning of Louis VIII, 400 years later, that the city became the recognised place for coronations, with a ceremonial ever more elaborate and charged with symbolism. By the time of Charles X, 25 kings had been crowned here. The most moving coronation was that of Charles VII on 17 July 1429, which took place in the middle of the Hundred Years' War in the presence of Joan of Arc; the Maid of Orléans had given Frenchmen the first inklings of national identity, and had persuaded the king to make his way to Reims, even though this involved him in crossing the hostile Burgundian territory of Philippe le Bon (the Good).

On 7 May 1945, in a modern technical college near the station, the document was signed which marked the surrender of Germany. Confirmed the day after in Berlin, this brought to an end World War II in Europe.

SIGHTS

Cathédrale Notre-Dame★★★

Place Cardinal Luçon. ◔*Open daily 7.30am–7.30pm; no visits during services.* ⬗*Guided multilingual tours on request.*

The present building was begun in 1211. It is one of the great cathedrals of France, built in the Lanceolate Gothic style pioneered at Chartres, but with more sophisticated ornamentation, its window tracery above all. The west front has wonderfully soaring lines and superb 13C sculpture, whose masterpiece is the world-famous Smiling Angel (in a splay of the north portal).

Inside is one of the greatest achievements of the Gothic, the west end of the nave, best seen towards the end of the afternoon when the sun lights up the two rose windows.

Reims was occupied by the German army from 3–12 September 1914, and for four years remained in the battle zone.

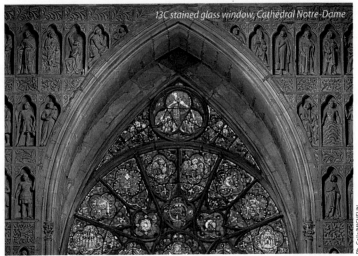
13C stained glass window, Cathedral Notre-Dame

Ph. Gajic/MICHELIN

By the end of the war, out of a total of 14 130 houses, only 60 remained habitable. The cathedral, one of the country's most precious buildings in terms of both artistic and historic value, was in ruins. The artillery bombardments of 19 September 1914 and April 1917 had been particularly destructive. The skilful restoration has largely been financed by the Rockefeller Foundation.

Palais du Tau★★

2 pl. du Cardinal-Luçon. ⏰*Open early May–early Sept Tue–Sun 9.30am– 6.30pm; rest of the year 9.30am– 12.30pm, 2–5.30pm.* ⏰*Closed 1 Jan, 1 May, 1 and 11 Nov, 25 Dec.* 🔄*Guided tours (1hr15min) of the palace available (in French); reserve 1 week in advance; guided tours (2hr30min) of palace and cathedral; reserve 2 weeks in advance.* 🎫*7€.* 📞*03 26 47 81 79. http://palais-tau.monuments-nationaux.fr.*

Dating from 1690, the former palace of the bishops of Reims was built by Mansart and Robert de Cotte. In it is housed some of the cathedral's original statuary and tapestries, among them two huge 15C Arras tapestries depicting scenes from the life of Clovis.

The treasury has many objects of outstanding interest, such as the 9C

Champagne

Though covering only 2% of the total area planted with vines in France, this northernmost of the country's wine-growing regions is perhaps its most prestigious. The product was known in Roman times, when it was a still wine. It was Dom Pérignon (1638–1715), cellar-master of Hautvillers Abbey (Abbaye de Hautevilliers), who had the idea of making it sparkle by means of double fermentation, a process carried out today by the use of cane sugar and yeasts. The vines are spread over an area totalling 30 000ha/74 000 acres, on the lower slopes of the chalk escarpment of the Côte de l'Île-de-France for preference. The most renowned vineyards are the Montagne de Reims (robust, full-bodied wines), the valley of the Marne (fruity wines with plenty of bouquet) and the Côte des Blancs (fresh and elegant wines). Champagne is a blended, branded wine, the prestige of the great labels dependent on the expertise of the master-blenders. Some 215 million bottles are produced in an average year, with over 75 million of them for export.

Talisman of Charlemagne, the 11C cut-glass Holy Thorn reliquary, the 12C coronation chalice, the St Ursula reliquary with its cornelian casket, the Holy Ampulla reliquary, and a collar of the Order of the Holy Ghost.

Basilique St-Rémi★★

Place Chanoine Ladame. ◷*Open daily 8am–7pm. Son-et-Lumière shows Jul–Sept Sat 9.30pm.* ⊚*No charge.* ☞*Guided tours on request.*
Dating from 1007, this is the city's most venerable church, though restorations have left little that is Romanesque and less that is Carolingian. The west front was rebuilt during a major restoration in 1170; it is remarkable for its Romanesque south tower. The façade of the south transept with its statue of St Michael was reconstructed in the 14C and 15C.

The sombre interior (**intérieur★★★**) is remarkable for its length (122m/400ft) in proportion to its width (26m/85ft). The oldest part of the church is the 11C transept. In the 12C, the choir was rebuilt in the Early Gothic manner and the whole nave given Gothic vaulting.

ADDRESSES

⌂ STAY

⊜ **Ardenn Hôtel** – *6 r. Caqué.* ☎*03 26 47 42 38. www.ardennhotel.fr. Closed Dec–early Jan. 14 rooms.* ⊡*5.50€.*
This hotel, behind an attractive brick façade in a quiet little town-centre street, has tastefully decorated rooms and smiling service.

⊜⊜ **Crystal** – *86 pl. Drouet-d'Erlon.* ☎*03 26 88 44 44. www.hotel-crystal.fr. 31 rooms.* ⊡*9€.* A haven of greenery right in the centre of town is the main sales argument of this 1920s house. The renovated bedrooms all have excellent bedding. Breakfast is served in a delightful flowered courtyard/garden in summer.

⊜⊜ **Hôtel La Cathédrale** – *20 r. Libergier.* ☎*03 26 47 28 46. 14 rooms.* ⊡*7€.* This smart, welcoming hotel stands in a street lead ingto the cathedral has small bright and cheerful rooms with comfortable beds, while the breakfast room is decorated with old engravings.

⊜⊜ **Hôtel Continental** – *93 pl. Drouet-d'Erlon.* ☎*03 26 40 39 35. www.grandhotelcontinental.com. Closed 21 Dec–7 Jan. 50 rooms.* ⊡*13€.*
The attractive façade of this central hotel adorns one of the city's liveliest squares. The rooms, in varying styles, are reached by a splendid staircase. Elegant Belle Epoque sitting rooms.

⊜⊜ **Grand Hôtel du Nord** – *75 pl. Drouet-d'Erlon.* ☎*03 26 47 39 03. www. hotel-nord-reims.com. Closed Christmas period. 50 rooms.* ⊡*9€.* Recently renovated rooms with all mod-cons in a 1920s building set in a pedestrians-only square. The rooms facing the back are quieter. Many restaurants nearby.

⊜⊜⊜ **Hôtel Porte Mars** – *2 pl. de la République.* ☎*03 26 40 28 35. www. hotelportemars.com. 24 rooms.* ⊡*11€.* Drink tea in the cosy sitting room, or enjoy a drink in the sophisticated bar. A delicious breakfast is served in the attractive glass-roofed dining room decorated with photographs and old mirrors. The comfortable, well sound-proofed rooms all have a personal touch.

⊻ EAT

⊜⊜ **Brasserie Le Boulingrin** – *48 r. Mars.* ☎*03 26 40 96 22. www.boulingrin. fr. Closed Sun.* This Art Deco-style restaurant dating from 1925 has become an institution in Reims life. The owner is much in evidence, overseeing the operations and creating a congenial atmosphere. The menu is inventive and the prices reasonable.

⊜⊜ **Café du Palais** – *14 pl. Myron-Herrick.* ☎*03 26 47 52 54. www. cafedupalais.fr. Closed Mon eve and Sun.* This lively café near the cathedral was founded in 1930. With its original glass roof and a warm red décor, it serves generous portions of salad and other daily dishes, which are much appreciated, as are the home-made pastries. You can also enjoy a reasonably priced glass of champagne.

Da Nello – *39 r. Cérès.* *03 26 47 33 25. Closed Aug.* A Mediterranean welcome awaits you at this Italian restaurant where the tables look onto the kitchen and the pizzas are baked in the oven in the centre of the room. Fresh pasta, grilled dishes and daily specials according to what the market has to offer… and all served with an authentic Italian accent.

La Table Anna – *6 r. Gambetta.* *03 26 89 12 12. www.latableanna. com. Closed Mon.* Champagne takes pride of place in the window of this establishment next door to the music conservatory. Some of the paintings adorning the walls are the work of the owner. Traditional dishes renewed with the seasons.

La Vigneraie – *14 r. de Thillois.* *03 26 88 67 27. www.vigneraie.com.* La Vigneraie boasts a fantastic collection of carafes. Tasty classical menu and fine wine list. Excellent value-for-money.

Au Petit Comptoir – *17 r. de Mars.* *03 26 40 58 58. Closed 1st half Aug, 24–31 Dec, Sun, Mon.* This imposing restaurant with its wooden terrace is right behind the town hall. Inside there is, the black and white décor and studied lighting lend a cosy atmosphere. Traditional cooking and spit-roast dishes.

NIGHTLIFE

Place Drouet-d'Erlon – This square is the prime starting point for anyone wanting to go out on the town. There is something for everyone, whether you are looking for a bar, pub, restaurant, tearoom or brasserie.

La Chaise au Plafond – *190 ave d'Épernay.* *03 26 06 09 61.* Founded in 1910, this bar and tobacconists is famous for the chair that has remained stuck to the ceiling ever since a shell hit the establishment on 12 September 1914. Terrace in summer. Selection of 150 cigars (Cuban, Honduran or from Santo Domingo).

CHOCOLATIERS

Deléans – *20 r. Cérès.* *03 26 47 56 35. Closed Aug.* Cocoa-based specialities have been made here in the old-fashioned way since 1874. Try Néluskos (chocolate-coated cherries in cognac) and *petits bouchons de champagne* enclosed in a giant champagne cork made of chocolate.

Fossier – *25 cours JB Langlet.* *03 26 47 59 84.* Founded in 1756, the biscuit- and chocolate-maker Fossier creates the ultimate in Reims confectionery. Pay a visit to the shop and factory and learn how to *piouler* (stir) your glass of champagne correctly!

La Petite Friande – *15 cours JB Langlet.* *03 26 47 50 44.* For over 170 years, the establishment has prided itself on being the specialists in authentic bouchons de champagne, made with marc de champagne. Another of their delicious creations are *bulles à la vieille fine de la Marne*.

CALENDAR

Fêtes Johanniques – *2nd weekend in June.* 2 000 walk-ons in period costume accompany Joan of Arc and Charles VII during a massive street festival.

Flâneries musicales d'été – *Jun–Jul.* Over 150 street concerts throughout the town, including shows by major international stars in some of the town's most prestigious and unlikely venues.

CHAMPAGNE HOUSES

Several of the world's most renowned champagne makers have their cellars in Reims, and offer guided tours, tastings and discount purchases.

Mumm 34 r. du Champ-de-Mars. www.mumm.com.

Piper-Heidsieck 51 bd Henry-Vasnier. www.piper-heidsieck.com

Pommery 5 pl. du Gén.-Gouraud. www.pommery.com.

Ruinart 4 r. des Crayères. www.ruinart.com.

Taittinger 9 pl. St-Nicaise. www.taittinger.fr.

Veuve Clicquot-Ponsardin 1 pl. des Droits-de-l'Homme. www.veuve-clicquot.fr.

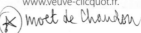
moet de Chandon

Rocroi★

Champagne-Ardenne

First laid out in the 16C in a clearing in the Ardennes forest, Rocroi is a typical Renaissance fortified town.

A BIT OF HISTORY

After the principality of Sedan had been incorporated into France in 1642, the death of Richelieu and the ill health of Louis XIII made a long period of uncertain rule by a regent seem likely. The prospect whetted the expansionist appetites of Philip IV of Spain, for whom the capture of Rocroi would open the way to Paris via the valleys of the Aisne and the Marne.

On 19 May 1643, three days after the death of Louis XIII, a bold manœuvre by the Duke d'Enghien – the future **Grand Condé** – routed the redoubtable Spanish infantry which never succeeded in regrouping. This, the first French victory over the Spaniards for more than a century, reverberated around Europe (it is commemorated by a monument in the leafy countryside 3km/1.8mi to the south). Fortune now began to smile on France, and Mazarin was able to implement Richelieu's foreign policy, using the generation of officers trained by the far-sighted Cardinal.

- ▶ **Population:** 2 420
- ◔ **Michelin Map:** 306 J 3
- ▣ **Info:** Place d'Armes.
  ℰ03 24 54 20 06.
  www.otrocroi.com.
- ▷ **Location:** The small town stands close to the Belgian border.
- ◉ **Don't Miss:** Vauban's ramparts are a fine example of the great engineer's mastery of his art.

Later, after his involvement in the disturbances known as the Fronde, Condé went over to the Spaniards, and, in 1658, was responsible for capturing Rocroi for them. But in the following year, the Treaty of the Pyrenees gave the fortress town back to France and Condé to his king.

VISIT
Ramparts

The ramparts **(remparts)** of Rocroi were improved by **Vauban**.

With their glacis, bastions, demi-lunes and deep defensive ditches they are a fine example of the great engineer's mastery of his art.

Fortified town of Rocroi

©Rene Mattes/World Pictures/Photoshot

Troyes★★★
Champagne-Ardenne

The lively centre of this distinguished old trading town is a charming collection of picturesque half-timbered houses, many beautifully restored.

A BIT OF HISTORY

Today Troyes shares with Reims the distinction of being one of the capitals of the province of Champagne, though historically the city looks southeast towards Burgundy rather than northwards to the Ardennes. The town developed in the Seine valley on the great trade route between Italy and the cities of Flanders. It had a considerable Jewish population, among them the influential scholar Rashi (1050–1105).

In the Middle Ages the town hosted two huge annual fairs, each lasting for three whole months, and attracting merchants and craftsmen from all over Europe. But by the end of the 14C the pattern of commercial exchanges had changed, and these great gatherings fell into decline.

Troyes has long been (and is still) France's most important centre of hosiery manufacture. The industry was introduced here at the very beginning of the 16C, followed by cloth-making, dyeing, paper-making. The city's wealth enabled it to overcome the great fire of 1524; houses and churches were quickly rebuilt in a style showing both the Italianate influence of the artists who came here from Fontainebleau around 1540 as well as the persistence of local, medieval traditions.

SIGHTS
Le Vieux Troyes★★

The outline of the old part of the city bears a curious resemblance to a champagne cork, with the area around the cathedral forming the head.

The majority of the old houses are timber-framed, with vertical members held together by horizontal beams rather than by timbers set obliquely or in the

▸ **Population:** 128 945
⌘ **Michelin Map:** 313 E 4
▸ **Info:** 16 bd Carnot (by the station) and r. Mignard (pedestrian zone, opposite Saint Jean church). ℘03 25 82 62 70. www.ot-troyes.fr.
▸ **Location:** The town is on the border of Champagne and Burgundy, and is at the meeting of autoroutes A5 (from Paris) and A26 (from Calais). Rue de la Republique is the main street, and Place Alexandre Israël is the town centre, where activities are organised throughout the year.
▸ **Parking:** If you are visiting the old town, park the car behind the town hall (place Alexandre-Israël) or along boulevard Gambetta.
▸ **Don't Miss:** Allow time for a leisurely stroll in the lanes of Vieux Troyes. For shopping bargains, visit the big factory outlet malls on the edge of town.
▸ **Timing:** Allow 4hr to visit Vieux Troyes.

Guided Tours

Guided tours, including audio tours, can be booked all year round at the tourist office, who also sell the useful **Pass'Troyes** (15€). *Ask at the tourist office.*

form of a St Andrew's cross as elsewhere in France. The most elegant infill is the characteristic local chequer-board pattern made from brick, slate or chalk rather than the cob or daub commonly employed.

The streets with the best examples of such houses are Rue Champeaux, Ruelle des Chats, Rue de Vauluisant, as well as the Cour du Mortier d'Or.

Maison du Boulanger and Tourelle de l'Orfèvre, Le Vieux Troyes

B. Brillion/MICHELIN

Maison de l'Outil et de la Pensée ouvrière★★

7 r. de la Trinité. ⏱*Open Jun–Sept Tue–Sat 10am–6pm, Mon 1pm–6pm.* ⏱*Closed Mon morning from Oct–May, 1 Jan and 25 Dec.* ⬳*6.50€.* ✆*03 25 73 28 26. www.maison-de-l-outil.com.*
Housed in the Hôtel du Mauroy, it is a fine architectural setting for the fascinating range of objects displayed.
The dignity of labour is celebrated here in the subtle but never gratuitous diversity of forms as much as in the individual character and highly specialised function of each object. Though some are conventionally beautiful or pleasingly ornamented, one is more touched in the end by the way in which tools like hammers have been shaped over time by the hand that has used them as well as by the material they have been in contact with.

Église Ste-Madeleine

This church is Troyes' oldest place of worship. Much rebuilt in the 16C, it is famous for the rood screen (**jubé★★**) made by Jean Gailde; this has scalloped ogee arches with no intermediate supports, fine glass (**verrières★**) – the Passion, the Creation, a Jesse Tree – as well as a statue of St Martha (**statue de Sainte Marthe★**) of striking gravity.

Musée de Vauluisant★

4 r. Vauluisant. ⏱*Open Jun–Sept daily 10am–1pm, 2pm–6pm; rest of the year Wed–Sun 10am–noon, 2–6pm.* ⏱*Closed public holidays.* ⬳*3€ (under 25 years no charge). No charge 1st Sun in the month (except during special exhibits).* ✆*03 25 73 05 85.*
The fine 16C Renaissance **Hôtel de Vauluisant★** contains a museum of **local art** and a **museum of hosiery** with exhibits depicting the industry's evolution, including historic looms and other machinery.

Cathédrale St-Pierre et St-Paul★★

The cathedral was begun in 1208 and continued until the 17C, enabling the regional Gothic style to be traced over the whole period of its evolution. The building has remarkable proportions, exceptionally rich decoration and a beautiful nave. The stained-glass windows (**vitraux★★**) of the cathedral cover a total area of 1 500sq m/16 000sq ft. One of the supreme achievements of this art form, they transform the building into a cage of glass.

Musée d'Art Moderne★★

Place Saint-Pierre. ♿⏱*Open Tue–Sat 11am–6pm.* ⏱*Closed public holidays.* ⬳*5€.* ✆*03 25 76 26 80.*
This is the collection built up since 1939 by Pierre and Denise Lévy, noted hosiery manufacturers. It comprises thousands of items dating from 1850–1950, many of them donated to the State and now on display in the former Bishops' Palace.
Particularly well represented here are the **Fauves**, who, together with Braque, Dufy, Matisse and Van Dongen "made colour roar". Derain too, one of the first to appreciate the art of Africa, is very much present, as is Maurice Marinot, a local artist and glass-maker.

ADDITIONAL SIGHTS

Basilique St-Urbain★ – 13C Gothic architecture.
Église St-Pantaléon★ – Collection of religious statuary

Musée St-Loup *(1 r. Chrestien de Troyes)*– Fine art and **archaeology**★ **Pharmacie Musée**★ **de l'Hôtel-Dieu** *(Quai des Comtes de Champagne Troyes)* – Rich collection of 18C earthenware

ADDRESSES

🛏 STAY

🍽 **Les Comtes de Champagne** – *56 r. de la Monnaie.* 🕿*03 25 73 11 70. 36 rooms.* 🍴*6€.* It is said that the four 12C houses which make up this hotel used to belong to the counts of Champagne who minted their coins here. Renovated rooms; those with kitchen facilities could be ideal for families. The impressive fireplace in the breakfast room testifies to the age of the premises.

🍽 **Motel Savinien** – *87 r. Fontaine, at Ste-Savinien, 3km/1.8mi W of city centre.* 🕿*03 25 79 24 90. www.motelsavinien. com. Closed Sun and Mon. 49 rooms.* 🍴*9€.* This conveniently placed motel by the ring road on the west of the city centre is a large, quiet, well-maintained 1970s building. Rooms are practical, regularly updated. There's a sauna, jacuzzi and small gym. Traditional cuisine served on the terrace.

🍽 **De La Bonne Fermière** – *Pl. de l'Église - 10450 Bréviandes, 5 km/3mi S of Troyes.* 🕿*03 25 82 45 65. 13 rooms.* 🍴*7€.* This peaceful little hotel has just been given a new look with gay springtime colours and new beds. Friendly service and excellent value.

🍴 EAT

🍽 **Auberge de la Cray'Othe** – *31 Grande-Rue, 10190 Messon, 12km/7. mi W of Troyes on N 60, Sens direction and D 83 to the left.* 🕿*03 25 70 31 12. Closed 2 weeks in Jan, 2 weeks in Sept. Booking necessary.* This beautiful farm houses a pleasant restaurant decorated with paintings of the village and surrounding area. Connoisseurs will love the authentic local dishes such as coq au cidre du pays d'Othe and the tasty farmhouse terrines.

🍽 **Aux Crieurs de Vin** – *4–6 pl. Jean-Jaurès.* 🕿*03 25 40 01 01. Closed Sun and Mon.* Wine connoisseurs will appreciate this establishment, which is part wine and spirits shop, part atmospheric pre-1940s style bistro. The cuisine will also please enthusiasts, with produce fresh from the market and a good choice of fish.

🍽 **Bistro DuPont** – *5 pl. Charles-de-Gaulle,10150 Pont-Ste-Marie, 3km/1.8mi NE of Troyes on N 77.* 🕿*03 25 80 90 99. Closed Sun eve and Mon.* Flowers and smiles from the staff provide a fine welcome. In a simple but carefully planned setting, the cheap and cheerful dishes suit the style of the bistro. Terrace in summer.

🍽 **Le Bistroquet** – *Pl. Langevin.* 🕿*03 25 73 65 65. Closed Sun except lunch from Sept–Jun.* This restaurant is situated in the centre of the pedestrianised part of Troyes, and is reminiscent of a Parisian brasserie. The large dining room is attractively lit by a decorated glass ceiling, and has leather seats, indoor plants and a lively atmosphere. All dishes are based on fresh ingredients. Terrace with shrubs and garden lights.

🛍 SHOPPING

Specialities – First and foremost, andouillettes (chitterling sausages)… grilled, unaccompanied or drizzled with olive oil flavoured with browned fines herbes and garlic. Try them with mustard au vin de champagne or Meaux mustard and accompanied by mashed potatoes, kidney beans or fried onion rings, dipped in milk or beer, then in flour. Other specialities include Chaource cheese, cider or champagne choucroute, rosé des Riceys, and cacibel (aperitif made with cider, blackcurrant and honey).

Market – Daily market in the Place St-Remy halls. The main market is held on Saturdays. There is another in the Chartreux area on Wed and on Sun morning. A country market is held every third Wed of the month on Boulevard Jules-Guesde.

La Boucherie Moderne – *Halle de l'Hôtel-de-Ville.* ☎*03 25 73 32 61/03 25 73 32 64.* Stock up on andouillettes made by Gilbert Lemelle, the largest French manufacturer of these sausages.

Charcuterie Audry-Chantal – *Halles de l'Hôtel-de-Ville-Case 37.* ☎*03 25 73 27 74. Closed 3 weeks in Jul and 2 weeks in Feb.* A good place to buy real home-made Troyes andouillettes (chitterling sausages).

Jean-Pierre-Ozérée – *Halles de l'Hôtel-de-Ville.* ☎*03 25 73 72 25.* Maturing of cheeses, including Chaource, Mussy and Langres. A useful alternative if you don't have time to go to the production site yourself.

Le Palais du Chocolat – *2 r. de la Monnaie.* ☎*03 25 73 35 73. www.pascal-caffet.com. Closed Sun afternoon.* An emporium of chocolate, as well as ice cream, sorbets and pastries. Among the specialities are *tuiles chocolatées et aux amandes* (chocolate almond thins), *cristallines de Troyes* and liquorice *ganache* which taste all the better in this magnificent setting.

Marques Avenue – *114 bd de Dijon,* ☎*03 25 82 00 72. Closed Sun.* With 120 boutiques, Marques Avenue is the biggest centre for discount fashion stores in Europe. Here you will find all the big brand names, both French and foreign.

Marques City – *Pont-Ste-Marie. www.marquescity.com. Closed Sun.* Stores offering almost 200 labels at discount prices in a mall of 15 000sq m/ 19 940sq yd, ranging across sportswear, formal wear and quality accessories. Three restaurants on site.

McArthur Glen – *Voie des Bois - 10150 Pont-Ste-Marie.* ☎*03 25 70 47 10. Closed Sun and 1 May.* Opened in 1995, the village includes 84 end-of-line shops along an outside covered gallery.

Patrick Maury – *28 r. du Gén.-de-Gaulle.* ☎*03 25 73 06 84. Closed Sun, Mon.* Opposite the market you will find this tiny boutique prized for its specialities. Andouillette de Troyes is of course the star buy, but black pudding and other home-made charcuterie come a close second.

🎭 NIGHTLIFE

Le Bougnat des Pouilles – *29 r. Paillot-de-Montabert.* ☎*03 25 73 59 85.* The high-quality vintages in this wine bar are sought out by the young proprietor himself, among the smaller producers in the region. The walls are often hung with exhibitions of painting and photography. The atmosphere is very peaceful and the music an easygoing blend of jazz, blues and world music. Concerts twice a month.

Le Chihuahua – *8 r. Charbonnet.* ☎*03 25 73 33 53.* This fashionable cellar bar also has dancing. Each Thursday a theme night takes place (e.g. tequila, techno) and a rock concert is organised once a month. The barman's Tex-Mex cocktails are brilliant.

La Chope – *64 ave du Gén.-de-Gaulle.* ☎*03 25 73 11 99.* Wide selection of beers, whiskies and cocktails.

La Cocktaileraie – *56 r. Jaillant-Deschainets, BP 4102.* ☎*03 25 73 77 04.* The clientele of this smart bar ranges from businessmen discussing stock options and the Dow Jones to young lovers whispering sweetnothings. A hundred or so cocktails are on offer, around 45 whiskies and many prestigious champagnes, as well as ice cream. A small reception room can be hired for private parties and meetings.

Le Tricasse – *16 r. Paillot-de-Montabert.* ☎*03 25 73 14 80. Closed Sun.* This most famous of Troyes' nightspots is in a smart area and offers a glorious mix of music, from jazz to salsa to house (DJ every Saturday night). It is frequented by students from the business school and engineers, among others. Rum, champagne, cocktails and wines are the house specialities.

🎭 SHOWTIME

Théâtre de Champagne – *R. Louis-Mary.* ☎*03 25 76 27 60 / 61. Performances Mon–Fri 10am–12.30pm, 2–6pm, Sat 10am–12.30pm, 2–5pm. Closed Jul–Aug.* Opera, comedy, arthouse theatre, variety shows.

Théâtre de la Madeleine – *R. Jules-Lebocey.* ☎*03 25 43 32 10. Performances Mon–Sat 10am–12.30pm, 2–6pm.* Arthouse theatre, comedy, variety shows.

Metz★★★

Lorraine

From the limestone escarpment of the Côtes de Moselle high above Metz, the Lorraine plateau can be seen stretching away eastwards towards the German frontier. The city itself lies at the meeting point of the Moselle with the Seille, a strategic site whose importance was appreciated by the Romans; it was here that their great highways leading from the Channel coast to the Rhine and from Trier to Italy were linked, their course marked today by Metz' busy shopping street, Rue Serpenoise.

A BIT OF HISTORY

In the 4C, as a response to the threat posed by the Germanic tribes to the east, fortifications were built, together with a basilica which later became the church of a monastery, the original Church of St-Pierre-aux-Nonnains or St Peter of the Noviciates. In the early part of the Middle Ages, the city was the residence of the Merovingian rulers of Eastern Gaul (Austrasia); it then became the capital of the kingdom of Lotharingia (Lorraine), before being attached to the Holy Roman Empire. In the 12C Metz declared itself the capital of a republican city-state, with an elected High Magistrate as ruler. But in 1552, together with Verdun and Toul, it was annexed by a French kingdom seeking to push its frontier eastwards, and its role henceforth was that of a fortress-town standing guard over the border.

1871–1918–1944

On 6 August 1870, the Prussian armies conquered the city, which became part of the newly declared German Empire. The city lost a quarter of its population, people who chose to resettle in France; artists left and so did many businessmen, at the very moment when industry was expanding rapidly. Metz's loss was Nancy's gain.

The town began to take on a Germanic character. In 1898 the cathedral was given a neo-Gothic portal, complete with a statue of the Prophet Daniel looking uncommonly like Kaiser Wilhelm II (though his moustache was subsequently clipped). With its surrounding forts, Metz became the centre of the greatest fortified camp in the world. From 1902–08 the area around the station was rebuilt; the station itself was constructed in a style which mixed Rhenish neo-Romanesque and Second Reich symbolism (the Emperor himself designed the bell-tower); an imposing central post office rose nearby, together with hotels providing accomodation for the officers of the garrison. Metz was in fact the linchpin of the Schlieffen Plan,

> ▸ **Population:** 322 526
> ◔ **Michelin Map:** 307 I 4
> 🅱 **Info:** Place d'Armes.
> 📞03 87 55 53 76. http://tourisme.mairie-metz.fr.
> ▣ **Location:** Metz is a major junction at the heart of Lorraine, with good rail, road and air links, only 50km/31mi from the German border. Much of the historic centre is traffic-free.
> 🅿 **Parking:** Use one of the eight underground car parks, of which two are open 24hr.
> ◔ **Timing:** Bus services *(from ;l. de la République; 📞03 87 76 31 11)* operate all over Metz and the vicinity. **Visi'Pass** is a one-day ticket (⊜3.30€).

Guided Tours

Guided tours around Metz are available Mon–Sat (except public hols) at 3pm and 4pm. Enquire at the tourist office, which has designed visits for disabled visitors so that they can discover the town, its monuments and museum.
♿Wheelchairs loaned.

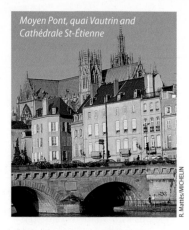
Moyen Pont, quai Vautrin and Cathédrale St-Étienne

R. Mattes/MICHELIN

the strategy to be followed in the event of a future war with France; this plan envisaged the adoption of a defensive posture to the south of the city coupled with a vast turning movement to the northwest, which would sweep through Belgium and then descend on Paris. In 1914 this plan all but succeeded; the German armies marched steadily forward for six weeks, coming within 50km/30mi of Paris, only to be thrown back by Marshal Joffre at the Miracle of the Marne.

In the inter-war period, the ring of forts around Metz was incorporated into the Maginot Line. Their defensive strength was such that the Allied armies took two and a half months to eject their German occupants in the autumn of 1944.

SIGHTS

Cathédrale St-Étienne★★★

The cathedral grew out of the joining together around 1240 of two churches which up to then had been separated by an alleyway.

The 13C and 14C interior recalls the Gothic style of Champagne; its relative narrowness combines with the modest height of the aisles to exaggerate the loftiness of the nave which does in fact reach 41.77m/137ft. The late Gothic chancel, crossing and transepts were completed at the beginning of the 16C.

The cathedral is known as "God's Lantern" (Lanterne du Bon Dieu) due to its stained-glass windows (**verrières★★★**). The rose window of the west front is 14C work, the lower part of the north transept window 15C, and the upper part of this window together with the glass of the south transept and the chancel, 16C. Contemporary glass can be seen beneath the towers and above all in the north ambulatory and on the southwest side of the north transept (the *Earthly Paradise* by Chagall).

Musées de Metz Métropole La Cour d'Or★★

La Cour d'Or. ◔*Open Mon–Fri 9am–5pm, Sat–Sun and public holidays 10am–5pm.* ◔*Closed 1 and 6 Jan, Good Fri, 1 and 8 May, 14 Jul, 15 Aug, 1 and 11 Nov and 25 Dec.* ◉4.60€; *no charge first Sun in the month.* ✆*03 87 68 25 00. http://musees.ca2m.com/site.*

The museums are housed in the buildings of a former Carmelite convent (17C), a 15C tithe barn (Grenier de Chèvrement) and several link rooms and extensions. In the basements are the remains of ancient baths.

The complex uses the latest display techniques to present a fascinating survey of times past.

Section archéologique★★★

On display in the archaeological section are artefacts found in Metz and the surrounding area. The finds attest to the importance of the town, which was in turn Gaulish, a major crossroads in Gallo-Roman times, and a cultural centre under the Carolingian kings. The **Grenier de Chèvrement★** is a fine building (1457) used to store cereals given over as tithes.

Centre Pompidou-Metz

◔*Opening 2010.*

This is the first so-called 'decentralised' branch of Paris's famous Centre Pompidou to open outside Paris. It will exhibit artworks of the 20C and 21C to further its mission of promoting art in Europe. The building, with exhibits spread across three galleries, has a 77m/253ft-high spire. The exhibitions, most taken from the Musée National d'Art Moderne in Paris, are all temporary to allow for the continuing evolution of artistic styles that prove ripe for presentation. Until it opens, an adjacent building showcases the project's progress with 3D images, maps, multimedia displays, models and drawings. ⏱*Open Oct–Apr daily 11am–5pm.* ✆*03 87 63 73 59. www.centrepompidou-metz.fr.*

ADDITIONAL SIGHTS
Porte des Allemands★
Place St-Louis★

ADDRESSES

🛏 STAY

🍽 **Chambre d'hôte Bigare** – *23 r. Principale – 57530 Ars-Laquenexy, 9km/5.6mi E of Metz, Château-Salins direction then D 999.* ✆*03 87 38 13 88. 2 rooms.* If the bustle of city life doesn't suit you, a short journey will bring you to this friendly local village house. Simple rooms and reasonable prices.

🍽🛏 **Hôtel de la Cathédrale** – *25 pl. de la Chambre.* ✆*03 87 75 00 02. www. hotelcathedrale-metz.fr. 20 rooms.* ⌧*11€.* A charming hotel situated in a lovely 17C house, completely restored. The attractive rooms have cast iron or cane beds, old parquet flooring and furniture, some of which is oriental. Most rooms face the cathedral, just opposite.

🍴 EAT

🍽🛏 **La Gargouille** – *29 pl. de Chambre.* ✆*03 87 36 65 77. www.lagargouille.com. Closed Mon lunch, Tue eve and Wed.* Don't be fooled by the ordinary façade of this restaurant located down from the cathedral: behind it lies a sumptuous interior with velvet-covered seats, cosy little booths and 1900-style décor typical of the Nancy School, all making for a warm ambiance. The food is exceedingly refined: carpaccio de fois gras au sel de Guérande, or joue de bœuf sauce vigneronne. Highly professional service.

🍽🛏 **La Robe des Champs** – *14 en Nouvelle rue.* ✆*03 87 36 32 19 .* You can't miss the yellow façade and Provençal-style terrace of this pleasant bistro in a pedestrian town centre street. Potatoes, as the name infers ("in its jacket"), take pride of place in this friendly unpretentious establishment.

🍽🛏 **Restaurant du Fort** – *Allée du Fort – 57070 St-Julien-lès-Metz, 8km/5mi NE of Metz, Bouzonville direction on D3, then a minor road.* ✆*03 87 75 71 16. Closed 1–10 Jan, 24 Jul–9 Aug, Sun eve and Wed. Booking advisable at weekends.* At the end of a forest track you will be amazed to discover this 1870 fort, evidence of the Moselle's turbulent history. Part of it has been restored to create a restaurant offering Lorraine cuisine.

🍽🛏 **Restaurant du Pont-St-Marcel** – *1 r. du Pont-St-Marcel.* ✆*03 87 30 12 29.* A 17C restaurant not far from St Étienne's cathedral, standing on piles beside a branch of the Moselle. Inside, an amusing contemporary fresco depicts a 17C fairground scene, complete with acrobats and theatre. The staff wear costumes to serve the local cuisine.

🍽🛏 **L'Écluse** – *45 pl. de la Chambre.* ✆*03 87 75 42 18. Closed 1–15 Aug, Sat noon and Sun and Mon eves.* Refined modern style, with art on display, and well-prepared contemporary dishes.

🍽🛏 **Maire** – *1 r. du Pont-des-Morts.* ✆*03 87 32 43 12. www.restaurant-maire.com. Closed Wed lunch and Tue.* There is a superb view of the Moselle from this town-centre restaurant. Enjoy the chef's carefully prepared dishes, whether in the salmon-pink dining room with its pale wood furniture or on the terrace.

Nancy★★★

Lorraine

Capital of the industrial area of Lorraine, Nancy is sited on the low-lying land between the River Meurthe and the Moselle Heights (Côtes de Moselle).

A BIT OF HISTORY

The city was founded in the 11C but its history really begins in the 15C, when the Dukes of Lorraine asserted their independence, added Renaissance ornament to their Flamboyant Gothic palace, and to the north of the Triumphal Arch – Arc de Triomphe – the district now known as Vieux Nancy began to take shape.

In the 17C, the new town (ville neuve) was planned on a regular pattern by the artist Claude Gellée, known as **Claude Lorrain** (1600–82). Louis XIV 's architect Mansart designed the town hall (**Palais du Gouvernement★**) in 1699.

Ever since the Treaty of Munster in 1648, the Duchy of Lorraine had been in a precarious situation; an

▶ **Population:** 331 363
  Michelin Map: 307 I 6
▪ **Info:** 14 pl. Stanislas. ℰ03 83 35 22 41. www.ot-nancy.fr.
▶ **Location:** The city is reached on autoroutes A 31 and A 33. The Old Town is the historic heart of the city, centred on place St-Epvre. The handsome New Town is the area outside its original gates.
☺ **Don't Miss:** Place Stanislas.
🕐 **Timing:** Discover Nancy by taxi on one of five routes that features commentary recorded by the tourist office.

independent enclave in French territory, it still formed part of the Holy Roman Empire. Though French in language and culture, its people were proud of their independence and much attached to their princes.

In 1738, following the War of the Polish Succession, Duke François I, son of Leopold and husband of Maria-Theresa of Austria, found himself having to cede Lorraine in exchange for Tuscany.

In his place, Louis XV appointed, as ruler for life, his own father-in-law Stanislas Leszczynski, and by 1766 the Duchy had been painlessly incorporated into the French kingdom, a notable success for Cardinal Fleury's foreign policy. Stanislas was a man of peace, fond of his daughter the Queen of France, a lover of good living and of the opposite sex, and a passionate builder.

He set out to join together the old quarter of Nancy with the "New Town" by means of a set-piece of civic design in honour of his son-in-law. The great project was completed in the short space of three years, between 1752 and 1755.

Guided Tours

Audioguides with a recorded commentary are also available on the Art nouveau theme. Enquire at the tourist office (*see Orient Panel above*).

Pl. de la Carrière

ARC DE TRIOMPHE

PLACE

MUSÉE DES BEAUX-ARTS

STANISLAS

Hôtel de ville

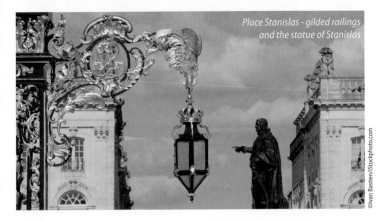

Place Stanislas - gilded railings
and the statue of Stanislas

©Ivan Bastien/iStockphoto.com

SIGHT

Place Stanislas★★★

Place Stanislas was added to the UNESCO World Heritage list in 1983.

In charge of the work were the architect Emmanuel Héré (1705–63) and Jean **Lamour**, a metal-worker of genius. Héré designed the City Hall (Hôtel de Ville) and the flanking buildings with their fine façades. To the north the square is defined by two further buildings, similar in general treatment, though with only one storey. The whole forms a space of exceptional elegance and clarity of structure, ornamented with urns and trophies and with balustrades to conceal the roofs. Further enclosure is achieved by Jean Lamour's brilliant ironwork. Perfectly integrated into the architectural concept, his **gilded railings** with their crests and floral decoration are of inimitable gracefulness.

ADDRESSES

🛏 STAY

🛏🛏 **Portes d'Or** – 21 r. Stanislas. 🖉03 83 35 42 34. www.hotel-lesportesdor.com. 20 rooms. 🍽6€. The main advantage of this hotel is its proximity to place Stanislas. The pastel-coloured rooms are not very large, but have modern furniture and are reasonably well equipped.

🛏🛏🛏 **Hôtel Crystal** – 5 r. Chanzy. 🖉03 83 17 54 00. 58 rooms. 🍽11.50€. This entirely renovated hotel near the station is a good place to stay in Nancy. Its modern, spacious rooms have been nicely arranged and decorated and feel welcoming. Cosy bar-lounge.

🍴 EAT

Rue des Maréchaux, by place Stanislas, justly nicknamed "r. gourmande", has some 40 different restaurants to suit all tastes and budgets.

🍽🍽 **Grand Café Foy** – 1 pl. Stanislas. 🖉03 83 32 21 44. Closed 29 Jul–21 Aug, Sun eve, Tue eve and Wed. Climb the lovely stone staircase to reach this first-floor restaurant above the café-brasserie of the same name in place Stanislas. The food is good and served in generous portions. Rustic décor with exposed beams.

🍽🍽 **Les Pissenlits** – 25, bis r. des Ponts. 🖉03 83 37 43 97. www.les-pissenlits.com. Closed 1–16 Aug, Sun and Mon. There's always a crowd in this bistro near the market. The atmosphere is relaxed, the cuisine innovative and diverse, and the décor pleasant with closely packed tables and blackboard.

🍽🍽 **Le V Four** – 10 r. St-Michel. 🖉03 83 32 49 48. Closed 1–7 Feb, 30 Aug–9 Sept, Sat lunch, Sun eve and Mon. It may be small, but this restaurant in the heart of the old city is popular among the locals, who enjoy its simple modern décor and its trendy cuisine. Terrace.

⊖⊜🍽 **Le Gastrolâtre** – *1 pl. Vaudémont. ℘03 83 35 51 94. Closed 1–6 May, 15–30 Aug, Christmas holidays, Mon lunch, Thu eve and Sun.* This popular bistro just behind place Stanislas is run with a master's hand by a media boss. Its mouth-watering menu and characterful cuisine combine local flavours with those from the south of France.

⊖⊜🍽 **Grenier à Sel** – *28 r. Gustave-Simon. ℘03 83 32 31 98. www.legrenier asel.eu. Closed Sun and Mon.* This restaurant is in a little-frequented street on the first floor of one of the oldest houses in town. In the large country-style dining room you can enjoy food with a modern flair.

🍸 NIGHTLIFE

L'Arquebuse – *13 r. Héré. ℘03 83 32 11 99. www.larq.fr.* This high-class bar with a refined décor has a good view of the place Stanislas. A wide choice of cocktails with atmospheric music and disco, attracting a mixed clientele of smart students and businessmen. The place to go after 2am.

L'Échanson – *9 r. de la Primatiale. ℘03 83 35 51 58. Closed Sun, Mon.* A pleasant little wine merchant that also serves as the local bistro. A dozen or so wines are available by the glass, which can be accompanied by a savoury snack.

🎭 SHOWTIME

Get hold of a programme!
The magazine *Spectacles à Nancy* will keep you informed.*www.spectacles-publications.com.*

Concerts And Stage Performances
The Opéra de Nancy et de Lorraine, Ballet de Nancy, Théâtre de la Manufacture, Centre dramatique national Nancy-Lorraine, Association de musique ancienne de Nancy, Ensemble Poirel, Orchestre symphonique et lyrique de Nancy, Association Lorraine de musique de chambre, Gradus Ad Musicam, La Psalette de Lorraine all put on numerous concerts and shows throughout the year.

Gastronomie en Musique – Ask the tourist office about these summer evening musical performances (*Thu, Fri and weekends in different areas of the city*).

Patrimoine en Musique – Classical concerts in city-centre churches in the afternoons.

CONFECTIONERY

Adam – *3 pl. St-Epvre. ℘03 83 32 04 69. Closed Mon.* This confectioner sells St-Epure, which is made of almond meringue, vanilla cream and crushed nougatine, together with a host of other sweet-tooth delights.

Confiserie Chocolaterie Alain Batt – *30, r. du Tapis-Vert. www.alainbatt.com. ℘03 83 35 70 00.* Before your very eyes, this confectioner will create macaroons and bergamotes de Nancy, plums in marzipan, Chardons de Lorraine, bergamot truffles and chocolates. Products to taste and buy.

Au Duché de Lorraine – *47 r. Henri-Poincaré. ℘03 83 30 13 83. Open daily.* Fans of the famous *bergamotes de Nancy* (hard sweets flavoured with citrus rind) and *macarons des Dominicains* will not be disappointed by this confectioner, established since 1840. Also on sale, delightful Lorraine gift boxes and baskets, all generously filled.

Maison des Sœurs Macarons – *21 r. Gambetta. ℘03 83 32 24 25. www.macaron-de-nancy.com.* The secret recipe for macaroons has been handed down within the family since the 18C. Other Lorraine specialities are available here: *bergamots* (a sweet made with essence of bergamot), *Berg'amours* (crystallized fruits), *Perles de Lorraine* (crystallized fruits with plum liqueur centres), *Florentines des sœurs*, (fondant-encased praline chocolates) *Babas du Roi*, gingerbread, etc.

Toul★

Lorraine

On the banks of the River Moselle, the handsome fortified town occupies a strategic position at the intersection of highways and waterways.

A BIT OF HISTORY

Together with Metz and Verdun, the city was one of the three Imperial Bishoprics which were annexed by Henri II in 1552 and were finally recognised as belonging to the French crown by the Peace of Westphalia in 1648.

Vauban built new ramparts round the city in 1700, (the Porte de Metz is all that remains today), which were subsequently improved at intervals so that on the eve of World War I Toul was acknowledgeed as one of the best defended strongholds in Europe.

SIGHTS

Cathédrale St-Étienne★★

Built from 1221 to 1496, cathedral has a very simple elevation. The highly pointed arches of the first five bays of the nave are in the High Gothic style of the 14C. The west front (**façade★★**), almost overloaded with architectural ornament, lost its statuary at the time of the French Revolution. The **cloisters★**, adorned with fine gargoyles, are among the most extensive in France.

▶ **Population:** 16 945
🖈 **Michelin Map:** 307 G 6
🗓 **Info:** Parvis de la Cathédrale. ✆03 83 64 11 69. www.ot-toul.fr.
◗ **Location:** The town is in Lorraine. The walled old quarter, almost enclosed by water, is entered by Porte de France on the west side or Porte de la Moselle on the east.

Musée d'Art et d'Histoire★

25 rue Gouvion Saint Cyr . ⊙Open Wed – Mon, 9.30– 18.30; Sat, Sun 2– 6pm. No charge except for large exhibitions ✆03 83 64 13 38.

Housed in the Hôtel-Dieu there are numerous collections tracing the history of Toul. There are 28 themed rooms which cover everything from the prehistoric period through the Middle Ages to recent history.

Église St-Gengoult★

This former Collegiate church , erected in the 13 C and 15C , is a fine example of Champagne Gothic architecture. The West front has an elegant doorway dating from the 15C.

Cloisters★★The Cloister dates from the the 16C and the outside decoration of the galleries is in Renaissance style.

Fortified town of Toul

©Guido Alberto Rossi/Tips Images

Verdun★★
Lorraine

This ancient stronghold occupies a strategic position on the Meuse. The Upper Town with its cathedral and citadel is poised on an outcrop overlooking the river.

A BIT OF HISTORY

The Gauls were the first to build a fortress here on the left bank of the Meuse. They were followed by the Romans, but Verdun entered the mainstream of history with the signing of the **Treaty of Verdun** in 843.

By its terms, Charlemagne's realm was divided up among his grandsons, contrary to their father's wish for its preservation as a single unit.

The Emperor, Lothair, received the central zone (Northern Italy, Provence, the Rhineland and the Low Countries); Louis, the Germanic countries, and Charles the Bald, Gaul. The repercussions have been felt throughout the centuries, and the treaty has been referred to as "the most significant in all the continent's history", partly because Louis was dissatisfied with his portion and launched what might be considered the first of all Franco-German wars in 858 following the death of Lothair.

The town was besieged in 1870 at the start of the Franco-Prussian War, then occupied for three years. In World War I,

▶ **Population:** 20 733
⏱ **Michelin Map:** 307 D 4
ℹ **Info:** Place de la Nation. ℘03 29 86 14 18. www.verdun-tourisme.com.
▷ **Location:** The town is in the north of France, 80km/50mi NW of Toul just off the A4 autoroute.

Verdun was the scene of some of the bloodiest fighting of the Western Front, in a battle that lasted 18 months (℄see *CHAMP DE BATAILLE DE VERDUN*).

SIGHT
Ville Haute★

The seat of a bishop, the fortified upper town rises in stages from the banks of the river.

The city's historic buildings include **Cathédrale Notre-Dame★**, laid out like the great Romanesque basilicas of the Rhineland, and the Bishop's Palace **(Palais épiscopal★)** constructed by Robert de Cotte in the 18C.

ADDITIONAL SIGHT

Citadelle Souterraine (Underground Citadel) – self-guided vehicle travels 7km/4.3mi of tunnels equipped to fulfil the needs of the army.

Palais épiscopal

R. Mattès/MICHELIN

Douaumont Ossuary

R. Mattès/MICHELIN

Champ de Bataille de Verdun★★★

Lorraine

The name of Verdun is indissolubly linked to the decisive struggle on which turned the outcome of the Great War (1914–1918). The gaze of the world was fixed for a year and a half on the paroxysm of violence endured by both sides, in a battle which brought forth the uttermost in steadfastness and courage.

Info: Place de la Nation, Verdun. ℘03 29 86 14 18. www.verdun-tourisme.com.

Location: The battlefields are 10km/6.2mi NE of Verdun.

A BIT OF HISTORY

At the outbreak of war in August 1914, Verdun lay a mere 40km/25mi from the Franco-German frontier. The 21 February 1916 dawned bright but cold.

A devastating bombardment preceded the Germans' frontal assault on the French lines. Within four days Douaumont Fort had fallen. This was the moment at which General Pétain took effective charge of the battle; by the time of his replacement in April 1917, it was clear that the German attempt to break the staying-power of the French army had failed. Verdun, the hinge of the whole Western Front, could not be taken.

A series of battles raged throughout March and April in the Argonne, around Les Éparges; and, closer to Verdun, on Hill 304 and the other eminence known chillingly as the Mort-Homme (Dead Man's Hill). On 11 July, the final German offensive ground to a halt in front of the Souville fort, a mere 5km/3mi from the city. The French counter-offensive began in October 1916. By 20 August 1917, the Hell of Verdun, which had cost the lives of over 700 000 men, was over.

Guided Tours

The *Circuit Découverte* is a bus tour of the battlefields (*2–6pm, starts from Verdun tourist office;* ⊜*29€*).

The Atlantic Coast region of France stretches from the estuary of the River Loire in the north to the mighty natural frontier of the Pyrénées to the south. It is bounded on the west by the apparently endless Atlantic coastline and to the east by the lush countryside of the Limousin, the Périgord and Gascony. It encompasses some of the modern region of the Pays de Loire, the whole of Poitou-Charentes and the western half of the Aquitaine.

Highlights

1 Science-based leisure park near Poitiers: **Futuroscope** (p151)

2 Medieval towers of the **Vieux Port** at **La Rochelle** (p159)

3 1C Roman arena at **Saintes** (p165)

4 **Église Monolithe**, a church hollowed out of rock at **St Émilion** (p162)

5 History theme park based round a castle, **Le Puy de Fou** (p156)

Geography – With the exception of the Pyrénées in the south, the region consists for the most part of a flat coastal plain, rising gently to the more undulating countryside in the east. In the north there are great marshy tracts like the Marais Poitevin and dunes bordering sandy beaches.

To the south is the Gironde, the name given to the broad estuary of the Garonne, and the Atlantic coast south of here runs in a straight line almost to Spain, interrupted only by the Bay of Arcachon. Behind the vast sandy beaches rise the highest sand dunes in Europe while inland is the Landes, an immense wooded area planted with with pine trees.

History – In Classical times the Roman province of Aquitania included all the Atlantic Coast region. Following the collapse of the Roman Empire, it came under the control of Visigoths and then Franks. During the medieval period the region passed to the English crown as part of Eleanor of Aquitaine's dowry and not till the end of the Hundred Years' War did it revert to France. During the Revolution there was less support here for the new Republic than in other areas of France.

Economy – The Poitou Charentes region is mainly agricultural and cereal production is very important, as are cattle rearing and dairy farming. Cognac is produced in the area around the town of the same name and exported worldwide.

The area around Bordeaux is renowned for its fine wines and the produce of the famous Châteaux are much sought after. The Landes area produces vast quantities of timber and is the largest maritime pine forest in Europe.

Angoulême★★

Angoulême has a walled historic Upper Town, which rises high aboce a more industrial modern Lower Town; narrow streets lace through the lofty Upper Town, lined with beautiful old buildings, and the ramparts give immense views. Angoulême is France's 'Cartoon Capital', and everywhere you'll see the influence of its celebrated *Festival international de la bande dessinée*, devoted to the art of the strip-cartoon.

▶ **Population:** 42 096
⊙ **Michelin Map:** 324 K-L-M 5-6
▯ **Info:** 7 bis r. du Chat. ✆05 45 95 16 84. www.angouleme-tourisme.com.
◐ **Location:** Angoulême is 115km/71.4mi S of Poitiers and 43km/26.7mi E of Cognac.
🚸 **Kids:** In this cartoon-crazy city, there are brilliant graffiti and *trompe l'oeil* everywhere. The tourist office has a map of some of the best, or find their locations online at www.toutenbd.com/murs_peints.

A BIT OF HISTORY

Famous residents: Angoulême boasts two famous **literary characters**: Jean-Louis Guez de Balzac (1597–1654), one of the original members of the Académie Française; and Honoré Balzac (1799–1850), a novelist and playwright who made Angoulême his home.

In 1806, 77-year-old **General Resnier** launched himself from the city's northern ramparts in a **flying-machine** of his own invention. The general suffered a broken leg and a plan for the invasion of England by this method was shelved.

Bande Dessinée (strip cartoon, often known simply as BD) is an important entertainment for adults and kids alike in France. Angoulême's cartoon festival owes its origins to an exhibition in 1972, "Dix Millions d'images". In 1974, a regular Salon de la bande dessinée was started, that attracted many top cartoonists. In 1996, it became the popular international festival held in January each year.

VISIT

Cathédrale St-Pierre★

18 r. Fénélon, Angoulême.
Extensively destroyed by the Calvinists, the cathedral was restored in 1634 and again from 1866 onwards.
The early 12C statuary of the west front (**façade★★**) is mostly intact; more elaborate than the other façades typical of the region around Angoulême, its themes include the Ascension and the Last Judgement. Particularly noteworthy among the 70 statues and low-reliefs are the superb Christ in Majesty surrounded by the Evangelists, the medallions of saints and a battle scene inspired by *La Chanson de Roland (Song of Roland)*.

🚸 Centre National de la Bande Dessinée et de l'Image – strip-cartoon centre

121 r. de Bordeaux. ♿⊙*Open Jul–Aug Mon, Wed and Fri 10am–6pm, Thu 10am–7pm, Sat–Sun, 14 Jul and 15 Aug 2–6pm; rest of the year Mon, Wed and Fri noon–6pm, Thu noon–7pm, Sat–Sun 2–6pm.* ⊙*Closed 1 Jan, Easter Monday, 1 May, Whit Monday.* ⊛*6€ (child free).* ✆*05 45 38 65 65. www.cnbdi.fr.*

Cathédrale St-Pierre

B. Kaufmann/MICHELIN

Arcachon★★

A century and a half ago, the site of Arcachon was no more than a pinewood. Today, it is one of the most popular resorts on the French Atlantic.

A BIT OF HISTORY

Arcachon was born when a couple of speculators, the **Pereire brothers**, laid a railway line to the coast in 1852. The resort quickly grew and was popular for both winter and summer holidays. It is divided into 'seasons' – a winter resort **(ville d'hiver★)**, with fine villas among the pines; a summer resort (ville d'été), with the seafront and attractive **Boulevard de la Mer★**; and the fashionable autumn and spring districts (ville d'automne and ville de printemps) with opulent houses near Pereire park.

SIGHTS

Bassn★ (Bay)

Bordered by the resorts of Arcachon, Andernos and the wooded dunes of the Cap Ferret peninsula, this vast airy bay, with Bird Island (Île aux Oiseaux) at its centre, extends over an area of 250sq km/96.5sq mi, four-fifths of which is exposed at low tide. With its great stretches of oyster beds totalling 18sq km/7sq mi in all, Arcachon is one of the main oyster-farming areas. Drive along the waterfront, or take a trip in a 'pinasse', one of the traditional boats

> ▶ **Population:** 12 153
> ⏱ **Michelin Map:** 335 D 6-7
> 🅸 **Info:** Esp. G. Pompidou
> 𝄞05 57 52 97 97.
> www.arcachon.com.
> ◗ **Location:** The resort fronts onto the vast Bassin d'Arcachon inlet. The town centre is near the main beach on Bd de la Plage and Ave Gambetta.

used by the oyster farmers (many excursions available from Thiers and Eyrac landing stages (Arcachon) and other landing stages around the Bassin. 𝄞05 57 72 28 28. www.bateliers-arcachon.com).

Dune du Pilat★★

7.5km/4.5mi S.

This hill of sand, the highest (114m/374ft) and longest (2 800m/3 062yd) in Europe, drops on its landward side almost sheer to the pine woodland. Its summit offers a thrilling view along the long, straight sands of the 230km/143mi **Côte d'Argent** (Silver Coast) with its splendid Atlantic rollers.

Every year the ocean deposits another 15cu m/529.7cu ft of sand per m of coastline, continually building up the dune which in 1774 swallowed up the church at Soulac. The **panorama★★** of ocean and forest is especially lovely at dusk.

Dune du Pilat

Ch. Faurie/MICHELIN

Col
d'Aubisque★★
Aubisque Pass

The main east–west axis of the Pyrénées is interrupted by a series of long narrow valleys running roughly north–south. Each of these valleys forms a distinct unit, with a characteristic landscape and way of life, which often have more in common with the lowlands to the north or even with Spain than with the valleys on either side. A number of high passes permit east–west communication; the Tourmalet Pass at 2 114m/6 936ft is the highest, but the Aubisque Pass (Col d'Aubisque at 1 709m/5 608ft), which separates the Béarn from the Bigorre country, is the most spectacular.

◔ **Michelin Map:** 342 J-K 5
◓ **Location:** The Aubisque Pass lies in the Pyrénées region, SW of Lourdes.

VISIT
From the southern summit of the pass (*TV relay station – 30min return on foot*) the immense **panorama**★★★ extends over rocky slopes to the gentler, man-made landscape of the valleys far below, as well as taking in the rock formations of the Cirque de Gourette, (from left to right, the Grand Gabizos, Pène Blanque and the Pic de Ger).

Aulnay★★

Originally in the province of Poitiers, Aulnay was apportioned to Saintonge when France was divided into *départements* by the Constituent Assembly on 22 December 1789. It is known for its magnificent 12C Romanesque church.

▷ **Population:** 1 467
◔ **Michelin Map:** 322 G 3
▤ **Info:** 290 av. de l'Église. ☏05 46 33 14 44. http://tourisme.aulnay.info.
◓ **Location:** The village of Aulnay sits inland from Rochefort in the northern part of the Atlantic Coast region.

SIGHT
Église St-Pierre★★
r. Haute de l'Église.
This fine Romanesque church stands among the cypresses of its ancient burial ground with its Gothic Hosanna Cross. It was built between 1140 and 1170 at a time when Eleanor of Aquitaine ruled southwestern France as queen first to Louis VII, then to Henry II of England. Its structure, notably its tribuneless triple nave, is essentially in the Romanesque style typical of the Poitou area, while its sculpture is characteristic of Saintonge.

Although somewhat marred by massive 15C buttresses, the west front is remarkable for its sumptuously decorated arches and its large-scale figure sculptures. In the left portal is a poignant representation of St Peter hanging upside-down on his cross. Considering himself unworthy of the same treatment as his Master, he demanded this even crueller form of crucifixion for himself; by lowering its centre of gravity, the cross could be made smaller, and thus less costly.

The doorway of the south transept has lofty corner columns and a great relieving arch; the second arch, supported by sitting atlantes and showing the Prophets and Apostles, is an achievement of the 13C Saintonge school of sculpture.

Within, the central window of the apse is famous for its unusually rich carving, characteristic of the level which decorative art had reached in the High Middle Ages. The capitals of the columns in the nave are also worthy of attention, as is the bell-tower with its 18C slate-clad spire; its lower levels are particularly attractive.

Biarritz★★★

With its splendid beaches of fine sand and high-quality facilities, golf courses and luxury hotel, this Basque Coast resort enjoys an international reputation. Biarritz is Europe's capital of surfing and teems with thousands of visitors coming to ride the waves year-round.

A BIT OF HISTORY

Over a century ago, Biarritz was a place of no particular distinction, its beaches attracting people from nearby Bayonne. Fame came suddenly, with the visits of Empress Eugénie and Napoleon III, followed by many of the illustrious names of the period. Queen Victoria was here in 1889 and after 1906 Biarritz became a favourite of Edward VII.

Now enhanced by modernisation, Biarritz continues to offer pleasures which never pall, its beaches, promenades and gardens to either side of the rocky promontory of the Plateau de l'Atalaye remain as attractive as ever. The orientation of the beaches also produce rollers that attract surfers.

▶ **Population:** 26 690
ⓒ **Michelin Map:** 324 C-D 2
🄸 **Info:** 1 Square d'Ixelles.
  ☎05 59 22 37 10.
  www.biarritz.fr.
ⓒ **Location:** Biarritz, Bayonne and Anglet form a single urban area, just north of the Spanish border.
ⓒ **Don't Miss:** The view of La Perspective, a promenade overlooking Plage des Basques, is one of the highlights of Biarritz.
👥 **Kids:** Musée de la Mar.

VISIT
Promenades
Pleasantly shaded and landscaped streets lead from the main beach (Grande Plage) to the Virgin's Rock **(Rocher de la Vierge★)**.
To the south is the viewpoint (Perspective de la Côte des Basques) offering an uninterrupted **view★★** towards the mountain peaks of the Basque Country.

Grande Plage

B.Kaufmann/MICHELIN

SIGHTS
Musée Bonnat★★
5 r. Jacques, Laffitte, Bayonne.
⚊🕐*Open Nov–Apr Wed–Mon
10am–12.30pm, 2–6pm; May–Oct
Wed–Mon 10am–6.30pm.* 🕐*Closed
public holidays.* ⊗*5.50€.* 🕿*05 59 59 08
52. www.museebonnat.bayonne.fr.*
This beautiful building houses works by
the artist and collector, Léon Bonnat, as
well as artwork and sculptures by artists
including Degas and Rubens.

Musée Basque★★
37 quai des Corsaires, Bayonne.
🕐*Open Jul–Aug 10am–6.30pm; rest
of the year Tue–Sun 10am–6.30pm,
2–6pm, Wed 6.30–9.30pm.* 🕐*Closed
public holidays.* ⊗*5.50€.* 🕿*05 59 59 08
98. www.musee-basque.com.*
One of the finest regional ethnographic
museums in France and probably the
best on Basque ethnography. Exhibits
cover agrictulture, seafaring and *pelota*
– a ball game.

Cathédrale Sainte-Marie de Bayonne★
r. Thiers, Biarritz. 🕐*Open 7am–
12.30pm, 3–7pm.* 🕿*05 59 59 17 82.
http://moulian.free.fr.*
Set in the historic quarter of Bayonne,
this Gothic-style building was built in
13–17C. The present cathedral replaced
a Romanesque one destroyed by fire
in 1258 and again in 1310. Admire the
cloisters★.

Musée de la Mer
Plateau de l'Atalaye, Biarritz. 🕐*Open
weekends, Feb and May 9.30am–6pm;
Jun and Sept 9.30am–7pm; Jul and
Aug 9.30am–midnight; rest of the year
9.30am–12.30pm, 2–6pm* 🕐*Closed
Mon in Nov–Mar.* ⊗*7.80€ (child 5€).*
🕿*05 59 22 33 34. www.museede
lamer.com.*
A remarkable aquarium, set on **Rocher
de la Vierge**★, this place also has an
outdoor pool on the top floor with seals
who perform for curious visitors! A great
place for all the family.

EXCURSIONS
Bayonne★★
Biarritz, Anglet and Bayonne merge
to form a single urban area of which
Bayonne, with its busy quaysides and
old streets, is the commercial centre.
Its harbour on the estuary of the Adour
handles maize, sulphur and chemical
products.
The picturesque Rue du Pont-Neuf is
flanked by arcades and tall houses.
Among them are many excellent pastry
shops and confectioners emphasise the
importance of the chocolate-making
industry which began here in the 17C.

Route Impériale des Cimes★
Bayonne to Hasparren 25km/15.5mi.
This section of Napoleon I's scenic
highway was part of an overall project
to link Bayonne with St-Jean-Pied-de-
Port for strategic reasons. It follows a
highly sinuous alignment and affords
fine **views**★ of the Basque coast and
countryside.

ADDRESSES

STAY

⊜⊜ **Hôtel Atalaye** – *6 r. des Goëlands,
Plateau de l'Atalaye.* 🕿*05 59 24 06 76.
www.hotelatalaye.com.* ⊡*5.75€.
24 rooms.* This imposing turn-of-the-
20C villa owes its name to the superb
Atalaye plateau overlooking the Atlantic
ocean. The rooms here are of a good
size – those with a sea view are the
most attractive. Free parking nearby.

⊜⊜ **Chambre d'hôte Maison
Berreterrenea** – *Quartier Arrauntz,
64480 Ustaritz. 20km/12.4mi SE of
Biarritz. Take the D 932, Arrauntz exit.*
🕿*05 59 93 05 13. 4 rooms.* Facing a cider
apple orchard, this 17C Basque house
dominates the Valley of the Nive. Now
a bed and breakfast, the house has
been sympathetically renovated in
traditional style, with whitewashed
stone walls. Simply furnished rooms
adorned with beams and old doors.

Hôtel Gardenia – *19 av. Carnot. ℘05 59 24 10 46. www.hotel-gardenia. com. Closed Dec–Feb. 19 rooms.* This central hotel with a pink façade has all the charm of a private home. Its quiet, attractive rooms are regularly redecorated and its reception and salon have just been refurbished. Reasonable prices considering the location.

Hôtel Maïtagaria – *34 av. Carnot. ℘05 59 24 26 65. www.hotel-maitagaria. com. Closed 1–15 Dec. 15 rooms.* A warm, friendly reception in this little hotel near the garden, just 500m/550yd from the beach. The rooms, of varying sizes, are bright and functional and were recently renovated. Small flower-filled garden in the back.

Le Petit Hôtel – *11 r. Gardères. ℘05 59 24 87 00. www.petithotel-biarritz.com. Closed fornight in Nov and Feb. 12 rooms.* This appealing hotel is ideally located for exploring the town or spending time on the beach. Its soundproofed rooms have been renovated in tones of blue or yellow; all have Internet access. The hotel has a seminar room above its restaurant, just 100m/110yd from the hotel.

⊊ EAT

La Goélette – *4 r. du Port-Vieux. ℘05 59 24 84 65.* Take a break from shopping and treat yourself to a meal in this pleasant restaurant surrounded by boutiques. The décor is inspired by the nearby sea – blue and white tones, fishing nets, and other nautical objects. Cuisine with an accent on fish and salads.

La Pizzeria des Arceaux – *20–24 av. Édouard-VII. ℘05 59 24 11 47.* This lively pizzeria near the city hall is particularly popular with a young, trendy crowd. Attractive décor with tile frescos and mirrors and an excellent choice of desserts.

Tikia – *1 pl. Ste-Eugénie. ℘05 59 24 71 66. Tikia* means 'small' in Basque. It's true that there's not much space in this little restaurant, but its attractive ambience makes it a pleasant place to linger. The décor has a cabin-type feel, with

varnished wood panelling on the walls, porthole-shaped mirrors and other marine knick-knacks. Giant kebabs on the menu.

Le Clos Basque – *12 r. Louis-Barthou. ℘05 59 24 24 96. Closed 16 Feb–5 Mar, 23 Jun–3 Jul, 19 Oct–6 Nov, Sun eve and Mon except in Jul–Aug.* Excellent local cuisine and a warm, friendly atmosphere mean that there's rarely a spare table in this popular restaurant. Exposed beams and *azulejos* tiles add an Iberian flavour to the décor.

Plaisir des Mets – *5 r. du Centre. ℘05 59 24 34 66. Closed 15–30 Jun, 15–30 Nov, Mon noon and Tue noon in Jul and Aug, Tue eve and Wed from Sept–Jun.* This small restaurant is situated near the market hall, just a short distance from the sea. The contemporary cuisine served here highlights seasonal, regional produce. Light, modern décor in restful shades of white and blue.

⊟ BARS AND ⊟ CAFÉS

Le Caveau – *4 r. Gambetta. ℘05 59 24 16 17. http://lecaveau-biarritz.com.* One of the trendiest disco bars in town, Le Caveau is popular with locals and visitors, as well as the inevitable stars on holiday. *The* place to be seen in Biarritz.

L'Impérial (Hôtel du Palais) – *1 av. de l'impératrice. ℘05 59 41 64 00. www. hotel-du-palais.com.* "La Villa Eugénie", the scene of Napoleon III's love affair with the Empress Eugénie, became the majestic Hôtel du Palais in 1893. Enjoy a glass of champagne and savour the atmosphere in the hotel's elegant bar, the Impérial, where a pianist makes the ambience complete from 7.30–11pm every evening.

La Santa Maria – *Espl. du Port-Vieux. ℘05 59 24 53 11.* The splendid view of the Rocher de la Vierge and the Port Vieux beach is one of the attractions of this little bar perched on a rock. A terrace, a few stools and a bar counter in a cave make this a pleasant, unpretentious spot where you can sample tapas while listening to the little orchestra.

🛒 SHOPPING

Cazaux et fils – *10 r. Broquedis.* ℘*05 59 22 36 03.* The Cazaux family has been involved in making ceramic pottery since the 18C. The boutique also offers personalised creations – every step can be undertaken according to the customer's wishes, from extracting the clay to hand-painting the finishing touches.

Fabrique de chistéras Gonzalez – *6 allée des Liserons. 64600 Anglet.* ℘*05 59 03 85 04.* Founded in 1887, the Gonzalez company produces hand-made *cestas* (wicker scoops that prolong the protective *pelota* glove). In one hour, you'll learn everything there is to know about the history and manufacture of *pelotas* and *cestas*.

Chocolats Henriet – *pl. Clémenceau.* ℘*05 59 24 24 15.* Established after World War II, Henriet is the local guiding light in chocolates and confectionery, featuring *calichous* (butter and cream caramels), and *rochers de Biarritz* (bitter chocolate, orange rinds, almonds). Proprietor Serge Couzigou, maître chocolatier, also created the Musée du Chocolat *(located 4 av. de la Marne).*

Maison Arostéguy – *5 av. Victor-Hugo.* ℘*05 59 24 00 52. www.arosteguy.com.* Founded in 1875, this famous Biarritz grocery store (formerly the 'Epicerie du Progrès') has kept its original walls, shelves and façade. The shop specialises in regional fare and also stocks many products difficult to find elsewhere: rare bottles of Bordeaux, prestigious Armagnacs, Basque products, flavoured teas and spices.

🎭 SHOWTIME

Casino Barrière de Biarritz – *1 av. Édouard-VII.* ℘*05 59 22 77 77. www.lucienbarriere.com.* Located on Grande Plage, this enormous casino has a table games room (roulette, black jack), a poker table and 220 slot machines as well as Le Café de la Plage brasserie, Le Quiniela Café, Le Baccara restaurant,

B-Pink bar and club, a show room (theatre, dance) and a ballroom.

Gare du Midi – *21 bis av. du Mar.-Foch.* ℘*05 59 22 44 66. www.entractes-organisations.com. Tickets available from the tourist office.* The city's main theatre, with a seating capacity of 1 400, puts on a range of plays, music concerts and ballets. It is also the home of the Biarritz Ballet company.

🏃 SPORT AND LEISURE

Euskal-Jaï Fernand Pujol – *r. Cino-del-Duca.* ℘*05 59 23 91 09.* This pelota Basque school organises competitions most Wed and Sat in summer.

Hippodrome des Fleurs – *av. du Lac Marion.* ℘*05 59 41 27 34. www.hippodrome-biarritz.com.* Horse races have been held here on July and August evenings for over fifty years. This trotters' hippodrome has an 800m/874.8yd cindered track with sharp bends.

Piscine municipale – *bd du Gén.-de-Gaulle.* ℘*05 59 22 52 52.* Located on the shore, this municipal complex features heated seawater pools as well as a Jacuzzi, a hammam and a sauna.

Thermes Marins – *80 r. de Madrid.* ℘*05 59 23 01 22. www.biarritz-thalasso.com.* This spa, featuring a leisure pool and Jacuzzi, offers affusion or underwater showers, seaweed treatment booths, massages and sea-air bath booths.

SURF SCHOOLS
Biarritz Paradise Surf School – *Plage Marbella.* ℘*06 14 76 01 18 . www.biarritzparadisesurfschool.com.* **École De Surf Jo Moraiz** – *r. des Landes de Cristobal.* ℘*05 9 41 22 09. www.jomoraiz.com.* **École de Surf Plums** – *5 pl. Clémenceau.* ℘*05 59 24 08 04.* **Tropical Euscadi** – *École de Surf Quiksilver. 29 bd Charles de Gaulle.* ℘*05 59 22 03 12. www.biarritz-boardriders.com.*

Bordeaux★★★

"Take Versailles, add Antwerp, and you have Bordeaux" was Victor Hugo's description of the city, impressed as he was by its 18C grandeur and its splendid tidal river. Bordeaux had, however, played an important role in the affairs of France long before Versailles had been envisioned. Capital of the Aquitaine region, made a UNESCO World Heritage Site in 2007, Bordeaux is a town full of history

A BIT OF HISTORY

A large settlement even before the Roman conquest, **Burdigala** (as it was called) was always an important trading port, but frequently attacked and seized by sea-going raiders.

From 7C, Good King Dagobert took effective control of the town and its region, creating the Duchy of Aquitaine. In 1152, when **Eleanor of Aquitaine** married Henry Plantagenet, Duke of Normandy, Count of Anjou, ruler of Touraine and Maine, the bride's dowry consisted of practically the whole of southwestern France. Two months later her new husband inherited the English crown, becoming Henry II of England. Bordeaux thus became part of the English kingdom, and so remained for three centuries.

It was the English demand for wine that began the city's tradition of seafaring, and promoted the expansion of the Bordeaux **vineyards**.

Even during the Hundred Years' War claret continued to flow north to England. In 1453, Bordeaux and Guyenne (Old English for Aquitaine) were won back for France in the final battle of the Hundred Years' War.

- ▶ **Population:** 232 260
- **Michelin Map:** 335 H 5
- **Info:** 12 cours du 30-Juillet. ℘05 56 00 66 00. www. bordeaux-tourisme.com.
- **Location:** Bordeaux is on the S bank of the wide River Gironde, about 48km/29.8mi from the Atlantic.
- **Parking:** There are car parks by the river, accessible from the ring road.
- **Don't Miss:** The extensive collection of paintings in the Musée des Beaux-Arts. Of course, there are Bordeaux's world-famous wines. Take an excursion to the Bordeaux Vineyards – you won't regret it.
- **Kids:** Croiseur Colbert – Take a tour of this anti-aircraft warship which was first launched in 1959 and has been berthed in Port de la Lune since 1993.

The French crown appointed **Intendants** to rebuild and govern Bordeaux as a well-planned city to replace the tangle of medieval streets. In the course of the 18C they succeeded in transforming Bordeaux, giving it the Classical face it wears today, with grandiose set-pieces of urban design: the quaysides, the Place de la Bourse, the great avenues, the Town Hall (Hôtel de Ville), and the Grand Théâtre.

During the French Revolution the Bordeaux *députés* formed the group known as the **Girondins**. Accused of conspiring against the Revolution, twenty-two of them were tried in May 1793 and executed.

In the 18C, goods from the Caribbean added to the huge volume of trade, further stimulating the development of this great port lying 98km/61mi inland.

Guided Tours

Guided tours run Jul–Aug daily at 10am and 3pm; rest of the year, at 10am only. ⬤6.70€. Enquire at the tourist office.

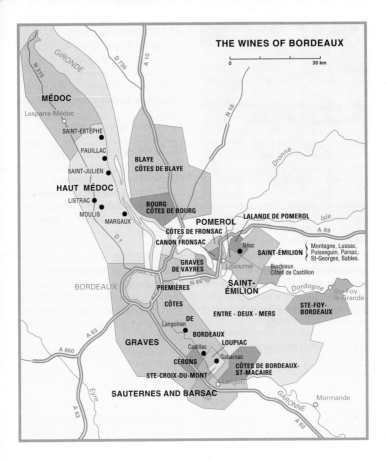

THE WINES OF BORDEAUX

0   30 km

GIRONDE

MÉDOC

Lesparre-Médoc

SAINT-ESTÈPHE

PAUILLAC

SAINT-JULIEN

HAUT MÉDOC

LISTRAC

MOULIS

MARGAUX

BLAYE
CÔTES DE BLAYE

BOURG
CÔTES DE BOURG

POMEROL

LALANDE DE POMEROL

CÔTES DE FRONSAC

CANON FRONSAC

Néac

Libourne

SAINT-ÉMILION

Montagne, Lussac,
Puisseguin, Parsac,
St-Georges, Sables.

Bordeaux
Côtes de Castillon

GRAVES
DE VAYRES

SAINT-
ÉMILION

BORDEAUX

PREMIÈRES

CÔTES

DE

Langoiran

BORDEAUX

Cadillac

GRAVES

CÉRONS

STE-CROIX-DU-MONT

Gabarnac

LOUPIAC

CÔTES DE BORDEAUX-
ST-MACAIRE

Langon

SAUTERNES AND BARSAC

ENTRE - DEUX - MERS

STE-FOY-
BORDEAUX

Ste-Foy
la-Grande

Dordogne

GARONNE

Marmande

Dronne

Isle

SIGHTS
VIEUX BORDEAUX

The old town has been undergoing extensive restoration in an effort to return the ancient ochre stonework of its 18C buildings to its original splendour. The restored buildings include those along the **quayside** following the bend of the Garonne for over half a mile (1km).

Grand-Théâtre★★

pl. de la Comédie. 🔊Guided tours *(1hr) according to the rehearsal schedule, visitors must book.* ∞5€. *Tourist office.* ✆05 56 00 85 95. *www.opera-bordeaux.com.*
This theatre, one of the finest in France, has recently been restored. Its architect was Victor Louis (1731–1802), a proponent of the Louis XVI style; here

he succeeded in creating a combined theatre and concert hall which recalls Antiquity not only in its sheer scale but also in its restrained use of decoration. A colonnade, one of his favourite devices, runs around the building; in front of the main façade, surmounted by 12 huge statues of muses and goddesses.
The interior too is a triumph, not only because of the great staircase, but also in the auditorium with its pillars, ramps and cantilevered boxes.
The design of the balconies, including the type of wood chosen, was carried out with the acoustic quality of this magnificent space in mind.

Place du Parlement★

A good example of the urban planning carried out in the reign of Louis XV, the square has a number of houses with

Fontaine des Girondins

A. Thuillier/MICHELIN

Musée des Beaux-Arts★★ *(Jardin de la Mairie, 20 cours d'Albret)*.

Cathédrale St-André★

Basilique St-Michel★ *(pl. Meynard)*

Place de la Bourse★ *(pl. de la Bourse, Mériadeck)*

Église Ste-Croix – façade★ *(1 pl. Jacques Ellul)*

Musée d'Aquitaine★★ *(20 cours Pasteur)*

Musée d'Art contemporain★ *(7 r. Ferrère)* – **Entrepôt Lainé**★★

Croiseur Colbert★ – a post-Second World War cruiser. *(quai des Chartrons)*

EXCURSIONS

The Bordeaux Vineyards★

The Bordeaux wine region which extends over approximately 135 000 ha/333 585 acres in the Gironde *département* is the largest producer of quality wines in the world.

The areas to the north produce red wines: Médoc on the west bank of the Gironde with Bourg on the east bank, and St-Émilion and Pomerol north of the Dordogne. The remaining area produces white wines: Entre-Deux-Mers between the Dordogne and the Garonne, and Graves and Sauternes to the south.

Haut Médoc

It boasts the most prestigious "châteaux" with a wine-making tradition dating back to the reign of Louis XIV. Some of the châteaux and the famous cellars are open to visitors, in particular Château Margaux, **Château Mouton-Rothschild**★ and Château Lafite.

St-Émilion★★

The region is famous for its full-bodied and fragrant red wines produced under the strict control of the Jurade, a guild founded in the Middle Ages which was reconvened in 1948. *See ST-ÉMILION.*

Sauternes

The vineyards on the slopes of the lower valley of the Ciron produce renowned sweet white wines, in particular Château Yquem.

groundfloor arcades, transom windows and decorative masks. The harmony and unity of the square is emphasised by the balcony running the whole length of the façades.

Quartier des Chartrons★

This old neighbourhood, behind the quayside devoted to the wine trade and ships' chandlers, became fashionable in the 18C when the city's great families built their town houses here. Some of the streets (Rue Notre-Dame, Cours de la Martinique, Cours Xavier Arnozan) have many fine dwellings with classical façades, attics, wrought-iron balconies (balconsa) and transom windows with entablatures.

Esplanade des Quinconces

The sheer size (about 126 000sq m/ 150 700sq yd) of this esplanade is impressive. It was laid out on the site of the old Château de la Trompette during the Restoration (early 19C).

Monument aux Girondins

pl. des Quincones.

It consists of a column (50m/164ft high) topped by Liberty casting off her chains and two bronze **fountains**★ (**fontaines**★) symbolising the Triumph of the Republic (facing the Grand Théâtre) and the Triumph of Concord.

ADDRESSES

STAY

Hôtel Acanthe – *12 r. St-Rémi.* *05 56 81 66 58. www.acanthe-hotel-bordeaux.com. 20 rooms. 5.50€.*
A central location and very reasonable prices are strong points of this recently renovated hotel. The bright rooms are big enough and well sound-proofed, and the reception is agreeable.

Hôtel Notre-Dame – *36 r. Notre-Dame.* *05 56 52 88 24. www.hotelnotre dame.com. 21 rooms. 6€.*
An unpretentious little family hotel in an 18C house just behind the Quai des Chatrons. Rooms small but well-kept; reasonable prices.

Hôtel Opéra – *35 r. de l'Esprit-des-Lois.* *05 56 81 41 27. 27 rooms. 6€.*
Near the Grand Théâtre et the Allées de Tourny, here's a modest little family hotel. The reception is courteous and the rooms are functional. Those on the street are well sound-proofed. Good value for the euro.

Hôtel Continental – *10 r. Montesquieu.* *05 56 52 66 00. www. hotel-le-continental.com. 50 rooms. 7€.* In the old city, here's a venerable 18C mansion with a fine staircase in the hall. Breakfast room under a glass roof. Modern rooms with waxed wood furnishings.

Hôtel Presse – *6 r. de la Porte-Dijeaux.* *05 56 48 53 88. www.hotel delapresse.com. 27 rooms. 8€.* In the pedestrian shopping quarter of the old city, this is a nice little hotel despite the rather difficult access by automobile. Superb stairway with crimson carpets. Modern, functional, yet cosy rooms.

EAT

Bar Cave de la Monnaie – *34 r. Porte-la-Monnaie.* *05 56 31 12 33. www.latupinalatupina.com. Closed Sun.* This very young wine bar decorated with photos of old Bordeaux bistros has an original flair. Customers choose their dishes first (omelettes or salads), then they help themselves to a glass of Bordeaux from one of four taps in the wall. Affordable prices.

Chez Mémère – *11 r. de la Devise.* *05 56 81 88 20.* Under the vaulted ceiling of this 16C workshop, discover the flavour and ambience of a fine meal chez mémère (at granny's): garbure landaise (soup), agneau de Pauillac, encornets frais aux piments d'Espelette... and, at the end of the week, la sanguette, a sort of black pudding made of poultry blood.

Lou Magret – *62 r. St-Rémi.* *05 56 44 77 94. Closed 7-21 Jul, Sun and public holidays.* If overwhelmed by the choice of restaurants in this street, try this pleasant establishment whose speciality is canard de Chalosse, duck served grilled or with a delicious sauce. No-frills décor and outdoor terrace.

La Table du Pain – *6 pl. du Parlement.* *05 56 81 01 00.* A wide selection of sandwiches, toasts and salads is offered at this restaurant with stone walls, old shelves and waxed pine furnishings.

Le Bistro du Musée – *37 pl. Pey-Berland.* *05 56 52 99 69. Closed 2 weeks Christmas, 3 weeks in Aug and Sun.* This bistro with a pretty green wood entrance makes a promising impression from the start. Thoughtful décor with exposed stone walls, oak parquet, moleskin seats and wine paraphernalia. Southwest cuisine and a fine Bordeaux wine menu.

SHOWTIME

L'Onyx – *11 r. Fernand-Philippart, Quartier St-Pierre.* *05 56 44 26 12. www. theatreonyx.net. Closed Jul–Sept. 12.50€.* The city's oldest café-theatre, L'Onyx is an essential stop for local culture.

La Boîte à Jouer – *50 r. Lombard.* *05 56 50 37 37. Performances 8.30pm. Closed Jul–Sept.* This theatre has two small rooms (60 and 45 seats) where lesser regional, national or international troupes specialised in contemporary or musical theatre perform.

Opéra de Bordeaux-Grand-Théâtre – *pl. de la Comédie.* *05 56 00 85 95. www.opera-bordeaux.com.* The Grand Théâtre de Bordeaux is one of the most handsome of France. Symphonies, operas and ballets are performed here under excellent acoustic conditions.

Théâtre Fémina – *20 r. de Grassi.* *℘05 56 79 06 69.* With 1100 seats, this handsome edifice sets the stage for plays, comedies, operettas, dance and concerts.

🛒 SHOPPING

Librairie Mollat – *15 r. Vital-Carles.* *℘05 56 56 40 40. www.mollat.com.* France's first independent bookstore is still a veritable regional institution.

Baillardran Canelés – *Galerie des Grands-Hommes.* *℘05 56 79 05 89.* Located in the Grands-Hommes market, this boutique makes delicious *canelés*, the small brown Bordelais cakes, irresistibly delicate and caramelised, that take on the shape of the ribbed (canelé) cake tins they're baked in. Crisp outside, they're soft and spongy inside.

Confiserie Cadio-Badie – *26 allées de Tourny.* *℘05 56 44 24 22. www. cadiotbadie.com. Closed 2 weeks in Aug, Sun and, public holidays except Christmas and Easter.* You can't help but be charmed by the old-fashioned style of this appealing old-fashioned boutique founded in 1826. Their truffes and Armagnac-flavoured *bouchons bordelais* are worth a special trip.

Chocolaterie Saunion *56 cours Georges-Clemenceau.* *℘05 56 48 05 75. Closed 15–22 Aug, Sun and Mon morning, public holidays except Christmas, New Year and Easter.* One of the most illustrious chocolate confectioners of Bordeaux – a must.

Conseil Interprofessionnel des Vins de Bordeaux – *1 cours du XXX Juillet.* *℘05 56 00 22 66. www.vins-bordeaux.fr. Closed weekends and public holidays.* This is where you'll find ample information about Bordeaux wines and vineyards – workshops, tastings. Several different wine cellars are to be found around this centre, including La Vinothèque Bordeaux (8 cours du XXX Juillet), L'intendant (2 allées de Tourny) and Bordeaux Magnum (3 r. Gobineau).

Darricau – *7 pl. Gambetta.* *℘05 56 44 21 49. www.darricau.com. Closed 1–15 Aug and public holidays.* Since the turn of the 20C, this chocolatier pampers the city with the irresistible *pavé Gambetta* (praline with raisins soaked in wine), Bordeaux bottle-shaped chocolates (*confits de sauterne* or *de médoc*), la *cadichonne* (crunchy vanilla) and *niniches* (soft caramel with dark chocolate).

Château de La Brède★

In the peaceful countryside of the Graves area along the Garonne River, this **château**, protected by its moat, still keeps its aristocratic 15C appearance. It was the birthplace of **Charles Montesquieu (1689–1755), Baron de la Brède – a magistrate of Bordeaux.**

A BIT OF HISTORY

Montesquieu, a country gentleman, wrote extensively (*Persian Letters* – 1724) and travelled widely, notably to England, where he spent two decisive years (1729–31), returning with that arguably somewhat idealised notion of English constitutionalism prevalent among French political thinkers of the 18C.

  Michelin Map: 335 H 6
Info: Avenue du Château, 33650 La Brède. *℘05 56 20 20 49. www.chateau labrede.com.*
Location: The castle lies S of Bordeaux, along the A 62, exit 1.1.

Twenty years of hard writing led to the publication in 1748 of his *L'Esprit des Lois* (The Nature of Laws), in which he expanded the theory of the separation of legislative, executive and judicial powers, sole guarantee of the citizen's liberty. Its 31 volumes are hardly read today but with them, political writings entered the mainstream of French literary history.

VISIT

av. du Château, 33650 La Brède.
⚒🔊Guided tours (30min) end Feb–18
Dec 9am–noon (group tours), 2–5.30pm
(hours may extend according to
season). ✆7€.

In the château, the bedroom **(chambre)**
with its original furnishings and library
(bibliothèque) comprising some 7 000
volumes help to evoke the life and work
of this sympathetic figure.

Cognac★

For many years Cognac was a river
port on the calm waters of the
Charente, exporting salt and, from
the 11C, wine. In 1570, it was one of
the four strongholds conceded to
the Protestants under the Treaty of
St-Germain. Place Francois I, a busy
square with an ornamental fountain,
links the old part of Cognac, on the
slope above the River Charente, with
the sprawling modern town.

A BIT OF HISTORY

Of all the different kinds of spirits, it is
cognac which has acquired a universal
reputation. Early in the 17C local vintners started to distil wines that travelled
badly, in order to help turnover, reduce
excise dues and facilitate storage. The
taste for the product spread to Holland,
Scandinavia and Britain, whose long
association with brandy is reflected in
some of the great names of Cognac,
Hine, Martell, Hennessy.
A century later it was realised that ageing
improved the quality of the spirit.

▸ **Population:** 19 409
♿ **Michelin Map:** 324 I 5
🚹 **Info:** 16 r. du 14-juillet.
 ✆05 45 82 10 71. www.
 tourism-cognac.com.
▶ **Location:** Cognac is 43km/
 26.7mi W of Angoulême.
😊 **Don't Miss:** A visit to one
 of the distilleries.

Cognac was divided into regions in 1887;
today they comprise Grande Champagne, Petite Champagne, Borderies, Fins
Bois, Bons Bois and Bois Ordinaires,
reflecting, in that order, a decreasing
proportion of chalk in the soil, an increasing earthiness of taste – *goût de terroir*
– and ability to mature rapidly.
The making of cognac has given rise to
a very distinct way of life.
People here have a fine sense of irony
and a love of independence which has
expressed itself in revolts against salt-
tax, in peasant rebellions at the time of
Louis XIV and in the disturbances of the
Wars of Religion.

Fins Bois vineyards

M. Thierry/MICHELIN

Cognac Production

The production of cognac is the result of a two-stage distillation process, using the special still of the region. The 90 000ha/220 000 acres of vineyards yield a white wine which is light, flowery and quite acid; it takes nine litres of it to make one of brandy. It is then kept in barrels made of porous oak from the Limoges district for at least two and a half years, during which time the brandy absorbs tannin and resins from the wood, and oxygen from the atmosphere, to which it loses 2 1/2% of its volume per annum – the "angels' portion", equivalent to 2 million bottles a year!

Other cognac houses with cellars open to visitors include: Camus, Otard and Prince Hubert de Polignac

SIGHTS

Quartier Ancien

In the streets of the old part of the town on the west bank are a number of fascinating buildings. The Grande-Rue has a fine half-timbered example dating from the 15C, the Rue Saulnier a number of 16C houses with rusticated stonework and elaborate doorways and windows, while in the Rue de l'Îsle d'Or is the Hôtel de l'Échevinage (House of the Magistrates), distinguished by its corner niches.

The château was rebuilt by John the Good in 1450; its riverside façade has an austere air, enlivened somewhat by the King's Balcony of 1515, a grand loggia resting on a bracket carved in the shape of a salamander, the emblem of François I who was born here in 1494.

Les Chais

Guided tours (45min–1hr30min). The cellars and storerooms **(chais)** spread out along the riverside quays, near the port and in the suburbs, house the casks in which the slow alchemy between spirit and oak occurs, bestowing its distinctive subtlety to the brandy of Cognac.

Hennessy

1 quai Hennessy. Guided tours (1hr15min) Jun–Sept daily 10am–6pm; Mar–May and Oct–Dec daily 10am–5pm; Closed 1 May. 6€. 05 45 35 72 68. www.hennessy.com.

The business was founded in 1765 by a captain of Irish origin serving in Louis XV's Irish Brigade. His descendants still head the company today. A Cooperage Museum **(Musée de la Tonnellerie)** is devoted to the manufacture of brandy casks.

Rémy Martin

Domaine de Merpins, rte de Pons. Guided tours by train (1hr30min) Jul–Aug daily 10am–5.30pm; Apr–Jun and Sept–Oct daily 10am–11am, 1.30–4.30pm. Closed 1 May. Reservations recommended. 5€. 05 45 35 76 66. www.remy.com.

The distillery, founded in 1724, creates its cognac exclusively from the prestigious Grande Champagne and Petite Champagne vintages.

Martell

pl. Edouard-Martell. Guided tours (1hr) Apr–Oct Mon–Fri 9.30am–5pm, Sat–Sun and public holidays 11am–5pm. 4€. 05 45 36 33 33. www.martell.com.

Founded in 1715 it is the oldest of the famous cognac distilleries. Three rooms of the founder's residence have been restored and convey the working environment of an entrepreneur in the early 18C.

ADDITIONAL SIGHT

Musée d'Art et d'Histoire de Cognac (48 bd Denfert-Rochereau).

Futuroscope★★

This vast science-orientated leisure park offers a range of exciting shows, games and entertainments based on the theme of the screen image. There are restaurants, shops, "experiences" such as "fly me to the moon" and "the future is wild".

⚇ VISIT

🕐 *Open daily 7 Feb–15 Nov and 19 Dec–early Jan 10am–8pm; weekends 21 Nov–18 Dec 22–29 Nov, 5–8 and 12–31 Dec 10am–8pm; Evening Show 7.30pm (subject to change).* 🎫 *35€ (child 25€).* Numerous attractions, include **Lac enchanté** and its **Théâtre Alphanumérique** which present productions incorporating the technology of the future. **Kinémax, Omnimax, Solido, Showscan** and **Imax 3D** show films using 3D films, hemispherical cinema,

- 🕐 **Michelin Map:** 322 I 4
- 🛈 **Info:** Futuroscope Destination, BP 3030, 86130 Jaunay-Clan. ☎05 49 49 11 12. www.futuroscope. com/eng.
- ▶ **Location:** The Park is on the northern outskirts of Poitiers.
- 🕐 **Timing:** Plenty to keep the family busy for a couple of days.
- ⚇ **Kids:** Much of the park is geared especially to youngsters. Look out for the magic shows.

etc.). **Images-Studio★★★**, a vast glass structure, shows what goes on behind the scenes.

Marais Poitevin★

The vast Poitou marshlands occupy what was once a wide bay, the Golfe du Poitou. It is now a conservation area extending over three *départements*. Under clear, luminous skies, its meadows are bordered by slender poplar and willow. The boats of the marshlanders glide on a network of waterways.

GEOGRAPHY

The marsh rests on a bed of hardened marine silts; it is drained by an extensive network of channels and protected from floods and high water by dikes and sluices. The bay is in the process of silting up and evolving into a marsh. The work of reclamation, involving the digging of drainage channels, the building of sluices and the parcelling out of the new-won lands, was begun by the monks from the abbeys as early as the 11C, and continued, once the Wars of Religion were over, by Henri IV.

- 🕐 **Michelin Map:** 316 H-I 8-9 and 324 D-G 2
- ▶ **Location:** The region lies N and NE of La Rochelle. It is divided into the Dry Marsh, where the Atlantic winds blow keenly, and the Wet Marsh, further inland.
- ☺ **Don't Miss:** Enjoy a boat trip on the waterchannels, or a walk in the Parc Ornithologique at Le Petit Buisson.

VISIT

The marsh is linked to the ocean by a bay **(anse d'Aiguillon)**. It is protected from the waves by a headland **(Pointe d'Arçay)** and its sandbanks, and by the Aiguillon dike built by a team of Dutch engineers.

The bay makes a grand sight at high water, but only when the tide is out does the waterbody reveal its full interest.

Pau★★

Overlooking the Gave de Pau torrent, the town has guarded an important route to Spain since Roman times. Since 1450 it has been the capital of the Béarn country, in touch with both the lowlands and the high mountains of this ancient southwestern province of France.

▶ **Population:** 83 903
◐ **Michelin Map:** 342 J 3
▯ **Info:** Place Royale.
   ✆05 59 27 27 08.
   www.pau-pyrenees.com.
◐ **Location:** Pau lies just off the A64 between Biarritz and Toulouse.
▯ **Parking:** On arrival head for Place Clemenceau or Plade de Verdun in the city centre, and park the car.

A BIT OF HISTORY
The Béarn and its people

The province has an attractively varied landscape of hills, vineyards, orchards and pasture. Houses are large, with steep slate roofs.

Gaston IV Fébus (1331–91), an authoritarian ruler who surrounded himself with men of letters; was the first to fortify Pau. **Jean II d'Albret** acquired the Foix country through his marriage to Catherine de Foix in 1484, but was obliged to abandon southern Navarre to the King of Spain. In 1527, his son Henri II married Marguerite d'Angoulême, the sister of François I: it was she who brought the art of the Renaissance to the castle and, fired with Reformation zeal, made the place one of the intellectual centres of Europe. Their daughter, **Jeanne d'Albret**, married Antoine de Bourbon, a descendant of Louis IX; this enabled her own son Henry of Navarre (the future Henri IV) to garner the inheritance of the House of Valois on the extinction of the line, thereby "incorporating France into Gascony by way of the Béarn" (Henri IV).

SIGHT
Boulevard des Pyrénées★★

From this splendid panoramic avenue running along a high ridge between the château and the park, there is a famous **view★★★** over the valley to the Pyrénéan foothills, and, in clear weather, far beyond, to the Pic du Midi de Bigorre and the Pic d'Anie.

ADDITIONAL SIGHTS

Château★★ *(2 r. du Châteaux)* – **tapestry collection★★★**
Musée des Beaux-Arts★ *(r. Mathieu Lalanne)*

Château de Pau

©Emmanuelle Bonzami/Bigstockphoto.com

Poitiers★★

Key events in France's history have occurred in and around this city and the medieval districts in its heart have much of interest to sightseers.

A BIT OF HISTORY

Poitiers was established in Gallo-Roman times on the promontory overlooking a bend in the River Clain, a site which commanded the "Gate of Poitou", the almost imperceptible rise in the land some 30km/18.6mi south, that divides the Paris Basin from Aquitaine. It was here in 732 that Charles Martel (688–741) won a great victory against invading Arab forces at **Moussais-la-Bataille** on the banks of the Clain, thereby saving Europe from Islamic rule.

Poitiers was under English domination twice: in the 12C and the 14C. On 19 September 1356, a famous episode in Hundred Years' War took place at

- ▶ **Population:** 88 776
- ◔ **Michelin Map:** 322 H-I 5
- ▯ **Info:** 45 pl. Charles-de-Gaulle. ℰ05 49 41 21 24. www.ot-poitiers.fr.
- ◐ **Location:** The city is 102km/64mi S of Tours. The old town centre sits on a promontory almost surrounded by the rivers Boivre and Clain.
- ▲▲ **Kids:** Just 12km/7.4mi from Poitiers, the science-themed leisure park Futuroscope is popular with children (ℰ see FUTUROSCOPE).

Nouaillé-Maupertuis on the steep banks of the River Miosson. Jean II le Bon (the Good) was fighting with the French forces, who were defeated.

The French king surrendered and was taken to London, where he remained in comfortable exile. The result was the signing four years later of the Treaty of Brétigny under which the French agreed to give Poitiers to the English. In 1372 Bertrand du Guesclin retook the town, presenting it to the king's representative, Duke Jean de Berry, brother of Charles V.

In 1418, the fleeing Charles VII set up his court and parliament here and four years later he was proclaimed king. In March 1429, in the Gothic Great Hall **(Grande Salle★)** of Poitiers' recently rebuilt Law Courts **(Palais de Justice)**, Joan of Arc was subjected to a humiliating investigation by an ecclesiastical commission.

In the 16C the city played host to Rabelais, then Calvin and the writers of the Pléiade. In 1569, the place was besieged for seven weeks by a Protestant army under Coligny. In the 18C, under the rule of the centrally appointed governors known as Intendants, Poitiers became a tranquil provincial capital.

SIGHTS
Baptistère St-Jean★
r. Jean Jaurés. Open varying hours, call ahead. 05 49 41 21 24.
This is one of France's most venerable Christian buildings. It goes back to the 4C, when St Hilary was elected Bishop of Poitiers, 27 years after the Edict of Constantine. Hilary played a leading role in the conversion of Gaul.

The narthex and baptistery proper have the characteristic architecture of 4C Gaul. The narthex was restored in the 10C and is polygonal in form; there are panels of Roman brickwork under its windows, and beneath the gables are strange pilasters with capitals carved in low relief.

Inside are marble columns and arcades with richly decorated capitals. Right up until the 17C, the octagonal pool was the city's sole place of baptism, originally by total immersion.

Église St-Hilaire-le-Grand★★
r. du Doyenne.
This great Romanesque edifice was built in 1049; it was an important staging-post on the pilgrimage route to Santiago de Compostela and in architectural terms is Poitiers' most interesting church.

In 1100, it was given stone vaults to replace the original wooden roof which had been destroyed by fire.

The distance it was possible to span in stone was naturally shorter than in timber, and the designer thus had to reduce the width of the nave and increase the number of aisles; he set up a double row of columns linked ingeniously with the original walls and carrying a series of domes.

The final arrangement is the unusual one of a nave flanked by three aisles on either side.

Église Notre-Dame-la-Grande★★
pl. Charles-de-Gaulle.
The church is a good example of the local version of the Romanesque style as it had developed around 1140. Its harmonious appearance is due to the great height of its rib-vaulted aisles. It has a splendid 12C west **front★★★**, richly decorated with sculpture. Six round columns hold up the choir vault, which was painted in the 12C with a fresco depicting the Virgin in Majesty and Christ in Glory.

Palais de Justice
pl. Alphonse-Petit. Open Mon–Fri 8.45am–noon, 1.45–5.30pm. Closed public holidays. No charge. 05 49 50 22 00.
The **Grande Salle★** of Poitiers' recently rebuilt Law Courts was where Joan of Arc was questioned about her visions and her instructions from God. The vast hall, scene of solemn audiences, great trials and the sessions of the Provincial Estates, was built under the Plantagenets and restored by Jean de Berry. It has a great gable wall with

monumental chimneys, a balcony and Flamboyant windows.

ADDITIONAL SIGHTS
Cathédrale St-Pierre★
(Poitou-Charente)

ADDRESSES

🏠 STAY

🛏🍽 **Chambre d'hôte Château de Vaumoret** – *r. du Breuil Mingot. 10km/6.2mi NE of Poitiers. Take the D3 towards La Roche-Posay, then the D 18 to Sèvres-Anxaumont.* 🕿 *05 49 61 32 11. 3 rooms.* Although only a short distance from Poitiers, this B&B is surrounded by peaceful countryside. Housed in a delightful 17C château in grounds of 15ha/37 acres, the guestrooms here are attractively furnished in traditional style. The perfect place to unwind.

🛏🍽 **Hôtel Gibautel** – *rte de Nouaillé.* 🕿 *05 49 46 16 16. 36 rooms.* This modern hotel situated opposite a clinic on the outskirts of Poitiers has small, modern and well-equipped rooms.

🛏🍽🍽 **Hôtel Château de Périgny** – *Périgny, 86190 Vouillé. 17km/12mi NW of Poitiers via the N 149 and a secondary road.* 🕿 *05 49 51 80 43. 39 rooms.* Right in the middle of a park, this 15C château is a haven of peace and tranquillity. The rooms are furnished in period or modern style; those in the annexe are a little more basic. Attractive patio-terrace. Contemporary cuisine.

🍴 EAT
ST-BENOÎT
🍽🍽 **Le Chalet de Venise** – *6 r. du square (le bourg).* 🕿 *05 49 88 45 07.* This charming restaurant is situated just outside Poitiers in the village of St-Benoît. The outdoor terrace overlooking a peaceful garden with a stream is the perfect spot for a meal in summer, while the comfortable dining room has a cosy ambience in winter.

Musée Ste-Croix★★ *(3 bis, r. Jean-Jaurés)* – archaeology, ethnology, fine arts.
Église Ste-Radegonde★
(1 r. Sainte-Croix)

🍽🍽 **L'Orée des Bois** – *13, r. Naintré.* 🕿 *05 49 57 11 44. http://oreedesbois. objectis.net. Closed Sun (Nov–Apr) and Mon.* This building covered in Virginia creeper is a restful place for a meal away from the bustle of the city centre. There are two country-style dining rooms, one with a fireplace. Traditional local fare.

POITIERS
🍽🍽 **Les Bons Enfants** – *11 bis r. Cloche-Perse.* 🕿 *05 49 41 49 82. Closed 20–29 Feb, Sun eve and Mon.* Amidst the many schools of this neighbourhood, this little restaurant with a green façade boasts a large painting of a group of late 19C schoolchildren. The restaurant specialises in regional cuisine. Friendly ambience.

🍽🍽 **Maxime** – *4 r. St-Nicholas.* 🕿 *05 49 41 09 55. Closed 13 Jul–18 Aug, Sat (except eve Nov–Feb) and Sun.* Situated near the Musée de Chièvres in a quiet street in the city centre, this restaurant serves traditional French cuisine. Attractive mix of red and yellow hues in the contemporary-style dining room.

🍽🍽🍽 **Poitevin** – *76 r. Carnot.* 🕿 *05 49 88 35 04. Closed first half Apr, early–late Jul, 22 Dec–5 Jan and Sun eve.* The accent is on traditional regional cuisine in this busy restaurant which is popular with locals. Sample specialities such as *mouclade charentaise* or *farci poitevin* in one of four comfortable contemporary-style dining rooms.

MARKET
The main food market takes place *(Mon–Sat)* in the market hall near Église Notre-Dame-la-Grande. There is an excellent choice of fruit and vegetables, fish, meat, cheese and bread.

Le **Puy du Fou★★★**

This impressive theme park, based around a real château and its grounds, takes visitors on an adventure through 2 000 years of Vendean history. On summer evenings its château sparkles under the lights of a famous *Son et Lumière*; by day the museum, Écomusée de la Vendée★★, evokes the past of the Vendée region, while various attractions along a trail (Grand Parcours★★) lure visitors into the 12ha/29.6 acres of grounds. Puy du Fou is Latin for "beech hill".

- 🕭 **Michelin Map:** 316 K 6
- 🛈 **Info:** 30 r. Georges Clemenceau, BP 25, 85 590 Les Epesses. ✆0820 09 10 10. www.puydufou.com.
- ▷ **Location:** Puy du Fou is at Les Epesses, SW of Cholet.
- 🕐 **Timing:** There is a hotel and restaurant on the site, ideal for an unhurried visit including the evening show.

VISIT
👥 **Grand Parc★★**
🕐*Opening times vary, call ahead.* ✆*02 51 64 11 11.* ☞*Admission fees vary during the year.*
Numerous paths surround the château, skirting lakes or passing through dense chestnut woods, with many attractions.

Château
It is likely that the original castle, built in the 15C and 16C, was never completed; it was in any case partly destroyed during the Wars of the Vendée. There remains a fine late Renaissance pavilion at the end of the courtyard, preceded by a peristyle with engaged Ionic columns. This now serves as an entrance. The left wing of the château is built over a long gallery.

Cinéscénie★★★
🕐*Show lasts 1hr 45min. Fri and Sat 10pm, but check ahead. Reservations necessary.* ✆*02 51 64 11 11.*
The terrace below the rear façade of the château, together with the ornamental lake below it, makes an agreeable background for the spectacular *"Cinéscénie"* in which "Jacques Maupillier, peasant of the Vendée" directs a company of 700 actors and 50 horsemen in a dazzling show. The history of the Vendée is re-lived with the help of an impressive array of special effects, fountains, fireworks, laser and other lighting displays.

Cinéscénie

©Puy du fou

Rochefort★★

Rochefort takes pride in an illustrious maritime past. There is still something exotic in the air around the arsenal, where great expeditions were masterminded.

A BIT OF HISTORY

In 1665, Colbert chose a site 22km/13.7mi up the River Charente and commissioned Vauban to extend the defences of the fort already built there. Though the place had few natural advantages as a port, the presence of easily fortifiable islands and promontories facilitated the task.

Seven years later, the work, which included a harbour for the navy, was complete, and by 1690 Rochefort rivalled the naval bases of Toulon and Brest. The increasing draught of modern vessels led to the harbour's obsolescence and it closed in 1926.

VISIT

Rochefort's history has left many richly ornamented houses; the former rope-walk (**corderie★★**), 374m/1 200ft long; the great timber hall built by naval carpenters (now a covered market and conference centre), and the Sun Gateway (Porte du Soleil) which formed the entrance to Colbert's **Arsenal**. Admirers of the writer Pierre Loti (1850–1923), a native of Rochefort and lover of the exotic, should pause at the **Maison de Pierre Loti★**

▶ **Population:** 26 299
⚓ **Michelin Map:** 324 E 4
Info: Avenue Sadi-Carnot.
℘05 46 99 08 60.
www.paysrochefortais-tourisme.com.
▶ **Location:** Rochefort is 38km/23.6mi SE of La Rochelle.
Don't Miss: The Arsenal district.

(🗪guided tours (45min); 7.65€), now a museum evocative of his travels.

ADDITIONAL SIGHTS

Musée de l'Ancienne Ecole de Médecine Navale★ (25 r. de l'Admiral Meyer)

Musée d'Art et d'Histoire★ (63 av. Charles de Gaulle)

Corderie Royale
©alexandre neumann/Bigstockphoto.com

Pierre Loti (1850–1923)

The author Pierre Loti, (real name Julien Viaud), was born in Rochefort at no 141 of the street that now bears his nom-de-plume. Loti, a much-travelled naval officer, accomplished sportsman and something of a dandy with a distinguished bearing, was also a novelist of great sensitivity and an exceptional story-teller. Inspired by his voyages to exotic destinations, he wrote *Pêcheur d'Islande* (Iceland Fisherman), *Aziyadé*, *Ramuntcho* and *Madame Chrysanthème*, books that were instrumental in his acceptance as a member of the élite Académie Française young at the age of 41.

Maison de Pierre Loti, Rochefort

Château de La **Rochefoucauld**★★

This elegant Renaissance château, reminiscent of the Loire, stands outside a pucturesque village of the same name.

A BIT OF HISTORY

The property is the seat of a noble family which gave the name François to all its first-born sons and which produced many a very distinguished soldier, statesman, artist and churchman. **François VI** (1613–1680) established his reputation as the greatest of France's maxim-writers. In his younger days, he had been a brave soldier but a somewhat inept plotter; he had been imprisoned by Richelieu, fought on the wrong side in the Fronde and was almost blinded by a blast from a harquebus (the first gun fired from the shoulder).

With a perception of the world sharpened by an understandable pessimism, he produced the *Maxims* for which he is famous, for example: "Hypocrisy is the tribute vice pays to virtue", and "We are all brave enough to bear other people's misfortunes."

VISIT

The first fortification here was a wooden structure built by Foucauld, the youngest

- 🕯 **Michelin Map:** 324 M 5
- 🛈 **Info:** 1 r. des Tanneurs.
  ✆05 45 63 07 42.
  www.chateau-la-rochefoucauld.com.
- ▶ **Location:** The château and village are in the Charente, NE of Angoulême.

brother of the Viscount of Limoges, in 980 and named Foucauld's Rock.

During the following century a stone keep with a surrounding wall was constructed and the medieval works were completed by five towers, later raised in height to demonstrate the power of the Rochefoucauld family.

In 1520 François II de la Rochefoucauld and his wife Anne de Polignac transformed the severe fortress into a sophisticated Renaissance residence, albeit retaining the medieval towers, with a chapel, a terrace and 16C façades. They also added galeries and a staircase based on a design by Leonardo da Vinci which had been given to Anne by King François I.

Château de La Rochefoucauld

©Tom Dautlich/iStockphoto.com

La Rochelle★★★

The port of La Rochelle is a lively place, much frequented by artists and tourists. It owes its origin to the fort built in the 11C during the centuries of English rule.

A BIT OF HISTORY

La Rochelle was one of the first places in France where the Reformation took hold. After the St Bartholomew's Day Massacre (1572), La Rochelle became one of the main centres of Protestant resistance.

The religious freedoms secured by the Edict of Nantes in 1598 brought several years of peace. By 1627, however, the town's continued adherence to Protestantism had become intolerable to Richelieu, not least because of its English connection. Richelieu personally directed a siege of La Rochelle that took 15 months to starve the town into submission. 23 000 citizens perished. The 5 000 who survived were spared, though a number of their leaders, including the mayor, Jean Guiton, were banished for a period of several months.

La Rochelle contributed more than its share to the opening up of the world beyond Europe; in the 15C, it was from here that the first colonists embarked for Canada and Jean de Béthencourt sailed to discover the Canary Islands; in the 16C, the La Rochelle fishing fleet operated in the rich fishing grounds off Newfoundland.

Other explorers to set out from here were René-Robert Cavelier, Sieur de La Salle, who sailed down the Mississippi to the Gulf of Mexico in 1681–2, and René Caillié, the first European to get back from Timbuktu alive.

La Rochelle's shipowners profited from international trade, and above all with the West Indies, where they owned vast plantations; they drew wealth, too, from the triangular trade involving the selling cloth to Africa, transporting African slaves to the Americas, and bringing American products to Europe.

▶ **Population:** 177 196
Michelin Map: 324 D 3
Info: 2 Quai Georges Simenon, Le Gabut.
℘05 46 41 14 68. www.holidays-la-rochelle.co.uk.
Location: On the west coast of France, easily reached from Bordeaux, Poitiers and Nantes. The town centre lies around the Vieux Port.
Timing: Francofolies is La Rochelle's huge popular music festival celebrating French music and culture for about a week around 14 July.
Kids: Aquarium (quai Louis Prunier; www.aquarium-larochelle.com); Musée des Automates (℘see Additional Sights).

VISIT

Vieux Port★★

The old port was originally laid out by Eleanor of Aquitaine; its entrance is guarded by two towers, probably built by the English in the 14C and once forming part of the town's ring of fortifications. **La Tour St Nicolas★** (℘open daily; ℘closed 1 Jan, 1 May, and 25 Dec; ℘4.60€, or 10€ ticket combined with the Tour de la Chaine and Tour de la Lanterne; ℘05 46 34 11 81) to the east has rested on its foundation of oak piles for six centuries; 42m/137.8ft high and with immensely thick walls, it is a fortress in its own right.

Vieux Ville ★★

The 18C **Porte de la Grosse-Horloge★** leads into the Old Town.

As well as timber-framed medieval houses and fine Renaissance residences, there are substantial 18C stone townhouses adorned with astonishing gargoyles. The splendid **Hôtel de Ville★**, built in Tuscan style, has a courtyard **façade★** of 1606, with an arcaded gallery.

ADDITIONAL SIGHTS

Museum d'Histoire Naturelle★★
(28 r. Albert 1er)
Musée du Nouveau-Monde★
Musée des Beaux-Arts *(10 r. Fleuriau)*
Musée d'Orbigny-Bernon★ *(2 r. Saint-Côme)* – local history, ceramics
Tour de la Lanterne★ *(esplanade St Jean d'Acre)*
🧍‍♂️🧍 **Musée des Automates**★
(r. La Désirée) – automatic figures in lifelike set-pieces

Parc Charruyer★
(av. Maurice Demas).

EXCURSION
Île de Ré★

The island, which is also known as White Island and has been linked to the mainland by a viaduct since 1988, is a popular resort. Part of the salt-marshes to the north has been set aside as a bird sanctuary.

ADDRESSES

🏨 STAY

🛏️🛏️🛏️🛏️ **Hôtel Les Brises** – *chemin digue Richelieu (av. P.-Vincent).* ☎️*05 46 43 89 37. www.hotellesbrises. com. 48 rooms.* 🍴*11€.* How delightful to open one's windows in the morning, contemplate the ocean and breathe the sea air. This 1960s hotel is well situated between earth and water. Lovely views.

🛏️🛏️🛏️🛏️ **Hôtel Champlain – France et Angleterre** – *30 r. Rambaud.* ☎️*05 46 41 23 99. www.hotelchamplain.com. 36 rooms.* 🍴*12€.* A spot of the country in the city. On a busy street near the historic district, this old 16C convent features a discreet, pleasant garden – a marvellous place to unwind after a busy day in town. In this genteel setting, the rooms, some quite spacious, are decorated with period pieces.

🛏️🛏️🛏️🛏️ **Hôtel de la Monnaie** – *3 r. de la Monnaie.* ☎️*05 46 50 65 65. 35 rooms. www.hotel-monnaie.com.* 🍴*13€.* Right behind the Tour de la Lanterne, this splendid 17C mansion, where coins used to be made, is an agreeable address. You'll appreciate the serenity of the rooms between courtyard and garden, as well as their modern furnishings and spaciousness.

🍴 EAT

🍴🍴 **André** – *pl. de la Chaîne.* ☎️*05 46 41 28 24.* A visit to La Rochelle is not complete without a meal at André! On the old docks, facing the Tour de la Chaîne, this enormous restaurant comprises a dozen bistro-style dining rooms where customers sit elbow to elbow to feast on seafood. Nautical ambience and marine paintings.

🍴🍴 **Le Boute-en-Train** – *7 r. des Bonnes-Femmes.* ☎️*05 46 41 73 74. Closed Sun, Mon.* Near the markets, this charming restaurant serves a variety of quiches and food fresh from the marketplace. Children's drawings adorn the walls of the bistro dining room… grab a crayon and add to their collection. Other customers may prefer to visit the vaulted cellar to choose their bottle of wine.

🍴 **À Côté de chez Fred** – *32–34 r. St-Nicolas. Closed Sun, Mon.* ☎️*05 46 41 65 76. Reservations recommended.* Here the fish couldn't be fresher! This little restaurant gets its provisions from its neighbour and sister… the fishmonger. Result: a slate menu that changes as the fishing boats come to moor and an authentic atmosphere just behind the docks.

🍴🍴 **Le Mistral** *10 pl. Coureauleurs, in the Le Gabut district.* ☎️*05 46 41 24 42. Closed Sun.* This wood-clad house is located a stone's throw from the tourist office. The maritime-style dining room is on the first floor; the terrace, on the same level, overlooks the old fishing port.

🍴🍴 **Le Petit Rochelais** – *25 r. St-Jean-du-Pérot. Closed Sun.* ☎️*05 46 41 28 43.* An inviting atmosphere complements the traditional French cuisine prepared with brio, cooked fresh each day and served with enjoyable wines.

🍷 BARS AND 🍸 CAFÉS

Café de la Paix – *54 r. Chaudrier.* ☏*05 46 41 39 79.* Behind its carved wood façade, this big café covered with mirrors and mouldings has a long history. A hospital in 1709, a theatre during the Revolution, since 1900 it has been a café popular with visiting artists such as Colette.

Cave de la Guignette – *8 r. St-Nicolas.* ☏*05 46 41 05 75.* This charming and colourful wine bar used to be the watering hole of the local fishermen (who have since changed towns).

Try the house speciality, *Guignette*, an aperitif made of wine and fruit.

🏃 LEISURE ACTIVITIES

Casino de la Rochelle – *allée du Mail.* ☏*05 46 34 12 75. www.lucienbarriere.com.* This Casino awaits with 160 slot machines, a poker room, a bar, a restaurant and a discotheque. From 9pm you can also try your hand at traditional blackjack or roulette. Coaching sessions are also on offer here, but don't get too carried away!

Château de **Roquetaillade**★★

This imposing medieval castle, built in 1306, is part of a compound made up of two forts dating from the 12C and the 14C within a single walled enclosure.

VISIT

🔎 Guided tours (1hr) Jul–Aug 10.30am–7pm; mid-Apr–Jun and Sept–Oct 2.30–6pm; Nov–mid-Apr Sun, public holidays and school holidays 2.30–5pm. Last admission 1hr before closing. ◷Closed 25 Dec. ≈6.50€. ☏05 56 76 14 16. www.chateau deroquetaillade.com.
Six enormous round towers, crenellated and pierced with arrow slits, frame a rectangular main structure. In the courtyard stands a powerful square keep and its

⏱ **Michelin Map:** 335 J 8
🅘 **Info:** 33210 Mazères.
☏05 56 76 14 16. http://chateauroquetaillade.free.fr.
▶ **Location:** The château is S of Langon on the River Garonne, on the edge of the Landes region.

turret. There are also vast vaulted rooms and monumental chimneys.
Inside, the decorative paintings and the furnishings are a good example of the restoration of medieval buildings by Viollet-le-Duc during the Second Empire.

Château de La Roquetaillade

©Photononstop/Tips Images

St-Émilion★★

St-Émilion offers both simple and sophisticated attractions to art lovers and gourmets alike.
The town is divided into two hill sites with the Royal Castle and Deanery (Doyenné) symbolising the age-old rivalry between the civil and religious authorities. Its sun-baked, pantile-roofed stone houses nestle in an **amphitheatre**★★ on the slope of a limestone plateau. Apart from its wines, the town is known for its strange underground church.

▸ **Population:** 2 124
◔ **Michelin Map:** 335 K 5
▮ **Info:** Le Doyenné, Place des Créneaux. ✆05 57 55 28 28. www.saint-emilion-tourisme.com.
◖ **Location:** The town is 10km/6.2mi E of Libourne. It has to be explored on foot, so wear comfortable shoes suitable for steep cobbled lanes. Place du Marché is the focal point.

VISIT
Église Monolithe★
r. du Clocher.
This extraordinary underground church was hollowed out of a single rock between the 8C and the 12C. It's an impressive size: the nave and two aisles are 38m/124.6ft long, 20m/65.6ft wide and 11m/36ft high.

Guided Tours

The Catacombes, St Émilion's Hermitage, Chapelle de la Trinité and the Église Monolithe can all be visited by guided tour (45min) from the tourist office (▨5.50€).

St-Jean-de-Luz★★

A popular beach resort and harbour town at the mouth of the river Nivelle, St-Jean-de-Luz is one of the principal centres of the French Basque country.

▸ **Population:** 13 579
◔ **Michelin Map:**342 C 2
▮ **Info:** Bd. Victor Hugo. ✆05 59 26 03 16. www.saint-jean-de-luz.com.
◖ **Location:** The town is on the Atlantic seafront just S of Biarritz, close to the Spanish border. The centre is on the right bank of the Nivelle.
◉ **Don't Miss:** Be sure to explore the port area. .

A BIT OF HISTORY
The main event to occur in the town was the marriage of Louis XIV of France to the infanta of Spain Maria-Theresa. The wedding was initially held up by the king's passion for Marie Mancini, but in the end was solemnised here, on 9 June 1660.
The king had been staying since 8 May in an imposing dwelling belonging to the ship-owner Lohobiague, which ever since has been known as the **Maison Louis-XIV**★ (*guided tours (30min) daily from 10.30am; ✆05 59 26 01 56).* The interior is particularly interesting, with a sturdy staircase built by ships'

carpenters, 18C furniture in the drawing room and fine panelling in the dining room. Maria-Theresa was lodged in an elegant brick and stone house now known as the **Maison de l'infante**, nearby. For a while in this brief period, St-Jean-de-Luz became in effect the capital of France. Court and government moved here, and days and nights were spent in feasting and revelry.

SIGHTS
The Port and Barre district

This is the original St-Jean-de-Luz. As early as the 11C, its sailors were hunting whale off Labrador. By the 15C, their quarry had changed to the abundant cod of the great fishing grounds off Newfoundland. When the Treaty of Utrecht forbade this activity, they turned to piracy, creating a fearsome reputation for their home port. Eventually they returned to more law-abiding ways, fishing for sardines off the coasts of Portugal and Morocco and for tuna off Senegal and Mauritania.

The part of the town known as **La Barre** was where the ship-owners lived; its growth was intimately linked to the fortunes of its fleet. The 16C and 17C brought good times, though the place was burned down by the Spaniards in 1558, then ravaged by high tides in 1749 and 1785. Among the fine old houses, the most venerable is the one which survived the 1558 fire, once the property of Carquiou Kailu.

Église St-Jean Baptiste★★
r. Gambetta.

Work on enlarging the church, began in 1649, had still not been completed when the royal wedding took place here in 1660. It is the finest church in the French Basque country, with a resplendent 17C gilded altarpiece **(retable★)** attributed to Martin de Bidache, a painted wooden ceiling and oak-built galleries on several levels. The main altar is raised above the sacristy, a feature of churches in the Basque provinces of Labourd (in France) and Guipuzcoa (in Spain).

EXCURSIONS
Corniche basque★★
14km/8.7mi S, then extending S to Hendaye.

The Socoa cliff **(Falaise de Socoa★)**, an unusual example of coastal relief, is best seen at low tide. Following the submersion of the former coastline by the waters released by the melting of the Quaternary glaciers, the beds of highly laminated schists were attacked by wave action; the strata dip sharply seaward, the

St-Jean-de-Luz

S. Sauvignier/MICHELIN

projecting sharp saw-tooth ridges of the more resistant rock from the wave-cut platform at the foot of the cliffs.

La Rhune ★★
14km/8.7mi SE, then as far as Sare.

Towards the end of the 6C, the Basques were probably pushed northwards by the Visigoths. Those of their number who settled in the plains of Aquitaine intermarried with local people, eventually becoming the Gascons. Those who remained in the mountains, however, kept their independence and their enigmatic language, thus guaranteeing their very distinct identity.

The mountain called La Rhune ("good grazing" in Basque) is one of the symbols of the Basque country; its **summit** *(accessible by rack-and-pinion railway)* rises to a height of 905m/2 969ft, offering a wonderful **panorama★★★** of the Bay of Biscay, the Landes and the ancient provinces of Labourd, Navarre and Guipuzcoa.

At the foot of the mountain lie the villages of **Ascain★** and **Sare★**, both with many characteristically Basque features. The houses are timber-framed; the white rendering of the walls makes a pleasant contrast to the reddish-brown colour usually applied to the timber, while the cemeteries adjoining the churches have the typical discoidal tombstones arranged in a circle.

If visitors are lucky, they may see the local people dancing the chaste but passionate fandango or taking part in pigeon-hunts.

St-Savin★★

St-Savin lies among the pasturelands of the eastern border of the old province of Poitou, an area of sandy clay soils known as Les Brandes. Its former abbey church still draws many visitors in spite of the depredations of the centuries. It is now difficult to imagine how the place must have looked in its days of glory before the Hundred Years' War, when the whole interior glowed with Romanesque wall-paintings, when none of the furnishings had been removed, and when the impact of insensitive restoration had not been felt.

VISIT
L'Abbatiale★★

1 pl. du Castel. ○*Open all day. Use discretion in visiting during religious services.* ━*Guided tours (1hr15min plus 30min for the film); call in advance.* ○*Closed Jan, 11 Nov, 25 and 31 Dec.* ⊜*6€.* ℘*05 62 97 02 23.*

The abbey church was mostly built in the space of 50 years, between 1040 and 1090. The base of the tower dates from the 11C; above it rise two storeys added

> ▸ **Population:** 925
> ⏱ **Michelin Map:** 322 L 5
> ▯ **Info:** Place Peyramale, Lourdes. ℘05 62 42 7 40. www.lourdes-info tourisme.com.
> ◖ **Location:** The abbey is on the west bank of the River Gartemps, 42km/26mi E of Poitiers.

in the 12C and a slender 14C steeple (rebuilt in the middle of the 19C). Inside, tall columns divide the nave from the transepts, and in the six chapels which open off the choir and transepts are Romanesque altar-tables still with their original carved inscriptions.

The fame of St-Savin rests on its Romanesque **murals**★★★, the finest in the whole of France. They seem to have been painted around 1100 by a single team of artists over a period of only three to four years. Some of the paintings have withstood the ravages of time better than others; they include a monumental treatment of the *Apocalypse* (in the narthex), the *Creation* (nave), and the *Book of Abraham*.

Saintes★★

With its plane trees, white houses and red-tiled roofs, Saintes has a curiously Mediterranean feel. This pleasant regional capital on the River Charente has a rich cultural and historical heritage.

A BIT OF HISTORY

Saintes was already a regional capital in Roman times, with a bridge over the Charente aligned on today's Rue Victor-Hugo.

In the Middle Ages, the town was an important stop on the pilgrims' route to Santiago de Compostela.

Two great religious establishments developed on its outskirts, St-Eutrope

> ▸ **Population:** 26 531
> ⏱ **Michelin Map:** 324 G 5
> ▯ **Info:** 62 cours National. ℘05 46 74 23 82. www.ot-saintes.fr.
> ◖ **Location:** Saintes is just off the A10 autoroute between Cognac and Royan. Main streets include Avenue Gambetta, Cours National and Cours Lemercier.

on the west bank of the river, the Abbey for Women (Abbaye aux Dames) on the east bank. The historic core of the town has been restored and pedestrianised.

Old Town along the Charente

M. Thierry/MICHELIN

SIGHTS
The Arena and the Arch of Germanicus★

The arch was built in AD 19 at a point on the east bank of the Charente where the roads from Poitiers and Limoges converged on the Roman bridge.

An archaeological museum houses objects saved when the ruins of the Roman city were demolished. To the west, on the slopes of the west bank of the river, is an amphitheatre (**arènes**★), one of the oldest (1C AD) in the Roman world.

Église St-Eutrope

On the west bank, the crypt (**crypte**) of this church once served as a parish church (**église inférieure**★) to the pilgrimage church above. This upper part of the building was monastic in origin.

Abbaye aux Dames

11 pl. de l'Abbaye. ○*Open Apr–Sept daily 10am–12.30pm, 2–7pm; Oct–Mar 2–6pm;* ○*Closed 24 Dec–4 Jan;* ∞*2€.* ℘*05 46 97 48 48. www.abbayeaux dames.org.*

The church (**église**★) of the Abbaye aux Dames is a notable achievement of Romanesque local style, with fine carving in excellent local stone.

La **Haute Soule**★★

One of the original seven Basque provinces, the Upper Soule has retained the dances and folk traditions most characteristic of the region.

VISIT

This is ideal country for forest walks (and cross-country skiing) in rough terrain. At **Ahusquy**, a mountain inn stands in a panoramic **site**★★. At **Col d'Aphanize**, wild horses graze on the slopes around the pass. The

- **Michelin Map:** F-G-H 4-5
- **Location:** The region is in the high Pyrénées near the Spanish border.

pastureland here is the summer home of many flocks of sheep. **Forêt des Arbailles**★★ and **Fôret d'Iraty**★ are extensive beech forest covering the higher reaches. Care is needed when exploring the impressive gorges of **Crevasses d'Holçarté**★ *(on footpath GR 10)* and grandiose **Gorges de Kakouetta**★★ *(tiring and difficult path).*

The Auvergne forms the core of the Massif Central. It is a volcanic landscape unique in France, with mountains, lakes and rivers in deep gorges and whose great variety of relief makes for fine upland walking country, while the towns and villages of sombre granite have their own allure heightened by the presence of some of France's finest Romanesque churches. To the east an escarpment leads down to the sun drenched Rhône Valley with its mighty river charging down to the Mediterranean which could not be in greater contrast to the verdant, rugged uplands of the Auvergne.

Highlights

1 The Romanesque abbey of **La Chaise-Dieu** (p168)

2 Viaduc de Garabit at **St-Flour** (p187)

3 One of the main peaks of the Cantal Volcano **Puy Mary** (p184)

4 The huge Statue of the Virgin Mary at **Puy-en-Velay** (p182)

5 Le Quartier Thermal at **Vichy** (p190)

Geography - The volcanoes of the Auvergne vary from the classic cones of the Monts Dômes to the rugged shapes of the much-eroded Monts Dore. Mainly agricultural, the grazing grounds of the higher land complement the rich alluvial soils of the lower ground. The volcanic activity has created an array of lakes and other water- bodies; at Aydat a lava flow has blocked a valley trapping its waters, while the same effect has been produced at Chambon by a volcano erupting into the valley itself. Elsewhere the hollows produced by a series of volcanic explosions have filled with water while elsewhere lakes have formed inside a crater. Further east the valley of the River Rhône, and its tributary the Saône, seems to divide the ancient uplands to the west from the younger, folded rocks of the Alps to the east.

History - The Auvergne was named after the Arveni whose King, Vincingetorix, had the distinction of defeating Julius Caesar. The victory was shortlived, however, and the region was in turn ruled by Romans, Visigoths and Franks before becoming a Duchy and, later, a Province.

The Rhône Valley has long served as a communications corridor of great importance, linking northwestern Europe to the Mediterranean. For this reason the Romans founded Lyon and the chateaux perched on spurs high above the river provide further evidence of its importance.

Economy – In Auvergne, this is based mainly on tourism, *charcuterie*, cheese and the Michelin tyre plants. In the Rhône Valley the area around the great city of Lyon is marked by centuries of industrial activity. The taming of the Rhône means 2 000t barges can reach the city.

However, the improved waterway carries only a fraction of the total traffic using its corridor; it is supplemented by the A6 motorway, two national highways, a mainline railway on each bank and gas and oil pipelines.

Brioude★

Brioude is a bustling market town overlooking the lush plain of the River Allier.

SIGHT
Basilique St-Julien★★

pl. Grégoire-de-Tours. ⏱*Open daily 9am–noon, 2–5pm.* 💬*Guided tours available.* 🎟*No charge.* 📞*04 71 74 94 59. http://en.ot-brioude.fr/basilica.html.*
This vast Romanesque church was built at the spot where, according to tradition, Julian, a centurion of a Roman legion based at Vienne, was martyred in 304. For many years it attracted throngs of pilgrims on the road which, beyond Le Puy, passed through Langogne and Villefort, at the time the only route between the Auvergne and Languedoc. Work on the present building began with the narthex in 1060, and was completed in 1180 with the construction of the choir and east end. The nave was raised in height and given a ribvault in 1259.

The east end (**chevet★★**) is one of the final examples of Romanesque architecture in the Auvergne. Its five slate-roofed radiating chapels have richly decorated cornices and capitals, above which runs a band of mosaic masonry.

The south porch (**porche★**) has kept its typical Auvergne five-sided lintel, its wrought-iron strap-hinges and two fine bronze knockers. The warm colouring of the interior is due to the combination of sandstones and basalts of red, pink and brown hue. The nave is paved with cobblestones laid in the 16C and only recently exposed again.

The presence locally of both sandstones and marble was a distinct advantage to the four, possibly even six, masons' workshops responsible for the decoration of the church during the 12C and 13C. The capitals (**chapiteaux★★**) are exceptional; note particularly (in the south aisle near the entrance) an armed knight, perhaps a participant involved in the First Crusade (which had been preached at Clermont-Ferrand), together with a usurer (the sculptor's social comment on this curse of the Middle Ages).

▶ **Population:** 6 820
ⓖ **Michelin Map:** 331 C 2
🈁 **Info:** Le Doyenné, Pl. Lafayette. 📞04 71 74 97 49. www.ot-brioude.fr.
▶ **Location:** The town is midway along the road from Clermont-Ferrand to Le Puy en Velay.
⏱ **Timing:** Allow half a day to fully explore the St.Julien Basilica and the rest of the town.

Further up the south aisle are two 14C works, the Virgin Birth and Our Lord as a Leper. There are murals too, though not, unfortunately, very well preserved, but covering an area of around 140sq m/ 1 507sq ft.

There are two outstanding subjects, the figure of St Michael in the first bay of the nave, and the composition in the gallery of the narthex (south room): Christ in Glory, the Chosen and the Damned, the Virtues and the Vices and 100 angels, and, on the timber wall, a stunning 13C Fall of Satan.

EXCURSION
Lavaudieu★

10km/6.2mi SE.
The 11C Benedictine priory, attached to the great abbey at La Chaise-Dieu, has charming cloisters (**cloître★**) with timber-built galleries and 14C **frescoes★**in the chapel and refectory.

Frescoes, Basilique St-Julien

J. Damase/MICHELIN

La Chaise-Dieu★★

Set amid lush green countryside and rolling hills between Le Puy and Thiers, the ornate abbey comes as a magnificent surprise.

▶ **Population:** 778
⏱ **Michelin Map:** 331 E 2
ℹ **Info:** Pl. de la Mairie. ℘04 71 00 01 16. www. abbaye-chaise-dieu.com.
◐ **Location:** The village is 40km/25mi from Le Puy.

VISIT

Église abbatiale de St-Robert★★

🕑 *Open year-round; hours vary, so call ahead.* 🕑 *Closed Mon in Dec and Feb (except school holidays), 25 Dec, 1 Jan.* 👓*4€.* 💬*Guided tours available.*

Over 1 000m/3 280ft up on the high granite plateau of Livradois, **La Chaise-Dieu Abbey**, from the latin *Casa Dei* or House of God, was already a famous monastery in the 11C. Founded in 1043 by St Robert it had a thriving community of about 300 monks at the time of his death in 1067. In the 12C its importance was second only to that of Cluny and by the 13C it had 300 dependent congregations. The abbey's decline set in after 1518, when abbots were henceforth appointed by the king, with fiscal, rather than religious, considerations taking first place.

The granite west front with its twin towers (the spires have disappeared) speaks strongly of the abbey's former grandeur and austerity. Within, the structure is of a noble simplicity, a single-storeyed elevation. The **Monks' chancel**★★ was built from 1344 to 1352 by Pope Clement VI, (the former monk Pierre Roger who went on to become the fourth Avignon Pontiff), and who is buried here in the Choir. The 14 Flemish **tapestries**★★★ (1500–18) of wool, linen and silk, came from Arras and Brussels. The tapestries are hung over the richly carved 15C **stalls**★★, 144 in number. In the **Dance macabre (Dance of Death)**★ figures of the mighty are shown next to their likeness in death.

A great organ was installed at the west end in 1683 and enlarged in 1726; the organ-case **(buffet★)** is elaborately sculpted and contrasts with the spirit prevailing in the choir's architecture. Note also the gothic **cloisters**★.

Église abbatiale de St-Robert

J.Damase/MICHELIN

Clermont-Ferrand★★

The **site★★** of Clermont is unique; the old town, including the cathedral, is built on a volcano, whose black lava makes for an unusual townscape. To the north are the plateaux of Chanturgue and Les Côtes, once the site of a Gallic oppidum, and an example of the phenomenon known as relief inversion, which has protected them from erosion and left them standing out from the surrounding country. To the west are the summits of the Puys, the mountain range that gives Clermont its incomparable setting, perhaps best viewed from the Place de la Poterne with its pretty fountain (**Fontaine d'Amboise★**) of 1515.

A BIT OF HISTORY

Clermont was the great oppidum of the Arverni (the Celts who gave their name to the Auvergne). Here in the spring of 52BC, Julius Caesar and his legions were roundly defeated at the battle of Gergovie by the forces of the Gallic chieftain **Vercingétorix**, whose spirited equestrian statue by Bartholdi stands at one end of Clermont's Place de Jaude . Caesar soon returned, this time winning a decisive battle at Alésia (modern Alise Ste-Reine), and captured Vercingétorix who was taken to Rome where he was paraded in triumph and eventually ritually strangled after being imprisoned for six years in the Tulllianum in Rome. It was at Clermont on 28 November 1095 Pope Urban II launched **the First Crusade**. Clermont was also the town of the remarkable writer, mathematician, thinker and inventor **Blaise Pascal** ("The heart has its reasons that reason knows not" – Blaise Pascal 1623–62). Among other things, at 19 he invented an adding machine (*on display in Musée du Ranquet*).

▶ **Population:** 258 541
⚙ **Michelin Map:** 326 E-G 7-10
ℹ **Info:** Pl. de la Victoire.
   ☏04 73 98 65 00.
   www.clermont-fd.com.
▷ **Location:** Place de Jaude is the focal point for everything that's happening in the city, and is a good place to start.
◔ **Timing:** Allow at least 2hr for the cathedral.

SIGHTS
Basilique Notre-Dame du Port★★

5 r. Saint-Laurent. ☏*04 73 91 32 94.*
⚙*See Introduction: Art – Architecture.*
This is the finest of the larger Romanesque churches of the Lower Auvergne, unforgettable in its beautiful simplicity. It was built around 1150 over a crypt of the 11C.

Inside, the raised chancel (**chœur★★★**), admirably proportioned, is divided from the ambulatory by eight slender columns; their capitals (**chapiteaux★★**), together with those of the wall of the ambulatory, are among the finest in Auvergne. In the crypt is an ancient together with a Black Virgin which has been worshipped here since the 13C.

Rue Pascal

Lined with lava-built residences of somewhat severe aspect, this is one of the typical streets of the old town (**Vieux Clermont★★**).

Aerial view of Old Montferrand

J. Damase/MICHELIN

169

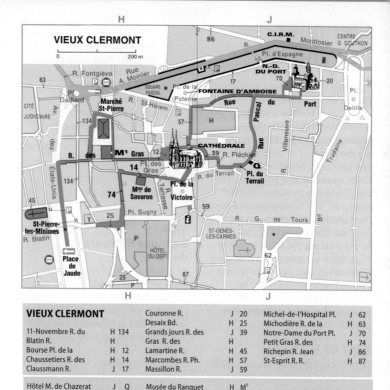

Guided Tours

The tourist office organises various walking tours around Clermont, the Port Walk or the Montferrand Walk. Ask at the tourist office for the *Parcours dans la ville* brochure.

Cathédrale Notre-Dame-de-l'Assomption★★

2 Avis.

Compare this building with Notre-Dame-du-Port: a revolutionary change in architectural style had occurred in the 100 years which separates the two. The stained-glass medallions (**vitraux**★★) of the 12–15C are copies of those in the Sainte-Chapelle in Paris. The **Treasury**★ (*guided tours Jul–Sept Mon, Wed & Fri 3pm; contact tourist office*) displays 12–19C collections of gold, silver and enamel ware.

L'Aventure Michelin

Montferrand quarter, near Parc des Sports Marcel Michelin at 32 r. du Clos Four, Cataroux industrial site, N of the city. Open Sept–Jun Tue–Sun 10am–6pm; Jul and Aug daily until 7pm. 8€. 04 73 98 60 60. www.aventure-michelin.com. Online reservations necessary.

An exhibition space opened at the end of March 2009 spanning 2 000sq m/ 21 528sq ft and two floors displays the workings of Michelin, past present and future. Visitors learn about the history of Michelin tyres, the Michelin Man (Bibendum) and can admire a replica of the Bréguet XIV aeroplane built by Michelin during World War I.

ADDITIONAL SIGHTS

Vieux Montferrand★★ (old town)
Musée d'Art Roger-Quilliot★★ *(pl. Louis-Deteix)*
Église St-Léger de Royat★ *(pl. Cohendy, Royat – 4km/2.5mi SW)*

The Capital of the Motor Tyre

Two men, Aristide Barbier and Édouard Daubrée came together around 1830 to make agricultural machinery as well as gunshot, and rubber belts and tubes. In 1889, their factory was taken over by brothers **André** and **Édouard Michelin**, the grandsons of Barbier. Building on their tradition of applying scientific method to the work of industry, the

PARIS-BORDEAUX 1895 — 1ʳᵉ VOITURE sur PNEUS MICHELIN

company has subsequently flourished through study of clients' needs, scrupulous observation of reality and previous experience. This process has led from the detachable bicycle tyre of 1891, the car tyre of 1895, the low-pressure "Confort" tyre of 1923, the "Metalic" of 1937, the radial tyre of 1946 (designated "X" in 1949), to the Michelin Energy tyre (1990s). This "green" tyre technology – based on reduced rolling resistance – enables fuel savings.

Issoire★★

This old Auvergne town is situated at the point where the Pavin valley meets the flatter fertile country of the southern Limagne. In 1540 the town became a notable centre of Protestantism. More recently it has acquired an industrial character, with important engineering works. But there is still an agreeable, provincial ambiance about the place that rewards even the shortest break.

ABBATIALE ST-AUSTREMOINE D'ISSOIRE★★

&⬆✎ *Guided tours (1hr30min) available.* 📞04 73 89 15 90.
Built around 1135, this is the largest Romanesque church in the Auvergne. It was extensively restored in the 19C (west front, roof, bell-tower, many of the capitals, the polychrome interior decoration).

The east end (**chevet★★**) is a fine example of Auvergne Romanesque, generously and harmoniously proportioned and rich in detail. Inside, an impression of strength and solidity, characteristic of these Auvergne churches, is given by the four great arches at the crossing

▶ **Population:** 13 559
🕐 **Michelin Map:** 326 G 9
📖 **Info:** Pl. du Général de Gaulle. 63500 Issoire. 📞04 73 89 15 90. www.sejours-issoire.com.
▶ **Location:** Climb up the clocktower for a superb view of the town and surrounding countryside. Then start your tour of the town. Most shops, restaurants and bars cluster around the tower and along the Main street.

East end of the abbey

S. Sauvignier/MICHELIN

and by the ambulatory with its ribbed vault. The influence of the Mozac School of sculpture is clearly seen in the capitals (**chapiteaux**★ – c. 1140) carved from the local volcanic rock; particularly fine are those showing the Last Supper and Christ washing the feet of the disciples.

In the narthex is a 15C mural of the **Last Judgement**★, a favourite subject of the time, here treated with great verve and a degree of satire.

Château de Lapalisse★★

The little crossroads town has grown up at the foot of the château which has commanded the crossing of the Besbre since the 11C. Its most famous owner was Jacques II de Chabannes (1470-1525), a Marshal of France who distinguished himself in the conquest of Milan but who was killed by a blast from a harquebus received during the Battle of Pavia.

VISIT

Guided tours (1hr) Apr–Sept daily 9am–noon, 2pm–6pm; Oct Sat and Sun only 9am–noon, 2–6pm. Reservations required. ☞5.50€. ℘04 70 99 37 58.

Little remains of the medieval castle. The present building, started at the beginning of the 16C, is very much in the style of the early Renaissance, the work of Florentine craftsmen brought from Italy by Jacques. The courtyard

- ▸ **Population:** 3 332
- ᴑ **Michelin Map:** 3 332
- ⓘ **Info:** 26 r. Winston Churchill, Lapalisse. ℘04 70 99 08 39.
- ◖ **Location:** Town and château are 25km/15.5mi NE of Vichy.

façade is enlivened by heraldic motifs and polychrome brickwork, by sandstone courses on the towers and around the windows, by bracketed lintels and mullioned windows, by medallions in the portal of the central tower, by foliated scrolls, pilasters and Corinthian capitals.

Inside, there is interesting Louis XIII furniture in the main reception room.

The **Salon doré**★★ has a coffered ceiling and 15C Flemish tapestries. The chapel, built in granite, is in Flamboyant style, and there is a fine timber ceiling in the service range (**communs**).

Château de Lapalisse

J. Damase/MICHELIN

Lyon★★★

Two millennia of history, a site at the meeting point of the Rhône and Saône corridors and an exceptionally enterprising population have combined to make Lyon France's second city. Its past periods of greatness, in Roman and Renaissance times, are matched by its present industrial, commercial and cultural dynamism. Truly the heart of the city, la Presqu'île offers great views of the quays of the Saône River and Vieux Lyon. Department stores, boutiques, cinemas and bars line rue de la République, well known for its 19C architecture. Stretching from north to south, rue du Président-Herriot and rue Paul-Chenavard are also good for shopping.

▸ **Population:** 1 348 832
⏣ **Michelin Map:** 327 H-I 5
▣ **Info:** 19 pl. Bellecour. ☎04 72 77 69 69. www.lyon-france.com.
◖ **Location:** Lyon lies 100km/62mi W of Cahambéry
▣ **Parking:** Lyon has many underground parking garages.
◉ **Don't Miss:** The Renaissance old quarter, Vieux Lyon, on the right bank of the Saône.
◷ **Timing:** You can spend anything from an afternoon to a few days here.

A BIT OF HISTORY

A Celtic, then Gallic settlement, Lyon was chosen as a base camp by Julius Caesar for his conquest of Gaul. Under Augustus it became the capital of the Roman Empire's "Three Gauls" (Aquitaine, Belgium and the province around Lyon) complementing the older province centred on Narbonne. Agrippa was responsible for choosing Lyon as the hub of the road system, constructed originally in pursuit of political ends. It was here that the great route coming north from Arles met the other highways from Saintes, Orléans and Rouen, from Geneva and Aosta, and from Chalon with its links to Amiens, Trier and Basle.

The manufacture of pottery became established here as early as the first century AD, only to move later to La Graufesenque on the Tarn (⏣ see MILLAU). The Amphitheatre of the Three Gauls on the hill, Colline de la Croix-Rousse, was joined by the Temple of Rome and of Augustus and by the Federal Sanctuary where the noisy annual assembly of the 60 tribes of Gaul was held under Roman supervision.

Christianity reached Lyon via Vienne by the middle of the 2C, brought by soldiers, traders and Greek missionaries. In 177, there were riots on the occasion of the annual assembly, and Saints Pothinus and Blandina, along with 48 others, became the city's first Christian martyrs. Twenty years later, Saint Irenaeus, head of the Church in Lyon, was to meet the same fate. According to St Gregory of Tours, the Gospel was reintroduced to Lyon around 250 by Roman missionaries, and, under Constantine, Christianity is supposed to have flourished here as in the other cities of the Empire.

The era of invention – Lyon played a leading role in science and technology at this time. Among its eminent citizens should be noted the following:

Marie-Joseph Jaquard who built a power-loom in 1804; **André Ampère,** inventor of the galvanometer, electromagnetism, and electrodynamics; **Barthélemy Thimonnier**, who invented the sewing machine in 1829; **Jean-Baptiste Guimet**, who, in 1834, succeeded in making the dye ultramarine; the **Lumière brothers**

Lyon City Card

This pass is valid for one, two or three days (18€, 27€, 36€ respectively). The pass offers itineraries for your visit. Contact the tourist office. Guided tours available, too.

(Auguste and Louis), the creators of cinematography; **Hector Guimard**, one of the founders of Art Nouveau in architecture, the designer of the entrances to the metro stations of Paris.

SIGHTS
La Colline de Fourvière
(Fourvière Hill)

The name of the hill is derived from the old forum *(Forum vetus)* which was still here in the reign of King Louis I in the 9C. Its site is now occupied by the pilgrimage chapel (with its Black Virgin) next to the basilica of 1870. Roman Lyon had numerous public buildings, including the imperial palace (the Capitol) giving onto the forum, a theatre and an odeon (both rebuilt) on the slope of the hill, baths, a circus building and several temples, as well as the amphitheatre on the east bank of the river.

The terrace to the north of the basilica forms a splendid **viewpoint** overlooking the confluence of the Rhône and Saône and encompassing the hills and Dauphiné plain over which the great city has spread.

Musée gallo-romain de Fourvière★★

17 r. Cléberg. &♿ ⏰*Open year-round Tue–Sun 10am–6pm.* ☞*Guided tours Sun 3pm.* ⏰*Closed 1 Jan, 1 May, 1 Nov, 25 Dec. On other public holidays call in advance.* ≈4€ *(free Thu).* ℘*04 72 38 49 30.*

The most striking exhibit is perhaps formed by the Claudian Tables **(Table Claudienne★★★)** of bronze, discovered in 1528. They record the speech made by Claudius in AD 48 which gave the citizens of Gaul the right to become senators. It is possible to compare this ponderous "official" version with the more witty and revealing transcription made by Tacitus.

Le Vieux Lyon (Old Lyon)★★★

The medieval and Renaissance quarter of Lyon, the precursor of today's city, extends along the west bank of the Saône at the foot of the Fourvière hill.

Of interest in the old town are the many passages or alleyways known as "traboules" – from the Latin trans ambulare meaning "walking through." The passageways run perpendicular to the streets and link the buildings by means of corridors with vaulted or coffered ceilings leading to inner courtyards.

Primatiale St-Jean★

Begun in 1192, today's church was preceded by a number of sanctuaries, including an early Christian baptistery, remains of which are on the north side of the building. The cathedral was enlarged in the reigns of Philippe Auguste and St Louis, beginning with the Romanesque east end. The 280 medallions adorning the west front were begun in 1310; in their wealth of detail and great variety they are comparable with those of Rouen cathedral or the chapel of the Papal Palace at Avignon, though the juxtaposition of the sacred, profane and grotesque is sometimes disconcerting. Inside, the chancel **(chœur★★)**, together with the apse, is the oldest part of the church. The apse, with its fluted pilasters below a blind arcade and a frieze of palm-leaves, is typical of Romanesque architecture of the Rhône valley. It is lit by a 13C stained-glass axial window with a fine medallion depicting the Redemption. There is a 14C astronomical clock **(horloge astronomique★)** with original ironwork.

Quartier St-Jean★★

Lyon was incorporated into the French kingdom at the beginning of the 14C. In the Middle Ages it was a border town facing the Dauphiné, Savoy, and the Holy Roman Empire. Charles VII made it a trading centre of European importance when he founded the twice-yearly fair in 1419. Louis XI introduced the weaving of raw silk imported from the Levant and from Italy, but local opposition led the only silk-mill to transfer its operations to Tours. Forty-four years later, Louis doubled the number of fairs; long-distance trade was encouraged and patterns of commercial activity

Basilique Notre-Dame de Fourvière, La Colline de Fourvière

developed which were far in advance of the time; accommodation at inns and hostels was improved, and clearing houses were set up, forerunners of the great bank founded in the 16C.

Trade flourished, and with it came a period of great prosperity for the city, its merchants, bankers and high officials. Lyon seethed with activity and ideas; its streets were lined with elegant Flamboyant Gothic façades with asymmetrical window patterns; behind them, down narrow alleys, lay courtyards like the ones at 11 and 58 rue St-Jean. More numerous are houses of Renaissance date, decorated with Italianate motifs (polygonal turrets, superimposed galleries, basket-handle arches and corner signs like the figure of the ox at the junction of rue du Bœuf – Hôtel Paterin (4 r. de la Juiverie), sculpted in the 16C by John of Bologna.

The **Hôtel de Gadagne**★ houses the **Musée historique de Lyon**★ *(1 pl. du Petit Collège; www. museegadagne.com)* and the **Musée international de la Marionnette**★ *(as for the Musée historique de Lyon),* the latter created by Laurent Mourget (1769–1844), whose

Guignol is the very embodiment of the spirit of the Lyon populace.

With the development of the characteristic forms of the French Renaissance come superimposed orders, as in the Hôtel Bullioud *(8 r. de la Juiverie)* with its gallery and corner pavilions by the local architect **Philibert Delorme**. Printing had been invented in Korea in 1403, then again at Mainz in 1447 and made its first appearance on the banks of the Saône in 1485. The world of the transcriber or of the illuminator would never be the same again. The spread of books transformed Europe with its diffusion of learning, in literature,

GALLO-ROMAIN LYON

science and technology and accounts of voyages. The Reformation, born from widespread reading of the Bible, came about some 50 years after the invention of the printing press.

This was also the age of Louise Labé, known as la "Belle Cordière" (Rope-maker's wife), whose salon became a centre for literature and the arts; among those writing was the Lyon poet Maurice Scève.

By 1548 there were almost 400 printers working in the city, including Sébastien Gryphe, Guillaume Rouille and Étienne Dolet, the publisher of Marot and of Rabelais; the latter served as a doctor at the Pont-du-Rhône hospital for three years, carrying on a correspondence with Erasmus and Du Bellay. It was Du Bellay who published **Rabelais**' *Pantagruel* in 1532 and Gargantua in 1534 to coincide with the Lyon fairs.

It was here that the Florentine Angelo Benedetto produced white porcelain. Other manufacturers were active too, including Julio Gambiu, who moved away to Nevers around 1565.

Musée de l'Imprimerie★★

13 r. de la Poulaillerie. 🚻🕐*Open Wed–Sun 9.30am–noon, 2–6pm.* 🕐*Closed public holidays.* 👓*3.80€.* 📞*04 78 37 65 98. www.imprimerie.lyon.fr.*

The museum traces the evolution of printing from its very beginnings in Lyon, from the first wood engravings to the discovery of typography and to photocomposition.

La Presqu'île (Lyon's Peninsula)

The modern centre of the city is sited on a long tongue of alluvial material brought down by the Rhône. The formation of the "Peninsula" has shifted the junction of the two rivers 4km/2.5mi southwards since Roman times.

The area was first of all a military encampment, then its proximity to the two rivers made it a favourable place for trading and warehousing. Finally it became the very core of the city; its development along Classical lines begun under Henri IV and Louis XIII

was continued in the 18C and 19C, until the urban area spread outwards to the modern suburbs and beyond. The great city's character comes across not only in the busy Rue de la République, with its fine 19C façades and elegant shops, but also in the pleasantly shaded Place de la République, with its trees and fountains.

Place Bellecour

Planned by Henri IV in 1609, the project could not be started until 50 years later, when the city had finally succeeded in purchasing the land.

The designer was Robert de Cotte, who arranged the avenues of trees on the south side of the square in such a way as to disguise its irregular shape. The buildings lining the square were razed during the Terror in retribution for the city's resistance to the Convention. "Lyon is no more," it was triumphantly proclaimed at the time, but the square was rebuilt in the 19C.

Hôtel-Dieu

1 pl. de l'Hôpital.

The plans for this, one of the kingdom's most important buildings, were drawn up by Soufflot in 1740. It marks a significant stage in the evolution of French architecture with its long façade facing the Rhône, its projecting central section with Ionic columns and its dome rising from a square base and crowned with a square lantern. The way in which the transoms of the windows are decorated with linen motifs evokes its function as a hospital. A balustrade relieves the great length of the main façade and disguises the low roofs.

Place des Terreaux

This is sited where the Saône flowed into the Rhône in Roman times. The older inhabitants of the city are particularly fond of the square with its fountain (**fontaine**★) by Bartholdi, which has four eager horses representing rivers bounding oceanwards. The town hall dates from the reign of Louis XIII, although its façade was rebuilt by Robert de Cotte after a fire and is typically 18C,

La Presq'île

J. Damase/MICHELIN

with a dome and a rounded tympanum supported by atlantes.

Musée des Beaux-Arts★★

20 pl. des Terreaux. Open Wed–Sun *10am–6pm (Fri 10.30am–6pm).* Closed public holidays. 6€. 04 72 10 17 40. www.mba-lyon.fr.
The museum presents a remarkable survey of art through the centuries throughout the world. Its collections are organised into five separate departments: painting, sculpture, art objects, antiquities and graphic art. The highlights of the selection of European painting include 35 **Impressionist** works, **The Ascension**★ by Perugino, an imposing *St Francis* by Zurbaràn, and *The Adoration of the Magi* by Rubens. Also illustrated is the evolution of French painting from the 17C (Philippe de Champaigne) to the 19C (*Femme au perroquet* by Delacroix) and 20C (*Corbeille de Fruit* by Chagall).
There is a very fine collection of ancient art: temple doors from Mehamoud (Egyptian section); a remarkable kore (statue of a young girl) from the Acropolis (Ancient Greece).

Musée des Tissus et Musée des Arts Décoratifs★★★

34 r. de la Charité. Textile Museum: *Tue–Sun 10am–5.30pm; Decorative Arts Museum: Tue–Sun 10am–noon, 2–5.30pm* Closed public holidays,

Easter, Whitsun. 6€. 04 78 38 42 00. www.musee-des-tissus.com.
Apart from its exhibits devoted to very early examples of the weaver's art, the collection consists mostly of Lyon silk from the 17C onwards, by masters such as Philippe de Lasalle. There are Louis XV lampas and embroidered satins, embroidery and cut velvets of the Empire and Restoration periods. On the slopes of the hill, Colline de la Croix-Rousse, is a network of covered passageways called *traboules*, once used to protect the precious sheets of silk. They proved useful during the French

Lampas silk

Basset, Caillure/Courtesy Musée des Tissus, Lyon

Revolution, too, and were much used by the Resistance in World War II.

ADDITIONAL SIGHTS
Musée des Confluences★★
(86 quai Perrache)
Centre d'Histoire de la Résistance et de la Déportation★
(14 av. Berthelot)
Musée des Hospices civils –

pharmacy★ *(in Hôtel Dieu)*
Basilique St-Martin d'Ainay – capitals★ *(pl. d'Ainay, 11 r. Bourgelat)*
Église St-Nizier – Virgin with the Infant Jésus★ *(pl. St Nizier)*
Église St-Paul – Lantern-tower★
(r. St Paul)
Montée de Garillan★ *(hill)*
Parc de la Tête d'Or★ *(bd des Belges)*
Place Rouville – view★.

Massif Du Ézenc★★★

These dramatic volcanic uplands in the southern part of the Velay region form the watershed between Atlantic and Mediterranean. They lie at the centre of a belt of igneous rocks cutting across the axis of the Cévennes.

> 🚶 **Michelin Map:** 331 H 4
> ▶ **Location:** The area lies SE of Le Puy-en-Velay.

WALKS
Mont Mézenc
2hr round trip on foot from the Croix de Boutières pass.
Two great lava flows extend downwards from the twin summits of the mountain, from which a vast **panorama**★★★ extends over the Velay. Quite close at hand can be seen the village of Les Estables.

Gerbier de Jonc★★
1hr30min round-trip on foot.

Screes of bright phonolite clatter under the feet of the many who clamber to the summit of this lava pinnacle, from which there is a fine **view**★★.

Cascade du Ray-Pic★★
11km/6.8mi S of the Gerbier de Jonc – 1hr30min round trip on foot.
In a harsh setting formed by a succession of lava flows, the Bourges torrent drops in a series of falls. In the bed of the stream, dark basalt contrasts with lighter granite.

Lac d'Issarlès★
20km/12.4mi E of the Gerbier de Jonc.
This pretty, rounded lake with its blue waters occupies the crater of an extinct volcano, 138m/450ft deep.

Lac d'Issarlès

A. de Valroger/MICHELIN

Moulins★

Moulins, on the River Allier, is the quiet, charming capital of the Bourbonnais region dominated by the twin spires of its Flamboyant Gothic Cathedral and the Église du Sacré Coeur. Le Pal Amusement Park is well worth a visit – especially if you have children in tow. Activities on offer include horse riding, kayaking and golf.

A BIT OF HISTORY

The city was founded by the Bourbon lords at the end of the 11C. In time, the Bourbons rose to the rank of dukes. The 15C was the duchy's golden age, with many artists commissioned to work here. The independence of the Bourbonnais became an irritant to the king and François I took advantage of the supposed treason of Charles III, the Ninth Duke, to confiscate his estates. After a series of battles against the French forces, Charles was killed (1527) and the Bourbonnais attached to the French Crown.

SIGHT
Cathédrale Notre-Dame★

Pl. des Vosges (in the Cathedral).
Open year-round daily 9am–noon, 2–6pm. Guided tours available.
Closed 1 Jan, 1 May, 14 Jul, 25 Dec.
2€ donation suggested. 04 70 20 89 65.

From the 17C arcaded covered market there is a good view of the Cathedral, which has exemplary **stained glass windows**★★ depicting famous figures from the Bourbons' court. Among the works of art diplayed in the Cathedral is the **Triptych by the Master of Moulins**★★★, from about 1498 – a triumph of late-Gothic painting. The Master has never been conclusively identified. The poses of the figures

▶ **Population:** 21 892
Michelin Map: 326 H 3
Info: 11 r. François Péron. 04 70 44 14 14. www.pays-bourbon.com/ville-moulins.html.
Location: Moulins sits in the centre of the country, 60km/37mi N of Vichy and 60km/37mi S of Nevers.

J. Damase/MICHELIN

Central part of Triptych by the Master of Moulins

depicted suggest the Flemish School, while their faces recall the work of Florentine masters. Note also the **Jaquemart**★ (belltower). The **Mausolée du Duc de Montmorency**★ (*guided tours available; 04 70 48 51 18*) dating from 1585–1632, is not to be missed.

Orcival★★

Many houses in this tiny Auvergne village, famed for its Romanesque basilica, still have their original roof coverings of tiles cut from the phonolitic lavas of the nearby Roche Tuilière, the core of an ancient volcano. In summer the village becomes very busy with visitors who come here to admire the famous Basilica.

▶ **Population:** 244
♿ **Michelin Map:** 326 E 8
ℹ **Info:** Le Bourg.
  ☎04 73 65 89 77.
  www.terresdomes-
  sancy.com
▶ **Location:** The village is high in the Volcanoes Regional Park, SW of Clermont-Ferrand.

A BIT OF HISTORY
Founded by the monks of La Chaise-Dieu in the 12C, Orcival had become an important parish by the middle of the 13C and has been a centre of pilgrimage since that time. More recently it has been the home town of the ex-president of France (1974–81), Valéry Giscard d'Estaing.

SIGHT
Basilique Notre-Dame★★
🕐Open year-round. ✎Guided tours available; ask at the tourist office.

Illustration – ♿See Introduction: Art and Culture. Completed around 1130, this basilica is a fine example of the Auvergne Romanesque, with a many-tiered apse, powerful buttresses and massive arches. Inside, the majestic crossing is lit by 14 windows, while both chancel and crypt, the latter with a spacious ambulatory, are masterpieces of their kind.
In the chancel is a **Virgin Enthroned**★ still with its original gilt ornamentation; one side of the face (left) is that of an Auvergne peasant woman, the other (right) of a lady of society.

Pérouges★★

Tightly contained within the ramparts, the tortuous streets and ancient houses of the old town have formed the perfect setting for many a period film including , "The Three Musketeers"and "Monsieur Vincent".

▶ **Population:** 1 103
♿ **Michelin Map:** 328 E 5
ℹ **Info:** Entrance of the Cité.
  ☎04 74 46 70 84.
  www.perouges.org.
▶ **Location:** 25km/15.5mi NE of Lyon.

SIGHT
Cité ancienne★★
On its hilltop site dominating the Ain valley, this fortified town was originally founded by settlers who came from Perugia in central Italy long before Caesar's invasion of Gaul. It was virtually rebuilt in its entirety after the war of 1468 with Savoy.
The older buildings are timber-framed with projecting upper storeys.
The modest artisans' houses contrast with those of the richer townsfolk and gentry, which have mullioned windows and basket-handle arches.

The Upper Gate **(Porte d'en Haut★)** is the principal entrance to the town; the main square, the **Place de la Halle★★★**, has a splendid old hostelry and the **Musée du Vieux-Pérouges** which contains many local artifacts, a restored weaver's workshop and a medieval garden with medicinal herbs.
Nearby, there is also a wonderful old lime tree, the Liberty Tree, planted in in the place des Tilleuls during 1792 as a symbol of the Revolution.

Le Puy de Dôme★★★

At 1 465m/4 806ft, this peak is the highest of the peaks in the volcanic landscape known as the Puys. The Gauls erected a sanctuary to their god Lug here and the Romans built a temple to Mercury. In 1648, Pascal conducted an experiment here proving Torricelli's theory about atmospheric weight, taking readings of the height of a column of mercury while his brother-in-law simultaneously did the same in Clermont-Ferrand; the difference was a decisive 8.4cm/3.3in.

Michelin Map: 326 E 8

Info: Place de la Victoire, Clermont-Ferrand. *℘*04 73 98 65 00. www.clermont-fd.com.

Location: It is easy to drive almost to the summit (there is a car park), but more spectacular is the shuttle service running between Clermont-Ferrand and Le Puy de Dôme.

Kids: Nearby Vulcania is an entertaining volcano-themed leisure park *(rte de Mazayes, Saint-Ours-les Roches; ℘0820 827 828; ⊙21€; child 15€).*

VISIT

Panorama★★★

From the summit there is a vast panorama over the city of Clermont-Ferrand, the Grande Limagne basin and the Puys themselves. The Puys, or the Monts Dômes as they are sometimes known, extend over an area 30km/18.6mi long and 5km/3mi wide; in it, there are a total of 112 extinct volcanoes, all more than 50 000 years old.

If visibility is good, the view extends over 11 départements. At sunset the view is the most spectacular.

Puy de Pariou and Puy de Dôme

J. Damase/MICHELIN

Le **Puy de Sancy**★★★

The Puy de Sancy, the highest peak in central France, rises to 1 885m/6 184ft from the set of extinct volcanoes called the Mont Dore massif, one of the most picturesque areas in the Auvergne.

VISIT
Panorama★★★
1hr30min to the summit and back on foot by a rough path from the top station of the cable railway.
With the heights of the Mont Dore massif in the foreground, the immense views extend northeastwards over the Puys and to the Cantal massif in the south. The hedged fields of the valley bottoms give way, between 1 100–1 400m (3 600–4 600ft), to a forest of beech,

- ⛷ **Michelin Map:** 326 D 9
- ▷ **Location:** Le Puy de Sancy is 48km/30mi SW of Clermont-Ferrand. Sancy station sits 4km/2.5mi along D 983. Take the cable-car ride (3min), then 20min on foot to the summit.

spruce and fir, while the landscape as a whole is enhanced by the presence of volcanic lakes.

Besse-en-Chandesse★
On the eastern slopes of the massif.
This is a mountain village, made of lava, with picturesque **streets** and houses, a barbican and a little **church**★ with sturdy columns and rough capitals.

Le **Puy-en-Velay**★★★

The town occupies one of the most amazing sites in France, its most striking landmark being the huge **statue of the Virgin Mary** atop a tall column of volcanic rock. Le Puy has been famous for pilgrimages since Bishop Gotescalk made one of the first pilgrimages to Santiago de Compostella from here in 962. It is also known for its fine lace.

VISIT
Rocher Corneille
This is an outlier of the volcano of which the Rocher St-Michel was the vent. It is topped by a 16m/52ft statue of Notre-Dame of France made in 1860 from more than two hundred melted-down cannons captured at the Siege of Sebastopol during the Crimean War. Reached by a steep path, the terrace at the foot of the statue offers the best viewpoint over the extraordinary **site**★★★ of Le Puy.

- ▸ **Population:** 20 490
- ⛷ **Michelin Map:** 331 F 3
- 🗊 **Info:** Place du Clauzel. 𝄞04 71 09 38 41.
- ▷ **Location:** Le Puy-en-Velay lies 75km/46.5mi SW of Saint Etienne. In the summer there is a tourist train that introduces you to the many curiosities of Puy-en-Velay.
- 🕲 **Don't Miss:** The fantastic views from the upper rim of the basin, especially during sunset or the lively Saturday market at Place du Breuil.

La Cité Épiscopale (Cathedral Quarter)★★★
The city's growth dates from the 11C, when it took over the urban functions of nearby St-Paulien and when it formed an important destination on the pilgrimage road to Santiago de Compostela in Spain.

Chapelle St-Michel-d'Aiguilhe and Rocher Corneille

J.Damase/MICHELIN

The cathedral's fortifications are evidence of the bishops' quarrels with the local lords over sovereignty and taxes raised from the pilgrims.

In the centre of the old town, the area around the cathedral has a sombre air, with its buildings of granite and lava, narrow arcaded entranceways, mullioned windows, heavy iron grilles and paving stones.

Cathédrale Notre-Dame★★★

Guided tours available; contact the tourist office. ℰ04 71 09 38 41. *www.cathedraledupuy.org.*

The first building to occupy the site was a Roman temple. This was followed around 430 by a sanctuary dedicated to the Virgin Mary, built at the same time as Santa Maria Maggiore at Rome. Rebuilding and extension took place from the 10C on, and in the 19C major restoration was carried out.

The lofty west front rises from its monumental steps to dominate the Rue des Taules. The windows in the third storey mark the extension to the nave which took place at the end of the 12C and which is supported on massive arcading. The overall impression is a highly ornamental one, due to the pierced or blind Romanesque arches, the use of polychrome granite and basalt stonework, the mosaics in the gables and the columns with carved lava capitals.

The steps continue to rise, giving a good view of the carved doors of the Golden Doorway (Porte Dorée) with, on the left, a depiction of the Nativity, and on the right, Christ's Passion. In the 10C and 11C, the apse was rebuilt and the transepts and first two bays of the nave erected. At the beginning of the 12C the two adjacent bays were built and vaulted with splendid domes. The two last bays were added at the end of the 12C.

Dating from the 11C and 12C, the cathedral **Cloisters** ★★ have polychrome mosaics, an allegorical Romanesque frieze at the base of the roof, a fine 12C wrought-iron **grille**★ and, in the Reliquary Chapel (Chapelle des Reliques), a celebrated Renaissance fresco depicting the Liberal Arts.

It also qualifies as one of the starting points of the pilgrim route to Santiago de Compostela.

Chapelle St-Michel-d'Aiguilhe★★

🕐*Open daily May–Sept 9am–6.30pm (mid-Jul–Aug 6.45pm); mid-Mar–Apr and Oct–mid-Nov 9.30am–noon, 2–5.30pm; Feb–mid-Mar 2–5pm.* 🕐*Closed 1 Jan and 25 Dec.* ⊜3€. ℰ04 71 09 50 03. *www.rochersaintmichel.fr.*

Lace

Lace-making was widespread in the area around Le Puy as early as the 17C, though its high point was reached in the 19C, in part due to the efforts of Théodore Falcon (1804–56), who encouraged high standards in both design and quality. Before World War I, bobbin lace and needlepoint lace were equally popular, but after 1919, the former (also known as pillow lace) became dominant, with threads of linen, silk and wool used to form patterns of great variety and delicacy.

268 steps lead to the chapel perched on its 82m/270ft lava pinnacle. Arabesques and polychrome mosaics of Byzantine inspiration decorate the chapel doorway. Inside, the complex vaulting gives some indication of the difficulties the 11C architect had to overcome in transforming the original Carolingian sanctuary; one of his contributions was the addition of a gallery to the narthex. Note two capitals re-used in the smaller gallery, the 10C murals in the apse depicting the heavenly kingdom, and a Romanesque Christ-reliquary carved in wood.

ADDITIONAL SIGHTS

Trésor de la Cathédrale★★ (Treasury).

Trésor d'art Religieux★★ (Religious Art Collection in the cloisters).

Musée Crozatier *(Jardin Henri Vinay)* – with a **Lace collection**★ of great richness.

EXCURSIONS
Château de Polignac
5km/3mi NW. www.ot-lepuyenvelay. fr/hist/pol.html.

There is a striking view of this medieval fortress from the N 102 main road. Its defences were so strong that its lords were known as the "Kings of the Mountain". From the 17C to the 19C, their descendants held prominent positions in political and diplomatic life.

Lac du Bouchet★
21km/13mi SW.

The clear waters of the lake, surrounded by coniferous woodland, occupy the almost perfectly circular crater of an ancient volcano. Around it stretch the extensive Devès uplands, formed by a series of fissure-eruptions and overlying the even older granite foundation of the landscape.

Le **Puy Mary**★★★

At 1 787m/5 863ft, Puy Mary is one of the main peaks of the once immense Cantal volcano, which had a circumference of 60km/37mi and a cone rising to 3 000m/10 000ft. It is also the most visited natural reserve of the Auvergne region and has to be managed very sensitively. As a consequence, the local authoriies have implemented "Operation Grand Site: Puy Mary – Volcan du Cantal".

 Michelin Map: 330 E 4

Location: These peaks are NE from the town of Aurillac. The summit is reached by a steep path from Pas-de-Peyrol – 1hr30min round-trip on foot.

GEOGRAPHY

Sharp ridges divide the country up into a series of amphitheatres, in each of which the same set of activities is carefully staged. Meadows and cropland fill the valley bottoms, where the villages are

Ridge along Le Puy Mary

J. Damase/MICHELIN

also sited, though in areas less exposed to the sun there are birchwoods, grown for fuel. On the middle slopes are beeches, used for a range of purposes, and recently planted conifers. Higher still come the upland pastures, dotted with stone-built huts used until lately as summer-dwellings by shepherds or for cheese-making. Known as burons, they are planted round with ash-trees, a useful source of fodder in times of drought.

The basaltic lava (unlike the trachytes of Mont Dore) yields rich herbage which is grazed by the reddish Salers cattle, who in their turn yield the milk for the famous Cantal cheese.

VISIT

Panorama★★★

Glacial action has decapitated the volcano and worn it down. The view from the top takes in a landscape punctuated by the remains of volcanic vents and lava flows which seem to have only just cooled. The **Pas-de-Peyrol**★★ too affords fine views.

ACTIVITIES

The authorities are determined that any development in the area should be compatible with the concept of sustainable tourism. While a large range of sport and leisure facilities is offered to suit all tastes and interests, they are closely monitored and must fit in with the long term plans for the site. *For further details see: www.puymary.fr.*

Mountain Biking

This is ideal territory to explore on two wheels and if you do not have your own machine then mountain bike rental and even guided tours can be obtained.

Horse Riding

If you prefer four legs then various circuits both on horseback and even by donkey are available.

Other Activities

Hiking, hang-gliding, canyoning, cross-country skiing, fishing, rock climbing and white-water sports.

Riom★★

The old town of Riom, market centre of the Limagne district, still reflects the splendour of bygone days with its black stone houses and fountains.

▸ **Population:** 18 548
◉ **Michelin Map:** 326 F 7
▣ **Info:** 27 place de la Fédération. ℘04 73 38 59 45. www.riom.net.
▶ **Location:** Riom is 63km/39mi NW of St-Flour along the A 72/E 70.
☺ **Don't Miss:** Be sure to have a leisurely wander in the Old Town.

SIGHTS

Quartier Ancien (Old Town)

The medieval town is was the capital of the Duchy of Auvergne, then in the 16C and 17C an administrative and legal centre, giving it a heritage of fine houses. Note the 16C **Maison des Consuls**★ (5 r. de l'Hôtel de Ville); and the Renaissance **clock tower** and 16C **Hôtel Guimoneau**★ in Rue de l'Horloge. A ring of boulevards is built on the former ramparts enclosing the Old Town.

Rue du Commerce

The modern sculptures made of lava contrast with the traditional decoration of the houses using the same material (no 36 has 17C caryatids). 16C **Église Notre-Dame-du-Marthuret**★, houses the splendid late 14C sculpture – **Virgin with a bird**★★★, a masterpiece of harmonious proportion with a graceful Madonna and infant Jesus holding a bird in his hand.

ADDITIONAL SIGHTS

Ste-Chapelle★ (r. Jean de Berry) – remarkable 15C stained glass windows.
Musée régional d'Auvergne★ (10 bis r. Delille)– folk art and local customs.
Musée Francisque Mandet★ (14 r. de l'Hôtel de Ville) – 17–18C French and Flemish painting and decorative arts.

EXCURSIONS

Église de Mozac★

2km/1.2mi W.

This ancient abbey was founded towards the end of the 7C by St Calminus, becoming subordinated to Cluny in 1095. Until its collapse in 1460, the abbey church was one of the finest in Auvergne. Of the building of 1095, all that remains are arches and pillars and the north aisle, together with the 47 capitals (**chapiteaux**★★) which are the oldest and perhaps the most beautiful in the whole of the province. They are products of a workshop which was active from the end of the 11C until the middle of the 12C and which enjoyed considerable influence. Those depicting Jonah (1st bay of the nave), the Apocalypse (on the ground in the choir), and the Centaur (third pillar on the left), are justly famous, but it is the capital showing the Resurrection which is truly outstanding (on the ground at the end of the nave).

The Shrine of St Calminus (**châsse de Saint Calmin**★★) in champlevé enamel is an exquisite example of Limoges work with chased and gilded inlay figures.

Église de Marsat

3km/1.8mi SW.

The church here has one of Auvergne's great works of medieval art, a 12C **Black Virgin**★★ (in the choir of the north chapel). Few will be untouched by this depiction of Mary as a simple countrywoman, holding out the Child in a maternal gesture of great dignity.

Château de Tournoël★★

8km/5mi W.

This is one of the province's most celebrated castles. It dominates the town of Volvic, famous for its lava quarry and, of course, its spring water (on sale worldwide), whose exceptional purity is due to the filtering effect of one of the lava flows from the Puy-de-la-Nugère. Picturesquely perched on a crag, the castle dates from the turn of the 13C and was first owned by Guy II the Count of Auvergne. It has two keeps, one round, one square, joined together by ancillary buildings now in ruins. Mullioned windows of Renaissance date look down onto the courtyard, some of them blocked up to avoid the payment of window tax.

Gour de Tazenat★

22km/14mi NE.

This lovely upland lake (32ha/79 acres, 60m/196.8ft deep) in its wooded setting marks the northern limit of the Auvergne volcanoes, one of whose craters it now fills.

St-Flour★★

Occupying a spectacular site★★, St-Flour comprises two little towns; one perched on a huge rock; the other a modern, busy place at its foot. Although all the interest is in the Upper Town, it is more convenient to park, eat and stay in the Lower Town.

> ▶ **Population:** 6 625
> ⊙ **Michelin Map:** 330 G 4
> ▤ **Info:** 17 bis, pl. Armes.
>   ✆04 71 60 22 50 .
>   www.saint-flour.com.
> ◐ **Location:** St-Flour is
>   63km/39mi SE of Riom
>   along the A 72/E 70.

VISIT

At the eastern end of the Upper Town with its old lava-built houses stands the 15C **cathedral**★. From the Terrasse des Roches nearby there are extensive **views** over the rich grasslands of the Planèze de St-Flour, an inclined plateau.

EXCURSIONS

Viaduc de Garabit★★

12km/7.4mi S.

This daring steel structure carries the Clermont-Ferrand-Millau railway across the Truyère valley with its many hydro-electric works built in the **gorges**★★ gouged in the granite plateaux. Its central arch is 116m/381ft across. The viaduct was built from 1882–1884 by Gustave Eiffel.

Site du Château d'Alleuze★★

26km/16mi W from Garabit via the Mallet viewpoint and the Grandval Dam.

The square keep and round towers of this most romantic of ruins loom menacingly over the lake held back by the Grandval Dam.

Viaduc de Garabit

J. Damase/MICHELIN

Église de
St-Nectaire★★

This little Romanesque church enjoys a spectacular location on the eastern slopes of the Dore mountains (Monts Dore). Built around 1160 as a dependency of the great Chaise-Dieu monastery, it suffered much damage during the French Revolution, and underwent major restoration in 1875.

- **Michelin Map:** 326 E 9
- **Info:** Les Grands Thermes, St-Nectaire.
  04 73 88 50 86.
  www.ville-saint-nectaire.fr.
- **Location:** The church dominates St-Nectaire-le-Haut. The lower village, St-Nectaire-le-Bas, is a thermal spa, spreading along a green valley.

VISIT

Pl. de l'Eglise. Open daily Apr–Oct 9am–7pm; Nov–Mar 10am–12.30pm, 2–6pm. Guided tours available on request. 04 73 88 50 67.

The church has a number of notable features, including a massive **narthex**. The 103 **capitals**★★ (most are 12C) are justly famous. The treasury **(trésor**★★ – north transept) houses a statue of Notre-Dame-du-Mont-Cornadore (a Virgin in Majesty of the 12C), **a reliquary bust of St Baudime**★★, a 12C Limoges masterpiece, as well as a reliquary arm of St Nectaire in repoussé silver and a pair of Limoges book-plates of about 1170.

EXCURSION
Château de Murol★★

6km/3.7mi E.

The ruined castle rises from a basalt platform formed by a lava flow from the Tartaret volcano. The site with its polygonal keep was fortified as early as the 12C because of its strategic position between Auvergne and Cantal. At the end of the 14C, it became one of the main seigneurial residences of the province; Guillaume de Murol was responsible for those features which still distinguish the stronghold today (internal courtyard, main tower, and north and east walls) and which serve to remind us both of the medieval obsession with security and of the fiercely guarded independence of the Auvergnat nobility.

A century later, the castle was brought into line with Renaissance tastes. However, the Wars of Religion led to the place being modernised in a military sense, with the building of bastions, watch-towers, as well as an outer wall rising directly from the cliff, all reinforcing the site's natural defensive ability to withstand bombardment or sapping. Now impregnable, the fortress was spared by Richelieu's demolition programme, but fell into ruin in the 19C.

LES MONTS DORE

The Monts Dore consist of three major Volcanoes: the Puy de Sancy (see PUY DE SANCY), the Puy de l'Aiguiller and the Banne d'Ordanche which together with their secondary cones form a region characterised by rugged mountains whose steep, grassy upper slopes provide summer pasture for cattle. Traditionally these animals produced the famous St. Nectaire cheese although nowadays beef cattle are also fattened here before they are taken to the autumn markets.

The Monts Dore are also very popular with those seeking outdoor pursuits and hiking, paragliding, canoeing and sailing can all be found here. During the winter there are also plenty of skiing opportunities.

The mighty River Dordogne rises on the Puy de Sancy, beginning as two separate streams the Dore and the Dogne, and plunges down its slopes before becoming the meandering giant which flows through the verdant countryside of the Corrèze, the Lot and the Aquitaine Region to the west before finally reaching the Gironde estuary north of Bordeaux.

Salers★★

High up among the vast grazing-grounds of the volcanic Cantal uplands, Salers has long been a market centre and staging-post for travellers. The tiny town has a maze of tortuous streets leading to the main square.

VISIT

This square (**Grande-Place★★**) is something of a stage-set, overlooked by the corner-towers and turrets of the grandiose 16C lava-built **houses** of the local notables. The Renaissance **Ancien Bailliage** has typically Auvergnat window-mouldings and angle-towers, while the **Hôtel de la Ronade** has a five-storey Gothic turret.

▶ **Population:** 401
Michelin Map: 330 C 4
Info: Pl. Tyssandier d'Escous. ✆04 71 40 70 68. www.pays-de-salers.com.
Location: In the heart of the Cantal region, the village is 43km/26.7mi north of Aurillac.
Don't Miss: Salers is also a locally produced tasty farmhouse cheese made from unpasteurised cows' milk.

The church (**église★**) has a 12C porch and, inside, a fine 15C polychrome sculpture of the **Entombment★**.

Forêt de Tronçais★★★

This splendid oak forest, "one of the finest in France, indeed in Europe" (JL Reed), lies at the southeastern end of the great plains of central France, bounded by the rivers Allier and Cher.

A BIT OF HISTORY

Today's forest covers a total area of 10 954ha/27 067 acres. It passed into the hands of the French Crown when François I put an end to the independence of the Bourbonnais in 1527.

A steady process of deterioration set in which was reversed by the great Colbert in 1670; anxious to maintain the supply of ship timber for the expanding French navy, he instituted measures for the conservation and renewal of the woodland. However, in 1788 an iron foundry was opened, and to satisfy its demands for charcoal, two-thirds of the area was converted from high forest to a coppice regime.

In 1832 a new policy of conservation was adopted, and since 1928 six blocks of high forest totalling 650ha/1 606 acres

Michelin Map: 326 D 3
Info: Pl. du Champ-de-Foire, Cérilly. ✆04 70 67 55 89. http://paysdetroncais.free.fr.
Location: The forest lies N of Montluçon, and is easily reached on autoroute A71. For information on tourist activities, contact the Association du Pays de Tronçais in Cérilly. ✆04 70 67 55 89.

have been managed on a long rotation of 225 years.

VISIT

The forest consists largely of sessile oak. The finest stands are called the **Hauts-Massifs★★★**; here there are a number of exceptional trees with their own names, some more than 300 years old. East of the Gardien clearing are the Carré, Émile-Guillaumin and Charles-Louis-Philippe oaks, and to the west of the Buffévent clearing in the Richebout block are other venerable trees called Jacques-Chevalier, de la Sentinelle and des Jumeaux.

Forêt de Tronçais

©World Pictures/Photoshot

The Tronçais region straddles the boundary between the north and south of France. To the north is the langue d'oïl, four-wheeled carts, and slate or flat-tiled roofs; to the south, the langue d'oc, two-wheeled carts, and pantiled roofs in the Roman fashion.

ADDITIONAL SIGHTS

Séries de l'Ouest★ – Western forest stands.
Futaie Colbert★ – Colbert Stand
Étangs de St-Bonnet★
Pirota et Saloup★ – ponds

Vichy★★★

Pleasantly sited in the Allier valley, and well endowed with lush parks and luxurious thermal establishments, as well as high-quality entertainment, racing, a casino and good shopping, Vichy is a world-famous spa town. The virtues of the waters drew visitors here in Roman times and again from the 17C onwards.

A BIT OF HISTORY

The Roman spa town here was relatively small. In medieval times, the river crossing was commanded by a castle and later the town grew during the reign of Henri IV.

It began to flourish as a spa resort from the 17C onwards and the renowned letter writer Madame de Sévigné came here during the latter part of the century soon to be followed by the daughters of Louis XV. It was the visits of Napoleon III during the 1860s however, which really placed Vichy in the top rank of spa towns.

More recently, Vichy gave its name to the Nazi collaborationist government of France led by Marshal Pétain, whose regime ruled the country from Vichy

▶ **Population:** 26 528
⚅ **Michelin Map:** 326 H 6
🚇 **Info:** 19 rue du Parc.
   ℰ04 70 98 23 83.
   www2.ville-vichy.fr.
▷ **Location:** The town is 70km/43.mi NE of Clermont-Ferrand.

under close German supervision from 12 July 1940 until 20 August 1944.

Vichy's reputation was somewhat tarnished by this episode but its fortunes were revived by the damming of the Allier in the 1960s which created a town centre lake for watersports.

SIGHT
Le Quartier Thermal (Spa)★

The florid spa architecture of the second half of the 19C is well represented by a number of constructions such as the Grand Casino of 1865, the Napoleon Gallery (Galerie Napoléon) of 1857, the covered galleries bordering the park (Parc des Sources), which formed part of the 1889 Paris Universal Exhibition before being re-erected here, and the Great Baths (Grand établissement thermal) of 1900.

Vienne★★

Vienne is favoured with a sunny site★ on the east bank of the Rhône. The town overlooks the bend formed by the river as it makes its way through the crystalline rocks marking the last outcrops of the Massif Central.

▶ **Population:** 29 500
⦿ **Michelin Map:** 333 C 4
▤ **Info:** Cours Brillier.
　 ✆04 74 53 80 30.
　 www.vienne-tourisme.com.
◗ **Location:** Vienne lies 38km/24mi S of Lyon.

A BIT OF HISTORY

Originally the capital of the Allobroges tribe, Vienne came under Roman rule 60 years before Caesar's conquest of Gaul. In the 3C and 4C, the city was the centre of the vast province known as the Viennoise stretching from Lake Geneva to the mouth of the Rhône. Great public buildings were erected at the foot of Mount Pipet, opposite **St-Romain-en-Gal**, the Gallo-Roman city (**cité gallo-romaine★**) with its houses and shops. In the 5C, Vienne became the capital of the Burgundians, who ruled over the east bank of the Rhône before being chased away by the Franks in 532. Ruled subsequently by its archbishops, the city became the object of the rivalry between the Kingdom of France and the Holy Roman Empire, until its final incorporation into France at the same time as the Dauphiné, in 1349.

SIGHTS

Temple d'Auguste et de Livie★★

pl. Charles de Gaulle.

This Classical temple was first built in the reign of Emperor Augustus shortly before the beginning of the Christian era; it seems likely that it was then reconstructed, somewhat carelessly, under Claudius, about 50 years later. At the time it would have dominated the Forum to the east. It has been well preserved through successive re-use as a public building of various kinds (church, Jacobin club, tribunal, museum, library), and subsequently through its restoration by Prosper Mérimée in 1850.

The 16 Corinthian columns rise from a podium rather than directly from the ground in the Greek manner. In the pediment are traces of a bronze inscription to the glory of Augustus and Livia.

Cathédrale St-Maurice ★★

pl. Saint Maurice. ◷*Open daily 10am–6pm.* ⦸*No charge.* ✆*04 74 53 80 30 www.cathedraledevienne.com.*
Built from the 12–16C, the cathedral combines Romanesque and Gothic elements. Only 35 years after its completion, the cathedral suffered much mutilation during the Wars of Religion. It underwent extensive restoration in the 19C (vaults, arching of the portals, rose window). But much remains to be admired, including the fine Renaissance window in the south aisle *(to the right of the choir)*, the 13C low-relief between the sixth and seventh chapels in the north aisle depicting Herod and the Magi, and the rare 11C Bishop's Throne *(in the apse behind the high altar)*.

ADDITIONAL SIGHTS

Théâtre romain★ *(r. du Cirque)*
Église et Cloître St-André-le-Bas★ *(pl.du Jeu de Paume)*
Musée Lapidaire St-Pierre★ *(pl. Saint-Pierre)*

Temple d'Auguste et de Livie
J. Damase/MICHELIN

BRITTANY

Populated by Celts since its birth, Brittany retains many affinities with the other Celtic lands fringing the Atlantic. Its identity, quite distinct from that of the rest of France, is expressed in its language (Breton akin to Welsh), traditions and landscape. The province's long and mysterious past makes itself felt in the abundance of prehistoric remains, menhirs, dolmens and megaliths. Granite distinguishes Breton building whether in church or castle, harbour wall or humble house, and is used to great effect.

Highlights

1. Megaliths at **Carnac** (p197)
2. Walled town of Concarneau: **Ville Close** (p198)
3. Breton monumental parish close: **St-Thégonnec** (p212)
4. Spectacular coastal landscape: **Pointe-du-Raz** (p209)
5. Small inland sea near Vannes: **Golfe de Morbihan** (p216)

Geography – Brittany has an extraordinarily indented coastline, called "Armor" (country near the sea) by the Gauls. Its cliffs, rocky headlands and offshore islands are battered by Atlantic breakers, while its narrow drowned valleys, abers, and sandy bays are washed by tides of exceptional range. Inland is the "Argoat" (country of the wood), once thickly afforested, now a mixture of bocage, heath and moor.

History – The Channel coast is punctuated by historic towns, elegant resorts, dramatic corniches and headlands. The original Celts were subjugated by the Romans in the 1C AD, but fresh waves of Celtic settlers arrived here from Cornwall following the collapse of the Roman Empire and the country remained anarchic until 799, when Charlemagne took control.

The Duchy of Brittany was soon established and independence achieved in AD 845. Although later Dukes paid homage to the French monarch, this autonomy was retained till the late 15C following the marriage of Anne of Brittany to the King. The Bretons were enthusiastic supporters of the Revolution and helped put down those Royalists who revolted against the new state.

Economy – Much of France's fishing fleet operates from Brittany. Other industries include food processing and car manufacturing. Tourism is vitally important to the region and many summer visitors are attracted to the resorts on the Atlantic and Channel coasts.

Beach at la Baule

S. Sauvignier/MICHELIN

La Baule★★★

Perhaps the ultimate in modern seafront development on the French Atlantic, the resort of La Baule is today one of Europe's major resorts and considered to have one of its most beautiful beaches. It was only in 1879 that construction of the town began, after 400ha/1 000 acres of maritime pines had been planted to halt the steady encroachment of sand dunes. The older houses retain much of their original charm and stand mostly hidden behind the more recent constructions along the shaded and well laid-out avenues. Water sports, tennis, a casino and golf make this one of the most popular seaside resorts on the Atlantic Coast.

▶ **Population:** 15 830.
◔ **Michelin Map:** 316 B 4
▤ **Info:** 8 pl. de la Victoire.
  ℰ02 40 24 34 44.
  www.labaule.fr.
◗ **Location:** The resort stands on the N bank of the wide Loire estuary. It is reached on autoroute A11 and then by expressway from Nantes.

VISIT

Miles of beautiful and well-frequented sandy beaches are protected by the headlands, Pointes de **Penchâteau** and **Chémoulin** to the northwest and southeast respectively. The elegant promenade lined with modern buildings stretches for about 7km/4.3mi. Numerous hotels and apartment complexes, some comfortable, others luxurious in the proximity of delight-

ful resorts such as **Le Croisica, Le Pouliguen★** and **Pornichet★**, with their pleasure-boat harbours, make La Baule, together with its neighbour **La Baule-les-Pins★★**, the ideal spot for discovering the splendour of the "Côte d'Amour" and the **Guérande Peninsula**.

La Côte Sauvage

This Wild Coast is on the mainland (the other is on Belle-Île, ◔*see BELLE-ÎLE*) and stretches from Pointe du Croisic in the west to Pointe de Penchâteau in the east. Skirted by a road and footpaths, the coastline alternates rocky parts with great sandy bays and numerous caves accessible only at low tide such as the cave of the Korrigans, the little elves of Breton legends.

Belle-Île★★★

The name alone is enticing, but the island's beauty surpasses expectations. This, the largest of the Breton islands, is a schist plateau measuring about 84sq km/32sq mi; 17 km/10.5mi long and 5–10km/3–6mi wide. Valleys cut deep into the high rocks, forming beaches and harbours. Farmland alternates with wild heath, and whitewashed houses stand in lush fields.

A BIT OF HISTORY

Belle-Île's interest lies as much in its history as in its wonderful coastline. It is a story of constant attack and defence. In the Middle Ages the island belonged to the Counts of Cornouaille and was often raided by pirates (French as well as Dutch and English) because of its wealth in grain.

From 16C the island was constantly in danger of an English attack, and the fortifications were substantially increased. The island's proximity to the French coast gave it great strategic importance. In 1696, the English took the nearby islands of Houat and Hoëdic and at one point landed on Belle-Île itself. Over the next decades, the English fleet was a ceaseless threat, and eventually took Belle-Île's citadel in the Seven Years' War. By the 1763 Treaty of Paris England gave back Belle-Île.

> ▶ **Population:** 4 489
> ⏱ **Michelin Map:**
>   308 L-M 10-11
> ℹ **Info:** Quai Bonnelle, Le Palais. ℘02 97 31 81 93. www.belle-ile.com.
> ◖ **Location:** Regular car ferries linking Quibéron (Brittany) and Le Palais in 45min are operated by SMN (℘08 20 05 60 00. www.smn-navigation.fr). Passenger-only speed-boats operate in summer between Le Palais and Lorient (Brittany) in 60min.

SIGHTS
Le Palais

This is the island's capital, known to locals simply as 'Palais'. Most of the island's amenities are to be found here. The natural harbour is dominated by the imposing citadel and fortifications, known as **Citadelle Vauban**★ (⏱ open Apr–Oct daily 9.30am–6pm; Jul and Aug daily 9am–7pm; Nov-Mar: daily 9.30am–noon, 2-5pm. ⬅6.10€ (child 3.05€); no charge 3rd weekend in Sept. ℘02 97 31 84 17). The proximity of Belle-Île to the ports of the south coast of Brittany and the mouth of the Loire gave it great importance in the fight for the control of the high seas conducted by England

Aiguilles de Port-Coton

G. Targat/MICHELIN

and France. In 1658 the island came into the hands of chancellor Fouquet. He consolidated the defences and installed 200 new batteries.

From 1682, the great military engineer Vauban adapted the citadel following improvements in the technology of war, converting an old chapel into a powder-magazine with a projecting roof to fend off broadsides, rebuilding the old arsenal as well as laying out an officers' walk with a gallery giving fine seaviews.

Côte Sauvage★★★

The Côte Sauvage, literally "wild coast", runs from the Pointe des Poulains to the Pointe de Talud. Battered by the Atlantic waves, the schists of which the island's plateau is composed, have been formed into spectacular coastal scenes.

Port-Donnant★★ has a splendid sandy beach between high cliffs but is known for its great rollers and perilous currents.

The **Aiguilles de Port-Coton**★★ are pyramids hollowed out into caverns and grottoes. The different colours of the rock have been exposed by the action of the sea.

ADDITIONAL SIGHTS

Sauzon★
Pointe des Poulains★★
Port-Goulphar★

Brest★

A very ancient port built on a magificent natural roadstead that, being nowhere less than 10m/33ft deep, is almost an inland sea, Brest remains wedded to its maritime tradition.

A BIT OF HISTORY

Although used as a port by Gauls and then Romans, the importance of Brest was firmly established from 13C onwards. A French garrison moved in and has been there ever since.

At the beginning of the 17C, Richelieu's wish was to have French naval forces which could be permanently ready for action. He founded the naval dockyard and its first warship was launched in 1634. The Rue de Siam, running in a straight line between the arsenal and

> ▶ **Population:** 149 630
> ⊙ **Michelin Map:** 308 A 4, E 4-5
> ▯ **Info:** Place de la Liberté. ✆ 02 98 44 24 96. www.brest-metropole-tourisme.fr.
> ◗ **Location:** The town is 71km/42mi N of Quimper.
> ♟ **Kids:** One of the town's principal attractions is the giant Océanopolis centre.

Place de la Liberté, formed the main axis of the ancient town and its fame was spread world-wide by the sailors who frequented it. The town had to be completely rebuilt after World War II, in which it suffered four years of air attack and a 43-day siege.

Ships of the French fleet and Brest castle

R. Mattés/MICHELIN

King penguins in Océanopolis
Océanopolis

SIGHTS
👥👤 Océanopolis★★★
Port de Plaisance du Moulin Blanc.
♿🕐*Hours vary for each exhibition; call ahead.* 👓*16.20€ (child 11€).* ☎*02 98 34 40 40. www.oceanopolis.com.*
In this ultra-modern building, shaped like a giant crab, visitors discover the marine life of Brittany's coastal waters in the saltwater aquariums (downstairs), and the many sea birds of the coast in their nesting places on the cliff face (entrance level).

Christ washing the disciples' feet, the Calvary, Plougastel-Daoulas
MICHELIN

Cours Dajot★
This fine promenade was laid out in 1769 on the old ramparts. It gives splendid **views**★★ of the activity of the port and of the great roadstead of 150sq km/ 58sq mi.

Musée des Beaux Arts★
24 r. Traverse. 🕐*Open Tue–Sat 10am– noon, 2–6pm, Sun 2–6pm.* 🕐*Closed public holidays (except 14 Jul and 15 Aug).* 👓*4€.* ☎*02 98 00 87 96.*
The collections illustrate the advances made by the painters of the Pont-Aven School, for example *Yellow Sea (Mer jaune)* by Lacombe, as well as a curious study of the town of Ys (👆*see QUIMPER*), Manet's *Parrots*, and *Bouquet of Roses* by Suzanne Valadon.

EXCURSIONS
Calvaire de Plougastel-Daoulas★★
11km/6.8mi E, S of the church.
The calvary was built from 1602 to 1604 by the Priget brothers to mark an outbreak of plague four years earlier. Its 180 figures are sculpted in the round; a certain stiffness of posture is set off by the size of the heads and the vigorous expressions.
The 28 scenes illustrate the life of Christ (the Nativity, the Washing of Feet) and above all the Passion (Arrest and Scourging) and the Resurrection.

The Abers★
The term *aber* is of Celtic origin and is found in Scottish and Welsh place names such as Aberdeen, Aberdour, Aberystwyth, Abersoch.
In Brittany *abers* are picturesque, fairly shallow estuaries on the low, rocky northwest coast of Finistère. Harbours are suitable only for yachts and other sailing craft.
The entrance to the **aber Wrac'h** is guarded by the small seaside resort of the same name near which there are fine views of the lighthouse on Vierge Island, the tallest in France (82.5m/270ft). A **scenic road**★ runs along the rugged coastline through a number of charming resorts.

Carnac★

In the bleak Breton countryside just north of the little town of Carnac are some of the world's most remarkable megalithic remains.

VISIT
Megaliths★★
The area containing the megaliths is divided up by roads and a number of stones have been lost, but altogether it comprises 2 792 menhirs, arranged in 10 or 11 lines – *alignements* – including the **alignements du Ménec**★★ with 1 169 menhirs, the **alignements de Kermario**★ with 1 029 and the **alignements de Kerlescan**★ with 594. There are also dolmens (burial places), cromlechs (semicircles) and tumuli (mounds). Megalithic culture flourished from about 4 670 to 2 000 BC. It was the creation of a settled population growing crops and with domestic animals (in contrast to the hunter-gatherers of Paleolithic times), who produced polished objects, pottery and basket-work and who traded in flints. The inhabitants of Carnac had commercial relations with people from Belgium and from Grand-Pressigny in the north of Poitou.

Markings on the megaliths resemble abstract art in contrast to the figurative cave-art of the Upper Paleolithic, and the orientation of the lines in a west-north-east direction adds to their enigmatic character. Various theories have been advanced about their likely religious or astronomical significance.

The tumuli and dolmens which appeared 40 centuries before the birth of Christ are collective burial-places, and the mounds covering them, a thousand years older

▷ **Population:** 4 450
⟳ **Michelin Map:** 308 M 9
🏠 **Info:** 74 av.. des Druides. ℘02 97 52 13 52. www.ot-carnac.fr.
◉ **Location:** Although its fame is considerable, the site is surprisingly small. It is located at the base of the Quiberon Peninsula.

than the pyramids, may be "Mankind's most ancient built monuments."

Four thousand centuries previously, the Carnac area was inhabited by prehistoric people, and, during the Lower Paleolithic, by nomads, contemporaries of the nomads of Tautavel, Terra Amata and the Ardèche Valley. In 5C BC, the Celts moved here. In Gallo-Roman times there was the great villa of the Bosseno.

Later, the area was repopulated by immigrants from Britain and by monks from Ireland.

ADDITIONAL SIGHTS
Église St-Cornély★ – fine 17C Renaissance church In the centre of the village with good 17–19C decoration.
Musée de Préhistoire J.-Miln-Z.-Le-Rouzic★★ *(10 pl. de la Chapelle;* ♿🕑*open Apr–Jun and Sept Wed–Mon 10am–12.30pm, 2–6pm; Jul–Aug daily 10am–6pm; Oct–Mar Wed–Mon 10am–12.30pm, 2–5pm;* 🕑*closed 1 Jan, 5–31Jan, 1 May, 25 Dec;* 🎫*5€ (child 2.50€);* ℘*02 97 52 22 04; www.museedecarnac.com).*
Tumulus St-Michel★ *(*🕑*open daily 9am–7pm;* 🎫*no charge).*

Alignements du Ménec

J. Malburet/MICHELIN

Concarneau★

The growth of Concarneau is based on its importance as a fishing port. Trawlers and cargo-boats moor in the inner harbour up the estuary of the Moros, while the outer harbour is lively with pleasure craft. There are many vegetable and fish canneries and plenty of bustle as the catch is sold in the early morning at the "criée" (fish auction market).

▶ **Population:** 19 453
◔ **Michelin Map:** 308 H 7
🛈 **Info:** Quai d'Aiguillon, ℰ02 98 97 0144. www.tourismeconcarneau.fr.
⊙ **Location:** The town is S of Quimper, in western Brittany.
⊘ **Don't Miss:** La Criée, the fish auction.

SIGHT
Ville close (Walled Town)★★

On its islet in the bay, this was one of the strongholds of the ancient county of Cornouaille; as at Dinan and Guérande, its walls proclaim the determination of the citizens to maintain their independence, particularly in times of trouble (as during the War of the Breton Succession in 1341).

The English nevertheless seized the place in 1342, and were thrown out only by Du Guesclin in 1373.

The granite ramparts (**remparts**) (ⓞ open mid-Jun–mid-Sept daily 10am–8pm; rest of year until 5pm; ♿access to the ramparts is prohibited if weather conditions are not favourable and during the Filets bleus festival (15–19 Aug); ⊚0.80€ high season, no charge low season) with their typically Breton corbelled machicolations, were started at the beginning of the 14C and completed at the end of the 15C. They were improved by Vauban at the end of the 17C at a time when England once more posed a threat to these coasts; he lowered the height of the towers and built gun emplacements into them.

The interior of the town gate is of the same period. It has impressive crenellations, regular stonework and gables. A Fishing Museum, **Musée de la Pêche**★ (♿ⓞ open Jul–Aug daily 9.30am–8pm; Apr–Sept daily 10am–6pm; Feb–Oct and Christmas holidays 10am–noon, 2–6pm; ⓞ closed last 3 weeks of Jan; ⊚6€, child 4€; ℰ02 98 97 10 20), is nearby.

At the heart of the walled town, Rue Vauban and Rue St-Guénolé are a demonstration of how medieval marketplaces arose more or less spontaneously through a simple widening of the street.

Concarneau

H. Le Gac/MICHELIN

Dinan★★

Dinan is a gem of a town, surrounded by ramparts and guarded by a castle.

A BIT OF HISTORY

The great hero of the town is **Bertrand du Guesclin** (c. 1315–80), redoubtable warrior. Jean le Bon (John the Good) had been taken prisoner by the English at the Battle of Poitiers in 1356.

During the four years of captivity he spent in England he became aware of the extent to which feudal rights imposed limitations on royal power, and conceived the idea of a body of knights attached to the monarch. In pursuit of this aim, he took Du Guesclin into his service shortly after his release and return to France.

This middle-aged knight had until then experienced little but rebuffs and difficulties due to his modest ancestry, lack of means and exceptionally ugly appearance. John's successor, Charles V, kept him on, doubtless in view of his great popularity and reckless bravery and his implacable hatred of the English (which at one point in his youth had led him to support Charles of Blois).

In 1366, after ridding France of the "Free Companies" (marauding bands of mercenaries), he was made High Constable of France. He freed Périgord from English rule in 1370 and Normandy in 1378. In 1379 he handed his sword to the king rather than use it against his rebellious Breton compatriots. In 1380 he died beneath the walls of Châteauneuf-de-Randon in the south.

SIGHTS

La Vieille Ville

The houses of the old town cluster together behind the 2.5km/1.5mi long circuit of walls, built by the Dukes of Brittany in the 14C in order to protect to defend their domain against the Normans, the English, and, after the accession of Louis XI, the French.

> ▶ **Population:** 10 907
> 🚗 **Michelin Map:** 309 J 4
> ℹ **Info:** 9 r. du Château, 𝄞 02 96 87 69 76. www.dinan-tourisme.com.
> ▶ **Location:** Dinan is at the top of the Rance estuary, about 30km/18.6mi S of St-Malo.

Château★

Place du Guesclin. 🕐*Open Jun–Sept daily 10am–6.30pm; Oct–Dec and Feb–May daily 1.30–5.30pm.* ⊙*4€.* 𝄞*02 96 87 58 72.*

Begun by Duke John IV about the middle of the 14C. Its 15C towers project outwards in order to facilitate enfilading fire. The exceptionally fine machicolations of Duchess Anne's Keep (Donjon de la Duchesse Anne) are of interest.

Basilique St-Sauveur

Place St.Sauveur.

The west front is much influenced by the Poitiers version of the Romanesque. In the north aisle is the Evangelists' Window, a fine example of late-15C Breton glass, famous for its yellows. In the north transept is the cenotaph containing the heart of Du Guesclin.

Vieilles maisons

Duke John was happy to let Dinan run its own affairs, and the town's prosperity is reflected in the rebuilding of many old timber houses in stone. A most picturesque townscape results from the many buildings with overhanging upper storeys, angle-posts, half-timbering, arcades and granite side-walls.

The most interesting houses are on Rue de l'Apport (the 15C Mère Pourcel House), **Place des Merciers★** (triangular gables and porches), **Rue du Jerzual★** which links the main part of the town with the port (15C and 16C shops where craftsmen have worked for six centuries) and on Place Du Guesclin (17C and 18C town houses).

Dinard★★★

On the magnificent estuary of the River Rance opposite St Malo, Dinard, once a small fishing village, is an elegant resort with sheltered sandy beaches and luxuriant Mediterranean vegetation flourishing in the mild climate.

A BIT OF HISTORY

The resort came into being when a wealthy American called Coppinger built himself a château here in 1850. He was followed two years later by a British family, who in turn attracted many of their fellow-countrymen.

By the end of the 19C its reputation rivalled that of Brighton; sumptuous villas and luxurious hotels abounded, frequented by an international smart set. Nowadays many of Dinard's grand hotels are no more than a memory, but plenty of well-tended villas remain to tell of past glories.

▶ **Population:** 9 918
Michelin Map: 309 J 3
Info: 2 bd. Féart.
℘02 99 46 94 12.
www.ot-dinard.com.
▷ **Location:** This smart resort is on the left bank of the Rance across from St Malo.

VISIT
Seashore

Promenades lead from **Plage de l'Écluse**★ (or **Grande Plage**), a fine sandy beach bordered by hotels, the casino and convention centre, to the Plage du Prieuré, giving fine views over the coast and the Rance estuary. From the **Pointe du Moulinet**★★, the view extends as far as Cap Fréhel to the west and the ramparts of St-Malo to the east. In summer, the **Promenade du Clair de Lune**★ with its pretty parterres and Mediterranean plants forms an attractive setting for evening concerts.

Fougères★★

In the 19C Fougères was the most industrialised town in Brittany, having abandoned cloth-making in favour of shoe production.
The area formed part of the frontier region taken from the Franks in AD 850 by **Nominoé** (*see VANNES*).

VISIT
Château de Fougères★★

pl. Pierre Symon. ◷*Open mid-Jun–mid-Sept: 9am–7pm, rest of year 10am–noon, 2–5pm.* ◷*Closed Jan and 25 Dec.* ⊙*4.10€.* ℘*02 99 99 79 59.*
It is set on an easily defended rocky promontory protected by a meander.

Guided Tours

Guided tours of the town: Information at the tourist office.

▶ **Population:** 21 779
Michelin Map: 309 O 4
Info: 2 r. Nationale.
℘02 99 94 12 20.
www.ot-fougeres.fr.
▷ **Location:** The town is on the eastern edge of Brittany.
◷ **Timing:** Allow at least an hour to visit the castle, and another hour to enjoy the church and gardens.

The first fortifications date from the 10C. Baron Raoul II began to rebuild in stone in 1173. In the 13C the castle's mighty towers served to protect Brittany from Capetian France.
After its important role in the War of the Breton Succession (*see JOSSELIN*) in the 14C, the castle was partly demolished by Richelieu.

Cap **Fréhel**★★★

This is one of the grandest capes on the Breton coast. Its red, black and grey cliffs rise vertically from the sea and are fringed with reefs on which the swell breaks heavily.

Cap Fréhel - an ornithological reserve

Y.Tierny/MICHELIN

VISIT

This cape is one of the most magnificent sights the Breton coast has to offer.

- **Michelin Map:** 309 I 2
- **Info:** 7 r. St-Gouéno, St-Brieuc. ℘08 25 00 22 22.
- **Location:** It is between St-Brieuc and Dinard, on the Emerald Coast.
- **Parking:** There is vehicle access Jun–Sept 8am–8pm (⊜2€).
- **Timing:** Take a walk to the lighthouse, just 30min there and back.

The action of the waves has worn away the softer rocks around, and the great cliff of red sandstone rises 70m/230ft above the reefs.

Th**e panorama**★★★ from the clifftop is superb, taking in the Channel Islands and the Cotentin Peninsula.

Guérande★

Standing on a plateau overlooking the salt marshes and secure behind its circle of ramparts, Guérande has kept its appearance as a proud medieval town.

SIGHTS
Remparts★

Begun in 1343, the ramparts were completed in 1476 and remain unbreached. They were flanked by six towers and pierced by four fortified gateways. In the 18C the Governor of Brittany had the moats filled in, although the north and west sections still contain water.

Collégiale St-Aubin★
pl. St.Aubin

Built between the 12C and the 16C, the church has a striking west front in granite. Embedded in a buttress on the right is an **outdoor pulpit**. Inside, the **capitals** are decorated with grotesque

- **Population:** 13 603
- **Michelin Map:** 316 B 4
- **Info:** 1 pl. du Marché au Bois. ℘02 40 24 96 71. www.ot-guerande.fr
- **Location:** The town lies behind beach resort La Baule.
- **Timing:** Explore this interesting district of salt-marshes, beaches and busy fishing ports.

figures and foliage. The chancel is lit by a magnificent **stained-glass window**.

Presqu'île de Guérande★

In the Roman era, a great sea gulf stretched between the rocky island, Ile de Batz, and the Guérande ridge.
Just a channel remains open opposite Le Croisic through which the sea flows at high tide.

Château de
Josselin★★

This famous stronghold of the Rohan family, who have owned the castle for more than 500 years and still live here in the private apartments, has stood guard over the crossing of the Oust for 900 years and seen many battles.

- **Michelin Map:** 308 P 7
- **Info:** Place de la Congregation. ℘02 97 22 36 43. www.pays-de-josselin-tourisme.com.
- **Location:** The chateau is in the heart of the inland village of Josselin, W of Rennes.

A BIT OF HISTORY

The **War of the Breton Succession**, which started in 1341, set rival heirs to the Duchy against each other, Jeanne de Penthièvre, granddaughter of Jean II of Brittany, and Jean de Montfort, Jean III's half-brother. The struggle, long and confused, overlapped with the early stages of the Hundred Years' War. Jeanne was married to Charles de Blois and her claim, supported by the Valois rulers of France, was based on established Breton custom. The ousted De Montfort allied himself to the Plantagenets who had won the great naval battle of Sluys the previous year. He was able to persuade them to set a terrible example by laying waste the area around Tréguier; this action took place during the period which also saw the triumph of English arms at Crécy and Calais.

The garrison at Josselin faced the defenders of Ploërmel Castle, 12km7.4mi to the east; between them they ravaged the countryside without any decisive outcome. A solution to the impasse was sought by arranging a contest between 30 knights from each camp. The **Battle of the Thirty** took place in 1351, halfway between the two towns. Ploërmel's champions consisted of four Bretons, six Germans and 20 Englishmen. Josselin emerged victorious, but even this dramatic settling of accounts did not prove decisive.

The war was finally brought to an end in 1364 by the death of Charles de Blois at the Battle of Auray. In 1365 de Montfort was acknowledged as ruler of the Duchy, albeit subject to the Capetian kings of France.

VISIT

Guided tours (45min) daily mid-Jul–Aug 11am–6pm; Sept 2–6pm; Oct, weekends and school hols 2–5pm; 4 Apr–13 Jul 2–6pm. ≈6.80€. ℘02 97 22 36 45.

The medieval robustness of the massive walls overlooking the river contrasts with the refinement of the upper parts belonging to the reconstruction of the 15–16C. The marriage of Anne of Brittany to Charles VIII of France in 1491 had led to a lessening of tension between the Duchy and the French kingdom, and John of Laval was able to rebuild the old castle in accordance with the new ideas of Renaissance architecture. What had been a fortress now became a palace. The transformation is particularly evident in the courtyard, where the **façade★★** featuring an ornate roof **balustrade** has a splendid variety of motifs: pinnacles, tracery and mouldings. Inside there is an innovative staircase with straight ramps.

In the 17C the keep and five of the towers were demolished on the orders of Richelieu who announced with cruel irony "I have just thrown a fine ball among your skittles, Monsieur". A park was laid out in 1760, and in 1882 the castle was restored.

ADDITIONAL SIGHTS

Basilique Notre-Dame-du-Roncier★ (pl. A. de Rohan)
Mausoleum★ of Olivier de Clisson (located in the Basilique)

Kernascléden★★

The small village has a beautiful church with remarkable 15C frescoes.

SIGHT
Church★★

Built in granite between 1430 and 1455, the church typifies the Breton version of Flamboyant Gothic. It has two **porches** on the south side (one of them with statues of the **Apostles**★). Inside there is a fine window at the east end. The

▶ **Population:** 355
🕐 **Michelin Map:** 308 L 6
▷ **Location:** The village is about 34km/21mi N of the coastal town of Lorient.

frescoes★★ are striking: the choir vault depicts 24 scenes from the Life of the Virgin; in the north transept, note particularly the folds of the clothes of the celestial choir; in the south transept is the Passion, and a Dance of Death.

Locronan★★

The little town once flourished on the manufacture of sailcloth. Traces of its golden age are to be found in its fine main square.

SIGHTS
Place de l'Église★★

This little square with its well is like many others in Brittany, having grown up over the centuries in a haphazard way without any overall plan, but with a unity due to the consistent use of granite. Because of the strength of the westerly winds, the walls on that side of the weavers' houses are windowless. In the 17C many of the houses were given an additional storey in stone. The lofts are lit by means of dormer windows let into the roof.

Église St-Ronan et Chapelle du Penity★★

This is a 15C pilgrimage church with stone vaults. The plain east end, normal in Brittany at the time, lets more light into what would otherwise be a somewhat dark interior.

Behind the altar, the main window has fine 15C stained glass depicting scenes from the Passion. The pulpit (**chaire**★) of 1707 has panels illustrating the life of St Ronan.

The chapel (Chapelle du Penity) in the south aisle has a 16C altarpiece with a low relief (**bas-relief**★) of the Last

▶ **Population:** 799.
🕐 **Michelin Map:** 308 F 6
🛈 **Info:** Place de la Mairie. 📞02 98 91 70 14.
▷ **Location:** Locronan is sited at the foot of its granite hill at the meeting point of the roads from Quimper to Châteaulin and from Crozon to Douarnenez.
🅿 **Parking:** Cars must be left outside the village.
✪ **Don't Miss:** The beautiful main square is a must.

Supper, a St Michael in armour (on the pillar) weighing souls, and an early 15C effigy of St Ronan, carved from the dark kersanton stone.

Buildings on the main square were once the homes of makers of sailcloth

G.Targat/MICHELIN

Nantes★★★

Nantes is Brittany's largest city, sited at the point at which the mighty Loire becomes tidal. The presence of islets (inhabited from the 17C on) in the river had long facilitated the building of bridges, making Nantes the focus of trade and movement between Lower Brittany and Poitou.

A BIT OF HISTORY

In the 9C, the city was disputed between Nominoé, the first Duke of Brittany, and the Franks to the east. In 939, it was chosen as his capital by King Alain Barbe-Torte (Crookbeard). By the 14C, Nantes had become a trading port, with a fleet of 1 300 ships, but it was only in the 15C, under Duke François II, that the city reached its full importance. It was in its cathedral, on 13 April 1598, that Henri IV signed the **Edict of Nantes**, establishing equality between Catholics and Protestants, and granting privileges to the latter regarding the right to maintain fortified strongholds. Louis XIV revoked the Edict in 1685, provoking the Huguenot exodus to England, Holland and Germany and depriving France of some of its most valuable craftsmen.

In the early 18C Nantes grew rich on the 'triangle' of trade importing sugar cane from the West Indies, exporting manufactured goods to Africa, and shipping of slaves from Africa to the West Indies. Nantes became France's premier port until the loss of French territories abroad and the abolition of slavery. The

> ▶ **Population:** 544 932
> ⟳ **Michelin Map:** 316 G 4
> 🛈 **Info:** 3 cours Olivier de Clisson. ℰ08 92 46 40 44. www.nantes-tourisme.com.
> ▷ **Location:** Three tramway lines and over 60 bus routes make for easy movement throughout the city.
> 🕓 **Timing:** You'll need at least 3hr to visit the château and the surrounding sights.
> 🅿 **Parking:** It is not easy to move around Nantes by car. Find parking in one of several lots surrounding the downtown area and move around the city by tramway, bus or foot.
> ⊚ **Don't Miss:** Find a bar or restaurant in the Ste-Croix neighborhood for an authentic Nantes evening.
> ▲▲ **Kids:** Planète Sauvage at Port-St-Père.

substitution of sugar-beet for cane sugar and the increasing size of ships further led to the old port's decline. However, in the 19C and 20C the construction of larger downstream harbour facilities has contributed towards Nantes' continuing prosperity.

SIGHTS

Château des Ducs de Bretagne★★

4 pl. Marc Elder ⟳*Open daily.* **Castle courtyard and ramparts** *Jul–Aug daily 9am–8pm (Sat 11pm); Sept–Jun 10am–7pm.* **Museum** *Jul–Aug daily 9.30am–7 pm; Sept–Jun 10am–6pm (no admission after 6pm).* ⟳*Closed Tue (till 7 Jun, Mon from 9 Jun, 1 Nov, 25 Dec, 1 Jan, 1 May.* **Evening events** *mid-May–mid-Sept, the courtyard, ramparts and moat gardens are open until 11 pm – a chance to enjoy the Castle's illuminations. From mid-Jul–mid-Aug, open air concerts on Tue at 8 pm.* ⊜*Entrance is free to the Castle courtyard, ramparts and moat gardens.*

Un bon vin blanc

This expression, well known for being part of a phonetics exercise for Anglo-Saxon learners of French – literally "a fine white wine" – adequately describes the local Muscadet, dry but not too sharp, perfect with seafood. The vineyards are located to the south and east of Nantes, alongside or near the Sèvre and towards Ancenis on the banks of the Loire.

Museum 5€. &0811 46 46 44 (when in France), 00 33 2 51 17 49 48 (from abroad). www.chateau-nantes.fr

"God's teeth! No small beer, these dukes of Brittany!" exclaimed Henri IV on seeing this massive stronghold for the first time.

The castle was much rebuilt and strengthened from 1466 on by Duke François II who saw in it the guarantee of his independence from Louis XI. His daughter Anne of Brittany continued the work.

The great edifice is defended by deep ditches of considerable width, which could be flooded when necessary, and by six stout towers with characteristically Breton pyramidal machicolations. The interior reflects the castle's role as a palace of government and residence, known for its high life of feasts and jousting.

Many of its features are of great interest, like the Golden Crown Tower (**Tour de la Couronne d'or**★★), the main building (Grand Logis) with its massive dormer windows, the Governor's Major Palace (Grand Gouvernement) rebuilt at the end of the 17C, and the well (**puits**★★) with its wrought-iron well-head incorporating ducal crown motifs.

There are two museums in the castle: the **Musée d'Art populaire**★ featuring Breton coiffes, dress and furniture, the Musée des Salorges, a maritime museum *(reorganisation in progress)*. Temporary exhibitions of the latter's collections are held in the Horse-shoe Tower (Tour du Fer-à-Cheval).

Cathédrale St-Pierre et St-Paul
pl. St-Pierre

Although the building of the cathedral extended over a period of 450 years, it has a great unity of style.

The use of a white calcareous tufa in the **interior**★★ enhances the impression of boldness and purity of line resulting from the mouldings of the pillars which soar without a break in their flight up into the keystones of the vaults.

Tomb of François II, Cathédrale St-Pierre-et-St-Paul

A. de Valroger/MICHELIN

In the south transept of the cathedral is the exceptionally fine tomb of François II (**tombeau de François II**★★ – 1502).

ADDITIONAL SIGHTS
Musée des Beaux-Arts★★
(10 r. Georges Clemenceau)
Muséum d'Histoire Naturelle★★ *(le Square Loius-Bureau, pl. de la Monnaie)*
The 19C Town★ *(pl. Royale, pl. Grasilin, passage Pommeraye, etc.)*
Palais Dobrée★ *18 r. Voltaire*
Musée Jules-Verne★ *(3 r. de l'Hermitage)*
Musée archéologique★ *(18 r. Dobrée)*
Jardin des Plantes★ *(pl. Charles Leroux)*
Ancienne Île Feydeau *(r. Kervégan opposite pl. du Commerce)*

EXCURSIONS
👥 **Planète Sauvage**★★
20km/12.4mi SW, on D 758.
www.planetesauvage.com.
This safari park at the heart of the Pays de Retz has over 1 500 animals roaming free in its 140ha/350-acre enclosure. The visit includes two circuits: one to be toured on foot, the other by car.

Île d'**Ouessant**★★

Most of the island's male residents are professional seamen, many in the Navy. The few fishermen trap lobsters. The population lives in scattered hamlets or in the little capital of Lampaul, with its tiny harbour and the mausoleum where the Proella crosses representing those lost at sea are assembled.

GEOGRAPHY

The island is a fragment of the Léon plateau on the mainland, 25km/15.5mi away. Two outcrops of granite running northeast–southwest enclose a sunken area of mica-schist much eroded by the sea to form bays to the southwest (Baie de Lampaul) and to the northeast (Baie du Stiff). Where there is shelter from the wind, camellias, aloes and agaves can grow, but the characteristic vegetation of the island is heather and dwarf gorse. The meagre grasses nourish a small flock of sheep. The cliffs of Ushant and its neighbouring islands house numbers of migrating and nesting birds.

VISIT

For all ferry information, reservations, crossing times and prices, contact **Compagnie Maritime Penn**

Phare du Stiff

©Stefano Ginella/Bigstockphoto.com

▶ **Population:** 1 062
Michelin Map: 308 A 4
Info: Bourg de Lampaul. 02 98 48 85 83.
Location: The island is open to pedestrians and cyclists only, and reached from the coast of Brittany by a 15min flight from Brest or by ferry from Brest (2hr15min), Le Conquet (30min–1hr) or Camaret (1hr15min).
Timing: Almost all ferry crossings are early in the morning.

Ar Bed (*02 98 80 80 80; www. pennarbed.com*). For flight information and bookings, contact **Finistair**: *02 98 84 64 87. www.finistair.fr.*

Côte Sauvage★★★

4hr round-trip on foot starting at Lampaul.

The headlands and inlets of Ushant's rocky northwestern coastline have a rugged and dramatic beauty. The most spectacular locations include Keller Island (Île de Keller), Penn-ar-Ru-Meur and the Cadoran islet (Îlot de Cadoran).

The 300 or so vessels which pass each day are guided by five great lighthouses. The one at **Creac'h**, which houses the **Centre d'Interpretation des Phares et Balises** (*open daily Apr–Sept 10.30am–6.30pm; Nov–Dec 1.30–5pm, Jan–Mar and Oct 1.30–5.30pm, excl. holidays; closed winter holidays, Easter and 1 Nov; 02 98 48 80 70*), a historical museum on lighthouses and beacons, is the most powerful in the world; together wth its counterpart at Land's End in Cornwall it marks the western limit of the English Channel. The light at **Stiff** with its towers built by Vauban in 1695 gives a splendid **view**★★ over the rolling sea. The lighthouses play a vital role: over the last hundred years over 50 wrecks have been recorded.

Pointe de
Penhir★★★

Penhir Point is the most impressive of the four headlands of the Crozon Peninsula, which has some of the finest coastal landscapes in the whole of Brittany.

VISIT

The high cliffs and deep inlets of the peninsula are the result of the faulting and fracturing of this part of the Armorican plateau.

The processes of coastal erosion have worn away the sandstone matrix from which the cliffs were formed, exposing the seams of quartzite. In rough weather, the violence of the waves crashing against the variously coloured rocks makes a magnificent spectacle.

Offshore, the line of isolated rocks known as the Tas de Pois marks where

- **Michelin Map:** 308 D 5
- **Location:** Crozon Peninsula (Presqu'île de Crozon) lies between the Brest roadstead to the N and Douarnenez Bay to the S.

the ancient coastline used to be; there is an unusual view of them from the grassy strip called the Chambre Verte.

OTHER SITES ON THE CROZON PENINSULA

Pointe des Espagnols★★ *(15.5km/ 10mi via D 8 and D 355 at Carnaret)*
Pointe de Dinan★★ *(18.5km/11.5mi via D 8 and D 308 at Crozon)*
Grottes de Morgat★ *(16km/10mi via D 8 and D 887 at Crozon)*
Cap de la Chèvre★ *23km/14.5mi via D 8, at Crozon D 887 then D 255 at Morgat.*

Quimper★★

Quimper is in Brittany's far west and is the capital of Finistère. It lies in a pretty valley at the junction (*kemper* in Breton) of two rivers, the Steir and the Odet.

A BIT OF HISTORY

The town was first of all a Gaulish foundation, sited on the north bank of the Odet estuary 16km/10mi inland at the tidal limit.

Towards the end of the 5C BC, Celts sailed over from Britain (hence the area's name of Cornouaille, i.e. Cornwall) and drove out the original inhabitants. This was the era of the legendary King Gradlon and of the fabulous city of Ys which is supposed to have sunk beneath the waves of Douarnenez Bay.

The town had a long tradition of making faience (fine earthenware), and is a centre of Breton folk art.

- **Population:** 120 441
- **Michelin Map:** 308 G 6-7
- **Info:** 7 r. de la Déesse. ℘02 98 53 04 05. www.quimper-tourisme.com.
- **Location:** A large ring-road skirts the town. The old centre lies between the two rivers close to the confluence.

VISIT
Cathédrale St-Corentin★★

Place St. Corentin. Open Mon–Sat 9.30am–noon, 1.30–6.30pm, Sun morning only.

The choir being out of alignment with the nave is particularly striking. This is due to using the foundations of earlier buildings on the site. The choir itself is remarkable for deeply moulded pillars, an imposing triforium and the design of the vault spanning both the ambulatory and radiating chapels.

Le Vieux Quimper★

The medieval town lies between the cathedral and the Odet and its tributary, the Steyr. There are fine old houses with granite ground floors and timber-framed projecting upper storeys, notably in the Rue Kereona.

Musée des Beaux-Arts★★

40 pl. St-Corentin. &⊙*Open Jul–Aug 10am–7pm; Apr–Jun Wed–Mon 10am–noon, 2–6pm; Nov–Mar Wed–Sat 10am–noon, 2–6pm, Sun 2–6pm. Guided tours available on Sat and daily in summer.* ⊙*Closed 1 Jan, 1 May, 1 and 11 Nov and 25 Dec.* ≈*4.50€.* ℘*02 98 95 45 20. www.musee-beaux arts.quimper.fr.*

This Fine Arts Museum contains a collection of paintings representing European painting from the 14C to the present. The museum has its own unique atmosphere, largely due to the mixing of natural and artificial lighting, in which it is possible to view the works in – quite literally – a new light.

On the ground floor, two rooms are devoted to 19C Breton painting: *A Marriage in Brittany* by Leleux; *A Street in Morlaix* by Noël; *Potato Harvest* by Simon; *Widow on Sein Island* by Renouf; *Flight of King Gradlon* by Luminais and *Fouesnant Rebels* by Girardet. One room is devoted to **Max Jacob** (1876–1944), who was born and grew up in Quimper.

Pointe du Raz

A. de Valroger/MICHELIN

His life and work are evoked through literature, memorabilia, drawings, gouaches, and in particular a series of portraits signed by his friends Picasso, Cocteau and others.

At the centre of the first floor, the architect J P Philippon designed an area fitted in pale beech wood to set 23 paintings from the dining room of the Hôtel de l'Épée, executed by the painter Lemordant (1878–1968). The area around the edges displays the work of different European Schools up to the contemporary period: Flemish (Rubens, Van Schriek); Italian (Bartolo di Fredi); Spanish; and French. Note in particular works by Boucher, Fragonard, Van Loo, *View of the Château de Pierrefonds* by Corot and *View of Quimper Harbour* by Boudin.

ADDITIONAL SIGHTS

Musée Départemental Breton★ *(1 r. de Roi Gradion;* ⊙*open Jun–Sept daily 9am–6pm; Oct–May Tue–Sat, 9am–noon, 2–5pm, Sun 2–5pm;* ⊙*closed Easter Mon, 1 and 8 May, 25 Dec;* ≈*4€, no charge Sun pm (Oct–May);* ℘*02 98 95 21 60. http:// museedepartementalbreton.fr)* – local history.

Musée de la Faïence★ *(r. Haute; guided tours 10.30am, 2pm, 4pm;* ≈*5€;* ℘*02 98 90 09 36; www.hb-henriot.com).*

EXCURSION

La Cornouaille★★

Although the area today is limited to the coast and immediate hinterland west of its capital Quimper, Cornouaille was once the Duchy of medieval Brittany, stretching as far north as Morlaix. Brittany's "Cornwall" juts out into the Atlantic just like its counterpart across the Channel. The spectacular coastline with its two peninsulas, **Presqu'île de Penmarch**★ and **Cap Sizun**★★, culminates in the breathtaking **Pointe du Raz**★★★.

Pointe du
Raz★★★

Raz Point is one of France's most spectacular coastal landscapes. Its jagged cliffs, battered by the waves and seamed with caves, rise to over 70m/220ft.

VISIT

The **view**★★ extends over the fearsome Raz de Sein with its multitude of reefs and rocky islands (on the outermost of which is sited the lighthouse, Phare de la Vieille). The outline of the Île de Sein can be seen on the horizon. To the north lies the headland, Pointe du Van, perhaps less impressive, but having the distinct advantage of being off the tourists' beaten track.

HIKE

A coastal path *(difficult in places, 1hr30min round trip on foot;* to be *avoided in bad weather or high winds)*

- **Michelin Map:** 308 C 6
- **Location:** The point is at the farthest tip of Brittany's Cornouaille peninsula, about 51km/32mi W of Quimper.
- **Timing:** Allow at least an hour to reach the Pointe from Quimper and a further 15min from parking area to the far end.

leads round the Point; the sheer walls of the Plogoff Inferno (Enfer de Plogoff) dropping down to the boiling ocean are particularly impressive *(safety rope)*. To the north of the Point, **baie des Trépassés** cuts into the schists; it was from here that the bodies of Druids are supposed to have been taken over to Île de Sein for burial.

Rennes★★

The city of artistic, architectural and historical interest, founded by the Gauls, became capital of Brittany in the 16C.

A BIT OF HISTORY
Du Guesclin's Beginnings (14C)
See DINAN.

Bertrand Du Guesclin was born in a castle (no longer in existence) southwest of Dinan. The eldest of 10 children, he entered a tournament at Rennes at age 17 and unseated several opponents. From this humble victory, he went on to defeat far greater opponents during the Hundred Years' War. In the service of France, he freed Périgord from English rule in 1370 and Normandy in 1378.

Great Fire of 1720
In the 18C there was no running water in the town and therefore, no way of fighting fires. In December 1720 an

- **Population:** 272 263
- **Michelin Map:** 309 L-M 6
- **Info:** 11 r. St Yves. 02 99 67 11 11. www. tourisme-rennes.com.
- **Location:** Rennes, capital of Brittany, is skirted by a large ring road. The old centre lies on the right bank of the River Vilaine where it is joined by the Ille-et-Rance canal. The tourist office runs guided tours.

accidental fire caused by a lamp falling into a carpenter's shavings destroyed much of the town.

Architect Jacques Gabriel's rebuilding plan resulted in the fine rectangular street pattern and uniform granite houses of today.

SIGHTS
Palais du Parlement★★
Pl. du Parlemont. ‎Guided tours
Mon–Fri. ⏰*Closed 1 Jan, 1 May, 25 Dec.*
‎*6.10€. Call tourist office in advance.*
This is the former seat of the Breton
Parliament. The splendid south
front of the building is an early and
characteristically severe example of the
Classical style of architecture.

Le Vieux Rennes★
The old town was devastated in 1720
by a great fire that raged for eight days
and engulfed almost 1 000 houses.
Enough buildings were spared to
make a walk through the old part of
Rennes an architecturally rewarding
experience. The medieval houses crowd
picturesquely together in the narrow
streets, identifiable, like the Early
Renaissance (pre-1580) houses among
them, by their timber construction,
their projecting upper floors and
their sculptured decoration. No 3 r.
St-Guillaume, called the **Du Guesclin**
House (although it actually dates from
a later period than the Breton hero),
has a deeply carved door flanked by
figures of St Sebastian and one of his
tormentors.
In the 17C, oversailing upper floors were
abandoned and ground-floor walls
sometimes built in granite; exuberant
timber patterning still found favour.
The city's notables had houses built in
which the granite ground floor supports
one or two upper floors with walls of
tufa or Charentes limestone. The **Hôtel
de Brie**★ *(8 r. du Chapitre)* is of such
refinement that it has been attributed
to Mansart.
After the great fire, the streets were
realigned and widened and lined with
new buildings with granite ground
floors, frequently in the form of arcades,
and upper floors of stone.

ADDITIONAL SIGHTS
Musée des Beaux-Arts★ *(20 quai
Emile Zola)* – fine picture collection.
Cathédrale St-Pierre –
(r. de la Monnaie) – **interior**★;
altarpiece★★.

St-Malo★★★

**The site★★★ of the walled town of St
Malo on the east bank of the Rance
is unique in France, making the
ancient port one of the country's
great tourist attractions.**

A BIT OF HISTORY
The town's prosperity began in the 16C.
In 1534, **Jacques Cartier** had set out
from here on the voyage which led to
the discovery and naming of Canada;
very soon a thriving commerce had
begun, based on furs and fish. Local
ship-owners began to build themselves
fine manor houses in the surrounding
countryside, as well as tall timber-built
residences in the town itself. By the
1660s their boats were trading in the
Pacific, and their ever-increasing wealth
enabled them to build in granite. Parisian
architectural fashions began to prevail
over local traditions. Anticipating the

▸ **Population:** 50 675
◉ **Michelin Map:** 309 J 3
▯ **Info:** Esplanade St-Vincent.
  ✆08 25 135 200. www.
  saint-malo-tourisme.com.
◗ **Location:** St Malo is on
  Brittany's N coast. The
  walled town projects
  into the waters of the
  English Channel.
▯ **Parking:** Park near the
  port by the Esplanade
  St-Vincent.
◷ **Timing:** Starting at the
  Esplanade St-Vincent, it
  is possible to walk right
  around the town on top of
  the ramparts in about 2hr.
  Spend another 2hr seeing
  the château and cathedral.
▮ **Kids:** Le Grand Aquarium.

coming naval rivalry between England and France, Colbert became aware of the vulnerability of his country's western coasts; in 1689, Vauban was commissioned to strengthen the defences of St-Malo.

In the 19C, the invention of floating docks ended the advantage which the great tidal range of the port had long given its ship-builders and -repairers.

SIGHTS

Old Town and Ramparts★★★

From the ramparts there are fine views of the Rance valley and towards Dinard on the far side of the estuary. Within the walls is the old town, almost entirely rebuilt in their original form after near-total destruction in 1944. Solid walls of granite, relieved by horizontal bands between each storey, steep mansard roofs and formidable chimney stacks combine to give an effect of harsh dignity and strong identity. The houses along the Rue de Dinan and those facing the walls are particularly fine.

Château★★

Espl. Felicité Lamennais
This still has the façades of the 17C and 18C barracks.

Cathédrale St-Vincent

Pl. J. de Chantion
The nave vault of 1160 is one of the oldest in Brittany, albeit rebuilt after the last war. Note the **stained-glass windows**★ by Jean Le Moal.

Le Grand Aquarium★★

av. du Général Patton. ⏲*Open daily Apr–Jun and Sept 10am–7pm; mid-Jul–mid-Aug 9.30am–10pm; early Jul and late Aug 9.30am–8pm; rest of the year 10am–6pm.* ⏲*Closed mornings of 25 Dec and 1 Jan, 2 weeks in Jan, 2 weeks Nov (call to check).* ✆*15.50€; child 9.50€.* ☎*02 99 21 19 00. www.aquarium-st-malo.com.*
The aquarium offers a fascinating experience as well as presenting collections of great scientific interest, as visitors trace the history of great sailors from St-Malo. Attractions are of special

St-Malo

H. Le Gac/MICHELIN

interest include the ring **(Anneau)**, a remarkable round aquarium containing 600 000 litres in which shoals of pelagic species of fish swim endlessly; and a life-size reconstruction of a sunken wreck **(Vaisseau englouti)** with sharks.

ADDITIONAL SIGHTS

Musée d'Histoire de la Ville et d'Ethnographie du Pays Malouin★ *(espl. Felicité Lamennais)* – history of the town and its famous men.
Quic-en-Groigne Tower★ *(pl. Vauban)*– wax museum.
Fort National★ *(Parame Beach opposite Château)*

EXCURSION

🚶🏊 Côte d'Émeraude★★★

The name Emerald Coast has been given to Brittany's picturesque northern shore from Cancale **(headland – Pointe du Grouin**★★**)** to **Le Val André**★★ and includes some famous beaches: Dinard, St-Lunaire, Paramé etc. and the city of privateers, St Malo.The Emerald Coast scenic road runs through the major resorts (Dinard, St-Malo) and offers detours to the tips of the numerous headlands, including **Fort de Latte**★★, **Cap Fréhel**★★★ and **Cap d'Erquy**★from which the views of the jagged coastline are in places quite spectacular.

The coast is bisected by the Rance estuary on which it is possible to make an enjoyable boat excursion between Dinan and St Malo.

St-Pol-de-Léon★

St-Pol is one of the main market-gardening centres of the rich band of fertile soils running all round the Breton coast from St-Malo to St-Nazaire. Where the wind can be kept out, the otherwise mild climate allows excellent crops of vegetables to be grown, artichokes, onions, early potatoes, cauliflowers, salad vegetables… eagerly bought in the markets of Paris and on the far side of the English Channel. Mechanisation means that much of the characteristic pattern of tiny fields bounded by stone walls is doomed to disappear.

SIGHTS
Chapelle du Kreisker★
2 r. Verderel.
The chapel was rebuilt around 1375; in the 15C, when the coastal towns were prospering from their sea-borne trade, it housed the meetings of the town council. In about 1430, Duke John V of Brittany tried to introduce the Gothic style into Brittany in order to boost his prestige. But the response of the Breton architects was to adapt Flamboyant Gothic to local ways; they shunned highly designed and decorated façades which were difficult to reconcile with the dour qualities of the granites of the region, and favoured a flattened apse.

They thereby eliminated the problems caused by vaults with a circular or polygonal plan, as well as enabling the interior to be lit by a single large window. In addition, the use of a coffered ceiling and a lightweight slate roof allowed them to dispense with flying buttresses.

The chapel was subsequently enlarged, and, between 1436–1439, given its belfry (**clocher★★**), the finest in the province. Interest in it has increased owing to the loss of the tower of Notre-Dame-du-Mur at Morlaix on which it is supposed to have been modelled. In its vertical emphasis, it is reminiscent of the churches of Normandy; it has a pointed

▶ **Population:** 7 121
◔ **Michelin Map:** 308 H
▯ **Info:** Place de l'Evêché. ℘02 98 15 05 69. www.saintpoldeleon.fr.
◐ **Location:** The town is in western Brittany, close to the port of Roscoff.

steeple and pinnacles so delicate they had to be tied into the main structure by braces to enable them to resist the force of the wind.

Ancienne Cathédrale★
R. de Morlaix.
The old cathedral was erected on 12C foundations in the 13C and 14C. This fine building with its characteristically Breton balustraded belfry was restored by the Dukes of Brittany from 1431 onwards. Seven bays of the nave still have their original vaults; the nave itself was built in Caen stone, a clear indication of Norman influence. Norman too is the inspection gallery which runs below the triforium.

In the north side of the chancel, below the funerary niches, are a number of wooden reliquaries with skulls dug up in a nearby cemetery, while in the sanctuary a palm tree carved in wood contains a ciborium for the Host (1770).

EXCURSION
Roscoff★
5km/3mi N.
The harbour town with its fishing fleet and important export trade (vegetables) to Britain also has ferry services linking Brittany to Plymouth and Cork. It is a flourishing resort and a medical centre using sea-water treatment.

Not far from the harbour in the town centre is the church of **Notre-Dame-de-Kroaz-Batz**★ with its remarkable lantern-turret belfry (**clocher★**) of Renaissance date. Inside, four alabaster **statues**★ grace the altarpiece of one of the altars in the south aisle.

Enclos Paroissial de
St-Thégonnec★★

The parish close at St-Thégonnec is among the most famous of these typically Breton monumental groupings of church, cemetery, calvary and ossuary.

VISIT

The magnificent 17C parish close at St-Thégonnec was to be the last of the great parish closes of Brittany. By good fortune, the village has managed to preserve it in fine condition.

Although of older origin, parish closes began to develop in this form during the second half of the 16C. They formed a useful tool for the Catholic Church, trying to promote a veneration of apostles and saints in opposition to Brittany's heritage of local cults. Their effectiveness was increased by the presentation of their subject matter somewhat in the manner of a strip cartoon, with exaggerated features and dramatic gestures.

This parish close is approached through a Renaissance triumphal arch (**porte triomphale**★) (1587), lavishly decorated with cannon balls, shells, pilasters and little lanterns. The calvary (**calvaire**★★) dates from 1610. It is the work of Rolland Doré, and the last of its type to be carved from the mica-rich igneous rock known as **kersanton**. On the lower arm of the cross are figures of angels collecting Christ's blood, while the base shows scenes of the Passion and Resurrection. Note particularly the depiction of Christ's tormentors and also the symbolic use of clothing, with Our Lord and His followers dressed according to Christian tradition, while the representatives of worldly power wear the fashions of the time of Henri IV. The funerary chapel (**chapelle funéraire**★) of 1676 illustrates traditional decorative motifs in the province (altarpiece with spiral columns and a Holy Sepulchre in painted oak).

The 15C church (**église**★) was rebuilt and refurnished several times in the 17C

⌚ **Michelin Map:** 308 H 3
▶ **Location:** The village lies 12km/7.4mi SW of the town of Morlaix, in northern Brittany.

and early 18C. The pulpit (**chaire**★★) has a polygonal base (1683) carved by master carpenters from the naval yards at Brest, as well as a fine medallion at the back and a Louis XV sounding-board.

EXCURSION
Enclos Paroissial de Guimiliau★★
8km/5mi SW.

This example of a parish close pre-dates the one at St-Thégonnec by some 30 years. The calvary (**calvaire**★★, 1581) has an attractively naïve quality; its 200 figures are full of a sense of vigorous movement and are carved in a robust way which recalls the sculpture of the Romanesque period. Also of interest is the terrifying sculpture showing the Gates of Hell, with the struggling figure of Catel Gollet (Lost Kate in Breton), the flirtatious serving-girl who failed to reveal all at Confession. The funerary chapel of 1642 has an outdoor pulpit of earlier (15C) date.

The church (**église**★) has a Renaissance **porch**★★ dating from 1606; the arching

Scene from the Passion on the Calvary

R. Mattès/MICHELIN

depicts scenes from the Old and the New Testaments. Panelled vaulting is a feature of the interior, which has a Baroque baptistery **(baptistère★★)** with a canopy and spiral columns decorated with pampres and foliage. With its sculpted panels of about 1675, the pulpit **(chaire★)** is also in the Baroque style.

Tréguier★★

Tréguier is a little medieval city, overlooking the wide estuary of the Jaudy and Guindy rivers, one of the drowned valleys known as abers which are so characteristic of the Breton coast.

A BIT OF HISTORY

The place was converted to Christianity in the 6C by St Tugdual, a monk of Welsh origin, and soon became the seat of a bishop. The most popular Breton saint, **Saint-Ives** (1253–1303), lived here; he was often depicted in the act of even-handedly dispensing justice between rich and poor alike and hence became the patron saint of lawyers.

The town and its surroundings were no strangers to misfortune. In 1345–47 the area was devastated by the English allies of Jean de Montfort in retribution for having supported Jeanne de Penthièvre in the War of the Breton Succession. In 1592 it was pillaged by the Catholic Leaguers for having taken the part of Henri IV, then punished again in 1789 for its oppostion to taxes and reforms introduced at the French Revolution.

▶ **Population:** 2 679
☼ **Michelin Map:** 309 C 2
▪ **Info:** 67 r. Ernest Renan. ✆02 96 92 22 33. www.paysdetreguier.com.
◐ **Location:** The town lies half-way between Lannion and Paimpol.

SIGHTS
Cathédrale St-Tugdual★★
🕐 *Open Jul–Aug daily 9.30am–6.30pm; low season 10am–noon, 2–6pm.*
🕐 *Closed Sun morning.* 👓*3€ (Oct–Mar no charge).* ✆*02 96 92 22 33.*
Begun in 1339, this is one of the finest buildings of its kind in Brittany, Anglo-Norman in style in spite of the use of the local granite. The exterior is notable for its Romanesque Hastings Tower (Tour d'Hastings) and the balustrades adorning the slate roofs, as well as for the two porches on the south side; the larger one with its statues of the Apostles is known as the People's Porch (Porche du Peuple), the other with its much-eroded statuary is the Bell Porch (Porche des Cloches).

Cathédrale St-Tugdual - the cloisters are divided by forty Flamboyant arcades made from granite from Île Grande and Pluzumet

J. Malburet/MICHELIN

Within, the Lanceolate version of the Gothic survives in the three-storeyed elevation. A frieze sculpted in white tufa runs underneath the blind triforium, while in the south transept there is a graceful window (**Grande Verrière**★) with Flamboyant Gothic lancets (**fenêtre**★) adorned with a depiction of the Mystic Vine symbolising the Church in Brittany. In the ambulatory is a 13C wooden figure of Christ, and the nave has a copy of the tomb of St Ives built by Duke John V.

The cathedral's **cloisters (cloître)**★ of 1458 are among the few to survive in Brittany. Timber-roofed and with a carved frieze, it has 48 elegant arches giving onto a hydrangea-planted courtyard.

Vannes★★

Vannes is a pleasant city in the shape of an amphitheatre at the highest point to which tides flow at the head of the Morbihan Gulf. The picturesque old town, enclosed in its ramparts and grouped around the Cathedral, is a pedestrian zone where elegant shops have established themselves in old half-timbered town houses.

A BIT OF HISTORY

In pre-Roman times, it was the capital of the **Veneti** tribe.

One of Gaul's most powerful peoples, they were intrepid sailors, crossing the seas to trade with the inhabitants of the British Isles. They nevertheless suffered a terrible defeat at sea in 56 BC at the hands of the Romans, losing 200 ships in a single day. As a result, Brittany's fate was to remain a backwater for a very long time.

In the 9C, Vannes was where Breton unity was achieved under Nominoé, who made Vannes his capital.

SIGHTS

Vieille Ville (Old Town)★★

Surrounded by ramparts (**remparts**★), the area around the cathedral, the successor to a much more ancient place of worship, still has the air of a medieval town.

Among the old half-timbered houses built over a granite ground floor with pillars, arcades and lintels is a 14C market hall known as **La Cohue**★. Its upper floor served as the ducal law-

> ▶ **Population:** 51 759
> ⚙ **Michelin Map:** 308 O 9
> 🅸 **Info:** 1 rue Thiers (moving right of the river end 2009). ℰ08 25 13 56 10. www.tourisme-vannes.com.
> ▶ **Location:** Vannes is a lively, popular resort on the SE coast of Brittany. The historic centre is by the cathedral and Pl. Henri IV.
> 😊 **Don't Miss:** A boat trip on the Gulf.
> 👥 **Kids:** Adults and kids will love the Aquarium du Golf.

court right up until 1796, the ground floor as a market until 1840.

There are fine houses bordering **Place Henri IV**★ and in the adjoining streets. Note the timber cross-braces, corbelling, granite pilasters and 16C slate-hung gables.

Stained-glass window depicting Joan of Arc, Cathédrale Saint-Pierre

A. Coupe/MICHELIN

Cathédrale St-Pierre★

r. des Chanoines.

Of robust granite construction, it has a north aisle with a balustraded terrace and sharply pointed granite gables in Breton Flamboyant style separating the chapels. Inside, the 15C nave is covered by a heavy ribbed vault of the 18C, concealing the original timber roof. Note in particular the stunning **stained-glass windows**★ and statuary.

Hôtel de Ville

Place Maurice-Marchais. ℘*02 97 01 60 00. www.mairie-vannes.fr.*

This building in the Renaissance style, erected at the end of the 19C, stands in *place Maurice-Marchais*, which is adorned with the equestrian **statue** of the Constable de Richemont, one of the great figures of the 15C – for it was he who created and commanded the French army which defeated the English at the end of the Hundred Years' War. He became Duke of Brittany, succeeding his brother in 1457, but died the following year.

Ramparts★

After crossing from the *Promenade de la Garenne* you will get a **view**★★ of the most picturesque corner of Vannes, with the stream (the Marle) that flows at the foot of the ramparts (built in the 13C on top of Gallo-Roman ruins and remodelled repeatedly until the 17C), the formal gardens and the cathedral in the background. A small bridge, leading to Porte Poterne, overlooks some old **wash-houses**★ with very unusual roofing.

EXCURSIONS

Golfe du Morbihan★★

This little inland sea was formed when the land sank and the sea-level rose as a result of the melting of the great Quaternary glaciers, drowning the valleys occupied by the Vannes and Auray rivers. The indented coastline and the play of the tides around the countless islands make this one of Brittany's most fascinating maritime landscapes.

Golfe de Morbihan en bateau★★★ (boat trips)

The best way to see the gulf is by boat. About 40 islands are privately owned and inhabited. The largest are Île d'Arz and the Île aux Moines, both communes. The Île d'Arz is about 3.5km/2mi long and has several megalithic monuments. The Île aux Moines is 7km/4.3mi long and the most populous. It is a particularly quiet and restful resort where camelias and mimosas grow amongst the palm trees.

Wash-houses along the ramparts

J. Malburet/MICHELIN

Tumulus Mané-er-Hroech, Locmariaquer

G. Targat/MICHELIN

👥 Aquarium du Golfe★

Parc du Golfe du Morbihan. ⚐ ⏰ Open daily Jul–Aug 9am–7.30pm; rest of the year 2pm–6pm (except public holidays 10am–noon, 2–6pm); Apr–Jun and Sept 10am–noon, 2pm–6pm. Ticket office closes 30min before closing time. ⏰ Closed 1 Jan and 25 Dec. 🎟️10.30€; child 7.20€. ✆02 97 40 67 40. www.aquarium-du-golfe.com.

More than 50 pools, in which the relevant natural environment has been reconstructed, house about 1 000 fish from all over the world (cold seas, warm seas, freshwater), which make up an incredible kaleidoscope of colour. In one 35 000l/7 700gal tank, a coral reef has been recreated and is home to numerous species of fish which habitually frequent this environment. A huge aquarium contains several varieties of shark and an exceptional sight: a huge 3m/9.8ft-long sawfish!

Château de Suscinio★
Sarzeau

This was once the summer residence of the Dukes of Brittany. There is a rare 13C decorated tiled floor (accessible via a spiral staircase with 94 steps). The massive buildings lining the courtyard are now partly ruined.

A gun-emplacement at the foot of the northwest tower may well date from the time of the War of the Breton Succession.

Port-Navalo★

The little port and seaside resort guards the entrance to the Gulf. There are fine views.

Ensemble Mégalithique de Locmariaquer★★

This group of megaliths is an important part of a programme of conservation and restoration of megalithic sites. Three megaliths can be found on this site: the **Grand Menhir brisé** (probably broken on purpose into five pieces, after it had served as a landmark for sailors); the **Table des Marchands** (a recently restored dolmen as well as the tumulus underneath) and the **Tumulus d'Er-Grah** (excavations are underway here).

Presqu'île de Quiberon★

Quiberon used to be an island, but over the years sand has accumulated north of Penthièvre Fort to form an isthmus linking it to the mainland. The peninsula's rocky and windswept western shore is known as the **Côte Sauvage** (Wild Coast), but to the east there are sheltered sandy beaches. The ferries for **Belle-Île**★★ leave from Quiberon harbour.

Cairn de Gavrinis★★

The tumulus, 6m/19.6ft high and 50m/164ft round, is made of stones piled on hillock. It comprises a gallery with carved symbols leading to a funeral chamber.

BURGUNDY JURA

Burgundy's unity is based more on history than on geography. Fortunately located on the trade route linking northern Europe to the Mediterranean, the territory was consolidated by its great Dukes in the 15C. It comrpises a number of *pays* of varying character, though its heartland lies in the limestone plâteaux stretching eastwards from the Auxerre area and terminating in escarpments, which drop down to the Saône valley. To the east the Jura's limestone uplands run in a great arc for some 240km/150mi from Rhine to Rhône, corresponding roughly to the old province of Franche-Comté.

Highlights

1 Flemish-Burgundian Hospital, Hôtel Dieu, at **Beaune** *(p222)*

2 6C BC grave goods **Trésor de Vix** *(p227)*

3 The Benedictine **Abbaye de Cluny** *(p228)*

4 17C Ducal Palace at **Dijon** *(p230)*

5 The 1C **Abbaye de Fontennay** *(p233)*

Geography – Of the Burgundian escarpments La Côte is the most renowned, with its slopes producing some of the world's finest wines.

To the north is the Morvan, a granite massif of poor soils, with scattered hamlets and extensive forests. Further north and west the Nivernais stretches to the Loire and to the south the lower reaches of the Saône are bordered by the broad Bresse plain. The limestone uplands of the Jura were folded into long parallel ridges and valleys by the pressure exerted on them in the Alpine-building period (⚙ *see p240*). This is a verdant landscape with extensive forests and vast upland pastures.

History – Burgundy was independent of France in the Middle Ages, but by the 15C the powerful Dukes had extended their rule to include the Jura. Later, however, the Duchy became a province of the Holy Roman Empire, annexed by France in 1674.

Economy – The name Burgundy has been synonymous with fine wines since the 14C. The region also produces cheese, cereals and poultry, although tourism is increasingly important.

In the Jura region, world-famous cheeses are produced, along with the yellow wine of Arbois.

Château d'Ancy-le-Franc★★
Burgundy

This dignified château marks the end of the early, Italian-influenced French Renaissance in all its brilliance.

- **Michelin Map:** 319
- **Info:** 18 pl. Clermont-Tonnerre. ✆03 86 75 14 63. www.chateau-ancy.com.
- **Location:** The château stands in N Burgundy countryside, SE of Tonnerre.

VISIT

Open late Mar–mid-Nov Tue–Sun. 9€. Guided tours (50min) late Mar–mid-Nov Tue–Sun 10.30am, 11.30am, 2pm, 3pm, 4pm; Apr–Sept at 5pm. 8€.

Designed by Sebastian Serlio, Italian architect invited to France in 1541 by François I, the château was begun in 1546 and completed 50 years later.

The exterior gives an impression of great order, combining symmetry with a masterly handling of spaces and surfaces according to the rules of the Golden Section. The courtyard is particularly subtle, with deeply sunken twin pilasters topped by Corinthian capitals and separating scalloped niches.

The interior is equally fine. The Judith Room has a coffered ceiling painted by a pupil of Primaticcio, Cornelius van Haarlem. There are ancient bindings in the library, secret cabinets from Italy, dell'Abbate's *Battle of Pharsalus* and oval medallions by Primaticcio representing the Liberal Arts.

Arc-et-Senans★★
Burgundy

Erected 1775–80, the Classical buildings of the former royal saltworks are an extraordinary essay in utopian town planning of the early Industrial Age. They are now on UNESCO's World Heritage List.

- **Population:** 1 277
- **Michelin Map:** 321 E 4.
- **Info:** Institut Claude-Nicolas Ledoux. ✆03 81 54 45 45. www.salineroyale.com.
- **Location:** The royal saltworks of Arc-et-Senans are located in Jura, not far from the River Loue. They are situated SW of Besançon and N of Arbois.

A BIT OF HISTORY

In 1773, the King's Counsel decreed the royal saltworks should be built at Arc-et-Senans, drawing on the salt waters of Salins. Only the cross-axis and half the first ring of buildings envisaged by the visionary French architect architect **Claude-Nicolas Ledoux** (1736–1806), inspector general of other saltworks, were actually completed; what we see today is however enough to evoke the idea of an ideal 18C city. His plan was ambitious; a whole town laid out in concentric circles with the Director's Residence at the centre, flanked by storehouses (Bâtiments des sels), offices and workshops, and extending out to include a church, a market, public baths and recreational facilities. Ledoux's vision makes him one of the forerunners of modern architecture and urban design and while the enterprise was never really viable, being closed down in 1895, the amazing buildings of the *Saline Royale* remain.

VISIT
Saline Royale
(Royal Saltworks)★★
The complex today consists of the gatehouse, Director's Residence, courtyard, coopers' building and salt storehouses. The **gatehouse**, which features a peristyle of eight Doric columns, now houses the reception and a book shop. Badly damaged by fire in 1918 and a subsequent dynamite attack, the **Director's Residence** has been the object of much needed restoration; its rooms are now used for conferences. Its basement contains a display on the saltwork operations. The semicircular **courtyard** is today a lawn; firewood was once unloaded for storage here. In the **coopers' building** architectural models, photographs and prints depict Ledoux' ideas about an ideal society. On the first floor, there is a display of toll-houses. The old **salt storehouses** have been converted into venues for concerts and other events.

Autun★★

Burgundy

Flanked by wooded hills, this dignified country town in northern Burgundy has a cathedral, museums and Roman remains that bear witness to its past.

A BIT OF HISTORY
Autun was founded by the Emperor Augustus, half a century after Caesar's conquest of Gaul. Rome itself was taken as the model for the new town; its walls (6km/4mi in length) soon sheltered fine civic buildings (a theatre, an amphitheatre) and a thriving commercial life. From their stronghold at Bibracte on Mont Beuvray 29km/18mi away to the west, the Gallic Aedui tribe watched the city's growth with fascination and ended up

▶ **Population:** 16 420
🕭 **Michelin Map:** 320 F 8
🗊 **Info:** 13 r. Général Demetz.
  📞03 85 86 80 38. www.
  autun-tourisme.com.
◗ **Location:** The cathedral,
  ramparts and Roman
  remains are all within easy
  walking distance of the
  tourist office and central
  Place du Champs du Mars.

moving there themselves. In the Middle Ages the city consolidated itself on the upper part of its site.

SIGHT
Cathédrale St-Lazare★★
The great sandstone edifice was built from 1120–1146 and named after the friend of Christ whom He raised from the dead and whose relics had supposedly been brought here from Marseille shortly before. Though its external appearance was altered by the addition of a tower and steeple in the 15C, it remains essentially a building of the Burgundian Romanesque style; its barrel-vaulted nave having slightly pointed arches (an early example) and a blind triforium designed to enliven an otherwise bare wall. With a gallery identical to that of the city's Roman Arroux Gate (Porte d'Arroux), this triforium is evidence of the continuing Roman influence well into the 12C.

View of the town

G. Corbic/MICHELIN

The glory of the cathedral is its 12C Burgundian sculpture, most of it the achievement of Master Gislebertus, who came from Vézelay in 1125 and worked here for 20 years. The **tympanum (tympan)**★★★ over the central doorway dates from about 1135 and has the Last Judgement as its subject. It exhibits supreme mastery of technique and the boldness of its design outshines all other contemporary work. Look carefully, for example, at the joy of the saved, the agony of the damned and the use of scale in the treatment of the figure of Christ, the Apostles and other figures. The same mastery is evident in the **capitals (chapiteaux)**★★ in the nave and the chapter-house, where more capitals (originally in the choir) are displayed at eye-level.

ADDITIONAL SIGHTS
Musée Rolin★ *(5 r. des Bancs)*
Porte St-André★ *(Gallo-Roman gate)*
Roman Theatre *(vestiges of the largest theatre in Gaul)*

Auxerre★★
Burgundy

A port on the River Yonne, surrounded by rustic, wooded farm country and hillsides planted with vines and orchards, the city was once an important staging-post on the great Roman highway which led from Lyon to Boulogne via Autun and Lutetia (Paris).

- **Population:** 37 790
- **Michelin Map:** 319 E-F-G 5
- **Info:** 1 et 2 quai de la République. ℘03 86 52 06 19. www.ot-auxerre.fr.
- **Location:** Boulevard 11 Novembre encloses the central area where the sights are located.

VISIT
Abbaye St-Germain★
2 bis, Place Saint-Germain. Open Jun–Sept Wed–Mon 10am–12.30pm, 2–6.30pm; Oct–May Wed–Mon 10am–noon, 2–6pm. Closed 1 Jan, 1 May, 1, 11 Nov, 25 Dec. 4.30€. ℘03 86 18 05 50. www.auxerre.culture.gouv.fr.
The city's famous Benedictine abbey is named after bishop St Germanus (378–448), born in Auxerre. A small basilica was probably erected over the saint's tomb in the 6C by Clothilde, the wife of King Clovis. It was extended in 841 to include an outer nave and a crypt.
The abbey crypt **(crypte**★) houses a raised cavity which was hollowed out in the 9C to hide the tomb from raiding Norsemen. In addition there is a false tomb designed to lead them astray. In part of the crypt dating from Merovingian times (6C), there are two oak beams on Gallo-Roman columns and also a 5C monogram of Christ. From the Carolingian period (8–10C) there is a **fresco** showing the bishops of Auxerre, floor-tiling, and most moving of all, a capital based crudely on the Ionian Order, proof of the aesthetic poverty of the time. The mid-12C bell-tower, was isolated from the rest of the building by the destruction of several bays in the 19C.

ADDITIONAL SIGHT
Cathédrale St-Étienne★★ *(pl. Saint Étienne)* **crypt, treasury**★, **stained glass**★.

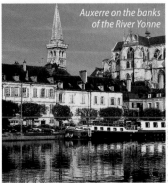
Auxerre on the banks of the River Yonne
S. Sauvignier/MICHELIN

Beaune★★

Burgundy

At the heart of one of the world's greatest wine regions, Beaune is also renowned for its artistic heritage. Fortified in 1368, it was the residence of the Dukes of Burgundy before they moved to Dijon.

A BIT OF HISTORY

The vine was first planted here in Gallo-Roman times; the area devoted to it increased in the Middle Ages thanks to the clearing of woodland by the monasteries. The reputation of Burgundy wines grew in the 15C along with the rise of its Ducal court.

Few careers have been as meteoric as that of **Nicolas Rolin** (1377–1461). Born into a bourgeois family, he became a successful lawyer, then counsellor to John the Fearless. In 1422 he was promoted to Chancellor by Duke Philip the Good. While expertly promoting the interests of his master, he also acquired fortune and power for himself to an unprecedented degree. It was he who detached Burgundy from its alliance with England, reconciling her with France by the Treaty of Arras. In 1443, Rolin and his wife founded the **Hôtel-Dieu** to be a free hospital and guaranteed it an income from 1 300ha/3 200-acre of land between Aloxe-Corton and Meursault. Yet in 1457 Rolin fell from favour; he died at Autun four years later.

SIGHT

Hôtel-Dieu (Hospices de Beaune)★★★

r. de l'Hôtel-Dieu. ♿ ⏱*Open daily 24 Mar–18 Nov 9am–6.30pm; 19 Nov–23 Mar 9am–11.30am, 2–5.30pm.* ⊜*6€.* ℘*03 80 24 45 00.*

For 520 years, Rolin's foundation cared for the sick, from 1451–1971. It has come down to us intact. With its fine architecture, its elegant decoration (ironwork, gabled dormers, weathervanes), its multi-coloured glazed tiles and its old well, it seems more a palace than a place for the poor. Although the internal courtyard

▶ **Population:** 21 289
⛪ **Michelin Map:** 320 I-J 6-7
🛈 **Info:** 6 bd Perpreuil. ℘03 80 26 21 30. www.ot-beaune.fr.
◖ **Location:** Central Beaune is enclosed by a fast-moving ring-road in anti-clockwise direction – so any turn on the left leads into the centre. Focal point is the Hôtel-Dieu and the main square in front of it, Place des Halles.
🅿 **Parking:** It's easier to park just outside the ramparts than try to find a space within the walled town.

in Flemish-Burgundian style, the pharmacy, the nuns' quarters and the kitchens are fascinating, it is the Great Hall (Grand'Salle) which most completely evokes the spiritual dimension of the hospitals of yesteryear. It remained in service up to 1959. One end of the Grand' Salle is arranged as a place of worship, so that the sick could attend services without leaving their beds. The **Polyptych of the Last Judgement**★★★ was displayed here. Rolin himself commissioned this work from Rogier van der Weyden to go over the altar of the Great Hall. The master, with the help of assistants, completed it between 1443–1451. In its expression of emotion at this crucial moment and in its perfection of detail (which can be inspected with the aid of a giant magnifying-glass), it is one of the greatest of Gothic paintings. At the time, its masterly evocation of the outcome to be expected from the living of a blameless life must have been reassuring, too.

On the third Sunday in November the auction takes place in Beaune of the wines of the Hospices.

ADDITIONAL SIGHTS

Musée du vin de Bourgogne★
(Hôtel des Ducs, r. d'Enfer)
Collégiale Notre-Dame★

Côte de Nuits
Hautes-côtes de Nuits
Côte de Beaune
Hautes-côtes de Beaune
Côte Chalonnaise
Main crus

0   5 km

Walking Tours

The tourist office has information about many different tours and excursions in town and to the vineyards.

tapestries★★ (pl. Notre-Dame)
Hôtel de la Rochepot★ (24 bd Foch)

EXCURSION
Vineyard road★

The prestigious vineyards of the Côte d'Or stretch mainly north and (much less) south from Beaune. Explore the famous names, and stop for tastings, on picturesque back roads, for example at Meursault, Vougeot and Gevrey-Chambertin.

ADDRESSES

🏠 STAY

👄👄**Chambre d'Hôte Le Meix des Hospices** – R. Basse, Demigny, 10km/6.2mi S of Beaune by D 18. ℰ03 85 49 98 49. 4 rooms. This former hospice annexe consists of several outbuildings arranged around a square courtyard. The quiet, simple rooms, one of which is set up beneath the eaves, are sparsely appointed with modern furniture. The dining room features exposed beams, stone flooring and a fireplace.

👄👄**Hôtel du Parc** – 13 r. du Golf, 21200 Levernois, 5km/3mi SW of Beaune by rte de Verdun-sur-le-Doubs, D 970 then D 111L. ℰ03 80 24 63 00. www.hotelleparc.fr. Closed 25 Jan–12 Mar. 17 rooms. ⊆8€. Covered with Virginia Creeper and bursting with flowers in summertime, this hotel is quite simply charming. The two buildings are separated by a small patio. Bright, sober accommodation. The park at the back looks out over peaceful meadows.

👄👄🛏🛏**Hostellerie du Château de Bellecroix** – 20 Chemin de Bellecroix, Chagny, 18km/11mi SW of Beaune by N 74 then N 6. ℰ03 85 87 13 86. www. chateau-bellecroix.com. Closed 15 Dec–15 Feb. 20 rooms. ⊆15€. The two towers of this 18C château stand amid wooded parkland. Nearby lie the turrets of a former 12C Knights Templar commandery belonging to the Order of Malta. The bedrooms are appointed with antique furniture. There are some fine replicas of medieval wainscoting in the dining hall.

👄👄🛏🛏**Hôtel Le Cep** – 27 r. Maufoux. ℰ03 80 22 35 48. www.cep.abcsalles. com. 56 rooms. ⊆22€. Ravishing 16C house in the old quarter. The bedrooms, decorated in old-fashioned style, carry the names of famous vintages from the Côte-d'Or. Breakfast is served in the vaulted cellar or, weather permitting, in the courtyard with its pretty Renaissance arcades and medallions.

🍽/EAT

👄👄**Caveau des Arches** – 10 Bd Perpreuil. ℰ03 80 22 10 37. www.caveau-des-arches.com. Closed Aug; Sun & Mon. In summer remember to bring a cardigan with you as the vaulted dining rooms of this restaurant set up on the ramparts can be somewhat chilly. Admire the ruins of an old bridge which once gave access to the city. Traditional Burgundy cooking.

👄👄**Ma Cuisine** – Passage Ste-Hélène. ℰ03 80 22 30 22. Closed August; Wed, Sat and Sun. Located along a tiny street, this small dining room sports the colours of Provence. Regional wines on the wine list.

👄👄**Le P'tit Paradis** – 25 r. Paradis. ℰ03 80 24 91 00. Closed 13–21 Aug; Sun–Mon. The pretty dining room and terrace border a flowering garden. Contemporary cuisine incorporates regional flourishes, and wines are selected from boutique producers.

👄👄🛏 **Le Bénaton** – 25 Faubourg Bretonnière. ℰ03 80 22 00 26. www. lebenaton.com. Closed Apr–Nov all day Wed, Thu & Sat for lunch; 1 Dec–31 Mar Wed & Thu. Small restaurant far from the madding crowd with a pretty covered terrace for the summer days. Pleasant dining room with stone walls and bright decorative hues. Attractive quality/price ratio for light yet delicious meals made with fresh seasonal produce.

⛾ CAFÉS

Bouché – *1 pl. Monge. ℰ03 80 22 10 35. www.chocolatier-bouche.com. Closed Mon.* Step inside this pretty tea room and you'll find lovely gift boxes ready to fill with tantalising house specialities, among them chocolate "snails", candied chestnuts and candied fruits. At table, you'll have to choose between *tarte vigneronne, millefeuille,* or any of the 20 or so specially created sweets.

Palais des Gourmets – *14 pl. Carnot. ℰ03 80 22 13 39.* This delightful *patisserie*-tea room serves many a local delicacy, including *cassissines* (blackcurrant fruit jelly flavoured with blackcurrant liqueur), *roulés au cointreau* (pancakes with a Cointreau filling) and chocolate medallions depicting the Hôtel-Dieu.

☻ NIGHTLIFE

Le Bistrot Bourguignon – *8 r. Monge. ℰ03 80 22 23 24. www.restaurant-lebistrotbourguignon.com. Closed Sun, Mon.* Relax on the charming terrace or sink into one of the comfortable armchairs inside this old house, sipping a glass of excellent wine to the strains of a few popular songs.

Place Carnot – This large, recently restored square has many outdoor cafés where you can sit in the sun all day. The perfect place to have breakfast, lunch or dinner!

☙ FOR WINE LOVERS

L'Athenaeum de la Vigne et du Vin – *5 r. de l'Hôtel-Dieu. ℰ03 80 25 08 40. www.athenaeumfr.com.* This bookshop has earned quite a reputation as the ultimate authority on the art of oenology, Burgundy and fine gastronomy. It also presents a collection of miscellaneous items related to wine: corkscrews, glasses and cellarman's knives.

Cave Patriarche Père and Fils – *5–7 r. du Collège. ℰ03 80 24 53 79. www.patriarche.com. Closed public holidays.* Burgundy's largest cellars (15 000sq m/ 18 000sq yd) are housed in a former convent dating from the 14C and 16C. Guided tours and tasting sessions of 13 different wines.

Caves de La Reine Pédauque – *2 Faubourg St-Nicolas. ℰ03 80 25 00 00. Closed public holidays.* After exploring the 18C vaulted cellars, visitors may take part in a wine tasting session around an imposing round marble table! An opportunity not to be missed!

La Cave des Cordeliers – *6 r. de l'Hôtel-Dieu. ℰ03 80 25 08 85. Closed public holidays.* The Couvent des Cordeliers, built in 1242, provides a splendid backdrop to these wine cellars, which you can visit before tasting six fine Burgundy wines. In the courtyard, note the 1580 low relief depicting the Adoration of the Magi.

Le Comptoir Viticole – *1 r. Samuel-Legay. ℰ03 80 22 15 73. www.comptoirviticole.com.* Wine buffs and amateur vignerons will adore this shop, which sells all manner of devices related to winemaking: bottling machines, corkscrews, bottle racks, jeroboams, balthasars...

Marché aux Vins – *2 r. Nicolas-Rolin. ℰ03 80 25 08 20. www.marcheauxvins. com. Open daily 9.30am–11.30am, 2–5.30pm; Jul–Aug daily 9.30am–5.30pm. 10€.* Housed in Beaune's oldest church (13C and 14C) opposite the famous hospice, this wine market offers 18 wines of between 3 and 15 years of age, to be sipped and relished slowly. If requested, a cellar containing some extremely rare vintages, which have been maturing since 1911, can also be opened to visitors.

Vins de Bourgogne Denis-Perret – *Place Carnot. ℰ03 80 22 35 47. www.denisperret.fr. Closed Sun.* Five wine-growers and a group of landowners have teamed up to offer you some of the most prestigious names from the Burgundy region— Romanée-Conti, Clos-Vougeot, Montrachet, Chambertin. Such a rich selection could easily leave you speechless but, not to worry, for several young oenologists are there to help you make your choice and to suggest the best dishes to go with each wine.

Briare

Burgundy

Briare is a busy town on the banks of the Loire, known for its ceramic floor mosaics and its stoneware.

SIGHT
Pont-Canal★

The Loire was used by river traffic from the 14–19C, but the navigation companies found it difficult to cope with the river's irregular flow on the one hand, and shallowness on the other.

To rectify this, and as part of his policy of economic unification, Henri IV began building the Briare Canal in 1604; completed in 1642, it linked the basins of the Loire and the Seine via its junction with the River Loing at Montargis. It was the first connecting canal in Europe.

The Loire Lateral Canal (1822–38) extends it south to Digoin. It crosses the Loire at Briare on an aqueduct built 1890–94 (58 years after those at Le Guétin and Digoin). The channel is the longest in the world (662.7m/2 174ft). It rests on 15 granite piers designed by Gustave Eiffel; their loading is constant, irrespective of the presence of barges or the weight of their cargo, a nice illustration of Archimedes' principle.

▶ **Population:** 6 070
◔ **Michelin Map:** 318 N 6
▤ **Info:** Place Charles de Gaulle. ℘02 38 31 24 51. www.briare-le-canal.com.
◑ **Location:** The Briare canal lies SE of Orleans and north of Bourges.

Chalon-sur-Saône★

Burgundy

Chalon is the urban centre for the fertile lowlands bordering the Saône River as it makes its way between the Jura and the Massif Central. Its most famous son is the father of photogrpahy, Joseph Nicéphore Niepce (1765-1833)

A BIT OF HISTORY

The river is fed by a number of canals; at Corre it is joined by the Eastern Canal (Canal de l'Est – completed 1882), at Pontailler by the canal from the Marne (1907), at St-Jean-de-Losne by both the Rhine-Rhône Canal (1833) and the Burgundy Canal (1832).

But it is only at Chalon, where it is joined by the Central Canal (completed 1790), that it becomes one of Europe's great commercial waterways, flowing south to join the Rhône at Lyon. Long before the present age, however, the Saône had been an important commercial route; a large number of amphora bases were found at Chalon, proof that wine was imported here from Naples before the introduction of the vine to Burgundy by the Romans.

Since the 18C the banks of the river have been a favoured site for industry, which includes the heavy engineering firm Schneider du Creusot as well as electrical works and nuclear power plants.

▶ **Population:** 62 452
◔ **Michelin Map:** 320 J 9
▤ **Info:** 4 place du Port Villiers. ℘03 85 48 37 97. www.uk.chalon-sur-saone.net
◑ **Location:** Chalon-sur-Saône, which is listed as a "Town of Art and History", offers discovery tours conducted by guide-lecturers approved by the Ministry of Culture and Communication.

The Origins of Photography – Joseph Nicéphore Niepce (1765–1833) was a native of Chalon. His restlessly inventive disposition had already led him to design an internal combustion engine in 1807. He lacked talent as a draughtsman, but was fascinated by lithography. At the age of 48 he set himself the task of recording images through the spontaneous action of light. He was already familiar with the optics of the camera obscura which had been studied by the Arab physicist El Hazen (11C), by Leonardo da Vinci and by various 18C men of science, among them Jacques Charles, the husband of Lamartine's Elvire.

After three years' work he succeeded in making and fixing a positive image, and on 28 May 1816 he sent his brother a print made at his home in St-Loup-de-Varennes (7km/4.3mi south); this was the very first photograph.

Daguerre popularised Niepce's discovery and others developed it (e.g. Fox Talbot and Bayard). Progressive refinement and invention have led from Niepce's simple apparatus to photography as an art form, to the Hasselblad used in lunar exploration and to the snapshots in the family album.

SIGHT
Musée Nicéphore Niépce★★

28 quai des Messageries. ◯*Open Sept–Jun Wed–Mon 9.30am–11.45am, 2–5.45pm; Jul–Aug Wed–Mon 10am–6pm.* ◯*Closed public holidays.* *No charge.* *Guided tours; 1st and 3rd Sun, 2nd and 4th Fri of the month 3pm;* *6€).* *03 85 48 41 98. www.museeniepce.com.*

The museum is housed in the 18C Hôtel des Messageries on the banks of the Saône. The rich collection comprises photographs and early photographic equipment, including the earliest cameras ever made which were used by Joseph Nicéphore Niepce, as well as his first heliographs. There are also works by well-known contemporaries of Niepce in the world of photography.

Châtillon-sur-Seine★

Burgundy

Châtillon occupied a strategic location on the ancient north–south trade route. It was here that the Seine ceased to be navigable; as a result, the place developed all the facilities that transhipment needed, and grew prosperous on the merchandise being exchanged between Cornwall and Etruria – amber, tin, coral, ceramics.

▸ **Population:** 6 269
⚲ **Michelin Map:** 320 H 2.
▯ **Info:** 9–11 r. de la Libération. *03 80 81 57 57. www.pays-chatillonnais.fr.*
▸ **Location:** The town is in a rural area 83km/51.5mi N of Dijon.

A BIT OF HISTORY

Two major events in Chatillon's history are seperated by exactly 100 years. In 1814 a Congress was held here between France and her enemies.

Napoleon rejected the terms, fighting resumed and the downfall of the Empire soon followed. In 1914 General Joffre set up his Headquarters here and issued the famous order which led to the halting of the German advance by French troops.

SIGHT
Le Trésor de Vix★★

Found in the tomb of a young Celtic queen, 6C BC grave goods (the treasure of Vix) can be found on display in the **Abbaye Notre-Dame de Châtillon** (*r. de l'Abbaye; for information and opening times, contact tourist office*).

Cluny★★

Burgundy

The conditions for the future renown and prosperity of the great **Abbaye de Cluny**★★ existed at the very moment of its foundation.

A BIT OF HISTORY

The abbey, founded 910, deep in forest, far removed from the centres of power in either France or Germany, was subject to no authority other than that of the Pope himself. It answered – like its daughter houses and other dependencies – to no one but its elected abbot. It thus became a powerful instrument for the Papacy.

Cluny's development was rapid, its prestige immense, and its influence preeminent. In under a century, the abbey had amassed considerable power as well as much property and already had 1 184 daughter- and dependent houses. One hundred and fifty years later their numbers had risen to 3 000, scattered all over Europe. For two and a half centuries this capital of monasticism found leaders of exceptional calibre, some of

▶ **Population:** 4 376
◔ **Michelin Map:** 320 H 11
▮ **Info:** 6 r. Merciere. ℘03 85 59 05 34. www.cluny-tourisme.com.
◑ **Location:** A climb to the top of the Tour des Fromage gives the best view of the town and its historic structures.
ℙ **Parking:** Plenty of parking available at pl. de l'Abbaye and pl. du Marche.
◔ **Timing:** Tour of the abbey, then stroll around the town.

whom ruled for up to 60 years. The decline of the order began in the 13C, but its prosperity lasted until the 18C.

SIGHT

Abbaye Bénédictine de Cluny

Palais Jean de Bourbon. ◔*Open daily May–Aug 9.30am–6.30pm; Sept–Apr 9.30am–noon, 1.30–5pm.* ◔*Closed*

CLUNY ABBEY

0   50 m

Musée Ochier ★

Hôtel de Ville

Rue Porte des Prés

HARAS NATIONAL

Barabans

Espace K. J. Conant

Narthex

BASILICA

Place du Marché

Clocher de l'Eau Bénite ★★

Ch^lle St Martial

Place de l'Abbaye

Galilee Passage

St Hughes' Stables

Pope Gelasius Façade

Clock Tower

Ch^lle Bourbon

Ch^lle St Étienne

R. du 11 Août 1944

R. Municipale

Cloisters

FORMER ABBEY

Existing buildings

No longer exists

Farinier

public holidays. ⊚*7€.* ℘*03 85 59 15 93.* *http://cluny.monuments-nationaux.fr.*

The abbey church, started 1088, was completed in 1130. It was destroyed during the Revolution. All that remains are the lower parts of two towers; the bell-tower known as "the Holy Water" (**Eau bénite★★**), a superb octagon, and another known as the Clock Tower (Tour de l'Horloge); of the great transept, the south arm with its two chapels and an octagonal vault (32m/105ft high); of the minor transept, the chapel (Chapelle de Bourbon) with sculpted heads of the Prophets. Reduced in height, the flour store (Farinier) has a fine 13C timber roof, and eight capitals from the abbey. The abbey buildings were rebuilt in the 18C.

EXCURSION
Château de Cormatin★★
13km /8mi N of Cluny. ◔ *Guided tours (45min) daily; call for times.* ⊚*9€.* ℘*03 85 50 16 55. www.chateaude cormatin.com.*

Dijon★★★

Burgundy

Close to some of the world's finest vineyards, Dijon, former capital city of the Dukes of Burgundy, straddles important north–south and east–west communication routes and has a remarkable artistic heritage.

A BIT OF HISTORY
Dijon had been the capital of Burgundy ever since the rule of Robert the Pious at the beginning of the 11C. In 1361 Philippe de Rouvres died without an heir, leaving the duchy without a ruler. In 1363, the French King Jean II le Bon (the Good) handed the duchy to his son Philippe, the first of an illustrious line of Valois Dukes who made the Burgundian court at Dijon one of the most brilliant of Europe.

Philippe became Duke in 1364, at the same time as his brother Charles V le Sage (the Wise) was acceding to the

---

> **Walking Tours**
>
> The tourist office has details of a choice of guided tours including a Guided Tour of the Abbey (approx 60min; ⊚6.50€) starting from the Museum of Art and Archaeology in the Abbey complex.

The château (*4km/2.5mi N of Taizé*), probably built by Jacques II Androuet du Cerceau, is a good example of the Henri IV style (late 16–early 17C): the monumental gates framed by antique orders, the basement built of stone and the windows decorated with mouldings. The mannerist style which evolved in the literary salons under Louis XIII (1610–43) reached its peak with the gilding and the lapis-lazuli decoration of the St Cecilia Room (**Cabinet Ste-Cécile★★★**).

- ▸ **Population:** 236 953
- ⚅ **Michelin Map:** 320 K 5-6
- ▤ **Info:** 11 r. des Forges. ℘0892 70 05 58. www.dijon-tourism.com.
- ◗ **Location:** The core of the city is around Place de la Liberation. Make use of the free shuttle buses called *Diviaciti* which run in the city centre from 7am–8pm Monday to Saturday.
- ▣ **Parking:** There are plenty of car parks around the perimeter of the city centre, and metered street parking within the city.
- ◔ **Timing:** There is a choice of guided tours; ask at the tourist office.

throne of France. Thus from this time Burgundy and France were closely

City of Dijon from above

B. Kaufmann/MICHELIN

entwined. Philippe stood out as the most able of four royal brothers; cool, analytical on the one hand, well-named "le Hardi" (the Bold) on the other. His marriage in 1369 to Margaret of Flanders made him the most powerful prince of Christian Europe.

Anxious to provide a worthy burial place for himself and his successors, he founded the Champmol Charterhouse in Dijon in 1383, and set out to attract to the city the best sculptors, painters, goldsmiths and illuminators from his possessions in Flanders. His successor **Jean sans Peur** (John the Fearless) was assassinated in 1419. **Philippe le Bon** (the Good) inherited the title. From this time on, Burgundy saw its cultural importance waning in favour of the Netherlands and Flanders, where Renaissance ideas were blossoming. Nevertheless, artistic production continued throughout his 48-year reign. At the same time, Nicolas Rolin, the Duke's Chancellor, was establishing the Hôtel-Dieu at Beaune.

The boundaries of the Burgundian state had never been more extensive nor the life of its court more exuberant; on his wedding day in 1429, Philip founded the Order of the Golden Fleece; never had the French king and his court, lurking in relative obscurity at Bourges, been more pitiful. But Burgundy's alliance with England had become unpopular just as Joan of Arc was awakening national sentiment. Philip decided it was prudent to submit himself to the authority of the

French king, marking the beginning of the end of the Hundred Years' War.

Charles le Téméraire (the Bold) succeeded in 1467; he was the last and perhaps the most renowned of all the Valois Dukes of Burgundy. He squandered its resources in the search for glory. Charles' death in 1477 marked the end of the great days of the Burgundian dynasty, but in the same year Mary of Burgundy, Charles' daughter, married Maximilian, Holy Roman Emperor. She was to be the mother of **Philippe le Beau** (the Fair), who in turn fathered the future Emperor Charles V. The recovery of Burgundy and the other lands making up her dowry cost France more than two and a half centuries of struggle.

LA VILLE DUCALE (THE DUCAL CITY)

Palais des ducs et des États de Bourgogne★★

pl. des Ducs-de-Bourgogne. ⏱*Open Mon–Fri 8.45am–12.15am, Sat 9.30am–12.30pm.* ✆*03 80 74 52 71. Fax 03 80 74 53 40.* ✉*No charge.*

The ducal palace had been neglected since the death of Charles the Bold. In the 17C, it was restored and adapted and given a setting of dignified Classical buildings. At the time the city was keen to emphasise its parliamentary role and needed a suitable building in which the States-General of Burgundy could meet in session. Plans were drawn up by Mansart. The exterior of the Great Hall of the States-General (Salle des États) recalls the Marble Court (Cour de Marbre) at Versailles. By contrast, the east wing with its peristyle anticipates the architectural style of the 18C.

Mansart was also responsible for the semicircular Place de la Libération (formerly Place Royale). With its arcades crowned by an elegant stone balustrade, it is designed to show off the main courtyard of the palace.

Musée des Beaux-Arts★★

Cour de Bar entrance, Palais des Etats de Bourgogne. &♿⏰*Open May–Oct Wed –Mon 9.30am–6pm; Nov–Apr Wed– Mon 10am–5pm.* ⏰*Closed public holidays.* ☎*No charge.* ✆*03 80 74 52 09. http://dijoon.free.fr/mba/acc-mba.htm.* The Fine Arts Museum is housed in the former ducal palace and in the east wing of the palace of the States-General.

Salle des Gardes★★★

Palais des Etats de Bourgogne. On the first floor, in the former Banqueting Hall. This is the ducal palace's most important interior. Its centrepiece is formed by two tombs which before the French Revolution were in the chapel of the Champmol Charterhouse. The tomb of Philip the Bold was designed by Jean de Marville; its decoration was in the hands of Claus Sluter followed by his nephew Claus de Werve who succeeded in softening somewhat the severity of Marville's conception. Flamboyant Gothic inventiveness and exuberance are expressed in the procession of hooded mourners making its way around the cloisters formed by the four sides of the monument.

ADDRESSES

🛏 STAY

🛏**Hôtel Victor Hugo** – *23 r. des Fleurs.* ✆*03 80 43 63 45. http://hotelvictor hugo-dijon.com. 25 rooms.* ⚏*6€.* You will appreciate the thoughtful service at this traditional hotel. The rooms with their white roughcast walls are simple and quiet, despite their location near the town centre.

Nearby, the tomb (**tombeau★★★**) of John the Fearless and Margaret of Bavaria is similar in style. There are also two altarpieces dazzling in the richness of their decoration: one, sculpted by Jacques de Baerze and painted and gilded by Broederlam, shows **Saints and Martyrs★★★**; the other, depicting the Crucifixion, has famous paintings by Broederlam on the reverse side of its panels. A portrait of Philip the Good by Rogier van der Weyden (born in Tournai, a pupil of Van Eyck and perhaps of Campin too, then teacher to Memling) is remarkable for its psychological insight. In an adjoining room is a fine Nativity of 1425 by the Master of Flémalle.

Ancienne Chartreuse de Champmol★

Enter at 1 Boulevard Chanoine-Kir. Follow signs for "Puits de Moïse". ⏰*Open 10am–6pm.* ☎*No charge.* ✆*03 80 42 48 01.* All that is left of the Charterhouse is Moses' Well (**Puits de Moise★★**) and the chapel doorway (**portail de la chapelle★**), both the work of Claus Sluter, the foremost among the sculptors of the Dijon School. Born in Holland, he learnt his skills in Brabant and worked in Dijon from 1385–1404. Moses' Well was originally the pedestal of a Calvary. Six great statues of Moses and the Prophets face outwards from the hexagonal base; their treatment shows a striking realism, notably in the folds of the clothing. The statues of Philip the Bold and Margaret of Flanders in the chapel doorway are thought to be actual portraits.

🛏 **Jacquemart** – *32 r. Verrerie.* ✆*03 80 60 09 60. www.hotel-lejacquemart.fr. 31 rooms.* ⚏*5.95€.* Simple, family-style rooms in a 17C building.

🛏🛏 **Hôtel Wilson** – *pl. Wilson.* ✆*03 80 66 82 50. www.wilson-hotel.com. 27 rooms.* ⚏*12€.* This former post house has retained its traditional charm. The rooms are prettily decorated with light wood furniture. Exposed beams and luminosity make for a cosy atmosphere where one immediately feels at home.

⬤/EAT

La Mère Folle – *102 r. Berbisey. ✆03 80 50 19 76. Closed public holidays.* This small restaurant in the town centre offers regional specialities on its menu such as *escargots, œufs en meurette,* and *sandre au Chablis.* Convivial atmosphere, good service and 1930s-style décor.

Le Bistro des Halles – *10 r. Bannelier. ✆03 80 49 94 15. Closed Sun and Mon.* A typical bistrot a stone's throw from the covered market. Choose one of the dishes chalked up on a slate and enjoy the warm and friendly ambience.

Les Deux Fontaines – *16 pl. de la République. ✆03 80 60 86 45. Closed 1 Jan, 10–25 August, 25 Dec, Sun and Mon.* Whitwashed walls, old banquettes, wood tables plastered with advertisements of yesteryear: it all makes for a nostalgic trip to bistros past.

La Dame d'Aquitaine – *23 pl. Bossuet. ✆03 80 30 45 65. www.la damedaquitaine.fr. Closed Mon for lunch and Sun.* In the town centre, a porch, a paved courtyard and a long flight of steps will take you down to a superb vaulted dining hall dating back to the 13C. The décor is typically medieval, complete with tapestries, stained glass, sculpted columns and imposing chandeliers. Regional cuisine.

TEAROOMS

Comptoir des Colonies – *12 pl. François-Rude. ✆03 80 30 28 22.* Teas, coffees roasted in-house and hot chocolate await you in this colonial-style tea shop, which also has a leather and mahogany salon and a large sunny terrace.

La Causerie des Mondes – *16 r. Vauban. ✆03 80 49 96 59. Closed Mon.* Jute-covered walls, and Asiatic-themed décor, with a backdrop of mood music makes for an exotic atmosphere in this pleasant tearoom. More than 70 imported teas, 20 house-roasted coffees, chocolates and cakes to tempt you.

🎭 NIGHTLIFE

THEATRES AND OPERA

Comedians and actors regularly ply the stages of the Théâtre du Sablier (*r. des Trois Forgerons*), the Théâtre du Parvis-St-Jean (*r. Danton*) and the Bistro de la Scène (*r. d'Auxonne*). In May the city hosts the Rencontres Internationales du Théâtre. The Théâtre National Dijon-Bourgogne is directed by François Chattot. Classical music, opera and dance productions are held at the Auditorium and at the Opéra de Dijon (*pl. du Théâtre*).

L'Agora Café – *10 pl. de la Libération. ✆03 80 30 99 42. Closed Sun, Mon.* A piano-bar located in a former 16C convent chapel. Wide selection of whiskies, beers and cocktails in a quiet, convivial atmosphere. Piano performances on Saturday evenings. Patio open in summer.

Le Caveau de la Porte Guillaume – *pl. Darcy. ✆03 80 50 80 50. www.hotel-nord. fr. Closed 20 Dec–5 Jan.* Bordering the Hotel du Nord, this wine bar is an ideal spot for sampling the delights of the region, by the glass or by the bottle.

🛒 SHOPPING

Marché des Halles – *r. Odebert.* Constructed by Gustave Eiffel in 1868, this market conatains a sensory delight of cheeses, flowers and meat produce.

Pain d'Epices Mulot et Petitjean – *13 pl. Bossuet. ✆ 03 80 30 07 10. www.mulotpetitjean.fr.* This long-standing establishment, which originated in 1796, specialises in all forms of gingerbread: round biscuits filled with jam, crunchy *gimblettes* with almonds, and sweetmeats.

Nicot Yves – *48 r. Jean-Jacques-Rousseau. ✆03 80 73 29 88.* The proprietor, M Nicot, nurtures a veritable passion for wines in this shop. He also runs a school offering courses in wine tasting and oenology.

Boutique Amora-Maille – *32 r. de la Liberté. ✆03 80 30 41 02. www. maille.com.* Opened in 1845, this shop specialises in Maille mustards and vinegars of Dijon.

Abbaye de
Fontenay★★★
Burgundy

Tucked away in its lonely valley near the River Brenne, Fontenay is very evocative of the self-sufficient life of a Cistercian abbey of the 12C.

A BIT OF HISTORY
St Bernard (1091–1153), unhappy with the wealth and power of Cluny, found greater asceticism and spirituality at the abbey of **Cîteaux,** 23km/14mi south of Dijon. He was made responsible for establishing the abbey at **Clairvaux** on the River Aube; then, in 1118, at the age of 27, he founded **Fontenay**, his "second daughter".

- **Michelin Map:** 320 G 4
- **Info:** ℘03 80 92 15 00. www.abbayede fontenay.com.
- **Location:** The abbey is next to Montbard, in northern Burgundy.

VISIT
Ancienne Abbaye
Open daily mid-Nov–Mar 10am–noon, 2–5pm; Apr–Jun and Sept–Oct 10am–6pm; Jul–Aug 10am–7pm. ℘*03 80 92 15 00.*
The abbey church (**église abbatiale**) was built between 1139–1147. It is the first example of the "monastic simplicity" characteristic of the architecture promoted by St Bernard, and is laid out in a straightforward way, with a square chancel and chapels of square plan.

Cascade du
Hérisson★★★
Burgundy

High up at the foot of the cirque of Chaux-de-Dombief is little Lake Bonlieu, drained by the River Hérisson (hedgehog). The river crosses the narrow Frasnois plateau, then, in the space of 3km/1.8mi drops via a series of rapids and falls through its famous wooded gorge to the Champagnole plain 200m/650ft below. The falls are dramatic after wet weather, much less so after a dry period.

The path climbs over a series of limestone outcrops laid down over a period of 35 million years during Jurassic times; it is they that form the succession of splendid falls, the **Éventail**★★★ (Fan Falls), the **Grand Saut**★★ (Great Leap), Château Garnier, the **Saut de la Forge**★ and Saut Girard.

- **Michelin Map:** 321 F 7
- **Info:** 36 Grande-r., Clairvaux-les-Lacs. ℘03 84 25 27 47. www.juralacs.com
- **Location:** The falls are E of Lons-les-Saunier. They are approached by road from the villages of Bonlieu, Doucier or Ilay, and then reached on foot.
- **Parking:** From Doucier, parking is available at the Jacquard Mill (*fee*), from Ilay, you can leave the car near the Auberge du Hérisson.
- **Don't Miss:** Most impressive of the falls is **Cascade du Grand Saut**★★.

Walking Tours
Follow the marked **Sentier des Cascades** footpath which starts 8km/5mi E of Doucier as far as the Ilay crossroads (3hr round-trip).

Nevers★

Burgundy

From the red sandstone bridge spanning the Loire, there is a fine view of the old town of Nevers set in terraces on its limestone hill. Its tall town houses with their roofs of slate and tile are dominated by the high square tower of the great cathedral and the graceful silhouette of the ducal palace.

A BIT OF HISTORY

Nevers was known for its pottery in the Middle Ages. Artistic pottery seems to have been brought here in the 1560s by Italian craftsmen. In the time of Louis XIII and Louis XIV the town was a centre of faience production, with 12 manufactories and producing some of the finest Blue Persian work ever made. There is a fine **collection**★ of Nevers pottery in the museum **(musée municipal)**. Nevers flourished as a port until the 19C when the Loire ceased to be navigable.

Following her visionary experiences at Lourdes, Bernadette Soubirous came to Nevers in 1866 to enter the convent of **St-Gildard**★ here.

▶ **Population:** 100 556
𝒸 **Michelin Map:** 319 B 10
 Info: Palais Ducal r. Sabatier. ℘03 86 68 46 00. www.nevers-tourisme.com.
 Location: Long established as a stopover on the upper Loire highway, the centre of town clusters on the E bank.

SIGHTS
Palais Ducal★
r. Sabatier.
The former residence of the Dukes of Nevers is a fine example of French Renaissance architecture.

Église St-Étienne★
This splendid Romanesque church has a magnificently tiered east end and a beautiful overall pattern of windows in the style of the great abbey church of Cluny. The height of the interior is particularly impressive for a building of its date (1063–97).

Sens★★

Burgundy

The once-important old town is girded by boulevards that replaced the ancient ramparts. In the city centre stands the first of France's great Gothic cathedrals.

A BIT OF HISTORY
The tribe of the Senones, who gave the town its name, was of the most powerful in Gaul. In 390BC they even invaded Italy and seized Rome.

Its central position in relation to Burgundy, Champagne and the Île-de-France gave Sens considerable importance for centuries; for a long time it was the Bishop of Sens who crowned French kings.

▶ **Population:** 26 904
𝒸 **Michelin Map:** 319 C 2
 Info: Place Jean-Jaurès. ℘03 86 65 19 49. www.office-de-tourisme-sens.com.
 Location: Approach the town from the W for the finest views. The town centre is around the cathedral. There's good shopping along pedestrianised Grande-Rue, and outdoor cafe tables in Place de la République.
 Don't Miss: The great Gothic cathedral.

SIGHT
Cathédrale St-Étienne★★

148 r. de la Résistance. ☞Guided tours available; contact tourist office. ℘03 86 83 88 90. http://catholique-sens-auxerre.cef.fr.

In its general conception this is the very first of France's great Gothic cathedrals, its foundations laid in the years 1128–30, though most building took place between 1140–1168.

The influence of the Romanesque can still be discerned in a number of features, like the slightly pointed "Burgundian" arches of the nave, a series of twin openings at tribune level with a false gallery, as yet no triforium, and, in the side chapels, a combination of rounded and pointed arches. But it is the Gothic which is decisive. There is use throughout of quadripartite vaulting; the choir has sexpartite vaults of square plan resting on massive pillars alternating with slender columns, and the ambulatory has pointed arches, still awkwardly asymmetrical.

Following the collapse of the south tower of the west front in 1268, the building was restored and altered, with the probable addition of flying buttresses. In the 13C and 14C, the clerestory windows were given extra height; then, in the 15C and 16C, the transepts were built in Flamboyant style.

Outside, the decorative features include the pier of the central portal, the famous statue of St Stephen, and the Flamboyant gable of the north portal.

Inside, the eye is drawn to the **stained glass**★★; which is 12C in the ambulatory and north side of the choir, while the Jesse Tree and St Nicholas in the south transept and the rose window of the north transept are all Renaissance works by master glaziers from Troyes. The ambulatory, the chapels opening off it, and the choir all have very fine grilles of wrought and gilded ironwork (18C).

Vézelay★★★
Burgundy

The quiet and picturesque little village of Vézelay climbs a steep slope among the northern foothills of the Morvan countryside, overlooking the Cure valley. Its fame is due to the majestic basilica which numbers among the greatest treasures of France.

- ▶ **Population:** 492
- ⚙ **Michelin Map:** 319 F 7
- ▤ **Info:** R. St-Étienne. ℘03 86 33 23 69. www.vezelaytourisme.com.
- ▷ **Location:** Vézelay is W of Avallon. Grande-Rue leads up to the basilica from Place du Champ-de-Foire at the foot of the village.

A BIT OF HISTORY

The Celts were the first to settle this hilltop site. In 878 an abbey was founded here, and in 1050 it was dedicated to Mary Magdalene, whose remains were supposedly here, and the place soon became one of France's great pilgrimage destinations. It suffered destruction by fire more than once.

It was here that St Bernard preached the Second Crusade in 1146. In 1279, however, the monks of St-Maximin in Provence claimed to have discovered the bones of Mary Magdalene in a cave; the certification of the relics as authentic led to the decline of Vézelay as a place of pilgrimage; it was pillaged by the Huguenots, razed at the time of the French Revolution and given its coup de grâce by lightning.

In 1840, Prosper Mérimée, who was in charge of the national survey of the country's heritage, came to Vézelay; recognising the value and significance of the ruin, he appointed the young Viollet-le-Duc as architect in charge of its restoration.

Aerial view of Vézelay with Basilique Ste-Marie-Madeleine

J. Damase/MICHELIN

SIGHT
Basilique Ste-Marie-Madeleine★★★

Pl. de la Basilique. ⊙*Closed during Church services.* ⊖*No charge.* ℘*03 86 33 39 50.* *http://vezelay.cef.fr.*
First built between 1096–1104 and restored following the fire of 1120. The principal external features are the fine Romanesque body of the church (to which flying buttresses were added in the 13C), St Antony's Tower (Tour St-Antoine), and a particularly harmonious chevet with radiating chapels. From the terrace, there is a fine **view**★ over the valley of the River Cure.

In the dimly lit narthex (1140–60) is the marvellous tympanum (**tympan★★★**) of the central doorway, dating from around 1125. Proportion is used to reinforce the meaning of the composition; for example, the figure of Christ is of superhuman size.
The Romanesque nave is unusually large and well lit. The greatest contribution to the basilica's decoration is made by the many capitals (**chapiteaux★★★**) adorning the pillars; these were sculpted from 1106 onwards. The magnificent Gothic **choir** (1185–1215) seems to have been influenced by the great new churches of the North of France.

Besançon★★
Jura

The capital of the Franche-Comté occupies a superb site★★★ on a meander of the River Doubs, overlooked by a rocky outcrop on which Vauban built a fortress which has resulted in the town being an outstanding example of 17C military architecture. The birthplace of the writer Victor Hugo, Besançon is also known for its many museums and fine architecture.

A BIT OF HISTORY
A 2C triumphal arch called the Black Gate (Porte Noire) survives from a Gallo-Roman settlement (Vesontio) first mentioned by Julius Caesar as the home of

▶ **Population:** 122 623
  Michelin Map: 321 G 3
Info: 2 pl. de la 1ére-Armée-Française. ℘03 81 80 92 55. www.besancon-tourisme.com.
Location: The historic centre of town lies within the circle (la boucle) of the Doubs river. Shops and restaurants can be found on Grande-Rue, near the bridges. The modern town is on lower ground across the river.
Timing: Allow several hours to appreate everything.

the Gaulish *Sequani* tribe: the modern Grande-Rue still follows the course of its main street in the heart of old Besançon. Later the town became an important archbishopric.

The city is closely connected with the Holy Roman Empire and was given the title of Imperial Free City in 1184. Through inheritance and marriages, in 15–16C the town – like the rest of Franche-Comté – became part of the Austro-Spanish empire. It marked a high point in the province's commercial life, illustrated by the rise of the Granvelle family. Although born into the humblest of peasant families, the son Perrenot was given an education, rose rapidly, becoming Chancellor to Charles V, and built himself the Palais Granvelle. In 1674 Louis XIV conquered the Franche-Comté, made Besançon its capital and had Vauban construct the citadel.

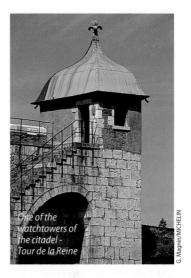

One of the watchtowers of the citadel - Tour de la Reine

G. Magnin/MICHELIN

SIGHTS

Palais Granvelle★

Grande-Rue.

This fine example of civil architecture of the 16C has a three-storey façade, divided by five horizontal bands of decoration, and a high mansard roof with crowstep gables. Its proportions and decorative details are those of the Early Renaissance (basket-handle arches, mouldings) while other features are quite new (Tuscan columns, and the superposition of Ionic and composite orders).

Citadel and Museums★★

99 r. des Fusillés-de-la-Résistance.
🕐*Open 25 Oct–28 Mar 10am–5pm; 29 Mar–4 Jul 9am–6pm; early Jul–Aug 9am–7pm; Sept–24 Oct 9am–6pm.*
🕐*Closed 25 Dec, 1 Jan.* ⊚*8.20€ (low season 6.80€).* 📞*03 81 87 83 33. www.citadelle.com.*

From 1675–1711 Vauban constructed this mighty fortress. Its great mass is best appreciated from the sentry-walk along the encircling ramparts. The building houses a zoo and several museums: Musée d'Histoire naturelle, Aquarium, Insectarium, Climatorium, Noctarium.

Musée des Beaux-Arts et d'Archéologie★★

1 pl. de la Révolution. 📞*03 81 87 80 49. www.musee-arts-besancon.org.*
🕐*Open Mon, Wed–Fri 9.30am–noon, 2–6pm; Sat–Sun 9.30am–6pm.*
🕐*Closed 1 Jan, 1 May, 1 Nov, 25 Dec.*
⊚*5€ (free on Sun).*

The museum houses a diverse collection of artistic, historical and archaeological displays. Most important is the priceless 14–17C art collection of the Granvelle family. A room on the first floor provides plenty of evidence of the long tradition of clock-and-watch-making in the Franche-Comté. Most of the great clock-making firms are represented at Besançon. Many of the important advances in the art from 17C to the present have been made here or nearby.

ADDITIONAL SIGHTS

Cathédrale St-Jean Painting of the Virgin with Saints★, **St-Jean Rose Window★** (Rose de St-Jean), **Astronomical Clock★ (Horloge astronomique)** *(r. du Chapitre)* **Folk Museum (Musée comtois) and Resistance and Deportation Museum** *(r. des fusillés)* **Préfecture★** *(8 bis r. Charles Nodier)*

Bourg-en-Bresse★★

Jura

Bourg is the capital of the Bresse area, famous in France for its high-quality poultry, which bears its own label of authentification.
It is situated to the west of the Jura Mountains on the River Reyssouze, a tributary of the Saône.

> ▶ **Population:** 40 972
> ⚲ **Michelin Map:**
> 328 C-D-E 34
> 🔲 **Info:** 6 av. Alsace Lorraine.
> 📞04 74 22 49 40.
> www.bourg-en-bresse.org.
> ◖ **Location:** The main attraction is the church at Brou, about 2km/1.2mi SE of the town centre.

A BIT OF HISTORY

Little is known about Bourg until it was awarded the status of a free town in 1250. Passed between Savoy and France several times, it finally became French in 1601.

"Fortune infortune fort une" – The sad motto of **Margaret of Austria** (1480–1530) can be translated (less poetically) as "Fate very hard on one woman." As a child of two, Margaret lost her mother, Mary of Burgundy. At three, she was chosen by Louis XI as the wife of the Dauphin Charles VIII because of her Burgundian inheritance; a form of wedding took place. Then, at the age of 11, she was repudiated by the Crown and the marriage annulled. At the age of 21 she married John of Castile who died after less than a year. At 24 she re-married, this time to Philibert le Beau. He too soon died. From then on Margaret's life was devoted to prayer and to quietly caring for the domains she had inherited. Her rule was marked by diplomacy, prudence and wisdom. As a result, in 1508 her father, the Emperor Maximilian, made her Regent of the Low Countries. Margaret, still only 26 years old, moved to Brussels, but also set about transforming the humble priory of Brou into a monastery, partly to fulfill a vow made 24 years earlier by her mother-in-law, Margaret of Bourbon, partly to symbolise her love for her husband.

SIGHT

Monastère royal de Brou★★

63 bd de Brou. ◷*Open Apr–Jun 9am–12.30pm, 2–6pm; Jul–Sept 9am–6pm; Oct–Mar 9am–noon, 2–5pm.* ◷*Closed public holidays.* ☞*7€.* ⚑ *Guided tours available.* 📞*04 74 22 83 83. www.brou.monuments-nationaux.fr.*
The church – now de-consecrated – was built from 1513–32 in exuberant Flamboyant Gothic style. The work was undertaken by a Flemish master builder and a team of artists and craftsmen, mostly from Flanders, where Margaret was now living. The interior decoration was already much influenced by the Renaissance. In the elegant nave built of pale stone from the Jura, a finely sculptured balustrade was substituted for the more usual triforium. The stone rood screen (**jubé★★**) has three basket-handle arches and is profusely decorated with leaves, cable-moulding and scrolls.
The 74 choir stalls (**stalles★★**) were built by local carpenters. An array of statuettes represents Biblical figures. In the Margaret of Austria chapel (**Oratoire★★★**) an altarpiece is a masterwork of amazing craftsmanship. There are also superb stained-glass windows (**vitraux★★**). The three tombs (**tombeaux★★★**) give the church its truly regal character. On the right is that of Margaret of Bourbon, in a Gothic niche with Flamboyant decoration. Philibert the Fair's elaborate tomb is completely Renaissance in character. Margaret of Austria's tomb forms part of the parclose screen; she is first shown lying in state on a black marble slab, then, underneath, in her shroud. Its richly carved canopy incorporates her motto.

ADDITIONAL SIGHT

Musée★ *(in the monastery)* – painting, sculpture, decorative arts.

Saut du Doubs

A. De. Valroger/MICHELIN

Saut du
Doubs★★★
Jura

- **Michelin Map:** 321 K 4
- **Info:** 5 r. Pierre Berçot, Villers-le-Lac. ℰ03 81 68 00 98. www.villers-le-lac-info.org.
- **Location:** The falls are in eastern Burgundy, close to the Swiss border.
- **Timing:** Follow a footpath through the woods to reach the main viewpoint (*45min return*); beyond, a very steep path descends to the lake itself, from where there is another most impressive view of the falls crashing down into the narrow defile.

The gorges of the River Doubs downstream from Villers-le-Lac mark the frontier between France and Switzerland. The river has cut down deeply into the highly folded Jurassic limestone, but here its course has been blocked by eroded material to form Lake Chaillexon (Lac de Chaillexon). Its waters escape from the lake over the 28m/92ft high Doubs Falls (Saut de Doubs). The falls are less interesting after a long period of dry weather.

Grand
Colombier★★★
Jura

- **Michelin Map:** 328 H 5
- **Info:** R. de la Mairie, Culoz, ℰ04 79 87 00 30. http://culoz.interarb.com/colom.
- **Location:** It's possible to drive almost to the top. Leave the car in the car park and continue to the summit on foot. It's a tough climb.
- **Don't Miss:** The road from Virieu-le-Petit to Culoz.

At 1 571m/5 154ft the Grand Colombier forms the highest point in the Bugey area. The viewpoint at the summit is one of the finest in the whole of the Jura.

VISIT
From Virieu-le-Petit to Culoz
29km/18mi.
The road rises steeply (maximum gradient 19%), passing first through splendid fir-woods. At the summit, with its cross and triangulation-point, there is the widest of panoramas, taking in the Jura, the Dombes plateau, the valley of the Rhône, the Massif Central and the Alps.

In the distance the Grand Fenestrez, crowned by an observatory (**Observatoire★★**) rears up from the Culoz plain, which can be reached by car via a boldly designed hairpin road.

Diagram showing the typical structure of the folded Jura

The synclines form valleys (vals) running parallel to each other, separated by anticlinal ridges (monts). Transversal valleys (cluses) cut across anticlines to link two main valleys. A high-level depression (combe) occupies a hollowed-out ridge: it has steep inward-facing scarps (crêts).

Lons-le-Saunier★

Jura

The capital of the Jura is a spa town with an interesting heritage, and makes a good base for excursions to the vineyards or the Jura plateau. The local *Vin Jaune* or yellow wine is similar in taste to dry sherry.

▶ **Population:** 18 483
○ **Michelin Map:** 321 D 6
▣ **Info:** Place du 11-novembre. ℘03 84 24 65 01. www.ville-lons-le-saunier.fr.
◖ **Location:** Near the Swiss border. Its centre is Place de la Liberté.

SIGHT
Rue du Commerce★

The town was ravaged by fire between 25 June–4 July 1636 when it was attacked by Condé on Richelieu's orders. Seven years later, the population was amnestied by Mazarin and allowed to return. The Rue du Commerce was rebuilt in accordance with a detailed plan in the second half of the 17C; it is elegantly laid out on a slight curve and is famous for its great variety of shops with their attractive displays.

What might have been a monotonous piece of planning reflects instead a local love of independence and appreciation of good design. Note particularly the high roofs with their mansards and tall chimneys, the 146 stone arcades (some of them of Romanesque date) of many different shapes and sizes, the trapdoors leading to the cellars, sculpted heads, and balconies and window decoration in wrought iron.

No 24 is the birthplace of Rouget de l'Isle, composer of the *Marseillaise*, the French national anthem and a museum in the Hôtel-de-Ville has a collection of his songs. A statue of the great man by Bartholdi, (the designer of the Statue of Liberty in New York Harbour), can be found on the Promenade de la Chevalerie. Erected in 1882, it was declared a National Monument in 1992 for the bi-centennial celebrations of the *Marseillaise* song.

EXCURSION
Cirque de Baume★★★

19km/11.8mi E.

This is one of the most spectacular of the blind valleys characteristic of the western rim of the Jura.

The action of water has been particularly significant here in undermining the upper beds of limestone, which have caved in, thus creating the impressive gorge we see today. The viewpoint at Roches de Baume (*near the D 471*) gives splendid prospects over this great natural amphitheatre with its 200m/650ft walls marking the boundary between the high plateau of the western Jura and the Bresse plain.

Pontarlier

Jura

Between the 13–17C this proud upland town, which still commands the internationally important Besançon-Lausanne highway, was the capital of the area known as the Baroichage. This statelet, consisting of Pontarlier and the 18 surrounding villages, enjoyed an independent regime of republican character which was only extinguished by Louis XIV's conquest of the Franche-Comté. Today, Pontarlier is a busy resort and commercial centre.

EXCURSIONS

Cluse de Pontarlier★★
5km/3mi S.

The Jura has many such cluses – lateral clefts through the high ridges separating two valleys that facilitates communication between valley communities. This example, with the road and railway tightly squeezed together in the narrow defile, is strategically located on the route to Switzerland and overlooked by the Larmont and Joux forts high above (the Cluse de Joux is one of the Jura's most beautiful cluses).

▶ **Population:** 18 360
Michelin Map: 321 i 5
Info: 14 bis r. de la Gare. ℘03 81 46 48 33. www.pontarlier.org.
▶ **Location:** The town lies near the Swiss border at the foot of the Jura mountains.

The Château de Joux is a spectacular site site which exhibits the evolution of defensive structures from the Middle Ages to the late 19C.

Lac de St-Point★
8km/5mi S.

Nearly 7km/4.3mi long and covering 398ha/983 acres, it is the largest lake in the Jura, fed by the waters of the River Doubs and attractively sited among mountain pastures and firwoods.

Source de la Loue★★★
16km/10mi W.

The River Loue rises in one of the blind valleys that penetrate deeply into the high plateau of the Jura. In its setting of high cliffs and luxuriant vegetation, it is one of the region's finest natural sites.

Chapelle de Ronchamp★★

Haute-Saône (by Jura)

Built by **Le Corbusier** (1887–1965), the Chapelle Notre-Dame-du-Haut on its hilltop site is one of few great works of religious architecture produced by the early 20C Modern Movement. The characteristically Corbusian use of fluid appears here to great effect.

VISIT

The apparent simplicity of the building's curving lines and asymmetrical surfaces can be deceptive, as can the architect's subtle use of light falling from the "periscopes" in the side chapels, fil-

Michelin Map: 314 H 6
Info: Rue Chapelle, Ronchamp. ℘03 84 20 65 13. www.chapellede ronchamp.fr.
▶ **Location:** Ronchamp is a small former mining town bordering Alsace.

tering in from the base of the convex vault or streaming through the irregular wall-openings which constitute the building's main decoration. Only slowly does one come to appreciate the fusion of feeling and technology which is the measure of the greatness of this unique work of art.

CHÂTEAUX OF THE LOIRE

Rising far to the southeast in the Massif Central, France's longest river, the Loire, was once a busy waterway. Many of the towns along its banks bear traces of this former activity: from Orléans, once the Loire's foremost port, Blois, Tours, Langeais and Saumur. As with other great rivers, navigation was never easy and, once the railways came, the Loire was left to its caprices. Nowadays the region is famous for its magnificent Renaissance châteaux, which adorn the banks of the Loire's tributaries, the Indre and the Cher.

Highlights

1 Exceptional tapestry at Angers **Tenture de l'Apocalypse** *(p245)*

2 French Gothic style: **d'Azay le Rideau** *(p247)*

3 First of France's Classical palaces: **Chambord** *(p250)*

4 Château partly built on a bridge: **Chenonceau** *(p251)*

5 Formal gardens (Jardins) at **Villandry** *(p265)*

Geography – This "garden of France", as the Loire Valley has been called, has also been called "a home-spun cloak with golden fringes", a reference to the contrast between the fertile valleys of the Loire and its tributaries and the low plâteaux that separate them. From Orléans onwards the Loire exercises its greatest attraction, with gentle landscapes and soft light.

History – Following the withdrawal of the Romans the Franks occupied the region. Viking incursions affected Tours and Angers during the 9C, but until the 12C most of the area was held by powerful barons. After 1202 King Philippe-Auguste was able to take charge following the seizure of the territory from King John of England. In the late medieval period the region was involved in the Hundred Years' War with much of the Loire falling into English hands again. During the 16C, however, the great château-building period began as part of the new ways of thinking about art and architecture ushered in by the Renaissance and exemplified by the magnificent edifices at Chenonceau, Azay, Blois and Chambord, their elegance and architectural exhuberance contrasting with the sterner fortresses of an earlier age, like the great castle at Angers. Other buildings have white tufa walls and slate roofs; around Amboise and Tours are are trogloditic dwellings.

Economy – The Loire Valley is a major agricultural region, cultivating vines, cereals, rapeseed, sugarbeet and sunflowers. Manufacturing is important with the production of car parts, ball bearings and tyres, made possible partly by the establishment of three nuclear power plants and partly by excellent communications. Tourism, also vitally important, is based on the châteaux and the great Cathedrals of Orléans and Tours.

Amboise★★

Amboise is a bridge-town, built at the foot of an escarpment already fortified in Gallo-Roman times, on which stand the proud remains of its great château which appears at its most picturesque when viewed from the north side of the river.

SIGHTS
Château★★

🕐 Open daily Jul and Aug 9am–7pm; Apr–Jun 9am–6.30pm; 1 Sept–1 Nov daily 9am–6pm; Mar and 2–15 Nov 9am–5.30pm; 16 Nov–31 Jan 9am–12.30pm, 2–4.45pm; Feb 9am–12.30pm, 1.30–5pm. 🕐 Closed 1 Jan, 25 Dec. ☞9.50€. ✆08 20 20 50 50. www.chateau-amboise.com.

The 15C saw the Golden Age of Amboise. Charles VIII was born here in 1470; from his 22nd year onwards he carried on the work begun by his father, Louis XI. By the time he left on his Italian campaign, work was well in hand on a number of projects: the round towers, the great Gothic roof of the wing overlooking the Loire, and the Flamboyant St-Hubert Chapel, which served as an oratory for Anne of Brittany and has particularly fine Flemish door panels. In 1496 Charles returned from Italy, bringing with him not only works of art but a whole retinue of artists, architects, sculptors, cabinet-makers and gardeners. With these Italians came a taste for Antiquity and a decorative sense unknown at the time in France (doorways resembling triumphal arches, inlaid ceilings, superimposed arches, etc.). Charles' liking for luxury enhanced the prestige of the monarchy; his promotion of the artistic ideas of the Renaissance was continued by Louis XII and even more by François I, under whom château life became a whirl of princely gaiety with festivals, entertainments, hunting parties. However, this first French château of the Renaissance was destined to disappear; partly demolished by the troops of Louis XIII, it was further dismantled on the orders of Napoleon's Senate. Now it is known only from an engraving by Du Cerceau.

▶ **Population:** 11 460
⏱ **Michelin Map:** 317-O 4
ℹ **Info:** Quai du Gén.-de-Gaulle. ✆02 47 57 09 28. www.amboise-valdeloire.com.
◐ **Location:** The busy town centre rises from the S bank of the Loire.
🅿 **Parking:** There is metered parking on Quai du Gén.-de-Gaulle, the main road beside the river.
👫 **Kids:** On the edge of town there are sights kids will love, including touring the Parc des Mini-Châteaux (La Menaudière – D31; ✆0 2 47 23 44 57; www.mini-chateaux.com) and marvelling at the 44m/144.3ft-high Chinese pagoda at the Parc de la Pagode de Chanteloup (Route de Blere; ✆02 47 57 20 97; www.pagode-chanteloup.com).

Tour – From the **terrace**, there is a fine view of the Loire Valley and the slate-blue roofs of the town. Inside, the **Royal Apartments** are the only part of the château that escaped demolition from 1806–1810. The tour of the interior takes

Château's Salle du Conseil
B.Kaufmann/MICHELIN

in the **Salle des Gardes nobles**, or guard room; the **Salle des tambourineurs**, which features interesting furniture and a 16C Brussels tapestry, **Homage to Alexander the Great**; the **Salle du conseil**, also known as the Hall of State, where the king presided over the State Council (which decided policies of the realm); and **Henry II's bedchamber**, adorned with trompe-l'oeil decoration. Visit the two towers, **Tour des Minimes** and **Tour Herutault**, the latter of which leads directly to the town of Amboise. Laid out in informal English style, the pleasant **gardens** are worth seeing.

Clos-Lucé★

Very near the Château. ◷*Open daily Jul and Aug 9am–8pm; Feb–Mar, Apr–Jun and Sept–Oct 9am–7pm; Nov–Dec 9am–6pm; Jan 10am–5pm.* ◷*Closed 1 Jan, 25 Dec.* ₪*12€ (winter 9€).* ₢*02 47 57 00 73. www.vinci-closluce.com.*

To this manor house of red brick with stone dressings François I invited **Leonardo da Vinci** in 1516. The great Florentine was then age 64. At Amboise he neither painted nor taught, devoting himself instead to organising royal festivities, designing a château at Romorantin, planning the drainage of the Sologne and amusing himself designing mechanical inventions some of which now have been constructed in a display of "fabuleuses machines".

Angers★★★

This dynamic and cultured city on the river Maine was once the capital of a mighty Plantagenet kingdom encompassing all of England and half of France.

A BIT OF HISTORY

On 9 June 1129, Geoffrey Plantagenet married William the Conqueror's granddaughter Mathilda, whose inheritance of both Normandy and England made her the most desirable of brides. Twenty-three years later another significant marriage took place, between Henry II, Geoffrey's son, and Eleanor of Aquitaine, the divorced wife of Louis VII.

Two months later Henry became King of England, thereby extending the frontiers of the Angevin state to Scotland in the north and the Basque country in the south. By contrast, the Capetian kingdom to the east cut a sorry figure; its capital, Paris, seeming little more than an overgrown village in comparison with Angers.

In 1203, with the 81-year-old Eleanor living in retirement at Fontevraud, King Philippe Auguste succeeded in incorporating Anjou into the French

- ▶ **Population:** 226 843
- ⚲ **Michelin Map:** 317 E-F-G 4
- 🛈 **Info:** 7 place du Président-Kennedy. ₢02 41 23 50 00. www.angers-tourisme.com.
- ▷ **Location:** A fun way to discover the city is a tour on the Petit Train, which drives around to all the main sights. There are also Taxi Tours, and guided Discovery Tours on foot. Ask at the tourist office for details.
- 🅿 **Parking:** Parking is available by the château on Esplanade du Port-Ligny.
- ⊛ **Don't Miss:** The 14C Tenture de l'Apocalypse and other historic tapestries.
- ◷ **Timing:** After visiting the château (2hr), allow at least half a day to walk through the streets of the Old Town.

kingdom, together with Normandy, Maine, Touraine and Poitou, all territories of John Lackland. In 1471, King **René** let Anjou pass into the hands of Louis XI.

SIGHTS
Château★★★

2 Promenade du Bout-du-Monde *Open daily May–early Sept 9.30am–6.30pm; early Sept–Apr 10am–5.30pm. Last admission 45min before closing. Closed Jan 1, May 1, Nov 1 and 11, Dec 25. Guided tours available (2hr). 6€ (reduced due to fire; normally 8€), no charge 1st Sun in the month from Oct–Mar. 02 41 86 48 77. www.monum.fr.*

Built by Louis IX from 1228 to 1238 on the surviving Roman foundations, this splendid fortress was intended to counter any threat from the nearby Dukes of Brittany. With 17 towers in alternating courses of dark schist and white freestone they must have constituted a formidable deterrent. The moats were dug in 1485 by Louis XI. During the Wars of Religion (1562–1598), the towers were reduced in height and terraces added to give the defenders a clear field of fire.

A purpose-built gallery at the heart of the château displays the **Tenture de l'Apocalypse**★★★, a tapestry, originally 168m/550ft long and 5m/16ft high, the oldest and most important to have been preserved. Jean Lurçat (1892–1966) who discovered it in 1938 and whose artistic career was inspired by it, called it "one of the greatest works of Western art". The 76 extant scenes are based on the Apocalypse of St John, and are impressive in their masterly scale, composition and design. Commissioned by the Duke of Anjou Louis I, this superb tapestry was executed in 1375–1380 by master weaver **Nicolas Bataille**.

In the Governor's Lodging, a fine collection of Flemish tapestries includes the 16C *Lady at the Organ* and *Penthesilea* and the richly coloured late 15C three-part *Tenture de la Passion et Tapisseries mille-fleurs*★★ with graceful angels carrying the instruments of the Passion.

Cathédrale St-Maurice★★

The cathedral stands in a charming district of old houses.

The characteristically elegant Angevin vault is notable in the 12C vaulting of the nave, with its transverse arches with double roll mouldings by Normand le Doué. By the end of the century the vaulting has become lighter; the number of ribs increases, springing from slender

Château d'Angers

Studio 3 Bis/MICHELIN

columns, as in the choir and transepts. At the beginning of the 13C it reaches its peak of development: lateral support is dispensed with; the structure dissolves into a graceful web of liernes, as in the hospital ward of the former **hôpital St-Jean★** (St John's Hospital), resting on a small number of slim columns, as in the early 13C ceiling of the choir of the Église St-Serge .

Musée Jean-Lurçat et de la Tapisserie contemporaine★★

4 bd. Arago. ♿🕐*Open Jun–Sept daily 10am–7pm; Oct–Jun Tue–Sun 10am–noon, 2–6pm.* 🕐*Closed 1 Jan, 1*

ADDRESSES

🛏 STAY

⊝⊝**Chambre d'hôte Grand Talon** – *3 rte des Chapelles. 49800 Andard, 11km/6.8mi E of Angers on N 147 (towards Saumur) then D 113.* 📞*02 41 80 42 85.* *3 rooms.* This elegant 18C house just outside Angers, decked out with leafy vines of Virginia creeper, is a haven of peace. You can picnic in the park, or relax in the lovely square courtyard. The rooms are pretty and the owners extend a very warm welcome.

⊝⊝**Hôtel Cavier** – *La Croix-Cadeau – 49240 Avrillé, 8km/5mi NW of Angers on N 162.* 📞*02 41 42 30 45. 43 rooms.* ⊠*10€.* The sails of this 18C windmill still turn! Inside its old stone walls is the dining room, near the original machinery. Modern bedrooms in a recent wing. Terrace next to the outdoor pool.

⊝⊝**Hôtel Mail** – *8 r. des Ursules.* 📞*02 41 25 05 25. www.hotel-du-mail.com. 26 rooms.* ⊠*9€.* The thick walls of this former Ursuline convent in a peaceful street prevent the noise from the nearby town centre from penetrating. The fairly spacious rooms have a personal touch and are under the sloping roof on the top floor.

⊝⊝**Le Progrès** – *26 r. Denis-Papin.* 📞*02 41 88 10 14. w ww.hotelleprogres. com. Closed 7–15 Aug, 24 Dec–3 Jan. 41 rooms.* ⊠*7.50€.* Conveniently located near the train station, this is

May, 14 Jul, 1 and 11 Nov, 25 Dec;⊜*4€.* 📞*02 41 05 38 00 . www.angers.fr.* The former St John's Hospital, founded 1174 and in use for 680 years, now houses the **Musée Jean-Lurçat**. In the hospital ward with its Angevin vaulting is Lurçat's series of tapestries known as **Le Chant du Monde★★** (The Song of the World), ten huge compositions symbolising the contradictions of the modern world. Lurçat's achievement marked the revival of the art of tapestry.

ADDITIONAL SIGHT
Romanesque arcade★★ (in the prefecture)

a friendly place with modern, well-lit and practical rooms. Before setting out to tour the château, enjoy your coffee in the breakfast room, with its décor inspired by the bright colours of Provence.

🍴 EAT

⊝**La Ferme** – *2 pl. Freppel.* 📞*02 41 87 09 90. www.la-ferme.fr. Closed 24 Dec–6 Jan and Aug, Sun eve and Wed. Reservations required.* A well-known restaurant near the cathedral, where you can enjoy traditional local cooking in a simple setting. The terrace is one of the nicest in town.

⊝⊝**Provence Caffé** – *9 pl. du Ralliement .* 📞*02 41 87 44 15. Closed, Aug, 24 Dec–15 Jan, Sun and Mon. Reservations required.* This popular restaurant next to the Hôtel St-Julien is often full both at lunchtime and in the evenings. The patron is from the south of France and the menu reflects this, with its Mediterranean flavours. The dining room has a Provençal atmosphere too. Carefully prepared cuisine at moderate prices.

⊝⊝**Le Relais** – *9 r. de la Gare.* 📞*02 41 88 42 51. Closed Aug, 24 Dec–4 Jan, Sun and Mon.* The woodwork and the murals in this charming tavern recall the vineyard and the harvest. The traditional cooking is satisfying and simple, at affordable prices.

🛒SHOPPING

Maison du Vin de l'Anjou – *5 bis, pl. Kennedy. ☎02 41 88 81 13. www. vinsdeloire.fr.* In the centre of town, near the château, this wine shop offers a good selection of Anjou and Saumur wines, which you can taste.

La Petite Marquise – *22 r. des Lices. ☎02 41 87 43 01.* Does *Quernons d'Ardoise* mean anything to you? If you don't know about this delicious local speciality of nougatine and chocolate made to look like roof slates, then head to this little shop where they were first created.

🚶 OUTDOOR LEISURE ACTIVITIES

Maison de l'Environnement – This nature information centre organises various activities including environment-awareness courses.

Public Gardens and Parks – Jardin des Plantes, Jardin du Mail, Jardin Médiéval, French-style gardens in the moat and Parcs de l'étang St-Nicolas on the outskirts of town. *Open daily.*

Boat Trips – Possibilities include a combined tourist-train ride and mini boat trip on the River Maine or a candlelit dinner/cruise. *Batellerie promenade l'Union, cale de la Savatte. 49100 Angers. ☎02 41 42 12 12.*

Château d'Azay-le-Rideau★★★

Sitting in a verdant setting where the waters of the Indre act as reflecting pools, this castle was built for financier Gilles Berthelot from 1518–1529.

VISIT

🕐*Open daily Apr–Sept daily 9.30am–6pm (Jul and Aug 7pm); Oct–Mar 10am–12.30pm, 2–5.30pm. Last admission 45min before closing.* 🕐*Closed 1 Jan, 1 May, 25 Dec. ✆8€. ☎02 47 45 42 04. www.azay-le-rideau. monuments-nationaux.frmonum.fr.*

The château d'Azay-le-Rideau was built in French Gothic style. Its defences (machicolated cornice, pepperpot towers and turrets) are purely decorative. By contrast, the interior shows Italianate influences.

The decoration includes Florentine shells in the gable of the great dormer window, pilasters, moulded entablatures and above all the grand staircase with straight flights and rectangular landings. The interior is also notable for the French-style ceiling in the dining room and the chimney piece in the François I Room.

- 🔧 **Michelin Map:** 31 I 5
- 🛈 **Info:** 4 r. du Château. ☎02 47 45 44 40. www. ot-paysazaylerideau.fr.
- ▶ **Location:** Azay lies about 25km/15.5mi from Tours in the direction of Chinon.
- 🕐 **Timing:** Allow 45min for the castle and 1hr for the park.

Château d'Azay-le-Rideau

B. Kaufmann/MICHELIN

Blois★★

Blois looks northwards to the Beauce and south to the Sologne, and is situated at that point on the Loire at which the limestone landscapes around Orléans give way almost imperceptibly to the chalk country of Touraine downstream. Originally defended by a medieval castle, the town was transformed from 1503 onwards when the kings moved there from Amboise, bringing in their train all the trades devoted to satisfying the royal taste for luxury.

SIGHT
Château★★★

○*Open daily Apr–Sept 9am–6pm; Sept–Mar 9am–12.30pm, 2–5.30pm. Last admission 30min before closing.* ○*Closed 1 Jan and 25 Dec.* ⊜*6.50€.* ℘*02 54 90 33 32. www.ville-blois.fr.* ○*For Illustration, see p79.*

The whole development of secular French architecture from feudalism to the Classicism of Louis XIII's reign can be traced at Blois.

The medieval remains include the round towers, spiral stairways and steep-pitched roofs of the Foix Tower and the Chamber of the States-General of 1205; with its panelled ceiling, this is where the States-General held its Assemblies in 1576 and 1588.

▶ **Population:** 49 171
⚙ **Michelin Map:** 318 C-D-E-F 5-6-7
🛈 **Info:** 23 pl. du Château. ℘02 54 90 41 41. www. bloispaysdechambord.com
▶ **Location:** The town climbs gently from the Loire, the château sitting at the very top.
😊 **Don't Miss:** Be sure to stroll in the old quarter, which rises behind the town centre.
👪 **Kids:** Across the square from the château, the Magic Museum (1 pl. du Château ℘02 54 90 33 33; ⊜8€ (child 5€); www. maisondelamagie.fr) will entertain young ones.

The transition from the Gothic to the Renaissance is evident in the Charles of Orléans Gallery and particularly in the Louis XII Wing of 1498–1501. Louis had been born at Blois in 1462 and, together with Anne of Brittany, carried out a number of improvements including the construction of a new wing.

This was right up to date with its triumphal arch doorways, Italianate arabesque decoration applied to the three Gothic pillars on the courtyard side, and the use of galleries to link

Blois old town viewed from the Loire

S. Sauvignier/MICHELIN

rooms rather than having them run directly into one another.

Built only 15 years later, possibly by Claude de France, the François I wing exemplifies the preoccupation with ornamentation that swept in with the first phase of the French Renaissance. The work remained incomplete but the new taste for sumptuous decoration is very apparent, not only in the Façade des Loges (built 7m/23ft in front of the old rampart) with its still-irregular fenestration, but also in Pierre Trinquart's François I staircase; though somewhat over-restored in the view of some archaeologists, this is a richly decorated masterpiece with openings between its buttresses forming a series of balconies. The much-modified interior includes, on the first floor, Catherine de Medici's study with its secret cupboards, and on the second floor, Henri III's apartments, scene of the murder of Henri de Guise. The King's brother employed François Mansart, who, however, failed to deploy the full range of his talents, his work here being stiff rather than dignified. Building stopped when the birth of Louis XIV put paid to his uncle's hopes of succeeding to the throne.

ADDRESSES

STAY

⊜ ⊜ **Hôtel Anne de Bretagne** – *31 av. J.-Laigret.* ✆*02 54 78 05 38 . Closed 9 Jan–6 Feb. 28 rooms.*⊇ *6.50€.* This small family hotel is near the castle and the terraced Jardin du Roi. The rooms are decorated in attractive colours and well soundproofed; those on the third floor are under the sloping roof.

⊜ ⊜ ⊜ **Chambre d'hôte La Villa Médicis** – *1 r. St-Denis, Macé, 41000 St-Denis-sur-Loire. 4km/2.5mi NE of Blois on N 152 towards Orléans.* ✆*02 54 74 46 38 .Reservations required in winter. 6 rooms.* Marie de Medici came to take the waters at the springs in the park in which this 19C villa was built, as a hotel for spa patrons at the time.

⚭ EAT

⊜ ⊜ **Au Bouchon Lyonnais** – *25 r. des Violettes.* ✆*02 54 74 12 87. Closed 20 Dec–10 Jan and Sun, except public holidays. Reservations recommended.* Located just at the bottom of the hill crowned by the château, this restaurant is a favourite with residents of Blois, who enjoy the rustic décor with exposed beams and stone walls. The menu features regional fare.

⊜ ⊜ **Au Rendez-vous des Pêcheurs** – *27 r. Foix.* ✆*02 54 74 67 48. Closed 2–14 Jan, 29 Jul–20 Aug, Mon lunchtime and Sun. Reservations recommended.* A provincial-style bistro in the old part of Blois. Stained-glass windows filter the light in the quiet dining room. Fish features prominently among the fresh market produce on the menu.

⊜ ⊜ ⊜ **Le Bistrot du Cuisinier** – *20 quai Villebois-Mareuil .* ✆*02 54 78 06 70.* You'll find a real bistro atmosphere here, simple and relaxed, and from the front dining room there is a splendid view of Blois and the Loire.

🛒 SHOPPING

Rue du Commerce and the adjacent streets in the pleasant pedestrian-only town centre (*r. du Rebrousse-Pénil, r. St-Martin*) offer all kinds of shops.

SON ET LUMIÈRE

👥 *Shows are put on nightly at the château from Easter–Sept from 10pm. The Wed show is in English. 7€ (child 3€).* ✆*02 54 90 33 32. www.ville-blois.fr.* Alain Decaux of the Académie Française wrote the texts that retrace the history of Blois – "a thousand years' history spanning ten centuries of splendour" – and they are read by famous French actors including Michael Lonsdale, Fabrice Luchini, Robert Hossein, Pierre Arditi and Henri Virlojeux. Enormous projectors, combining photographs with special lighting effects, and the very latest in sound transmission systems make for a lively, entertaining and visually stimulating show, despite there being no live actors participating in the show.

Château de
Brissac★★

The château, set in a fine park shaded by magnificent **cedar trees**★, is unusual both for its height and for the juxtaposition of two buildings, one of which was intended to replace the other rather than stand next to it.

- ⏱ **Michelin Map:** 317 G 4
- **Info:** 8 pl. de la République, Brissac-Quincé. ☎02 41 91 21 50. www.otbrissac-loire-aubance.fr.
- ▶ **Location:** Brissac lies 18km/11.2mi from Angers.
- **Don't Miss:** Be sure to see the tapestries inside the château.

VISIT
🎧Guided tours (45min) Jul–Aug Wed–Mon 10am–6pm; Mar 28–Oct 10am–12.15pm, 2–6pm; Nov–27 Mar; ring for details. ☎8.80€. ☎02 41 91 22 21. www.brissac.net.

As the original building had been damaged during the Wars of Religion, Duke Charles de Cossé commissioned a new residence designed by Jacques Corbineau, the architect responsible for the citadel at Port-Louis in Lorient. Work ceased on his death in 1621 and the château was left as we see it today. There is an unfinished main façade flanked by medieval towers. The central pavilion and the left wing are abundantly ornamented with rusticated pilasters and statues in niches. The right wing, which would have replaced the Gothic tower, was never built.

The 17C French painted **ceilings** are often embellished with sculptures; the walls are hung with superb **tapestries**. The Louis XIII staircase leads to the imposing guard room (Salle des Gardes), to the bedchamber where Louis XIII and his mother, Marie de' Medici, had a short-lived reconciliation after the Battle of Ponts-de Cé (1620), and to the Hunt Room (Chambre des Chasses) hung with magnificent 16C Flemish tapestries.

North of Brissac, on the road to Angers, stands a fine windmill with a chamber hollowed out at ground level.

Château de
Chambord★★★

The first of France's great Classical palaces, Chambord stands in a vast park enclosed by a 32km/19.8mi wall. Beyond stretches the forest of Sologne, teeming with the game that the rulers of France have long loved to hunt.

- ⏱ **Michelin Map:** 318 G 6
- **Info:** pl. Saint Louis, Chambord. ☎02 54 33 39 16. www.chambord.org.
- ▶ **Location:** The château is S of the Loire, between Beaugency and Blois, at the end of a long avenue through woodland.
- 🕐 **Timing:** Allow at least 2hr for the château.
- **Don't Miss:** Two particularly outstanding features of this immense château are the double spiral staircase and the roof terrace.

A BIT OF HISTORY
At the age of 21, François I had just returned in triumph from his victory over the Swiss at Marignano which had given him possession of the Duchy of Milan. Dissatisfied with the old royal residence at Blois in spite of the improvements he had made, he had a vision of a dream castle to be built four leagues away

on the forest edge. Leonardo da Vinci may have helped with the plans for this fabulous edifice; its feudal keep and corner towers belied its purpose as a palace of pleasure and status symbol for a Renaissance prince. The château was begun in 1519; later Philibert Delorme, Jean Bullant and the great Mansart all worked on it.

Hardly had Chambord started to rise from its foundations when the king suffered defeat and captivity at Pavia in 1525. On his return to France he judged it more suitable for a monarch to live close to his capital, at either Fontainebleau or St-Germain-en-Laye.

VISIT

⏱*Open Jan–Mar and Oct–Dec 9am5.15pm; Apr–10 Jul and 17 Aug–Sept until 6.15pm; 11 Jul–16 Aug until 7.30pm; last entry 30min before closing.* ⏱*Closed 1 Jan, 1 May, 25 Dec.* ⊚*8.50€.* *Guided tours (5 languages) on request.* ☎*02 54 50 40 00. www.chambord.org.*

From the entrance there is a fine view of the keep linked to the corner towers by two arcades surmounted by galleries.

A gallery was added to the façade towards the end of the reign of François i at the same time as the two spiral staircases in the north corners of the courtyard.

The château's famous double staircase, undoubtedly conceived by Leonardo da Vinci, is justly famous for its interlocking spirals opening onto internal loggias and for its vaults adorned with salamanders, François' crest. The extraordinary roof terrace was where the king and his entourage spent much of their time watching tournaments and festivals or the start and return of the hunt; its nooks and crannies lent themselves to the confidences, intrigues and assignations of courtly life, played out against this fantastic background of pepperpot turrets, chimney stacks, dormers peeping from the roofs, false windows embellished with shells, all decorated with inset slatework and dominated by the splendid lantern.

The state rooms contain rich furnishings: wood panelling, tapestries, furniture, portraits and hunting collections.

Château de
Chenonceau★★★

Chenonceau is a jewel of Renaissance architecture built 1513–1521 on the site of a fortified mill on the River Cher by Thomas Bohier, François I's treasurer. It is a rectangular building with corner-towers; it stands on two piers of the former mill resting on the bed of the Cher. The library and the chapel are projecting structures to the left. Catherine de Medici's two-storeyed gallery is built on the elegant 60m/197ft multi-arched bridge spanning the river and provides one of the region's iconic views .

- ♿ **Michelin Map:** 317 P 5
- ℹ **Info:** 1 r. Bretonneau.
  ☎02 47 23 94 45.
- ▶ **Location:** 14km/8.7mi S of Amboise, the château straddles the River Cher. The main entrance is on the N bank.
- ⏱ **Timing:** Allow at least 2hr for the château, the gardens and a riverbank stroll

A BIT OF HISTORY

Over the years the place has been in the charge of six women, of whom three marked it strongly with their personality. Catherine Briçonnet was the wife of Thomas Bohier. In his absence she supervised much of the building work. It is to her that we owe the central hall giving onto all the other rooms; its axial vault, broken by keystones, is a masterpiece. Another innovation is the introduction into the Loire Valley of an Italian staircase, that is, one that substitutes ramps for Gothic spirals, and is consequently much better adapted for receptions. However, here the returns are still curved and provided with steps.

In 1556 Diane de Poitiers commissioned Philibert Delorme, who had previously worked for her at Anet, to design the flower garden (to the east) as well as the bridge across the Cher.

Three years later, on the death of Henri II, Catherine de' Medici humiliated the former favourite by forcing her to exchange Chenonceau for Chaumont. Later, she added the two extra storeys to the bridge, laid out the gardens to the west and gave the windows their elaborate pediments.

VISIT

🕐 *Open daily Jul–Aug and public holidays 9am–8pm; Jun and Sept 9am–7.30pm; 1–23 Oct 9am–6.30pm; 24 Oct–4 Nov 9am–6pm; 5 Nov–6 Feb 9.30–5pm; 7 Feb–15 Mar 9.30–6pm; 16 Mar–31 Mar 9.30–7pm; Apr–May 9am–7pm.* 🎫*10€.* 📞*02 47 23 90 07.*
There is much to see within the château; a fine fireplace by **Jean Goujon** (in the Salle Diane de Poitiers), the Library of 1521, the ceiling of the Green Cabinet (Cabinet Vert), the portrait of Diane by Primaticcio, the tapestries and mantelpiece of the Salon Louis XIV, a fine Renaissance creation with its wealth of scrolls, baskets of fruit, cornucopias and fantastic beasts.

Château de
Cheverny★★★

Cheverny was built between 1604 and 1634 with that simplicity and distinction characteristic of the Classical architecture of the reigns of Henri IV and Louis XIII.

VISIT

🕐 *Open Jul–Aug daily 9.15am–6.45pm; Apr–Jun and Sept daily 9.15am–6.15pm; Oct daily 9.45am–5.30pm; Nov–Mar daily 9.45am–5pm; "feeding the dogs" early Apr–mid-Sept daily 5pm; mid-Sept–Mar Wed–Fri and Mon 3pm.* 🕐*Closed public holidays.* 🎫*7.40€ (château and park).* 📞*02 54 79 96 29. www.chateau-cheverny.com.The main façade is built in stone from* **Bourré** *(28km/17.4mi SW), which whitens and hardens with age.*

The elevation is strictly symmetrical, extending to either side of the well containing the staircase, and terminated by massive corner pavilions with square domes. The prominent slate roofs are in Louis XIII style, pierced with mansards

- ⛪ **Michelin Map:** 318 F 7
- ℹ️ **Info:** 12 r. des Chenes des Dames, Cour-Cheverny. 📞02 54 79 95 63.
- ▶ **Location:** 17km/10.5mi S of Blois, the château can be seen from afar.
- 🕐 **Timing:** It will take about 1hr to visit the château, but if the weather is fine, allow some time to walk and relax in the beautiful gardens.
- 👪 **Kids:** There's a permanent exhibition on the cartoon character Tintin.

and bull's-eye windows. The first-floor windows are crowned with scrolls; between them are medallions of Roman emperors (Julius Caesar in the central pediment). The elegant doorway is adorned with two concentric collars. The state rooms, served by a majestic Louis XIII ramped staircase with massive balustrades and rich sculptural decoration, contain a fine collection of furniture from the 17–19C.

Main façade, Château de Cheverny

Studio 3bis/MICHELIN

Chinon★★

Chinon occupies a sunny site on the Vienne, surrounded by the fertile Veron countryside, and known for the mildness of its climate.

SIGHTS
Le Vieux Chinon★★
The old town has kept its medieval and Renaissance appearance. The old gabled houses with corner turrets and the 16C and 17C mansions, most of them in white tufa, make up a most evocative townscape. Many fine old buildings stand in its main street Rue Voltaire, including the Gothic dwelling where Richard the Lionheart is supposed to have died in 1199.

At the crossroads **(Grand Carroi★★)** the oldest houses of all press closely together. On her arrival from Vaucouleurs on Sunday 6 March 1429, **Joan of Arc** is thought to have used the coping of the well-head here to dismount from her horse. The following day she picked out the Dauphin (the heir apparent) hiding among his courtiers, and declared, "You are the heir of France and true son of the king, Lieutenant of the King of Heaven who is King of France".

Château★★
◓*Open daily Apr–Sept daily 9am–7pm; Oct–Mar 9.30am–5pm.* ◓*Closed 1 Jan and 25 Dec.* ◉*6€ (3€ during restoration).* ℘*02 47 93 13 45.*

▸ **Population:** 8 716
⌖ **Michelin Map:** 317 J 5
ℹ **Info:** Place d'Hofheim.
℘02 47 93 17 85.
www.chinon.com.
▷ **Location:** Chinon is 45km/28mi W of Tours.
◔ **Timing:** Allow at least 2hr to explore the château and the town. Walking tours of varying distances as well as other leisure activities including boat and balloon trips are available; ask at the tourist office.

The spur overlooking the town was the site of a Gallic oppidum, then of a fortress, long before Henry II of England (born at Le Mans in 1133) built the present castle to protect Anjou from Capetian designs. The castle was taken by Philippe Auguste in 1205 from John Lackland; it subsequently became a royal residence, was strengthened by Charles VII, but then abandoned by the court at the end of the 15C and gradually dismantled.

The remains of the castle include, to the east, St George's Fort (Fort St-Georges), watching over the most vulnerable approach, the Middle Castle (Château du Milieu) which has a 14C clock tower, the royal apartments and gardens, and finally the Coudray Fort (Fort de Coudray) at the far end of the spur.

Fontevraud L'Abbaye★★

Fontevraud Abbey, close to the hearts of the Plantagenets, stands on the borders of Anjou, Tourraine and Poitou. Despite the ravages of history, it remains the largest group of monastic buildings in France, having retained some interesting features typical of Anjou architecture, in particular the lofty vaulting of the abbey church and the impressive kitchen. There is a good view of the Abbey from the Loudun road on the south side of the village.

- ⚙ **Michelin Map:** 317 J 5
- ▯ **Info:** Place Saint-Michel. ✆02 41 51 79 45. www.cote-saumuroise. com. www.abbaye-fontrevaud.com
- ◗ **Location:** The abbey occupies the heart of the village of the same name, which is 15km/9.3mi SE of Saumur, close to the Loire and Vienne rivers.
- ◷ **Timing:** Allow 2hr to make the most of your visit.

A BIT OF HISTORY

The Order of Fontevraud was founded in 1099 following the failure in France of Pope Gregory's reform, which had been designed to enhance both the competence and the respectability of the clergy.

The success of the new Order was immediate and it quickly took on an aristocratic character accommodating both sexes. It was presided over by an abbess at a time when the growing cult of the Virgin Mary was influencing the status of womanhood and the abbesses, who were members of noble families, procured rich gifts and powerful protection for the abbey. The Plantagenets chose the abbey as their last resting place and Eleanor of Aquitaine, her husband Henry II and her son Richard the Lionheart were buried here. Later, the hearts of John Lackland (King John) and his son Henry III, who built Westminster Abbey, were transferred to the Crypt.

Église Abbatiale★★

The Abbey Church has a vast nave with delicately carved capitals and is roofed by a series of domes, characteristic of churches found in the south west of France. Built several decades earlier than the nave, the transept and chancel are reminiscent of the Benedictine plan: an ambulatory and radiating chapels where the luminosity and repetition of vertical lines signify the aspiration to reach up to heaven.

In the transept crossing are a number of Plantagenet tombs (**gisants des Plantagenêts★**), good examples of Gothic funerary sculpture. The figures of Henry Plantagenet, Richard the Lionheart and Eleanor of Aquitaine are in painted tufa, while the figure of Isabel of Angoulême, John Lackland's wife, is of polychrome wood.

The **Cuisine (kitchen)★★** is a highly individual structure (27m/89ft high), dating from around 1160 and restored in 1902. It is a rare example of a Romanesque kitchen, with a tiled roof characteristic of the Poitiers area.

Fontevraud abbey kitchen

S. Sauvignier/MICHELIN

Château de
Langeais★★

The castle is built on a promontory,
beneath the high walls of which are
nestled the town's white houses.

A BIT OF HISTORY
The great Angevin ruler Foulques Nerra
built a sturdy keep to command the Loire
Valley. Completed in 994, now in ruins in
the park of the château, it is considered
to be the oldest such building in the
whole of France.
The château itself was built to protect
France from Brittany. In 1491 the
marriage of Charles VIII of France and
Anne of Brittany ended the threat.

VISIT
Open Jul–Aug 9am–7pm; Apr–Jun
Sept and Oct–12 Nov 9.30am–6.30pm;
13 Nov–Jan 10am–5pm; Feb–Mar
9.30am–5.30pm. Guided tours (50min)
available. Closed 25 Dec. 8.20€.
02 47 96 72 60.
Seen from outside, the château still looks
like a medieval fortress, with drawbridge,
towers, battlemented sentry-walk and
almost windowless walls. But the façade

- **Michelin Map:** 317 L 5
- **Info:** Pl. du 14-juillet,
  Langeais. 02 47 96
  58 22. www.chateau-de-
  langeais.com.
- **Location:** The town and
  château are on the right
  bank of the Loire between
  Tours and Saumur,
  approached by taking the
  left bank road and crossing
  the river into the town.

facing the courtyard has the features of
a Renaissance country house, including
pointed dormers, turrets, sculptures
and mullioned windows. Inside, the
apartments (**appartements★★★**) have
kept their medieval layout, one room
commanding the next through narrow
doors and laid out along diagonal lines.
The last owner, Jacques Siegfried (a
mill- and ship-owner and banker from
Le Havre), refurnished the interior very
expertly, and Langeais gives a good
impression of aristocratic life in the early
Renaissance period. The rooms contain
fine tapestries. In the Charles VIII Room
is a 17C clock with a single hand.

Loches★★

Modern Loches lies mostly on the
left bank of the Indre, at the foot of
the fortified bluff that dominates the
valley and that set natural limits to
the growth of the medieval town.

SIGHT
Cité médiévale★★
The medieval town is contained within a
continuous wall some 1 000m/1 100 yd
long in which there are only two gates.
To the south, the great square keep
(**donjon★★**) (open 22 Mar–Sept
daily 9am–7pm; Oct–21 Mar daily
9.30am–5pm; closed 1 Jan and 25
Dec; 7€; 02 47 59 07 86) was built
by the Counts of Anjou in the 11C on
even earlier foundations. In the 13C,

- **Population:** 6 328
- **Michelin Map:** 317 O 6
- **Info:** Pl. de la Marne.
  02 47 91 82 82.
  www.loches-touraine-
  cotesud.com
- **Location:** Loches lies
  on the River Indre,
  49km/30.4mi SE of Tours.
- **Don't Miss:** The public
  gardens by the Indre give
  a wonderful view of the
  fortress and château.

it was strengthened by wide ditches
hewn into the solid rock, by buttress
towers and the Martelet Tower with
its impressive dungeons, then given

Detail of the Château de Loches

B. Kaufmann/MICHELIN

additional accommodation including service buildings.

In the centre of the old town is a church, **Église St-Ours**★, with its Angevin porch built around a Romanesque portal, and pyramid vaults in its nave.

To the north is the **Château**★★ (🕐*same as for the* **donjon**★★; ⊚*7€.* ☏*02 47 59 01 32)*, begun at the end of the 14C as an extension of the 13C watchtower known as Agnes Sorèl's Tower **(Tour Agnès Sorel)**. Part of the royal apartments are medieval (Vieux logis), part Renaissance

(Nouveau logis). It was in the great hall of the Vieux Logis on 3 and 5 June 1429 that Joan of Arc persuaded the Dauphin to undertake his coronation journey to Reims.

There is a tiny Flamboyant oratory dedicated to Anne of Brittany decorated with the ermine of Brittany and the girdle of St Francis, and, in the Charles VIII Room, a recumbent figure **(gisant d'Agnès Sorel**★) of Charles VII's "Lady of Beauty".

Le **Mans**★★

Le Mans, a large modern provincial capital, hosts several fairs and events every year, most famously the 24hr Grand Prix, the *"24 Heures de Mans"*.

A BIT OF HISTORY

An old town, enclosed by ramparts in the 4C, Le Mans was part of the Plantagenet estates. It has long been the site of trade fairs and festivals, which today include a Spring Fair (late Mar–early Apr), a great Four-Day Fair (mid-Sept), an Onion Fair (first Fri in Sept). As a result, Le Mans has a long gastronomic tradition; local specialities include potted pork

▸ **Population:** 189 107

⚙ **Michelin Map:** 310 K 6

🛈 **Info:** Hôtel des Ursulines, 19 bis, r. de l'Étoile. ☏02 43 28 17 22. www.ville-lemans.fr.

◖ **Location:** The city centre is the old quarter on the left bank of the Sarthe.

🅿 **Parking:** There is usually plenty of parking space in Place des Jacobins.

(rillettes), plump pullets (poulardes), capons (chapons) accompanied by cider, as well as the delicious reinette apple.

SIGHTS

Vieux Mans★★

The historic centre of Le Mans stands on the site of a Celtic settlement, overlooking the lowlands on either side of the Sarthe. This part of the city is still enclosed within its 4C Gallo-Roman ramparts, some of the few extant in western France.

Cathédrale St-Julien★★

This magnificent building makes a fine spectacle from Place des Jacobins. Its Gothic **chevet**★★★, supported on intricate Y-shaped two-tier buttresses, is a spectacular demonstration of the boldness and ambition of its architect. The transition from nave to choir is one of the clearest demonstrations anywhere – even for the architecturally uninitiated – of the great technical and stylistic changes which took place over a period of some 160 years. The arches of the south porch are pleasingly decorated, and the doorway (**portail**★★) has splendid statue-columns. The Gothic choir was completed in 1254. The whole is lit on three levels by 13C stained-glass windows (**verrières**★★) ; in the chapels opening out onto the outer ambulatory, in the inner ambulatory and in the clerestory. Note how in the south

transept (1385–92) the junction has been effected between the Gothic choir and the older, Romanesque transept.

Churches

Several of Le Mans' churches are worth a visit, including: **Église de la Couture**★ (22 r. Berthelot); **Église Ste-Jeanne d'Arc**★ (pl. Georg-Washington) and **Notre-Dame de L'Épau**★ (r. de l'Esterel).

MUSEUMS

Le Mans has its fair share of museums: discover old Le Mans with historical maps and pictures at **Musée de la Reine Bérengère**★ (7–3 r. de la Reine-Bérengère au Mans; ℘02 43 47 38 51); visit the half-timbered 16C house **Maison du Pilier Rouge** (Grand Rue); admire the paintings at **Musée de Tessé**★ (2 av. de Paderborn-au-Mans; ℘02 43 47 38 51).

An interesting museum in Le Mans circuit is the **Musée de l'Automobile de la Sarthe**★★ (442 r. de Laigne-au-Mans, 5km/3mi S; ℘02 43 72 72 24; www.museeauto24h.sarthe.com).

The museum displays 115 vehicles in a modern and instructive setting. The section on racing cars, especially winners of the 24hr Grand Prix race, presents a superb collection of outstanding cars.

River Sarthe at Le Mans

Studio 3bis/MICHELIN

Orléans★

Orléans grew up on the great bend in the Loire between the rich cornfields of the Beauce to the north and the heaths and forests of the Sologne to the south. For a time the city was the capital of France. Place du Martroi, with its statue of Joan of Arc, is the centre of the historic town.

▶ **Population:** 263 292
▶ **Michelin Map:** 318 i 4
▶ **Info:** 2 pl. de l'Etape. ℘02 38 24 05 05. www.tourisme-orleans.com.
▶ **Location:** The city occupies a site at the Loire's closest point to Paris, and is easily reached by excellent road and rail links.

A BIT OF HISTORY

The **Siege of 1428–29** was one of the great episodes in the history of France, marking the country's rebirth after a period of despair. It began on 12 October 1428, as the Earl of Salisbury attempted to take the bridge over the Loire and thus link up with the other English forces in central and southern France.

Lasting almost seven months, the siege was the scene of one of the first-ever (albeit inconclusive) artillery duels. On 29 April 1429, **Joan of Arc** arrived from Chinon (⚑see CHINON); she skirted Orléans to the south and entered the city by the Burgundy Gate (Porte de Bourgogne), several days in advance of the army advancing along the north bank of the river. By 7 May, victory seemed assured, and on the 8 May the English capitulated.

Statue of Joan of Arc

Alexander Wallnöfer/stock.xchng

In Orléans, Joan enjoyed the hospitality of Jacques Boucher, whose fine half-timbered dwelling with its **museum** is known as **Maison de Jeanne d'Arc**★ (3 pl. de Gaulle; ℘02 38 52 99 89; www.jeannedarc.com.fr/maison/maison.htm).

SIGHTS
Cathédrale Ste-Croix★
r. Adolphe Crespin

Construction of the cathedral lasted from the 13C to the 16C. The nave was torn down by the Huguenots in 1568, but rebuilt in composite Gothic style by **Henri IV**, mindful of the city's loyalty to him. The woodwork **(boiseries★★)** of the choir stalls (1706) includes splendidly carved medallions and panels adorning the high backs.

Musée des Beaux-Arts★★
1 r. Ferdinand Rabier, Pl. Ste-Croix. &Open Tue–Sun 10am–6pm. Closed public holidays. ⚑3€; no charge 1st Sun in the month. ℘02 38 79 21 55. www.orleans.fr.

This museum houses some of the richest collections in France, especially of French painting from the 16–20C, including Courbet, Boudin and Gauguin.

ADDITIONAL SIGHTS
Musée historique★ (Hôtel Cabu, Sq. Abbé des Noyers)
Musée des Sciences naturelles★ (2 r. Marcel Proust)
Parc Floral de la Source★★ (at Olivet)

Abbaye de St-Benoît-sur-Loire★★

Enthralling by its majestic size, exquisite harmony and utter simplicity, Fleury Abbey at St-Benoît-sur-Loire is justly one of the most famous Romanesque buildings in France.

A BIT OF HISTORY

In around AD 675, the original abbey was founded here on a river terrace well above flood level was presented with the remains of St Benedict and of his sister, St Scholastica, brought from Monte Cassino in Italy.

Hitherto known as Fleury Abbey, the monastery rededicated itself to the founder of Western monasticism (St Benedict is St-Benoît in French).

The abbey's influence waxed at the beginning of the 9C with the appointment of Theodulf by the Emperor Charlemagne; this great abbot served his master by introducing the study of the Scriptures and of Roman law, and by promoting the conservation of ancient texts.

VISIT
Basilique★★

⏲ *Open 9am–10.30am, 1–2.15, 4–6pm.*
⏲ *Closed mornings during religious festivals, first Fri of month and Holy Week* ✆ *02 38 35 72 43.*
www.abbaye-fleury.com.

Built between 1067 and 1108, the Romanesque basilica has a fine crypt (**crypte★**) with a double ambulatory and a massive central pillar containing the relics of St Benedict. The choir (**chœur★★**) is remarkable for its paving (a Roman mosaic brought here from Italy) and for the elegant arcading. Outside, the belfry porch (**clocher-porche★★**) is one of the finest examples of Romanesque art in France. Originally free-standing, it was joined to the basilica when the nave was extended in the middle of the 12C.

⏲ **Michelin Map:** 318 K 5
📖 **Info:** 44 r. Orléanais.
✆ 02 38 35 79 00.
▶ **Location:** The abbey is at the village of St-Benoît, beside the Loire between Gien and Orléans.
A pretty way to approach it is along the riverside road, D 60.
◉ **Don't Miss:** In addition to the abbey, be sure to visit the lovely church of nearby Germigny-des-Près.
🕐 **Timing:** Allow about 2hr for the basilica and village.

Porch of the basilicaLoire
Studio 3bis/MICHELIN

EXCURSIONS
Germigny-des-Prés★
5.5km/3.4mi NW.

The much-restored church is the oratory (**oratoire**) which Abbot Theodulf built for himself. It is a typical example of Carolingian architecture of the 9C, with an unusual plan, alabaster window-panes filtering the light, and a remarkable **mosaic★★**.

Saumur★★

Dominated by its imposing château on a chalky spur overlooking the meeting-point of the Thouet with the Loire, Saumur is especially famous for its fine wines.

A BIT OF HISTORY

The town owed its early prosperity to the wooden bridge which crossed the Loire via two islands (the Île d'Offrand and the Île Millocheau, now joined together). It formed the only crossing point over the river between Tours and Ponts-de-Cé downstream from Angers, at the time of pilgrimages to Santiago de Compostela. In the 13C, the monks from the Abbaye de St Florent undertook to replace the original structure by one of stone, constructed at the rate of one arch a year. Though often carried away by floods, this bridge was always rebuilt. Like all the towns along the great river such as Decize, Nevers, La Charité, Cosne, Gien, Orléans and Blois, Saumur's site was chosen, regardless of orientation, on whichever bank offered the better protection from high waters. The attractive old houses facing the Loire have walls of pale tufa and steeply pitched slate roofs.

Saumur's long association with the horse began in 1763, when the crack corps known as the Carabiniers Regiment was sent here, under the command of Louis XV's brother ("Monsieur"). It was a time when the refinement of riding technique which had begun under de Pluvinel (Louis XIII's Master of the Horse) had become fashionable among the aristocracy. The National Equitation Centre (École Nationale d'Équitation) was founded in 1972, incorporating the famous **Cadre Noir** (Black Squad) which had originally consisted solely of army instructors. This aspect of the town's identity is evoked in the museum in the château, and in the **Musée de la Cavalerie**★ (pl. Charles de Foucauld; ℘ 41 83 69 23; ⏰ open Mon–Thu 9am–noon, 2–5pm, Sat–Sun 2–6pm; http://museecavalerie.free.fr/cariboost1), which has displays on post-18C military

- ▶ **Population:** 857
- ⏣ **Michelin Map:** 317 i 5
- ▯ **Info:** Place de la Bilange. ℘02 41 40 20 60. www.ot-saumur.fr.
- ◖ **Location:** Saumur straddles the Loire about midway between Angers and Tours, also taking in an island in midstream. The town centre is on the S side of the river, around Place St-Pierre. For an overview, take a 45min ride on the 'little tourist train' (summer only, 6€).
- ◔ **Don't Miss:** One of the equestrian shows that take place throughout the year; a stroll around the Old Town; a boat excursion on the Loire.
- ▤▪ **Kids:** Zoo de Doué (⏰ see Excursions).

history and on the development of horsemanship.

In addition, is the **Musée des Blindés**★★ (♿ ⏰ open May–Sept daily 9.30am–6.30pm; Oct–Apr daily 10am–5pm; last admission 1hr before closing; ⏰ closed 1 Jan and 25 Dec; ◉6€; ℘02 41 53 06 99; www.musee-des-blindes.asso.fr), with displays of armoured vehicles both French and foreign from 1918 onwards.

SIGHT
Château★★

⏰Open Jul–Aug Tue–Sun 10am–6pm; Apr–Jun and Sept–4 Nov Tue–Sun 10am–1pm, 2–5.30pm. ◗◗Guided tours (30min) Jul–Aug 10.15am, 11.15am, 12.15pm, 12.15pm, 3pm, 3.45pm, 4.45pm. ◉3€. Free visit to the exterior. ℘02 41 40 24 40. www.saumur.fr.

In the 14C, the château was rebuilt on the foundations of the medieval fortress originally erected by Philippe Auguste and Louis IX. As a consequence, it has a somewhat irregular layout. In the

15C, with the return of more peaceful times following the end of the Hundred Years' War, Good King René endowed his "castle of love" with sumptuous decorative detail in late Gothic style. The château is shown in this state, albeit in a somewhat idealised landscape, in one of the miniatures from the *Très Riches Heures du Duc de Berry*. In the late 16C, at the time of the Wars of Religion, the place was refortified, as Saumur was one of the strongholds of French Protestantism.

There are two museums in the château: the **Musée du Cheval**★ with fascinating collections of riding equipment and a number of pictures (including work by Stubbs), and the **Musée des Arts décoratifs**★★, which has a fine display of works of art from the Middle Ages and Renaissance, including a collection of faience and French porcelain from the 17C and 18C. During the Military Tattoo (Carrousel) held in July, the Musée des Blindés presents a number of armoured vehicles restored at the school and driven by cadets.

EXCURSION
👥👤 Zoo de Doué★★
20km/12.4mi SW of Saumur. ⏰*Open early Feb–Oct daily.* 🎟*16€ (child 10€).* *www.zoodoue.fr.*

The zoo is situated on the western edge of Doué-la-Fontaine on the road to Cholet (D 960). Some 500 animals roam more or less freely in this remarkable cave setting enhanced by acacia trees and bamboo groves, cascades and rocky overhangs. Visitors can walk among the birds of prey in the vulture pen (fosse aux charognards) while in the large quarry reserved for leopards (canyon aux léopards), there are observation posts to view three sets of cats: snow leopards, Persian leopards and jaguars. A school of penguins disport themselves in a creek (crique aux manchots). A gallery (Galerie des Faluns) gives a glimpse of the fauna which existed on the site some ten million years ago.

Tours★★

With a civilised air, under dazzling Loire valley skies, built in bright white tufa and roofed in black slate, the ancient city of Tours makes a perfect base for excursions into the châteaux country.

A BIT OF HISTORY
The place originated in Gallich times, becoming an important centre of trade and administration under the Romans in the 1C AD. Throughout the Middle Ages it was an important religious centre and was the capital of Tours (Touraine) county; indeed Tours became the capital of France during the reign of Louis XI.

SIGHTS
Château★
25 av. André Malraux.
Not comparable in grandeur to the more typical Loire châteaux, this is a

▸ **Population:** 297 631
🖉 **Michelin Map:** 317 N 4
ℹ **Info:** 78 r. Bernard-Palissy.
📞 02 47 70 37 37.
www.ligeris.com.
▶ **Location:** Tours spans the Loire and fills the isthmus between the Loire and its tributary the Cher. The Old Town lies along the left bank of the Loire, reaching from the lively Place Plumereau area to the peaceful Cathedral district.

heterogeneous collection of buildings from the 4–19C. The lower parts of the wall on the west side go back to Roman times and here too is the 11C residence of the Counts of Anjou; the Guise Tower (Tour de Guise) with its machicolations and pepper-pot roof is of the 13–15C, while the dormer-windowed Governor's Lodging (Logis du Gouverneur) is 15C and other additions were made as recently as the 17–19C.

Cathédrale St-Gatien★★

Following a fire, the cathedral was rebuilt from 1235 onwards. The work lasted all of 250 years. As a result it demonstrates the complete evolution of the Gothic style, from a chevet in the early phase, to a Flamboyant west front, and even a lantern crowning the twin towers that is characteristic of the Early Renaissance. The stained glass ranges in date from the 13C (high windows in the chancel) via the 14C (transept rose windows) to the 15C (rose window of the west front).

La Psalette★

Open Apr daily 10am–12.30pm, 2–5.30pm, Sun morning by appt; May–Aug daily 9.30am–12.30pm, 2–6pm, Sun morning by appt; Sept–Mar, Wed–Sat 10am–12.30pm, 2–5.30pm, Sun afternoon only. Closed 1 Jan, 1 May and 25 Dec. 3€. 02 47 47 05 19. la-psalette.monuments-nationaux.fr.
This is the name given to the cathedral cloisters where canons and choir-master used to meet. The tiny Archive Room (Salle des Archives) of 1520 and the vaulted Library (Librairie) are reached by means of a spiral staircase, Gothic in structure but Renaissance in the way in which it is detailed.

Place Plumereau★

This busy and picturesque square is located at the old "meeting of the ways" (carroi); it is bordered by fine 15C residences built of stone and timber. On the corner with the Rue du Change and the Rue de la Monnaie is a carved corner post with a somewhat mutilated depiction of the Circumcision.

Musée des Beaux-Arts★★

18 pl. François Sicard. Open Wed–Sun 9am–12.45pm, 2–6pm. Closed 1 Jan, 1 May, 14 Jul, 1 and 11 Nov, 25 Dec. 4€. 02 47 05 68 73.
In the former Bishops' Palace (17–18C), its rooms are beautifully decorated with Louis XVI panelling and silk hangings made locally. It houses works of art from the châteaux at Richelieu and Chanteloup (now the site of the Parc de la Pagode, *see AMBOISE – Orient Panel*) as well as from the great abbeys of Touraine. The collection of paintings consists mostly of French works of the 19–20C, but there are also two outstanding Mantegnas, a Resurrection and Christ in the Garden of Olives (late 15C).

Musée du Compagnonnage★★

Entrance via 8 r. Nationale and a walkway. Open mid-Jun–mid-Sept daily 9am–12.30pm, 2–6pm; rest of the year Wed–Mon 9am–noon, 2–6pm. Last entry 30min before closing. Closed public holidays. 5€. 02 47 21 62 20. www.musee-du-compagnonnage.info.
The city long prided itself on its craftsmen, and even at the end of the 19C there were still three guilds jealously guarding their traditions. The museum contains many fine examples of the work of master craftsmen, such as roofers and slaters, blacksmiths and locksmiths, saddlers and carpenters.

ADDITIONAL SIGHTS

Rue Briçonnet★
Place Grégoire-de-Tours★
Hôtel Gouin★ *(26 r. du Commerce)*
Musée de la Société archéologique de Touraine★
(26 r. du Commerce)
L'Historial de Touraine★
(in the castle) *(25 quai d'Orléans)*
Jardin de Beaune-Semblançay★
(28 r. Nationale)
Musée des Équipages militaires et du Train★ *(r. du Plat d'Etain, Quartier Beaumont)*

ADDRESSES

STAY

⊜⊜ **Chambre d'hôte Le Moulin Hodoux** – *37230 Luynes, 14km/8.7mi W of Tours on N 152 and minor road. ℘02 47 55 76 27. 5 rooms*. In a peaceful country setting not far from Tours, near the castle at Luynes, this 18–19C watermill provides comfortable, well-equipped rooms. In the lovely garden there are tables, chairs and a barbecue, as well as a swimming pool.

⊜⊜ **Hôtel Le Cygne** – *6 r. du Cygne. ℘02 47 66 66 41. Closed Christmas. 16 rooms. ⏢7€*. One of Tours' oldest hotels (18C). Rooms have been renovated, but their character has been preserved. In winter, a fine 16C fireplace warms the little lounge. There is a pleasant family atmosphere.

⊜⊜ **Hôtel du Relais St-Éloi** – *8 r. Giraudeau. ℘02 47 38 18 19. 56 rooms. ⏢8.50€*. Recent building with small, practical rooms. Some, with a mezzanine, are particularly suitable for families. No-frills décor and regular maintenance. Modern dining room, but traditional culinary repertoire.

⊜⊜⊜⊜ **Central Hôtel** – *21 r. Berthelot. ℘02 47 05 46 44. 37 rooms. ⏢13€*. A quiet, comfortable hotel in the old part of Tours, near the busy pedestrian-only districts. The staff are reserved but pleasant. There is a small, peaceful garden behind the hotel and you can eat breakfast on the terrace.

⊽ EAT

⊜ **Bistrot de la Tranchée** – *103 av. Tranchée. ℘02 47 41 09 08. Closed Aug, Sun and Mon.* Dark wood panelling, bottles of wine, comfortable wall sofas and old-fashioned pizza ovens make up the décor of this pleasant bistro. Enjoy a good selection of small dishes typical to this type of restaurant. Definitely worth a visit.

⊜⊜ **Cap Sud** – *88 r. Colbert. ℘02 47 05 24 81. Closed 12 Aug–7 Sept, 24 Dec–8 Jan, weekends and Mon.* This little restaurant has a Mediterranean atmosphere, both in its warm décor and up-to-date cuisine. Short, well-selecetd wine list.

⊜⊜ **Léonard de Vinci** – *19 r. de la Monnaie. ℘02 47 61 07 88. Closed Sun eve and Mon. Reservations required in eve.* A taste of Tuscany in the heart of the Touraine. This Italian restaurant's claim to fame is that it doesn't serve pizzas! A chance to discover different Italian dishes, in a décor that highlights models of Leonardo da Vinci's inventions.

⊜⊜⊜⊜ **La Roche Le Roy** – *55 rte de St-Avertin. ℘02 47 27 22 00. Closed Feb school holidays (zone B), 1–25 Aug, Sun and Mon.* The restaurant in this Touraine manor house was created under a lucky star and will be much appreciated by gourmets. Sample the cooking, which varies with the seasons, in the intimate dining room or the pretty enclosed courtyard in summer.

⊽ CAFÉS

Le Vieux Mûrier – *11 pl. Plumereau – ℘02 47 61 04 77. Closed Sun, Mon.* This is one of the oldest cafés in place Plumereau and it has that extra hint of character that is so often missing from modern establishments.

🛒 SHOPPING

Markets – **Second-hand goods:** 1st and 3rd Fri of the month r. *de Bordeaux*; 4th Sun in the month, bd Bérange; Wed and Sat mornings, *pl. de la Victoire*. **Flowers** –Wed and Sat, all day, *bd Béranger*.

Au Vieux Four – *7 pl. des Petites-Boucheries. ℘02 47 66 62 33. www. auvieuxfour-mahou.com. Closed Sun and Mon.* This boulangerie and museum reveals the secrets of traditional bread-making.

La Chocolatière – *6 r. de la Scellerie, ℘02 47 05 66 75. www.la-chocolatiere. com. Closed Mon.* 'Le pavé de Tours' is one of the great specialities of the exceptional maker of pâtisseries, confectionery and top-of-the-range chocolates.

Château de
Valençay★★

Vast and superbly proportioned, richly furnished, and standing in an exquisite park, this is a place dedicated to the good life.

A BIT OF HISTORY

The original medieval castle was rebuilt in the 16C and the defensive features were retained as decoration. In 1803, the estate was acquired by **Charles-Maurice de Talleyrand-Périgord** (1754–1838), paid for mostly by Napoleon, at the time still First Consul.

For almost quarter of a century, the château served as a glittering background to international diplomacy conducted by its owner, who held high offices of state from the time of Louis XVI to the Restoration.

- **Michelin Map:** 318 G 9 X.
- **Info:** Château de Valençay. ℘02 54 00 10 66. www.chateaux-france.com.
- **Location:** The château is on D 956, between Tours and Vierzon.
- **Timing:** Many events are held here, notably the re-enactments of 19C life in period costume in the afternoons, and evening Son et Lumière shows.

VISIT

Open Jul–Aug 9.30am–7pm; Jun 9.30–6.30; May and Sept 10am–6pm; Oct–Nov 8 10.30am–5.30pm, 28 Mar–Apr 10.30am–6pm. ⬛*10€ château and show.* ℘*02 54 00 10 66.*

Inside are opulent furnishings of the Régence and Empire periods, including 18C Savonnerie carpets and the round table from the Congress of Vienna.

Vendôme★★

At the foot of a steep bluff, which is crowned by a castle, the River Loir divides into several channels. Vendôme stands on a group of islands crowded with bell-towers, gables and steep slate roofs.

SIGHT
Ancienne Abbaye de la Trinité★

Founded in 1040 by Geoffroy Martel, Count of Anjou, the Benedictine abbey expanded considerably and became one of the most powerful in France. Pilgrims flocked here to venerate the supposed Holy Tear Christ shed at Lazarus' tomb and which Martel brought back from a Crusade.

The Flamboyant Gothic **abbey church★★** has a remarkable west front, which contrasts with the plain Romanesque tower. The transept, all that is left of the 11C building, leads to the chancel and ambulatory with its five

- **Population:** 18 510
- **Michelin Map:** 318 D 5
- **Info:** Hotel du Saillant, Parc Ronsard. ℘02 54 77 05 07. www.chateaux-valdeloire.com/Vendome.html.
- **Location:** The River Loir, flows parallel to the Loire, to its N. The town's setting is complicated and unusual, the islands fitting together like a jigsaw puzzle. Rue Poterie runs north–south across the town centre.

radiating chapels. In the 14C chancel are fine late 15C stalls **(stalles★)** decorated with naïve scenes. The axial chapel contains a window dating from 1140 depicting the Virgin and Child (Majesté Notre-Dame).

Jardins et Château de
Villandry★★★

In 1536, Jean Le Breton, who had been France's ambassador in Italy, rebuilt the château here on the foundations of an earlier one. The new building had a number of features which made it unusual in Touraine: ditches and canals, an esplanade and a terrace, rectangular pavilions in place of round towers, and, above all, its gardens.

VISIT

Château★★

⏰ Open daily Jul and Aug 9am–6.30pm; end Mar–Jun and Sept–24 Oct 9am–6pm; 1–28 Mar 9am–5.30pm; 7–end Feb and 25 Oct–15 Nov 9am–5pm; 19–31 Dec 9am–4.30 and 1–4 Jan 9.30am–4.30pm. ⏰Closed 5 Jan–6 Feb and 16 Nov–18 Dec.
◂ Guided tours (2hr) available (call for times) except in Feb, Dec and Sun May–Sept (during which time you can take a self-guided tour with a leaflet). ⊗9€ (château and gardens). ℰ02 47 50 02 09. www.chateauvillandry.com.
The interior is distinguished by Louis XV panelling in the Great Salon and Dining Room, by the fine ramped staircase in wrought iron, and by a surprising 13C Mudejar ceiling from Spain, brought here by Joachim de Carvallo (1869–1936).

Jardins★★★

⏰Same as for the château.
In 1906, Dr Carvallo, founder of the French Historic Houses Association (Demeure Historique), bought the Villandry estate and began to restore the gardens. The plan of the gardens shows both the influence of the agricultural writer **Olivier de Serres**, and the synthesis of the monastery garden with the Italian garden proposed by Jacques II Androuet du Cerceau.
Covering a total area of 7ha/17.3 acres, the gardens have many fascinating features. There are three terraces, one above the other, separated by

---

♿ **Michelin Map:** 317 M 4
ℹ **Info:** Le Potager, Villandry. ℰ02 47 50 12 66. www.chateauvillandry.com.
▶ **Location:** Coming from Langeais, take D 16, which has scenic views. Coming from Tours, take D 288, which crosses the Loire at Savonnières.
👁 **Don't Miss:** The 13 Mudejar ceiling in the château.
🕐 **Timing:** The château tour takes 2hr. Allow another 1hr to stroll through the gardens.

---

shady avenues of limes and vines; the highest is the water garden with its mirror-like stretch of water, then comes an ornamental garden with box clipped into patterns symbolising the varieties of love: tragic (sword and dagger blades), fickle (butterflies and fans), tender (masks and hearts), and passionate (broken hearts). Finally there is a kitchen garden with 85 000 plants contained in clipped-box beds. The use of the humblest of vegetables (cabbage, celery), chosen for their culinary value, symbolism, therapeutic value or colour, is here raised to an art form of great delicacy and seasonal interest.

Gardens, Château de Villandry

Studio 3bis/MICHELIN

CORSICA

Kallisté, the name given to Corsica by the ancient Greeks, means "most beautiful"; even today the French refer to it as L'Île de Beauté. This mountainous island lies some 170km/105.6mi off the coast of mainland France. With its intense light, its superbly varied and dramatic coast and its wild and rugged interior, it is a place of distinct natural identity, enhanced by the succession of peoples who have been attracted here to settle or to rule; these have included megalith builders and mysterious Torreans, Greeks and Romans, Pisans and Genoese, French and British, though the somewhat absurd interlude of the Anglo-Corsican Viceroyalty of 1794–96 seems to have left little trace.

Highlights

1 Sheer rock walls rising above pines in **Aiguilles de Bavella** (p268)

2 The upper town **(Ville Haute)** of **Bonifacio** perched on high cliffs (p270)

3 Finger of mountains pointing into the sea: **Cap Corse** (p270)

4 Pisan-style striped church: **San Michele de Murato** (p272)

5 Jagged granite rocks on the coast at Porto **Calanches de Piana** (p273)

Geography – The gulfs of Corsica's west coast are of extraordinary beauty, the jagged headlands and precipitous porphyry cliffs rising from the Golfe de Porto being especially memorable. The Cap Corse promontory prolongs

the island's backbone of schistic rocks 40km/25mi northwards into the sea.

The coastal plains of Bastia and Aléria to the east constitute the only substantial areas of flat land. The interior is penetrated by a network of narrow and winding roads as well as by a remarkable 1m/3ft-gauge railway. Here are villages of tall granite houses overlooking deep gorges, as well as forests of oak, Corsican pine and sweet chestnut. Above the tree line rise the high bare summits, all the more imposing because of their proximity to the sea.

History – Remarkably Corsica has been part of France only since the late 19C and before that it had a succession of occupiers including Greeks, Romans, Byzantines, Saracens (who gave the island its symbol, the Moor's Head) and finally the Genoese. During the War of Independence in the 19C the nationalist movement, led by the Cosican hero Pasquale Paoli, had some success but despite the support of the British during the rather absurd Anglo-Corsican Viceroyalty of 1794–96, the island was absorbed into France in 1796. Corsica's most famous son is, of course, Napoleon Bonaparte and he is celebrated in every town.

Economy – Corsica is an unspoilt Mediterranean island and this, allied with beautiful mountains, a magnificent coastline and an agreeable climate attracts the many tourists who are the mainstay of the economy. The island does also produce honey, chestnuts, cheese, wine and sausages which are mostly exported to mainland France. The nationalist movement remains active, and in 2003, a referendum which would have given Corsica more independence was narrowly defeated.

Ajaccio★★

Ajaccio occupies a natural amphitheatre looking out over its splendid bay. The town was founded in 1492 by the Office of St George which governed Corsica on behalf of the Republic of Genoa. Native Corsicans were forbidden residence there until 1553, when, in the course of the first French intervention in the island, it was taken by the legendary military adventurer Sampierro Corso (1498–1567), born in the village of Bastelica, 25km/15.5mi to the northeast.

▶ **Population:** 60 000
Michelin Map: 345 A-B 7-8
Info: 3 bd. du Roi-Jérôme, 20181 Ajaccio (Aiacciu). &04 95 51 53 03. www.ajaccio-tourisme.com.
Location: Ajaccio is on the W coast of Corsica, 82.4km/51mi SW of Corte along the N 193. Place Foch is the heart of town; most places of interest are nearby. The tourist office has information on guided tours.

A BIT OF HISTORY

It was here, at 1am on 13 September 1943, that the first Free French forces to land on the territory of France disembarked from the submarine *Casabianca*, under Commander L'Herminier.

Ajaccio's historic importance is due above all to its being the birthplace of **Napolon Bonaparte**. The town continues to revere the memory of its "glorious child prodigy". Born on 15 August 1769, the son of Charles-Marie Bonaparte and Letizia Romolino, he entered the military school at Brienne (*Aube*) at the age of 10. At 27 he married Josephine Tascher de la Pagerie, widow of General Beauharnais, before directing the Italian campaign (Battle of Arcole) and, two years later, the expedition to Egypt. In 1804, taking the title of Napoleon I, he crowned himself Emperor of the French. On 26 August the following year he launched the *Grande Armée* (Grand Army) against Austria from the encampment at Boulogne whence he had threatened England with invasion. By 1807, at the age of 38, he dominated Europe.

It was then, however, that coalitions originally formed to resist the French Revolution were turned against the Empire. England was deeply involved in them all, in the colonies and on the high seas as well as in Europe. Though bloated and prematurely aged, Napoleon rose to the challenge, never more formidable than from 1809 on, the years of struggle against the Fifth and Sixth Coalitions. But France and her Emperor were out of touch with a changed Europe. There was now a strong desire for national independence among the peoples of Europe. The Napoleonic Age was brought to a close on 18 June 1815 by the Battle of Waterloo. On 15 July Bonaparte sailed to exile on St Helena, where he died on 5 May 1821.

SIGHTS

Salon Napoleonien

Hôtel de Ville, Place Foch. &Open mid-Jun–mid-Sept Mon–Fri 9am–11.45am, 2–5.45pm; mid-Sept–mid-Jun Mon–Fri 9am–11.45, 2–4.45pm. 2.30€. &04 95 51 52 62.

Situated in the Hôtel de Ville, this early 19C Restoration-style room displays

Napoleon statue on de Gaulle Square, Ajaccio

© Fotosearch Stock Photography

paintings and sculptures relating to the Imperial era in addition to coins and medals also from the period. Here, too, is currently housed the permanent collection of the **Musée Fesch** *(50 r. Cardinal Fesch; ℘04 95 21 48 17)* while the it undergoes refurbishment (due to be completed Jun 2010).

Maison Bonaparte

r. St-Charles ◷*Open Apr–Sept Tue–Sun 9am–noon, 2–6pm; Oct–Mar Tue–Sun 10am–noon, 2–5pm.* ✆*5€.* ℘*04 95 21 43 89. www.musees-nationaux-napoleoniens.org*

A typical house of the Genoese quarter, the Bonaparte family moved here from Italy in 1743. Napoleon is supposed to have been born on a couch in the antechamber on the first floor.

The family enjoyed a reasonable standard of living. In May 1793, the Bonapartes, loyal to Republican ideas, were forced by the followers of Pascal Paoli to abandon the house, which was sacked and the adjoining family properties laid waste. On her return to Ajaccio in 1798, Napoleon's mother put the house back in order with the help of her half-brother, Abbot Fesch (a future cardinal). The work was financed in part by a grant from the Directory, in part by sums sent to his brother Joseph by Napoleon (now in Egypt), enabling him to acquire the upper storeys and the adjoining house.

On his return from Egypt on 29 September 1799, Bonaparte stopped off at Ajaccio to see the family home. He is supposed to have slept in the alcove on the second floor. After six days he slipped away via a trap-door, never to see his birthplace again. A diverse collection of memorabilia is displayed.

Place Maréchal-Foch

This fine square, the focus of Ajaccio's outdoor social life, is shaded by palm trees; its upper part is dominated by a marble statue by Laboureur of Napoleon as First Consul.

Aiguilles de
Bavella★★★

This is one of the most dramatic locations in Corsica. From the Bavella Pass, Col de Bavella, there is an awesome view of the jagged Bavella or Asinao Peaks in a spectacular, stark setting; the changing light plays on the sheer rock walls rising above the pine trees at the base.

VISIT
Forêt de Bavella★★

The dense forest growing at an altitude of 500m–1 300m (1 640ft/4 265ft) has been damaged repeatedly by fire and has been extensively replanted with maritime and laricio pines, cedars and fir trees. A hunting preserve shelters herds of wild sheep which can be glimpsed perched high up on the sheer rocks. Just before the pass are low buildings

- Ⓖ **Michelin Map:** 345 E 9
- ⓘ **Info:** There is no tourist office nearby, but the Mairie (town hall, ℘04 95 78 66 87) in Zonza can assist with information. For more on this region of Corsica, see www.alta-rocca.com.
- Ⓛ **Location:** The Aiguilles rise above the Col de Bavella, the mountain pass on D268, which runs from Sartène in SW Corsica to Solenzara on the southeast coast. The nearest community is Zonza.

formerly used as sheep-pens, and an inn, **Auberge du Col**, which is the starting-point for hikes around the pass to the Trou de la Bombe and La Pianona.

Col de Bavella

The mountain ridge crowning the island is indented by the Bavella Pass (alt 1 218m/3 996ft) marked by a cross and the statue of **Notre-Dame-des Neiges**. The setting and the panorama over the summits are spectacular. To the west the Bavella Peaks rise above the forest of twisted pine trees while to the east the rock wall of Calanca Murata and the jagged ridge of red rock of Punta Tafonata di Paliri stand out against the backdrop of the Tyrrhenian Sea.

Walks

The Bavella Pass is the starting point for many walks and trails for all levels of ability, and is on the long-distance path GR20, which traverses the island.

Bonifacio★★★

Projecting into the sea on Corsica's southern tip, the old town occupies the top of a high wedge of rock with exceptional views, while the harbour and new town at the foot of the cliff is the busy centre of commerce and actiivity.

▶ **Population:** 2 683

♿ **Michelin Map:** 345 D-E 11

🛈 **Info:** 2 r. Fred Scamaroni. ☏ 04 95 73 11 88. www.bonifacio.fr.

▶ **Location:** From the harbour, steps lead up to Old Town.

A BIT OF HISTORY

Greek and Roman remains have been found at Bonifacio but the town's history really begins when Bonifacio, Marquis of Tuscany, gave it his name. The strategic position controlling of the Western Mediterranean was appreciated by the Genoese, who took it in 1187.

Upper town

J.L. Gallo/MICHELIN

The town was besieged many times, most notably in 1420 by King Alfonso V of Aragon. Legend has it that his soldiers cut the famous stairway of 187 steps into the cliff-face in the course of a single night.

VISIT
Site★★★
Bonifacio is magnificently sited on a long, narrow promontory protecting its "fjord" in the far south of Corsica and it is reached from the rest of the island across a vast, arid plain.

The town is divided in two, the **"Marine"**★, the port quarter offering a safe anchorage for warships, fishing boats and pleasure craft, and the Upper Town **(ville haute★★)** overlooking the sea from 60m/200ft-high cliffs.

Its old houses, many of them with four or five storeys, are joined together by what appear to be flying buttresses but are in fact rainwater channels feeding the town's cisterns. The great loggia of the Church of Ste-Marie-Majeure is built over a cistern with a capacity of 650cu m (c. 140 000 gal); under Genoese rule this is where the affairs of the town were deliberated upon by four elders, who were elected for three months at a time. Twice a week the *podesta*, the mayor, who lived opposite, would mete out justice from here.

EXCURSION
Grotte du Sdragonato★
45min by boat.
The dragon's cave is dimly lit by a shaft in the shape of Corsica in reverse. 12km/7.4mi away across the sometimes choppy waters of the Bonifacio Straits (Bouches de Bonifacio) is Sardinia. The trip gives good views of the high limestone cliffs of the promontory and of the King of Aragon's steps.

Cap Corse★★★

Cap Corse is the finger of mountain range which prolongs the island's ridge of schistous rock 40km/24.8mi into the sea.

A BIT OF HISTORY
A Seafaring People – In contrast to the rest of the Corsican population, local inhabitants responded to the call of the sea and took up trade and travel to distant lands. In the 19C they set up the first trading-posts in North Africa. A large number emigrated to South America; many became prosperous and built great houses in colonial or Renaissance style in their native village. These styles have influenced the architecture of the region.

This northernmost part of Corsica is in fact its sunniest and is ideal for walking and cycling. The east side of the the Cap has small villages like Erbalunga nestling in coves while on the west side the villages of Nonza and Canari are on higher ground.

- **Michelin Map:** 345 F 1-2
- **Info:** Port de Plaisance, Macinaggio. 04 95 35 40 34. www.ot-rogliano-macinaggio.com.
- **Location:** Cap Corse can be reached from either the east or the W coast. The city of Bastia stands at the base of the 'finger' on the east coast.
- **Don't Miss:** Make time to visit the superb covered market, near the Old Port, daily except Monday.
- **Timing:** Take a picturesque corniche road to discover villages clinging to defensive sites, tiny sandy beaches, and marinas nestling in an inlet.

Bastia, Cap Corse

A. de Valroger/MICHELIN

Corte★

Corte owes its fame to its site★ among gorges and ravines, as well as to two great men, Gaffori and Paoli, who were instrumental in making it one of the strongholds of Corsican patriotism.

> ▶ **Population:** 6 350
>   **Michelin Map:** 345 D 6
>   **Info:** Citadelle de Corté.
>   ℘04 95 46 26 70.
>   www.corte-tourisme.com.
> ▶ **Location:** Corte sits high in the rocky interior of the island.

A BIT OF HISTORY

Jean-Pierre Gaffori (1704–53) was born here. He was a member of the Triumvirate elected as "Protectors of the Nation", who took up arms against Genoa. In 1746, supported by his indomitable wife Faustine, he succeeded in wresting the town from the Genoese. In 1750 they returned, taking the citadel but failing to overcome the resolute defence of the old town; Gaffori's house still bears the marks made by the Genoese guns.

In June 1751, Gaffori was made "General of the Nation" and granted executive power. But two years later he was killed in an ambush, betrayed by his brother. After this assassination, an appeal was made for **Pascal Paoli** (1725–1807), then in exile in Italy, to return to his native land. He was proclaimed "General of the Nation" in his turn. By 1764, the island was united under his leadership, with only the Genoese coastal forts holding out against him. For 14 years he made Corte his capital, drew up a constitution, founded a

university, minted money, reformed the system of justice, encouraged industry and stimulated agricultural production.

Having failed to put down the Corsicans' long struggle for independence (1729-69) the Republic of Genoa requested the intervention of France. A mission of conciliation arrived, headed by the future French Governor, Marbeuf. Paoli unwisely prevaricated and was bypassed by events; on 15 May 1768, by the Treaty of Versailles, Genoa provisionally gave up its rights over the island to France. Paoli proclaimed a mass uprising, but was defeated at **Ponte Nuovo** on 8 May 1769.

Paoli went into exile, spent mostly in England, where he was lionised by the court of George III. Amnestied at the outbreak of the French Revolution, he met with a triumphal reception in Paris before returning to Corsica. Later, after his denunciation as a counter-

271

revolutionary, he sought aid from the English. Nelson's victories over the French at St-Florent, Bastia and Calvi did not however fulfil Paoli's hopes of independence under the English crown, but led to the shortlived Anglo-Corsican kingdom and renewed exile in London for Paoli. He died there in 1807.

SIGHT
Ville Haute★

Dominated by the citadel (**citadelle**★) perched high up on its rock, old Corte, with its cobbled, stepped streets and tall houses, still has the air of the island's capital it once was.

In the Place Paoli stands the statue of the great man, in bronze. Further up is the Place Gaffori, where, behind the monument to the General of the Nation, is his house. A ramp opposite the National Palace (Palais National) leads to a viewpoint (**belvedère**★) on a peak standing out from the main promontory on which the citadel is built. It offers a fine view of the town in its setting bordered by the river valley, Gorges du Tavignano.

EXCUSION
Église San Michele de Murato★★
Michelin map 345-E-4

The church and village of Murato are 54.6km/34mi NE of Corte along the D 5. On its hilltop site just north of the village of Murato in the Bevinco valley, this 13C Romanesque church is Pisan in style, of uneven stripes of beautiful green serpentine and white limestone blocks.

Filitosa★★

This fascinating site was discovered in 1946; the beginnings of Corsican history are all visible here, from the Neolithic (6000–2000 BC), to the Megalithic (3000–1000 BC) and the Torreen (1500-800 BC), and finally to the Roman.

SIGHT
Station Préhistorique★★

⏱Apr–mid-Oct: 9am–7pm. Preferably in the middle of the day: good light to study the sculptures and engravings. Sound recordings in 4 languages. ⬭5€. ☎04 95 74 00 91.

By the path leading to the prehistoric site stands the superb menhir known as Filitosa V bearing, in front, a long sword and an oblique dagger, and behind, anatomical or clothing details.

A stone wall built by the Megalithic people encloses the site. Within it, four striking groups of monuments testify to the domination exercised by the Torreens: the East Monument (**Monument Est**) which they filled in; the remains of huts (**cabanes**) which they re-used, the circular Central

- ♿ **Michelin Map:** 345 C 9
- ▯ **Info:** Place St Marcel. ☎95 37 18 07. www.frotsi-corse.com.
- ▷ **Location:** The site, over-looking the Taravo valley, is located in the commune of Sollacaro, 17km/10.5mi N of Propriano, in southern Corsica.

Monument (**Monument central**), and the fragments of menhir-statues. The latter had been made by the Megalithic people; the Torreens cut them up and re-used them, face downwards, in the construction of the Central Monument, doubtless to signal their supremacy.

Some of them, however, have been stood upright again, and Filitosa IX and XIII frame the way into the Central Monument. The West Monument (**Monument Ouest**) is Torreen, and is built on Megalithic foundations.

The five menhir-statues near an age-old olive-tree on the far slope of the valley mark the end of the Megalithic period in this area.

Golfe de **Porto**★

The Bay of Porto is one of the most splendid destinations on the Corsican coast, owing to its sheer size, range of colours and varied natural sights. Imposing cliffs of red granite contrast with the deep-blue waters. The area is part of a nature park, Parc naturel régional de Corse, listed as a World Heritage Site.

EXCURSIONS
Calanches de Piana★★★
Boat trips (1hr30min) leaving from Porto. ⏱*Easter–Oct: departure 2pm, 4pm, 6pm.*
The deep creeks *(calanche)* dominating the Bay of Porto are remarkable; the chaotic landscape is shaped by erosion of the granite, jagged rocks and spherical cavities known as "taffoni".
A road (D 81), which runs through the calanche for 2km/1.2mi, affords splendid viewpoints over the rock piles and the sea. Starting from the terrace of the **Chalet des Roches bleues**, several walks lasting about one hour allow visitors to

- ♿ **Michelin Map:** 345 A-B 6
- 🏢 **Info:** Qtr. de la Marine, ℘04 95 26 10 55. www.porto-tourisme.com.
- ▶ **Location:** The Gulf is the large bay on the shores of which the town of Porto stands, in western Corsica.

admire at close range the distinctive form of some of the rocks: the Turtle, the Bishop, a human head (Tête de Poincaré) and a castle.

Réserve Naturelle de Scandola★★★
The Scandola Peninsula (Presqu'île de Scandola) rises to a height of 560m/1 837ft between the Punta Rossa to the south and the Punta Nera to the north. The majestic massif is of volcanic origin. The large cavities known locally as **"taffoni"**, piercing the bare rocks along the coast, are an integral feature of the picturesque landscape of Corsica.

Sartène★

The writer Prosper Mérimée thought Sartène, 305m/1 000ft above the Bay of Valinco, the "most Corsican of Corsican towns".

SIGHTS
Place de la Libération
The shady square is the focus of local life. It is overlooked by the **Église Ste-Marie**, built in granite. To the left of the main entrance are the chains and the heavy cross of oak borne by Catenacciu, the anonymous red-robed penitential figure at the centre of the nocturnal procession on Good Friday. This procession **(procession du Catenacciu★★)** is probably the island's most ancient ceremony.

- ▸ **Population:** 3 410
- ♿ **Michelin Map:** 345 C 10
- 🏢 **Info:** Place de la Libération. ℘04 95 77 74 01. www.sartene.fr.
- ▶ **Location:** The town is 51km/31.7mi NW of Bonifacio.

Vieille ville (Old Town)★★
Go through the arch of the town hall (Hôtel de ville) and take the street opposite (Rue des Frères-Bartoli). The narrow stone-flagged alleyways, some stepped or vaulted, are lined by tall granite-built houses with a fortress-like air. The **Quartier de Santa Ann★★★** has this kind of characteristic townscape.

DORDOGNE BERRY LIMOUSIN

The Dordogne, with its hills, its mature and varied agricultural landscapes, its deciduous woodlands and its mellow stone buildings is not unlike parts of southern England, albeit with a more genial climate and a general atmosphere of good living. Little touched by industrialisation or mass tourism, the regions of Berry and Limousin seem to represent the quintessence of rural France. Berry centres on Bourges which, with its great cathedral, was once the seat of the French court. The Limousin is the name of the old province around Limoges forming the northwestern extremity of the Massif Central.

Highlights

1 Palace of wealthy financier, Jacques Coeur, at **Bourges** (p276)
2 Tranquil riverside village and Abbey **Brantôme** (p280)
3 Medieval bridge with towers at Cahors **Pont Valentré** (p293)
4 World famous prehistoric cave painting at **Grotte de Lascaux** (p284)
5 Pilgrimage site clinging to a cliff **Rocamadour** (p299)

Geography – The Dordogne incorporates the Périgord region which forms a plateau dissected by the Dordogne; along the banks grow maize, tobacco, sunflowers and cereals. In Quercy the thick layers of Jurassic limestone form *causses,* covered by scrubby oaks and carob trees, which are dissected by dry valleys and spectacular canyons.

The vast limestone plateau, which forms Berry's heartland, is devoted to arable farming making a contrast with the *bocage* of the Boischaut and the Brenne marshlands. Much of the Limousin is quiet countryside drained by rivers flowing westwards to the Dordogne and the Saintonge. In contrast is the Montagne, its name derived more from the rigour of the climate than the altitude since nowhere does it rise above 1 000m/3 280 ft.

History – The Dordogne area has been settled since the very earliest times as evidenced by its renowned cave paintings at Lascaux and Font-de-Gaume. As well as stunning examples of medieval settlement, such as Rocamadour, there are numerous reminders of Anglo-French struggle, from the planned towns, or *bastides* like Monpazier, Domme, Villefranche-du-Périgord and Beaumont to rugged strongholds such as Beynac and Castelnaud. The Limousin and the Berry, like the Dordogne, were both part of Aquitania in Roman times and were later ruled by the Franks. Also contested during the Hundred Years' War, they were eventually annexed to France during the reign of Henry IV.

Economy – The climate of the Dordogne enables the production of maize, tobacco, sunflowers, cereals and foie-gras, while the Lot Valley, west of Cahors, is renowned for its 'black' red wine. Tourism is very important and the area is much loved by northern Europeans. Berry and Limousin are largely rural; agriculture is the mainstay of both, but tourism is important and the Porcelain industry at Limoges is as prominent today as ever.

This section also covers towns in **Quercy**

Bourges★★★

Berry

The centre of Bourges is a majestic ensemble of dignified medieval buildings, dominated by the magnificent cathedral, a striking symbol of the town's rich past.

A BIT OF HISTORY

Bourges was already a place of some importance at the time of the conquest of Gaul; in 52 BC it was sacked by Julius Caesar, who is supposed to have massacred 40 000 of its inhabitants. In the 4C the city became the capital of the Roman province of Avaricum. Its significance increased over the years, but only at the end of the 14C did it take on a national role, under Jean de Berry. He made Bourges a centre of the arts to rival Dijon and Avignon, commissioning works like the Très Riches Heures, perhaps the most exquisite miniatures ever painted.

VISIT

Cathédrale St-Étienne★★★

⏲Open Apr–Sept 8.30am–7.15 (9pm Jul–Aug); Oct–Mar 9am–5.45pm.
No charge. ✆02 48 65 49 44.

In the 12C, Bourges was the seat of an archbishopric linked by tradition to the royal territories to the north, whereas the regions to the south west came under the sphere of influence of the Angevin

> ▶ **Population:** 94 731
> Ⓒ **Michelin Map:** 323 K 4-6
> ▣ **Info:** 21 r. Victor Hugo. ✆02 48 23 02 60. www.bourges-tourisme.com.
> ▶ **Location:** A 45min ride on the P'tit train touristique gives you a good look at the city's history and architecture (Apr–mid-Nov daily, every 15min in front of the tourist office). There are also 2hr guided tours offered by the tourist office (ↄsee sidebar, p276).

kingdom. The great new cathedrals of the Île-de-France were taking shape, and the Archbishop, Henri de Sully, Primate of Aquitaine, dreamed of a similar great edifice for his city.

In drawing up his plans, the anonymous architect exploited all the new techniques of the Gothic in order to control and direct the thrusts exerted by and on his great structure. Other innovations of his included leaving out the transepts, retaining six sexpartite bays and incorporating the Romanesque portals of the old cathedral into the north and south doorways of the new building.

By 1200 the crypt was completed, by 1215, the choir. In 1220 the great nave

Stained-glass window depicting Joseph's dream, Cathédrale St-Étienne

S. Sauvignier/MICHELIN

Guided Tours

The tourist office offers 2hr discovery tours of the Gallo-Roman town (including a visit to the temple of Vesone, otherwise closed to the public) or the medieval and Renaissance town (including a visit to the Hôtel la Joubertie and the Tour Mataguerre, which are also not normally open to the public). Jun–Sept Mon–Sat. ₰8€

with its splendid row of two-tiered flying buttresses was ready. Over-enthusiastic restoration at the start of the 19C included the remodelling of the external gables and the unfortunate addition of round windows, balustrades and pinnacles.

The huge west front has five doorways, anticipating the nave and four aisles adorned with the radiating motifs of the High Gothic (mid 13–14C) style; they were begun in 1230. Ten years later the two right-hand portals were in place. By 1250, the central portal (*Last Judgement*) had been finished. But 60 years later, subsidence made it necessary to prop up the South Tower by means of a massive pillar-buttress and to strengthen the west front. This was to no avail; on 31 December 1506, the north tower fell into ruins. Guillaume Pellevoysin, the new architect, worked for 30 years on its replacement and on the construction of the two left-hand portals; he included many architectural and decorative features of the Early Renaissance.

The east end (**chevet**) has the Gothic windows of the lower church inserted between the base of the chapels and the buttresses. Three-sided chapels radiate out from the outer ambulatory, while the inner ambulatory is spanned by the first tier of the double flying buttresses; the upper spans pierce the structure to hold the vault of the choir in place. The Lanceolate Gothic style here reaches a high point in its development.

Inside, the nave and four aisles (**nefs**), completed in 1270, make a striking impression by virtue of their great height and the light filtering through the stained glass. The outer aisles, lined by chapels, are already 9m/29.5ft from floor to vault, the inner aisles, with a blind triforium, reach 21m/68.9ft, while the nave rises to a full 37.1m/121.7ft. With no gallery, and limited by the great size of its arches it is covered by a sexpartite vault; the alternating sequence of major and minor piers is cunningly disguised by the shafts wrapped around the columns. Beneath the choir a crypt (**crypte★★**) of the same layout takes up a 6m/19.6ft change in level of the ground. A fine example of a 13C crypt, it has an outer ambulatory with triangular vaulting and arcades mounted on twisted diagonal arches to allow the keystones to be set properly. ➣Guided tours (45min); Apr–Sept 9.45–11.45am, 2–5.30pm; May2–Jun 9.30–11.30am, 14–17.30pm; Jly–Aug 9.30am–12.30pm, 2–6pm; Oct–Mar 9.30–11.30am, 2–4.45pm ©Closed 1 Jan, 1 May, 1 and 11 Nov, 25 Dec. ₰7€ (includes entrance to North tower). 9€ combined ticket with Palais Jacques-Cœur. ℘02 48 65 49 44.

The stained glass (**vitraux★★★**) – some of the finest in the whole of France – demonstrates the whole evolution of the art of glass-making between the 12C and 17C. The 13C windows in the choir recall the techniques of the master glass-makers of Chartres. The great nave is illuminated by light streaming in through all its windows.

Palais Jacques Cœur★★

10 bis, r. Jacques Cœur. ➣Guided tours (1hr); call for times. ©Open May 2–Jun 9.30am–noon, 2–6.15pm; Jul–Aug 9.30am–12.30pm, 2–6.30pm; Sept–Apr 9.30am–noon, 2–5.15pm. Last entry 1hr before closing. ©Closed 1 Jan, 1 May, 1 and 11 Nov, 25 Dec. ₰7€. ℘02 48 24 79 42. www.palais-jacques-coeur.monuments-nationaux.fr.

The son of a Bourges fur-trader, **Jacques Cœur** (1395–1456) started out as a goldsmith, first at the court of Jean de Berry, then with Charles VII. He soon became aware of the economic recovery just beginning and of the opportunities opening up in the Mediterranean. Before long he had many commercial interests and he supplied the royal court with luxury goods and became the king's Minister of Finance. At the peak of his career at the age of 50 he decided to build himself a worthy residence.

His palace, begun in 1445, was completed in the short space of 10 years. It shows how the will to build had revived after the stagnation due to war and also demonstrates the success of the Flamboyant Gothic style. It is a sumptuous building, incorporating certain pioneering comforts like a bath-house and an arcaded courtyard. Other innovations it contributed to the evolution of late-medieval domestic architecture included the provision of a large number of rooms with independent access, sculptures indicating the purpose of the rooms served by the various staircases, and, in the chapel, two oratories reserved for the proprietor and his wife.

ADDITIONAL SIGHTS

Hôtel Cujas★ **(Musée du Berry)** *(4 r. des Arènes)*
Hôtel Lallemant★ **(Musée des arts**

Detail of the wall decoration Palais Jacques-Cœur

décoratifs) *(5 r. Bouronneaux)*
Hotel des Échevins (Musée Maurice-Estève)★ *(r. Edouard Branly)*
Jardin des Prés-Fichaux★ *(bd de la République)*

ADDRESSES

🛏 STAY

🍴🛏 **Chambre d'hôte Château de Bel Air** – *Lieu-dit le Grand-Chemin, Arcay. 16km/10mi S of Bourges on the D 73. ✆02 48 25 36 72. 6 rooms.* Surrounded by spacious grounds, this 19C château is both calm and comfortable. The vast entrance hall leads to the dining room with its massive fireplace. Large rooms on the upper floor.

🛏🛏 **Hôtel Christina** – *5 r. Halle. ✆02 48 70 56 50. 71 rooms.* This hotel is the perfect base for discovering the city centre. Two categories of well-maintained bedrooms are available: cosy and chic, or smaller and functional.

🛏🛏 **Hôtel Les Tilleuls** – *7 pl. Pyrotechnie. ✆02 48 20 49 04. Closed 26 Dec–3 Jan. 39 rooms.* Situated in a quiet part of town, this hotel offers guests accommodation in the main building and an annex, where the rooms are less spacious, more basic, but with the benefit of air-conditioning. Children's play area in the garden. Solarium.

🛏🛏🛏 **Best Western Hôtel d'Angleterre** – *1 pl. des Quatre-Piliers. ✆02 48 24 68 51. 30 rooms.* The city's former court of justice is located close to the Palais Jacques-Cœur. All necessary creature comforts in the bedrooms (most with air-conditioning), where the décor is sober yet modern.

🍴 EAT

🛏🛏 **Le Bourbonnoux** – *44 r. Bourbonnoux. ✆02 48 24 14 76. Closed 10 days Feb, 10 days Easter, second-half Aug, Sun eve Nov–Jun, Sat lunch, Fri.* The restaurant is in a street lined with craft shops, just a few steps away from St-Étienne Cathedral. The welcome is warm and the dining room is pleasantly decorated with bright colours and exposed beams. Popular with locals.

⊖⊖ **Le Bistro Gourmand** – *5 pl. de la Barre. ℘02 48 70 63 37. Reservations recommended.* A delightful bistro specialising in regional and Lyonnais cuisine. The sober décor here is enhanced by gentle candlelight.

⊖⊖ **La Courcillière** – *r. de Babylone. ℘02 48 24 41 91. Closed Wed, Tue eve.* Located in the Les Marais district just a stone's throw from the city centre, this pleasant, rustic restaurant has a terrace by the water facing the gardens. Down-to-earth and reasonably priced cuisine.

⊖⊖ **D'Antan Sancerrois** – *50 r. Bourbonnoux. ℘02 48 65 96 26. Closed Jan 1, Aug 5–23, Dec 23–Jan 5, Sun, Mon.* This pretty bistro used to be home to a 15C alderman who kept company with the Duchesse de Berry. The handsome rustic décor features an amusing collection of porcelain tureen lids. Traditional fare and good service.

▼ BARS AND CAFÉS

Pub des Jacobins – *Enclos des Jacobins. ℘02 48 24 61 78. Closed Sun.* This piano-bar is whole-heartedly devoted to jazz, as demonstrated by the photos of musicians covering the walls. Top-quality concerts are held here once a month. The pub specialises in cocktails.

Pub Jacques Cœur – *1 r. d'Auron. ℘02 48 70 72 88.* This 16C half-timbered residence, now a pub, was built on the site where Jacques Cœur, a wealthy and influential 15C merchant and councillor to King Charles VII, was born. Sloping and lopsided, this antique building is the most photographed of Bourges. Concerts are frequently held here.

☼ ENTERTAINMENT

Maison de la Culture de Bourges – *pl. André-Malraux. ℘02 48 67 74 70. www. mcbourges.com. Closed 13 Jul–20 Aug and 1 May.* Opened by André Malraux, then Minister of Culture, this was the first Maison de la Culture in France. This lively and popular venue hosts plays, dance performances and classical music and jazz concerts. Cinema and café.

Les Nuits Lumières de Bourges – *℘02 48 23 02 60. Every eve in Jul–Aug and during the Printemps de Bourges festival; May–Jun, Sept Thu–Sat.* A walk through the historic city centre at night to view illuminated buildings (2hr30min). Blue lanterns mark the way.

☆☆ LEISURE ACTIVITIES

Base de Voile du Val-d'Auron – *23 chemin Grand Mazières. ℘02 48 20 07 65. Closed Oct–Apr and Mon.* This watersports centre at the Val d'Auron Lake (85ha/210 acres) offers swimming, canoeing, fishing, rowing, and more.

☒ SHOPPING

The main shopping area is in the pedestrianised area that includes rue Coursarlor and rue Mirebeau (near the Palais Jacques-Cœur), and rue Bourbonnoux and rue Moyenne (near the cathedral).

Markets – Every Sat morning, the listed **Halle au Blé** comes to life with 200 stallholders selling all types of food. A permanent daily market is also held at the **Halle St-Bonnet**, selling fresh seasonal produce, local cheeses and other regional specialities. On Sun mornings, stalls selling bric-a-brac, inexpensive clothes, etc. add to the charm of this popular market.

La Maison des Forestines – *3 pl. Cujas. ℘02 48 24 00 24.* This chocolate/confectionery business founded in 1825 occupies an attractive Haussmann-style building. The shop, with its coffered ceiling and superb Gien china, produces irresistible house specialities such as the Forestine, a chocolate praline with a satiny sugar coating and the Richelieu, a nougatine filled with an almond and pistachio creme.

Épicerie du Berry – *41 r. Moyenne (Îlot Victor-Hugo). ℘02 48 70 02 38.* This small boutique at the foot of the cathedral only sells regional products such as *sablés de Nançais* (a type of shortcake biscuit), pasta from La Chapelle de St-Ursin, tortillons (goat's cheese pastries) and Monin syrups.

Château de
Meillant★★

Berry

This château is a fine example of how stylistic change was allied to the growing desire for domestic comfort towards the end of the 15C, to transform what had been a typical medieval castle into an agreeable country residence.

VISIT

🚶 *Guided tours (45min) Jul–Aug 9.30am–6pm; Sept–Jun 9.30am–noon, 2–6pm.* 🎫*7€.* 📞*02 48 63 32 05.*
The medieval south front lapped by the waters of a moat is the only remnant of the old fortress built in the early 14C by Étienne de Sancerre; the towers retain their narrow loopholes although the wall-walk has been demolished. The

♿ **Michelin Map:**323 I 6
▶ **Location:** The castle is located 39km/24.2mi S of Bourges.

ornate east façade, which is in a different style recalling that of the châteaux of the Loire, includes two projecting stair turrets in the late-Gothic style featuring a pierced balustrade at the base of the roof, dormer windows adorned with carvings, chimneys with elaborate Gothic balustrades, and in particular the splendidly decorated tower (Tour du Lion) by Giocondo, one of Michelangelo's assistants.

The interior, notably the formal dining room (Grande Salle à Manger) and the Bishop of Amboise's chamber, is furnished with period pieces, fireplaces, tapestries and carpets.

Abbaye de
Noirlac★★

Berry

Between the River Cher and the Meillant Forest, this 12-14C abbey is one of the best preserved medieval monasteries in France. It occupies an exceptional setting for the Gregorian chants, concerts and cultural events that take place here.

VISIT

🕐*Open daily Apr–Sept daily 10am–6.30pm; Apr–Jun and Sept 9.45am–2.30pm, 2–6.30pm; Feb–Mar and Oct–23 Dec 2–5pm.* 🕐*Closed various dates during Dec–Jan; call for specific dates.* 🎫*7€.* 🚶*Guided tours available in six languages.* 📞*02 48 62 01 01. www.abbayedenoirlac.fr.*
The perfect simplicity of the abbey church (**église abbatiale**) dates from

♿ **Michelin Map:** 323 K 6
📋 **Info:** Place de la République, St Amand-Montrond.
📞02 48 96 16 86.
▶ **Location:** The abbey is just outside the town of St Amand-Montrond.
🕐 **Timing:** Allow a couple of hours to look around the Abbey and then enjoy a relaxing lunch at the Auberge de l'Abbaye on site!

1150–60. It follows the plan of the great abbey at Clairvaux. The modern glass is the work of Jean-Pierre Raynaud, aided by craftsmen from Chartres and Bourges. The Gothic cloisters were added in the 13C.

Beynac-et-Cazenac★★

Dordogne

One of the great castles of Périgord, **Château de Beynac** is famous for its history, its architecture and for its panoramic setting on top of a rugged rock face.

VISIT

ⓘ*Open daily Jun–Sept 10am–6.30pm; Oct–Feb 10am–dusk; Dec–Feb noon–dusk.* ✆*Call for admission price information.* ☏*05 53 29 50 40.*

Defended on the north side by double walls, the castle looms over the river from a precipitous height of 150m/492ft. Crouching benath its cliff is a tiny village, once the home of poet Paul Eluard. A square keep existed here as early as 1115; it was strengthened at the time of

- ◔ **Michelin Map:** 329 H 6
- ▣ **Info:** ⓘ *See SARLAT-LE-CANÉDA.*
- ◖ **Location:** The castle and village are on the N bank of the Dordogne, 12km/7.4mi S of Sarlat.
- ◉ **Don't Miss:** As well as the château, the beautiful Renaissance village at the foot of the cliff is also worth visiting.

the great rivalry between the Capetians and the Plantagenets.

During the Hundred Years' War, the Dordogne frequently marked the border between French and English territory; stirring times for Beynac, face to face with its rival Castelnaud on the cliffs opposite.

Brantôme★★

Dordogne

Brantôme lies in the midst of lush, smiling countryside, in the charming Vallée de la Dronne, north of the town of Périgueux. Its old abbey and picturesque setting make it one of the most delightful little places in Périgord.

A BIT OF HISTORY

Pierre de Bourdeilles (1540–1614) was commendatory abbot here. In 1589 he retired to the abbey after a fall from a horse, having also fallen from favour at court as the Bourbons replaced the Valois. Under the nom-de-plume of Brantôme, this former courtier and soldier of fortune amused himself with his memoirs, published posthumously as

- ▸ **Population:** 2 080
- ◔ **Michelin Map:** 329 E 3
- ▣ **Info:** Abbaye de Brantôme. ☏05 53 05 80 52. www.ville-brantome.fr.
- ◖ **Location:** A boat trip on the river is the perfect way to appreciate the town and its setting.

Mémoires de Messire Pierre de Bourdeilles comprising the *Lives of Illustrious Ladies, Lives of Gallant Ladies, Lives of French Illustrious Men and the Great Leaders,* and *Lives of Foreign Illustrious Men and the Great Leaders.*

VISIT

This riverside village has old dwellings with slate roofs built like manor houses, a crooked bridge seen across the tranquil surface of the water, and great trees growing on the lawns of its lovely gardens. The 18C abbey has a fine west front and a Romanesque **bell-tower★★**.

Guided Tours

Guided tours (1hr) of the abbey and its bell-tower: mid-Jun–mid-Sept Wed–Mon. ✆6€. ☏05 53 05 80 63.

Domme - the bastide high above the Dordogne

J. Damase/MICHELIN

Domme★★

Dordogne

One of the many medieval forti-fied towns *(bastides)* founded in southwest France by both French and English, Domme was laid out by Philippe le Hardi (the Bold) in 1281. The normal rectangular plan of such settlements was here distorted in order to fit it to the rocky crag over-looking the Dordogne 145m/475.7ft below.

A BIT OF HISTORY
A Royal Bastide

Domme was founded by Philip the Bold in 1283 in order to keep watch on the Dordogne Valley and check the desire for expansion of the English established in Gascony. The king granted the town important privileges including that of minting coins and Domme played an important role during the Hundred Years War. In the 17C, its wine-growing and river-trading activities were thriving and its markets were renowned throug-hout the region.

▶ **Population:** 987
Michelin Map: 329 i 7
Info: Place de la Halle.
℘05 53 31 71 00.
www.ot-domme.com.
▶ **Location:** The village is S of the River Dordogne, 12km/7.4mi from Sarlat.

VISIT
Panorama★★★

There are splendid views over the alluvial valley of the Dordogne from the Barre belvedere or, better still, from the cliff-top walk (Promenade des Falaises – *no para-pet*) just below the public gardens.

All around is an opulent landscape of castles, well-wooded slopes dotted with stone-built villages, lush meadows, wal-nut trees, and corn.

American writer Henry Miller described the area as perhaps the nearest thing to Paradise on earth.

Les **Eyzies-de-Tayac**★★

Dordogne

The village occupies a grandiose setting of steep cliffs crowned with evergreen oak and juniper, at the confluence of two rivers. In the base of the cliffs are caves that were prehistoric habitations, where the art and crafts of our distant ancestors can still be seen.

▶ **Population:** 909
 Michelin Map: 329 H 6
 Info: Pl. de la Mairie. ℘05 53 06 97 05. www.leseyzies.com.
 Location: The village is in the heart of the Dordogne region, 20km/12.4mi from Sarlat.
 Don't Miss: The best of the many fascinating sites are Grotte de Font-de-Gaume, Grotte du Grand Roc, and the Musée National de la Préhistoire.
 Timing: The sites are not all in the village – they are mostly spread along the Vézère valley. It is rewarding to spend a full day in the area.
 Kids: Prehisto-Parc near Les Eyzies.

PREHISTORY

The **Upper Palaeolithic** is the period from 35 000–10 000 BC. Skeletons dating from the early part of this period were found at Cro-Magnon in the Dordogne in 1868. Cro-Magnon people were tall, with nimble hands and clearly possessed of great inventiveness, the first examples of modern man, Homo sapiens. Another branch of the same species were the people known as the Chancelade race, remains of whom were discovered at Chancelade near Périgueux in 1888.

The Aurignacian and **Perigordian** cultures – the latter is marked by long migration periods – though contemporary, do not seem to have been in contact with each other and differ in a number of respects, although both are characterised by a continuous improvement in tool-making and the development of hunting techniques which allowed time to be set aside for the creation of works of art (line-drawings and paintings). Aurignacian industry (*see* **Aurignac** *in the Miichelin Green Guide French Atlantic Coast*) brought forth very finely knapped flints, gravers and scrapers and perforated batons made from reindeer horn. The culture reached its peak about 25 000 years ago; its achievements can be seen in the in the cave at La Grèze and in the shelter **(Abri du Poisson)**, all of which mark the beginnings of human activity in the lower Vézère valley.

Solutrean culture, named after the rock near Mâcon (Roche de **Solutré**★★) is well represented in the Dordogne. It is characterised by the manufacture of fine flint blades and weapons with serrated points and by the appearance of needles.

CAPITAL OF PREHISTORY

There are almost 200 prehistoric sites in the Dordogne, more than half of them in the vicinity of Les Eyzies. The area has easily accessible natural **caves** and shelters as well as rock projections forming a natural habitat. Prehistoric people have left many traces of their activities. Two thousand years before civilisations arose along the Tigris and the Nile, the valley of the Vézère was inhabited by accomplished artists who carved in ivory and reindeer horn and painted on cave walls.

ADDITIONAL SIGHTS

Grotte du Grand-Roc★★
Laugeri-basse, 24620 Les Eyzies de Tayac Guided tours (30min) Jul and Aug 9.30am–7pm; Mar–Jun and Sept–Oct and school holidays 10am–6pm; Feb and 1–11 Nov Mon–Fri 10am–6pm. 7.50€. ℘05 53 06 92 70. www.grandroc.com. Rock formations.

Outside Musée National
de la Préhistoire

J.Damase/MICHELIN

Musée National de la Préhistoire★
24620 Les Eyzies de Tayac. ⏱*Open Jul
and Aug daily 9.30am–6.30pm; Jun
and Sept Wed–Mon 9.30am–6pm;
Oct–May Wed–Mon 9.30am–12.30pm,
2.30–5.30pm.* 🚶*Call for guided
tours.* ⏱*Closed 1 Jan and 25 Dec.*
💶*5€ Mon–Sat, 3€ Sun, no charge
1st Sun in the month.* 📞*05 53 06 45
65. www.musee-prehistoire-eyzies.fr.*
Comprehensive displays in an old 13C
fortress with good views.
Grotte de Font-de-Gaume ★ *Just
outside village on road to St-Cyprien;
footpath to cave entrance.* ⏱*Open*
*Thu–Tue Apr–Sept 9am–noon, 2–6pm;
Mar and Oct 9.30am–noon, 2–5.30pm;
Nov–Feb 10am–noon, 2–5pm. Last
departure 1hr30min before closing.*
🚶*G guided tours, call in advance.*
⏱*Closed Jan 1, Nov 1 and 11, Dec 25.*
💶*5.50€.* 📞*05 53 06 86 00.* Many
multicoloured paintings.
Laugerie-Haute *On D47 where it
turns away from the Vézère.* 🚶*
Guided tours by appointment; call for
other opening times.* ⏱*Closed public
holidays.* 💶*6.10€. Information at the
Grotte de Font-de-Gaume.* 📞*05 53 06
86 00 – 7 000 years of civilisation.*

Château de
Hautefort★★
Dordogne

The elegant château rises up proudly
on its hilltop site, overlooking its
extensive and well-kept grounds.

VISIT
♿🚶 *Guided tours daily (1hr) Jun–
Sept 9.30am–7pm; Apr–May 10am–
12.30pm, 2–6.30pm; Feb–Mar and Oct
2–6pm; 1–11 Nov, weekends and public
holidays 2–6pm. Last admission 1hr
before closing.* 💶*8.50€. Garden:
self-guided visits.* 📞*05 53 50 51 23.
www.chateau-hautefort.com*

♿ **Michelin Map:** 329 H 4
🛈 **Info:** Place René-
    Lavaud, Hautefort.
    📞05 53 50 40 27.
▷ **Location:** The castle is
    41km/25.4mi E of
    Périgueux.
🔍 **Don't Miss:** Superb
    timberwork in the north-
    west tower.

In the 16C, an ancient fortress was
strengthened, and a century later,
reconstructed in Renaissance and
Classical style. It has been further
restored since a fire in 1968. The interior

Château de Hautefort

J.P. Clapham/MICHELIN

has fine Flemish tapestries saved from the flames, a 17C Felletin landscape, good pieces of furniture and unusual paved floors. The tower has magnificent chestnut timberwork (**charpente★★**).

Grotte de
Lascaux

Dordogne

The world-famous cave paintings of Lascaux were discovered by accident on 12 September 1940 by a young man looking for his dog which had disappeared down a hole.

VISIT

Open Mar–Oct daily; Nov–Dec Tue–Sun. ℘05 53 05 65 65 or 05 53 51 95 03. www.culture.gouv.fr/culture/arcnat/lascaux/en.

The actual Lascaux cave, carved out of the Périgord Noir limestone, is nowadays closed to the public. However, a replica, known as Lascaux II, is open for visits at Montignac, just 200m/656ft away.

THE PAINTINGS

Most of the paintings in the cave appear to date from the end of the Aurignacian

- **Michelin Map:** 329 I 5
- **Info:** Place Bertran-de-Born, Montignac. ℘05 53 51 82 60. www.bienvenue-montignac.com.
- **Location:** The cave is situated 2km/1.2mi S of the village of Montignac, and 26km/16mi S of Sarlat.
- **Timing:** Lascaux II is open for guided visits.

period, others from the Magdalenian. They cover the walls and roofs of the cave with a bestiary of bulls, cows, horses, deer and bison, depicted with such skill as to justify Abbot Breuil's epithet "the Sistine Chapel of prehistoric times".

Unfortunately, the damage caused by visitors was such that the caves were closed to the public and a full-size replica was constructed.

Périgueux★★
Dordogne

This ancient town, with its distinctive domed churches, is attractively sited in the valley of the River Isle.

A BIT OF HISTORY

Five distinct historical periods have contributed to the formation of this ancient town.

First was the Gaulish settlement which prospered in Roman times under the name of Vesunna; its site, the "Cité", is marked by the amphitheatre gardens and St Stephen's Church (St-Étienne).

In the Middle Ages, the quarter known as "Puy St-Front" became established on a rise to the north; the cathedral was built here and the area became the heart of Périgueux, eventually in 1251 absorbing the older Cité.

In the 18C, the provincial governors, the Intendants, were responsible for a planned northward extension of the city, which linked the two districts by means of broad streets lined with public buildings.

At the end of the 19C, the station area was developed, and more recently vast modern suburbs have grown up on the outskirts.

▶ **Population:** 63 539
⬤ **Michelin Map:** 329 F 4
Info: 26 pl. Francheville, Tour Mataguerre. ℘05 53 53 10 63. www.tourisme-perigueux.fr.
◖ **Location:** Périgueux is 49km/30mi N of Bergerac.
ℙ **Parking:** Underground car parks at place Montaigne, place Francheville and Esplanade du Théâtre.

Guided Tours

The tourist office offers 2hr discovery tours of the Gallo-Roman town (incl. temple of Vesone, otherwise ⊶) or the medieval and Renaissance town (incl. Hôtel la Joubertie and the Tour Mataguerre, otherwise ⊶). *Jun–Sept Mon–Sat.* ⊜*6.50€.*

SIGHTS
St-Étienne-de-la-Cité★

Two of the domes of the original sanctuary have survived. The earlier is thought to have been built in 1117. The second dome, half a century later, is altogether lighter.

Cathédrale St-Front seen from the bank of the Isle

B. Kaufmann/MICHELIN

Cathédrale St-Front★

Of the original early Romanesque church there remain only two small octagonal domes at the eastern end of the nave. The church was an important stopping-place for pilgrims on their way to Santiago de Compostela since it was here that the remains of St Front, the apostle of Périgord, could be seen. His tomb dates from 1077. The cathedral was virtually rebuilt from 1852 onwards by Abadie, the architect who designed the Sacré-Cœur in Paris.

ADDITIONAL SIGHTS

Quartier du Puy-St-Front★
Rue Limogeanne★
Musée du Périgord★ (22 cours Tourny)

ADDRESSES

🏨 STAY

🛏🛏 **Comfort Hôtel Régina** – 14 r. Denis-Papin (opposite the train station). ☎05 53 08 40 44. 41 rooms. It is easy to spot this hotel, thanks to its yellow façade. The rooms are small, functional and colourful. Buffet breakfast, friendly service and good location.

🛏🛏 **Hôtel-Restaurant L'Écluse** – at Antonne-et-Trigonant, 10km/6.2mi NE of Périgueux. ☎05 53 06 00 04. 43 rooms. The River Isle flows gently past the hotel's small waterfront. Rooms on the main façade have balconies which overlook the river. Dine on the terrace in summer.

🍴 EAT

🍽 **Au Bien Bon** – 15 r. des Places. ☎05 53 09 69 91. Closed Feb school holidays, early Nov, Sat lunch, Sun, Mon and public holidays. The menu here is firmly influenced by seasonal local products. Dine in the rustic interior or outdoors on the summer terrace.

🍽 **Au Temps de Vivre** – 10 r. St-Silain. ☎05 53 09 87 18. Closed eves (except summer 7pm–9.30pm), Sun and Mon. Reservations recommended. Tucked away in a pleasant street in the old town, this restaurant serves daily specials, plus savoury and sweet pies. In the afternoon, tea and pastries are served here. The décor includes attractive wooden tables and painted chairs.

🍽🍽 **Le Clos Saint-Front** – 5 r. de la Vertu. ☎05 53 46 78 58. This old house, with its exposed beams, fireplace and Louis XVI furniture, is now home to an elegant restaurant which is resolutely devoted to Périgourdine cuisine with an inventive twist. Attractive summer terrace with shade provided by linden, banana and liquidambar trees.

🍽🍽 **Hercule Poireau** – 2 r. de la Nation. ☎05 53 08 90 76. Closed 24–27 Dec, 31 Dec–3 Jan, Sat–Sun. In a vaulted 16C cellar, this place is popular with locals, who come here for the varied menu, which includes several healthy options.

🛍 SHOPPING

Le Relais des Caves – 44 r. du Prés.-Wilson. ☎05 53 09 75 00. The friendly proprietor sells a wide selection of wines from across France, including a few very special vintages. Other local specialities such as fruit preserved in Bergerac wine, wine jam and foie gras are also sold here.

Stéphane Malard – 8 r. de la Sagesse. ☎05 53 08 75 10. Behind the window arcades of his shop, Stéphane sells the region's finest delicacies, including confits, foies gras, duck magret and wines. What he doesn't prepare himself, he sources with the greatest care.

Markets – pl. de Clautre: Wed and Sat morning; pl. de la Clautre (food), pl. Bugeaud and pl. Franche-Ville (clothing): every morning; pl. du Coderc (food); duck and goose product market (marché au gras) from Dec–Feb.

Sarlat-la-Canéda★★★

Dordogne

This attractive old Dordogne market town has narrow medieval streets lined with restored Gothic and Renaissance houses.

A BIT OF HISTORY

Sarlat is the capital of the Périgord Noir (Black Périgord) country, a fortunate and abundant region between the Dordogne and Vézère rivers.

The town grew up around the Benedictine abbey founded in the middle of the 9C. The wealth of the surrounding countryside poured into the town, enabling it to support a prosperous population of merchants, clerics and lawyers. Sarlat reached its peak during the 13C and 14C. The town long played host to fairs and markets, which still takes place every Saturday, when the stalls are loaded with seasonal produce, poultry, cereals, horses, nuts, geese, foie gras, truffles and other goods.

OLD SARLAT★★★

Sarlat's old district was cut into two in the 19C by the Traverse (rue de la République).

The town houses are quite unique: built with quality ashlar-work in a fine golden-hued limestone, with interior courtyards; the roofing, made of heavy limestone slabs (*lauzes*), necessitated a steeply pitched framework so that the enormous weight (500kg per sq m – about 102lb per sq ft) could be supported on thick walls. Over the years new floors were added: a medieval ground floor, a High Gothic or Renaissance upper floor and Classical roof cresting and lantern turrets.

This architectural unit escaped modern developments and was chosen as one of the new experimental national restoration projects, the goal of which was to preserve the old quarters of France's towns and cities. The project, begun in 1964, has allowed the charm

▷ **Population:** 9 909
⊚ **Michelin Map:** 329 I 6
▣ **Info:** Rue Tourny.
 ℰ05 53 31 45 45.
 www.ot-sarlat-perigord.fr.
▷ **Location:** The town is on a north–south axis, accessible by avenues Thiers and Gambetta. In the summer; the old town is closed to motor vehicles during the day.
🅿 **Parking:** There are plenty of car parks; spaces also in the old town, except Sat.
⊛ **Don't Miss:** Saturday market, which fills the town centre with a glorious array of local produce.

of this small medieval town to be recreated.

Cathédrale St-Sacerdos

St Sacerdos' Church was built here in the 12C. In 1504 Bishop Armand de Gontaut-Biron had the church razed, in order to build a cathedral. However, the bishop left Sarlat in 1519 and the construction work was not completed for more than a century.

Typical house in old Sarlat

S. Sauvignier/MICHELIN

287

Beaulieu-sur-Dordogne★★

Limousin

Rising from the RIver Dordogne, picturesq ue Beaulieu has a fine church and former abbey.

SIGHT

Église St-Pierre★★

⏱*Open daily 8am–7pm (summer 7am–8pm).* ✆*05 55 91 18 78.* 🔊*Guided tours available Jul–Aug 10am–noon, 2.30–6pm.* ✆*01 46 51 39 30.*

This is the beautiful church of a former Benedictine abbey. Its **doorway (portail)**★★, dating from 1125, has as its theme the opening stages of the Last Judgement, with the dead being summoned from their graves. The

▶ **Population:** 1 265
♿ **Michelin Map:** 329 M-6
🛈 **Info:** Place Marbot.
✆05 55 91 09 94.
www.otbeaulieu19.fr.
▶ **Location:** Beaulieu is in the Limousin region, some distance upriver from the popular Dordogne resorts.

ecstasy of the Apostles, the magnificence of the Cross and of the instruments of the Passion, the display of Christ's wounds and the subjugation of Evil represented by monsters, all proclaim the imminence of judgement. The Treasury in the north transept houses a remarkable 12C Romanesque **figure of the Virgin**★ in a 13C shrine.

Collonges-La-Rouge★★

Limousin

Collonges-la-Rouge boasts mansions, old houses and a Romanesque church built of red sandstone; the surrounding countryside dotted with nut orchards and vineyards. In the 13C the village was granted franchises and other privileges by the county of Turenne. In the 16C it became a holiday centre for county dignitaries who built charming mansions and residences flanked by towers and turrets.

VISIT

The exclusive use of the traditional building stone and the balanced proportions of the various structures give a harmonious character to the town. Some are of special interest: the **Maison de la Sirène** (⏱*open Easter–All Saints Day 10am–noon, 3–6pm;* 💶*2€; contact Mme Foucher;* ✆*05 55 84 08*

▶ **Population:** 379
♿ **Michelin Map:** 329 K 5
🛈 **Info:** Place de l'Ancienne-Gare. ✆05 55 25 47 57.
▶ **Location:** 20km/12.4mi SE of Brive, in the Limousin region.
🅿 **Parking:** Cars are not allowed in the village in summer. Use the car park by the old station.

03) with an elegant carved porch; the imposing mansion **Hôtel des Ramades de Friac;** the **Château de Benge;** and the elegant **Castel de Vassinhac**★.

Église

The church dates back to the 11C; it was fortified during the Wars of Religion. The tympanum **(tympan**★**)** carved from the local white limestone is an unusual feature of this red sandstone structure. The bell-tower **(clocher**★**)** is a fine example of the Limousin Romanesque style.

Le Dorat★★

Limousin

Le Dorat lies in the gently rolling countryside of the old province of Marche, whose patchwork of pastureland feeds the yellowish-fawn Limousin cattle bought and sold in the great market at **St-Yrieix-la-Perche** 41km/25.4mi south of Limoges. The little town has a collegiate church of impressive size and harmonious proportions.

> ▸ **Population:** 1 963
> ⬥ **Michelin Map:** 325 D 3
> ▯ **Info:** 17 place de la Collégiale. ✆05 55 60 76 81.
> ◖ **Location:** Le Dorat is in a rural location 58km/36mi N of Limoges.

SIGHT

Collégiale St-Pierre★★

🕙*Open year-round daily.* 🗣️ *Guided tours Mon–Sat except public holidays 10am–noon, 2.30–6pm.* ✆*05 55 60 72 20.* 👝*No charge.*

The great edifice was rebuilt in Romanesque style over a period of 50 years beginning in 1112.

It is firmly rooted in its region by virtue of its siting, the coarse granite from which it is built, and by a number of characteristic Limousin features. These include the massive square west tower flanked by bell-turrets, the portal with its scalloped archivolts, the openwork lantern (inspired by the one built 50 years earlier at St-Junien 45km/28mi south but vastly more original), and the mouldings used in the arches and arcades throughout the building.

The late 11C crypt **(crypte)**, dedicated to St Anne, has crudely hewn columns and simple capitals, only one of which is sculpted, openwork barrel vaulting in granite in the ambulatory and groined vaults in the chapels.

Compared with the crypt in the church at Uzerche it shows the architectural progress achieved within a period of 50 years.

Limoges★

Limousin

A dynamic regional capital with a long history, and a great tradition of high-quality enamel, ceramics and porcelain.

> ▸ **Population:** 173 299
> ⬥ **Michelin Map:** 325 E 5-6
> ▯ **Info:** 12 bd de Fleurus. ✆05 55 34 46 87. www.tourismelimoges.com.
> ◖ **Location:** The town is circled by an expressway. The town centre lies on the N bank of the River Vienne, and is divided into two districts, Ville and Cité. The centre of activity is Ville.
> ☻ **Don't Miss:** The picturesque Rue de la Boucherie area; the Adrien-Dubouchée porcelain museum.
> 👥 **Kids:** The Aquarium de Limousin is not only for kids, but they'll love it (www.aquariumdulimousin.com).

A BIT OF HISTORY

Limoges originated as a ford over the River Vienne at a meeting-point of Roman highways, but remained a small provincial centre, specialising in ceramics, until the early 19C, when the manufacture of porcelain moved here from St-Yrieix *(40km/25mi S)* where there were kaolin deposits but no workforce. It became a prestigious industry, the town's name synonymous with the highest quality porcelain. The town was the birthplace of the impressionist Auguste Renoir (1841–1919).

Limoges Enamel

In the 12C Limoges became an important centre of production, partly due to the variety of minerals found in the area. The technique consists of crushing leadglass, coloured with metal oxides, applying it to a metal surface, then heating it to a temperature of up to 800°C/1 472°F, resulting in a crystalline effect. In the 12C Limoges specialised in champlevé enamels, in which the enamel is poured into grooves let into a copper surface, then polished level with the metal. In the 14C painted enamels made their appearance. In the reign of François I, Léonard Limosin was made Director and enamels of great brilliance and colour were produced.

SIGHTS

Musée Municipal de l'Évêché – Musée de l'Émail (Enamel Museum)★

Place de la Cathédrale. Open Jul–Sept: daily 10am–noon, 2–6pm. Rest of year: closing at 5pm, and closed Tue. Closed public holidays. No charge. 05 55 45 98 10.

The museum is housed in the former Bishops' Palace and features a stunning collection of some 300 *champlevé or cloisonné* enamels *(ground floor)* by Limoges masters. The palace gardens, **Jardins de l'Évêché**★, include a themed and a "wild" garden.

Musée Adrien-Dubouché★★

8 bis pl. Winston Churchill. Open Wed–Mon 10am–12.25pm, 2–5.40pm. Closed Jan 1, May 1, Dec 25. Audioguides (3 languages). 4.50€. 05 55 33 08 50. www.musee-adriendubouche.fr.

This remarkable collection of international importance features items illustrating the evolution of pottery from ancient times to today, with many examples of the finest Limoges ware.

Ville and Cité

Early in its history, Limoges developed two rival centres, known as Cité and Ville (or Château). Overlooking the Vienne, **La Cité** is the historic core of Limoges. It spreads out around the **Cathédrale St-Étienne**★ which has a fine portal **(portail St-Jean**★) and which has kept its **rood screen**★ of 1533, now located at the west end of the nave. In the chancel are a number of **tombs**★.

The **Château** quarter, or Ville, serves as the modern centre of Limoges, with busy shopping streets. **St-Michel-des-Lions**★ is an old hall-church that has retained its original rectangular plan.

Pont St-Étienne over the Vienne and Cathédrale St-Étienne

S. Sauvignier/MICHELIN

ADDRESSES

STAY

Hôtel de la Paix – *25 pl. Jourdan.* ✆*05 55 34 36 00. 31 rooms.* This Napoleon III-style hotel in the heart of the city features an entertaining phonographic collection. Bright and airy bedrooms, some with wicker furnishings. Friendly atmosphere.

Hôtel Jeanne-d'Arc – *17 av. du Gén.-de-Gaulle.* ✆*05 55 77 67 77. www.hoteljeannedarc-limoges. Closed 21 Dec–8 Jan. 50 rooms.* ⌑*8€.* This pleasant, well-located hotel is close to the city's famous train station. The well-mantained bedrooms and pleasant breakfast room have managed to retain their old French charm.

EAT

Le Bœuf à la Mode – *60 r. François-Chenieux.* ✆*05 55 77 73 95. www. leboeuf-alamode.com. Closed Sat lunch, Sun and public holidays.* If you love meat, then this is definitely the place for you! Excellent cuisine served in a friendly and traditional ambience.

Chez Alphonse – *5 pl. de la Motte.* ✆*05 55 34 34 14. Closed Mon eve, Sun and public holidays.* Tucked away behind the *halles,* this bistro is a popular local haunt. Tables decorated with chequered tablecloths and a menu which is written up on the blackboard.

L'Escapade du Gourmet – *5 r. des 71ème-Mobiles.* ✆*05 55 32 40 26. Closed 10–26 Aug, Sat lunch, Sun and Mon.* A Belle-Époque décor of wood, frescoes, moulded ceilings and coloured glass is the backdrop to this popular traditional restaurant located between the château and the Cité Episcopale. Classical French cuisine. Good-value-for-money.

Le Pont St-Étienne – *8 pl. de Compostelle.* ✆*05 55 30 52 54.; Reservations required at weekends.* Attractive bay windows with views of the old stone bridge and the river. The à la carte menu features a number of imaginatively named dishes. Summer terrace.

Les Petits Ventres – *20 r. de la Boucherie.* ✆*05 55 34 22 90. Closed 6–20 Apr, 6–23 Sept, Feb–2 Mar, Sun and Mon.* Classic, high quality French cuisine is to the fore in these two typical 15C houses, run by two enthusiastic owners. Traditional dishes based on liver, tongue, pig's trotters, tripe, etc.

BARS AND CAFÉS

Brasserie Artisanale St Martial – *8 pl. Denis-Dussoubs.* ✆*05 55 79 37 98.* This brewery (in the true sense of the term), perpetuates an old local tradition. Beer has been brewed in the region since the 18C; in the 19C there were no fewer than 50 brewers in the Limoges area.

Café des Anciennes Majorettes de la Baule – *27 r. Haute-Vienne.* ✆*05 55 34 34 16. Closed Mon, and mid-Jul–mid-Aug.* This renowned local bar is the venue for regular concerts and plays.

L'Irlandais – *2 r. Haute-Cité.* ✆*05 55 32 46 47.* This lively Irish pub is run by a fisherman from Brittany who has travelled the world and established a bakery and a pub in Ireland, and a concert violinist who has played in royal circles. Over recent years they've hosted jazz, Celtic music and other concerts here.

SHOPPING

Most of the city's shops are located in the area around the castle. The main boutiques selling porcelain are along boulevard Louis-Blanc and along the streets heading west from the city centre.

Le Pavillon de la Porcelaine – *Av. du Prés.-John-Kennedy* – ✆*05 55 30 21 86. www.haviland-limoges.com.* Factory outlet of Haviland, makers of prestigious porcelain sets. A wide choice of tableware on sale.

Paul Buforn – *4 pl. de la Cité.* ✆*06 37 25 62 62.* Skilled enameller.

Buissières – *27 r. Jean-Jaurès.* ✆*05 55 34 10 44. At t*his chic confectioner's, the Art-Deco décor is almost worth a visit on its own. Chocolates, pastries and desserts, including the house speciality black chocolate with chestnut cream.

Oradour-sur-Glane★★

Limousin

Scene of a horrific massacre, Oradour was chosen by the Germans for its very innocence and insignificance in order to terrorise ordinary French people.

A BIT OF HISTORY

This small country town where the 642 inhabitants were massacred in a revenge attack by retreating Germans on 10 June 1944 is preserved unchanged as a fascinating and deeply moving memorial.

VISIT

Access to the ruins of the martyred village via the Centre de la Memoire. The centre offers a permanent exhibit dedicated to the rise of Nazism and the massacre of the villagers. ⏲ *Open 15 May–15 Sept 9am–7pm; Mar–May 14*

- ▶ **Population:** 2 025
- **Michelin Map:** 325 D 5
- **Info:** Place du Champs-de-Foire. ✆ 05 55 03 13 73.
- **Location:** The site is located 24km/15mi NW of Limoges.
- **Don't Miss:** The Centre de la Mémoire, at the entrance to the ruined village.

and Sept 16–Oct 9am–6pm; Feb, Nov–mid-Dec 9am–5pm. Last admission 1hr before closing. 👓6€. ✆ *05 55 43 04 30.* The stark walls of the burnt-out village have been kept as an eloquent reminder. Harassed by the Resistance, the troops made a characteristically brutal example of this entirely innocent place, massacring its inhabitants (men, women and children), and laying waste the village itself. The victims are buried in the village cemetery; a memorial commemorates the terrible deed.

Solignac★★

Limousin

The 12C abbey church, robust and harmonious, has multiple domes. As well as being among the last of their kind to be built in Aquitaine, are some of the finest examples to be seen. There is an extraordinarily deformed dome over the choir and one of ovoid shape covering the north transept.

SIGHT
Eglise Abbatiale★★

Founded in 632 by St Eligius and rebuilt around 1175, the abbey church shows Limoges influence in its use of granite,

- ▶ **Population:** 1 367
- **Michelin Map:** 325 E 6
- **Info:** Place Georges Dubreuil. ✆ 05 55 00 42 31.
- **Location:** Solignac is 10km/6.2mi S of Limoges.

but its domes are based on the ones at Souillac in Quercy.
From the steps of the porch, there is a view of the interior, beautifully proportioned. Among the last of their kind, the pointed arches and pendentives are some of the finest examples in the region.

Château de
Bonaguil★★

Quercy

This majestic fortress on the border of Périgord Noir (Black Périgord, so-called because of its extensive woods) and Quercy, makes a stunning sight. It exemplifies the state of military architecture of the late 15C and of the 16C.

VISIT

🕐*Open daily Feb–Mar and Nov weekends and school holidays 10.30am–12.30pm, 2–5pm; Apr–May, Oct and Dec–Jan school holidays until 5.30pm; Jun–Sept until 6pm; Jul–Aug 10am–7pm.* 🕐*Closed 25 Dec and 1 Jan.* ∞6€. ✆05 53 71 90 33. www.bonaguil.org.

The castle was enlarged in 1445 around the existing 13C keep, and further extended between 1482 and 1520. It is unusual in that underneath its old-fashioned appearance of a traditional stronghold it is actually remarkably well adapted to the new firearms then coming into use, and thus has loopholes for both cannon and muskets. Furthermore, it was conceived not as an offensive establishment but as a place of refuge, able to withstand any attack, with its firearms used in a purely defensive role. In 1480–1520 this was something new, and anticipated the idea of the fort.

- 🕐 **Michelin Map:** 336 i 2
- 🛈 **Info:** Place de la Truffière, Puy-l'Eveque. ✆05 65 21 37 63.
- ▶ **Location:** The château is in the countryside, 54km/33.5mi W of Cahors.

Cahors★★

Quercy

Impressively sited on a promontory almost completely surrounded by a bend in the River Lot, Cahors enjoyed fame and fortune in the Middle Ages and is a pleasant country town today. Cahors is well known for its 'black' wine.

SIGHTS
Pont Valentré★★

The city's merchants were responsible for building this superb six-arched stone bridge; its construction lasted from 1308 to 1378. Its fortifications are a reminder of the importance attached to the defence of Cahors by Philippe le Bel (the Fair), whose relationship with the city was based on an act of pariage (equality between a feudal lord and a town).

Cathédrale St-Étienne★
pl. Chapou.
The cathedral is one of the first of the domed churches of Aquitaine. The 13C

- ▶ **Population:** 20 000
- 🕐 **Michelin Map:** 337 E 5
- 🛈 **Info:** Place Mittérand. ✆05 65 53 20 65. www.quercy-tourisme. com/cahors.
- ▶ **Location:** The ancient axis of Boulevard Gambetta is a lively central promenade. The old quarter lies on its east side. For a different perspective on the town, take a boat trip on the Lot.
- 🅿 **Parking:** Several car parks around the town centre.
- 🕐 **Timing:** Allow 1 day to explore the town and the nearby villages and vistas of the Lot valley.
- 📷 **Don't Miss:** Pont Valentré.

north door **(portail nord★★)** shows Christ beginning to rise and the angels are stilling the fears of the disciples.

Pont Valentré

S. Sauvignier/MICHELIN

ADDRESSES

🖾 STAY

⊜ Chambre d'hôte Le Clos des Dryades – *46090 Vers. 19km/11.8mi NE of Cahors on the D653, towards St-Cirq-Lapopie and the D49 road to Cours.* ℘*05 65 31 44 50. 5 rooms, 3 gîtes.* Nestled deep in the woods, this house with its tiled roof is the perfect place to get away from it all. The rooms are comfortable and the large swimming pool is a great place to cool off on a hot summer's day. Two self-catering cottages are also available.

⊜ Hôtel Les Chalets – *46090 Vers, 14km/9mi E of Cahors on the D 653.* ℘*05 65 31 40 83. Closed Jan, Sun eve and Mon Oct–Apr. 23 rooms.* This small modern hotel situated in an attractive leafy setting is particularly welcoming. The bedrooms, with balconies or small gardens, overlook the river. A quiet and peaceful retreat, with gentle background noise courtesy of a waterfall. Swimming pool in summer.

⊜⊜ Hôtel A l'Escargot – *5 bd Gambetta.* ℘*05 65 35 07 66. Closed Feb school hols, Dec and Sun out of season. 9 rooms.* Near the Tour Jean-XXI, this hotel occupies the old palace built by the pontiff's family. Functional bedrooms with colourful furnishings, plus a renovated breakfast room.

🍽 EAT

⊜⊜ Auberge du Vieux Douelle – *46140 Douelle, 8km/5mi W of Cahors on the D8.* ℘*05 65 20 02 03. http:// aubergeduvieuxdoulle.new.fr.* The dining room in the vaulted cellar of this popular inn, known locally as "Chez Malique", is decked out with bright red tablecloths. Meats are grilled over a wood fire; salads and a buffet are also available. Terrace and pool in the summer. A few rooms available.

⊜⊜ Le Dousil – *124 r. Nationale.* ℘*05 65 53 19 67. Closed Sun and Mon.* This wine bar near the town's covered market offers an extensive list of over 100 vintages. The décor includes a traditional zinc counter and stone walls. The menu includes a choice of sandwiches, *charcuterie* and daily specials.

⊜⊜ La Garenne – *In Saint-Henri, 7km/4.5mi N towards Brive.* ℘*05 65 35 40 67. Closed Feb–15 Mar, Mon eve and Tue eve (except Jul–Aug) and Wed.* This typically Quercy-style building once served as a stable. Cosy interior décor featuring exposed beams, stone walls, attractive, locally made furniture and typical country objects. The main attraction here is the delicious regional cuisine.

😊🍽 **Le Rendez-Vous** – *49 r.
Clément-Marot.* 📞*05 65 22 65 10.
Closed 28 Mar–14 May, Sun and Mon.
Reservations recommended.* Located
close to the cathedral, Le Rendez-
Vous has developed a reputation for
modern cuisine. The mix of colourful
contemporary décor and old stonework
combine well in the dining room and
mezzanine extension.

🛒 SHOPPING

Market – A traditional market is held
on Wednesday and Saturday mornings
at **Place Chapou**, with farmers' stalls
selling a range of local produce.

Les Délices du Valentré – *21 bd Léon-
Gambetta.* 📞*05 65 35 09 86.* Try the
Coque de Cahors, a *brioche* with candied
citron and flavoured with orange water,
and *Cabecou,* a chocolate sweet.

🤸 LEISURE ACTIVITIES

L'Archipel – *Quai Ludo-Rollès.
Watersports and leisure centre.* 📞*05 65
35 05 86/31 38. www.payscahors.fr. Closed
mid-Sept–mid-Jun.* This summer pool
offers lots of fun activities, including
slides, massage, bubble baths, fountains
and games.

Alliance Nautique Cahors – *Port Bullier.*
📞*06 80 14 96 77. Open Easter–
15 Sept. 30min: 18€; 1hr: 28€.* Hire an
easy-to-handle electric boat to explore
the River Lot. No permit required.

EVENTS

Festival de Blues – *mid-Jul.* 📞*05 65 20
88 60.*

Festival du Quercy Blanc – *late
Jul–mid-Aug.* 📞*05 65 31 83 12.*

Figeac★★

Quercy

A sprawling commercial town on
the north bank of the Célé, Figeac
developed at the point where the
Auvergne meets the Upper Quercy.
It had a prestigious past, shown in
the architecture of its tall sandstone
townhouses.

▶ **Population:** 9 606
◉ **Michelin Map:** 337 i 4
▤ **Info:** Hôtel de la Monnaie,
pl. Vival. 📞05 65 34 06 25.
www.tourisme-figeac.com
◖ **Location:** The heart of
town rises from the River
Célé near Pont Gambetta.

A BIT OF HISTORY

Jean-François Champollion – Champollion, the outstanding Orientalist,
whose brilliance enabled Egyptology
to make such great strides, was born at
Figeac in December 1790. He set himself the task of deciphering a polished
basalt tablet which had been discovered
in 1799 by members of Napoleon's expedition to Egypt near Rosetta in the northwest Nile delta, from which it derives
its name – the Rosetta Stone.
In Figeac, at the **Place des Écritures**, a
replica of the Rosetta Stone covers the
square.

SIGHTS

Le Vieux Figeac★

The old quarter, surrounded by
boulevards tracing the line of the former
moats, has kept its medieval town plan
with its narrow and tortuous alleys.
The buildings, of elegant beige
sandstone, exemplify the architecture
of the 13C, 14C and 15C. Generally
the ground floor was opened by large
pointed arches and the first floor had
a gallery of arcaded bays. Underneath
the flat tiled roof was the soleilho,
an open attic, which was used to dry
laundry, store wood, grow plants, etc.
Its openings were separated by columns
or pillars in wood or stone, sometimes
even brick, which held up the roof. Other
noticeable period architectural features

The Rosetta Stone

During the reigns of the first Ptolemaic kings (332–80 BC), Egyptian priests recorded the decrees issued at the end of their synods on basalt tablets which were then displayed in the main temples. The Rosetta Stone is one of these tablets, carved in 196 BC. By this time, the members of the clergy were the only people to be taught hieroglyphics, hence the need for a translation into three languages so that the decrees would be understood also by those people who used demotic script in Memphis and Greek in Alexandria. The content of the decrees was both political and economic, defining the respective powers of the clergy and the monarch, the extent of fiscal privileges and the nature of laws and taxes among other things. This is illustrated by the following extracts from the Rosetta Stone: "whereas king PTOLEMY…, the son of King Ptolemy and Queen Arsinoe, the Gods Philopatores, has been a benefactor both to the temples and to those who dwell in them, … he has dedicated to the temples revenues in money and corn and has undertaken much outlay to bring Egypt into prosperity, and to establish the temples, and has been generous with all his own means; and of the revenues and taxes levied in Egypt some he has wholly remitted and others has lightened, in order that the people and the others might be in prosperity during his reign; …he has directed that the gods shall continue to enjoy the revenues of the temples and the yearly allowances given to them, both of corn and money, likewise also the revenues assigned to the gods from vine land and from gardens and other properties which belonged to the gods in his father's time."

Translation courtesy of the British Museum, London.

to be discovered during your tour of the old quarter are: corbelled towers, doorways, spiral staircases and some of the top storeys, which are half-timbered and of brick.

Hôtel de la Monnaie★

Place Vival (First Floor of tourist office).
Open Jul–Aug daily 10am–7pm; May–Jun and Sept Mon–Sat 9am–12.30pm, 2–6pm, Sun 10am–1pm; Oct–Apr Mon–Sat except public holidays 9am–noon, 2–6pm. Closed 1 May. 2€. 05 65 34 06 25.
Museum with Gothic architecture.

ADDRESSES

STAY

Champollion – 3 pl. Champollion. 05 65 34 04 37. 10 rooms. The memory of the famous Egyptologist is everywhere in the centre of town, including this hotel, the town's medieval meat market. Although on the small side, the bedrooms are modern and well-maintained.

Musée Champollion★

Place Champollion. Open Apr–May and Jun Tue–Sun (excluding public holidays) 10.30am–12.30pm, 2–6pm; Jul and Aug daily 10.30am–6pm; Nov–Mar Tue–Sun 2–5.30pm. Closed 1 Jan, 1 May, 25 Dec. 4€. 05 65 50 31 08. www.ville-figeac.fr/musee.
Museum devoted to Jean-François Champollion. Permanent exhibits include hieroglyphs and letters written by Champollion to his brother. Learn how and why people started writing.

Grand Hôtel Pont d'Or – 2 av. Jean-Jaurès. 05 65 50 95 00. www.hotelpontdor.com. 32 rooms. A welcoming stone house on the banks of the Célé, with some rooms offering balconies overlooking the river. A yellow and orange colour scheme, contemporary furniture and immaculate bathrooms. Fitness room and rooftop swimming pool. In summer, breakfast is served on the riverside terrace.

⊕/ EAT

◉🛢 **À l'Escargot** – *2 bis av. Jean-Jaurès.* ☎*05 65 34 23 84. Closed 16 Dec–14 Feb and Thu. Reservations recommended.* The regular clientele of this unassuming restaurant flock here for the simple, family-style fare and friendly ambience.

◉🛢🛢 **La Dînée du Viguier** – *r. Boutaric.* ☎*05 65 50 08 08. Closed 18 Jan–9 Feb, 15–23 Nov, Sun eve out of season, Sat lunch and Mon.* The restaurant in the Château Viguier du Roy combines medieval décor (high ceilings, painted beams and stone fireplace) with contemporary cuisine.

◉🛢🛢 **Ferme-Auberge Domaine des Villedieu** – *46100 Boussac, 8km/5mi SW of Figeac on the D 13 and then the D 41.* ☎*05 65 40 06 63. Reservations required.* An enchanting 18C farmhouse deep in the country. In keeping with their farming background, the owners serve their own produce in the wood-floored dining room and on the outdoor terrace. The restored farm buildings have been converted into a number of attractive guestrooms.

🏃 LEISURE ACTIVITIES

Domaine de Loisirs du Surgié – *Chemin Moulin Surgie.* ☎*05 65 34 59 00. www.domainedesurgie.com. Open May–Sept 11am–8pm.* This large (14ha/34.5 acre) outdoor watersports and leisure area is on the banks of the River Célé to the northeast of Figeac.

🛒 SHOPPING

Market – The town's weekly market is held on Sat (the largest one is the last Sat of the month). Evening markets are held on Thu in July and August.

Gouffre de Padirac★★

Quercy

Padirac Chasm, (Gouffre de Padirac), provides access to wonderful galleries hollowed out of the limestone mass of the Gramat plateau, (Causse de Gramat), by a subterranean river. A tour of this mysterious river and the vast caves adorned with limestone concretions leave visitors with a striking impression of this fascinating phenomenon.

A BIT OF HISTORY

The chasm served as a refuge for the people living on the causse during the Hundred Years' War and the Wars of Religion, but it would appear that it was towards the end of the 19C, following a violent flooding of the river, that a practicable line of communication opened between the bottom of the well and the underground galleries.

The speleologist, **Edouard A Martel**, was the first to discover the passage, in 1892. He then undertook nine expeditions and finally reached the Hall of the Great Dome.

⚬ **Michelin Map:** 337 G 2

ℹ **Info:** All local tourist offices in the Dordogne and surrounding region have information about the Gouffre.

▶ **Location:** The Gouffre lies about 2km/1.2mi from the village of Padirac, in the Lot département.

Padirac was opened to tourists for the first time, in 1898. Since then, numerous speleological expeditinos have uncovered 22km/13.6mi of underground galleries. The 1947 expedition proved by fluorescein colouring of the water that the Padirac river reappears above gound 11km/6.8mi away where the Lombard rises and at St George's spring in the Montvalent Amphitheatre near the Dordogne.

During the expeditions of 1984 and 1985, a prehistoric site was discovered, with bones of mammoths, bison, bears and other animals, all of which were found to date from between 150 000 and 200 000 years ago. Among the bones were chipped flints dating from between 30 000 and 50 000 years ago.

Thanks to the efforts of **Guy de Lavaur** (1903–86), the total known length of the subterranean network at Padirac rose from 2km/1.2mi to 15km/9.3mi.

VISIT

Exhibited in the entrance hall are copies of some of the bones found in the prehistoric site.

The chasm *(1hr30min)* itself is like a gigantic well of striking width (99m/324.8ft around its rim) and depth (75m/246ft to the rubble cone formed by the collapse of the original roof). With its walls covered in vegetation and the overflow from stalagmites, it is one of the most atmospheric of France's underground domains.

The underground river flows 103m/338ft beneath the surface of the plateau, to reappear on the surface near the natural amphitheatre at Montvalent 11km /6.8mi away on the Dordogne. Some 5km/3mi of its main channel and tributaries have been explored.

The Grand Pilier, Grande Pendeloque of the Lac de la Pluie and the **Salle du Grand Dôme** are among the most striking of all natural monuments of the underground world.

Grotte du
Pech-Merle★★★
Quercy

Sited high above the River Célé just before it flows into the Lot, the Pech-Merle cave is one of the most fascinating in terms of prehistory and speleology.

- **Michelin Map:** 337 F 4
- **Info:** Place du Sombral. St. Cirq-Lapopie. ☎05 65 31 29 06. www.saint-cirqlapopie.com
- **Location:** The cave is located 7km/4.3mi N of St. Cirq-Lapopie and 32km/19.8mi E of Cahors.

VISIT

Guided tours (1hr) 5 Apr–3 Nov 9.30am–noon, 1.30–5pm. Tour limited to 700 visitors per day (reservations recommended 3 days in advance in Jul and Aug). ☎7.50€. ☎05 65 31 27 05. www.pechmerle.com.

On the lower level of the cave **(grotte)** are paintings of a fish, two horses covered in coloured dots, and of "negative hands" (made by stencilling around hands placed flat against the rock).

Something like a three-dimensional effect is produced by the way in which the Late Perigordian artists integrated their work with the irregularities of the rock surface. There are also representations of bisons and mammoths, as well as petrified human footprints from the Early Magdalenian. The upper level has strange, disc-like concretions, "cave pearls", and eccentrics with protuberances defying the laws of gravity.

Prehistoric painting in Grotte du Pech-Merle

E. Larribère/MICHELIN

Town of Rocamadour

E. Larribère/MICHELIN

Rocamadour★★★

Quercy

Clinging dramatically to the sheer cliffs of the gorge cut by the little River Alzou, the tiny medieval town of Rocamadour is one of the most visited places in the Dordogne. All around stretches the **Causse de Gramat**★, a vast limestone plateau, known as good sheep country and for its pâté de foie gras.

A BIT OF HISTORY

Long ago, Rocamadour was chosen by a hermit, Saint Amadour, as his place of retreat. From the 12C onwards, and above all during the 13C, Rocamadour was one of the most popular places of pilgrimage in the whole of Christendom. Just as they do today, souvenir stalls tempted the throngs of tourists, among them Henry III of England, who experienced a miraculous cure here.

VISIT

A stairway with 216 steps leads to the Place St-Amadour (**or Parvis des églises**) around which are grouped seven sanctuaries, including the Chapel of Notre-Dame or Miraculous Chapel. The stream of pilgrims eventually dried up, unsurprisingly, in view of the destruction which was caused by the great rock-fall of 1476 and completed

▶ **Population:** 614
⊚ **Michelin Map:** 337 F 3
▤ **Info:** The tourist office is at L'Hospitalet. ℘05 65 33 22 00.
◖ **Location:** Rocamadour itself is approached through a separate small community, almost joined on to it, called L'Hospitalet. You can only enter Rocamadour on foot, so park on the plateau and walk into town (or pay and take the elevator) or take the little train (fee). To reach Place St-Amadour (and the seven sanctuaries), take the stairway at Via Sancta or the elevator.
⊜ **Don't Miss:** View Rocamadour from the Hospitalet belvedere *(2km/1.2mi NE)*, or from the Couzou road. The castle, rising 125m/410ft above the valley floor.

by the Huguenots a century later. In the 19C, the place was restored by the Bishops of Cahors in an attempt to revive the pilgrimages.

FRENCH ALPS

Stretching from the Mediterranean to Lake Geneva, the French Alps display all the varieties of mountain scenery, from the sublimity of bare rock and eternal snow to the animation of densely settled valleys. Nowhere more than among these incomparable mountains does human habitat show such close adaptation to natural conditions. Centuries of endurance and ingenuity have overcome formidable obstacles and brought all possible resources into play, not only settling valley floors, but pushing grazing and cultivation to its highest limits and developing widely varied local traditions of living and building.

Highlights

1 Sea of ice above Chamonix **Mer de Glace** (p305)
2 Spectacular view of Grenoble from **Fort de la Bastille** (p306)
3 High road through the Alps **Route des Grandes Alpes** (p309)
4 Natural fortress: **Massif du Vercors** (p315)
5 Europe's most spectacular gorge **Grand Canyon du Verdon** (p316)

Geography – The north of the French Alps is marked by the great sweep of Lake Geneva. To the south rise the Alps of Savoy, first the Chablais and Faucigny country and beyond that the famous peaks and glaciers around the

great white mountain, Mont-Blanc. Westward lie other graceful stretches of water, Lake Annecy and Le Bourget Lake. An important communication route is formed by the Sub-Alpine Furrow, a broad and prosperous valley in which Grenoble sits, and the western rampart of the Alps is formed by a succession of massifs including the Vercors. Briançon is close to the Italian border and further south still the scene is often one of striking severity, bare rock rising from vegetation of Mediterranean character. The stark summit of Mount Ventoux overlooks the Comtat plain, while eastwards lie the Pre-Alps and high plateaux of Provence.

History – The Alps have been inhabited since the stone-age, but it was the Romans who first made an impact on the region as they sought to control the trade routes through the mountains. After the Romans the area was subject to Barbarian invasions before eventually becoming the County of Savoy which, during the 15C, was integrated with Piedmont and became the Duchy of Savoy. After the Revolution Savoy was made a french *département* although by 1815 it had been restored to King Victor Emmanuel I of Sardinia who was also the Duke of Savoy. Following a plebiscite in 1860 Savoy reverted to France.

Economy – Traditionally the Alps were an area of cattle rearing. Now year-round tourism is very important with many activities available in summer as well as the traditional winter sports such as skiing. The richness of the natural heritage of the French Alps is reflected in the number of National Parks (Mercantour, Écrins, Vanoise) and Regional Parks (Vercors, Queyras) set up to protect these incomparable landscapes and enhance the visitors' experience of them.

Annecy★★★

Lakeside Annecy enjoys an exquisitely beautiful setting of water and mountains, and has a picturesque old centre clustered around the river Thiou.

A BIT OF HISTORY

Ancient lake settlement, then a hillside Gallo-Roman town, Annecy moved back downhill in the Middle Ages to its present site by the Thiou, whose rapid waters powered its many mills.

In the 16C Annecy became the regional capital, displacing Geneva, and in the 17C was the home of the influential **St Francis of Sales**, bitter opponent of the Calvinism, which had spread throughout the region.

SIGHTS

Le Vieil Annecy (Old Annecy)★★

The picturesque old town, largely pedestrianised and renovated, lies on the banks of the Thiou as it flows from the lake. Its arcaded houses, Italianate wells and colourful markets *(Tue, Wed and Sun mornings)* give immense charm. **Rue Ste-Claire**★ is especially attractive with arcades and gabled houses. The **Palais de l'Isle**★ rising from the midst of the river offers the most famous view of Old Annecy.

▶ **Population:** 50 350

Michelin Map: 328 j-k 5

Info: Centre Bonlieu, 1 r. J.-Jaurès, 74000 Annecy. ℘04 50 45 00 33. www.lac-annecy.com.

Location: The town is 39.4km/24.5mi NE of Lac du Bourget. The pedestrianised Old Annecy is the heart of the city.

Parking: You won't need the car; leave it at the central Bonlieu car park, or park at the train station.

Don't Miss: A boat trip on the lake is a must.

Timing: On market days (Tue, Wed, Sun), visit Old Annecy in the morning, when it is in full swing. The tourist office has information on guided tours.

Overlooking the old town, the **château**★ (*open Jun–Sept daily 10.30am–6pm; Oct–May Wed–Mon 10am–noon, 2–5pm; last admission 45min before closing; closed main public holidays; 4.80€; ℘04 50 33 87 30*), former residence of the lords of Geneva, retains its defensive character. It houses a museum and an observatory.

Talloires

Fr.Isler/MICHELIN

Le Lac (The Lake)★★★

Open Apr–end Oct: several types of boat trips with commentaries (1hr). 12€. May–mid-Sept: boats stopping at various places (2hr). 15.40€. Lunch trip and dinner-dance on board the MS Libellule. Times and reservations: Compagnie des Bateaux du lac d'Annecy, 04 50 51 08 40. www.annecy-croisieres.com.

A road runs around the edge of this lovely lake, giving wonderful views. Fine vista from the **Avenue d'Albigny**, in Annecy. There are several pleasant small resorts on the lakeside, notably **Talloires**★★★, overlooking the narrows dividing the Grand Lac to the north from the Petit Lac to the south.

ADDITIONAL SIGHTS

Jardins de l'Europe★ *(av. d'Albigny) –* arboretum
Musée de la Cloche★ *214 rte du Piron – 14C to 19C bells – at Sevrier (5km/3mi S).*

Lac du
Bourget★★

Enclosed within an impressive mountain setting, this is France's largest (18km/11.2mi long by 3.5km/2.2mi wide), deepest (145m/476ft) and most celebrated natural lake, lying in a glaciated valley between the Jura and the Alps. On its eastern shore is the elegant spa town of Aix-les-Bains and the best view of the Lake can be enjoyed from a little further north at La Chamobtte.

A BIT OF HISTORY

The lake and its banks form a rich and unusual habitat for wildlife. In its waters live around 50 varieties of fish, including pollans, migratory members of the salmon family, crayfish. Its varied birdlife includes 300 cormorants which winter on the west bank at La Grande Cale. The poet Lamartine (1790–1867) wrote movingly about the beauty of the lake, and of Mme Lulie Charles Julie whom he met here in October 1816. The popular spa Aix-les-Bains is one of the best-equipped resorts in the Alps, and has been known for its health-giving waters for over 2 000 years. Queen Victoria visited here three times.

- **Michelin Map:** 333 H-i 3-4
- **Info:** Place Maurice Mollard, Aix-les-Bains. 04 79 88 68 00. www.aixlesbains.com or www.bourgetdulac.com.
- **Location:** The lake is is 39.4km/24.5mi SW of Annecy. The ideal base for a tour of the lake is Aix-les-Bains, a famous resort with lively streets, opulent hotels near the spa baths, and an attractive lakeshore.

VISIT

Abbaye royale de Hautecombe★★

On the west bank of the lake. Open Wed–Mon 10am–11.15am, 2–5pm. Audioguide (5 languages) available in 04 79 54 58 80.

Jutting into the lake, the abbey (founded 1125) houses the tombs of 42 princely members of the House of Savoy. The abbey's little harbour has an unusual 12C building **(grange batelière)** with covered moorings, allowing goods to be unloaded and stored under the same roof.

Briançon★★

The highest town in Europe
(1 321m/4 334ft), Briançon is best
viewed from the terraces of the
UNESCO site, la Fort de Salettes
(the fortress), where stands the
9m/29.5ft-high statue of **France** ★
sculpted by **Antoine Bourdelle**.

▶ **Population:** 12 000
◉ **Michelin Map:** 334 H 3
▣ **Info:** 1 place du Temple.
✆04 92 21 08 50.
www.ot-briancon.fr.
◐ **Location:** Briançon lies
118km/73.3mi SE of
Grenoble. After arriving at
the town, follow signs to
'Briançon Vauban' to find
the Old Town.

A BIT OF HISTORY

Since ancient times, two great routes
into Italy have met here, one coming
from the Romanche valley via the Col
de Lautaret, the other following the
Durance up from Embrun. The strategic
value of the site was appreciated by the
Gauls. It seems likely that the survivors
of the Germanic tribes routed by the
Roman general Marius outside Aix-
en-Provence found their way here,
and Briançon may have provided a
refuge too for some of the persecuted
members of the Vaudois, a 15C sect. The
town played an important commercial
and military role, the latter enhanced by
the presence of great rock bars lending
themselves naturally to fortification.
The forts (Dauphin, Sallettes, les Trois-
Têtes, Anjou, Randouillet) built by Vauban in the 17C proved their effectiveness
in the year of Waterloo, when General
Eberlé's triumphant resistance here held
off the invading Austro-Sardinians for
three months.

SIGHT

Ville Haute★★ (Upper Town)

In January 1692, the War of the League
of Augsburg had been raging for six
years; mercenaries in the pay of Vittorio-
Amadeo II, Duke of Savoy, invaded the
Dauphiné and torched Briançon – only
two houses out of 258 escaped the fire.
Vauban was working in Burgundy, but
was immediately dispatched by Louis
XIV to Briançon (which he knew already)
with a brief to rebuild the town and
make it impregnable. A week sufficed for
the great engineer to draw up his plans,
but age and ill health made it impossible
for him to supervise their execution, and
he was to deplore a number of modifications and compromises made to his
project.
With its gate (Porte Pignerol) and its
fortified church, Briançon-Vauban, in

Briançon's Old Town can be
entered through Porte d'Embrun

E. Baret/MICHELIN

contrast to the lower town Briançon-Ste-Catherine, still has the look of a frontier town of Louis XIV's reign, while its narrow, steeply sloping streets, especially the **Grande Gargouille**★

(also known as the Grande Rue), express the drama of its precipitous site.
To the east of town, the **Pont d'Asfeld**★ (bridge) was built in 1734. It, too, is part of the town's collection of UNESCO sites.

Chambéry★★

The well-restored old centre recaptures something of Chambéry's past splendour as the capital of Savoy.

SIGHTS
Château de Chambéry
This fortress was occupied by the counts of Savoy in 1285, who expanded it during the 14C to serve as their residence and seat of administration. The **Sainte-Chapelle**★, adjoined to the château displays Flamboyant Gothic architecture (• guided tours (1hr) daily; ∞4€ ℘04 79 70 15 94).

Musée Savoisien★
sq. Lannoy de Bissy. ◷Open Wed–Mon 10am–noon, 2–6pm. ◷Closed public holidays. ∞3.20€; no charge 1st Sun in the month. ℘04 79 33 44 48.
Here can be found exhibits of prehistory, religious art and regional ethnography.

- ▸ **Population:** 113 460
- ⟡ **Michelin Map:** 333 i 3-4
- ▯ **Info:** 24 bd de la Colonne, ℘04 79 33 42 47. www.chambery-tourisme.com.
- ▻ **Location:** The town is in the Alps, 10km/6.2mi S of Lac du Bourget.
- ◉ **Don't Miss:** The many fascinating trompe-l'œil decorations around the town.

Fontaine des Éléphants (Elephants' Fountain)
r. de Boigne.
This famous – and originally disliked – landmark was erected in 1838. The shape of the Savoyan cross is achieved by the truncation in a column of the forelimbs of four elephants.

Chamonix-Mont-Blanc★★★

Chamonix is France's mountaineering capital. It lies at the foot of the famous 3 000m/9 842ft Chamonix Needles (Aiguilles de Chamonix) at a point where the glacial valley of the Arve widens out. All around are the high mountains of the Mont Blanc Massif; this is the most renowned of the massifs of the French Alps, because of its dramatic relief, crystalline rocks and glacial morphology. The dome of the great White Mountain is visible from the town.

- ▸ **Population:** 9 830
- ⟡ **Michelin Map:** 328 M-O 5
- ▯ **Info:** 85 pl. du Triangle de l'Amitié. ℘04 50 53 00 24. www.chamonix.com.
- ▻ **Location:** Chamonix is 101km/63mi east of Annecy.
- ◷ **Timing:** The resort is very crowded during school holidays, so try to come at some other time. Always reserve your rides up the Aiguille du Midi and Montenvers, and be sure to check the weather in advance.

Mer de Glace

J.-L. Gallo/MICHELIN

SIGHT

The tongue of the 7km/4.3mi-long Glacier des Bossons hangs 500m/1 650ft above the valley on the approach to Chamonix. The Geneva naturalist **Horace Benedict de Saussure** based himself here in the course of his scientific studies in Savoy. In 1760, he offered a reward for the first ascent of Mont-Blanc. On 8 August 1786 Dr Michel Paccard and Jacques Balmat reached the summit, thereby inaugurating the age of mountaineering, as well as the development of the town as an Alpine resort.

EXCURSIONS

By cable-car or rack railway

Aiguille du Midi★★★

Cable Car: *Runs daily mid-Dec–early Nov every 30, 15 or 10min at peak periods; see website for more specific details: http://www.compagniedumontblanc. fr/pages/excursion_schedules.html. Trip in two stages: Chamonix–Plan de l'Aiguille and Plan de l'Aiguille–Aiguille du Midi. ≈40€ round-trip. Central ticket office: 100 place de l'Aiguille du Midi, Chamonix. ℘04 50 53 22 75. Allow at least 2hr round-trip on the cable-car.* **Rack Railway:** *20 Dec–26 Apr 9am–4pm, hourly; 27 Apr–May 8.30am–5pm, every 30min.*

The **panorama**★★★, especially from the central peak (3 842m/12 605ft), is staggering, taking in Mont-Blanc, Mont-Maudit, the Grandes Jorasses, and the dome of the Goûter whose buttresses are buried in 30m/100ft of ice.

The **Vallée Blanche**, also known as the Giant's Glacier (Glacier du Géant), can be reached by taking the cable-car *(téléférique)* to Pointe Helbronner. From here can be seen the glacial cirques with their flanks worn down by the incessant attacks of the ice.

Mer de Glace★★★

2hr30min by rack railway and cable-car. The view from the upper station of the railway built in 1908 takes in the whole of this "sea of ice". The glacier is 7km/4.3mi long, in places 200m/656ft thick, and moves 90m/295.2ft a year. The rocky material it carries with it scores and scratches the mountain walls on either side as well as giving the glacier its characteristic rather grimy appearance (as the ice evaporates grit is left on the surface). At the foot of the glacier this material is deposited, forming a terminal moraine.

Beyond, the eye is led from one peak to another; this **panorama**★★★ is one of the most beautiful in the region.

OTHER PANORAMAS AROUND CHAMONIX

Summit of the Brévent★★★

2 525m/8 284ft Brévent.

Brévent to Planpraz

2 525m/8 284ft Brévent,
2 000m/6561.6ft Planpraz.

La Flégère Viewpoint★★
2 396m/2 861ft. By téléférique.
**Aiguille des
Grands-Montets**★★★
3 295m/12 875ft.

Bellevue★★ **(Les Houches)**
1 000m/3 281ft. Cable-car to Bellevue.
Nid d'Aigle★★
*2 372m/7 782ft. Glacier de Bionnassay –
leave from St-Gervais-les-Bains.*

Grenoble★★

Undisputed capital of the French Alps, Grenoble is a flourishing modern city of broad boulevards at the confluence of the Drac and Isère rivers.

A BIT OF HISTORY
The vast quantities of material brought down by the restless River Drac ("that most brutal, most violent of Alpine tributaries" R Blanchard) formed an alluvial fan on which by the late 3C a fortified Roman town was sited.
Development of the town was held back by the precarious nature of its communication links; though Grenoble was well-sited on the roads leading from the Rhône valley to Turin and Cannes, frequent floods and challenging gradients made travelling an uncertain business. In the reign of Henri IV the city was captured by Lesdiguières, commander of the armies of Piedmont and Savoy, who re-fortified it.
Later fortifications, the Enceinte Haxo, doubled the area of the city to the south.

SIGHTS
Fort de la Bastille
Access by cable car. Allow 1hr.
See box for details.

> **Population:** 419 334
> **Michelin Map:** 336 H 6 -7
> **Info:** 14 r. de la République.
> *04 76 42 41 41.*
> www.grenoble-isere.info.
> **Location:** Main routes into town follow the two rivers. The city centre is on the south bank of the Isère, about 2km/1.2mi east of the confluence.
> **Don't Miss:** A walk along the heights of the Bastille is a highlight of any trip.
> **Timing:** The Notre-Dame district comes to life in the evening.

The fort was built in the 16C to protect the approaches to the city, and strengthened in the 19C. It has the best **view**★★★ over the town in its magnificent setting.

Vieille ville (Old Town)★
The Roman town lay close to the present-day Place Granette (celebrated by Stendhal) and on either side of the Grande-Rue, itself a Roman road. By the 13C the town had spread northeastwards as far as the Isère, where today a number of courtyards and porches dating from

Getting to Fort de la Bastille
Open Jan, Feb, Nov, Dec Mon–Tue 11am–6.30pm, Wed–Fri and Sun 10.45am–6.30pm, Sat 10.45am–11:45pm; Mar, same as above except Sun until 7.25pm; Apr, May and Oct Mon 11am–7.25pm, Tue 11am–11.45pm, Wed–Sat 9.30am–11.45pm, Sun 9.30am–7.30pm; Jun Mon 11am–11.45pm, Tue–Sat 9.30am–11.45pm, Sun 9.15am–7.25pm; Jul–Aug Mon 11am–12.15am, Tue–Sun 9.15am–12.15am; Sept Mon 11am–11.45pm, Tue–Sat 9.30am–11.45pm, Sun 9.30am–11.25pm. 6.50€ round-trip, 4.40€ single. Max 6 persons per car. 04 76 44 33 65. www.bastille-grenoble.fr.

Grenoble cable car - an unofficial emblem of the city

Fr. Isler/MICHELIN

the 16C can be found (no 8 Rue Broche-rie, nos 8 and 10 Rue Chenoise).

Musée de Grenoble★★★

&⊙Open Wed–Mon 10am–6.30pm. ⊙Closed public holidays. ⊜5€, no charge 1st Sun in the month. ℘04 76 63 44 44. www.museedegrenoble.fr.

On the bank of the Isère in the heart of the old town, this Fine Arts museum has a remarkably plain and sober appearance. Huge windows look out on massive sculptures which enhance the parvis and the Parc Michallon, outside the north building.

This is one of France's most important provincial museums, with painting from 16C to 20C, including an exceptionally rich collection of modern art. The collections include fine modern works like Matisse's *Interior with Aubergines*

and Picasso's *Woman Reading* as well as Old Masters like de Champaigne's *John the Baptist*, Rubens' *Pope Gregory surrounded by Saints* or de La Tour's *St Jerome*. Most art movements after 1945 are represented: Abstraction lyrique, New Realism, "Supports-surfaces", Pop Art and Minimalism.

ADDITIONAL SIGHTS

Église-musée St-Laurent (*on the outskirts*) – Merovingian **crypt**★
Cathédrale – unusual 14C Flamboyant **ciborium**★ in polychrome stone
Musée Dauphinois★ (*30 r. Maurice Gignoux*). **Musée de la Résistance et de la Déportation**★ (*14 r. Hébert*).
Palais de Justice (Law Courts)★ (*pl. Firmin Gautier*) – combining Renaissance and Flamboyant Gothic styles.

L'Oisans★★★

L'Oisans is the second highest massif in France after Mont Blanc. Its population is grouped in villages sited on high terraces reached by spectacular narrow roads.

EXCURSIONS
Les Écrins

These bare mountains between the valleys of the Romanche, Drac and Durance look down on more than

- ◐ **Michelin Map:** 333 J 7.
- ◑ **Location:** The region is largely within the Parc National des Écrins, between the rivers Romanche and Drac.

100sq km/38.6sq mi of glaciers. The Route des Grandes Alpes (◐ *see ROUTE DES GRANDES ALPES*) gives fine views of the north and east faces of the massif (from the Col du Galibier, the Oratoire du Chazelet, and from La Grave), cut by isolated valleys with their typical way of life and served by long cul-de-sac roads; the best-known is the valley of the Vénéon leading to La Bérarde.

Bassin du Bourg d'Oisans★

Until the 13C the fertile basin was a glacial lake, now filled in by material brought down by the Romanche and its tributary, the Vénéon. This is the economic centre of the region.

Vallée du Vénéon★★★

▶ *31km/19mi from Bourg-d'Oisans to La Bérarde*

The road up to La Bérarde is a lesson in glacial geomorphology made more dramatic by the scale of the great U-shaped valley and the ruggedness of its high granite walls, moraines, waterfalls in hanging valleys, and compact little villages, before reaching La Bérarde, now a climbing centre.

Route des Grandes Alpes★★★

Among the many routes inviting visitors to explore the French Alps, this high-altitude road is the most famous. Rarely far from the frontier, the Great Alpine Road links Lake Geneva with the Riviera, crossing 25 passes in all as it leaps from valley to valley. The route is open from end to end during the summer months only.

EXCURSIONS

734km/458mi
Thonon-les-Bains★★

From the Place du Château the view extends over the great sweep of Lake Geneva (**Lac Léman★★★**). On the Swiss shore to the north rise the terraces of the great Lavaux vineyard, and beyond are the mountains of the Vaudois Alps (to the east) and the Jura. Saint Francis

> ⚓ **Michelin Map:** 332, 334, 340 and 341
> ▯ **Info:** Association Grande Traversée des Alpes, 14 r. de la République. ℘04 76 42 41 41. www.grande-traversee-alpes.com.
> ▶ **Location:** Streching 600km/372.8mi from Thonon-le-Bains to Menton, the route crosses 16 mountain passes.

of Sales once preached in St Hippolytus' Church (Église St-Hippolyte); its vault (**voûte★**) has retained its original stucco and 18 painted medallions, together with the stucco decoration of its false pillars (visible from the adjoining basilica), all done by the Italian craftsmen who restored the interior in Rococo style in the 18C. The road rises in a series of steps through the damp beech woodland of the gorges cut by the River Dranse de Morzine. This marks the transition between the gently rolling hill country fringing the great lake and the **Chablais★★** massif, a complex of high ridges and peaks, with rich pastures grazed by Abondance cattle.

The most spectacular part of the route is known as the Devil's Bridge Gorge (**Gorges du Pont du Diable★★**), marked by a number of rock-falls, one of which has formed the bridge attributed to the Evil One.

Port of Thonon-les-Bains

M.-H. Carcanague/MICHELIN

Morzine★★

▷ *33km/20.5mi SE of Thonon*

The valleys around the resort are dotted with hamlets; the chalets have patterned balconies. All around grow sombre forests of spruce.

After the pass at Les Gets, the small industrial town of Tanninges marks the beginning of the **Faucigny**★★ country. Drained by the Giffre, this is a landscape of pastures and sprucewoods, fashioned by the action of glacial moraines on calcareous rocks deposited here far from their point of origin.

Cluses

▷ *29km/18mi SW of Morzine*

The town commands the most important lateral valley *(cluse)* in the French Alps. The River Arve has cut down directly through the folded rocks of the **Aravis** range to make its gorge. Clocks and watches and precision metal products are made here.

The upland Sallanches basin is bounded to the north by the dramatic peaks of a number of ranges, but dominating all is the great mass of Mont Blanc itself, the "Giant of the Alps".

La Clusaz★★

▷ *44km/27.3mi SW of Cluses*

The most important ski resort in the **Massif des Aravis** owes its name to the deep gorge or cluse, downstream of it, through which the Nom torrent gushes. The village, situated in the middle of pine forests and mountain pasture, is tightly huddled around the big church characterised by its onion-dome tower. The jagged outlines of the Aravis mountains can be seen in the distance.

In the summer, La Clusaz offers excellent walking, and in winter plenty of thrills for ski enthusiasts.

At the top of the climb out of the valley, Val d'Arly, the Notre-Dame de Bellecombe road gives good views, first of the whole Aravis massif, then of the wooded gorges cut by the Arly.

Col des Saisies

▷ *18km/11mi SE of La Clusaz*

At this point that the route leaves the Sub-Alpine Furrow (Sillon alpin); from here as far as St-Martin-d'Entraunes to the south of the Cayolle Pass (Col de Cayolle), its course lies entirely within the High Alps (Grandes Alpes).

The broad depression of the Saisies Pass, 1 633m/5 357.6ft high, is one of the most characteristic alpine grazing grounds to be seen along the route; it is browsed by sturdy little reddish-brown cattle as well as by the dark-brown Tarines breed and the white-spotted Abondances. The landscape is studded with innumerable chalets.

Beaufort

▷ *18km/11mi SE of Col des Saisies.*

This little crossroads town (its church has fine woodcarvings and interesting sculptures) has given its name to the **Beaufortain**★★ country, an area of folded limestone beds on a base of ancient crystalline rocks. Virtually continuous forest cover forms a background to sweeping alpine pastures. Above the 1 450m/4 757ft contour, the pastoral economy is marked by the seasonal movement of the herds up and down the slopes. The village of **Boudin**★ *(7km/4.3mi S)* is particularly picturesque.

Cormet de Roselend★

▷ *20km/12.4mi SE of Beaufort*

This long valley, 1 900m/6 200ft high, links the Roselend and Chapieux valleys. It is a vast, treeless, lonely place, dotted with rocks and a few shepherds' huts. A rushing mountain stream descends the steep valley, **Vallée des Chapieux**★, in a series of abrupt steps towards **Bourg-St-Maurice**. This strategically sited town commands the routes coming down from the Beaufortain country and the Little St Bernard (Petit-St-Bernard) and Iseran Passes. Around it is the **Tarentaise**★★ country of the upper Isère valley where transhumance is still practised. By the time the route reaches Ste-Foy in the upper Tarentaise, the landscape has become more

Two-Day Programme

By driving hard it is indeed possible to get from Thonon to Menton in two days, but to do so would be to deprive oneself of a number of sights that in themselves would make the trip worthwhile; they include Chamonix with the Aiguille du Midi and the Vallée Blanche, La Grave and the splendid viewpoint at Le Chazelet, St-Véran.

Five-Day Programme

Thonon-Beaufort:
144km/89.4mi –allow 5hr30min including sightseeing.
Beaufort-Val d'Isère: *71km/44mi – allow 3hr including sightseeing.*
Val d'Isère-Briançon:
180km/111.8mi – allow 7hr30min including sightseeing.
Briançon-Barcelonnette:
133km/82.6mi – allow 6hr30min including sightseeing.
Barcelonnette-Menton:
206km/128mi – allow 6hr including sightseeing.

mountainous in character. The Tignes valley (Val de Tignes) is characterised by gorges and glacial bars; the avalanche protection works are impressive, as is the **Tignes Dam**★★, a major engineering feat of the 1950s.

Val d'Isère★★★

▶ *50km/31mi SE of Cormet de Roseland*

In its high valley 1 000m/3 281ft above Bourg-St-Maurice, this is the most important town in the upper Tarentaise. With an excellent sunshine record, the resort is surrounded by splendid mountain landscapes; to the south and west are the glaciers and peaks (several rising to more than 3 500m/11 483ft) of the Vanoise National Park, much favoured by walkers.

As the road climbs amid the crystalline massifs, it gives views of the imposing peaks of the Gran Paradiso in Italy to the left and of the Vanoise massif (Grande Motte peak) to the right.

Col d'Iseran★

▶ *16km/10mi SE of Val d'Isère*

2 770m/9 088ft. The road across this high pass is the only link between the Tarentaise and the **Maurienne** country to the south which centres on the long valley of the River Arc. Industry is more important here than agriculture. The location of settlements has been determined by the sharp breaks in slope marked by glacial bars.

Modane

▶ *55.5km/34.5mi SW of Col d'Iseran*

This is a border town at the French end of rail and road tunnels into Italy. At Valloire, the route once more enters the ancient Hercynian mountains and begins to climb towards the Galibier Pass.

Col du Galibier★★★

▶ *52km/32.3mi SW of Modane*

2 642m/8 668ft. From the viewing table there is a superb panorama which takes in the Maurienne country (to the north), and the Pelvoux region (to the south), which is separated from the Briançonnais country by the high ridge of the Massif des Écrins. The pass marks the dividing line between the northern and southern part of the French Alps.

At the pass, **Col du Lautaret**★★, with its fine views of the Meije mountains, turn right in the direction of La Grave in the Romanche valley, then turn left at the entrance to the second tunnel.

Col du Galibier

©Claudio Giovanni Colombo/Dreamstime.com

Oratoire du Chazelet★★★

◐ *23km/14.3mi W of Col du Galibier*

From the viewing table, the view extends over the high peaks of the Écrins National Park from the Col des Ruillans on the right to the broken ridges of the Meije (including le Doigt de Dieu – The Finger of God – at 3 974m/13 025ft). The upper course of the glacier, fed by frequent snowfall, is of a staggering whiteness.

La Grave★

◐ *5km/3mi E of Oratoire du Chazelet*

The village has a particularly fine **site**★★ in the Romanche valley at the foot of the Meije. A two-stage cable-car ride takes the visitor to a height of 3 200m/10 500ft at the col on the western flank of Mont du Râteau, from where there are unforgettable views over the Meije and the Écrins glaciers.

Back at the Col du Lauteret, the route now enters the southern part of the French Alps. At Monêtier in the Guisanne valley, it re-enters the sedimentary zone of the High Alps; oak, beech and ash reappear, the valleys open out and the whole landscape takes on a lighter air.

Briançon★★

38km/23.6mi SE of La Grave.
◔ *See BRIANÇON*

Col d'Izoard★★

◐ *14km/8.7mi SE of Briançon*

2 361m/7 746ft. The pass is in a desolate setting fringed by dramatic peaks. From the viewing tables magnificent views extend over the Briançonnais to the north and the Queyras country to the south.

The road descends in a series of hairpin bends through a strange landscape of screes and jagged rocks known as the **Casse Déserte**★★. At this high altitude, the processes of erosion are greatly accelerated by the extremes of temperature to which the rocks are exposed.

The high **Queyras**★★ country is centred on the valley of the River Guil. Closed off downstream from the outside world by a series of narrow gorges, and cut

off from main communication routes, it has fine examples of alpine houses. Above Château-Queyras, the valley sides are sharply differentiated; the gentler south-facing slopes are covered with well-watered meadows, while the north-facing slopes grow only larches and Arolla pines.

Saint-Véran★★

◐ *34km/21mi SE of Col d'Izoard*

Lying between the 1 990m/6 528.8ft contour and the 2 040m/6 693ft contour, this is the highest village in France and the third highest in Europe. Its chalets, timber-built on a basement of schist, are a unique example of adaptation to the rigours of a high-altitude mountain life which combines arable cultivation and grazing, forestry, and the exercise of craft skills during the long winters. The south-facing dwellings are sited in groups, most with hay-barns and balconies on which cereals are ripened. The village has a strange sculpture showing Christ's Agony.

La Meije from the Oratoire du Chazelet
D. Hée/MICHELIN

The little town of **Guillestre**, with its church characterised by a beautiful **porch**★ is situated at the end of the **Combe du Queyras**★★, a canyon carved out by the clear waters of the Guil.

Embrun★

◆ *51km/31.6mi SE of Saint-Véran*

High up on its terrace overlooking the River Durance as it emerges from the mountains, the little town was once the seat of an archbishop. From the Place de l'Archevêché there are fine views over the valley slopes with their well-cultivated terraced fields. The torrents entering the main valley have spread their debris over its floor in alluvial fans. The upper slopes are gouged by deep ravines, while dominating the scene are sombre high mountain crests.

The former **Notre-Dame Cathedral**, the finest church in the whole of the Dauphiné Alps, dates from the 12C. It has fine black-and-white marble stonework and the **north porch**★ is supported on pretty pink columns.

Col de Vars

◆ *38.5km/24mi E via N 94/D 902*

2 111m/6 893ft. This pass forms the gateway to the Ubaye valley. The valley floor, littered with boulders and studded with ponds, is grazed by sheep.

Beyond the pass, the south-facing slopes with their scattered hamlets are given over to stock-farming. In its upper reaches, the River Ubaye has cut deeply into the dark schists. Near La Condamine, the 19C Fort Tournoux seems part of the high rock on which it is built. After Jausiers, the route enters the Barcelonnette basin; the valley pastures are interspersed with woodland and the scene becomes more cheerful.

Barcelonnette★

◆ *31km/19mi SW of Col de Vars*

The little capital of the Ubaye district was laid out as a bastide on a regular plan in 1231 by Raimond Béranger, Count of Barcelona. It belonged to the House of Savoy until passing to France under the provisions of the Treaty of Utrecht in 1713. On the edge of town are the houses of the "Barcelonnettes" or "Mexicans", locals who made their fortunes in the textile trade in Mexico before returning home. A museum, **Musée de la Vallée**, traces the history of the migrations.

The road climbs around the flank of Mont Pelat, the highest (3 035m/10 164ft) peak in the Provence Alps.

Col de la Cayolle★★

◆ *30km/18.6mi SE of Barcelonnette*

2 327m/7 635ft. This pass links the Ubaye country and the Upper Verdon to the upper reaches of the Var. From the top there are views over the deep valley of the Var towards the Grasse Pre-Alps in the far distance.

THE UPPER VALLEY OF THE RIVER VAR★★

The source of the Var is on the left as the road drops away from the pass to follow the river through the sombre mountains. At **St-Martin-d'Entraunes** *(20km/12.4mi S of Col de la Cayolle)*, the route passes from the High Alps into the sedimentary zone, the Pre-Alps of **Provence**. Downstream from **Villeneuve d'Entraunes** *(4.4km/2.7mi SE of St-Martin-d'Entraunes)*, water coursing through drainage channels draws attention to the changes that take place in the landscape of the countryside around **Guillaumes** *(7.5km/4.6mi SE of Villeneuve d'Entraunes)*.

Gorges de Daluis★★

◆ *3.5km/2mi S of Guillaumes*

These deep gorges have been cut by the river into thick beds of red porphyry and Urgonian limestone, giving striking colour effects. The road from **Guillaumes** to **Beuil** leads to the **Gorges du Cians** in the upper stretch of the river Var.

The road climbs steadily to the **Col de Valberg** offering views of the different sides of the valley: woody to the north, compared to the southern one covered with vineyards and fruit trees. The descent towards **Roubion** from the **Col de**

Couilloie (1 678m/5 503ft) reveals the valleys of **La Vionèse** and **La Tinée**. After the impressive **site**★★ of **Roubion** (the village is perched 1 300m/4 264ft up on a ridge), the road travels through a red schistose landscape, enlivened by several waterfalls.

Roure★

◉ *12.4km/7.7mi E of Roubion*
This village is characterised by its architectural unity: houses with red schist walls and limestone tile roofs *(lauze)*. The route then follows the river Vionèse until it flows into the river Tinée at **St-Sauveur-sur-Tinée**. Outside the village, on the left, a small road leads to the striking **site**★ of **Ramplas**, a village built on a ridge.

La Bolline

◉ *22km/13.7mi SE of Roure via D2205/D2265*
This pleasant summer resort is situated in the middle of a chestnut grove.

La Colmiane

◉ *8km/5mi E of La Bolline*
The chalets and hotels of this winter sports resort are set amidst a wonderful larch forest. From the **Col de St-Martin**, there is a possibility of taking a chairlift up to the **Pic de Colmiane**★★ (beautiful **panorama**★★ from the top).

St-Martin-Vésubie★

◉ *8.4km/5.2mi E of La Colmiane*
A baroque church and channeled stream flowing down the Rue du Docteur-Cagnoli characterise this famous mountaineering centre from which visitors can go rambling in the **Vallon du Boréon**★★ or the **Vallon de la Madone de Fenestre**★.

La Bollène-Vésubie

◉ *16km/10mi SE of St-Martin-Vésubie*
The concentric streets of this peaceful village, in the middle of a beautiful chestnut grove, converge on the church, which crowns the hill. The forest, Fôret de Turini★★, which spreads across the valleys of the Vésubie and of the Bévéra,

demarcates the southern border of the Parc national du Mercantour.

Le Massif de l'Authion★★

◉ *32.5km/20.2mi SE of La Bollène-Vésubie*
North of the **Col de Turini**, this massif constitutes a wonderful natural fortress which seems to stand guard over the roads between the Vésubie and Roya valleys. This strategic value has caused it to be, throughout the centuries, the stage for several conflicts. In April 1945, it was the last sector of France to be liberated. A stele commemorates the fierceness of the combat.
After crossing the forest of Turini, the river Bévéra winds its way towards the **Gorges du Piaon**★★ where the corniche road overlooks the river. Before reaching the gorges, the road goes through **Moulinet**, a charming village set in a verdant valley before passing the **Chapelle de Notre-Dame-La-Menour** with its Renaissance façade on the left.

Sospel★

◉ *28.6km/17.7mi SE of Le Massif de l'Authion.*
This Alpine resort was once a bishopric, during the Great Schism and a stop on the Salt Road linking Turin with the coast. Old houses line both banks of the Bévéra which is traversed by an ancient fortified bridge.
On the Nice road, 1km/0.6mi from the centre of the village, stands the **Fort St-Roch** one of the last elements of the "Alpine Maginot line" built in the 1930s.
The road follows the old railway line which used to link Sospel to Menton, along the course of the Merlanson, a tributary of the Bévéra. On the opposite side of the valley, the road to Nice via the **Col de Braus** winds its way, amidst olive groves, towards the capital of the French Riviera.

Menton★★

◉ *21km/13mi SE of Sospel.*
◉ *See MENTON*

Sisteron★★

The lofty citadel of Sisteron, sternly
guarding a narrow ravine and looking down on the clustered lanes of
the 14C town, still makes an impressive spectacle despite the battering
it took from Allied bombing raids
during 1944.

GEOGRAPHY

Sisteron lies on the Route Napoleon
and the River Durance and is the main
mountain gateway to Provence.
The town is situated between the
Laragne valley to the north and the
valley of the middle Durance to the
south. As well as marking the historic
boundary between Dauphiné and
Provence, this is also the northern limit
of the cultivation of the olive.

▶ **Population:** 6 964
🚗 **Michelin Map:** 334 D 7
📋 **Info:** Place de la République. ℘04 92 61 36 50.
www.sisteron.com.
🔵 **Location:** Sisteron is
located on the Route
Napoléon between Gap
and Digne.

SIGHT
Citadelle★

🕐*Open daily Apr–11 Nov 9am–7pm
(Jul–Aug 7.30pm; Apr, May, Oct
6.30pm).* ⊗*4.80€.* ℘*04 92 61 06 00.*
Following Second World War bombing
in August 1944, little remains of the
fortress other than the 12C keep and 16C
ramparts, with excellent **views**★.

Massif de la
Vanoise★★★

Numerous Neolithic monuments,
cairns and stone roads high on
the mountains show that this
magnificent landscape has been a
centre of human activity for many
tens of thousands of years. Today it
is a skiing area of world importance.

GEOGRAPHY

This famous massif lies between the
valleys of the Arc and the Isère. It was
proclaimed a national park in 1963 and
consists of two concentric areas.
The outer zone (1 450sq km/560sq mi)
includes some of the largest skiing
resorts in the world, including the
Three Valleys (les 3 Vallées – Courchevel,
Méribel, Les Menuires-Val Thorens),
and l'Espace Killy (Tignes and Val
d'Isère). The central zone (530sq km/
204.6sq mi), accessible to ramblers, is a
remarkable natural site subject to strict
regulations.
La Vanoise Massif, which is dotted with
charming villages and lovely forests,
remains nonetheless a high mountain

🚗 **Michelin Map:** 333 M-N-
O 4-5-6
📋 **Info:** Maison de la Vanoise,
Termignon. ℘04 79 20 51
67. www.vanoise.com.
🔵 **Location:** The Vanoise
extends from the Isère
valley in the north to the
Arc valley in the south, and
to the east runs up to the
Italian border.

area: 107 summits exceed 3 000m/9
842.5ft and the glaciers cover a total
surface of 88sq km/34sq mi. The massif
is noted for its diverse fauna (marmots,
ibexes, chamois) and flora (around 2 000
species).

VISIT

Val-d'Isère★★★ – a prestigious winter
sports resort with an impressive views.
Rocher de Bellevarde★★★ – 🚠 *Access
by cable railway.* Views of the Tarentaise
and Mont-Blanc.
Refuge de Prariond★★ – *2hr round-
trip on foot.* A pleasant walk with
varied landscapes (gorges, rock faces).

Réserve naturelle de la Grande Sassière★★ – A backdrop of lakes and glaciers frames Tignes Dam.
The park boasts a wealth of animal and plant species which may be easily observed. From the Saut car park, walks to **Lac de la Sassière★★** *(1hr on foot)* and the **Glacier de Rhême-Golette★★** (2hr30min), at an altitude of 3 000m/9 842.5ft.

Tignes★★★ – *Alt. 2 100m/6 889.7ft.* Resort around a lake in a **site★★** dominated by the breath-taking view of the Grande Motte Glacier (3 656m/11 994.7ft). Seasoned ramblers may want to tackle **Col du Palet★★**, **Pointe du Chardonnet★★★** (⏢*very steep slope*) or the **Col de la Croix des Frêtes★★**, the **Lac du Grattaleu★**, **Col de Tourne★**.

Peisey-Nancroix★ – This village, nestling in the lush **Vallée de Ponturin★**, opens onto the park and is linked to the skiing area of Les Arcs.

Lac de la Plagne★★ – *4hr round-trip on foot*. A route in a delightful, flowery setting, at the foot of the Bellecôte summit, 3 417m/11 269ft) and Mont Pourri (3 779m/12 398ft).

Pralognan★ – *Alt. 1 410m/4 626ft.* One of the main stopping-places for ramblers in La Vanoise Massif.

Col de la Vanoise★★ – *Alt. 2 517m/8 260ft. 4hr round-trip.* Views of the Grande Casse (3 855m/12 647.6ft).

Col d'Aussois★★★ – *Alt. 2 916m/9 567ft. Ascent 5hr.* Sweeping panorama. These two passes may also be reached from Termignon and Aussois en Maurienne.

La Saulire★★ – *Alt. 2 738m/8 983ft.* 🚡 *Access by cable-car.* View of La Vanoise Massif and the Oisans.

Réserve naturelle de Tuéda★ – Beautiful pine forest by Tuéda Lake.

Cime de Caron★★★ – *Alt. 3 198m/10 550ft.* 🚡 *2hr 30min round-trip by cable-car and cable railway.* Panorama of the Écrins, Tarentaise and Mont-Blanc.

Massif du
Vercors★★★

Rising above Grenoble like a fortress, the massive limestone plateau of the Vercors forms the largest regional park in the northern Alps.

GEOGRAPHY

The Vercors is the most extensive of the Pre-Alpine massifs. Protected by sheer cliffs, it is a natural citadel, inside which grow fine forests of beech and conifers interspersed with lush pasturelands. In places, the immensely thick limestone has been cut into by the rivers to form deep and spectacular gorges.

A BIT OF HISTORY

In 1944, the Resistance in these mountains numbered several thousand. In June of that year, the Wehrmacht stepped up its assault on the Resistance, and

🕪 **Michelin Map:** 332 F-G 2-3
🈺 **Info:** La-Chapelle-en-Vercors. ☏04 75 48 22 54. www.vercors.fr; www.vercors.com.
▶ **Location:** The area is to the W and SW of Grenoble.

brought in parachute troops on 21 July. With many of their number lost, the surviving members of the Resistance were given the order to disperse on 23 July. 700 of the inhabitants and defenders of the Vercors had died; several of its villages lay in ruins.
North of the rebuilt village of **Vassieux-en-Vercors** is a National Cemetery with the graves of some of those who died during that terrible summer, and at the Col de Lachan stands a monument to the fallen (Mémorial du Vercors).

Grands Goulets

S. Sauvignier/MICHELIN

One of the finest sights in the Vercors. The road clings dizzily to a vast limestone wall rising 600m/1 968.5ft above the upper valley of the Cholet.

Grands Goulets★★★

▶ *17.7km/11mi SE of Combe Laval*
An epic piece of construction dating from 1851, the narrow road was hewn directly into the rock. From its upper section it is possible to see the river beginning the process of eroding an as yet intact geological formation. The village of Les Barraques-en-Vercors was destroyed by enemy action in 1944.

Col de Rousset★★

▶ *22.6km/14mi S of Grands Goulets.*
Go to the southern entrance to the
disused tunnel
The pass marks the climatic as well as the morphological boundary between the northern and southern Alps. There are spectacular views, not only of the road twisting its way downwards, but also of the great limestone walls protecting the Vercors, of the Die valley 960m/3 149.6ft below, and of a succession of bare ridges extending into the far distance.

EXCURSIONS
Gorges de la Bourne★★★

▶ *18.7km/11.6mi N of Vassieux-en-Vercors*
The unusually regular walls of the gorge open out downstream. its entrance is marked by the old cloth town of Pont-en-Royans with its houses clinging picturesquely to the rock face.

Combe Laval★★★

▶ *24.6km/15.3mi SW of Gorges de la Bourne.*

Grand Canyon du
Verdon★★★

The modest-looking River Verdon has cut Europe's most spectacular canyon through a remote, wild landscape.

GEOGRAPHY
The canyon extends 26km/16mi from the meeting-point of the Verdon with the Jabron in the east to where it flows into Ste-Croix Lake in the west at the Galetas bridge.
The opposite rims of the canyon are between 200–1 500m (656–4 921ft) apart. Its depth varies from 250–600m (820–1 968.5ft), while the width of its floor ranges from 8–90m (26–295ft). The dizzy height of the canyon's walls

♿ **Michelin Map:** 334 E-F 10
ℹ **Info:** Maison des Gorges du Verdon, La Palusur-Verdon. ℘04 92 77 32 02. www.lapaludsurverdon.com.
▶ **Location:** The gorge is best reached from Castellane on the east side or Moustiers-Ste-Marie on the west. On the north side, the canyon can be followed on D 952 and D 23, while the spectacular D 71 (the Corniche Sublime) runs along the south side.
🕐 **Timing:** The road on either side is slow and tiring, so make sure you allow a full day.

impresses on one the sheer scale of the Jurassic sedimentation, in terms of both time and the quantity of material deposited.

VISIT

La Corniche Sublime★★★
South bank scenic route.
The steep and twisting (20km/12.4mi) road was engineered so as to open up the most spectacular views. They include: the **Balcons de la Mescla**★★★ overlooking the swirling waters where the Verdon is joined by the Artuby; the bridge, Pont de l'Artubya, linking sheer walls of rock; the Fayet tunnels above the Étroit des Cavaliers (Knights' Narrows), and the **Falaise des Cavaliers**★ (Knights' Cliff) 300m/982.2ft high.

La route des Crêtes★★★
North bank scenic route.
The road (23km/14.3mi long) links a series of viewpoints overlooking the most spectacular section of the canyon. Further eastwards, the viewpoint known as the **Point Sublime**★★★ dominates the downstream section of the canyon and the impressive narrows, the **Couloir de Samson**★★★.

Castellane★
 See ROUTE NAPOLÉON.

Moustiers-Ste-Marie★★
The small town is the centre for the Valensole plateau. It has an extraordinary **site**★★ at the foot of a cleft in the limestone cliff, across which a knight returning from the Crusades stretched the chain which can still be seen today. The church has a **tower**★ with arcading in Lombard style. Faience was introduced here in 1679; the most sought-after pieces were fired at high temperatures (*see LIMOGES*) and have charming hunting scenes in blue.

Yvoire★★

This picturesque village bedecked with flowers has retained its medieval character. It enjoys a magnificent site on the shores of Lake Geneva (Lac Léman), at the tip of a headland separating the Petit Lac and the Grand Lac, and has a very popular marina.

SIGHTS

Village Médieval (Old Town)★
Pedestrian access only.
Rebuilt in the 14C on the site of a former fortress, Yvoire has kept part of its original ramparts including two gates protected by towers and its castle (*closed to the public*) with a massive square keep framed by turrets.

The bustling streets lined with old houses and craft shops lead to delightful squares decked with flowers which afford fine views of the lake. From the end of the pier there are views of Switzerland and the Jura mountains.

▸ **Population:** 639

 Michelin Map: 328 K 2

 Info: Place de la Mairie. ℘04 50 72 80 21.

 Location: Approach the town from Douvaine, passing through the village of Nernier, or come from Exevenex.

 Parking: Parking is available just outside the town wall on the Thonon road.

Jardin des Cinq-Sens★
Le Labyrinthe. *Open 18 Apr–May, Sept and 1–4 Oct, daily 11am–6pm; Jun–Aug daily 10am–7pm.* 10€. *℘04 50 72 88 80. www.jardin5sens.net.*
The former kitchen garden of the castle has been turned into a reconstruction of a medieval enclosed garden, situated in the centre of Yvoire's Old Town.

FRENCH RIVIERA

The Riviera's abundant sunshine, exotic vegetation and dramatic combination of sea and mountains have made it a fashionable place of pleasure since its "discovery" in the 19C. The coast is densely built up; the resorts linked by triple corniche roads. Further north are the Maritime Alps, dissected by the upper valleys of the Var, Tinée, Vésubie and Roya. To the west of Nice the coast flattens out, forming wide bays with fine beaches, before again rising beyond Cannes to higher ground.

Highlights

1 The fascinating old quarter of Nice: **Le Vieux Nice** *(p327)*
2 Ancient village in natural amphitheatre: **Saorge** *(p337)*
3 Stunning red porphyry outcrop: **Massif de L'Estérel** *(p319)*
4 The capital of the city of Monaco: **Le Rocher** *(p323)*
5 Exciting drives and fine views: **Corniches de la Riviera** *(p330)*

Geography – The bustle of the coast is in contrast to the quieter charm of the interior, with its olive groves, spectacular gorges and hill-villages.

Between Nice and Menton, the Pre-Alps plunge into the sea while the limestone plâteaux of the Provence tableland are separated from the sea by two massifs, Estérel and Maures. Its coastline has great promontories extending into the sea defining wide bays like that of the Gulf of St-Tropez. The Toulon coast is characterised by vertical cliffs, a number of attractive beaches; to the north rise the limestone heights of the Provençal Ranges.

History – Although preceded by the Ligurians and Greeks, the Romans had established themselves in the region by the 1C AD and evidence of their presence can be seen today at Fréjus and Cimiez (Nice). In the Middle Ages Provence changed hands several times and did not become part of France until the late 15C. Nice remained part of Savoy and was not restored to France until 1860.

Economy – The Riviera is dominated by tourism, which began in the 19C.

This most important industry is why Nice, the largest city in the region, has France's second-busiest airport. After tourism, the best-known industry on the Riviera is perfume.

Cannes★★★

A charming old quarter, chic town centre and glamorous beachside promenade make Cannes one of the most enjoyable places on the Riviera. Spread out between the Suquet Heights and La Croisette Point on the shore of La Napoule Bay, Cannes also owes its popularity to an exceptionally beautiful setting.

A BIT OF HISTORY

In 1834, the former Lord Chancellor of England, Lord Henry Brougham, was on his way to Italy when he was prevented from entering the County of Nice, then part of Italy, because of a cholera epidemic. Forced to wait, he made an overnight stop at a fishing village called Cannes. Enchanted by the place, he built a villa here and returned to it every winter, establishing a trend among the English aristocracy and stimulating Cannes' first period of growth, ultimately leading to its establishment as a holiday resort.

SIGHTS

Boulevard de la Croisette ★★

Locals and visitors congregate along this wide, attractive seafront road, with delightful gardens along its centre. To one side extends the resort's splendid sandy beach and broad promenade, while the landward side of the boulevard is lined with the dignified and impeccably maintained façades of four luxury 'palace' hotels and exclusive boutiques. At the eastern end of La Croisette is a marina, busy with yachts and pleasure craft, and at its western end another, overlooked by the Festival and Conference Centre (Palais des Festivals et des Congrès). It is here that the **Cannes Film Festival** is held every May – the town's most spectacular and prestigious event.

Le Suquet

Le Suquet, the old town area of Cannes, climbs a steep hill beside the Old Port. The lower streets of this area are today the centre for nightlife and restaurants.

▶ **Population:** 70 450

◉ **Michelin Map:** 341 B-D 5 AND P-Q 5

🛈 **Info:** Palais des Festivals, 1 La Croisette. ℘04 92 99 84 22; and at the railway station (Gare SNCF). ℘04 93 99 19 77. www.cannes.fr.

▶ **Location:** Cannes is situated 34.4km/21.3mi along the coast SW of Nice. As a town it is surprisingly extensive; the heart of town, and most of the sights, are in a narrow strip close to the sea, while the centre of the action is the Palais des Festivals et des Congrès.

🚩 **Don't Miss:** The superb covered market, near the Old Port, (Tue–Sun).

🕐 **Timing:** Allow yourself at least 2hr to visit Le Suquet.

TOURS AND TRANSPORTATION

TAM – ℘0800 06 01 06. www.cg06.fr/transport/transports-tam.html. These buses operate between Cannes and Nice, including a direct service to the airport. **Train Station** – SNCF Gare de Cannes. ℘0891 70 30 00. www.ter-sncf.com/paca. This train station is served by local and national trains including TGV and regional TER trains (service between Mandelieu-La-Napoule and Vintimille). **Trans Côte d'Azur** – Quai Laubeuf. ℘04 92 98 71 30. www.trans-cote-azur.com. Regular service to the Île Ste-Marguerite (15min), plus seasonal tours to l'Île de Porquerolles, Monaco, Saint-Tropez, San Remo, la Corniche d'Or, etc.

From a terrace in front of the Tour du Mont Chevalier, there is a fine **view**★ over beach and bay, the Lérins Islands and the Estérel Heights. The 11C Cannes castle today houses the remarkable

Musée de la Castre ★★ *(Le Suquet; ℰ04 93 38 55 26;* ☞guided tous (1hr) available), an eclectic 19C private collection of exceptional ethnographic artefacts taken from cultures around the world.

EXCURSION
Massif de L'Estérel★★★
40km/24.8mi W by N 98.

The massif's jagged relief of volcanic rock (red porphyry) worn by erosion dips vertically into the deep blue sea between La Napoule and St-Raphael. The rugged coastline is fringed with rocks, islets and reefs. From **Mont Vinaigre**★★★, its highest peak (alt 618m/2 027.5ft), a vast panorama unfolds over the surrounding area. The pine and cork-oak forests clothing the wild and lonely massif have been ravaged by fire in recent years.

ADDRESSES

🏨 STAY

🛏 **Hôtel Alnea** – *20 r. Jean de Riouffe. ℰ04 93 68 77 77. www.hotel-alnea.com. Closed 3 weeks in Dec. 14 rooms. �릴7€.* A family run establishment with simple but well kept rooms decorated with colourful. Located just a couple of minutes from La Croisette in the heart of Cannes.

🛏 **Hôtel Appia** – *6 r. Marceau. ℰ04 93 06 59 59. www.appia-hotel.com. Closed 21 Nov–28 Dec, 5–14 Jan. 32 rooms. ⊿7€.* Practicality takes precedence over comfort in this downtown hotel where the well-kept, smallish rooms are both air-conditioned and soundproofed. Pristine bathrooms.

🛏🛏 **Villa l'Églantier** – *14 r. Campestra. ℰ04 93 68 22 43. 3 rooms.* Impressive white villa dating from 1920, surrounded by palm trees and other exotic species, dominating the city of Cannes. The large, peaceful rooms are all extended by a terrace or a balcony.

🍴 EAT

🍽 **Le Côte d'Azur** – *3 r. Jean-Daumas. ℰ04 93 38 60 02. Closed evenings and Sun.* Modest restaurant with a friendly ambience and cosy setting with period furnishings. The traditional cooking attracts a great many locals. Low prices guaranteed.

🍽🍽 **Aux Bons Enfants** – *80 r. Meynadier. Closed 1 Dec–2 Jan.* Simplicity, generosity and congeniality are the hallmarks of this informal establishment where there's no telephone and customers are required to pay in cash. A true locals' hangout since 1935, with tasty Mediterranean food.

🍽🍽 **Le Comptoir des Vins** – *13 Boulevard de la République. ℰ04 93 68 13 26. Closed a fortnight in Feb and a fortnight in Sept; all Sun.* This handsomely stocked wine boutique leads to a colourful dining area where light snacks can be served, washed down with a glass of wine.

🍽🍽🍽 **Le Caveau 30** – *45 r. Félix-Faure. ℰ04 93 39 06 33. www.lecaveau30. com.* Large restaurant comprising two dining rooms done up in the style of a 1930 brasserie. The terrace overlooks a shaded square popular among boules players. Fish and seafood are the specialities of the house.

🍽🍽🍽 **Fred l'écailler** – *7 Place de l'Étang. ℰ04 93 43 15 85. http://fred lecailler.com.* A large neon sign marks the entrance to this rustic-style restaurant whose walls are draped with fishing nets. The tiny square affords a glimpse of village life with its bustling activity and daily games of pétanque. Fine selection of freshly caught fish and seafood.

🍽🍽🍽 **Au Poisson Grillé** – *8 Quai St-Pierre, Vieux Port. ℰ04 93 39 44 68. www.poisson-grille.com.* Appropriately located in the old port, this fish restaurant was opened back in 1949. It serves grilled fish alongside many other Mediterranean dishes, in a warm setting of varnished wood evoking the interior of a luxury cabin. Attentive service at affordable prices.

NIGHTLIFE

The best way to get to know this glamorous city is to frequent its luxury hotel bars: order a cocktail on the terrace of the Carlton hotel, on the beach of the Majestic or in the piano-bar of the Martinez.

L'Amiral – *73 bd. de la Croisette.* ℘*04 92 98 73 00. www.hotel-martinez.com.* Attached to the Martinez Hotel, this bar is by far the most popular meeting place along the coast. It owes its reputation to the head barman and to Jimmy, the American piano player. Live music every evening from 8pm.

SHOPPING

Market – *Marché de Forville; Tue–Sun 7am–1pm.* Fine stalls displaying fresh regional produce. **Allées de la Liberté** – Flower market every morning. Popular flea market on Saturdays. **Shopping streets** – *r. Meynadie.* Tempting window displays of food and craftwork in lively pedestrian area. Rue d'Antibes: luxury clothes and luggage. **Cannolive** – *16 r. Vénizelos.* ℘*04 93 39 08 19.* This shop boasts an incredible choice of Provençal products: household linen, *tapenades*, crockery, *santons*, soap, and even Lérina liqueur from the nearby islands.

LEISURE ACTIVITIES

Watersports Plongée Club de Cannes *(46 rue Clémenceau;* ℘*04 9338 6757).*
Beaches – Not all the beaches on La Croisette charge a fee (details of prices are listed at the top of the steps), or belong to a hotel (located opposite). There are also three free beaches, one of which is located behind the Palais du Festival. The other public beaches lie west of the old port, on Boulevard Jean-Hibert and Boulevard du Midi, at Port Canto and on Boulevard Gazagnaire beyond La Pointe.

Ponton Majestic Ski Nautique – *10 Boulevard de la Croisette.* ℘*04 92 98 77 47. http://majesticskiclub.online.fr.* Water-skiing and parasailing.

CALENDAR OF EVENTS

Cannes International Film Festival – 11 days in May; free open-air cinema on the beach. ℘*01 53 59 61 00. www.festival-cannes.com.*
Nuits Misicales du Suquet – Mid–late July; classical concerts on the esplanade in front of the Église du Suquet. ℘*04 92 99 33 83. www.nuitsdusuquet-cannes.com.*

Les Îles de Lérins★★

The peaceful islands *(boat service from Cannes)* **are clad in a rich vegetation of pines, cypresses and eucalyptus and have a fascinating historic and archaeological heritage. The fine view back to the coast of the mainland stretches from Cap Roux to Cap d'Antibes.**

VISIT

Île Ste-Marguerite★★
Regular boat service from Cannes (Quai des Îles, Vieux Port). ℘*04 92 98 71 36.*
There are fine **forest walks** as well as through the botanical collection and

- **Michelin Map:** 341 D 6
- **Info:** See CANNES. ℘04 92 99 84 28. www.cannes-groupes.fr
- **Location:** The islands are just offshore from Cannes, with frequent boat departures from the Old Port.

along the avenue, Allée des eucalyptus géants. **Fort Royal** was built for coastal defence by Richelieu.
It served as a prison for Protestants, and also for the mysterious Man in the Iron Mask (1687–98). whose identity has never been established with certainty. From the terrace there is an extensive **view**★ of the coast.

Menton★★

Between mountain and Mediterranean, Menton stretches out agreeably on its sunny **site**★★ on the lower slopes of a picturesque natural amphitheatre of mountains. The town is known for its citrus groves and its dazzling annual Lemon Festival (during Carnival).

A BIT OF HISTORY

On the cliffs around are the remains of fortifications and human settlement going back to Neolithic times. The town was bought by the Grimaldi family of Monaco in the 14C, then incorporated into the French kingdom when the county of Nice was annexed.

SIGHTS

Hôtel de Ville

17 r. de la République.
℘04 92 10 50 00.
The town hall is a pretty building in Italianate style, with pilasters and Corinthian capitals and a cream-coloured cornice contrasting with the rosy rendering of the walls. The Registry Office **(Salle des mariages★)** was decorated by Cocteau in 1958 and can be visited duiring normal office hours for a small fee.

▶ **Population:** 28 812
◔ **Michelin Map:** 341 F 5
▧ **Info:** 8 av. Boyer. ℘04 92 41 76 76. www.menton.fr.
◖ **Location:** Menton is the last town on the French Riviera before the Italian border. It is divided into a modern beach resort and, lying behind, an old town.
☻ **Don't Miss:** The Tropical Garden **(jardin botanique exotique★★)** is outstanding. There are also many interesting Edwardian gardens in the **Garavan** district and nearby countryside.

Vieille Ville★★

Allow about 2hr.
The old town nestles underneath the hill just above r. Longue and r. St-Michel fragrant with orange trees, whose alignment marks the course of the Roman Via Giulia Augusta. **Parvis St-Michel★★** is a charming square in the Italian style, laid out on two levels by the Grimaldis, whose monogram can be seen in the pebble mosaic forming the paving. It is bordered by a number of houses in

Menton by night

E.Baret/MICHELIN

the local style, by a pink-walled chapel (Chapelle de la Conception), and by the **Basilique St-Michel** ★ (🕐*open Mon–Fri 10am–noon 3–5.15pm; Sat–Sun 5–5.15pm),* a fine Baroque building dating from the middle of the 17C, extensively restored after the earthquake of 1887.

ADDITIONAL SIGHTS
Promenade du Soleil★★
Musée des Beaux Arts★ *(Palais de Carnolès at 3 av. de la Madone)*

Principauté de
Monaco★★★

The Principality of Monaco, world-famous haunt of the super-rich, is a sovereign state covering an area of just 192ha/474 acres. Inhabited since prehistoric times and later a Greek settlement (5C BC) and a Roman port (1C AD), its history really began when the Grimaldi family bought it from the Republic of Genoa in 1308. Prince Rainier III ruled the principality from 1949–2005 with the assistance of a National Council. His only son Prince Albert then took power, but because he has no children, it seems certain that the line of succession will pass to Rainier's daughter, Princess Caroline.

SIGHTS
Le Rocher (The Rock)★★
This is the historic core of the principality, and its prestigious capital, the miniature city of Monaco. It is built on a rocky peninsula 60m/196.8ft above the sea.

👤👤 Musée Océanographique★★
av. St-Martin. ♿🕐*Open daily Oct–Mar 10am–6pm; Apr–Jun 9.30am–7pm; Jul–Aug 9.30am–7.30pm; Sept 9.30am–7pm.* 🕐*Closed day of F1 Grand Prix.* 💳*12.50€ (child 6€).*
📞*00 377 93 15 36 13. www.oceano.mc.*
The museum was founded by Prince Albert I, a leading light in the early days

EXCURSION
Roquebrune-Cap Martin★★
2km/1.2mi SW.
Roquebrune is a most picturesque hill-top village (**village perché**★★), where the tourist can stroll through the small streets towards the keep (**donjon**★) From the top, wonderful **panorama**★★ of the sea, Cap Martin, the Principality of Monaco and the Mont Agel.

▸ **Population:** 31 800
⏱ **Michelin Map:** 341 F 5
ℹ **Info:** 2a bd. des Moulins.
📞00 377 92 16 61 66.
www.visitmonaco.com.
◉ **Location:** The territory includes the Old Town or Monaco Ville on the Rock (Rocher de Monaco); the new town of Monte-Carlo and the port area at La Condamine linking the two.
🅿 **Parking:** Park in the underground garage (parking des Pêcheurs creusé) of Le Rocher, and take the lift up to the Old Town on the Rock.
🚩 **Don't Miss: The Musée Océanographique** ★★ or the **Palais Princier** ★
🕐 **Timing:** Allow 3hr in Old Monaco before visiting Monte-Carlo, where you can try your luck in the casino. November is especially busy, especially around the 19th, Monaco's National Day.
👤👤 **Kids:** Musée Océanographique; Collection des Voitures Anciennes; Musée National des Automates et Poupées d'Autrefois à Monaco.

of oceanography. The imposing rooms house the skeletons of large marine mammals, such as whales and sea-cows as well as stuffed specimens.

A splendid **aquarium**★★ teems with rare tropical and Mediterranean species of marine life. A live coral reef from the Red Sea is a unique exhibit. The museum is also a research centre, with exhibits of marine laboratories, the technology of underwater exploration and applied oceanography.

Cathédrale

av. St-Martin. ⏱*Open daily winter 8am–6pm; summer until 7pm.* ✎*12.50€.* ℘*00 377 93 30 87 70. www.cathedrale.mc.*

The neo-Romanesque building constructed with white stone from La Turbie between 1875 and 1903 contains a number of early paintings of the **Nice School**★★, including a St Nicholas altarpiece by Louis Bréa: 18 sections in glow-

ing colours surrounded by Renaissance carving of leaves and dolphins.

Palais Princier (Prince's Palace)★

Place du Palais. **State Rooms** ⏱*open daily Apr 10.30am–6pm; May–Sept 9.30am–6.30pm; Oct 10am–5.30pm.* ✎*7€.* **Museum of Napoleonic Souvenirs** ⏱*open Tue–Sun mid-Dec–May 10.30am–12.30pm, 2–5pm; Jun–Sept 9.30am–6.30pm; Oct–11 Nov 10am–5pm.* ⏱*Closed 25 Dec, 1 Jan.* ✎*4€.* 🎧*Guided audio tours (30min) available.* ℘*00 377 93 25 1831. www.palais.mc .*

The oldest parts of the Palace are 13C although the buildings on the south side are in 15-16C Italian Renaissance style. The formidable perimeter is built into the vertical rock and a monumental doorway with the Grimaldi Arms completes the the ensemble.

The palace overlooks a square called the **Place du Palais**★, ornamented with cannon presented by Louis XIV. With its medieval battlements and walls strengthened by Vauban, the palace makes a most picturesque composition.

The imposing gateway leads into the Court of Honour with its arcades; inside the Palace is the Throne Room and state apartments decorated with fine furniture and hung with signed portraits by Old Masters.

Monte-Carlo Opera House

B. Kaufmann/MICHELIN

Monte-Carlo★★★

Europe's gambling capital was launched by François Blanc, director of the casino in Bad Homburg in Germany. The place's success has led to building at a very high density indeed, but Monte-Carlo retains its attractiveness with its luxurious casino, its sumptuous villas, its de luxe shops and its pretty gardens. From the fine terrace (**terrasse★★**) of the Casino, the view extends from Monaco to the Bordighera headland in Italy.

Jardin Exotique★★

bd. du Jardin-Exotique. ⏰*Open daily mid-May–mid-Sept 9am–7pm; rest of the year 9am–6pm or until dusk.* 🎫*7€.* 📞*00 377 93 15 29 80. www.jardin-exotique.mc.*

The gardens cascade down a steep rock-face which has its own microclimate supporting a luxuriant variety of vegetation; there are many semi-desert species together with plants from the southern hemisphere.

👥 Collection des voitures anciennes★

Terrasses de Fontvieille. ♿⏰*Open daily 10am-6pm.* ⏰*Closed 25 Dec.* 🎫*6€ (child 3€).* 📞*00 377 92 05 28 56. www.palais.mc.*

Fine old carriages and vehicles from the royal collection are on display. There are also famous cars from the early 20C.

ADDITIONAL SIGHTS

Grotte de l'Observatoire★
(🔦*see Jardin exotique*)
Musée d'Anthropologie préhistorique★ *(56 bis, bd du Jardin exotique)*
Musée Napoléonien★ *(🔦see Palais Princier)*
👥 **Musée des Poupées et Automates★** *(17 av. Princesse-Grâce)*
Musée des Timbres et des Monnaies *(Terrasses de Fontvieille)*

ADDRESSES

🏨 STAY

🛏️ **Hôtel de France** – *6 r. de la Turbie.* 📞*00 377 93 30 24 64. www.monte-carlo.mc/france. 27 rooms.* 🍽️*9€.* Charming, soundproofed rooms decorated in Provençal hues and a modern breakfast lounge enhanced with metal and wood furniture.

🛏️ **Columbus Hôtel** – *23 Avenue des Papalins.* 📞*00 377 92 05 90 00. www.columbushotels.com. 181 rooms.* 🍽️*25€.* Clean, contemporary lines and a soothing palette are combined with cozy fabrics and warm wood furnishings. A lounge bar and Italian-style brasserie with terrace seating attract fashionable locals. Access to a private pool; the heliport is just a block away.

🛏️ **Metropôle** – *4 av. de la Madone.* 📞*00 377 93 15 15 15. www.metropole.com. 141 rooms.* 🍽️*37€.* This 1886 hotel got a complete facelift by the hot Parisian designer Jacques Garcia, with luxurious fabrics and timeless style. The outdoor pool and solarium have views overlooking the rooftops of the Place du Casino. The restaurant is managed by leading French chef Joël Robuchon.

🍽️ EAT

🍴 **Polpetta** – *2 r. Paradis.* 📞*00 377 93 50 67 84. Closed Sat lunch & Tue.* A small Italian restaurant offering three different settings in which to enjoy a tasty tagliatelle alla carbonara or vitello al funghi: the verandah giving onto the street, the rustic-style dining hall or the cosy, intimate room at the back.

🍴 **La Maison du Caviar** – *1 av. St-Charles.* 📞*00 377 93 30 80 06. Closed Sat lunch and Sun.* This prestigious house has been serving choice caviar to Monaco residents for the past 50 years. In an unusual setting made up of bottle racks and wooden panelling, you can also purchase salmon, foie gras or bœuf strogonoff. Definitely worth a visit.

🍴 **Vistamar** – *Hôtel Hermitage, Square Beaumarchais.* 📞*00 377 98 06 98 98. www.hotelhermitagemonte carlo.com. Closed for lunch Jul-Aug.*

An elegant restaurant specialising in fresh seafood, with one of the best panoramic views of the Principality from its top-floor terrace.

 Zebra Square – *Grimaldi Forum, 10 av. Princesse-Grâce. 00 377 99 99 25 50. Closed 3 weeks in Feb.* This stylish restaurant has the same sleek décor as its Parisian namesake, featuring modern fusion cuisine and panoramic views over the sea from the terrace. At night the bar is packed with a young and trendy crowd.

NIGHTLIFE

Casino de Monte-Carlo – *pl. du Casino. 00 377 98 06 21 21.www.montecarlocasinos.com. Open daily from 2pm.10€.* This is Europe's leading casino, with over a million euros in profits, attributed to gambling and not to slot machines as is the case in other casinos. The gambling salons and lavish dining hall Le Train Bleu, decorated in the style of the Orient-Express, are truly impressive. The terrace overlooking the sea is a haven of tranquillity, whether or not you have broken the bank!

Bar le Vistamar – *Hôtel Hermitage, Square Beaumarchais. 00 377 98 06 98 98. www.hotelhermitagemontecarlo.com.* This famous bar has been patronised by many celebrities over the years. Its superb terrace affords beautiful views of Monaco harbour. The specialities of the house are American cocktails, particularly with champagne!

Sass Café – *11 av. Princesse-Grace. 00 377 93 25 52 00. www.sasscafe.com.* Exclusive bar-restaurant with a cosy atmosphere where members of the local jet set drop in for a fancy vodka or champagne cocktail before meeting up at Jimmy'z.

Le Jimmy'z – *26 Princesse-Grâce. 00 377 92 16 20 00. Reservations recommended.* Formal evening wear is expected in this legendary small but select club where the wealthy love to congregate, whether they come from banking, advertising, fashion, film or the entertainment world. A unique, magic experience.

Stars'N'Bars – *6 Quai Antoine 1er. 00 377 97 97 95 95. www.starsnbars.com.* This is the great American bar-of-the-moment, more relaxed than the Principality's other establishments, and catering to a younger clientele eager to drink beer, eat a hamburger or two, play billiards, surf on the internet and dance the night away. The decoration features the paraphernalia of stars. Rock concerts are organised on a regular basis. Terrace with a view of Monaco harbour.

Grimaldi Forum – *10 av. Princesse-Grâce. 00 377 99 99 20 00. www.grimaldiforum.com.* This 1 800-seat auditorium plays host to headlining events throughout the year, including performances by the Monte Carlo Ballet and the Monte Carlo Philarmonic Orchestra.

BOAT TRIPS

 Aquavision – *Quai des Etats-Unis, Port Hercule. 00 377 92 16 15 15. Departures several times daily throughout the season.11€ (child 8€).* Views of the sea depths, and marine fauna and flora, with commentary in four languages.

SHOPPING

All the famous fashion brands have boutiques in Monte-Carlo. Find shops specialising in traditional goods in the narrow streets of the Rock *(Le Rocher)* opposite the palace. Boutique du Rocher in Avenue de la Madone is the official shop for local crafts.

CALENDAR OF EVENTS

Highlights of a packed calendar are

Monte-Carlo Rally – *held every year since 1911 (late Jan).*
Feast of Ste-Dévote – *Feast day of Monaco's Patron Saint (27 Jan).*
Sciaratù Carnival – *Monégasque festival (week of Mardi Gras).*
Spring Arts Festival – *Art, music, theatre and dance festival (Apr).*
Monaco Grand Prix – *Race in the Principality's winding streets (late May): 78 laps of a 3.34km/2.08mi circuit.*
National Day – *Picturesque procession and cultural displays (19 Nov).*

Nice★★★

Enclosed by an amphitheatre of hills, extending around a beautiful blue bay, the capital of the Riviera has artistic treasures, countless attractions, distinctive cuisine, a wonderful climate and a magnificent setting that has long attracted visitors year round.

A BIT OF HISTORY

Some 400 000 years ago, bands of elephant hunters made their encampments on the fossil beach at Terra Amata, 26m/85.3ft above the present level of the sea. In the 6C BC, Celto-Ligurians settled on the castle hill; a little later it was the turn of merchants and sailors from Marseille, who they established themselves around the harbour. These were followed by the Romans, who favoured the Cimiez district. In 1388, aided and abetted by the **Grimaldi** family, Count Amadeus VII of Savoy (1360–1391) incorporated Provence into his domain and made a triumphal entry into Nice.

As a result of the alliance of 1859 between France and Sardinia, Napoleon III undertook to help drive out the Austrians from the Lombardy and Veneto regions; in return, France was to receive from the House of Savoy the lands to the west of the Alps and around Nice, which had once been hers. A plebiscite produced an overwhelming vote in favour of a return to France (25 743 for, 260 against) and the ceremony of annexation took place on 14 June 1860.

SIGHTS

Le Vieux Nice★

The core of the city, huddling at the foot of the castle hill, has a lively, utterly Mediterranean character.

Château

The landscaped slopes of the castle hill, with their umbrella pines shading pleasant walks, reach a height of 92m/301.8ft. The summit provided

▶ **Population:** 888 784

Michelin Map: 341 E 5

Info: 5 Promenade des Anglais, and at Avenue Thiers (SNCF Train Station). *℘*08 92 70 74 07. www.nicetourisme.com.

Location: Start with the Promenade des Anglais – most visitors arrive along this seafront highway. At its eastern end is the Old Town (Le Vieux Nice), the château hill and the old port. North of it spreads the modern town, reaching to the Cimiez, the ancient Roman settlement.

Parking: Parking is difficult. As soon as possible, park in one of the many large underground car parks.

Don't Miss: A stroll along the Promenade des Anglais; the panorama from the château hill.

Timing: At least a full day is necessary to discover Nice. Spend the morning on the oceanfront and in Vieux Nice; reserve the afternoon for Cimiez, and, if you have time, choose an art museum according to your taste – Matisse, Chagall, or the Musée des Beaux-Arts, the Musée d'Art Moderne et d'Art Contemporain.

a place of refuge for the denizens of Cimiez at the time of the fall of the Roman Empire. In the 12C, the Counts of Provence built a castle here which was subsequently strengthened by the Angevin princes and the Dukes of Savoy but was demolished by Louis XIV in 1706. From the top there is a fine **view**★★ over the city, the Pre-Alps and the bay (Baie des Anges).

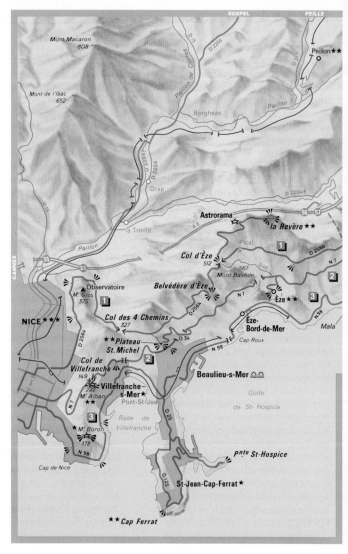

Place Garibaldi

The square is named after the great fighter for Italian unity who was born in Nice. The ochre walls and arcading of the buildings along its sides recall the urbane elegance characteristic of Piedmontese town planning in the 18C.

Cathédrale Ste-Reparate

pl. Rossetti. ℘04 93 62 34 40.
This is a fine example of the Baroque style as it developed in Nice. The west front, a pleasant mixture of greens and

yellows, is decorated with niches and medallions, topped by an imposing entablature and supported by buttress-pillars with composite capitals. The **interior**★ is enlivened by an elaborate cornice, and in the choir is a frieze outlined in white and gold and decorated with little figures of angels.

Église St-Jacques-le-Majeur★

r. Droite.
The west front recalls the Gesù church in Rome. Behind it lies a nave whose

severity is relieved by an abundance of sculpture. The barrel vault opens into side chapels containing loggias where the local nobility once worshipped.

Place Masséna

The linear park laid out on what was once the bed of the river Paillon is interrupted by this square begun in 1815. Its buildings with their façades rendered in reddish ochre and their arcades recall the planned urban spaces of Turin.

Site archéologique gallo-romain★

160 av. des Arènes de Cimiez. ♿⏰*Open Wed–Mon 10am–6pm.* ⏰*Closed 1 Jan, Easter Sunday, 1 May, 25 Dec.* 🎫*No charge.* ☛*Guided tours (1–2hr)* *(🎫3€).* ✆*04 93 81 59 57. www.musee-archeologique-nice.org.*

The Cimiez district originated in the Roman settlement whose growth soon eclipsed that of the older town laid out around the harbour. The archaeologi-

cal site consists mostly of medium-size amphitheatres and the area around the baths.

Monastère de Cimiez★

av. du Monastère. ✆*04 93 81 00 04.*
The monastery church possesses a Pietà of 1475 *(to the right of the entrance);* though an early work of Louis Bréa, and executed in Gothic style, it is one of his finest achievements, notably in its portrayal of the grieving Mary. To the left of the choir is a later work by the same artist, a Crucifixion (1512) which heralds the Renaissance.

Cap Ferrat

©Mgvuvan/Dreamstime.com

Musée Matisse★★

164 av. des Arènes. &Open
Wed–Mon 10am–6pm. Closed 1 Jan,
Easter, 1 May, 25 Dec. 4€; no charge
1st and 3rd Sun in the month. 04 93
81 08 08. www.musee-matisse-nice.org.
The museum is housed in the Villa des
Arènes; it traces the artist's evolution,
from a still-life *(Nature morte aux livres,
1890)* to the *Rococo Armchair (Fauteuil
de Rocaille, 1947)* and the *Blue Nude
(Nu bleu, 1952).*

Musée Marc-Chagall★★

av. Docteur Ménard. &Open May–
*Oct Wed–Mon 10am–6pm; Nov–Apr
Wed–Mon 10am–5pm.* Closed 1 Jan,
1 May, 25 Dec. 6.50€; free 1st Sun in
the month. 04 93 53 87 31.
www.musee-chagall.fr.
The museum was designed to display
the 17 great paintings making up the
artist's Biblical Message (painted between 1954 and 1967).

ADDITIONAL SIGHTS

Promenade des Anglais ★★
(Seafront)
Musée des Beaux-Arts ★★
(33 av. des Baumettes)
**Musée d'Art Moderne et d'Art
Contemporain**★★ *(Promenade
des Arts)*
**Musée d'Art et d'Histoire – Musée
Masséna**★ *(65 r. de France)*

**Palais des Arts, du Tourisme et
des Congrès**★ (Acropolis)
Chapelle de la Miséricorde★
(cours Saleya)
**Église St-Martin–St-Augustin –
interior**★ *(pl. Saint-Augustin)*

EXCURSION
Corniches de la Riviera★★★

*Circular tour of 41km/25.4mi –
allow 3hr.*
The Lower Corniche road skirts the
foot of Mont Boron, giving fine views
over Villefranche-sur-Mer and its
bay. The highly indented coastline
is the result of the recent folding
and subsequent drowning of the
limestone Pre-Alps.
Both **Cap Ferrat**★★ and nearby headland, Pointe St-Hospice, offer splendid
views of the Riviera with its corniche
roads; the village of Èze-Bord-de-Mer,
the fashionable resort of Beaulieu,
Cap d'Ail can all be identified, and
rising out of the sea in the distance is
Cap Martin.
Clinging like an eagle's nest to its inac-
cessible rock spike, **Èze**★★ seems the
very archetype of a hill village. It was
inhabited by the Ligurians and by the
Phoenicians, then fortified against raiders from the sea. In 1706 both the village and its castle were demolished on
the orders of Louis XIV, but it was rebuilt
after 1760.

ADDRESSES

STAY

⊜⊜ **Clair Hotel** – *23 bd Carnot, Impasse Terra Amata.* ℘*04 93 89 69 89. 10 rooms.* �*7.50€.* This converted schoolhouse near the archaeological museum has rooms all on one floor (in the old class-rooms) and a Mediterranean garden terrace where breakfast is served in the summer. Quiet neighbourhood, friendly, family-run atmosphere.

⊜⊜ **Star Hôtel** – *14 r. Biscarra.* ℘*04 93 85 19 03. www.hotel-star.com. Closed 15 Nov–24 Dec. 20 rooms.* �*6€.* Small hotel away from the bustling town centre offering simple accommo-dations, some with a balcony. Close to the Nice-Etoile shopping centre.

⊜⊜⊜⊜ **La Pérouse** – *11 Quai Rauba-Capéu.* ℘*04 93 62 34 63. www.hotel-la-perouse.com. 58 rooms.* �*21€.* A prime seaside location overlooking the Baie des Anges from the foot of the Château hill, this cosy Provençal-style hotel features a heated swimming pool and grill restaurant set within a garden against the rocky hill. The top floor terrace has panoramic views over the sea, a hot tub and fitness room.

EAT

Salade niçoise, socca, pan-bagnat, poutine, tourte aux blettes, beignets de fleurs de courgettes are just some of the distinctive local specialities to look out for, especially in Le Vieux Nice, the main restaurant district .

⊜ **La Tapenade** – *6 r. Ste-Réparate.* ℘*04 93 80 65 63. Closed Mon.* Curious décor re-creating a typical street from the south of France, with its shutters, terra-cotta flower pots and strings of garlic. Do not miss the surprising fresco painted on the ceiling. The warm, friendly owners will serve you a pizza, a tapenade or any other local speciality.

⊜⊜ **Lou Balico** – *20/22 av. St-Jean-Baptiste.* ℘*04 93 85 93 71. www.loubalico.com. Closed lunch in Jul-Aug.* Three generations of the same family have been serving classic Niçois dishes in this cosy dining room adorned with a piano and guest book with signatures from around the world.

⊜⊜ **L'Escalinada** – *22 r. Pairolière.* ℘*04 93 62 11 71. www.escalinada.fr. Closed 15 Nov–15 Dec.* Nestling in the old quarter, this charming restaurant offers attractively presented regional cuisine in a spruce dining room with rustic overtones. Friendly service.

⊜⊜ **Le Pain Quotidien** – *3 r. St-François-de-Paul (Cours Saleya).* ℘*04 93 62 94 32. Closed Tue.* This country-style restaurant specialising in brunch has long wooden tables where guests sit side-by-side, an original formula conducive to a friendly, convivial atmosphere. In addition to the bread baskets and tasty spreads of jam, honey and hazelnut, there is a wide selection of salads and open sandwiches.

⊜⊜ **La Table d'Alziari** – *4 r. François-Zanin.* ℘*04 93 80 34 03. Closed Sun–Mon.* Unpretentious family restaurant set up in a small alley of the old district. Typical dishes from Nice and the Provence area, chalked up on a slate, are served in a homey décor, together with wine recommended by the owner.

⊜⊜ **Grand Café de Turin** – *5 pl. Garibaldi.* ℘*04 93 62 29 52. www.cafedeturin.com. Closed Tue.* This brasserie, which is over 200 years old, has become an institution in Nice. It serves seafood dishes à la carte at reasonable prices throughout the day. Pleasant, welcoming setting, although a bit noisy on the terrace.

NIGHTLIFE

Casino Ruhl – *1 Promenade des Anglais.* ℘*04 97 03 12 22. www.lucienbarriere.com.* The casino boasts 300 slot machines and has facilities for French and English roulette, blackjack, stud poker, etc. American bar. Dinner is coupled with live performances on Fridays. Themed evenings on Thursdays.

Le Relais – *Hôtel Negresco, 37 Promenade des Anglais.* ℘*04 93 16 64 00.* The sumptuous decoration of this bar belonging to the legendary Negresco Hotel has remained the same since 1913: Brussels tapestry (1683), 18C paintings, replicas of the wall lamps adorning the Ballroom in Fontainebleau Château and a rug similar to that chosen by

Napoleon I for the King's Bedchamber in Rome. Piano bar every evening.

La Trappa – *2 r. Jules Gilly.* ℘*04 93 80 33 69.* A lively tapas bar with deep, comfortable settees and red walls awaits you at La Trappa, open since 1886. Sip a Cuban cocktail while you listen to Latin-American music (DJ weekends). Friendly atmosphere and local wine list.

Le Livingstone at Grand Hotel Aston – *12 av. Félix Faure.* ℘*04 92 17 53 00.* A chic rooftop bar providing panoramic vistas over the city.

🛒 SHOPPING

Shopping streets – The streets around Cathédrale Ste-Réparate have many shops selling typical Provençal fabrics *(r. Paradis and r. du Marché)*, arts and crafts *(r. du Pont-Vieux and r. de la Boucherie)*, olive oil and santons *(r. St-François-de-Paul)*.

Markets – There are street markets all over town, including: **Fish market** – *pl. St-François; Tue–Sun 6am–1pm;* **Flower market** – *Cours Saleya; Tue–Sun 6am–5.30pm;* **Marché aux Puces** (Flea market) – *pl. Robilante Tue–Sun 10am–6pm;* **Marché de la Brocante** (Antiques) – *Cours Saleya Mon 7.30am–6pm.* **Alziari** – *14 r. St-François-de-Paule.* ℘*04 93 85 76 92. www.alziari.com.fr.* One of the best addresses in town for olive oil and regional specialities.

La Maison de l'Olive – *18 r. Pairolière.* ℘*04 93 80 01 61.* Marseille soaps made from pure olive oil, lotions and scents for the body and home, and regional products such as dried tomatos, lemon jam, marinated capers and olives, and Provençal herbs and spices.

À l'Olivier – *7 r. St-François-de-Paule.* ℘*04 93 13 44 97. www.olivier-on-line. com.* Every brand of French olive oil with the AOC label is sold in this boutique, originally opened in 1822, in Nice since 2004. Also a fine selection of elegant glassware, dishes, tablecloths.

Confiserie Auer – *7 r. St-François-de-Paule.* ℘*04 93 85 77 98. www.maison-auer.com.* A gorgeous vintage boutique selling candied fruit and crystallised flowers from the Nice region, as well as chocolates, and calissons from Aix.

Confiserie Florian – *14 Quai Papacino.* ℘*04 93 55 43 50. www.confiseriefon-rian.com. Guided tours of the factory 9am–noon, 2–6.30pm.* Candied fruit, lemon, orange and grapefruit preserve, chocolates and sweets, crystallised petals and delicious jams made with rose, violet and jasmine blossom.

Maison Poilpot – Aux Parfums de Grasse – *10 r. St-Gaétan.* ℘*04 93 85 60 77.* This traditional perfumery produces more than 80 different fragrances, including popular Mediterranean scents such as mimosa, rose, violet and lemon.

L'Art Gourmand – *21 r. du Marché.* ℘*04 93 62 51 79.* This Old Nice boutique has nougats, calisson, candied fruit, cookies, pastries, ice cream and northern France specialities. There's a tea room decorated with murals.

CALENDAR OF EVENTS

There are many traditional festivals throughout the year. Ask at the Tourism Office for a complete schedule. Highlights include:

Nice Carnival – This colourful, 2-week extravaganza attracts huge crowds. Events, culminating at Mardi Gras (Shrove Tuesday), include fancy dress, processions, lavish floats, 'battles' where armfuls of flowers and confetti are thrown, and a firework display.

Cougourdons Festival – Cougourdons are dried, painted gourds. The city of Nice pays homage to these vegetables (in the same family as melon, pumplin, squash, cucumber) in early April.

Fête de la Mer et de la St-Pierre – Celebrating the sea and St-Peter on the port and Quai des Etats-Unis the last weekend in June.

Nice Jazz Festival – The Roman amphitheatre is the venue for the jazz festival in the last two weeks of July, attended by leading performers from all over the world. *Cimiez Arenas and Gardens.* ℘*08 92 68 36 22. www.nicejazzfestival.fr.*

Route Napoléon★★

This scenic highway follows the route taken by Napoleon on his return from Elba in 1815. it leads from the Riviera northwest through the Pre-Alps and is marked along its length by the flying eagle symbol inspired by Napoleon's remark: "The eagle will fly from steeple to steeple until he reaches the towers of Notre-Dame".

Michelin Map: 341 B 5-D 6

Info: ℘04 76 68 15 16. www.route-napoleon.com.

Location: The route starts at Golfe-Juan and ends at Grenoble. The highway following the route is mainly the D 6085.

A BIT OF HISTORY

The Emperor escaped from Elba on 26 February 1815, landing on the beach at Golfe-Juan on 1 March.

2 March: After a brief overnight stop at Cannes, Napoleon and his band halted outside Grasse and took to the mule tracks. The next night was spent at Seranon.

3 March: Midday halt at Castellane and overnight in Barrème.

4 March: The party rejoined the highway at Digne, and passed the night at the Château de Malijai.

5 March: The Emperor lunched at Sisteron, then continued. Overnight at Gap.

6 March: At Les Barraques, Napoleon declined the offer of the local peasants to join his force. Overnight at Corps.

7 March: Near Laffrey, the way was barred by troops. Ordered to fire, they hesitated, then broke ranks to shouts of "Vive l'Empereur!" Escorted by the men of the 7th Regiment, Napoleon made a triumphal entry into Grenoble at 7pm.

🚗 DRIVING TOUR

GOLFE-JUAN TO GRENOBLE
336km/208.7mi – allow a whole day.

Leading across the southern Pre-Alps to the long valley known as the Sub-Alpine Furrow, the route can be followed throughout the year.

▷ *Leave Golfe-Juan to the NE on Avenue de la Liberté (D 6007) for 5km/3mi until you reach Antibes.*

Antibes★★

The first settlement here was a trading-post founded by Greek merchants from Marseille in the 4C BC. Reconstructed in the 16C, the castle (**Château Grimaldi**) dates from the 12C, when it was built on the site of a Roman encampment to protect the coast from the incursions of Barbary pirates. Inside, the **Musée Picasso**★ *(Picasso Museum; 4 r. des Cordiers; ℘04 92 90 54 20)* has a superb selection of the master's works, including ceramics, drawings, prints and tapestries *(The Lobster, Two Nudes and a Mirror),* as well as paintings *(Still Life with Watermelon).* The town was purchased from the Grimaldi family by Henri IV because of its strategic position in relation to the Kingdom of Savoy. It was fortified first by François I, then by Vauban. To the west of the **Cap d'Antibes**★★ stretches the fine sandy beach of Golfe-Juan.

▷ *Go E until you hit D 635; follow it N onto La Provençale (A 8/E 80); continue on to Pénétrante Grasse Cannes (D 6185). Once you reach D 9, continue NW to Grasse. 28.5km/17.7mi.*

Grasse★★

Prettily located on the slopes of the Grasse Pre-Alps, the Old Town (**Vieille Ville**★) has picturesque streets lined with tall Provençal houses. Grasse's most famous son was **Jean-Honoré Fragonard** (1732–1806), a painter known for witty depictions of the frivolities of 18C court life. The Salle Fragonarda in the Villa-Musée Fragonard has two of the artist's self-portraits as well as his *Landscape with Washerwomen* and *Three Graces*. For the past three centuries, Grasse has been the world's most important centre of the perfume industry, with perfume manufacturers open to the public and two museums, the **Musée international de la Parfumerie** *(2 bd du Jeu de Ballon; www. museesdegrasse.com)* and the **Musée d'Art et d'Histoire de Provence** *(2 r. Mirabeau)*. To the north of the **Pas de la Faye** with its **view**★★ over mountains and Mediterranean, the road enters Upper Provence (Haute Provence) through the Seranon valley.

◯ *Leave Grasse NW onto av. Gaston de Fontmichel (D 6085); road becomes D 4085. Continue through La Garde and Chaudanne until you reach Castellane. 64km/39.7mi.*

Castellane★

The sheep-grazed valley in which the town is situated is overlooked by the "Roc", a limestone cliff 184m/604ft high. The Castellane Pre-Alps extend over a wide area; they consist of a series of bare ridges through which the River Asse has cut a deep valley.

To the north rise the Digne Pre-Alps, a harsh landscape with a meagre mantle of garrigue vegetation, deeply scored by the beds of torrents. A complex geological history has produced a series of folded ridges through which the rivers have cut deep gorges, as well as long crests of pale rock to the east and broad fertile valleys to the north.

◯ *Head NW on Boulevard Saint-Michel; continue towards D 4085. Bear left on to N 85 (direction Grenoble). Continue N through Châteauredon until you hit Digne-les-Bains. 52km/32mi.*

Digne-les-Bains★

Digne spreads out along its valley **site**★ at the foot of the rise on which its old town is situated. There are dramatic **views**★ of the whole area from the hill-top village of **Courbons**★, 6km/3.7mi to the north. In the Place General-de-Gaulle is a memorial to **Pierre Gassendi** (1592–1655), born at nearby Champtercier. This natural philosopher was provost of the cathedral here; much of his scientific work was devoted to studying the properties of sound.

At **Malijai**, the route enters the **Durance basin**, an alluvial plain 6km/3.7mi wide in places, lying between the Valensole plateau to the east and the Vaucluse to the west. The Durance is the great river of the southern Alps, tracing its meanders through the gravel terraces on which a prosperous agricultural pattern has developed, favoured by the mildness of the climate.

◯ *Leave Digne-les-Bains to the SW along N 1085 for 6km/3.7mi or so; at roundabout take 2nd exit onto N 85 (direction Grenoble). Follow N 85 as it winds NW and becomes D 4. At Briasc, move onto L'Autoroute du Val de Durance (A 51/E 712) heading N following Durance river. Sisteron is about 6km/3.7mi from Briasc.*

Sisteron★★ – ◔ *See SISTERON.*
◯ *Head out of Sisteron NW on A 51/E 712. The road merges into N 85. Bear NE until you reach Gap. 50.5km/31.4mi.*

Gap★

Gap is pleasantly sited in the valley carved out by the glacier which was the ancestor of the Durance. The town's prosperity was built on the rich soils of its agricultural hinterland, one of the most fertile areas of the southern Alps. Founded by the Gauls, Gap became a staging-post along the Roman road from Turin to Valence, then a fortified cathedral town.

The **Col Bayard** (1 246m/4 088ft) links the southern and northern Alps. From the viewing table at Chauvet on the south side of the pass the view extends over the valley around Gap. To the north is the beginning of the Sub-Alpine Furrow which the road enters by way of the Drac valley, hollowed out in the beds of schist by the action of the

Quaternary glaciers. This is an ancient highway, once travelled by merchants on their way to the fairs at St-Bonnet. Terraced villages line the route, their roofs tiled in brown stone. To the left are the precipitous slopes and savage peaks of the Dévoluy Massif, to the right the Valgaudemar valley threading its way deep into the Écrins National Park.

▷ *Leave Gap N by N 85; follow N 85 as it bears NE until you reach Corps. 39.6km/24.6mi.*

Corps

A small bustling town in the Sub-Alpine Furrow. The road passes through areas of well-cultivated farmland interrupted by glacial bars, one of which has been used in the siting of the Sautet Dam (**Barrage de Sautet**★★ – *5km/3mi W*), with its deep lake hemmed in by high canyon-like walls; far below its surface is the hidden confluence of the Drac with the Souloise. Around La Mure, the Trièves country is overlooked by the broad summit of Mont Aiguille (2 086m/6 844ft), also known as the "unclimbable mountain" though it was actually conquered as long ago as 1492.

▷ *Leave Corps NW by r. des Fosses (D 1085) and continue for 24.5km/15mi. Turn left at D 1085/r. de Breuil and keep following D 1085 for about 14km/9.3mi N, passing Lac de Pierre-Châtel, Lac de Petichet and Lac de Leffry until you reach Leffry.*

Laffrey★

Just south of the village lies the spot known as **"Prairie de la Rencontre★"**, where the vain attempt was made to bar Napoleon's progress northwards. The road now descends towards **Vizille**★ and Grenoble.

St-Tropez★★

After half a century of fame, the little town of St-Trop' (as the locals call it) is still in fashion, thanks to an exquisitely picturesque harbour, a stunning location, and a constant stream of artists, journalists and photographers.

VISIT

Celebrities can sometimes be spotted in St-Tropez and the atmosphere is created by an impressive array of luxury charter yachts moored in the picturesque harbour, which teems with life.

The old fishing village, which was discovered by writer **Guy de Maupassant** and his friend painter **Paul Signac**, and went on to attract Matisse and major Post-Impressionist artists as well as the writer **Colette**, remains a fashionable resort frequented by writers and artists and more recently by celebrities from the entertainment world.

Two *Bravades*, or "acts of defiance", take place each year in May. The first is a religious procession in honour of St-

▸ **Population:** 5 444
⟡ **Michelin Map:** 340 O 6
▤ **Info:** Quai Jean-Jaurès. ℘0892 68 48 28. www. ot-saint-tropez.com.
▷ **Location:** St-Tropez can be reached from W or S on the congested road that encircles the St-Tropez Peninsula. The easiest and most enjoyable way to approach is on the water, especially the short passenger ferry crossing from the marina resort of Port Grimaud, on the other side of the bay. The real centre of town is Place des Lices. For visitors, the focus is the quayside.
▣ **Parking:** Parking is difficult; use the large car parks on the edge of town.

Tropez, the second commemorates an event of local history which took place in 1637.

Musée de l'Annonciade★★
pl. Georges Grammont. ○*Open Jun–Sept Wed–Mon 10am–noon; Oct and Dec–May 10am–noon, 2–6pm.* ○*Closed 1 Jan, 1 May, Ascension Day, 25 Dec;* ▭*6€.* ℘*04 94 17 84 10.*
The museum, in an old house delightfully positioned on a bend in the quayside, has an impressive permanent collection, including post-Impressionist pictures of St-Tropez and also some remarkable temporary exhibitions.

EXCURSIONS
St-Tropez Peninsula★★
St-Tropez is located is on the north coast of the peninsula. Its east coast is fringed with popular sandy beaches, notably the famous **Plage de Pampelonne**. The south coast has some scenic rocky headlands. The interior is hilly and rustic, with small vineyards, pine copses and two charming old villages commanding wide views, **Ramatuelle** and smaller **Gassin**. A **footpath** extends around the coast of the whole peninsula.

Massif des Maures★★★
The long, low parallel ranges of the massif unfold from Fréjus to Hyères. Its fine forests of pine, cork oak and chestnut trees have often been devastated by fire. Chapels, monasteries and small villages are dotted in the hinterland, while the coast is fringed by coves, bays and small beach resorts.

ADDRESSES

☖ STAY
⊜ **Bello Visto** – *Place deï -Barri, Gassin, 8km/5mi SW of St-Tropez.* ℘*04 94 56 17 30. www.bello-visto.com. Closed Jan and Nov. 9 rooms.* ▭*8€.* There's truth in the name of this small family-run out-of-town hotel and restaurant at the top of Gassin village. Most rooms, like the terrace, profit from a "beautiful vista" over the Massif des Maures and the gulf of St-Tropez. Dining room with Provençal cuisine.

⊜⊜–⊜⊜⊜ **Hôtel Lou Cagnard** – *av. Paul-Roussel.* ℘*04 94 97 04 24. www.hotel-lou-cagnard.com. Closed 1 Nov–26 Dec. 19 rooms.* ▭*10€.* Enjoy breakfast in the shade of a mulberry tree in the tiny garden of this pretty Provençal house, just off Place des Lices. At night you'll be lulled to sleep by the chirping of cicadas. Modest prices, for St-Tropez.

⊜⊜⊜ **Hôtel de La Ponche** – *3 r. des Remparts.* ℘*04 94 97 02 53. www. laponche.com. Closed 2 Nov–3 Apr. 18 rooms.* ▭*19€.* The rooms of this cosy hotel occupy four village houses formerly belonging to fishermen; the blue one was a favourite of Romy Schneider's. The rooftop terraces nestle between the citadel and the bell-tower and the warm, bright hues, combined with considerate service, make the Hôtel Ponche an absolute must.

� EAT
⊜⊜ **Leï Salins** – *rte des Salins.* ℘*04 94 97 04 40. Closed 15 Oct–31 Mar.* Open-air beach restaurant offering a tasty bill of fare consisting of salads and grilled, freshly caught fish. Charming seaside location coupled with attractive surroundings.

⊜⊜⊜ **Leï Mouscardins** – *1 r. Portalet.* ℘*04 94 97 29 00. Closed Wed off-season.* Tucked away behind the harbor, near Tour du Portalet, this restaurant pays homage to Mediterranean tradition. It has a faithful following of food lovers, lured by its creative and lovingly prepared cuisine, presented to you in two dining rooms opening out onto St-Tropez Bay.

⊜⊜⊜ **Régis Restaurant** – *19 r. de la Citadelle.* ℘*04 94 97 15 53. Closed 1 Nov–10 Jan.* Pasta in all shapes and sizes, cooked in various ways, as well as sushi and wok stir-frys, attract a regular clientele to this restaurant located on a steep, narrow street in St-Tropez. The food is served on the terrace or inside one of the small dining areas decked out in white.

⊝⊜🍽 **La Table du Marché** – *38 r. Georges-Clemenceau. ✆04 94 97 85 20. www.christophe-leroy.com/table marchesttropez.* Gourmets will love this temple of gastronomy located near Place des Lices, open at all hours of the day. In addition to the restaurant offering traditional French cuisine, La Table du Marché is also known for its homemade pastries that can be purchased on the premises.

🎭 NIGHTLIFE

Bar du Château de la Messardière – *rte de Tahiti. ✆04 94 56 76 00.* This bar belongs to one of the Riviera's most prestigious hotels. Cosy ambience in the piano bar of this former 18C private residence.

Le Bar du Sube – *15 quai Suffren sur le Port. ✆04 94 97 30 04.* Right on the quayside, one of the most beautiful bars in town. Model boats decorate the comfortable interior.

Sénéquier – *quai Jean-Jaurès. ✆04 94 97 20 20.* The sidewalk terrace and crimson chairs of this tea room are

famous throughout the world – or so say the locals! Renowned personalities such as Jean Marais, Errol Flynn and Colette would come here for the many delights on offer.

🛒 SHOPPING

Markets – *Tue and Sat, Place des Lices.*
Shopping streets – *r. Clemenceau, r. Gambetta and r. Allard* offer an impressive selection of local arts and crafts: pottery, glassware, etc.

Les Sandales Tropéziennes – *16 r. Georges Clemenceau. ✆04 94 97 19 55.* The Rondini house has been crafting St-Tropez sandals since 1927. The distinctive, namesake model in natural leather is the most popular, but the snakeskin version sells well, too!

Le Petit Village – *at La Foux roundabout, follow signs to Grimaud/Cogolin. It is located at 500m/546yd on the left. ✆04 94 56 32 04.* This showroom brings together wines from eight prestigious vineyards on the St-Tropez peninsula, just off the busy La Foux intersection.

Saorge★★

The gorges★★ of the Upper Roya form a spectacular setting★★ for the village clinging to the steep south-facing slopes which rise abruptly from the river far below.

A BIT OF HISTORY

Saorge was originally a Ligurian settlement and then later a Roman colony. In the Middle Ages the town was said to be impregnable but it has yielded twice since: in 1794 to the French and in again in April 1945.

VISIT

Saorge is dominated by the belfries of its churches and monasteries, overlooking terraces and balconies, old houses with open-fronted drying lofts and roofs tiled with heavy stone slabs. A maze of stepped and tunnelled streets completes this highly picturesque townscape.

▶ **Population:** 396
⏱ **Michelin Map:** 341 G 4
▤ **Info:** Av. Docteur Joseph Davéo. ✆04 93 04 51 23. www.saorge.fr.
◑ **Location:** The village is high in the back country of the Riviera, close to the Italian border.

EXCURSION

Notre-Dame-des-Fontaines★★
17km/10.5mi NE via St-Dalmas-de-Tende, 4km/2.5mi E of La Brigue. ⚷The key to the chapel is kept at La Brigue.
In the 15C this church was an important piace for pilgrims.

Abbaye du
Thoronet★★

Of the "Three Cistercian Sisters of Provence" (the others are Silvacane and Sénanque), Le Thoronet is the earliest; it was founded in 1136, when St Bernard was still alive. It is one of the most characteristic of Cistercian abbeys, as well as one of the most austere.

VISIT

&⏱Open Apr–Oct Mon–Sat 10am–6.30pm, Sun 10am–noon, 2–6.30pm; Nov–Apr Mon–Sat 10am–1pm, 2–5pm, Sun 10am–noon, 2–5pm. ⏱Closed 1 Jan, 1 May, 1 and 11 Nov, 25 Dec. ⬤7€. ℘04 94 60 43 90/98. http://thoronet. monuments-nationaux.fr.

The plain architecture of the abbey is unrelieved by decoration, save in the

- ♿ **Michelin Map:** 340 M 5
- ▶ **Location:** The abbey is set deep in the Provençal back-country, close to the River Argens, between Brignoles and Draguignan. It can be reached from autoroute A 8, junction 13.

chapter-house, where just two roughly sculpted capitals relieve the prevailing rigour. The abbey **church**★ has a simple beauty. Built from 1160 onwards, it has remarkable stonework which was cut and assembled without the use of mortar (notably in the oven-vaulted apse). The **cloisters**★ of about 1175 have kept their four barrel-vaulted walks; the change of level is more obvious here than in the church and is still causing problems of subsidence.

Toulon★★

Backed by high hills whose summits are crowned by forts, Toulon is France's second most important naval base, set in one of the Mediterranean's most beautiful harbours. The Old Town of Toulon is located on the Old Port, or Vieille Darse, bounded to the east by Cours Lafayette, to the west by Rue Anatole-France and to the north by Rue Landrin. The greater Toulon area includes the towns surrounding the harbours (Grande Rade and Petite Rade) as well as the Bay of Lazaret formed by the peninsula of the Presqu'île de St-Mandrier. The Old Town is accessible to pedestrians only.

SIGHTS
La rade★★
Construction of Toulon's Old Port (Darse Vieille) began under Henri IV. Richelieu appreciated the strategic advantages of the roadstead and ordered the building of the first naval installations. In the reign

- ▶ **Population:** 519 640
- ♿ **Michelin Map:** 340 K 7
- ℹ **Info:** 334 av. de la République. ℘04 94 18 53 00. www.toulontourisme.com.
- ▶ **Location:** The city is 64km/39.7mi E of Marseille. Autoroute A 50 passes through the centre.
- 🅿 **Parking:** The largest parking areas are located on the Place d'Armes, Place de la Liberté/Palais Liberté, and at the Centre Mayol.
- ◉ **Don't Miss:** A boat trip around the immense natural harbour (rade) is especially enjoyable (1hr; 9€; ℘04 94 93 07 56). Also don't miss the winding streets of the Old Town and Old Port around the Arsenal and Quai Cronstadt.
- 👥 **Kids:** Musée de la Marine.

of Louis XIV, the base was extended and the New Port (Darse Neuve) laid out by Vauban. In the 19C, the Mourillon extension and the Castigneau basin were built, completing the naval base which had become the home port of the French Mediterranean Fleet.

Beyond the harbour lies the magnificent Outer Roadstead (Grande Rade), approached via the Inner Roads (Petite Rade), guarded to the north by the Royal Tower (Tour Royale) and the main jetty, to the south by Vieille Point; it is here that the naval base with all its installations and repair yards is located. The still-considerable remains of the French fleet had anchored here after the disaster of Mers-el-Kébir in 1940, when the Royal Navy had turned its guns on the ships of its defeated ally in order to prevent them falling into German hands. The same danger threatened in July 1942; in response to the Allied landings in North Africa, the Germans had swiftly overrun the hitherto-unoccupied part of France. Caught by surprise and unable to escape, 60 warships scuttled themselves, only a few submarines managing to make their way to the open sea.

View of Toulon from Mont Fanon

D. Chapuis/MICHELIN

Port★

To the west of the Quai Cronstedt (landing-stage for boat-trips) is the **Navy Museum** (Musée de la Marine). Once the entrance to the old Arsenal, its doorway is a Louis XV masterpiece; it is flanked by sculptures of Mars and Bellona and has marble columns with Doric capitals framing tableaux of maritime motifs. The balcony of the former **Town Hall** is supported by two splendidly muscular **Atlantes**★, the work of Pierre Puget.

Mont Faron★★★

This distinctive yet small massif, 584m/1916ft, rising behind the town is the easternmost of the limestone ranges which were raised up in Provence on the fringe of the great earth movements associated with the formation of the Alps in Tertiary times. A telepherique travels over pine clad slopes to the summit, an exciting experience, with thrilling views of Toulon, the inner and outer anchorages, the St-Mandrier and Cap Sicié Peninsulas and Bandol. (*bd Amiral Vence;* 6.60€; 04 94 92 68 25).

Musée-mémorial du Débarquement en Provence★

Summit of Mont Faron. ⚭ Open *Tue–Sun 10am–noon, 2–4.30pm.* 3.80€. 04 94 88 08 09.

From the tower, Tour Beaumont (507m /1 663ft), there are fine views inland as well as a magnificent seaward **panorama**★★★ over the Hyères Islands, the Toulon roadstead and the whole of the coast between Sanary and Bandol. The diorama explains the course of the landings which took place on the night of 14–15 August 1944, and of the subsequent liberation of the coast between Antheor and Marseille.

This second front supplemented the one already opened up by the Normandy landings, and forced the Wehrmacht to beat a rapid retreat to avoid being cut off.

ADDITIONAL SIGHTS

Corniche du Mont Faron★★ *(Corniche Road)*
🚹 **Musée de la Marine**★ *(pl. Monsenergue)*
Vieille ville★ (old town).
Navire de débarquement "La Dives" (landing craft)

Languedoc-Roussillon follows the arc of the coastal plain from the mighty River Rhône to the massive barrier of the Pyrénées. Adjoining the Languedoc-Roussillon on its western edge, the Midi-Pyrénées stretches from the mountains of the south to the Massif Central in the north. It is a hugely diverse area ranging from seaside resorts to mountain villages and rural hamlets, not to mention some large towns and cities in both regions.

Highlights

1 Restored Medieval walled city of **Carcassonne** *(p342)*

2 Fortified Templar settlement on the Causse: **La Couvertoirade** *(p361)*

3 The last stronghold of the Cathars: **Château de Montségur** *(p370)*

4 The magnificent meander of the **Cirque de Navacelles** *(p350)*

5 Abbey on an eagle's eyrie: **St Martin-du-Canigou** *(p354)*

Geography – Along the southern edge of the Massif Central stretch the Grands Causses and the corniche roads offer unforgettable views. The Cévennes to the east, consist of granite summits and deep, narrow valleys that merge with the scrubby *garrigues*. The plains of Lower Languedoc and Roussillon are bordered by a chain of brackish lakes, separated from the Mediterranean by sandy bars.

The south of the region is dominated by the huge natural barrier of the Pyrénées. To the west the Garonne flows through the heartland of the Midi-Pyrénées and to the north, the Lot meanders through the wine region of Cahors.

History – The Languedoc-Roussillon plain was used by Hannibal after he crossed the Pyrénées en-route to Rome (214 BC). By the 2C AD the Romans were in control but eventually the region was ruled by the Counts of Toulouse. Following the Cathar heresy, French kings took control; the region has been part of France since. Further west, Gascony and the Quercy all belonged to the English in the Middle Ages but later reverted to France.

Today – The Languedoc-Roussillon is characterised by its vineyards, which are the mainstay of local economy. Tourism is also important, and the coast between Agde and Argeles boasts several resorts. Around Toulouse the aerospace industry is key, while the rest of the Midi-Pyrénées is given over to agriculture and tourism.

Massif de L'Aigoual★★★

Languedoc-Roussillon

The immense forces involved in the formation of the Alps in the Tertiary era acted on the ancient granitic foundation of this landscape, uplifting it to form a massif which reaches its highest point at **Mont Aigoual**★★★ (1 567m/5 141ft). Subsequent erosion, all the more vigorous because of high precipitation and the low elevation of the surrounding country, has created a landscape of long straight ridges cut by deep ravines. These well-watered highlands make a striking contrast to the arid landscapes of the neighbouring *causses* where any rainfall is immediately absorbed by the porous limestone.

A BIT OF HISTORY

From 1875 onwards a massive programme of reafforestation was undertaken by the state; the forest today covers some 140sq km/54sq mi. Tree growth is particularly vigorous on the more exposed western slopes. In the last 20 years conifers have been

- 🕹 **Michelin Map:** 339 G 4
- 🛈 **Info:** Maison de l'Aigoual, L'Espérou. ✆04 67 82 64 67. www.causses-aigoual-cevennes.org.
- ▶ **Location:** Rising high at the heart of the Cévennes National Park, the Aigoual summit, 37km/23mi S of Florac, is reached on the steep D 118.
- 🕔 **Timing:** Choose a fine day for your visit – otherwise mist may reduce the view.

added to the beeches planted in the 19C. There are sweet chestnuts too, the traditional tree of the Cévennes, growing at altitudes of 600–900m/1 968.5–9 842.5ft.

VISIT

Panorama★★★

From the viewing table at the top of the meteorological station the view extends over the Causses and the Cévennes. The clearest days are in winter, when it is sometimes possible to see both Mont-Blanc (🕹*see MONT-BLANC)* and the Maladeta Massif in the Pyrénées.

Meteorolbgical station on top of Mount Aigoual

©macuazahn/Bigstockphoto.com

Principat d'
Andorra★★
Principality of Andorra

No mere tax-free shopping haven, this tiny Catalan-speaking nation in the high Pyrénées is also a wild, scenic land of lofty plateaus and precipitous valleys.

A BIT OF HISTORY
Andorra (with an area of just 464sq km/179sq mi) was through the centuries a possession of Catalan counts and bishops, and from 1278 was shared between the Count of Foix and the Bishop of Urgell ('co-principality'). In 1993 it was given the freedom to abandon its former feudal status and become an independent state. Despite a remote location, It is prospering with hydro-electric power and all-year-round tourism.

▶ **Population:** 71 822
⚲ **Michelin Map:** 343 G-H-i 9-10
▦ **Info:** 26 av. de l'Opéra 75001 Paris. ℰ01 42 61 50 55. www.tourisme-andorre.net.
▷ **Location:** There are few towns or roads. A single highway crosses the territory through the capital, Andorra La Vella.

SIGHTS
Andorra la Vella
The capital is a bustling commercial town. Away from the main road, the town's heart preserves quiet old streets. To the east it merges with Escales.

Port d'Envalira★★
This pass, highest in the Pyrénées (2 409m/7 903.5ft), marks the watershed between the Mediterranean and the Atlantic. There is a superb **panorama**.

Carcassonne★★★
Languedoc-Roussillon

Like a picture in a story book, Carcassonne's walled Cité seems to have been preserved untouched since the end of the Middle Ages.

A BIT OF HISTORY
The site of the Cité was first fortified by the Gauls; their entrenched camp served Roman, Visigoth and Frank in turn. In the 9C, Carcassonne became the capital of a county, then of a viscounty subject to the County of Toulouse. In common with the rest of the South of France it enjoyed a long period of prosperity which was brought to an end by the Crusade against the 'Albigensians' – Cathars. On 1 August 1209 the army of crusaders under Simon de Montfort arrived at the walls of Carcassonne and besieged the city. Within a fortnight, the attackers had seized the Viscount, Raymond-Roger

▶ **Population:** 43 950
⚲ **Michelin Map:** 344 E-F 3
▦ **Info:** 28 r. de Verdun. ℰ04 68 10 24 30. www.carcassonne-tourisme.com.
▷ **Location:** The walled medieval Cité stands on higher ground on the right bank of the River Aude. The Lower Town lies on lower ground on the left bank.
▣ **Parking:** When visiting the Cité, use the car parks outside the walls in front of the east gateway, Porte Narbonnaise.
⚯ **Don't Miss:** The view of the Cité from a distance, especially from autoroute A 1, is spectacular.
◔ **Timing:** Allow half a day to visit the fortified Cité.

CARCASSONNE
THE FORTIFIED TOWN

0   100m

Tour Notre-Dame

LOWER

BAILLEY

T. de Samson

Tour de la Charpenterie

T. du Moulin du Connétable

Watch tower

T. de la Chapelle

Tour du Major

Tour du Trésau

St-Gimer

T. de la Poudre

T. des Casernes

Tour de Bérard

CHÂTEAU COMTAL

T. de la Porte du Château

Barbacane du Château

Barbican

Tour de Guet

Porte Narbonnaise

Tour de la Justice

T. St-Paul

Pl. du Prado

Avant-porte de l'Aude

Porte d'Aude

Tour de la Peyre

Tour Wisigothe

BAILLEY

Tour de l'Inquisition

T. Carrée de l'Évêque

St-Nazaire

Tour de Balthazar

Tour de la Vade

T. Cahuzac

Tour dú Plô

Watch tower

UPPER

Théatre

Tour St-Nazaire

T. des Prisons

Tour Pouléto

T. Mipadre

T. du Grand Brulas

Barbican

T: Tour (Tower)

▬	5C - 7C	Visigoths
▬▬▬	8C - 13C	before Louis IX / Louis IX / Philip the Bold

Trencavel and the town capitulated. In 1240 his son tried to recapture his inheritance with the aid of the townspeople, but the attempt failed; Louis IX razed the fortifications and sentenced the inhabitants to seven years of exile for their treachery. After serving their term they were allowed to settle here again, but only on the far bank of the River Aude, which became today's Lower Town (Ville Basse). This was laid out in typical *bastide* fashion and the line of its ramparts is now marked by the ring of boulevards.

LA CITÉ★★★

The Cité is the upper town within its impressive ramparts. Louis IX restored and reinforced the Cité both to hold down France's new territorial acquisitions and to defend the kingdom against Spain. His son Philippe le Hardi (the Bold) strengthened the defences still further, making Carcassonne "the Virgin of Languedoc", in other words, impregnable. During the Hundred Years' War, the Black Prince, unwilling to risk a frontal assault, contented himself with burning the lower town to the ground. In 1659 Roussillon was incorporated into France, pushing the vulnerable frontier zone southward. This, together with the invention of modern artillery, meant that Carcassonne's strategic significance was now nil; abandonment and decay followed. Then, in the 19C, Romanticism brought the Middle Ages back into fashion; the writer **Prosper Mérimée**, with his taste for ruins, was made Government Inspector of Ancient Monuments; the architect **Viollet-le-Duc** surveyed the remains and in 1844 was put in charge of reconstructing the city. The restoration process lasted until

Guided Tours

There are several guided tour options in the Cité. Contact the tourist office for details. Château Comtal can only be visited as part of a guided tour.

1910, but – although visually impressive – was much criticised as historically inaccurate. Recent alterations, especially to the towers, are intended to correct some of these mistakes.

Fortifications

See Introduction: Art – Architecture: Miltary architecture.

Carcassonne's remarkable defences enable one to imagine what medieval siege warfare was like; they are a veritable catalogue of the architectural ingenuity that went into resisting an attack. There are drawbridges and fixed bridges with portcullises, towers with projecting "beaks" or open on the inside, protected at the top by hoardings and at the base by flared footings, curtain walls with a sentry-walk behind the crenellations, watch-turrets, arrow-slits, machicolations. Even if the attackers succeeded in breaking in, they could be pinned down by covering fire.

Château comtal de la cité

Open daily Apr–Sept 9.30am–6.30pm; Oct–Mar 9.30am–5pm.
Closed public holidays. ⊜8€.
Guided tours (45min) ⊜8€.
04 68 11 70 70. http://carcassonne. monuments-nationaux.fr.

Butting onto the Gallo-Roman ramparts, this was built in the 12C by the Viscounts, the Trencavels. A deep ditch and a barbican separate it from the interior.

Enceinte intérieure

The inner ramparts were first built in the 6C by the Visigoths, though altered and given extra height in the 13C. The original towers can be identified easily; they are slender, rounded on the outside and flat on the inside. The 13C additions include the remarkable "beaked" towers.

Enceinte extérieure

The outer ramparts were begun by Louis IX and completed by Philippe le Hardi (the Bold). Most of the towers are open on the inside; if taken by the attackers they would be difficult to defend against a counter-attack from within.

There are also completely enclosed towers acting as redoubts from which the defence could harass any attackers who had succeeded in gaining entry to the inner ward.

It is possible to date the fortifications by the way in which materials are used. The Gallo-Roman foundations are made up of large blocks fitted together without the use of mortar. The work of the Visigoths is characterised by the use of cube-shaped stones alternating with brick courses often laid in herring-bone fashion.

The Viscounts' buildings are constructed from yellowish sandstone laid rather crudely. The walls built by the kings of France are made up of rectangular stones laid in a regular fashion, smooth-faced under Louis IX, rusticated at the time of Philip the Bold in order to withstand impacts more easily. The curtain-walls and towers of the outer ramparts are unusual in that Roman or Visigothic work is visible at a higher level than the 13C walling. This is because additional work had to be carried out on the foundations when the ground level was lowered to form the outer ward.

Basilique St-Nazaire★

pl. de l'église. Open daily summer 9am–noon, 2–7pm; winter until 5pm.

The **stained glass**★★ and **statues**★★ in this basilica are well worth a visit. The church was first founded in 6C by Théoderic, de facto king of the Visigoths, and has undergone various modifications over the centuries, right up to the 20C. All that remains of the original church is the Romanesque nave.

ADDRESSES

🛏 STAY

Chambre d'hôte La Maison sur la Colline – *Mas de Sainte Croix, 1km/0.6mi S of la Cité on rte de Ste-Croix. 04 68 47 57 94. www.lamaisonsur lacolline.com. Closed 1 Dec–15 Feb. 5 rooms.* Perched on top of a hill, this restored old farm offers a spectacular view of the Cité from its garden. Rooms are spacious and furnished with old dyed objects, in a different colour for each room: blue, yellow, beige, white. Breakfast by the pool in summer.

Hôtel Espace Cité – *132 r. Trivalle. 04 68 25 24 24. www. hotelespacecite.fr. 48 rooms. 7.50€.* Modern hotel with attractive façade at the foot of the citadel. Rooms are functional and clean, without grand luxury but with plenty of light. Warm welcome. Great view of the city walls from the breakfast room.

Hôtel Le Donjon – *2 r. du Comte-Roger. 04 68 11 23 00. www. hotel-donjon.fr. 62 rooms. 12€.* Partly occupying a 15C orphanage at the heart of the Cité, this hotel combining old stonework and renovated décor offers three kinds of room to choose from: with white or rustic furniture in the main building, and modern style in the "Remparts" annex. Brasserie.

🍴 EAT

Le Bar à Vins – *6 r. du Plô. 04 68 47 38 38. Closed last fortnight in Jan.* Situated at the heart of the medieval Cité, this wine bar enjoys a charming shady garden offering a view of the St-Nazaire basilica. Tapas and fast food.

Auberge de Dame Carcas – *3 pl. du Château. 04 68 71 23 23. www.damecarcas.com.* A friendly establishment in the medieval Cité. The good-natured atmosphere and generous menu no doubt contribute to its success – the dining rooms on four levels are regularly packed with people. Carvery on ground floor.

La Tête de l'Art – *37 r. Trivalle. 04 68 47 36 36. Closed Sun.* Food and art go hand in hand in this restaurant specialising in pork dishes, which are served in rooms displaying works of modern painting and sculpture, in between figurines of the mascot itself.

Chez Fred – *31 bd Omer-Sarraut. 04 68 72 02 23. www.chez-fred.fr. Closed Sat, Sun & Mon for lunch.* This modern bistro not far from the station in the lower town is full of life. The cuisine vascillates between Andalusian dishes and daily menus. Food is served in a white-washed room or on the terrace in summer.

L'Écurie – *43 bd Barbès. 04 68 72 04 04. www.restaurant-lecurie. fr. Closed Sun evening.* This restaurant serving fine fare is located in magnificent old stables, where the old horses' stalls now separate the guests. This original setting and the garden-court which is pleasant in summer are popular with local residents, who count it among their favourite places to go.

🛍 SHOPPING

Cabanel – *72 allée d'Iéna. 04 68 25 02 58. Closed Sun.* This liqueur specialist has been here since 1868, selling a wide variety of unusual brews including Or-Kina (made from spices and plants), Micheline (its origins lost in medieval times), and Audoise (called the Cathars' liqueur). Selection of regional wines also available.

Marché aux fleurs, légumes and fruits – *Pl. Carnot. Open Tue, Thu & Sat 8am–12.30pm.* Flowers, fruit and vegetables market overlooked by a marble fountain.

CALENDAR OF EVENTS

Festival de la Cité – *Jul.* Culture festival.
L'Embrasement de la Cité – *14 Jul.* City illuminations.
Spectacles médiévaux "Carcassonne, terre d'histoire" – *Aug.* Medieval festival.
Tournois de chevalerie – *Aug.* Jousting tournament.

Grotte des
Demoiselles★★★

Languedoc-Roussillon

The cave, discovered in 1770, contains an enthralling underground landscape.

- **Michelin Map:** 339 H 5
- **Info:** Plan de l'Ormeau, Ganges. ✆04 67 73 00 56. www.ot-cevennes.com.
- **Location:** The caves are in the upper Hérault valley near the town of Ganges.

VISIT

Guided tours (1hr) Nov–Feb Mon–Sat 2–5.30pm, Sun 10am–noon, 2–5.30pm; Mar and Oct daily 10am–noon, 2–6pm; Apr–Jun and Sept daily 10am–7pm; Jul–Aug daily 10am–7.30pm. Last departure 1hr before closing time. 8.80€. ✆04 67 73 70 02. www.demoiselles.com.

Deposition of calcium carbonate within the cave has produced extraordinary forms, from stalactites and stalagmites and translucent draperies, to the great columns and huge organcase of this underground cathedral. The temperature in the caves is a constant 14°C/57°F.

Mont-Louis★

Languedoc-Roussillon

Mont-Louis occupies a strategic site at the meeting point of three valleys. To the north is the valley of the Aude; its broad upper course is known as the **Capcir**. To the southwest is the Sègre, a tributary of the Ebro, which here flows through the **Cerdagne**, an upland basin; its elevated position (1 200m/4 000ft) diminishes the apparent height of the surrounding peaks, and its high sunshine level led to the construction here in 1949 of the first "solar furnace" **(four solaire)** using parabolic mirrors. Finally, to the west, is the valley of the Têt, which flows out of the Lac des Bouillouses to form the **Conflent**, the major routeway linking the Cerdagne with Perpignan.

A BIT OF HISTORY

The site's importance was confirmed following the **Treaty of the Pyrénées** in 1659, which, by restoring Roussillon to the French crown, made the Pyrénées the legal as well as the natural boundary

- **Population:** 270
- **Michelin Map:** 344 D 7
- **Info:** 3 r. Lieutenant Pruneta. ✆04 68 04 21 97. http://mont-louis.net.
- **Location:** High in the Pyrénées, east of Font-Romeu and Andorra.

of France. Louis XIV set about giving his newly acquired lands some more solid protection than that afforded by a signature; the great Vauban carried out his survey of Roussillon and the Cerdagne in 1679, and, from 1681 onwards, directed the construction of Mont-Louis.

Thus came into being this austere little fortified town, completely contained by its massive ramparts **(remparts★)** and protected by its citadel.

SIGHT

Four Solaire (Solar Furnace)

Guided tours Nov–Jan 10am–4pm; Feb–mid-Jun, mid-Sept–Oct 10am–5pm; mid-Jun–mid-Sept 10am–6pm. 6€. ✆04 68 04 14 89. www.four-solaire.fr.

Installed as long ago as 1953, the solar furnace uses the sun's reflected light to generate heat and power. Its 546 mirrors focus on one point, where the temperature can reach 3 500°C/6 332°F.

Canal du Midi
Languedoc-Roussillon

It is hard to believe that this calm, beautiful, even elegant waterway, now so popular for leisurely boating holidays, was a daunting engineering achievement enabling the transport of industrial goods directly between the Mediterranean and the Atlantic.

- **Michelin Map:** 343 H-I 4, J-K 5 AND 339 A-K 1-3, A-F 9
- **Location:** The Canal runs from Sète on the Languedoc coast to Toulouse, then joins the Canal Lateral to the Garonne and then on to Bordeaux.

A BIT OF HISTORY
The notion of a canal between the Atlantic and the Mediterranean enabling shipping to avoid the long route via Gibraltar had preoccupied not only the Romans but also François I, Henri IV and Richelieu. The natural obstacles, however, seemed insurmountable.

Then in 1662, Pierre-Paul Riquet (1604–80) succeeded in interesting Colbert in overcoming them. The canal was to prove his ruin; all the work was carried out at his own expense and he died six months before the opening. The completed Canal du Midi is 240km/149mi long and has 103 locks; It proved a huge commercial success – too late for the great man.

Becoming obsolete in the late 19C, the canal provides a perfect illustration of pre-industrial techniques. It passed into state ownership in 1897 and today is used mainly by leisure craft. In 1996 it was named as a World Heritage Site by UNESCO.

Canal du Midi

D. Pazery/MICHELIN

Montpellier★★

Languedoc-Roussillon

One of the most charming and agreeable of French provincial cities, lively, cultured Montpellier successfully combines beautiful historical districts, 17C mansions and modern architecture.

A BIT OF HISTORY

By the 11C, Montpellier was an inland port served by the Maguelone lagoon and the Camargue canal. At the time of the first Crusades, there was already considerable trade with the Levant and Near East. Directly and indirectly this led to the founding here in 1137 of Europe's first medical school. It became a university in 1289.

The town passed by marriage into the hands of the King of Aragon, but was bought back by Philippe VI de Valois in 1349. A centre of Protestantism, it was much damaged in the Religious Wars. Louis XIV made it the capital of Lower Languedoc, and encouraged reconstruction, opening a period of high architectural achievement. In recent years too it has been noted for striking architecture, especially the Corum conference centre and the neo-Classical **Antigone district**★ linked to old Montpellier by the Triangle and Polygone shopping centres and also the new Odysseum district.

▶ **Population:** 244 300
◔ **Michelin Map:** 339 i 7
🗒 **Info:** 30 allée Jean-de-Lattre-de-Tassigny. ℘04 67 60 60 60. www.ot-montpellier.fr.
▷ **Location:** Montpellier is situated 92km/57mi NE up the coast from Narbonne. The heart of the town is the spacious traffic-free Place de la Comédie at its centre.
🅿 **Parking:** The city centre is largely traffic free. Leave the car in one of the big underground car parks, such as Parkings Antigone or Esplanade.
⊛ **Don't Miss: Jardin des Plantes** (Botanic Gardens, ⌕ *see Additional Sights*); a stroll in the **Antigone district**★.
🕐 **Timing:** The main atraction is just strolling and relaxing – allow at least a couple of hours for the Old Town. Think about combining your stay in the city with a trip to the nearby Mediterranean resorts of La Grande Motte, Carnon and Palavas.
👪 **Kids: Planétarium Galilée** (⌕ *see Additional Sights*).

Château d'eau, Promenade royale du Peyrou

A. Thuillier/MICHELIN

SIGHTS
Promenade royale du Peyrou★★
This handsome central park constructed to conceal water works, first laid out in 1688, gives a fine **view**★ over the Garrigue and the Cévennes.

Le Vieux Montpellier★★
In the 17C and 18C the medieval town centre was embellished with numerous fine mansions (hôtels), each with its own character but all conforming to common rules of taste.

Among the most impressive, **Hôtel des Trésoriers de la Bourse**★ has kept its fine staircase, and **Hôtel de Varennes**★ integrates Romanesque and Gothic elements.

City Pass

Ask at the tourist office about the City Card: a 24- (15€), 48- (22€) or 72- (28€) hour pass, giving free entry to many sites, discounts on leisure activities and travel.

ADDITIONAL SIGHTS
Musée Fabre★★ (39 bd. Bonne Nouvelle) – 17–20C fine arts, paintings
Musée Atger★ (Faculté de Médecine, 2 r. école de Médecine)
Musée Languedocien★ (7 r. Jacques Coeur) – art, history, archaeology
👥 **Planétarium Galilée** (100 Allée Ulysses – Odysseum)
Le Jardin des Plantes (1 bd Henri IV)

Narbonne★★
Languedoc-Roussillon

An agreeable provincial town near the Languedoc beaches, Narbonne retains vestiges of an exceptionally illustrious history.

A BIT OF HISTORY
The history of this ancient Mediterranean city is a long one, reaching back many centuries BC. After the defeat of Hannibal, the Roman Empire chose Narbonne to be the commercial centre of the Celtic province, with an artificial port created by diverting an arm of the river Aude. Finally it was made the capital of Gallia Narbonensis (today's Languedoc and Provence regions) and flourished right up to the end of the Empire and the arrival of the Visigoths, who made it the capital of their kingdom.

Trading activity continued (Muslim raiders found the city still worth looting in 793), and medieval shipping made use of the extensive shallow lagoons lining the coast behind the rampart of sand bars. However, in the 14C, the city's large and long-established Jewish community was expelled; the famous

▶ **Population:** 46 510
♿ **Michelin Map:** 344 i-J 3
ℹ **Info:** 31 r. Jean Jaurès. ☎ 04 68 65 15 60. www.mairie-narbonne.fr.
▶ **Location:** The town is SE of Béziers and east of Carcassonne.
🅿 **Parking:** The central area is a pedestrian zone. The two nearest car parks are on quai Victor-Hugo, and beneath cours Mirabeau.
👁 **Don't Miss:** The Palais des Archevêques.
🕐 **Timing:** In summer, it's best to explore early in the morning before it's too hot for comfort, then spend the afternoon at indoor venues like the museums.

port silted up, and the town's prosperity came to an abrupt end. The construction of the Canal du Midi in the 17C, the coming of the railway in the 19C, and the development of tourism on the Languedoc coast in the 20C halted the process of decline.

SIGHTS
Cathédrale St-Just★★
r. Armand Gautier. ⏰*Open daily Oct–Jun 9am–noon, 2–6pm; Jul–Sept 10am–7pm.* ✆*04 68 32 09 52.*
The present building was begun in 1272, but halted later in order to preserve the ramparts which would have been breached to build the nave. The choir remains, its vaulting reaching the dizzy height of 41m/135ft. The lofty cloisters (1349–1417) are built in crumbling limestone on the site of a Carolingian church. The cathedral **treasury** has a wonderful late 15C **Flemish Tapestry**★★ in silk and gold thread, a 10C ivory missal plaque and a rare marriage casket in rock crystal with intaglio decoration.

Palais des Archevêques
pl. de l'Hôtel de Ville. ⏰*Open daily Oct–Mar Tue–Sun 10am–noon, 2–5pm; Apr–Sept 10am–12.15pm, 2–6pm.* ⊚*5.20€.* ✆*04 68 90 30 30.*
Many building styles are represented here, from the 12C Old Palace (Palais Vieux), the 13C Madeleine Tower (donjon de la Madeleine) and Gilles Aycelin Tower **(donjon Gilles Aycelin★)**, the 14C St Martial Tower (tour St-Martial) and New Palace (Palais Neuf; ⏰*open daily Oct–Jun 9am–noon, 2–6pm; Jul–Sept 10am–7pm;* ✆*04 68 32 09 52)*, the 17C Archbishops' Residence (Résidence des Archevêques) with its Louis XIII staircase to the City Hall (Hôtel de Ville), with its 19C façade.

Museums
Among the many museums in Montpellier are: **Musée Archéologique**★★ *(390 rte de Pérols)*; **Musée d'Art et d'Histoire**★; *(pl. de l'Hôtel de Ville)*; and **Musée Lapidaire**★ *(pl.Lamourguier)*
Another attraction worthy of a visit is **Basilique St-Paul** *(r. Dupleix and r. de l'Hôtel Dieu)*, where there is a fine **chancel**★.

EXCURSION
Abbaye de Fontfroide★★
⏵ *15km/9.3mi SW.*
This former Cistercian abbey nestles in a quiet, restful corner of the countryside. The fine flame-coloured shades of yellow ochre and pink in the Corbières sandstone used to build the abbey enhance the serenity of the sight, particularly at sunset.

Cirque de Navacelles★★★
Languedoc-Roussillon

- 👤 **Michelin Map:** 339 G 5.
- ⏵ **Location:** The site is reached by turning off the road between Lodève and Ganges, in the Hérault département.

This spectacular 300m/984ft deep basin, separating the Causses – high plateaux – de Larzac and Blandas, marks the former course of the River Vis before it cut through the base of the meander.

VISIT
On the outer sweep of the meander great screes have been formed; the upper parts of the cliffs are made up of exceptionally thick beds, thinning out at the lower levels where traces remain of old buildings and terraces on the marl and clay deposits. On the valley floor a pretty single-arched bridge leads to the village of Navacelles, which once had a priory. The little settlement clings to a rocky outcrop in order to conserve as much as possible of the belt of cultivable land in the former bed of the river.
In contrast to the harsh conditions prevailing on the arid, windswept causses, the valley floor has a mild microclimate which allows figs to be grown.

Perpignan★★
Languedoc-Roussillon

A medieval town, Perpignan is lively and attractive, bursting with vibrant local culture. The town is located in the Pyrénées-Orientales department in SW France.

A BIT OF HISTORY
In the 13C the city prospered from growing trade with the eastern Mediterranean. In 1276, it became capital of Roussillon, part of the Catalan kingdom of Majorca. When the kingdom broke up, Roussillon became part of the principality of Catalonia. From 1463, the French crown tried in various ways to take possession of Roussillon, but met fierce resistance from the local inhabitants.

The province was briefly given to the monarchs of Spain, who fortified it heavily. Local people rebelled against Spanish rule too, and in 1640, Richelieu offered Roussillon a degree of autonomy if it would become part of France, which it agreed to do, leading to the Seige of Perpignan as the Spanish tried to retain the city. The French victory was ratified by the Treaty of the Pyrénées.

SIGHTS
Palais des Rois de Majorque★
4 r. des Archers. ⏱*Open daily Jun–Sept 10am–6pm; Oct–May 9am–5pm.* ⏱*Closed 1 Jan, 1 May, 1 Nov, 25 Dec.* ⏱*4€.* ℘*04 68 34 96 29.*

The origin of this characteristically Catalan palace lay in the desire of James I of Aragon to make his younger son ruler of the "Kingdom of Majorca" with its mainland seat in Perpignan. Flints and pebbles are used to make decorative patterns in the brickwork. See the great hall known as the Salle de Majorque, the lower Queen's Chapel (Chapelle de la Reine) with traces of medieval frescoes and the royal apartments.

▶ **Population:** 117 500
Michelin Map: 344 i 6
Info: Palais des Congrès, Pl. Armand Lanoux. ℘04 68 66 30 30. www.perpignantourisme.com.
Location: The most southerly city in mainland France, Perpignan lies on the banks of the River Têt and its tributary the Basse. The city centres on Place de la Loge and Place Arago.
Parking: There are plenty of car parks in the town, such as in Place Jean Payra, Cours Palmerole, Rue du Général Legrand, Place Arago, 1 av. Général de Gaulle. www.perpignan tourisme.com.

Rue de la Loge★
The civic buildings make a fine architectural group along Rue de la Loge. The **Loge de Mer**★ once housed the tribunal regulating Perpignan's sea-trade. Its walls are of the finest stonework with tall Gothic arches at ground level. The Town Hall (**Hôtel de Ville**★) has been rebuilt a number of times. The upper floor is made of bands of pebbles held in place by brick coursing. The Renaissance courtyard has arcades and 18C wrought-iron grilles. The **Députation**★ , once the seat of the Catalan "Corts"; has a high arched doorway and window-openings with delicate marble columns.

Le Castillet★
pl. de Verdun. ⏱*Open We–Mon Oct–Apr 11am–5.30pm; May–Sept 10am–6.30pm.* ⏱*Closed public holidays.* ⏱*4€.* ℘*04 68 35 42 05.*

This pink brick citadel dates from the reign of Peter IV of Aragon, while the adjacent Notre-Dame Gate was built during the occupation of the city by Louis XI. The **Casa Pairal** is now a Catalan folk museum, the **Joseph**

Deloncle Musée catalan des Arts et Traditions populaires.

Cathédrale St-Jean★
pl. Léon Gambetta. ○*Open daily 9am–noon, 3–7pm.* ✆*04 68 51 33 72.* Work on the cathedral was begun by Sancho of Aragon in 1324 but the building was completed only in 1509. The bell-tower is topped by an 18C wrought-iron cage housing a great 15C bell. Inside, the altarpieces of the high altar and the north chapels are fine work of the 15C and 16C. In an outside chapel is a touching carved wood **Crucifixion**★, known as the Devout Christ.

EXCURSIONS
Musée de Tautavel (Centre européen de préhistoire)★★
○ *av. Léon-Jean Grégory, Tautavel. 27km/16.7mi NW of Perpignan, 9.4km/ 5.8mi NE of Estagel.*
○*Open Apr–Jun and Sept 10am– 12.30pm, 2–6pm; Oct– Mar 10am–12.30pm, 2–5pm; Jul–Aug 10am–7pm.* ⊜*8€.* ✆*04 68 29 07 76.* After the discovery in in the 1970s of fragments of human skull at Tautavel, this little village gave its name to **"Tautavel man"**, hunters living about 450 000 years ago. Highlights of the

excellent museum are a reconstruction of his skeleton and a copy of the cave where ithe bones were found.

La Côte Vermeille★★
Between Argelès Beach and the Spanish border, small towns and ports huddle in bays along the mountainous coast. The picturesque port **Collioure**★★, below its royal castle, attracted artists of the Fauve School in the early 20C. **Banyuls** is famous for its sweet wine. In the hills above, the Madeloc Tower enjoys a wide **panorama**★★ of the Côte.

Fort de Salses★★
○ *20km/12.4mi N of Perpignan, A 9 autoroute.*

Rising strangely above the surrounding vine-covered plain north of Perpignan, this huge and intriguing brick fortress, originally 15C, was adapted by Vauban in the 17C to meet the demands of modern artillery.

SHOPPING
Clothing boutiques are found near r. Mailly. Avenue Gén.-de-Gaulle is also good for shopping, while the "r. des Olives" *(r. de l'Adjudant-Pilot-Paratilla)* is well known for fine foods.

Château de
Peyrepertuse★★★
Languedoc-Roussillon

The dramatic barrier of the Corbières was defended by a number of strongholds of which the ruins of the Château de Peyrepertuse, separated into two distinct castles on their rocky promontory, are the most imposing.

VISIT
○*Open daily Feb–Mar and Nov–Dec 10am–5pm; Apr–May and Oct 10am– 6.30pm; Jun and Sept 9am–7pm; Jul– Aug 9am–8.30pm.* ○*Closed for 3 weeks*

- ◔ **Michelin Map:** 344 G 5
- ○ **Location:** The site is 47km/29mi NW of Perpignan. On D 14, S of Duilhac, look out for the 3.5km/2mi narrow access road that leads to the site.
- ○ **Timing:** Allow 30min for walk up to the castle and back, and an hour to explore.

in Jan. ⊜*5€.* ✆*06 71 58 63 36. www.chateau-peyrepertuse.com.* The Lower Castle (Château Bas) to the east came under Aragonese rule in 1162. In 1240, it surrendered to the Seneschal of Carcassonne acting in the name of the King. Under the terms of the Treaty of Corbeil in 1258, it became part of the fortified French border facing Spanish Roussillon.

The northern curtain wall running to a dramatic point, together with the ruins of the main building, the keep and chapel, give an idea of the changes that took place over the centuries. On the far side of the open area separating the two castles, a monumental stairway has been hewn into the rock.

The royal castle raised on this western height is known as St George's Castle. It was built in the course of a single campaign, probably by Philip the Bold. There are remains of a cistern and a chapel. From its western extremity the view extends over the fortifications capping the neighbouring crests.

In 1659, the incorporation of Roussillon into France by the Treaty of the Pyrénées stripped Peyrepertuse of its strategic importance.

St-Guilhem-Le-Désert★★

Languedoc-Roussillon

In its remote and dramatic **site**★ where the Val de l'Infernet runs into the valley of the Hérault, this 9C **village**★grew up around an abbey founded by William of Aquitaine, one of Charlemagne's most valiant lieutenants.

SIGHTS
L'Abbaye et le Musée du Cloître★

◷*Open Jul–Aug Mon–Sat 9am–12.15pm, 2.30–6.30pm, Sun 9am–11am, 2.30–6.30pm; Sept–Jun Mon–Sat 9am–noon, 2–5.45pm, Sun 9am–11am, 2–5.45pm.*

This is a Romanesque structure of striking simplicity, famed for its possession of a fragment of the True Cross *(in the south transept)*. It has a doorway with dog-tooth moulding, and an apse with massive buttresses and an elegant little arcade. Inside, the width of apse and transept is the result of a rebuilding undertaken in the 11C.

Of the 11–12C cloisters, nothing remains apart from the ground floor of the north walk and part of the west walk.

The sculpted 13C capitals, which once graced the galleries, are now exhibited at the Cloisters Museum in New York.

▶ **Population:** 245
⚙ **Michelin Map:** 339 G 6 – Hérault
ℹ **Info:** Mairie de Saint-Guilhem-le-Désert. *℘*04 67 57 70 17.
◉ **Location:** The village in the Hérault gorge, and can be approached via Gignac and Aniane if coming from the E or S, via St-Félix and Montpeyroux if coming from the N or W.
🅿 **Parking:** All cars must be left in the village's large car park.

Grotte de Clamouse★★★

3km/1.8mi S. ◷*Open daily Jul–Aug 10am–7pm; until 6pm Jun and Sept; until 5pm Feb–May and Oct.* ◉*8.70€.* ◗*Guided tours (1hr). ℘04 67 57 71 05. www.clamouse.com.*

The caves, a UNESCO World Heritage Site, run beneath the Larzac plateau and were carved by an extensive network of underground streams. There are remarkable stalactites and stalagmites, but above all it are the splendid crystallisations in varied evocative shapes (flowers, bushes, bunches of grapes, etc.). ◉*Take a sweater; the temperature inside is 17°C/62.6°F.*

Abbaye de
St-Martin-du-Canigou★★

Languedoc-Roussillon

The abbey of St Martin on Mont Canigou, an eagle's eyrie at 1 055m/3 461ft above sea-level, is one of the great sights of the eastern Pyrénées.

VISIT

Site★★★

To appreciate St-Martin's unusual site, after reaching the abbey (30–50min on foot round-trip from Casteil – uphill walk), take a stairway to the left which climbs through the woods. Turn left past the water outlet. There is an impressive view of the abbey, which lies in the shadow of the Canigou until the late morning. It stands in an imposing site dominating the Casteil and Vernet valleys.

Abbey

Guided tours(1hr) in French Jun–Sept Mon–Sat 10am–noon, 2–5pm 4pm, Sun and religious holidays 10am–12.30pm; Oct–May Tue–Sat 10am–11am, 2–4pm, Sun and religious holidays 10am–12.30pm. 5€. 04 68 05 50 03. http:// stmartinducanigou.org.

Abbaye St-Martin-du-Canigou

M. Buffrad/MICHELIN

- **Michelin Map:** 344 F 7 – Pyrénées Orientales
- **Info:** Saint Martin du Canigous, Casteil. 04 68 05 50 03. http:// stmartinducanigou.org.
- **Location:** The abbey can be reached on foot from Casteil, or by jeep from Vernet-les-Bains (*11€* round-trip; 04 68 05 51 14). The abbey lies 2.5km/1.5mi S of Vernet-les-Bains.
- **Parking:** Park the car in Casteil, then follow a steep road uphill *(1hr round-trip)*.

This Romanesque abbey, built on a rocky pinnacle at an altitude of 1 094m/3 589ft from around 1001–1009, grew up around a monastic community founded here in the 11C. After falling into disuse at the Revolution in 1783, it was restored from 1902–1932 and extended from 1952–1972. At the beginning of the 20C, all that remained of the **cloisters** were three galleries with crude semicircular arches. As part of the restoration, a south gallery has been rebuilt overlooking the ravine using the marble capitals from an upper storey which was no longer extant.

The **lower church** (10C) dedicated to Notre-Dame-sous-Terre in accordance with an early Christian tradition, forms the crypt of the **upper church** (11C). The latter, consisting of three successive aisles with parallel barrel vaults, conveys an impression of great age with its rugged, simply carved capitals. On the north side of the chancel stands a bell-tower crowned by a crenellated platform. Near the church, two tombs have been hollowed out of the rock: the tomb of the founder, Count Gulfred de Cerdagne, which he dug out with his own hands, and that of one of his wives.

The abbey is now home to nuns and priests, who lead the tours, which are supposed to be in silence.

Prieuré de
Serrabone★★

Languedoc-Roussillon

In a wild and stony setting among austere mountains, this former priory contains superb Romanesque sculpture, its severity relieved by delicate pink marble.

VISIT

Boule d'Amont. ⏱*Open daily 10am–6pm.* ⏱*Closed 1 Jan, 1 May, 1 Nov, 25 Dec.* ⊜*3€.*
☏*04 68 84 09 30.*

The chapel gallery (**tribune**★★) of about 1080, originally intended to serve as the choir, was moved to the centre of the nave at the beginning of the 19C. It is

- ⚲ **Michelin Map:** 334 G 7 – Pyrénées Orientales
- ⧉ **Info:** 24 quai Sadi Carnot, Perpignan. ☏04 68 85 85 85. www.cg66.fr.
- ▶ **Location:** The steep winding road up to Serrabonne is a turning (near Ille-sur-Têt) off the mountain highway from Perpignan to Font-Romèu.

an unusual feature to have survived and has wonderful decoration in low relief as well as exceptionally richly carved capitals. A delightful south-facing **gallery**★ (Promenoir des Chanoines) overlooks the ravine far below.

Albi★★★

Midi-Pyrénées

From the bridges spanning the Tarn to the extraordinary cathedral, **Albi "the red"** is made of brick, which owes its rosy hue to the clays dug from the river's bed.

A BIT OF HISTORY

At the start of the 13C, the city was one of the centres of the dualist Cathar doctrine, dubbed the "Albigensian heresy" by a fearful Church.

The subsequent "Albigensian Crusade" of 1209 was directed on the spiritual side by St Dominic and commanded militarily by the fearsome Simon de Montfort; on the ground, armies moved in from north and east to commit the terrible atrocities of Béziers, Carcassonne, Minerve and Lavaur. The Capetian kings took advantage of the troubles from 1208–1229, to gain a foothold in Languedoc, but Catharism itself was finally stamped out only by the Inquisition and the ghastly funeral pyre at Montségur (⏍*see CHÂTEAU DE MONTSÉGUR*).

- ▶ **Population:** 47 800
- ⚲ **Michelin Map:** 338 D 6, E 7
- ⧉ **Info:** Palais de la Berbie, pl. Ste-Cécile, Albi. ☏05 63 49 48 80. www.albi-tourisme.fr.
- ▶ **Location:** Albi is 77km/47.8mi NE of Toulouse. The town was built around the cathedral and t better understand the massive proportions of the cathedral, view it from a distance, preferably the bridge across the Tarn (the Pont du 22-Août), or from one of the streets of Old Albi.
- ⏱ **Timing:** Start the day at "la Berbie" on Place Ste-Cécile, opposite the cathedral; sample some local specialities at "Pâtisserie Galy" (7 r. de Saunal); enjoy a boat trip on the river to appreciate the beauty of the city at its best.

SIGHTS
Cathédrale Ste-Cécile★★★

5 bd Sybille. &⌚*Open daily Jun–Sept 9am–6.30pm; Oct–May 9am–noon, 2–6.30pm.* ∞*3€.* ✆*05 63 43 23 43.*

Construction of the cathedral, extending over two centuries, began in 1282 at a time when work on the neighbouring Berbie Palace, the bishops' residence, and on that of the Dominicans at Toulouse, was already well advanced. For the bishops, the status of the church was inextricably linked to its temporal power and they therefore gave their cathedral the appearance of a fortress. In the 19C the formidable edifice acquired the three upper storeys of its keep-like bell-tower, its machicolations and its inspection gallery.

Inside, the perfect simplicity of the single broad nave with its Southern French Gothic side chapels passes almost unnoticed, such is the exuberance of the Flamboyant decorative scheme. The rood screen (**jubé**★★★), one of the few to have survived, is also one of the most sumptuous. In the 15C and 16C all the greater churches possessed such a screen; it separated the clergy, in the choir, from the lay worshippers in the nave; during services readings would be given from its gallery. This example dates from 1485, as does the screen closing off the choir (**chœur**) (&⌚*open daily Jun–*

Albi Pass

This visitors' card gives numerous discounts at sites and monuments, shops and attractions. Valid for a year, it costs 6.50€ from the tourist office.

Sept 9am–6.30pm, rest of year 9am–noon, 2–6.30pm; ∞*1€;* ✆*05 63 43 23 43);* its arches and gables, columns and arcading all show the extraordinary skill and attention to detail of the craftsmen who worked the white limestone. The naturalistic poses and facial expressions typical of Gothic art are here brought to a fine pitch. Old Testament figures are on the outside, those from the New Testament on the side of the choir, where there are two rows of 66 stalls. The vaults were painted from 1509 to 1512 by Bolognese artists; they repay study with binoculars.

The hallucinatory **Last Judgement** is a masterpiece of late 15C mural painting; it was unfortunately disfigured by the installation in the 17C of the great organ. But it is nevertheless possible to admire the upper part depicting the Heavenly Kingdom: on the left the Apostles, haloed in gold, and the saints as well as the elect bearing the book of their life held open; on the right the damned, punished by their sin itself.

CATHÉDRALE STE-CÉCILE

1	Judith	5	Esther	9	Chapelle Sainte-Croix
2	Prophet Zephaniah	6	Charlemagne	10	Painting of the Holy Family
3	Prophet Isaiah	7	Constantine	11	Chapelle du Rosaire
4	Prophet Jeremiah	8	Statue of Virgin and Child	12	Last Judgement

Palais de la Berbie★

🕐*Open year-round varying hours, call or see website for times.* 🕐*Closed 1 Jan, 1 May, 1 Nov, 25 Dec.* ⊜*5.50€.* 📞*05 63 49 48 70. www.mairie-albi.fr/arthisto/ lieux/museetl.html.*

The former Bishops' Palace houses the **Musée Toulouse-Lautrec★★**devoted to the life and art of Henri de Toulouse-Lautrec (1864–1901). The Collection was bequeathed to Albi by the artist's mother,

Comtesse Alphonse de Toulouse-Lautrec and other family members. Born in Albi at the Hôtel du Bosc, Toulouse-Lautrec was crippled in early life by two accidents. He is revealed here as one of the great painters of everyday life; his vision of the depravity and decadence of late 19C Paris is communicated with restraint and compassion (*Jane Avril, Mademoiselle Lucie Bellanger, Au bal de l'Élysée-Montmartre*).

ADDRESSES

🏠 STAY

🍴 **Chambre d'hôte à la Ferme "Naussens"** – *81150 Castanet.* 📞*05 63 55 22 56. Closed Nov–mid Apr. 5 rooms.* A warm and convivial welcome awaits at this farm in the midst of vines. Simple, traditional, family-style cooking using farm produce and washed down with their own wine.

🍴 **La Régence George V** – *27–29 av. du Maréchal-Joffre.* 📞*05 63 54 24 16. www.laregence-georgev.fr. 20 rooms.* ⊒*7€.* It is worth searching out this cosy establishment with its typical local style in the station district. Rooms are a generous size and some have a fireplace. At the first sign of fine weather, make the best of the pleasant shade of the little courtyard.

🍴 **Cantepau** – *9 r.Cantepau.* 📞*05 63 60 75 80. www.hotelcantepau. fr. 33 rooms.* Wicker furniture, subdued hues and fans give this hotel a colonial feel following its recent revamp.Friendly welcome.

🍴 **Hôtel Mercure** – *41 bis r. Porta.* 📞*05 63 47 66 66. 56 rooms.* ⊒*12€.* This modern hotel has an original setting, in an old 18C red-brick mill on the banks of the Tarn. The functional rooms offer a view of the river and cathedral.

🍴 EAT

🍴 **Salon de Thé de la Berbie** – *17 pl. Ste-Cécile.* 📞*05 63 54 13 86.* This attractive tea room, opposite the cathedral, serves a wide range of tea, coffee, pastries, ice cream sundaes and pancakes. Luncheon menu.

🍴 **Le Table du Sommelier** – *20 r. Porta.* 📞*05 63 46 20 10. www.latabledu sommelier.com. Closed Sun & Mon.* The proprietor sets the scene here perfectly, with cases of wine piled high in the entrance and rustic dining room with mezzanine floor. This wine-focused bistro serves refined cuisine using the freshest ingredients.

🍴 **Le Poisson d'Avril** – *17 r. d'Engueysse.* 📞*05 63 38 30 13. Closed Sun.* This restaurant in a typical old Albi house 200m/220yd from the cathedral has an unusual interior décor designed like the inside of a barrel, with wooden beams. Prices are moderate and food is not heavy.

🍴 **Le Robinson** – *142 r. Édouard-Branly.* 📞*05 63 46 15 69. Closed Jan–Mar; Mon & Tue.* This isle of green on the banks of the Tarn is acceible from the pont Neuf. Dating from the 1920's, the old-fashioned dance hall has an exuberant charm. The food is simple and the welcome warm.

🍴 **Jardin des Quatre Saisons** – *19 bd. de Strasbourg.* 📞*05 63 60 77 76. http://lejardindes4saisons.chez-alice.fr. Closed Sun for dinner and Mon.* A friendly welcome from the owners awaits, along with a good selection of wines and traditional cuisine. A little away from the centre, this remains a reliable favourite.

TOURS

Guided Tour of the Old Town (45min) organised by the tourist office, Jul–Aug Mon–Sat. Book at the tourist office**.
Walks** – Three walks allow the visitor to discover Albi : the circuit Pourpre (purple) goes through the heart of old Albi and takes in the main historic sites, characters

and monuments; the circuit Or (gold) focuses on the growth of Albi over two thousand years; the circuit Azur (azure) leads along the banks of the Tarn, taking in the Pont Vieux and the Pont Neuf, and provides some fine views of the town (these routes marked by explanatory signposts in three languages). Depart from the tourist office. Two more guided tours are available (45min): **Tour 1** explores the centre of the medieval city and **Tour 2** follows the life of Antoine Mégret d'Etigny (1719–1767), who masterminded the transformation of Auch during the 18C. Tickets and times available from the tourist office.

🛒 SHOPPING

In the streets of the Old Town (especially *rues Mariès, Ste-Cécile et Verdrusse*) are a variety of antique shops and boutiques. Also, visitors cannot miss the many shops selling local food and drink specialities, including foie gras, confits, anis biscuits and other pâtisserie.

L'Artisan Pastellier – *5 r. Puech-Bérenguier.* ℘*05 63 38 59 18. www.artisanpastellier.com.* Pastels were for centuries an important industry in the region. Near the Maison du vieil Alby, this shop is a poem in blue. Made from pastel leaves, this irresistible colour is used to shade local crafts and fabrics. Calligraphers and artists will also be in their element here among inks, paints and pastels of natural pigments.

Marché biologique (ORGANIC MARKET) – *pl. F.-Pelloutier.* **A BIG RANGE OF LOCAL ORGANIC PRODUCE. Markets**– *pl. Ste-Cécile.* A big market is held on Saturday on place Ste-Cécile: fruit, vegetables, foie gras (in season), mushrooms, garlic from Lautrec, charcuterie from Lacaune et Gaillac wines.

Patisserie Galy – *7 r. Saunal.* ℘*05 63 54 13 37. Closed Sat–Mon, public holidays.* One of the popular pastrycooks of the old quarter, with many local specialities (try out *navettes, gimblettes, croquants aux amandes*).

🏃 LEISURE ACTIVITIES

Boat Trip on the Tarn (Berges du Tarn) ℘*05 63 43 59 63. www.albi-croisieres. com. Open Jun–Sept daily 11am–11.45am. 6€.* The boat is a flat-bottomed barge, a *gabarre*, used for transporting goods until the 19C. Leaving the old harbour at the foot of the ramparts, the barge travels along the Tarn past the old Albi mills.

CALENDAR OF EVENTS

Carnaval – *Feb.* **Coupe de France des Circuits** – *Mar.* Motor Festival. **Marathon d'Albi** – *Apr.* **Free Organ Concerts in the Cathedral** – *Wed and Sun afternoons in Jul and Aug.* **Festival de Tarot** – *Aug.* **Le Grand Prix automobile d'Albi** – *Sept.*

Auch★

Midi-Pyrénées

Auch is an attractive, pleasantly busy local capital in the heart of Gascony.

A BIT OF HISTORY

Auch began in ancient times as a fortified Basque settlement beside the river Gers. For 2 000 years it served as a staging-post on the old Toulouse–Bordeaux highway; its position avoided the treacherously shifting course of the River Garonne to the north. It owes some fame to the story of *The Three Musketeers*

▶ **Population:** 21 838

🕭 **Michelin Map:** 336 E 6-7, C-D-E-F 8

🛈 **Info:** 1 r. Dessoles. ℘05 62 05 22 89. www.auch-tourisme.com.

▷ **Location:** Auch lies 76.4km/47.4mi W of Toulouse. The main streets converge on central Place de la Libération.

⚑ **Don't Miss:** The Escalier Monumental is a majestic flight of 232 steps linking the river to the town centre.

– the real d'Artagnan, Charles de Batz, was from this district.

SIGHTS
Cathédrale Ste-Marie★★
pl. de la République. Open daily. Closed during mass. ℘05 62 05 72 71. http://auch.paroisse.net.

The cathedral's ambulatory contains a masterly series of Renaissance **stained-glass windows (vitraux)** ★★, completed in 1517, and remarkable for their sophisticated use of colour (subtle nuances and gradations and half-tones, all in strong contrast to the pure colours, rigidly separated, of the Gothic), and for the way in which the central figure of each window is surrounded by vignettes elucidating its symbolism and prefiguration (a characteristic humanist device of the time). Adam and Eve, Jonah, and the Nativity are exceptionally fine.

The **choir stalls (stalles)** ★★★ (open daily Apr–Sept 8.30am–noon, 2–6pm; Oct–Mar 9.30am–noon, 2–5pm; 2€), are an inspired work completed in 1554, peopled by 1 500 different figures in an extraordinary wealth of detail. The backs are carved with representations

Stained-glass windows, Cathédrale Ste-Marie

of biblical and other personages; the faces crowding the dividers, elbow-rests, the panels and niches of the backs and the misericords provide an interest and stimulation which are inexhaustible. The opulence characteristic of the Flamboyant style survives in this work of the Renaissance.

Castres★
Midi-Pyrénées

This industrial town on the **Agout** river has fine 16–17C mansions, a Goya museum and makes a good base for exploring the Lacaune and Montagne Noire hill country. The Castres area is the French wool carding centre and its wool industry is second only to Roubaix-Tourncoing.

SIGHT
Musée Goya★
Hôtel de Ville. Open Sept–Jun Tue–Sun 9am–noon, 2–5pm; Jul–Aug daily 10am–6pm. Closed 1 Jan, May, 1 Nov, 25 Dec. 2.30€ summer; no charge 1st Sun in the month (Oct–May). ℘05 63 71 59 30.

▶ **Population:** 43 500
✦ **Michelin Map:** 338 E-F 9-10
▯ **Info:** 2 pl. de la République. ℘05 63 62 63 62. www.tourisme-castres.fr.
◐ **Location:** Castres is 70km/43.5mi E of Toulouse.

Set up on the second floor of the former episcopal palace (presently the Town Hall), this museum specialises in Spanish painting and possesses several outstanding works by Goya, namely *Self-Portrait*, *The Disasters of War*, *Francisco del Mazo* and *The Junta of the Philippines led* by Ferdinand VII.

Conques★★★

Midi-Pyrénées

This tiny medieval town has a splendid hillside **site**★★ best seen from the rock, Rocher du Bancarel (3km/1.8mi south).

▶ **Population:** 362
♿ **Michelin Map:** 338 G 3
ℹ **Info:** Le Bourg. ℘0820 82 08 03. www.conques.fr.
◐ **Location:** The village is just S of the River Lot, 43km/26.7mi E of Figeac.

SIGHTS

Église St-Foy★★

🚶 *Guided tours (45min) Apr–Sept daily.* ⊚*3.60€.*

Completely rebuilt between 1045 and 1060, this is one of the oldest Romanesque pilgrimage churches on the route to Santiago de Compostela.

Its abbey had a chapel and hospice at Roncesvalles to serve the pilgrims as they made their way across the Pyrénées. Within, the spacious nave is flooded with light from the south tribune windows. The dimensions of the transept are exceptional and the ambulatory with its annular barrel vault is also remarkable.

The tympanum (**tympan**★★★) above the west door with its wealth of sculpture forms a striking contrast to the overall plainness of the west front. Traces of the original colouring can still be made out. It shows how sculpture had evolved away from the static solemnity characteristic of Burgundy and Languedoc, towards the greater freshness and spontaneity evident in the capitals of the churches of the Auvergne. It may be that the weighing of souls taking place below the figure of Christ is an expression of the idea – entirely new at the beginning of the 12C – of the personal nature of the Last Judgement.

It seems likely that the tympanum was moved forward by the length of a bay and integrated with the west front in the 15C in order to extend the nave; this move would have led to the displacement of the statues in the north transept.

Trésor★★★

🕐 *Open daily Apr–Sept 9.30am–12.30pm, 2–6.30pm; Oct–Mar 10am–noon, 2-6pm.* ⊚*5.50€. Tickets available at the tourist office.*

The treasury is among the most important in Europe. Its most precious object is the reliquary statue of St Faith (Ste-Foy). The saint's relics had been brought to Conques at the end of the 9C, when they

Town of Conques

© Sylvain Cordier - Fotolia.com

were venerated by prisoners and by the blind. The statue was put together and added to over a long period; some of its features probably go back as far as the last years of the Roman Empire and consist of reused elements of Roman date (face-mask, intaglio work in precious stones, jewels); the gold and engraved crystal are of the Merovingian and Carolingian periods (7C–9C). At the close of the 10C the revered statue was renovated here at Conques and adorned with enamels, cabochons and other precious stones.

Four more of the treasures are of exceptional significance: the initial "A" given to the abbey, it is said, by Charlemagne (a fragment of the Holy Cross decorated in the 11C with intaglio work and with chased and gilded silver); two portable altars, one, St Faith's, in alabaster and chased silver, the other, Abbot Begon's, from the beginning of the 12C, in porphyry and silver inlaid with niello; and the reliquary of Pope Pascal with filigree work and diadems, also from the early 12C.

EXCURSION
Cordes-sur-Ciel★★★
The village is 69m/43mi SW of Conques and 25km/15.5mi NW of Albi. ℘05 63 56 00 52. www.cordes-sur-ciel.org.

Nestling at the top of the peak, Puech de Mordagne, Cordes occupies a most attractive **site**★★ overlooking the Cérou valley.

The superb row of **Gothic houses (maisons gothiques★★)** dating from the 13C and 14C testify to the wealthy past of this quaint little town. Notice the **Maison du Grand Fauconnier★** and the **Maison du Grand Veneur★**. For more than 50 years, artists and craftsmen have contributed to preserving and restoring local tradition.

La
Couvertoirade★
Midi-Pyrénées

High up on the lonely Larzac limestone plateau (*causse*), this old fortified settlement once belonged to the Knights Templar. It has many robustly built houses, typical of the region, with cisterns, outside stairways leading to the main floor, and a vaulted sheep-pen at ground level. Most date from the 17C.

VISIT
The towers and the sentry-walk of the **ramparts** are particularly interesting. Go through the north gateway and, taking great care, climb the steps at the foot of the Renaissance house, following the watch-path round to the left to the round tower for a view over the town and its main street, rue Droite. (◷*open daily Mar and Oct–mid-Nov 10am–noon, 2–5pm; Apr–Jun & Sept 10am–noon, 2–6pm; Jul & Aug 10am–7pm; ☞3€; ☞guided tours (40min); ☞5€).*

- ▸ **Population:** 153
- ◔ **Michelin Map:** 338 I 7
- ▯ **Info:** Service Accueil Tourisme, Mairie. ℘05 65 58 55 59. www.lacouvertoirade.com.
- ◖ **Location:** The village stands to one side of the highway, which crosses Larzac. Park outside the walls and walk through the main gateway. There may be a charge simply to enter the village on foot.

Also see the **fortified church** constructed in the 14C, which is an integal part of the town's defences and has two disc shaped steles showing different representations of the cross and a graveyard with unusual disc-shaped gravestones.

The fortress was built by the Templars in the 12 and 13C but the two upper floors have long since disappeared.

Foix★

Midi-Pyrénées

In the Middle Ages this hill town was important as the capital of the colourful Counts of Foix. Ruggedly set against a skyline of jagged peaks and three castle towers, it overlooks the Plantaurel hills. Its old narrow streets radiate from Rue de Labistour and Rue des Marchands, starkly contrasting with the 19C administrative area fanning out from the Allées de la Villote and the Champ de Mars.

- **Population:** 9 109
- **Michelin Map:** 343 H 7
- **Info:** 29 r. Delcassé. ☎05 61 65 12 12. www.ot-foix.fr.
- **Location:** The town stands on the Ariège between the high hills of the Plantaurel and the Pyrénées proper.

A BIT OF HISTORY

Once part of the Duchy of Aquitaine, the Foix region became a county in the 11C. At the conclusion of the Albigensian Crusade, the Counts, who had favoured the heresy, were obliged to submit to the King of France under the terms of the Treaty of Paris (1229). At the end of the 13C they inherited that other Pyrénéan statelet, the Béarn – which still enjoyed its independence – and decided to reside there. Their fondness for Foix, their ancestral home, was undimmed, although they failed to maintain it properly, and in the end had to dismantle much of its massive fortifications. But the three great towers remained intact, symbols of their pride, property and power. The greatest of the Counts was Gaston Febus (1331–91), a brilliant figure whose wide culture did not however stop him killing both his brother and his only son. Henri IV was a member of the family; his accession to the French throne in 1589 meant the formal union of the Pays de Foix with France.

Until the late 19C the Ariège river was panned for gold and many local iron foundries were supplied by the mine at La Rancié until 1931.

SIGHT

Panorama★

From the **Château** (🕐 open daily Sept–Oct and May–Jun 9.45am–noon, 2–6pm; Jul–Aug 9.45am–6.30pm; Nov– Apr 10.30am–noon, 2–6pm; 🕐 closed public holidays; ☜4.30€; ☎05 34 09 83 83) rock high above the river there are extensive views over the surrounding region. To the southwest are the green Plantaurel hills, characterised by their remarkably regular relief. To the south are the Pyrénées themselves; among the many summits are the Trois Seigneurs (2 199m/7 214.5ft) and St-Barthélemy (2 368m/7 769ft). Eastward lies the high and windy Sault plateau from which rise a number of pointed peaks resembling the one on which the Cathar fortress of Montségur is built.

EXCURSIONS

Grotte de Niaux★★

▷ Michelin map 343 H 8.

☜Guided tours (45min). ☜9.40€. ☎05 61 05 10 10 (reservations required). Located in the Vicdessos valley, this cave is famed for its remarkably well-preserved prehistoric wall drawings, in particular those depicting animals in the "Black Hall" (Salon noir); the pure, sober lines and high craftsmanship mark the summit of Magdalenian art.

Parc Pyrénéen de l'Art Préhistorique (Tarascon-sur-Ariège) ★★

▷ At Lacombe, on the road to Banat.

The park, devoted to cave paintings – there are some 12 decorated caves in the Ariège area – comprises a distinctive modern building housing a display area, the Grand Atelier, and an open space with exhibits featuring water and rock. An audio-tour of the Grand Atelier ives a comprehensive account of the discoveries of cave paintings.

Cirque de Gavarnie★★★

Midi-Pyrénées

Gavarnie's fame is due to its natural amphitheatre forming one of Europe's most magnificent mountain landscapes.

- **Michelin Map:** 342 L-M 6
- **Info:** OT Gavarnie Gèdre. ℘05 62 92 49 10. www.gavarnie.com.
- **Location:** Gavarnie is the upper end of a blind valley high in the Central Pyrénées.

VISIT

1hr30min round-trip on foot from the village; horses or donkeys can be hired.
The Cirque rises in a series of huge steps to a **crest** with a number of peaks over 3 000m/9 842.5ft. Innumerable falls cascade down the rock walls, the greatest of them (the **Grande Cascade**) 422m /1 384.5ft high. Downstream, the waters have carved a gorge; further downstream the landscape has serenity and charm to it.

Lourdes★★★

Midi-Pyrénées

This little market town, sited at the meeting point of mountain and plain, became a pilgrimage place of world renown in the 19C.

- **Population:** 16 300
- **Michelin Map:** 324 L 4
- **Info:** Place Peyramale. ℘05 62 42 77 40. www.lourdes-infotourisme.com.
- **Location:** The town is in the central Pyrénées area, 20km/12.4mi S of the town of Tarbes.
- **Don't Miss:** The grotto where Bernadette Soubirous had her visions (*see A Bit of History*).

GEOGRAPHY
The town's setting
The summit of the **Béout** mountain (*reached by cable-car then 45min round-trip on foot*) is littered with great erratic blocks that give some idea of the power of the Quaternary glaciers.
The **view★** is an object lesson in physical geography; it extends northwards from the exits of the Lavedan valleys over the morainic terraces through which the Pau torrent winds its sinuous course, to the glacial rock-bar on which the castle is sited, and finally to the great terminal moraine which forces the stream to make an abrupt turn to the west.

A BIT OF HISTORY
On 11 February 1858, a poor, lonely and sickly **Bernadette Soubirous** (1844–79), while preparing for her First Communion, had the first of the 18 visions that led to Lourdes' becoming a world-famous centre of the cult of Mary, with the grotto and its surroundings attracting pilgrims from all five continents, with a special place reserved for the lame and the sick, who come in the hope of a miraculous cure. In 1866, the building of the first sanctuary was begun, and in 1871 the upper basilica was constructed.
The grandiose Basilica of the Rosary was built in Romano-Byzantine style in 1889. Bernadette was canonised in 1933.

VISIT
Grotto area
Appropriate dress essential.
In the summer months the great local, national and international pilgrimages are held here. The degree of spirituality

A Typical Day During a Pilgrimage

Until 5am the only access, Entrée des Lacets, is to the Way to the Cross (Chemin du Calvaire). At 9am pilgrims gather at Esplanade du Rosaire for a celebration of the Virgin in Majesty (Easter–October). Then a ceremony for the sick is held in the grotto; a forest of candles twinkle along the alleyway and on the candelabrum in front of the grotto. Twenty outlets near the cave supply holy water to the faithful from the source which surged in front of Bernadette. The sick are immersed in marble pools. At 4.30pm a procession (Procession du Saint Sacrement) leaves from the grotto to the Esplanade du Rosaire, where the Blessing of the sick is celebrated. Finally at 8.45pm a candle-lit procession takes place from the grotto to the Esplanade and Parvis du Rosaire.

is evident in the scale of the ceremonial and the devotion of the participants.

Esplanade

500m/550yd long, the site of daily processions.

Basilica of the Rosary

1 av. Monseigneur Théas. ◷*Open daily.* ☛*Guided tours available.* ✆*No charge.*

In neo-Byzantine style. The two curving approach ramps have fixed the image of the great building in the popular mind.

Crypt

A realm of devotion, contemplation and silence.

Upper Basilica

Dedicated to the Immaculate Conception and with a vast nave of five bays.
St Pius X Underground Basilica: ellipse-shaped, one of the world's largest sanctuaries.

Grotto of the Miracles

The site of the visions, where the most moving manifestations of faith take place.

Fountains

Lourdes water collected by pilgrims.

Pools

Immersion of the sick.

Basilica of the Rosary

©Serge Villa/Dreamstime.com

Stations of the Cross
Overlooking the basilicas and the Pau torrent.

EXCURSIONS
Grottes de Bétharram★★
▶ *Saint-Pé-de-Bigorre. 14km/8.7mi W.*
🕐*Open 25 Mar–25 Oct daily 9am–noon, 1.30–5.30pm; 11 Feb–24 Mar Mon–Fri 2.30–4pm.* ✆*11.50€.*
📞*05 62 41 80 04. www.grottes-de-betharram.com.*
This is one of the most popular natural attractions in the Pyrénées area. The caves comprise five separate galleries, one above the other. The vast roofs of porous rock of the upper level, a striking column which is still growing and is a typical example of the evolution of stalagmites and stalactites, a collapsed pot-hole 80m/262ft deep, a narrow fissure through which the river flows are fascinating examples of concretions and underground erosion.

Pic de Pibeste★★★
▶ *2hr20min climb from Ouzous on D 202.*

This peak – alt 1 349m/4 426ft – provides one of the best viewpoints in the central Pyrénées.

ADDRESSES

🏠 STAY
🛏 **Cazaux** – *2 chemin Rochers.* 📞*05 62 94 22 65. http://hotelcazaux lourdes.site.voila.fr. Closed 9 Oct–8 Apr. 20 rooms.* ⌷*6€.* This small hotel just outside the town centre offers scrupulously kept, fresh-looking rooms, a friendly welcome and reasonable prices among other things. It is near the market.

🛏🛏 **Chambre d'hôte M. and Mme Vives** – *28 rte de Bartrès, Loubajac, 6km/3.7mi NW of Lourdes on D 940 towards Pau.* 📞*05 62 94 44 17. www.anousta.com. Closed mid-Nov–mid-Feb. 5 rooms.* If you like the countryside, peace and quiet and a farm atmosphere, then this is the place for you. Sheep, chickens and ducks are raised and consumed here against a stunning backdrop of the Pyrénées. Four rooms with beams and sloping ceilings, and two others with a terrace. Fine garden and children's play area.

🛏🛏 **Chambre d'hôte Les Rocailles** – *Omex, 4.5km/3mi SW of Lourdes on D 13 then D 213.* 📞*05 62 94 46 19. Closed Nov–Easter. 3 rooms.* You'll adore this sweet little place! The owner used to be a costume designer at the Paris Opera and has decorated this small stone house with taste and refinement. Warm woods blend harmoniously with shimmering fabrics.

🛏🛏🛏 **Chambre d'hôte Le Grand Cèdre** – *6 r. du Barry, St-Pé-de-Bigorre.* 📞*05 62 41 82 04. www.legrandcedre.fr. 4 rooms.* This lovely 17C manor is sure to charm you. Each room is in a different style: Art ddco, Louis XV, Henri II, Louis-Philippe. Dining room, music room and superb park with a glasshouese and a vegetable garden.

🛏🛏🛏 **Hôtel Solitude** – *3 passage St-Louis Ave.* 📞*05 62 42 71 71. Closed 6 Nov–31 Mar. 356 rooms.* This large imposing modern hotel on the banks of the Pau, a Pyrénéan stream, has a small rooftop swimming pool. The dining room is a rotunda and has a terrace overlooking the river. The rooms with their little red armchairs are comfortable. We recommend those on the side of the river.

🛏🛏🛏 **Mercure Hôtel Impérial** – *3 av. du Paradis.* 📞*05 62 94 06 30. www.mercure.com/gb/hotel-5445-mercure-lourdes-imperial/index.shtml. Closed 16 Dec–31 Jan. 93 rooms.* ⌷*12€.* This 1935 hotel, which has been completely renovated in its original Art Deco style, is near the cave. The rooms are pleasant and furnished in soothing mahogany tones. Large classic style dining room and drawing room opening onto a small garden.

🍴 EAT
🍽 **Pizza Da Marco** – *47 r. de la Grotte.* 📞*05 62 94 03 59.* This is a pleasant place, decorated with photos and engravings.

The pizzaïolo is set up in the front room, but it is nicer to sit in the other one. Crispy pizza and efficient service.

🍝🍷 **Le Magret** – *10 r. 4 Frères-Soulas. ℘ 05 62 94 20 55. www.lemagret.com. Closed 3 weeks in Jan & Mon.* This little restaurant occupies a rustic style dining room with exposed beams and straw-bottomed chairs. Pilgrims and locals alike can enjoy traditional southwest cuisine without pretention.

🍝🍷🍷 **Brasserie de l'hôtel de la Grotte** – *66 r. de la Grotte. ℘05 62 94 58 87. www.hotel-grotte.com. Closed 25 Oct–9 Apr. Reservations required.* Agreeable contemporary surroundings comprising ochre coloured dining room, veranda and terrace, and a menu to suit all budgets. Extravagant diners can decamp to the more formal adjacent restaurant.

🏃 LEISURE ACTIVITIES

Lac de Lourdes – *Leave town W along D 940 and turn left onto the path leading to the edge of the lake via l'Embarcadère restaurant.* Lying at an altitude of 421m/1 381.2ft, the 11m/36ft-deep glacial lake offers water sports facilities (non-supervised bathing), fishing and golf (Lourdes 18-hole golf course to the south). From the shores of the lake there are fine views of the Pyrénéan foothills. A footpath runs round the lake.

Grotte du
Mas-d'Azil★★

Midi-Pyrénées

This cave is one of the outstanding natural phenomena of southwestern France, as well as a very important prehistoric site.

A BIT OF HISTORY

In 1887 Édouard Piette discovered evidence of human habitation during the Azilian period, (9 500 BC). Research continued under Abbé Breuil, Mandement, Boule andCartailhac.

VISIT

Guided tours (45min) year round; call or see website for opening hours. 6.10€, includes museum visit. ℘05 61 69 97 71. www.grotte-masdazil.com. The River Arize has hollowed out a 420m/1 378ft tunnel through the Plantaurel heights, which once barred its way; a meandering dry valley to the east is testimony to its former course. The entrance to the tunnel is formed by a magnificent 65m/213.2ft arch, the exit by a much lower opening made in a sheer rock rising to a height of 140m/459.3ft. The site was first excavated by Edouard Piette (1827–1906), who, in 1887, discovered a human habitat

- 🅖 **Michelin Map:** 343 G 6
- ℹ **Info:** Mas d'Azil. ℘05 61 69 97 71. www.grotte-masdazil.com.
- ▶ **Location:** The site lies in the Ariège hills, 31km/ 19mi NW of Foix.

intermediate between the Magdalenian and the Neolithic: the Azilian. In this cave that Azilian industry was studied. Practised between 11 000 and 9 500 BC, it is characterised by miniaturised tools, flat harpoons made from stags' antlers, and the making of flattened pebbles. The latter carry enigmatic markings in a red paint made from calcined ferric oxide; they have been interpreted to be lunar or menstrual calendars, or possibly the beginnings of abstract numbering. The four floors of excavated galleries run for 2km/1.2mi through limestone, which is sufficiently homogeneous to prevent infiltration and propagation of moisture. Display cases contain artefacts from the Magdalenian (scrapers, chisels, needles, a moulding of a famous neighing horse) and Azilian periods (harpoons, coloured pebbles, miniature tools).

In the chamber, Salle Mandement, are the remains of animals (mammoths, bears) coated in rubble.

Pic du Midi de Bigorre★★★

Midi-Pyrénées

A vertiginous mountain road winds over the Tourmalet Pass (Col du Tourmalet). From the top (2 114m/6 935.7ft) a toll road leads to Les Laquets; from here a cable-car or a rough path (2hr round-trip) gives access to the summit of the Pic du Midi de Bigorre, now reduced in level to the 2 865m/9 400ft contour in order to accommodate the television transmitter.

VISIT

◔*Departures every 15min 1–12 Oct, 25 Oct–6 Nov, end Nov–Jan Wed–Mon, Feb–20 Apr, May Wed–Mon 10am–3.30pm, last descent 5.30pm; Jun–Sept 9am–4.30pm, last descent 7pm. ◓30€. ⊘Subject to change due to weather.*

Observatoire et Institut de Physique du Globe du Pic du Midi

The factors favouring the siting here of an observatory include the great height, the purity of the atmosphere and the all-round viewing possibilities. The observatory, founded by General

- **Michelin Map:** 342 M 5
- **Info:** ℘0825 00 2877. www.picdumidi.com.
- **Location:** The Pic is a landmark in the Gascon Pyrénées, rising SE of Lourdes.
- **Don't Miss:** The observatory for its **panorama**★★★ views of the Pyrénées.

Nansouty, was originally intended for botanical and meteorological studies, but the astronomical function was soon added. It was here in 1706 that the first observations were made of the solar corona during a total eclipse of the sun. At the beginning of the 20C, the great observatory dome and reflecting telescopes were added.

Today, it is used for lunar mapping and research into the solar corona, cosmic radiation and nocturnal luminescence.

Summit

At the summit, which can only be reached by cable-car (Level 4), a glassed in gallery and several terraces offer the most impressive panorama in the Pyrénées.

View from the summit

©8prm/Dreamstime.com

Millau★

Midi-Pyrénées

Millau huddles between two high limestone plateaux, the Causse du Larzac and the Causse Noir, at the meeting-point of the Tarn and the Dourbie. The site of a ford in ancient times, it acquired a bridge in the Middle Ages and became a trading centre of some importance. Today it is a lively provincial town, with a southern air, close to a remarkable modern viaduct soaring over the Tarn valley.

▶ **Population:** 21 339
◐ **Michelin Map:** 338 K 6
▤ **Info:** 1 pl. du Beffroi.
  ℘05 65 60 02 42.
  www.ot-millau.fr.
◑ **Location:** Millau, beside the Tarn at the northern edge of the Larzac plateau, is on autoroute A 75. All main roads lead directly to the centre of town.
◎ **Don't Miss:** Take a trip out of town to the Aire de Vision to see the beautiful 2.5km/1.5mi Millau Viaduct, part of the A 75 autoroute.

A BIT OF HISTORY

During the 1C AD, Millau, then known as Condatomagus, was a Roman centre for earthenware production with over 500 potters.

Terra sigillata ware – bright red-glazed pottery decorated with floral, geometric or historiated patterns of Hellenistic influence – were produced. As early as the 2C AD, the milk of the Larzac ewes was made into a gourmet blue cheese in the nearby caves at Roquefort. Their wool and skins were also turned to advantage, including the manufacture of fine gloves at Millau. Today Millau's gloves are still exported around the world and the industry has expanded into the designer market, producing gloves and shoes for well known high street labels as well as diverse leather goods and furnishings. In a sheltered valley with a mild climate, Millau's streets are attractive with plane trees, fountains and a bustling air.

EXCURSIONS
Chaos de Montpellier-le-Vieux★★★

◑ *18km/11.2mi NE – 2hr round-trip on foot.*

This extraordinary 'ruined city' in fact made entirely of natural rocks extends over some 120ha/300 acres and has a bewildering variety of rock formations (the Sphinx, the Elephant, the Gates of Mycaenae). The contrasting properties of the different rocks are further expressed in the tremendous diversity of vegetation.

Caves de Roquefort★

25km/15.5mi SW. ◐*Open Apr–mid-Jul 9.30am–noon, 1–5pm; mid-Jul–2 Aug; 3–23 Aug 9.30am–6pm; 24 Aug–1 Nov 9.30am–noon, 1.30–4.30pm; 2 Nov–29 Mar 10am–noon, 1.30–4.30pm.* ⊜*3€.* ℘*05 65 59 93 30. www.roquefort-societe.com.*

The name of the market town of Roquefort, located between Millau and St-Affrique, is synonymous with one of the most famous of French cheeses: the delicious blue-veined Roquefort. In accordance with AOC Roquefort regulations, all production of the cheese must take place underground, in natural caves in which the temperature and humidity are constant. Roquefort cheese is produced exclusively from full-fat, untreated ewes' milk and a minimum maturing period of three months is necessary for a good Roquefort.

Millau Viaduct/Millau Bridge★★★

This amazing cable-stayed construction, completed in 2004 and designed by the British architect Norman Foster, spans the 2km/1.2mi-wide Tarn Gorge near Millau. The world's tallest road bridge, it forms part of the A 71-A 75 Autoroute from Paris to Béziers.

Moissac★★

Midi-Pyrénées

Moissac is situated on a low rise overlooking the fertile flood plain near the meeting point of the Tarn with the Garonne. The place is famous for the white Chasselas dessert grape, which grows here in abundance.

SIGHT
Église St-Pierre★
See Illustration, p72.
The former Benedictine abbey church, founded in the 7C, was consecrated in 1063 and the **cloisters**★★ completed 35

▶ **Population:** 12 321
Michelin Map: 337 C 7
Info: 6 pl. Durand de Bredon. ℘05 63 04 01 85. www.moissac.fr.
Location: Follow the orange signs leading to the famous abbey.

years later. It subsequently served as a model for similar work all over Europe. The church's south doorway (**portail méridional**★★★) is one a great triumphs of Romanesque sculpture.

Montauban★

Midi-Pyrénées

On the boundary between the hillsides of Bas Quercy and the rich alluvial plains of the Garonne and the Tarn, the old bastide of Montauban, built with a geometric street layout, is an important crossroads and a good point of departure for excursions into the Aveyron gorges. The almost exclusive use of pink brick lends the buildings here a distinctive character, which is also found in most of the towns and villages in Bas Quercy and the Toulouse area.

▶ **Population:** 53 100
Michelin Map: 337 E 7
Info: 4 r. du Collège. ℘05 63 63 60 60. www. montauban-tourisme.com.
Location: The town is 55.3km/34.3mi N of Toulouse (autoroute A 62).

The ornate elements and warm tones of the brick soften the overall effect, which would otherwise be rather austere.

SIGHTS
Place Nationale★
The square, formerly the Place Royale, dates from the foundation of the town in the 12C.
After fire destroyed the wooden roofs or *couverts* above the galleries in 1614 and again in 1649, the arcades were rebuilt in brick in the 17C. The square features a double set of arcades with pointed or round-arched vaulting. The inner gallery was a covered passageway while the outer gallery was occupied by market stalls.

Musée Ingres★
19 r. de l'Hôtel-de-Ville. Open Jul–Aug daily 10am–noon, 1.30–6pm; late Oct–Palm Sunday Tue–Sat 10am–noon, 1.30–6pm, Sun 2–6pm; Palm Sunday–Jun and Sept–late Oct 10am–noon, 2–6pm. Closed public holidays. 4€; free 1st Sun in month. ℘05 63 22 12 91. www.amis-museeingres.com.
Devoted to Jean-Auguste-Dominique Ingres' works, the museum is housed in a former bishop's palace. The first floor features some of the artist's best examples of his paintings: *Ruggiero freeing Angelica, Ossian's Dream, Jesus among the Doctors*, along with a selection of his 4 000 **drawings**, displayed in rotation.

Château de
Montségur★
Midi-Pyrénées

It was on this fearsome peak that the last episode of the Albigensian Crusade took place, when its Cathar defenders were massacred and Languedoc eclipsed by the power of the French kingdom.

A BIT OF HISTORY

Catharism – the name is derived from a Greek word meaning "pure" – was based on the principle of the total separation of Good and Evil, of the spiritual from the material. Its adherents comprised ordinary believers and the *"Perfecti"*, the latter living lives of exemplary purity in the light of God. Their austerity contrasted sharply with the venality and laxity of the Catholic clergy.

At the beginning of the 13C the local **Cathars** built a castle here to replace an old, since-demolished fortress. Forty years later, following the ravages of the Albigensian Crusade against the Cathars, the stronghold was occupied by some 400 adherents to the faith, from whose ranks was drawn the fierce band which marched on Avignonet

>
> ▶ **Population:** 108
> ⏱ **Michelin Map:** 343
> 🛈 **Info:** Quartier le Sarrat.
>   ℘05 61 03 03 03.
>   www.montsegur.org.
> ◗ **Location:** The small village of Montségur is 56.6km/35mi N of Ax-les-Thermes, in the foothills of the eastern Pyrénées. It is dominated by its castle.

(70km/44mi north) to put to the sword the members of the Inquisition meeting there. This action sealed the fate of Montségur; in the absence of Louis IX, who was dealing with disturbances in Saintonge, Blanche of Castille ordered the Crusaders to put the castle to siege. On 2 March 1244, the resistance of the defenders was overcome, but 200 of the faithful refused to retract their beliefs, even after being granted a fortnight in which to consider the matter.

On 16 March, they were brought down from the mountain to be burnt on a huge pyre at a place known from then on as the Camp des Crémats ("Field of the Burnt Ones").

SIGHTS
Château
🕐*Open daily Feb and Dec 11am–4.30pm; Mar and Nov 10.30am–5.30pm; Apr 10am–6.30pm; May–Jun 10am–6.30pm; Jul–Aug 9am–7.30pm; Sept 9am–6.30pm; Oct 10am–6pm.*
🕐*Closed 25 Dec.* ◉*4.50€.*
Reaching an altitude of 1 207m/3 959ft, this imposing castle was rebuilt in a pentagonal shape due to the limestone rock.

Musée Historique et Archéologique
32, village. ℘*05 61 01 10 27.*
🕐*Same opening times as the château.*
As well as medieval period furniture and objects found in the vicinity of the castle, this museum also has two skeletons and a cast of the cross of Morency.

Inside Château de Montségur

©Raymond Thill/Fotolia.com

Massif de Néouvielle★★★

Midi-Pyrénées

The Massif de Néouvielle, forming part of the high central spine of the Pyrénées, is a veritable museum of glacial topography, with virtually all the features characterising such landscapes, from high, ice-smoothed cliffs and cirques separated by narrow ridges, to hanging valleys, rock-steps and a multitude of lakes and erratic boulders.

VISIT

The popular little mountain resort of **St-Lary-Soulan**★ is the starting-point for the spectacular **scenic route** *(46km /29mi round-trip)* rising up to 1 362m/4 435ft and leading, via dark fir-woods and many hairpin bends, to a dam (Barrage de **Cap de Long**★), and lakes (**Lac d'Oredon**★ and **Lac d'Aumar**★).

- ♿ **Michelin Map:** 342 M 5
- ℹ **Info:** 37 r. Vincent Mir. ℘05 62 39 50 81. www. saintlary.com.
- ▶ **Location:** This high mountain region is best approached from the town of Lanneman.

Massif de Néouvielle

M.-H. Carcanague/MICHELIN

Rodez★

Midi-Pyrénées

Once the capital of the Rouergue, Rodez is situated on the borders of two very different regions, the dry Causses plateaux and the well-watered Ségale hills. The ancient town stands on a rocky spur high above the meanders of the river Aveyron. Its layout reflects the medieval rivalry of secular and ecclesiastical power: the cathedral and castle districts were both fortified.

SIGHT
Cathédrale Notre-Dame★★
pl. d'Armes.
The 13C red sandstone edifice has a fortress-like west front, once a bastion

- ▶ **Population:** 23 900
- ♿ **Michelin Map:** 338 H 4
- ℹ **Info:** Place Foch. ℘05 65 75 76 77. www.ot-rodez.fr.
- ▶ **Location:** The town is on a meeting of highways between Languedoc and Auvergne.

in the city wall. It has Flamboyant Gothic portals and a **bell-tower** ★★★ that is magnificent.
The interior was completed in the 16C but still in the style of the 13C. Note the 15C former **rood screen**★ and the superb 17C carved wooden **organ case**★. The choir stalls **(stalles**★) are by André Sulpice (15C).

St-Bertrand-de-Comminges★★

Midi-Pyrénées

This is one of the most picturesque and charming villages in the Pyrénéan foothills, perched on an isolated hilltop, encircled by ancient ramparts and dominated by an imposing cathedral.

A BIT OF HISTORY

A substantial town was founded here in 72 BC by Pompey. In AD 585 the Burgundians descended on the place and laid it waste.

For centuries the site lay abandoned, until in 1073 St Bernard saw its potential for the building of a cathedral and monastery.

Here the rules of the religious reforms of Pope Gregory VII were applied, making the little city the spiritual centre of Comminges, endowing the awkwardly shaped county (sandwiched as it was between the territories belonging to the House of Foix-Béarn and dotted with enclaves) with a religious significance far outweighing its political importance.

Cloister, Cathédrale Ste-Marie-de-St-Bertrand de Comminges

H. Payelle/MICHELIN

▶ **Population:** 252

⏱ **Michelin Map:** 343 B 6

ℹ **Info:** 22 pl. Valentin-Abeille, Montréjeau. ℘05 61 95 80 22. http://otimontrejeau. ifrance.com

▶ **Location:** Saint-Bertrand lies S of autoroute A 64, junction 17. The cathedral – visible from afar – is the centre.

🅿 **Parking:** In July and August, access to the upper part of the village is closed. Park either under the trees in Grand Place and take the steps, or park near Porte Majou, from which a 'little train' (👓1€) makes the climb easy!

SIGHT

Cathédrale Ste-Marie-de-St-Bertrand de Comminges★

👓👓*Guided tours are organised by the tourist office:* ℘05 61 95 44 44. ℘05 61 89 04 91. www.cathedrale-saint-bertrand.org.

Medieval sculpture here reaches a high point in its development. The Romanesque portal of the cathedral is made up of several independently sculpted panels showing the Adoration of the Magi and a figure of St Bertrand without a halo (i.e. before his canonisation in 1218), recalling the work of the School of Toulouse at St Sernin.

The cloisters (cloîtreaa) are built over the 12–15C ramparts; the south side is open, giving fine views over the Upper Garonne countryside, and there is a famous pillar in primitive style with statues of the four Evangelists.

There are splendid **choir stalls**★★ of 1535 in Italian Renaissance style; features to note particularly include the bishop's throne, a Jesse Tree and a Madonna and Child.

Toulouse★★★

Midi-Pyrénées

A vibrant regional capital, attractive with its red-brick architecture, Toulouse is a lively university town with a thriving high-tech industrial sector and, at the same time, plenty of attractions for the visitor to enjoy.

A BIT OF HISTORY

Toulouse has long been the focus of very diverse influences. The city was the capital of the Visigothic kingdom, and enjoyed considerable prosperity between the 9C and 13C under the Raymond dynasty, whose court was considered to be one of the most cultured in Europe.

Their extensive territories were known as the "Langue d'Oc". In the 13C, the whole domain of the Raymonds – most of present-day Languedoc and parts of the Midi-Pyrénées and Provence – embraced Catharism. This stance gave the Capetian kings an opportunity, with the authority of the Pope, to launch the Albigensian Crusade against Catharism. The Crusade put an end to the power of the Raymonds, broke up their territories, and enabled the Capetian kings to push their frontier southwards into Languedoc.

In 1323, Europe's oldest literary society was founded here to further the cause of the language of southern France (Langue d'Oc). Later, in the 16C, the city flourished again because of a boom in what at the time was the most widely cultivated of all dye plants, woad, which yielded a blue-black colour.

As early as 1917, strategic industries like aircraft manufacturing were being set up in southwestern France, as far away as possible from the country's vulnerable eastern border. In the inter-war period,

▶ **Population:** 450 832
⚘ **Michelin Map:** 343 G 3
⚑ **Info:** Donjon du Capitole. ☏05 61 11 02 22. www.uk.toulouse-tourisme.com.
▶ **Location:** The city is enclosed by a circle of autoroutes and expressways, while the city centre, sitting on the right bank of the River Garonne around Place du Capitole, is also ringed by busy boulevards. The east side of the Place du Capitole is the main meeting place for local residents.
🅿 **Parking:** Cars can be parked free of charge in the "transit car parks" and you can then take the bus or metro into the city.
☺ **Don't Miss:** From the St-Michel bridge, there's a great view of the city, especially towards the end of the day when the sun picks up the warm red tones of the brickwork.
🕐 **Timing:** If you plan on visiting most of the museums, consider buying a Toulouse en Liberté City Pass. Take the 2hr guided tour of Toulouse first to get a better idea of where you want to spend your time in France's sixth-largest urban centre.

Toulouse became the starting-point of France's first scheduled air service. The city has remained the focus of France's aeronautics industry.

Toulouse en Liberté City Pass

This city pass entitles the bearer to discounts on dining, accommodation, entertainment, museum entry, car rental, excursions and shopping. Ask at the tourist office. Valid for 1 year: 10€ adult, 25€ family (2 adults, 2 children), 5€ child.

SIGHTS

Basilique St-Sernin★★★

pl. Saint-Sernin. ⏰*Open daily 10am–noon, 2–6pm.* **Crypts** *open Mon–Sat 10am–11.30am, 2.30–5pm; Sun 2.30–5pm.* ☏*05 61 21 70 18. www.basilique-st-sernin-toulouse.fr.*

The great church was built to honour the memory of the Gaulish martyr St Sernin (or Saturninus). A first phase of construction lasting from around 1080–1118 was in a mixture of brick and stone, a second phase in brick alone.

St-Sernin was one of a number of major Romanesque pilgrimage churches on the route to Compostela. St-Sernin's octagonal bell-tower is particularly characteristic of the area, with five levels of twin arches built in brick, the upper two of which are provided with little pediments.

Église des Jacobins★★

69 r. Pargaminières. ♿⏰*Open daily 9am–7pm.* ☏*05 61 22 21 92. www.jacobins.mairie-toulouse.fr.*

This was the first church of the Preaching Friars, an order founded in 1215 by St Dominic, and intended to help in the fight against Catharism. To the poverty demanded by St Francis of his followers, Dominic added a knowledge of theology and a training in eloquence which enabled his disciples to attempt to overcome their opponents in argument.

The church is the key building in the evolution from 1230 onwards of Southern French Gothic as influenced by the mendicant orders.

The size of the edifice, combined with the impossibility of providing it with external support (because of ownership and circulation problems), ruled out the construction of a single nave. The architect resorted to the expedient of a marvellous ribbed vault and the **"palm-tree"** of the chancel with its splendid array of 22 radiating arches. All this in 1292, 170 years before the great pointed vaults of the Late Gothic.

The tower dates from 1298. and became the model for the towers of the major churches of Southern France.

Capitole★

This is Toulouse's City Hall, its name being derived from the "capitouls" or consuls who administered the city when it was ruled by the Raymonds. With its Ionic pilasters and alternating use of brick and stone, it is a fine example of the urban architecture of the 18C.

Cathédrale St-Étienne★

pl. Saint-Etienne. ⏰*Open Mon–Sat 8am–7pm, Sun 9am–7pm.* ⬡*No charge.* ☏*05 61 52 03 82.*

There is a fascinating contrast here between the nave completed in 1212, a vast hall in the Mediterranean tradition designed to accommodate large numbers of people, and the chancel, begun 60 years later on the pattern of the Gothic churches of Northern France. The architect of this later addition was Jean Deschamps, who took it upon himself to propagate this style throughout Languedoc once it had become part of the Capetian realm.

The nave and chancel are not aligned on the same axis and hardly seem to form part of a whole.

The original plan had envisaged a more or less total reconstruction, but in the event the old nave was retained, and the link between it and the chancel cleverly improvised by some architectural virtuosity in what should have been the north transept.

Musée des Augustins★★

♿⏰*Open Thu–Tue 10am–6pm, Wed 10am–9pm.* ⏰*Closed 1 Jan, 1 May, 25 Dec.* ⬡*3€, free 1st Sun in the month.* ☏ *05 61 22 21 82. www.augustins.org.*

The museum is housed in the former convent, with a famous **Pietà** and superb collection of **Romanesque sculpture**★★★ (mostly 12C), much of it in grey Pyrénéan marble.

ADDITIONAL SIGHTS

Hôtel d'Assezat★★ *(pl. d'Assézat)*
Musée St-Raymond★★ *(pl. Saint-Sernin)*
Muséum d'Histoire Naturelle★★ (*35 allées Jules-Guesde*)
Musée Paul-Dupuy★ (*13 r. de la Pleau*)

ADDRESSES

STAY

Hôtel le Capitole – *10 r. Rivals.* *05 61 23 21 28. www.capitole-hotel. com. 33 rooms.* 8€. Situated very near to the Place du Capitole, this old mansion has a brick facade that has just been redone. Some of the spacious bedrooms are sparkling new, and half are air-conditioned. A bonus: breakfasts are served 'til noon.

Hôtel Castellane – *17 r. Castellane.* *05 61 62 18 82. www.castellanehotel. com. 53 rooms.* 8€. This small hotel close to the Capitole is slightly set back from the main thoroughfare. The simple, practical rooms are housed in three different buildings; some rooms are particularly well suited to families. Breakfast is served on the veranda.

Hôtel de France – *5 r. d'Austerlitz.* *05 61 21 88 24. www.hotel-france-toulouse.com. 64 rooms.* 8€ In business since 1910, this attractive hotel is situated a few steps from the Place Wilson. The rooms are of various sizes; though not luxurious, they are shipshape and affordable. Some of the largest come with a balcony.

Hôtel Ours Blanc – *25 pl. Victor-Hugo.* *05 61 23 14 55. www.hotel-oursblanc.com. 38 rooms.* 7€. Situated opposite the marché Victor-Hugo, this hotel has simple yet comfortable rooms (recently renovated) which are air conditioned and sound proofed; bright breakfast room with some attractive pictures embellishing its walls.

Hôtel St-Sernin – *2 r. St. Bernard.* *05 61 21 73 08. www.hotelstsernin. com.18 rooms.* 9€. Some rooms at this family hotel have fine views of the famous basilique St-Sernin; all are simply decorated with yellow or pale pink walls and well presented. Open fireplace in the breakfast room.

Hôtel Mermoz – *50 r. Matabiau.* *05 61 63 04 04. www.hotel-mermoz. com. 52 rooms.* 15€. The inner flower garden of this hotel near the city centre provides a haven of calm. Many decorative touches, notably portraits of pilots, bring aviation's early years to mind. Spacious rooms in 1930s style.

EAT

La Cave des Blanchers – *29 r. des Blanchers.* *05 61 22 47 47. Closed Tue.* An attractive spot, situated among other restaurants on a street which is very popular in the evenings. Vaulted ceiling and pink brick inside, while in summer diners can eat on the pavement terrace. Regional cuisine blending characteristic sweet and sour flavours.

La Faim des Haricots – *3 r. du Puit Vert.* *05 61 22 49 25. Closed Sun.* A mere stone's throw from the Capitole, this vegetarian restaurant gives diners a choice of varied, plentiful fixed-price menus at painless prices. The warm décor blends brick and yellow shades; the mezzanine is also very appealing.

Jean Chiche – *3 r. St-Pantaléon.* *05 61 21 80 80.* This pleasant patisserie and tearoom is close to the Capitole. The menu offers a choice of around a dozen light meals, plus cakes and ice creams.

Bon Vivre – *15 bis pl. Wilson.* *05 61 23 07 17. www.lebonvivre.com.* With its terrace giving onto Place Wilson and an attractive interior decorated with photos of Gers (where the proprietor was born), this is an appealing spot with a solid traditional menu.

Le Châteaubriand – *42 r. Pargaminières.* *05 61 21 50 58. www.restaurant-lechateaubriand.com. Closed Sun.* The atmosphere in this little restaurant in old Toulouse is particularly pleasant. Cosy interior with a parquet floor, red brick walls, a huge mirror and houseplants. Southwestern cooking on the menu.

Grand Café de l'Opéra – *1 pl. du Capitole -* *05 61 21 37 03. www.brasserieopera.com. Closed Sun.* The brasserie of the Grand Hôtel de l'Opéra is the essential place to go and see and be seen. The inviting décor, leather wall seats and autographed photos of the many artists who have spent time here create a special atmosphere. Cuisine of southwest France.

Le Mangevins – *46 r. Pharaon.* *05 61 52 79 16. Closed Aug & Sun.* In this local tavern where salted foie gras and beef are sold by weight, the bawdy, fun atmosphere is enhanced by ribald songs. There is no menu, but a set meal for hearty appetites. Anyone in search of peace and quiet should look elsewhere!

La Régalade – *16 r. Gambetta. 05 61 23 20 11. Closed Sat–Sun.* Located between the Capitole and the Garonne, this small restaurant's pink brick facade leads to a pleasant interior of exposed beams, modern art, wood furniture and bistro chairs. Bountiful traditional fare.

Brasserie "Beaux Arts" – *1 quai Daurade. 05 61 21 12 12. www.brasserielesbeauxarts.com.* The atmosphere of a 1930s brasserie is recreated here with bistro-style chairs, wall seats, retro lighting, wood panelling and mirrors. The cuisine, in keeping with the décor, features seafood, sauerkraut and a few regional specialities.

Colombier – *14 r. Bayard. 05 61 62 40 05. www.restaurant-le colombier.com. Closed Aug, last week in Dec, public hols & Sun.* Opened in 1874, this is an essential stopping point for culinary pilgrims in search of authentic cassoulet. Delightful dining room with pink bricks and wall paintings. Friendly and efficient service.

La Madeleine de Proust – *11 r. Riquet. 05 61 63 80 88. www. madeleinedeproust.com. Closed Sun.* Childhood memories inspire the original, carefully designed décor of this restaurant featuring yellow walls, waxed tables, antique toys, an old school desk, a time-worn cupboard. The cuisine gives the starring role to vegetables that have fallen out of common use.

L'Envers du Décor – *22 r. des Blanchers. 05 61 23 85 33. www. enversdudecor.info. Closed Sun; Mon–Tue for lunch.* Cuisine of the southwest with some exotic touches is served in this restaurant in a small, busy street not far from the Garonne. Dice, cards, and theatre contribute to the playful ambience; perhaps you will win yourself a second meal. Good luck!

En Marge – *8 r. Marge. 05 61 53 07 24. www.restaurantenmarge. com.* Excellent French cuisine located in the old district. Chef Frank Renimel produces a new menu every fortnight.

7 Place St-Sernin – *7 pl. St-Sernin. 05 62 30 05 30. www.7placesaintsernin.com. Closed Sat lunch, Sun.* This pretty 19C house typical of Toulouse stands opposite the basilica. Bright red and yellow Catalan colours, contemporary furniture and a display of paintings from a local art gallery garnish the dining room. Contemporary cuisine.

NIGHTLIFE

The bi-monthly magazine *Toulouse Cultures* lists all upcoming events.
Place du Capitole – The famous central square of the city is a pedestrian-only meeting place surrounded by alluring brasserie terraces.

Le Bibent – *5 pl. du Capitole. 05 61 23 89 03.* Classified as an historic monument due to its Belle Époque décor, this roomy café has a superb terrace giving onto the Place du Capitole.

Au Père Louis – *45 r. des Tourneurs. 05 61 21 33 45. Closed Sun & public holidays.* First opened in 1889 and now a registered historical building, this wine bar is a local institution. The portrait of Père Louis, the founding father, conspicuously observes goings-on from above; his debonair visage also adorns wine bottle labels. Wine is sipped around fat-bellied barrels; an appetising choice of open-faced sandwiches is available evenings.

SHOPPING

Markets – **Saturday mornings:** organic farmers' market in Place du Capitole. **Sunday morning:** farmers' market around Eglise St-Aubin; L'Inquet, a renowned flea market around the Basilique St-Sernin. **Wednesday and Friday** (Nov–Mar): geese, ducks and foie gras are sold in Place du Salin. **Shopping streets** – The main shopping streets are Rue d'Alsace-Lorraine, Rue Croix-Baragnon, Rue St-Antoine-du-T., Rue Boulbonne, Rue des Arts and the pedestrian sections of Rue St-Rome, Rue des Filatiers, Rue Baronie and Rue de la Pomme.

✦✦ LEISURE ACTIVITIES

Bateau Mouche Le Capitole – *Quai de la Daurade. ℘05 61 25 72 57. www. toulouse-croisieres.com. Depart Oct–Apr daily 10.30am, 3pm & 4.30pm (May–Sept also 6pm). 8€; Jul–Aug night cruises, 9pm, 10pm. 5€.* Embark upon this pleasure steamer for a cruise on the Garonne.

Péniche Baladine – *Quai de la Daurade. ℘ 05 61 80 22 26. www.bateaux-toulousains.com. Depart Oct–May Wed, Sat, Sun and public holidays; Jun–Sept and school holidays daily. Canal du Midi cruises (1hr15min) depart at 10.50am and 4pm; Garonne cruises (1hr15min) at 2.30pm, 5.30pm and 7pm. 8€.*

Parc Toulousain – on an island in the river Garonne, Parc Toulousain has 4 pools (3 outdoors); the Stadium; the Parc des Expositions and the Palais des Congrès.

CALENDAR OF EVENTS

Fête de la Violette – *mid-Feb. ℘05 61 11 02 22.* Growing, selling, exhibiting… the ideal opportunity to learn all about the flower that is the city's emblem.

Printemps du Rire – *late Mar–early Apr. ℘05 62 21 23 24. www.printemps-du-rire. com.* Spring comedy festival.

Le Marathon des mots – *mid-Jun. ℘05 61 99 64 01. www.lemarathondesmots. com.* Literary festival.

Piano aux Jacobins – *Sept. ℘05 61 22 40 05. www.pianojacobins.com.*

Le Printemps de Septembre – *Sept–Oct ℘05 61 14 23 51. www. printempsdeseptembre.com.* Festival of photography and visual arts.

Festival Occitania – *Sept–Oct. ℘05 61 11 24 87. http://festivaloccitania.com.* Regional culture celebrated through various media (cinema, poetry, song).

Le Marché de Noël – *Dec. ℘05 61 87 55 06. www.midexpo.fr.* Christmas market.

Villefranche-de-Rouergue★

Midi-Pyrénées

The ancient bastide of Villefranche, with its rooftops clustered around the foot of the massive tower of its church, lies at the bottom of a green valley surrounded by hills, at the confluence of the Aveyron and the Alzou.

▶ **Population:** 11 275
⚲ **Michelin Map:** 338 E 4
🛈 **Info:** Promenade de Guiraudet. ℘05 65 45 13 18. www.villefranche.com.
▷ **Location:** On the western edge of the Massif Central, the town is at a meeting point of three highways. The town centre is Place Notre-Dame, beside the church.

SIGHT
Bastide★

The old town on the north bank of the River Aveyron has kept many of the typical features of a planned urban foundation of the 13C. Its cobbled streets, connected by narrow alleyways, are laid out on a grid pattern, and there is a central square (**Place Notre-Dame★**) with covered walks, dominated by a large metal figure of Christ. The tall, severe houses are characteristic of the Rouergue area; a number of them have high open balconies with provision for drying grain. The President Raynal House (Maison du Président Raynal) with its 15C façade is particularly striking, and the Maison Dardennes has a fine galleried courtyard. The fortified church (**Église Notre-Dame★**) has splendid ironwork around the font.

EXCURSION
Chartreuse St-Sauveur★

▷ *Take D 922 towards Najac.*
15C Gothic charterhouse, with 'Great' and 'Small' cloisters.

Gorges du **Tarn★★★**

Tarn Gorges

The deep gorges cut by the Tarn through the harsh limestone plateaux (causses) to the south of the Massif Central make up one of France's most spectacular natural landscapes. The source of the Tarn lies high (1 575m/5 167ft) in the granitic uplands of Mount Lozère; tumbling torrent-like down the slopes of the Cévennes, the river then enters the most spectacular section of its course at **Florac**.

THE AREA

The Tarn River – 381km/237mi-long – flows through a gorges and canyons, joined by side valleys such as the Jonte and the Dourbie, in Millau.

Escape from the valley bottom is by means of roads that twist and turn up the precipitous slopes to join the roughly planed surface of the Causse Méjean; its porous limestone is deeply fissured and hollowed out to form the caves for which the region is famous.

Most visitors come here when the summer sun is beating down, but the scene is best appreciated in spring and autumn, when the vegetation is better able to assert itself and local life is flourishing. The spectacle of winter

- **Michelin Map:** 330 H-J 8-9 and 338 L-N 5
- **Info:** Le Bourg, Le Rozier. ℘05 65 62 60 89. www.officedetourisme-gorgesdutarn.com.
- **Location:** The River Tarn rises on Mont Lozère, and runs through the Cevennes before reaching the Causses country, where it has carved its plunging gorge between the limestone plateaux. The road runs at the top of the cliffs. There are small villages, notably Ste-Énimie, along the gorge, but no communities of any great size.
- **Don't Miss:** Pause at the Point Sublime to get the full picture of the Tarn gorge.
- **Timing:** The road along the gorge is narrow, difficult, and in season can be congested. Allow several hours to cover the full distance.

should not be missed, when every feature has its frosty outline.

The hostile landscape here has been humanised by centuries of determined human effort. Thus there are villages on the flatter patches of cultivable land which occur on the valley bottom and sides (Ste-Énimie, La Malène, Les Vignes) and the castles of lords and robber-barons on the more easily defended sites overlooking the river. On the plateau above are isolated farms based on the better soils of the little depressions known as dolinas; the drystone walls once made by piling up the boulders collected laboriously from the fields are now supplemented by electric fences, and the thoughtless forest clearance of the 19C is being made good by the planting of Austrian pines.

No trace of the underground realm of chasms (**Aven Armand★★★**) and

Tarn Gorge

A.Thuillier/MICHELIN

caverns is visible at the surface; those who venture into this unsuspected world are rewarded by the extraordinary spectacle presented by the dissolution of the limestone, and by the strange forms of the stalactites and stalagmites.

EXCURSIONS
Les Détroits (The Straits)★★
◗ *36km/22.3mi NE of Gorges du Tarn.*
This is the narrowest part of the valley, hemmed in by plunging cliffs of coloured limestone and slightly to the east of La Malène.

Cirque des Baumes★★★
◗ *2.4km/1.5mi NW of Les Détroits.*
Below Les Détroits, the gorge widens, forming a magnificent natural amphitheatre.

Le Point Sublime★★★
◗ *Just W of Cirque des Baumes.*
This splendid viewpoint above the Cirque des Baumes overlooks both the Tarn Canyon and the Tarn Causse.

Grotte de l'Aven Armand★★★
Tarn Gorges

One of the wonders of underground world, this immense cavern is reached down a 200m/656ft tunnel in the bleak Causse Méjean.

VISIT
👣 *Guided tours only, Jul–Aug 9.30am–6pm; 28 Mar–Jun and Sept–11 Nov 10am–noon, 1.30–5pm.* 👓*8.80€.* 🕿*04 66 45 61 31. www.aven-armand. com.* 🌡 *The temperature inside is 10ºC/50ºF.*
Deep within the arid limestone of the Causse Méjean, subterranean waters

- 🚹 **Michelin Map:** 338 M 5
- 🏳 **Info:** Pl. de Sully, Meyruies. 🕿04 66 45 60 33. www.aven-armand.com.
- ◗ **Location:** 43km/27mi NE of Millau, Aven Armrand is in the plateau country S of the Gorges du Tarn.

have created a vast cavern, 60m wide and 120m long (197 x 394ft), its floor littered with rock fallen from its roof. Four hundred stalagmites, some up to 30m/97.5ft high and christened the "Virgin Forest", make an extraordinary spectacle.

Stalagmites, Grotte de l'Aven Armand

A. Cassaigne/MICHELIN

NORMANDY

Taking its name from the Norsemen or Normans, this old dukedom extends from the edge of the Paris Basin towards the Breton peninsula. To many it is reminiscent of southern England with its shared heritage of glorious Norman architecture and lush, pastoral countryside. There is great diversity in the buildings here; Norman masons fashioned the fine Caen limestone into great churches while humbler structures were built from cob, chalk, pebbles in mortar, brick, timber, shingles and thatch.

Highlights

1 11C masterpiece of tapestry **The Bayeux Tapestry** (p381)
2 Castle above the Seine: **Château Gaillard** (p381)
3 The old town and picturesque port **Vieux Honfleur** (p394)
4 The Romanesque Benedictine abbey of **Mont-St-Michel** (p398)
5 Gothic architecture at **Rouen**'s Cathédrale Notre-Dame (p401)

Lower Normandy (Basse-Normandie) is built of the old rocks from the Primary era. In the north, the Cotentin Peninsula projects into the English Channel dividing the Bay of the Seine from the Gulf of St-Malo. To the southeast lies the *bocage* (pasture) – its hedgebanks offered excellent cover to the Germans in 1944. On either side of the Seine Valley extends **Upper Normandy** (Haute-Normandie), centred on the historic city of Rouen. To the south is the Pays d'Auge, quintessential *bocage* country, famous for its ciders, cheeses and calvados, while to the north stretches the vast chalk plain of the Pays de Caux, bordered by the Channel coast with its white cliffs and hanging valleys.

History – Originally occupied by Celts, by the 1C BC the Romans were establishing towns here. The collapse of the Roman Empire led to occupation by the Franks, but raiding Vikings took over c. 911. Normandy remained independent until 1204 before becoming a French dukedom subject to English control for long periods until 1469 when it became a province of France. The 15C–17C saw the discovery of new territories by Norman sailors, such as Quebec. More recently, on 6 June 1944, Normandy beaches were the scene of what became known as the "D-Day Landings".

Today – The major economies are dairy farming, agriculture and, in Upper Normandy, industry; products include calvados and cider. Tourism is also a major contributor to the economy.

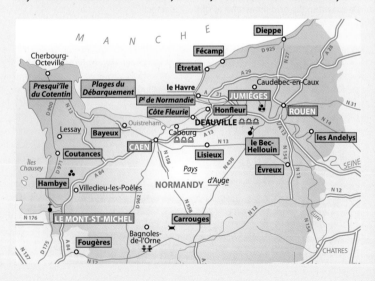

Les **Andelys**★★

The white castle rising beside Les Andelys commanded the Seine valley on the border of Normandy. Its strategic position was valued by Richard the Lionheart, Duke of Normandy as well as King of England. In 1196 he decided to break his agreement with the king of France, and construct a mighty fortress of his own. Within the year, so legend has it, the work was complete, and Richard was able to cry aloud "See my fine yearling!"

CHÂTEAU GAILLARD★★

Accessible by car from Grand Andelys or on foot (30min climb) from Petit Andelys. ○*Open 14 Mar–8 Nov Wed–Mon 10am–1pm, 2–6pm.* ○*Closed 1 May.* ◎*3€.* ◔*Guided tours 11am, 3pm, 4.30pm.* ◎*5€.*
Despite its 17 towers, 2.4m/8ft thick walls, three rings of defences and a moat, King Philippe Auguste succeeded in

▶ **Population:** 8 208
◔ **Michelin Map:** 304
🛈 **Info:** Rue Philippe Auguste. ☎02 32 54 41 93. http://office-tourisme. ville-andelys.fr.
◔ **Location:** Les Andelys lies 39km/24mi SE of Rouen. The château rises beside picturesque waterside Petit Andelys. Grand Andelys extends away from the river.

taking the castle in 1274 after a siege of only eight months. This victory enabled him to incorporate Normandy, Maine, Anjou and Touraine into the French kingdom. In 1419 Henry V of England took it back. La Hire, companion to Joan of Arc, won it again for France ten years later, only to lose it to Henry once more. It finally passed into French possession under Charles VII in 1449.

Bayeux★★

Charming with its half-timbered or stone houses, and known for its famous tapestry, Bayeux was also the first French town to be liberated at the end of WW II.

A BIT OF HISTORY

First a Roman town, then an early episcopal city until the 9C when it became a Norse speaking Viking city, Bayeux was the 'cradle of the Dukes of Normandy' and home of William, who invaded and conquered England.
Almost 900 years later the invasion came the other way when on 6 June 1944 the Allies landed on the Normandy beache.s On 7 June Bayeux became the first French town to be liberated and here on D-Day + 7, General de Gaulle made his first speech on French soil.

▶ **Population:** 14 446
◔ **Michelin Map:**303 H 4
🛈 **Info:** Pont St-Jean. ☎02 31 51 28 28. www.bayeux-tourism.com.
◔ **Location:** 30km/18.6mi from Caen, the town is just inland from the Omaha and Arromanches Landing Beaches.
👪 **Kids:** Special child-friendly audioguides are available to help youngsters enjoy the Bayeux Tapestry.

SIGHTS
👪 The Bayeux Tapestry (Tapisserie de la Reine Mathilde)★★★
Centre Guillaume Le Conquérant, r. de Nesmond. ♿○*Open daily 15 Mar–Apr and Sept–15 Nov 9am–6.30pm;*

Bayeux Tapestry scene – Duke William knights Harold; they set out for Bayeux.

May–Aug 9am–7pm; 16 Nov–14 Mar 9.30am–12.30pm, 2–6pm. ◷Closed 1 Jan, 2nd week in Jan, 25 Dec. ▧7.80€; child 3.80€ (ticket combined with the **Baron-Gérard Museum**). ✆02 31 51 25 50. www.tapisserie-bayeux.fr.

Beautifully displayed in specially designed premises, it is most likely that this extraordinary masterpiece of embroidery was made by talented nuns – in fact noble Saxon women who had chosen the convent – in England, soon after the Conquest in 1066. Using a style similar to today's strip cartoon, its 72 scenes, or pictures, recount the epic of the Norman invasion with striking truthfulness; in addition, it is an irreplaceable source of information on the ships, weapons, clothes and way of life of the mid-11C.

Cathédrale Notre-Dame★★

r. Lambert Leforestier. ◷Open daily Jan–Mar 8.30am–5pm; Apr–Jun and Oct–Dec 8.30am–6pm; Jul–Sept 8.30am–7pm. ☛Guided tours of Cathedral and Old Town Jul 3pm. ▧4€. ✆02 31 51 28 28.

Numerous changes contributed to this impressive edifice. The Romanesque vaulted crypt and lower nave date from the 11C. The 12C added intricate stonework including profusely decorated walls and cornerstonesand and rib-vaulting in the aisles. In the 13C, the High Gothic period, the superb chancel with radiating chapels and transepts with three-pointed arches and gallery with a fretwork design, were among many elegant additions. Later additions included side chapels (14C), frescoes and an octagonal storey over the crossing (15C).

The Norman Conquest

Edward the Confessor (c. 1003–1066) died without a clearly designated heir to the English throne. Harold Godwinson (c. 1022–1066) claimed that Edward had left England in Harold's 'protection' on his deathbed. William the Bastard, Duke of Normandy (Edward's distant cousin, c. 1028–1087), claimed that Harold had sworn on sacred relics at Bayeux to support his own claim to the throne and had therefore perjured himself of this oath. Having secured the support of Pope Alexander II and his barons by the promise of English lands and titles, and with the resources of the cities of Caen and Rouen at his disposal, William organised a punitive expedition in just seven months. The Norman fleet was assembled at **Dives**; its 600 ships carried 8 000 soldiers and cavalry who were landed on the coast at Pevensey Bay on 28 September 1066. On 14 October, William won the **Battle of Hastings**, the Saxon army routed and the claimant Harold dead. Duke William had become what history has renamed him, William the Conqueror. William was crowned King of England at a coronation ceremony in Westminster Abbey on 25 December. The situation was ambiguous: William was both King of England and Duke of Normandy; the latter title made him a vassal to the King of France. Difficulties soon arose, becoming more serious in 1152 due to the divorce of Louis VII and Eleanor of Aquitaine, only to be resolved at the end of the Hundred Years' War.

ADDRESSES

🏠 STAY

La Ferme des Châtaigniers – *Vienne-en-Bessin, 7.5km/4.6mi E of Bayeux via D 126.* ☎️*02 31 92 54 70. 3 rooms.* Set apart from the farmhouse, this converted farm building contains simple yet pleasant, comfortable rooms. Guests have the use of a fitted kitchen. Peace and quiet is guaranteed in this house set in the fields.

La Ferme de Fumichon – *Vaux-sur-Aure, 3km/1.8mi N of Bayeux via D 104.* ☎️*02 31 21 78 51. www.fermede fumichon.com. 4 rooms.* Once part of Longues-sur-Mer Abbey, this fortified 17C farm, with its square courtyard and characteristic porch, is today a dairy and cider-making farm. The attic rooms are plain but pleasant.

Hôtel Reine Mathilde – *23 r. Larcher.* ☎️*02 31 92 08 13. www.hotel-reinemathilde.com. Closed 15 Nov–15 Feb. 16 rooms.* ⊡*7€.* If you wish to stay in the old town, this small family hotel is conveniently situated a stone's throw from the cathedral and the famous tapestry. Exposed beams and light-wood furniture. Plain rooms, some of them with sloping ceilings.

Chambre d'hôte Manoir de Crépon – *Anne-Marie Poisson, Crépon, 14km/8.7mi NE of Bayeux via D12.* ☎️*02 31 22 21 27. www.manoirdecrepon. com. Closed 10 Jan–10 Feb. 4 rooms.* This 17C and 18C house is typical of the area, with its oxblood-coloured roughcast. You will like the stone floors and fireplaces, the vast, tastefully furnished bedrooms and the authentic atmosphere of the former kitchen converted into a breakfast room.

Hotel Le Bayeux – *9 r. Tardif.* ☎️*02 31 92 70 08. www.lebayeux. com. 30 rooms.* ⊡*7.50€.* Functional and well-kept facilities in a modern style, hidden in a quiet side street.

🍴 EAT

Hostellerie St-Martin – *6 pl. Edmond Paillaud, Creully.* ☎️*02 31 80 10 11. Closed 1–14 Jan.* Today it's a restaurant, but in olden times the large vaulted rooms dating from the 16C housed the village market. Exposed stone, a fireplace, sculptures and a view of the wine cellar make up the curious décor. Classic cuisine. A few bedrooms.

Le Petit Bistrot – *2 r. du Bienvenu.* ☎️*02 31 51 85 40. Closed Sun, Wed, Mon (low season).* An inventive cuisine prepared by a keen chef is the main attraction of this small establishment facing the cathedral. Original dishes inspired by Mediterranean cuisine are served in a Provençal-style décor with an ochre colour scheme, water colours and drawings.

Le Pommier – *38–40 r. des Cuisiniers.* ☎️*02 31 21 52 10. www. restaurantlepommier.com. Closed 14 Dec–18 Jan, Sun (Nov–Mar).* No place could be more centrally located, near the cathedral, its inviting apple-green façade announcing its rich Norman cuisine: smoked ham, *tripes à la mode de Caen*, cream sauces and, of course, apples. There are also vegetarian dishes. The vaulted dining-room with stone walls adds charming authenticity.

La Rapière – *53 r. St. Jean.* ☎️*02 31 21 05 45. Closed mid-Dec–mid-Jan, Wed & Thu.* A 15C house situated in old Bayeux. A lovely, rustic interior and tasty food using local produce.

🛒 SHOPPING

Naphtaline – *14, 16 parvis de la Cathédrale.* ☎️*02 31 21 50 03. www. naphtaline-bayeux.com. Closed Jan–Feb & Sun.* Three boutiques housed in a fine 18C building offer antique and modern lace, Bayeux porcelain and reproductions of traditional tapestries woven on Jaquard looms.

🍷 NIGHTLIFE

Café Inn – *67 r. St-Martin.* ☎️*02 31 21 11 37.* Coffee beans are roasted on the spot and 75 sorts of tea are served in a bustling ambiance. Light meals of salads, omelettes and quiches are offered as prelude to the delicious *Tarte Tatin*, an upside-down apple pie.

Abbaye du
Bec-Hellouin★★

This once-prestigious abbey produced two great archbishops of Canterbury.

A BIT OF HISTORY

In 1042 **Lanfranc** (1005–89) appeared at the abbey. This great yet humble man had been a distinguished teacher. Three years later, he started teaching again, making Le Bec one of the intellectual centres of the West.

After the Conquest, Lanfranc, who had become Duke William's Counsellor, was made Archbishop of Canterbury and Primate of all England. His successor at Le Bec was **St Anselm** (1033–1109), philosopher and theologian. His *Proslogion*, written here in 1078, is considered a great source of Western thought. In 1093 he became Archbishop of Canterbury. During the Revolution, the building was vandalised and the monks expelled.

- **Michelin Map:** 304 E 6
- **Info:** 1 r. du Général de Gaulle, Brionne. ℘02 32 45 70 51. www.tourisme cantondebrionne.com.
- **Location:** The abbey sits beside the Risle, S of the Seine, about 40km/25mi from Rouen.

VISIT

Open 7am–9pm. Guided tours (1hr) Jun–Sept Mon–Sat 10.30am, 11am, 3pm, 4pm and 5pm; Jun–Sept Sun and public holidays noon, 3pm, 4pm and 6pm; Oct–3 May Mon–Sat 11am, 3pm and 4pm, Sun and public holidays noon, 3pm and 4pm. ⊛5€. ℘02 32 43 72 60. www.abbayedubec.com

Since 1948, when Bec-Hellouin became a functioning abbey again, considerable reconstruction has taken place, particularly of the St-Nicolas Tower of 1467 and the Abbot's Lodging of 1735. But the great Abbey Church, whose 42m/140ft choir was one of the wonders of the Christian world, has gone, though its spiritual power is undiminished.

Caen★★★

Tough and enduring, the city of Caen rebuilt itself after being almost destroyed by bombing during World War II. Today the city proudly preserves an impressive historical legacy, while being committed to peace and the future.

A BIT OF HISTORY
Caen Stone

The light limestone quarried locally was used not only here but in great buildings of the Normans in England (Canterbury Cathedral, the White Tower at the Tower of London and Westminster Abbey).

The City of the Normans

After the invasions of the Norsemen in the 9C and 10C, and the establishment of the duchy of Normandy, Benedictines

- **Population:** 102 663
- **Michelin Map:** 303 E-J 3-4
- **Info:** Pl. St-Pierre. ℘02 31 27 14 14. www.tourisme.caen.fr.
- **Location:** The pedestrian precinct, between pl. St-Pierre and pl. de la République is very lively.
- **Don't Miss:** The Mémorial de la Paix and the Abbaye-aux-Hommes.
- **Timing:** Allow 2hr for the château and the nearby museums, 2hr for the abbeys, and 2hr for the Peace Memorial.

built the first major religious buildings in Normandy. Caen's architectural heritage reveals the affection felt for the city by William, Duke of Normandy, and his wife Mathilda, who chose this as their residence. They married in 1053, against Papal opposition, which arose because of they were cousins. This led to their excommunication until they made amends by William founding the Abbey for Men and Mathilda the Abbey for Women. When William left to conquer England, Mathilda became Regent and ruled the duchy herself.

"Caen the Crucible"

Chester Wilmot's pithy epithet evokes the sufferings undergone by the city in summer 1944. The first shells fell on Caen on D-Day itself (6 June 1944); the city burned for 11 days. Liberated by the Canadians on 9 July, it was then continuously bombarded for another month by the Germans. The inhabitants huddled in the abbey (Abbaye aux Hommes), the hospital (Hospice du Bon Sauveur) and the quarries at Fleury; the final shell fell on 20 August.

SIGHTS

Abbaye-aux-Hommes★★

Espl. Jean-Marie-Louvel. Guided *tours (1hr30min) daily 9.30am, 11am, 2.30pm and 4pm.* 2.40€.

The church of the **Abbey for Men** was founded by the Conqueror; it was begun in 1066 and took 12 years to build. The west front with its soaring towers (the octagonal spires were added in the 13C) dates from this time. The nave is vast; it is a fine example of Romanesque construction with great square bays divided in two by minor piers and with high galleries over the aisles. The clerestory was altered in the 12C when the timber roof was replaced by sexpartite vaulting.

The great lantern-tower over the crossing is probably the work of Lanfranc and William themselves; in its simple perfection it is a masterpiece of Romanesque art. The choir which was extended and altered in the 13C is a very early example of Norman Gothic which

set the standard for buildings all over the duchy.

Château Ducal★

Espl. du Château. Guided *tours Jul–Aug Fri.* No charge. 02 31 27 14 14.

This great fortress perched on a bluff overlooking the city was built by William in 1060, and subsequently strengthened and extended. From its ramparts there are extensive views over Caen. The château houses Caen's **Musée des Beaux-Arts**★★ (open *Wed–Mon 9.30am–6pm;* closed *public holidays;* 5€; 02 31 30 47 70), displaying a good collection of paintings spanning the 15C–20C.

Abbaye-aux-Dames ★★

Pl. Reine Mathilde. Guided *tours (1hr) daily 2.30pm and 4pm.* No charge. 02 31 06 98 98.

The Norman building, with its nave of nine bays, round-headed arches, and blind arcades in the triforium, was founded by Mathilda in 1062 as the church of the **Abbey for Women**. As at St Stephen's, the upper storey was altered when the timber roof was replaced by sexpartite vaulting.

The choir, with its spacious 11C groined vaults, has Mathilda's tomb at its centre.

Le Mémorial★★★

Espl. Général Eisenhower. Open *daily Feb–Dec (last admission 1hr15min before closing).* Closed *25 Dec.* Guided tours available. 16€. 02 31 06 06 45. www.memorial-caen.fr.

Le Mémorial is a "a museum for peace" housed in a former German bunker. With numerous arresting displays about conflict and war and much material of the destruction of Caen during the Liberation, it is a place of contemplation.

Musée de Normandie★★

Château. Open *Wed–Mon 9.30am–6pm.* Closed *public holidays.*

This great museum displays the history of the Normandy region, its culture and people.

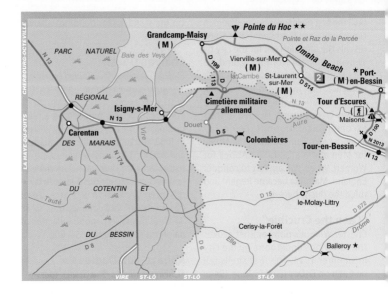

Église St-Pierre★

Pl. Saint Pierre.

Although only a parish church, St Peter's has frequently received generous endowments from wealthy citizens of Caen.

A mix of Gothic and Renaissance architecture make this church quite fascinating. The main church was built in 13–14C and the Renaissance **east end**★★ was added in the early 16C. Note the remarkable early 14C 75m (435ft)-high tower whose spire was restored after destruction in 1944.

Hotel d'Escoville★

Pl. Saint Pierre.

This is a fine example of a typical 16C town house in Caen, which has undergone various bouts of restoration over the years. The tourist office is now housed here.

Église St-Nicolas★

23 r. Saint-Nicolas.

Sometimes referred to as Saint-Nicolas-des-Champs, this 11C church is now disused.

ADDRESSES

▨ STAY

◄ **Hôtel St-Étienne** – *2 r. de l'Académie. ℘02 31 86 35 82. www.hotel-saint-etienne.com. 11 rooms. ⌑6.50€.*
This house, going back to the 1789 Revolution, is located in a quiet district close to the Abbaye-aux-Hommes. Note the fine wooden staircase with its beautiful patined woodwork and the smart bedrooms, some of them with fireplaces. Breakfast served in the dining room.

◄◄ **Hôtel Bernières** – *50 r. de Bernières. ℘02 31 86 01 26. www.hotelbernieres.com. 17 rooms. ⌑6€.*
Don't miss the discreet entrance of this hotel, with its convivial welcome, charming breakfast room and drawing room and delightful bedrooms.

◄◄◄ **Le Bristol** – *31 r. du 11-Novembre. ℘02 31 84 59 76. www.hotelbristolcaen.com. 24 rooms. ⌑8€.*
Those who prefer to be at a distance from the bustle of the centre will appreciate this hotel just a minute from the Orne and the racetrack. The bedrooms have modern, comfortable furnishings and WiFi.

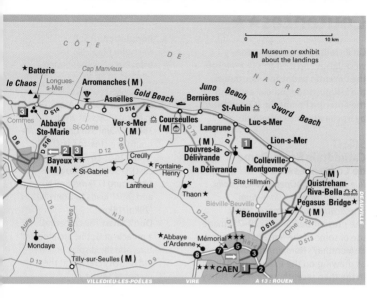

EAT

Le Bouchon du Vaugueux – *12 r. du Graindorge.* ☎*02 31 44 26 26. Closed Aug, fortnight in Jan, Sun–Mon.* This tavern (*bouchon*) is situated near the château and old Caen. Crowded tables add to the friendly ambience. Two fixed-price menus to be discovered on the slate *menu du jour.*

L'Insolite – *16 r. du Vaugueux.* ☎*02 31 43 83 87. www.restaurant-linsolite.com. Closed Sun–Mon except Jul–Aug, public holidays. Reservations recommded.* Take time to discover this half-timbered 16C house with its unusual décor combining rustic frescoes, mirrors and dried flowers. Fish and seafood dishes on the menu. Well-stocked cigar humidor.

P'tit B – *15 r. Vaugueux.* ☎*02 31 93 50 76.* Charming 17C house with a rustic interior artfully modernised, including a superb fireplace. Relaxed atmosphere, a view of the kitchen and seasonal dishes.

SHOPPING

Charcuterie Poupinet – *8 r. St-Jean.* ☎*02 31 86 07 25.* For authentic *tripes à la mode de Caen*, visit Poupinet, where you can buy this speciality in jars. Other regional specialities include pâtés, terrines, black puddings, pork ears in jelly, and more.

Stiffler – *72 r. St-Jean.* ☎*02 31 86 08 94. www.stifflertraiteur.com. Closed Mon, Tue.* This magnificent pastry shop offers such specialities as *charlotte aux fruits de saison, bavaroise au chocolat*, or *méringue aux amandes*. At the deli counter, find delicious, prepared dishes and salads for a quick lunch.

Markets – Marché St-Pierre (Sun) r. de Bayeux (Tue), bd Leroy (Wed, Sat), bd de la Guérinière (Thu), Marché St-Sauveur (Fri), Christmas Market (Dec).

LEISURE ACTIVITIES

Hippodrome de Caen – *La Prairie.* ☎*02 31 85 42 61. Closed Jul–Aug.* This racecourse, nearly 2km/1.2mi long, is located in the heart of Caen. On the second floor, the panoramic restaurant offers a lovely view of the city. Visits are organised on mornings when races are held (30 times a year).

Festyland – *bd Péripherique 50 N, exit for Carpiquet, 14650 Carpiquet.* ☎*02 31 75 04 04. www.festyland.com. Closed Oct–Mar. 14€ (child 12€).* This family leisure park has some 30 attractions. Three daily shows (including a circus show) for young children.

Coutances★★

On its hilltop overlooking the woodlands and pastures *(bocage)* of the Cotentin peninsula, Coutances, the religious and judicial centre of the Cotentin Peninsula, is dominated by its remarkable cathedral.

SIGHT
Cathédrale Notre-Dame de Coutances★★★

Rue Tancrède. ⏱*Open Mar–Oct daily 9am–7pm; Nov–Feb 9am–6pm. http://cathedralecoutances.free.fr.*

The present building (1220–75) made use of some of the remains of Geoffroy de Montbray's Norman cathedral, as well as drawing on the experience gained in the then recently completed abbey at Fécamp.

The west front is framed by two towers, whose soaring lines are emphasised by the tall, narrow corner turrets. The great octagonal lantern rises imposingly over the crossing; it, too, is flanked by turrets, and has strikingly delicate ribbing and slender openings. Within, the nave has clustered piers and highly moulded arches, a triforium with double openings and tall windows behind the typically

Lantern tower of the cathedral

J.P. Clapham/MICHELIN

- ▶ **Population:** 9 628
- **Michelin Map:** 303 D 5
- **Info:** Place Georges Leclerc. ✆02 33 19 08 10. www.ville-coutances.fr.
- **Location:** The town is in Normandy's far west, 76km/47.2mi S of Cherbourg at a crossroads: D 972 links it to St-Lô (29km/18mi east), D 900 heads towards Cherbourg (77km/48mi N) and D 971 leads to Granville (29km/18km S).
- **Don't Miss:** The cathedral, a miracle of Gothic architecture, and the display of old Nativity crèches at the manor of Saussey.
- **Timing:** Take 2hr to see the town and cathedral.
- **Kids:** The cathedral offers guided tours for children in July–August.

Norman balustraded inspection gallery.

The transept is in a more advanced style. Built in 1274, it is a masterpiece of ingenious construction. The columns of a second gallery support the ribs of the vault, and light floods in through 16 windows.

Jardin des Plantes★

2 r. Quesnel-Morinière. ⏱*Open Jul–mid-Sept 9am–11.30pm; Apr–Jun and last half Sept 9am–8pm; rest of the year 9am–5pm. Sound and light show in Jul–Aug.* ✆*No charge.* ✆*02 33 19 08 10.*

The garden's entrance is flanked by an old cider press on one side and the **Quesnel-Morinière Museum** *(✆02 33 07 07 88)* on the other. The terraced promenade traverses the sloping gardens with its many flower beds and pine trees. The obelisk in the centre commemorates a former mayor, Jean-Jaques Quesnel-Morinière.

Deauville★★★

Deauville owes its world-wide reputation as a luxury resort not only to its good facilities but also to the elegance of its social and sporting calendar.

EXCURSIONS
Corniche Normande★★
▷ *From Deauville–Trouville to Honfleur via the D 513 – 21km/13mi.*
This scenic route leads through typical Normandy countryside and affords fine views over the Seine Estuary.

Honfleur★★ – ᠖ See HONFLEUR.

Côte Fleurie★★
▷ *From Deauville–Trouville to Cabourg via the D 513 – 19km/11.8mi.*
The road passes through a number of attractive small resorts with excellent

▷ **Population:** 4 261
᠖ **Michelin Map:** 303 M 3
᠍ **Info:** Place de la Mairie.
℘02 31 14 40 00.
www.deauville.org.
▷ **Location:** Life centres on Place de Morny, the yachting harbour and Port Deauville.
᠗ **Don't Miss:** Regattas, golf and tennis championships, galas, the American Film Festival, international horse sales and horse racing, Deauville Grand Prix.

recreational facilities, among them **Villers-sur-Mer★★**, **Houlgate★★** and **Cabourg★★**.

Les Plages du
Débarquement★★

D-Day Landing Beaches

A mighty Allied armada of over 4 000 specially made craft, together with hundreds of warships and naval escorts, sailed from the south coast of England on the night of 5 June 1944. The following morning they arrived: it was D-Day. The liberation of France, and of Europe, had begun.

SIGHTS
The Normandy invasion, and its significance in European and world history, is marked all along this coastline by cemeteries, monuments and museums.

Omaha Beach
Here the US First Division made its first contact with French soil and here the bloodiest engagement of D-Day was fought. The 1962 film *The Longest Day* by Darryl Zanuck gives a realistic account of these dramatic events.

᠖ **Michelin Map:** 303 F-K 3-4
᠍ **Info:** There are information offices at several of the towns along the coast, or ᠖*see BAYEUX*.
▷ **Location:** The Landing Beaches are along the Normandy coast near Bayeux.

Utah Beach
This beach, northeast of Carentan, entered history following the landing of American forces on 6 June 1944. Despite murderous fire from the Germans, the American 4th Division managed on 12 June to link up with the forces who had landed at Omaha Beach.

EXCURSIONS
Pegasus Bridge
Sword Beach
Pointe du Hoc★★
St-Laurent military cemetery

Dieppe★★

The nearest seaside resort to Paris, Dieppe is sometimes referred to as Plage de Paris. Its famous sea-front lawns were laid out in 1863 by Empress Eugénie and Napoleon III.

A BIT OF HISTORY

Dieppe's history as a major port goes back to the 11C, the English wool trade, and the import of spices from the Orient. As early as the 14C, Dieppe sailors were landing on the coast of the Gulf of Guinea and Jean Cousin was exploring the South Atlantic. In 1402 **Jean de Béthencourt** founded the first European colony on the Canary Islands. **Jean Ango** (1480–1551), whose privateers once captured a fleet of 300 Portuguese vessels, equipped many a voyage of discovery to remote shores. The Parmentier brothers reached Sumatra and drew up charts of the globe.

In the 1608 the great explorer **Samuel de Champlain**, a Dieppe ship-owner, sailed out from Honfleur to found Quebec.

In more recent history, Dieppe was the scene of a failed Allied landing in 1942 codenamed Operation Jubilee. Despite careful planning there were many deaths and a massive loss of equipment.

SIGHTS

👪 ESTRAN Cité de la Mer★

37 r. de l'Asile Thomas. ⏱*Open daily 10am–noon, 2–6pm.* ⏺*5.80€ (child 3.50€).* ✆*02 35 06 93 20. http://estran citedelamer.free.fr.*

This museum is dedicated to the maritime history of Dieppe as a port.

Église St Jacques★

Pl. Saint-Jacques.
Begun in c. 1195, it has parts dating from the 14C, 15C and 16C.

- **Population:** 32 637
- **Michelin Map:** 304 G 2
- **Info:** Pont Jehan Ango. ✆02 32 14 40 60. www.dieppe.fr.
- **Location:** The town is on the Normandy coast close to the border with Picardy.
- **Kids:** ESTRAN Cité de la Mer.

Château-Musée de Dieppe (Dieppe Castle Museum)

r. de Chastes. ⏱*Open Oct–May Wed–Mon 10am–noon, 2–5pm; Jun–Sept until 6pm.* ⏱*Closed 1 Jan, 1 May, 1 Nov, 25 Dec.* ⏺*3€. www.musees-haute-normandie.fr.*

Housed in a 15C fortress, this museum's collection includes fine art, archaeology, ethnology, history, music and ceramics. About a thousand ivory items created by Dieppe craftsmen is also on display.

EXCURSIONS
Côte d'Albâtre (Alabaster Coast)★

From Dieppe to Étretat
104km/64.6mi
Sheer white cliffs cut into by dry valleys *(valleuses)* descend sandy beaches.

Little resorts – **Pourville-sur-Mer, Ste-Marguerite-sur-Mer** and **Veules-les-Roses** – are sited at the seaward end of a series of lush valleys.

In **Varangeville-sur-Mer**, the graveyard of the 11–15C church which overlooks the sea and shelters the tomb of the Cubist painter, **Georges Braque**, and the stained glass of Chapelle St-Dominique (on the outskirts) by the artist are of interest. In a gap in the cliffs halfway between Dieppe and Fécamp, **St-Valéry-en-Caux** is a fishing port and popular resort.

Étretat★★

Sited where a dry valley in the chalk country of the Caux region meets the sea, Étretat was a humble fishing village well into the 19C. It was then favoured by writers such as Maupassant and painters like Courbet and Eugène Isabey.

SIGHTS
Falaise d'Aval★★★
1hr round-trip on foot from the end of the promenade.

▶ *Take the steps and then the path to the clifftop known as Porte d'Aval.*

There are fine views of the magnificent Manneport Arch, the solitary 70m/229.6ft Needle (Aiguille), the long shingle beach and the Amont Cliff on the far side of the bay. The play of colours changes constantly with the time of day and conditions of sky and sea.

▶ **Population:** 1 531
 Michelin Map: 304 B 3
 Info: Place Maurice Guillard. ℰ02 35 27 05 21. www.etretat.net.
 Location: The town is 30km/18.6mi up the coast from Le Havre.
 Don't Miss: The amazing cliff views.

Falaise d'Amont★★
1hr round-trip on foot from the end of the promenade.
At the end of the promenade, the memorial was put up to mark the spot from which two aviators, Nungesser and Coli, were last glimpsed as they set out in their "White Bird" (*Oiseau Blanc*) on their attempt to make a non-stop westward crossing of the Atlantic (8 May 1927). It is not known how these brave men perished.

Évreux★★

The history of Évreux could read like a series of unmitigated disasters, from the burnings and sackings perpetrated by Vandals, Vikings and Plantagenets, to the more recent devastation wreaked from the air by Luftwaffe (in 1940) and Allied air forces (in 1944). But after each disaster, the townspeople have re-created prosperity from ruin. Evidence of this spirit can be seen in the promenade laid out on the old Roman rampart on the banks of the River Iton, and in the treatment of the Clock Tower (Tour de l'Horloge) which was built by Henry V in 1417, two years after his victory over the French at Agincourt.

SIGHT
Cathédrale Notre-Dame★
19 r. Charles Corbeau. Open Mon–Fri 8.30am–7pm; Sat–Sun 9am–7pm.

▶ **Population:** 48 152
 Michelin Map: 304 G 7
 Info: 1 ter Place de Gaulle. ℰ02 32 24 04 43. www.ot-pays-evreux.fr.
 Location: The town is 56km/35mi S of Rouen.

The cathedral, begun in the 12C, is essentially a harmonious Gothic building of the 13C. Much restoration had to take place after John the Good's siege in 1356 and during the reign of Louis XI (1461–83). In the 16C the aisles of the nave were rebuilt in Flamboyant style, and after World War II much of the upper part of the cathedral was replaced.
It has many beautiful 13–14C **stained-glass windows**★.

Fécamp★★

Today the fishing industry dominates Fécamp, but as early as the 11C the town had seen considerable monastic activity. Guy de Maupassant (1850–93) used the town as the setting for many of his short stories.

▶ **Population:** 21 027
◉ **Michelin Map:** 304 C 3
▯ **Info:** Quai Sadi Carnot.
  ✆02 35 28 51 01.
  www.fecamptourisme.com.
◐ **Location:** The town is on the N Normandy coast, 43km/27mi from Le Havre.

SIGHT

Abbatiale de la Sainte-Trinité★★

R. de la Fontaine.
http://abbaye-de-fecamp.com.
The ancient abbey church marks an important stage in the evolution of Gothic architecture in Normandy. Built mostly between 1168–1219, it was influenced by the developments in the Île de France (use of tribunes as in the churches derived from St-Denis outside Paris, the combination of flying buttresses and triforium pioneered at Chartres, which made the tribunes redundant and which here is seen in the south wall of the chancel).

Norman regionalism reasserts itself however in a number of ways: in the slender lantern-tower high above the crossing, and in the inspection gallery at the base of the triforium windows.
In the south transept chapel is a beautiful **Dormition of the Virgin**★.

ADDITIONAL SIGHTS

Palais Bénédictine★★ *(110 r. Alexandre le Grand)*
Musée des Terres-Neuvas et de la Pêche★ *(27 bd Albert)*
Musée des Arts et de l'Enfance★ *(21 r. Alexandre Legros)*

Abbaye d'Hambye★★

The 12C abbey of Hambye is charmingly sited in the green valley of the Sienne. Its ruins evoke the serenity of Benedictine life. The abbey is nearly as complete as Mont-St-Michel. The best-preserved buildings include the chapter house, the sacristy and the parlour.

◉ **Michelin Map:** 303 e 6
▯ **Info:** 43 place de la République, Villedieu.
  ✆02 33 61 05 69.
  www.ot-villedieu.fr.
◐ **Location:** 12km/7.4mi N of the town of Villedieu, in western Normandy.

VISIT

Église Abbatiale★★

Rte de l'Abbaye. ◐*Open Apr–Oct Wed–Mon 10am–noon, 2–6pm.*
◉*4.20€.* ✆*02 33 61 76 92.*
The abbey buildings are dominated by the church, with slender columns and sharply pointed arches around the

choir (1180–1200). The high bell-tower whose upper stage is pierced by round-headed arches was once crowned by a lantern. The monastic buildings frame former cloisters. The chapter-house is a masterpiece of Norman Gothic, divided into two by six central pillars, the final one gathers together the arches of the apse in a masterly way.

Le **Havre**★

Destroyed in World War II and rebuilt in a very striking modern style, this city is one of Europe's most important ports.

A BIT OF HISTORY

By 1517, the harbour at Harfleur *(8km/5mi E)* had silted up. To remedy this François I ordered the building of a new port, which was to be called "Havre-de-Grâce" (Harbour of Grace).

The marshy site selected by Admiral Bonnivet seemed unpromising, but his choice was a happy one since the tide remained at the flood two hours longer here than elsewhere. The port area subsequently spread some 20km/12.4mi upstream with a parallel industrial development of chemical, engineering and motor industries, shipyards and refineries.

The town and its region has an important **Impressionist** history and features in several Impressionist works, notably Claude Monet's *Terrace at Ste-Adresse* (in the Metropolitan Museum in New York), a key work. The old town and resort of **Ste-Adresse**★★ is still a pleasant place; from the clifftop at La Hève there are fine views out over the estuary and the English Channel.

Le Havre today comprises a large port and industrial area, the residential district of Ste-Adresse and the old port of Harfleur. The newer part of town

- ▶ **Population:** 179 052
- **Michelin Map:** 304 A 5
- **Info:** 186 bd Clemenceau. ℰ02 32 74 04 04. www.ville-lehavre.fr or www.lehavretourisme.com.
- **Location:** Le Havre is 42.6km/26.4mi SW of Fécamp.
- **Parking:** Between the Bassin du Commerce and the Espace Niemeyer (pl. du Gén.-de-Gaulle).
- **Don't Miss:** Avenue Foch is a fine promenade bordered by lawns and shaded by trees which opens onto the seafront by the Porte Océane.
- **Timing:** Spend 1hr walking around the modern town starting from the place du Géneral-de-Gaulle.

centres around the Espace Niemeyer, which provides a modern architectual facelift to the urban landscape on Place Gambetta.

SIGHTS
Quartier Moderne (Modern Town)★

During the bombing that preceded Le Havre's liberation on 13 September 1944, the old centre was obliterated

Le Volcan by Oscar Niemeyer, Basin du Commerce, Quartier Moderne

A. de Valroger/MICHELIN

393

and more than 4 000 people were killed; the besieged Germans completed the destruction by dynamiting the port.

The architect **Auguste Perret** (1874–1954), already famous for his innovative work with reinforced concrete, was given the task of rebuilding the devastated town from scratch.

His initial concept involved a vast deck covering all the new city's services (energy, pipelines, gas, traffic).

This bold scheme was rejected, so Perret laid out the town largely using the old street pattern, but in an uncompromisingly modern idiom which remains striking. Among the highlights of Perret's remarkable work are **Place de l'Hôtel de Ville**★, one of the largest squares in Europe; **Avenue Foch**★, with a vista down to the sea and **Église St-Joseph**★ *(134 bd François 1er;* 🕐*open daily 10am–6pm)*, whose interior walls are a lattice of stained glass.

Musée des Beaux-Arts André Malraux★

2 bd Clemenceau. www.ville-lehavre.fr.
This museum houses **works by Eugène Boudin**★ and **Raoul Dufy**.

Honfleur★★

Honfleur lies at the foot of the Côte de Grâce★★ **hill, overlooking the wide waters of the Seine estuary. With its old harbour, its church, its characterful old houses and lanes combining in a singular harmony, it is truly the most picturesque of ports.**

A BIT OF HISTORY

Many maritime ventures began on the quayside at Honfleur. Paulmier de Gouneville sailed from here to Brazil in 1503, and in 1506 Jean Denis explored the mouth of the St Lawrence River.

In 1608 Samuel de Champlain set out to found Quebec City and in 1681 La Salle started the voyage which was to make him the first European to descend the Mississippi all the way to the sea, thereby opening up those vast territories to which he gave the name Louisiana in honour of his king, Louis XIV.

Great artists have appreciated the soft light and breadth of sky over the Seine estuary as seen from Honfleur.

The town appealed to English watercolourist Bonington, locally born Eugène Boudin and later to Claude Monet and the other Impressionists. Erik Satie composed some of his music in Honfleur, and several distinguished writers have lived and worked here.

▶ **Population:** 8 177
⦿ **Michelin Map:** 303 N 3
🛈 **Info:** Quai Lepaulmier. 📞02 31 89 23 30. www.ot-honfleur.fr.
◐ **Location:** Honfleur is reached via the **Pont de Normandie**★★, soaring cable-stayed bridge crossing the Seine with a record-breaking main span 856m/2 808ft between 214m/705ft-high towers. The town is on the seafront at the mouth of the Seine. Its centre focuses on the old port.
⊙ **Don't Miss:** The picturesque lanes of the old quarter.
🕐 **Timing:** Make time in early morning or dusk to linger over the estuary views and the reflections of quayside houses in the harbour.

SIGHT
Le Vieux Honfleur (Old Honfleur)★★

The streets and quaysides of the ancient port are full of character. The old harbour (**Vieux Bassin**★★) shelters a fishing fleet as well as yachts and pleasure-craft.

A richly varied townscape is formed by the fine stone residences along the Quai St-Etienne, the narrow, slate-faced houses on the Quai Ste-Catherine, the church (Église St-Etienne), the Governor's House (Lieutenance), all seen against the foreground of masts and rigging. Nearby is the **Église Ste-Catherine**★ with its detached **bell-tower**★ *(r. des Logettes; ○open mid-Mar–mid-Nov Wed–Mon 10am–noon, 2–6pm; ○closed May, 14 Jul; ⊚2.10€; ℘02 31 89 11 83).* The church was rebuilt after the Hundred Years' War by the ships' carpenters. All around are houses built in like fashion, making up a fine group of timber buildings, unusual in Western Europe.

Rue Haute, a former pathway outside the fortifications, has kept many fine houses of brick, stone and timber once lived in by shipbuilders.

Musée Eugène Boudin

pl. Erick Satie. ○*Open mid-Mar–Sept Wed–Mon 10am–noon, 2–6pm; rest of the year Mon, Wed–Fri 2.30–5pm, Sat–Sun 10am–noon, 2.30–5pm.* ○*Closed 1 Jan–10 Feb, 1 May, 14 Jul, 25 Dec.* ⊚*3€.* ℘*02 31 89 54 00. www.ville-honfleur.fr.*

This museum houses temporary exhibitions of Impressionist works from Normandy. There is also a room devoted to the works of the French Impressionist Painter, Eugène Boudin (1824–1898).

ADDRESSES

🏠 STAY

⊖⊖ **Le Vieux Pressoir** – *route de Rouen, 14130 Surville/Pont l'Evêque. 13.5km/8.2mi from Honfleur via D 580, rte de Pont-Audemer then left on D 312. ℘02 31 64 34 82. 5 rooms.* Located in the heart of the countryside, this 18C wood-sided farm is meant for lovers of quietude and authenticity. Each room overflows with 19C and 20C furniture and objects discovered in second-hand shops. Children will be delighted with the duck pond.

⊖⊖⊟ **Le Belvédère** – *36 r. Émile-Renouf. ℘02 31 89 08 13. Closed Jan. 9 rooms.* ⊐*15€.* This venerable old house owes its name to the belvedere crowning the roof. The renovated bedrooms benefit from the ambient tranquillity. Mealtime, the glass-covered restaurant and small terrace offer an unbeatable view of the Pont de Normandie.

⊖⊖⊟ **Hôtel Otelinn** – *62 cours AlbertManuel. ℘02 31 89 41 77. www.kyriad.com. 50 rooms.* ⊐*8€.* At a distance from the city centre, this hotel has the considerable advantage of proposing rooms at reasonable prices. Small and functional, they make for an agreeable halt. A garden and a terrace give you the opportunity of basking in the gentle Norman sun.

⊖⊖⊟⊟ **Le Clos Deauville Saint-Gatien** – *4 r. des Brioleurs, 14130 St-Gatien-des-Bois. 9km/5.6mi S of Honfleur via D 579. ℘02 31 65 16 08. 58 rooms.* ⊐*13€.* The charm of the Norman countryside a few short miles from the shore characterises this half-timbered house nestled in a verdant setting. Comfortable, cosy rooms. Three pools, one covered, a sauna and a fitness room.

🍴 EAT

⊟ **Le Bistrot des Artistes** – *14 pl. Pierre Berthelot. ℘02 31 89 95 90. Closed Jan & Wed except Jul–Sept.* Antiques, paintings of the sea, photos of Honfleur and leatherette wall seats make up the décor of this restaurant with a Parisian bistro flair. Tables near the window have a lovely view of the Vieux Bassin. On the menu: salads and slices of bread with various toppings.

⊖⊖⊟ **Au P'tit Mareyeur** – *4 r. Haute. ℘02 31 98 84 23. www.auptitmareyeur. com. Closed Jan, Mon & Tue.* This minuscule restaurant right near the harbour has a decided maritime slant, in the kitchen as well as the dining area. The bill of fare changes often, but between the fixed-price menu and the suggestions du jour, fish and seafood fans can look forward to a delightful meal.

⊜⊜⊜ **Au Vieux Honfleur** – *13 quai St-Étienne.* ℘*02 31 89 15 31. www. auvieuxhonfleur.com.* This restaurant by the old harbour extends its terrace along the quay when the weather is fine. Al fresco or inside, nice and warm among bibelots, posters and paintings, you'll be able to savour Norman dishes and seafood while gazing upon the splendid basin.

🛒 SHOPPING

La Petite Chine – *14–16 r. du Dauphin.* ℘*02 31 89 36 52. Closed Mon.* Decorated in blue and yellow, Monet's favourite colours, this pretty little pastry shop and tearoom looks out on the wharf. Try the regional specialities: gingerbread, *tarte paysanne* (farmers' pie) and apples in calvados. Music and a library are at the customers' disposal.

Pom'cannelle – *60 quai Ste-Catherine.* ℘*02 31 89 55 25.* These home-made ices are an absolute must. In addition to liquorice and apricot, you must try this blissfully anti-dietetic concoction: ice cream flavoured with *confiture de lait*, a gooey milk caramel.

🏃 SPORT & LEISURE

Centre équestre du Ramier – *Chemin du Ramier, Équemauville. S of Honfleur.* ℘*02 31 89 49 97.* Located in the heart of the (authentic!) Norman countryside, this lovely riding centre has 15 training horses available. Rides last for 1hr–1hr30min.

Abbaye de
Jumièges★★★

The great abbey in its splendid setting on the Lower Seine forms one of the most evocative groups of ruins in France.

A BIT OF HISTORY

The abbey was founded in the 7C and within 50 years housed 700 monks and 1 500 lay-brothers. Its great wealth

- 🔹 **Michelin Map:** 304 E 5.
- 🔹 **Info:** Rue Guilllaume-le-Conquérant, Jumièges. ℘02 35 37 28 97. www.jumieges.fr.
- 🔹 **Location:** Jumièges is on a big loop of the River Seine just W of Rouen. The abbey is a ruin, in places open to the sky; consider this an outdoor venue and dress accordingly.
- 🔹 **Don't Miss:** Enjoy the view from the terrace over the garden.
- 🔹 **Timing:** Allow at least 1hr for the visit.

was based on the generosity of the Merovingian rulers and on tithes drawn from a vast area.

Destroyed by the Vikings, the abbey was raised again in the early 11C, but suffered in the Wars of Religion. The monks were scattered at the outbreak of the French Revolution.

In 1793 it was auctioned and a purchaser started dismantling it to re-use the stone, blowing up the chancel and lantern-tower in the process. In 1852 a new owner saved it from complete

Abbaye de Jumièges

A. de Valroger/MICHELIN

destruction, but by then the great edifice was already a ruin.

VISIT

🕐Open daily 15 Apr–15 Sept 9.30am–6.30pm; 16 Sept–14 Apr 9.30am–1pm, 2.30–5.30pm. 🕐Closed public holidays. ☜5€, free 1st Sun in the month (Nov–Mar). ✆02 35 37 24 02.

Lessay★

Lessay lies on the edge of moorland country whose harsh beauty was sung by Barbey d'Aurevilly (1808–89), who helped establish a distinct Norman literature. The town comes to life every September at the time of the Holy Cross Fair.

SIGHT
Église abbatiale★★

R. Hamet. ☜Guided tours Wed 3pm in summer. ☜4€. ✆02 33 45 14 34.
Founded in 1056, this is not only one of the most perfect examples of Romanesque architecture in Normandy, but also a tribute to the extraordinary skill and devotion of the chief architect of the Historic Monuments Institute, Yves Froidevaux, who rebuilt the church after its being blown up by the Wehrmacht in 1944.

From the east there is a fine view of the rounded apse backed by a flat gable and dominated by the massive tower.

Inside, there are the typically Norman features of great nave arches, triforium and inspection gallery running underneath the clerestory windows. But Lessay also marks the architectural transition from groined vaults (as used in the 11C aisles) to quadripartite vaults, used somewhat crudely in the choir (end of the 11C), then with greater confidence in the nave (beginning of the 12C). This revolutionary development led directly to the great achievements of Gothic architecture, with its high-flung vaults and walls of glass.

The most striking feature of the abbey is the west front of the **Église Notre-Dame** with its two magnificent towers, 43m/141ft high, the oldest and grandest of any Norman abbey.

The power of the building to move the beholder is enhanced by the absence of of vaults which permits the eye to soar freely skywards; the ruins seem to express spiritual qualities.

▶ **Population:** 2 021
🖮 **Michelin Map:** 303 C 4
🚹 **Info:** 11 pl. St-Cloud. ✆02 33 45 14 34. www.canton-lessay.com.
▶ **Location:** Lessay, a small town in the middle of the Cotentin Peninsula (☜see PRESQ'ÎLE DU COTENTIN in the Michelin Green Guide Normandy), grew up around the Benedictine abbey.

Église abbatiale
©Bart Parren/iStockphoto.com

CALENDAR OF EVENTS

La Foire de Sainte-Croix – 3 days in second week of Sept. Founded in the 11C, this popular trade fair attracts around 400 000 people with thousands of stalls. In fact, a huge section of the town effectively turns into a market-place!

Lisieux★★

Lisieux on the east bank of the Touques is the market centre of the prosperous Auge region. It is also a well-known pilgrimage centre.

A BIT OF HISTORY

The town is famous in France for **Ste Thérèse de Lisieux** (1873–97), canonised in 1925. Devout pilgrims come to the town to see her house, **Les Buissonnets** *(chemin du Paradis;* ⊙*open Palm Sunday–Sept 9am–noon, 2–6pm; Oct, Feb–Mar 10am–noon, 2–5pm; Nov–15 Dec 15 Jan–31 Jan 10am–noon, 2–4pm;* ℘*02 31 48 55 08; http://therese-de-lisieux.cef.fr)*, or attend services at the vast **Basilica** *(av. Jean XXIII)*, which is dedicated to her.

EXCURSIONS
Manor Houses of the Pays d'Auge
With its closely packed hedgerows, thatched cottages and old manors, the Pays d'Auge is a countryside of great charm. The farmhouses and manors of this tranquil landscape are set within an enclosure planted with apple trees and defined by a hedge.

All the buildings are timber-framed, from the house itself, to the cider-press, apple-store, stables and dairy grouped around it. Among the finest are the moated site at **Coupesarte** *(16km/10mi SW)* and **Château Crèvecœur**★ *(18km/11mi W)* with its museum devoted to the story of petroleum research (musée de la recherche pétrolière).

▶ **Population:** 22 100
⊙ **Michelin Map:** 303 N 5
ℹ **Info:** 11 R. d'Alençon.
℘02 31 48 18 10.
www.lisieux-tourisme.com.
◖ **Location:** The town is a short distance inland from Honfleur.

Le Mont-St-Michel★★★

Mont-St-Michel has been called "the Wonder of the Western World"; its extraordinary site, its rich and influential history and its glorious architecture combine to make it the most splendid of all the abbeys of France.

A BIT OF HISTORY

At the beginning of the 8C St Michael appeared to Aubert, the bishop of Avranches. Aubert founded an oratory on an island then known as Mont Tombe. This oratory was soon replaced by an abbey, which adopted the Benedictine Rule in the 10C, thereby assuring its importance. Two centuries later the Romanesque abbey reached its peak of development.

In the 13C, following a fire, a great rebuilding in Gothic style took place,

▶ **Population:** 41
⊙ **Michelin Map:** 303 C 8
ℹ **Info:** ℘02 33 60 14 30.
www.ot-montsaint michel.com.
◖ **Location:** Mont-St-Michel is a granite island about 900m/984yd round and 80m/262ft high. As the bay is already partially silted up, the mount is usually to be seen surrounded by huge sand banks which shift with the tides and often reshape the mouths of the neighbouring rivers. It is linked to the mainland by a causeway which was built in 1877.
🅿 **Parking:** Parking is available outside the Tour du Roi near the Porte de l'Avancée.

Mont-St-Michel

A. De Valroger/MICHELIN

known as *la Merveille* – the Marvel. Even though the English beseiged it during the Hundred Years' War, the Mount did not fall into the invaders' hands.

VISIT

L'Abbaye (Abbey)★★★

Rue de l'Abbaye. ○*Open daily May– Aug 9am–7pm; Sept–Apr 9.30am–6pm. Last admission 1hr before closing time.* ○*Closed 1 Jan, 1 May, 25 Dec.* ◉*8.50€.* ☞*Guided tours (1hr) available.* ✆*02 33 89 80 00.*

The architecture of the Abbey was determined by the constraints imposed by the rock on which it stands. Crowned as it is by the Abbey church and the buildings of the Merveille (c 1225), the result bears little resemblance to the conventionally planned Benedictine monastery.

Église★★

There is a striking contrast between the stern character of the Romanesque nave and the well-lit Flamboyant choir. The axis of the sanctuary is aligned on the rising sun on 8 May, the spring Feast of St Michael under the Eastern calendar.

La Merveille★★★

This is the group of buildings on the north side of the mount. The Guests' Hall (**salle des Hôtes**★) is a masterpiece of High Gothic. Suspended between sea and sky, the cloisters (**cloître**★★★), with their slim columns in pink granite arranged in a quincunx pattern, make a magic garden conducive to serenity and inner joy. The Refectory (**Réfectoire**★) is filled with light from its recessed windows. It hangs 45m/148ft high, a bold achievement on the part of its architect who was unable to use buttresses on the sheer rock-face. The vast Knights' Hall (**Salle des Chevaliers**★) is divided into four parts. It may be so named after the chivalric Order established here.

Jardins de l'Abbaye★

From the gardens there is a view of the north face of the mount, the "most beautiful wall in all the world", according to Victor Hugo.

ADDRESSES

🛏 STAY

BEAUVOIR

🍽 **Amaryllis Bed and Breakfast** – *Le Bas-Pays, Beauvoir. 2.5km/1.5mi S of Mont-St-Michel dir. Pontorson.* ✆*02 33 58 46 79. www.amaryllis-chambres-dhotes. fr. 5 rooms.* ⊇*4.70€.* This recently built stone house was designed as a B&B. The impeccably clean rooms feature well-equipped bathrooms and a furnished terrace.

🍽🍽🍽 **Les Vieilles Digues** – *Rte du Mont-St-Michel, Beauvoir. 3km/1.8mi S of Mont-St-Michel dir. Pontorson.* ✆*02 33 58 55 30. http://bnb-normandy.com. Closed Dec, Jan. 7 rooms.* This pretty stone house boasts spacious rooms

thoughtfully furnished with handsome pieces. The room with a view of Mont-St-Michel is, naturally, a favourite. Agreeable half-timbered breakfast room. Landscaped garden.

PONTORSON

🍽 **La Tour Brette** – *8 r. Couesnon, Pontorson. 9km/5.6mi S of Mont-St-Michel.* ✆*02 33 60 10 69. www.fraysse. phpnet.org. Closed 14–22 Mar, 1–20 Dec, Wed except Jul–Aug. 10 rooms.* ⊇*7€.* This small, centrally located hotel is named after the tower that used to protect Normandy from the Duchy of Brittany's assaults. The rooms are not very large but they've been recently renovated. Restaurant in a simple setting with a long, traditional menu.

Hôtel de Bretagne –
R. Couesnon, Pontorson. 4km/2.5mi S of Mont-St-Michel via D 976. 02 33 60 10 55. Closed 20 Jan–5 Feb. 12 rooms. 7€. Regional-style house. Admire the lovely 18C wood panels and the grey-marble fireplace in the first room. Cosy, typically British bar and spacious, pleasantly furnished rooms.

ROZ-SUR-COUESNON
Chambre d'hôte Bergerie –
La Poultière, Roz-sur-Couesnon. 16km/10mi SW of Mont-St-Michel via D 797, the coast road to St-Malo. 02 99 80 29 68. www.la-bergerie-mont-saint-michel.com. 5 rooms. Located in the former sheepfold, the rooms are comfortable and benefit from the peaceful atmosphere of the small hamlet. The kitchen set aside for guests is very much appreciated. A self-catering cottage is also available.

Chambre d'hôte Mme Gillet –
3 Le Val-St-Revert, Roz-sur-Couesnon. 15km/9.3mi SW of Mont-St-Michel via D 797, the coast road to St-Malo. 02 99 80 27 85. 3 rooms. This family house overlooks the bay and offers a beautiful view of Mont-St-Michel and the surrounding countryside.

¶/EAT
Pré Salé – *Restaurant belonging to the Hôtel Mercure – 2km/1.2mi S of Mont-St-Michel via D 976. 02 33 60 14 18. www.hotelmercure-montsaintmichel.com.com. Closed 12 Nov–6 Feb.* Located along the River Couesnon at the start of the dike, the Hôtel Mercure welcomes you into its bright dining room.Try the delicious salt-meadow (pré salé) meat from Mont-St-Michel Bay.

La Sirène – *located inside the walls. 02 33 60 08 60 – closed 1 Jan–9 Feb.* This crêperie was an inn for many years. The frosted-glass windows, their panes separated by metal mullions, confirm the genuine flavour of the place.

Rouen★★★

With its skyline of towers, spires and fine buildings, Rouen offers a wealth of artistic delights. Established at the lowest point on the Seine which could be successfully bridged, Rouen developed into a hugely successful port and industrial centre.

A BIT OF HISTORY
Rouen has been important since Roman times owing to its position as the lowest bridging-point on the Seine; the alignment of its two main streets (Rue du Gros-Horloge and Rue des Carmes) still reflects the layout of the early city. Although Rouen is the birthplace of a number of scientists, it is men of letters and artists who have contributed most to Rouen's fame. **Gustave Flaubert** (1821–80) was the son of Rouen's chief surgeon and lived in and around the city. His major works include *Madame Bovary* (1857), in which the village of Ry (20km /12.4mi east) is described under the name of Yonville.

▶ **Population:** 105 043
Michelin Map:304 G 5
Info: 25 pl. de la Cathédrale. 02 32 08 32 40. www.rouentourisme.com.
▶ **Location:** The city stands on both banks of a curve in the River Seine. The quays on the north bank and the surrounding streets are the city centre. The other bank of the river contains the city's administrative buildings, as well as extensive residential and commercial districts and shopping centres.
Don't Miss: Notre-Dame cathedral.
Timing: Take 1hr30min for the cathedral and 30min for a walk through Old Rouen with its beautiful 15C–18C half-timbered houses.

SIGHTS
Cathédrale Notre-Dame★★★
Pl. de la Catédrale. Open Nov–9 Mar
*Tue–Sat 7.30am–noon, 2–6pm, Mon
2–6pm, Sun and public holidays 8am–
6pm; 10 Mar–Oct Tue–Sat 7.30am–7pm,
Mon 2–7pm, Sun and public holidays
8am–6pm.* Closed 1 Jan, 1 May, 11
Nov. www.cathedrale-rouen.net.

This is one of the finest achievements of
the French Gothic; it was rebuilt after a
fire in 1200. Thanks to the generosity of
John Lackland, Duke of Normandy as
well as King of England, reconstruction
was swift; the transepts were
extended and the choir enlarged. The
spaciousness of the interior is striking.
The choir, with its 14 soaring pillars and
delicate triforium, is a masterpiece of
harmonious proportion.

The great edifice seems to have been
under repair for most of its existence
for varied reasons: the Hundred
Years' War, another fire in 1514, the
Religious Wars, the hurricane of 1683,
the French Revolution, the burning-
down of the spire in 1822 and the
aerial bombardment of the night of 19
April 1944. This most recent disaster
threatened the whole structure; indeed,
restoration work is still underway.

Vieux Rouen★★★
All around the cathedral and the Rue
du Gros Horloge approaching it is
Vieux Rouen. The old town's narrow
streets, many of them pedestrianised,
are lined with more than 800 timber-
framed houses, large and small, elegant
or picturesquely askew, all characteristic
examples of medieval building
techniques. Until 1520, the upper floors
jutted out for reasons of economy and
greater floor-space.

Bustling **Rue du Gros-Horloge★★**,
lined with old houses and given over to
pedestrians, is one of the city centre's
main attractions. **The Gros-Horloge
clock** on its arch has only one hand;
next to it is the belfry from the top of
which there is a fine view over the city
and its surroundings.

Rue St-Romain★★ is one of the most
fascinating streets, with many timber-
framed houses dating from the 15C to
the 18C. No 74 is a Gothic building with
15C windows.

Place du Vieux-Marché★
This modern complex on the edge of
the Old Town occupies the site where
Joan of Arc, aged 19, was burned at the
stake following her trial as a heretic; 25
years later she was rehabilitated. In the
centre of the square is the great Cross
of Rehabilitation, marking the place
where Joan of Arc was burnt. There
is also a covered market and a church
incorporating stained-glass windows
(**verrière★★**) of 16C date.

Église St-Maclou★★
Pl. Barthélemy. Open Fri–Mon
*Apr–Oct 10am–noon, 2–6pm; Nov–Mar
10am–noon, 2–5.30pm.* Closed 1 Jan,
25 Dec.

When compared with the cathedral,
the church provides striking evidence
of the evolution of the Gothic style. It
was begun in 1437 and is a fine example
of the Flamboyant style at its purest.
Nevertheless its decoration is of the
Renaissance (doors, stairs, gallery and
organ-case). At the north corner of
the west front is a fountain with two
manikins performing the same act as
their counterpart at Brussels, albeit with
somewhat less finesse.

Aître St-Maclou★★
r. Victor Hugo.
This is a rare example of a medieval
plague cemetery. It is enclosed by half-
timbered buildings decorated with
macabre carvings showing the Dance
of Death, skulls and crossbones, grave-
diggers' tools...

Église St-Ouen★★
135 r. Beauvoisine. Open Apr–Oct
*Tue–Thu, Sat–Sun 10am–noon,
2–6pm; Nov–Mar Tue–Thu, Sat–Sun
10am–noon, 2–5.30pm .* Closed 1
Jan, 25 Dec.

Built in the 14C, this former abbey
church marks the peak of achievement
of the High Gothic style. Its architect was
complete master of the forces acting

on his building, leading them at will via ogee arches on to flying buttresses weighted by pinnacles, thence to foundations beyond the walls. The structural problem solved, he was then able to concentrate on designing the shell of the building. With no structural role, walls could become windows, flooding the interior with light and thereby encouraging an increasingly literate congregation to follow the service with the missals now coming into use.

A few years on, and the Gothic had fulfilled its architectural potential; its final phase, the Flamboyant, delights in ornamental excess rather than innovation.

Musée des Beaux-Arts★★★

espl. Marcel Duchamp. 🔄🕐*Open Wed–Mon 10am–6pm.* 🕐*Closed public holidays.* 🎫*4€.* 🕿*02 35 71 28 40. www.rouen-musees.com.*

The museum has a magnificent collection of 15–20C painting, especially in the earlier period, as well as fine sculpture, and other pieces including furniture and gold-work. See Gérard David's *Virgin and Saints*, an oil painting on wood, one of the masterpieces of Flemish Primitive art, as well as several choice pieces from the French School: *Diana Bathing* by François Clouet, The *Concert*

of Angels by Philippe de Champaigne, and *Venus Arming Aeneas* by Nicolas Poussin. Other outstanding works from European countries are *The Adoration of the Shepherds* by Rubens, *St Barnabé Healing the Sick* by Veronese, and especially *Democritus* by Velasquez.

Musée de la Céramique★★

1 r. Faucon. 🕐*Open daily 10am–1pm, 2–6pm.* 🎫*2.30€; no charge 1st Sun in the month.* 🕿*02 35 07 31 74. www.rouen-musees.com*

The 17C Hotel d'Hocqueville houses this museum, which presents the history of Rouen pottery with outstanding faience collections. The work of **Masséot Abaquesne**, the first faïence-maker in Rouen in the mid-16C, is represented here. Rouen pottery enjoyed great popularity in the 18C. The liking for chinoiserie and lambrequin ornament, and a desire to replace metal plates and dishes with ceramics, helped assure Rouen's success with ewers, fountains, spice pots.

ADDITIONAL SIGHTS

Palais de Justice★★ *(36 r. aux juifs)*
Musée Le Secq des Tournelles★★ *(r. Jacques-Villon)*
Panorama★★★ from **Côte-Ste-Catherine Jardin des Plantes★** *(114 av. des Martyrs de la Résistance)*

ADDRESSES

🛏 STAY

🍴 **Hôtel des Carmes** – *33 pl. des Carmes.* 🕿*02 35 71 92 31. www.hoteldes carmes.com. 12 rooms.* 🛏*8.50€.* Situated in the town centre, not far from the cathedral, this hotel is an appealing halt. The delightfully decorated reception area hints of Bohemia, and the clutter-free bedrooms are charming and well fitted out. A very good address for budget-conscious travellers.

🍴 **Hôtel Versan** – *3 r. Jean-Lecanuet.* 🕿*02 35 07 77 07. www.rouen-hotel-versan.com. 34 rooms.* 🛏*9€.* A practical address on a busy boulevard not far

from the town hall. The rooms are all similar, functional and well equipped.

🍴 **Hôtel Dandy** – *93 r. Cauchoise.* 🕿*02 35 07 32 00. www.hotel-dandy-rouen.federal-hotel.com. Closed 26 Dec–2 Jan. 18 rooms.* 🛏*11€.* Situated in a pedestrian street downtown, close to place du Vieux-Marché, this little hotel decorated with care has a certain charm. The rooms, rather too cluttered for some tastes, are quite cosy. Breakfast served in a pretty little room.

🍴 EAT

🍴 **Les Maraîchers** – *37 pl. du V ieux-Marché.* 🕿*02 35 71 57 73. www.les-maraichers.fr.* A restaurant with Parisian bistro airs in a half-timbered house. Wall seats, a bar, tables set close to one another, old advertising plaques, hat and jug collections – nothing's missing! Improvised cuisine. Norman-style second dining room on the ground floor.

😐🍽 **Pascaline** – *5 r. de la Poterne. ✆02 35 71 18 30. www.pascaline.fr. Reservations recommended.* Located next to the courthouse, this restaurant with a bistro façade is very nice. Brasserie décor with handsome wood counters, long seats and yellow walls. Choice of attractive fixed-price menus.

🍽🍽🍽 **Le Beffroy** – *15 r. Beffroy. ✆02 35 71 55 27. Closed Sun eve and Tue. Reservations required.* This 16C Norman half-timbered house offers the choice between three pretty dining rooms, all equally inviting. A fine address for savouring plentiful fare prepared with quality ingredients.

🍽🍽🍽🍽 **La Couronne** – *31 pl. du Vieux-Marché. ✆02 35 71 40 90. www.lacouronne.com.fr.* The décor of this 14C house on the market place is simply superb: beams, carved woodwork, hearths and frescoes. It is said to be France's oldest inn. True or false? No one knows, but one thing is certain: their *canard rouennais* (Rouen-style duck) is superlative!

🎭 NIGHTLIFE

Le Bateau Ivre – *17 r. des Sapins. ✆02 35 70 09 05. http://bateauivre.rouen. free.fr. Closed Sun–Tue and Aug.* Ever on the lookout for new talents, this bar has been livening up Rouen night life for the past 20 years. Concerts Fridays and Saturdays, ballads and poetry Thursdays, café-theatre or French songs Tuesday evenings. A few programmes are available at the tourist office.

Bar de la Crosse – *53 r. de l'Hôpital. ✆02 35 70 16 68. Closed Sun, Mon, fortnight in Aug and public holidays.* When spending time in Rouen, pay a visit to this small, unpretentious bar. It owes its fine reputation to its singular atmosphere; between concerts and exhibits, laughter abounds, and it isn't unusual to see tourists and regulars chatting here like old friends.

La Taverne St-Amand – *11 r. St-Amand. ✆02 35 88 51 34. Closed 3 weeks in Aug & Sun.* Transformed into a bar 30 years ago, this 17C house attracts painters, writers, actors and other regular patrons. Convivial atmosphere.

🎭 SHOWTIME

Théâtre de l'Écharde – *16 r. Flahaut. ✆02 35 89 42 13. Tickets available at the theatre before performance.* Theatre with 100 seats where the troupe's creations and shows for young theatregoers are performed.

Théâtre des Deux Rives – *48 r. Louis Ricard. ✆02 35 70 22 82. www. cdr2rives.com. 18€. Ticket office open Tue–Sat 2–7pm. Closed Jul–Aug.* Classical and modern theatre.

🛒SHOPPING

Markets – Place Saint-Marc (Tue, Fri and Sat all day); Place des Emmurés (Tue and Sat all day); Place du Vieux-Marché (daily except Mon, mornings).

Faïencerie Augy-Carpentier – *26 r. St-Romain. ✆02 35 88 77 47.* The last handmade and hand-decorated earthenware workshop in Rouen! They offer copies of many traditional motifs on white and pink backgrounds, from blue monochrome to multicoloured, and from lambrequin to cornucopia. Personalised pieces available.

Maison Hardy – *22 pl. du Vieux-Marché. ✆02 35 71 81 55.* In this alluring delicatessen, the Hardis offer Rouen specialities such as terrine de canard, duck being a highly prized fowl in this city (also known for its mutton). Mr Hardi's andouilles de Vire and his Caen tripe cooked in calvados and cider, specialities from Normandy, have clinched his reputation.

Chocolatier Auzou – *163 r. du Gros-Horloge. ✆02 35 70 59 31. www.auzou-chocolat.fr.* Located in a half-timbered house, this renowned chocolatier will tempt you with his specialities, such as Les Larmes de Jeanne d'Arc (Joan of Arc's Tears: lightly roasted almonds covered with nougatine and chocolate) or L'Agneau Rouennais (a sort of sponge cake) and candied apples.

NORTHERN FRANCE AND PARIS

Paris is located at the centre of the Île-de-France (Island of France), from which the French state has grown due to its location defined by the rivers Seine, Aisne, Oise and Marne. Where its limestone plateaux have been cut into by the rivers, lush valleys have been formed, contrasting with the vast arable tracts of the Beauce, Vexin and Brie. A girdle of greenery surrounds the capital, made up of the great forests such as those of **Fontainebleau** and Rambouillet, into which merge the landscapes of leisure and pleasure. Further north, landscapes are open and high-yielding arable land is broken by a number of valleys, such as that of the Somme.

Highlights

1. Grand'Place and Place des Héros at Arras: **Les Places** (p409)
2. Rodin's bronze figures: **Monument des Bourgeois de Calais** (p413)
3. Railway carriage at Compiègne: **Clairière de l'Armistice** (p419)
4. Europe's only Disney resort: **Disneyland Paris** (p422)
5. French Classicism at its best: **Château de Versailles** (p475)

Geography – Northeast is Flanders, consisting largely of polderlands having much in common with the adjoining Low Countries. Inland is the *pays noir* of the coalfield or "Black country", stretching from Béthune to Valenciennes and running into the conurbation of Lille-Tourcoing-Roubaix.

The presence of a number of islands in the Seine made a convenient crossing point for the prehistoric North–South trade route. Under the Gauls, urban development was confined to the Île de la Cité, though Roman Lutetia spread into today's Latin Quarter.

History – The Capetian kings made Paris their capital, giving it the dominant role in the country's political and cultural life – exercised ever since.

At the centre of the Revolution and the establishment of Empire which followed, Paris soon became an imperial city. Managing to avoid a great deal of damage in World War I; during World War II it was occupied by the Germans. Away from the capital, the Île-de-France, together with Amiens, was the cradle of Gothic architecture; while to the north, Flanders has long been a battleground and was completely devastated during both World Wars.

Today – the whole region is part of a highly successful modern economy, which, while heavily industrialised, retains much woodland – especially around the capital – and there are huge tracts of agricultural land to the north, particularly in Picardy. Tourists flock to see the many attractions of Paris and the Île-de-France bolstering its already tourist economy.

In the *pays noir*, the coal industry has disappeared and, in its place, textile, processed food and car part industries provide much employment.

Amiens★★

The largest Gothic cathedral in France, one of the finest in the world, is the majestic centrepiece of the historic capital of Picardy.

A BIT OF HISTORY

Amiens' great legend is that of the Roman soldier who, passing near Amiens, sliced his cloak in two and gave half to a wretched beggar. Later becoming Bishop of Tours, the former soldier was eventually canonised as St Martin, patron saint of France. In 1477, on the death of Charles le Téméraire (the Bold) this ancient capital of Picardy became subject to the French Crown. In the 17C its textile industry prospered (Amiens velvet). The city suffered in both World Wars, in 1918 during the Ludendorff Offensive, and in 1940 during the Battle of France. Later attractively restored and now a university town, it is again a major centre for the arts and the economy.

SIGHTS

Cathédrale Notre-Dame★★★

pl. Notre Dame. ⏰*Open daily Apr–Sept 8.30am–6.30pm; Oct–Mar 8.30am–5.30pm.* ✎ *Guided tours available.* ⏍*5.50€.* ✆*03 22 71 60 50.*
A UNESCO World Heritage Site, this harmonious building was begun in 1220 and completed just 68 years later. The architect, Robert de Luzarches,

▶ **Population:** 136 105
🖫 **Michelin Map:** 301 G 8
🗉 **Info:** 40 pl. Notre-Dame. ✆03 22 71 60 50. www.amiens-tourisme.com.
◗ **Location:** After visiting the cathedral, stroll the shopping streets, especially rue du Hocquet and place du Don. Walk across the River Somme to explore the narrow streets of Quartier St-Leu, which contain craft and antique shops, cafés and restaurants.
🅿 **Parking:** Leave the car in place St Michel, next to the cathedral, or in Saint-Leu underground car park.
👥 **Kids:** Within the Hortillonnages, the Île aux Fagots has an aquarium and insectarium. Amiens is famous for its tradition of puppets: enjoy a show at the **Chés Cabotans** puppet theatre.

had all the stonework cut to its finished dimensions before it left the quarry, then simply assembled it on site.
The cathedral is in Gothic Lanceolate style, with three-storey elevations including a blind triforium in nave and transept. The wonderfully

Puppets

Amiens' puppet shows date back to about 1785. Known in Picardy dialect as **cabotans**, the puppets are carved out of wood and about 50cm/19.7in tall. The main character **Lafleur** is The King of St-Leu (the medieval quarter) and undoubtedly embodies all the spirit and character of the Picardy people. Since at least the 19C, this truculent, irreverent, bold character with his fiery temper has expressed plain common sense and acclaimed the proud nobility of the province in the language of his ancestors. Even from a distance, he is recognisable by his impressive stature, characteristic gait, and 18C valet's livery of fine red Amiens velvet. He is often accompanied by his wife **Sandrine** and his best friend Tchot Blaise. His motto is "Drink, walk and do nothing".

In the 19C, each of the 20 quarters in the city had its own puppet theatre. With the arrival of the cinema and sporting events at the turn of the 20C, however, the theatres gradually closed down.

Detail of the central doorway, Cathedral Notre-Dame

S. Sauvignier/MICHELIN

façade, including the 16C Sea Window (rose de la Mer), of the north transept; the 14C Window of the Winds (rose des Vents); and of the south transept, the 15C Window of Heaven (rose du Ciel). Inside, the wrought-iron choir screen dates from the 18C and the oak choir stalls from the beginning of the 16C. The third chapel of the north aisle houses a remarkable Romanesque Crucifixion probably influenced by oriental art. Christ's feet are nailed to the Cross separately; clad in a long robe, He wears His royal crown in glory. The figure was carved before the arrival in Paris of the relics of the Passion (including the Crown of Thorns) purchased by St Louis.

elegant nave is the highest in France (42.5m/139.4ft).

At an early date problems arose through water from the Somme penetrating the foundations; movement occurred along the length of the building, evidence of which can be seen in cracks in the nave near the transept. The weight of the vaults aggravated the effect; to remedy it, in the 16C a brace of Toledo steel was inserted into the triforium, heated red-hot, and allowed to cool. For four centuries it has served its purpose admirably. The building was further strengthened by increasing the number of buttresses at the east end and by adding side chapels in the form of double aisles to the nave in order to spread the downward forces as widely as possible.

The famous slender steeple rising above the crossing was built by the master carpenter Cardon in two years (1528–29). Much of the cathedral's decoration is of very high quality indeed: the sculpture of the west front (including the noble figure of Christ known as the "Beau Dieu"), and the rose windows of the main

Chés Cabotans Puppet Theatre

31 r. Édouard-David F. ◷*Puppet shows displayed year round except early Sept–mid-Oct, school holidays, Christmas and public holidays.* ⊜*10€.* ☏*03 22 22 30 90*

Visiting this theatre you will get to learn a bit about famous local characters such as Lafleur and his wife Sandrine. (☝*see Puppets sidebar p405*). While you may not understand everything that's said, why not watch one of the shows given in this miniature theatre where the characters express themselves in a mixture of Picardy dialect and French.

Hortillonnages★

Maison des hortillonnages, 54 bd de Beauvillé. ⊜*5.50€; child 4.55€.* ⛵*Boat trip (45min) daily Apr–Oct 2pm onwards.* ☏*03 22 92 12 18. www.visit-amiens.com.*

The small allotments known as **aires** which stretch over an area of 300ha/7491acres amid a network of canals or **rieux** fed by the many arms of the Somme, have been worked since the Middle Ages by market gardeners or *hortillons.* At present, fruit trees and flowers are tending to replace vegetables and the gardeners' sheds are becoming weekend holiday homes. Kids will enjoy the Île-aux-Fagots, where there is an **aquarium** and an **insectarium**.

City Pass

This pass offers coupons for guided tours, half-price entry to various entertainment event, recreational activities, restaurants and much more. 8€ from the tourist office.

ADDITIONAL SIGHT

Musée de Picardie★★ (48 r. de la République)

ADDRESSES

🏠 STAY

◻🍽🛏 **Hôtel Alsace-Lorraine** – 18 r. de la Morlière. ℰ03 22 91 35 71. www.alsace-lorraine.fr.st. 14 rooms. ⧉7€.
This comfortable, likeable little hotel hides behind an imposing carriage entrance a five-minute walk from the town centre and train station. Bedrooms, brightened with colourful fabrics, give onto the charming inner courtyard.

◻🍽🛏 **Hôtel Carlton** – 42 r. de Noyon. ℰ03 22 97 72 22. www.lecarlton.fr. 24 rooms. ⧉8.50€. Behind the attractive 19C façade discover a modern, plush interior. Every room features waxed furniture and murals. Their simple restaurant, Le Bistrot, serves grilled meats.

◻🍽🛏🛏 **Chambre d'hôte Le Petit Château** – 2 r. Grimaux, Dury. 6km/3.6mi S of Amiens via N 1 dir. Beauvais. ℰ03 22 95 29 52. www.le-petit-chateau.fr. 4 rooms. In the countryside, 10min from central Amiens, a massive 19C residence whose comfortable guest rooms are housed in an outbuilding. The owner is happy to show his collection of old automobiles.

🍴 EAT

◻ **Le Petit Poucet** – 52 r. des Trois-Cailloux. ℰ03 22 91 42 32. Closed Mon. This attractive establishment is very popular with the people of Amiens who come for a slice of quiche, a ficelle picarde (baked crepes, stuffed and rolled), or a mixed salad for lunch, a delectable chocolate for tea, or a box of divine pastries to enjoy at home.

◻🍽🛏🛏 **Le Bouchon** – 10 r. Alexandre Fatton. ℰ03 22 92 14 32. www.lebouchon.fr. Closed Sun eve. A Parisian-style bistro near the railway station specialising in typically Lyonnais dishes and traditional cuisine of the region; a relaxed, "no fuss" atmosphere.

◻🍽🛏🛏 **Les Marissons** – Pont de la Dodane, Quartier St.-Leu. ℰ03 22 92 96 66. www.les-marissons.fr. Closed Wed & Sat for lunch and Sun. The place to be in the Saint-Leu quarter is this old marine workshop transformed into a restaurant. The flowery mini-garden becomes a terrace in summer, while in winter diners sit under the sloping wooden frame in a pleasant décor of handsome beams and round tables.

GUIDED TOURS

Contact the tourist office for guided tours of the town in French, several times daily.
Barge Tours – explore the canals of St-Leu in traditional style. Depart from chemin du port Cappy.
ℰ03 22 76 12 12.

🍸 NIGHTLIFE

After dark, the Quai Belu canalside area in the St Leu quarter is the place for pubs, discos and nightlife.

Texas Café – 13 r. des Francs-Mûriers, Quartier St.-Leu. ℰ03 22 72 19 79. This enormous Confederate-themed 'saloon' of brick and wood is always crowded and popular. Before midnight, drink (beer and cocktails), dance and sing (karaoke). After midnight, it's a disco and dance venue.

🎭 SHOWTIME

"The cathedral in living colour" – ℰ03 22 22 58 90. www.amiens.fr/decouvrir/cathedrale. The artist Skertzò uses lighting to highlight the colourful entrance on the cathedral's west side. The presentation is held mid-Jun–Sept at dusk, and from during December at 7pm. Commentary in French and then English.

Comédie de Picardie – 62 r. des Jacobins. ℰ03 22 22 20 20. www.comdepic.com. This venerable old manor, entirely restored, houses a very pretty 400-seat theatre. The region's creative and dramatic hub, it produces 15 different shows for a total of 250 performances per season.

Maison de la Culture d'Amiens – pl. Léon-Gontier. ℰ03 22 97 79 79. www.maisondelaculture-amiens.com. Two halls (1 070 and 300 seats), a movie theatre devoted to art and experimental films and two exhibition rooms. This complex offers an unusually interesting and eclectic selection of events.

👥 **Théâtre de Marionnettes** – *Chés Cabotans d'Amiens, 31 r. Édouard-David, quartier St-Leu.* 📞*03 22 22 30 90. www. ches-cabotans-damiens.com.* This fascinating family-orientated show, established in 1933, takes place in a veritable miniature theatre with a beautifully designed set. The puppets all have their own history and language (French or Picard) plus remarkably expressive faces that can also be admired in the ground-floor exhibition.

🛒 SHOPPING

Atelier de Jean-Pierre Facquier – *67 r. du Don.* 📞*03 22 92 49 52.* Transforming them into traditional and invented wooden Picardy puppets, Monsieur Facquier carves life into pieces of wood before your eyes. Madame Facquier sews their clothes using fabric chosen with care. Each unique character is a genuine work of art.

Jean Trogneux – *1 r. Delambre & 2nd branch at Parvis de la Cathédrale.* 📞*03 22 71 17 17. www.trogneux.fr.* The city's speciality since the 16C, the Amiens macaroon, with its blend of almonds and honey, is ever popular. The Trogneux family, confectioners and chocolatiers for five generations, sell more than two million of them every year! The shop also carries a nice selection of local products.

Marché des Hortillons – The local market gardeners, who grow their produce in canal-bordered wetlands *(hortillonnages)*, come to market Saturday mornings at **Place Parmentier**. Once a year, on 3rd Sunday in June, a market is held as in years gone by: the gardeners, wearing traditional attire, come in flat-bottomed punts and unload their produce onto the docks.

Arras★★

The Abbey of St-Vaast formed the nucleus around which the capital of Artois grew in the Middle Ages. Between the 12C and 14C it gained privileges from the Counts of Artois encouraging an economy based on corn, banking and, especially, fabrics. The city prospered; poetic and literary societies thrived in which Arras' notables could enjoy hearing themselves lampooned by minstrels and entertainers. In the 15C, Artois passed into the hands of the Dukes of Burgundy, ensuring steady orders for its fine tapestries, which were notable for dealing realistically with secular themes.

A BIT OF HISTORY

The notorious **Maximilien Robespierre** was born in Arras in 1758 to a well-to-do legal family. He was called to the Bar before becoming a Deputy in 1789, a Republican in 1792, and a prominent member of the feared Committee of

- ▶ **Population:** 42 015
- ⏱ **Michelin Map:** 301 J 5-6
- 🅿 **Info:** Pl. des Héros. 📞03 21 51 26 95. www.ot-arras.fr.
- ▶ **Location:** Close to the English Channel, Arras is one of the main towns in northern France. Its centre is Place des Héros.
- ◉ **Don't Miss:** The 45min Historama film shown at the tourist office makes an interesting introduction to the town (€2.70€).

Public Safety in 1793. Determined and indifferent to favours, "Robespierre the Incorruptible" embodied the spirit of the French Revolution. Backed by Saint-Just and Couthon, he harried plotters and crushed deviationists, going so far as to take part in the condemnation of his allies, the Girondins. Discredited in the end by the consequences of his extremist ideology, on 27 July 1794 he himself fell victim to the guillotine to which he had condemned so many others.

SIGHTS

Ancienne Abbaye St-Vaast★★

In 667, a small chapel found itself the site of the building of a new abbey intended for Benedictine monks.

The chapel had been erected by St Vaast (453–540), whose remains were moved from Arras cathedral into the new abbey. It was St Auburt who began the abbey's development, which was completed by his successor and richly endowed by King Theodoric. Independent until 1778, the abbey enjoyed huge importance in the surrounding area.

After the French Revolution the monastery was used as a hospital and later a barracks. In 1838, part of it was turned into a museum; the bishop held residence in the other part. In 1833, the abbey church was rebuilt and now serves as Arras Cathedral, replacing the former Gothic building destroyed during the Revolution.

The abbey houses the **Musée des Beaux-Arts**★ (⊙ open Wed–Mon 9.30am–noon, 2–5.30pm; ⊙ closed public holidays; ℘ 03 21 71 26 43; www. musenor.com/gm/arras.htm). This museum displays a variety of medieval and archaeological artworks, paintings and ceramics.

Les Places★★ (Main Squares)

Dating from the 11C, the **Grand'Place**, **Place des Héros** and the **Rue de la Taillerie** linking them celebrate the city's status as an important regional market centre. Their present splendidly harmonious appearance is the fruit of the city fathers' purposeful civic design initiatives in the 17C and 18C.

The existing Spanish Plateresque buildings of the 16C and 17C (Arras was effectively under Spanish rule from 1492–1640) were given Flemish Baroque façades from 1635 onward.

The 155 brick and stone houses rest on 345 columns: their arcading sheltered traders and clients alike. With few projections, their regularly proportioned

Grand'Place
B.Kaufmann/MICHELIN

façades give an impression of great unity, relieved by a rich variety of detail. To the north of the Grand'Place a brick building with a stone-built ground floor is topped by a stepped gable, the only one of its kind. Arras' civic pride was symbolised by the construction of its Town Hall, **Hôtel de Ville**★ (pl. des Héros) in 1572; its bell-tower **(beffroi)** (⊙ open mid-Sept–mid-Mar Tue–Sat 9am–noon, 2–6pm, Mon 10am–noon, 2–6pm, Sun 10am–12.30pm, 2.30–6.30pm; 1 Apr–14 Sept Mon–Sat 9am–6.30pm, Sun 10am–1pm, 2.30–6.30pm; ⊙ closed 1 Jan, 25 Dec; ⚌2.70€; ℘03 21 51 26 95) blends Flemish Gothic with Henri II-style ornamentation. It was destroyed in World War I but rebuilt using the original plans in 1919.

EXCURSIONS

Vimy Canadian Memorial★

10km/6.2mi N.

A gripping sight that brings home some of the realities of the Great War. The summit of this chalky ridge was taken by the Canadian Expeditionary Force, part of the British Third Army, in April 1917.

It is crowned by the Canadian Memorial. There are extensive views over a farmed landscape dotted with the conical tips of coal mines. To the west are the cemetery and basilica of Notre-Dame-de-Lorette, and nearby, entrenchments and pitted landforms left by trench warfare, which can be visited.

Parc Astérix★★
Asterix Park

Asterix the Gaul, comical hero of the famous cartoon strip by Goscinny and Uderzo, is universally known and loved in France. He and his fellow characters provide the theme for this resort (50ha/123.5 acres). It is a fantasy world for all ages which offers a madcap journey into the past: carefully reconstructed 'historical' sections, various attractions and shows, as well as audiovisual displays add to the fun.

VISIT

Opening times vary annually. 10am–6pm 4 Apr–31 Aug daily; Sept Sat–Sun; Oct Sat–Sun; 26 Oct–4 Nov; 19–30 Dec Sat–Wed. 39€ (under-11 29€, child under-3 free). 0826 30 10 40 (0.15€/min). www.parcasterix.fr.
To explore this enchanting world, start at the Via Antiqua lined with stalls symbolising Asterix's journeys across Europe. Five areas illustrate various themes: the **Village Astérix** is a veritable Gallic village with its huts; the **Menhir Express**★ is the highlight of a Stone Age village built on piles (**Domaine Lacustre**); ten centuries of history are illustrated in the **Rue de Paris**; **Les Vikings** is a popular spot with thrilling

- **Michelin Map:** 305 G 6
- **Info:** BP8 60128 Plailly 60128. *See PARIS.*
- **Location:** By car: 30min from central Paris on autoroute A1; by Métro/RER train: line B3 from Châtelet or Gare du Nord stations (alight at Roissy-Charles-de-Gaulle 1 station); by coach: from Roissy coach station with Courriers Île-de-France (CIF; www.cif-bus.com.
- **Kids:** Camp de Petitbonum, Le Petit Train, Les Petits Drakkars, La Fôret Des Druides Au Pied du Grand Huit, La Petite Tempete, Les Petits Chars Tamponneurs.

attractions (**Goudurix**★); Icarus's flight (**Vol d'Icare**), Zeus' Thunder **Tonnerre de Zeus** and performing dolphins in an auditorium, **Theâtre de Poséidon,** are the main interests of the section on Ancient Greece (**La Grece**); in the Roman Empire (**L'Empire Romain**) roman legionnaries entertain in the arena and there is an exciting rollercoaster (**Les Espions de César**).

Beauvais★★

An extraordinary Gothic cathedral stands at the centre of this fortified city.

SIGHTS
Cathédrale St-Pierre★★★
R. Saint-Pierre. Open daily Nov–Apr 9am–12.15pm, 2–5.30pm; May–Jun and Sept–Oct 9am–12.15pm, 2–6.15pm; Jul–Aug 9am–6.15pm. 03 44 48 11 60. www.cathedrale-beauvais.fr.
The strange spireless building is the result of a long effort, technical and financial, which eventually ended in failure. In 1225 the Bishop of Beauvais

- **Population:** 55 481
- **Michelin Map:** 305 D 4
- **Information:** 1 r. Beauregard. 03 44 15 30 30. www.beauvais tourisme.fr.
- **Location:** Beauvais lies on the A16 in southern Picardy.
- **Don't Miss:** The astronomical clock in the cathedral, *L'Horloge astronomique,* which puts on a display at 40min past the hour 10.40am–11.40am, 2.40–4.40pm. 4€.

decided to build the biggest and highest cathedral of the age in honour of St Peter. Its vaults were to top 48m/157.5ft. But in 1272, ten years after completion, the vault collapsed; it was rebuilt but fell again in 1284. Work had to start immediately on strengthening the walls, increasing the number of flying buttresses at the east end and using external struts at the base of the roof, 40m/131.2ft above ground, concealing the sheer daring of the original enterprise.

The interior was treated similarly. In the southern bays, additional pillars underpinned the structure above. The windows were given more lancets to subdivide and strengthen them, glazing was added to the elevation, lightening it considerably.

After the Hundred Years' War, Martin Chambiges began the construction of the transepts and crossing. He designed the great gable and rose window of the south transept, then, instead of starting on the nave, he built the crossing tower. It was completed in 1539, a century later, but 11m/36ft higher, than the tower of Strasbourg Cathedral. With no nave to buttress it, however, the great structure collapsed in 1573.

The dizzying height of the vaults is still most impressive and there is much decorative work to admire, from the Renaissance doors of the south portal, to the **stained-glass windows (vitraux)**★★ created by the Beauvais workshops founded by Ingrand Leprince. There's also the remarkable **astronomical clock (horloge astronomique)**★.

ADDITIONAL SIGHTS

Église St-Étienne★ – Jesse Window (vitrail de l'Arbre de Jessé)★★★ (r. de l'Etamine)

Musée Départemental de l'Oise★ (1 r. du Musée)

Boulogne-sur-Mer★★

Hotel Ibis May 11, 2010

Considered the most attractive and interesting of the 'short crossing' Channel ports, Boulogne has a historic walled upper town built on the site of the Roman fortress with 13C ramparts, interesting shops and a traditional market in the lower town and a busy quayside where fishermen's wives sell their husbands' fresh catch at traditional tiled stalls.

A BIT OF HISTORY

Boulogne's location along the chalk cliffs facing the English coast made it a cross-Channel port at an early date. It was from here that Emperor Claudius set sail to conquer Britain; he even established regular boat services to Dover and built an enormous 12-storey landmark tower 200 Roman feet high (1 Roman ft = 2.96m), which stood until the 16C.

▶ **Population:** 44 273
◔ **Michelin Map:** 301 C 3
▤ **Info:** Parvis de Nausicaä. ℘03 21 10 88 10. www.tourisme-boulognesurmer.com.
▶ **Location:** The busy town centre is beside the ferry port. It runs uphill towards the historic Upper Town.
▣ **Parking:** There are car parks by the seafront – it's much easier than trying to park in town.
▣ **Don't Miss:** The quiet streets of Ville Haute within its ring of sturdy ramparts.
▣ **Kids:** Nausicaä is a family destination and kids will love it.

Fishing has long been the town's principal activity, the ship-owners' guild being regulated as early as 1203. Today's fleet ties up alongside the Quai

...ts catch of fresh fish the largest in continental Europe.

👥 SIGHTS
Nausicaä★★★

Bd Ste-Beuve.♿🕐*Open daily Sept–late Jan 9.30am–6.30pm; Jul–Aug 9.30am–7.30pm.* 🕐*Closed first 3 weeks in Jan, 25 Dec & 1 Jan (until 2pm).* 💶*16.50€ (child 10.80€).* 📞*03 21 30 98 98.*
www.nausicaa.fr.

Designated as the national sea life centre, Nausicaä is an extraordinary complex, at once educational and entertaining. There are many serious elements which have an overall theme of conservation but there are also amusements such as highly trained sea lions. Within the centre, there is a cinema, a shop, some restaurants and bar.

Calais

The proximity of the English coast – a mere 38km/23.6mi away – has always determined the destiny of Calais. It handles more passengers than any other in France and is the main port for ferry passengers arriving from the UK..

A BIT OF HISTORY

In May 1347, eight months after his victory at Crécy over Philippe VI which marked the beginning of the Hundred Years' War, Edward III succeeded in starving Calais into submission.
The town was to remain English for more than two centuries until the Duke of Guise seized it in January 1558. The loss of England's last possession in France provoked Mary Tudor's sad comment "When I am dead and opened, you shall find 'Calais' lying in my heart".
Almost entirely destroyed in World War II, Calais was rapidly rebuilt, and remained the principal entry point into France from Britain. The Channel Tunnel, passing beneath the sea from near Folkestone to Coquelles (3km/1.8mi S of Calais), was opened in 1994.

Ville haute★★

The upper town, Boulogne's historic district built on the site of the Roman fortress, is still surrounded by its 13C ramparts, which has a walkway on top with fine views.

ADDITIONAL SIGHTS
Colonne de la Grande Armée★★ *(av. de la Colonne, Wimille)*
Basilique Notre-Dame – dome★, crypt★ and **treasury**. *(2 pl. du Parvis Notre-Dame).*
Château-Musée★ *(r. de Bernet)*

EXCURSION
Côte d'Opale★ – 🚗*See CALAIS: Excursion.*

- ▶ **Population:** 74 888
- 🚗 **Michelin Map:** 301 E 2
- 📋 **Info:** 12 Bd Clemenceau. 📞03 21 96 62 40. www.ot-calais.fr.
- ▷ **Location:** Calais is in two sections: the larger Calais-Sud is the modern commercial heart of town, while smaller Calais-Nord is the older maritime area close to the port and beach.
- 🅿 **Parking:** There is plenty of metered street parking in Calais-Sud. Place d'Armes in Calais-Nord is a useful car parking area.
- 🔎 **Don't Miss:** Rodin's remarkable *Burghers of Calais*, outside the town hall.
- 🕐 **Timing:** As well as the sights, allow plenty of time to browse Calais' excellent shops. For a more serious shopping spree, visit Cité Europe, a large mall 3km/1.8mi S of town.

SIGHT
Monument des Bourgeois de Calais★★

In front of the Town Hall (Hôtel de ville).
Rodin's group of bronze figures (1888) commemorates the self-sacrificing action of Eustache de Saint-Pierre and his five fellow citizens; emaciated by the eight long months of siege, barefoot and clad in long robes, they came before Edward III offering themselves for execution provided the King spared their fellow-citizens. Edward accepted their plea and spared them too, doubtless with an eye to the governability of his new conquest. Rodin's huge talent comes over triumphantly in these vibrant figures, haughty in their humiliation. Other examples of this sculpture may be seen in London (near the Houses of Parliament), in New York (at the Metropolitan Museum of Art) and in Washington (at the Hirshhorn Museum and Sculpture Garden).

ADDITIONAL SIGHTS
Views★★ from the lighthouse (*Phare*)
Musée des Beaux Arts et de la Dentelle★ (*25 r. Richelieu*)

EXCURSION
CÔTE D'OPALE★

The road linking Calais and Boulogne takes the visitor along the most spectacular part of this coastline with its high chalk cliffs, heathlands and vast sandy beaches backed by grassy dunes.

Blériot-Plage
3km/1.8mi W of Calais.
The little resort has a fine beach stretching as far as Cap Blanc-Nez. On a cliff-top knoll is the obelisk commemorating the **Dover Patrol**, mounted continuously between 1914 and 1918 to protect the vital supply routes across the English Channel. At Les Baraques just to the west of the resort is a monument marking **Louis Blériot's** flight across the Channel in 1909.

Detail of the Burghers of Calais by Rodin, Hôtel de ville

Cap Blanc-Nez★★
11km/6.8mi W of Calais, along D 940.
From the top of the white cliffs the **view★** extends from Calais to Cap Gris-Nez and right across the Channel to the English coast.

Wissant
19km/12mi W of Calais, along D 940.
With its superb beach of fine hard sand, one of France's main centres for land yachting, Wissant enjoys its privileged position in the middle of the National Conservation Area which includes both Cap Gris-Nez and Cap Blanc-Nez.

Cap Gris-Nez★★
31km/19.2mi SW of Calais.
This lofty limestone headland makes a contrast with the chalk cliffs to the south. In fine weather, it gives a **view★** of the white cliffs of the English coast.

Wimereux
27km/16.7mi SW of Calais.
This sizeable family resort is pleasantly situated between Cap d'Alprech to the south and the cliffs running up to Cap Gris-Nez in the north.
From the raised seafront promenade there are fine views over the Channel and along the coast from the monument (**Colonne de la Grande Armée**) to the port of Boulogne.

Boulogne-sur-Mer★ –
See BOULOGNE-SUR-MER.

Château de
Chantilly★★★

A synonym for elegance, Chantilly evokes wonderful art collections, a great park and forest, and the cult of the horse as well as the château itself.

THE CHÂTEAU★★★

Open Wed–Mon 4 Apr–1 Nov 10am–6pm; 2 Nov–3 Apr 10.30am–5pm. Château and park 11€. Guided tours (30min). 03 44 27 31 80. www.chateaudechantilly.com.

Anne de Montmorency, the great Constable of France who served six monarchs (from Louis XII to Charles IX), had a Renaissance castle built here in 1528. The foundations of an earlier building (1386) were re-used. In 1560 the architect Jean Bullant designed a charming little château (Petit Château) to the south of the main building.

The Great Condé and his descendants later made the state rooms of the Petit Château into their living quarters; today, there is much to delight the eye, including Rococo woodwork, manuscripts, silver caskets and icons. The greatest treasure is in the Library *(Cabinet des Livres; Open daily 9.15am–5pm)*; this is the **Limbourg** brothers' sumptuously illuminated *Book of Hours for the Duke of Berry (Les Très*

- **Michelin Map:** 305 F-G 6
- **Info:** 60 av. du Maréchal Joffre. 03 44 67 37 37 www.chantilly-tourisme.com.
- **Location:** Chantilly is 50km/31mi N of Paris. When you arrive, the château is well signposted.
- **Timing:** Allow at least 2hr for the château.

Riches Heures du Duc de Berry) of about 1415, completed 60 years later by Jean Colombe (on display in reproduction).

Under Louis II of Bourbon, known as the Great Condé, Le Nôtre laid out the park and gardens; François Mansart redesigned the principal façade and the layout of the rooms.

During the French Revolution, the château was dismantled to first-floor level, the Petit Château was ruined and the park laid waste.

On the death of Louis-Joseph de Condé, the estate passed into the hands of the Duke of Aumale, who rebuilt the great edifice (1875–83) in a neo-Renaissance style.

The château houses a **museum**★★ *(open same hours as château; 7€, museum and park; 03 44 62 62 62)* – manuscripts, furniture, paintings, sculpture – whose wealth would prove difficult to rival today.

Château de Chantilly

D. Pazery/ MICHELIN

Grandes Écuries★★

These stables were built in 1721 by Jean Aubert for Louis-Henri of Bourbon, the Great Condé's great-grandson. Much admired in its time, it is the finest example of 18C building at Chantilly to have come down to us. The stables house the **Musée Vivant du Cheval et du Poney**★ (*open Wed–Mon 10am–6pm; contact for precise details; 10€; 03 44 27 31 80; www.musee vivantducheval.fr*), which has stalls from the time of the Duke of Aumale, historic harnessing, costumes, and all kinds of objects associated with equitation. Riding displays take place in the central rotunda. More than 3 000 horses are stabled and trained in and around Chantilly; race-meetings and hunts both perpetuate the tradition begun on 15 May 1834 when France's first great official race-meeting was held, and maintain Chantilly's reputation as the country's thoroughbred capital. The French Derby (*Prix du Jockey Club*) is held here every April.

Chartres★★★

Chartres' magnificent cathedral, the "Acropolis of France" (Rodin), still beckons to the pilgrim far off across the endless cornfields of the Beauce. The area was occupied by the Carnutes, and Druids once worshipped here; there is also evidence of the pagan cult of a holy spring, and possibly also of a mother-goddess, whom the first missionaries may have christianised as a forerunner of the Virgin Mary.

A BIT OF HISTORY

The picturesque old town (**le Vieux Chartres**★) lies at the point where the Eure cuts into the plain of the Beauce. Today, the old mill-races and laundry-houses have been restored, and a number of 17C houses have kept their embossed doorways topped by a bull's-eye. The most attractive townscape is to be found in the St-André quarter, by the riverbanks, and in Rue des Écuyers and Rue du Cygne. Loëns Granary (Grenier de Loëns) is a fine 12C building which once housed the tithes of grain and wine. Chartres attracted pilgrims at an early date, first of all to Our Lady of the Underground Chapel (*Notre-Dame-de-Sous-Terre*), then to the cathedral which Bishop Fulbert built in the 11C but which was burnt down in 1194.

> ▶ **Population:** 40 022
> 🚗 **Michelin Map:** 311 E 5
> ℹ **Info:** Place de la Cathédrale. 02 37 18 26 26. www.chartres-tourisme.com.
> ▷ **Location:** The cathedral dominates the old quarter, Quartier St-André.
> 🕐 **Timing:** Allow at least 2hr for the cathedral.

SIGHT
Cathédrale Notre-Dame★★★

pl. de la Cathédrale. Open daily 8.30am–7.30pm. Guided tours Nov–Mar 2.45pm; Apr–Oct Sun–Mon 2.45pm, Tue–Sat noon & 2.45pm. 02 37 21 75 02.

See *Introduction: Art – Architecture.* Reconstruction began immediately and was completed in the short space of 25 years. The north and south porches were added only 20 years later and the building consequently has a unity of style possessed by few other Gothic churches. Pilgrims have been coming here for eight centuries.

The new cathedral raised the Transitional Gothic style to new levels. The bays of the nave, previously square in plan, are now oblong and have sexpartite vaults; the arches of arcades and windows are more pointed; a round opening is inserted in the space above the highest windows; the structural functions of galleries are taken over by flying buttresses.

Cathédrale Notre-Dame

B. Kaufmann/MICHELIN

Gothic verticality reigns outside, too, but the architect wisely kept two Romanesque masterworks, the Old Bell Tower (Clocher vieux) of 1145 and the Royal Doorway, **Portail Royal**★★★, of the west front, with its long-bodied but intensely expressive sculpted figures. The cathedral's interior is subtly lit by its superb stained glass (**vitraux**★★★) which covers a total area of 2 700sq m/

Gallo-Roman
9C
11C-12C
13C

0   20 m

Chapelle St-Piat-14C
(Treasury)

Chapelle des
Martyrs

N

Ambulatory

Sacristy

Crypt

CHOIR

Parclose ★★

6   1

3   2

North arm   South arm
North   of transept   of transept   South
Doorway   TRANSEPT   Doorway

Access to Clocher Neuf

5

NAVE

4

Pavillon
de l'Horloge
16C

Clocher   Clocher
Neuf   Vieux

Portail Royal ★★★

CATHEDRAL

Hearting

8

9

10

11

7

CRYPT

1	Notre-Dame-de-la-Belle-Verrière	
2	St Fulbert's window	
3	Window of Peace	
4	Chapelle Vendôme	
5	Organ	
6	Vierge du Pilier	
7	Chapelle St-Martin	
8	Crypte St-Lubin	
9	Gallo-Roman wall	
10	Puits des Saints-Forts	
11	Chapelle Notre-Dame-de-Sous-Terre	

25 000sq ft and depicts 5 000 figures. Most of the windows date from the 12C and 13C and are the greatest achievement of this art form. "Chartres blue" is famous for the clarity and depth which can be seen in the wonderful Notre-Dame-de-la-Belle-Verrière Window *(first window on the south side of the ambulatory)*. In 1964, the American Society of Architects gave a window and in 1971 the German Friends of the Cathedral did likewise *(north transept)*.

ADDITIONAL SIGHTS
Musée des Beaux-Arts★ *(29 cloître Notre Dame)*
Église St-Pierre★ – **stained glass**★ *(5 pl. St-Pierre)*

ADDRESSES

STAY
◛◛ **Chambre d'hôte La Ferme du Château** – *Levesville, Bailleau-l'Évêque. 7km/4.3mi NW of Chartres via N 154 and D 134. ℰ02 37 22 97 02. http://mongite. fr/lafermeLevesville2008920lc0. Closed 25 Dec, 1 Jan. 3 rooms.* This elegant Beauce farm offers pretty, comfortable rooms that have been decorated with a light hand. Neighbouring a small château, the farm is very quiet and its kind, hospitable owners are very discreet.

◛◛◛◛ **Le Grand Monarque** – *22 pl. des Épars. ℰ02 37 18 15 15. www. bw-grand-monarque.com. 55 rooms. ⌑14€. Le Georges restaurant◛◛◛◛.* A 16C coaching inn at the heart of the city. The comfortable rooms have a personal touch; some are embellished with cheerfully flowered patterns and canopies while others are more sober. Snug dining room with wood carvings and works of art.

EAT
◛◛ **Le Café Serpente** – *2 r. du Cloître Notre-Dame. ℰ02 37 21 68 81.* A bicycle on the ceiling, posters on the walls and enamelled plaques in the stairwell comprise the décor of this thoroughly genial old café opposite the cathedral. On your plates: appetizing salads, brasserie fare and authentic cuisine at all hours.

◛◛◛ **Le Pichet** – *19 r. du Cheval-Blanc. ℰ02 37 21 08 35. http://le-pichet.com.* Just down the street from the cathedral, a very friendly little bistro that suits our tastes. Inside, there is a pleasant jumble of bric-a-brac: wooden chairs, a collection of coffeepots, pitchers, old street signs and other good stuff. The food is traditional French cuisine.

◛◛◛ **Le Tripot** – *11 pl. Jean-Moulin. ℰ02 37 36 60 11. Closed Aug, Sun–Mon & public holidays.* This house built in 1553 used to accommodate a *jeu de paume* (real tennis court) called 'Le Tripot' whose Latin motto meaning 'Belligerents: stay away' may still be seen above the front door. A timeless ultimatum! Well-preserved rustic interior and contemporary cuisine.

SHOPPING
Marché aux légumes et volailles – *Pl. Billard.* Each Saturday morning, the covered Vegetable and Poultry Market displays colourful stands featuring authentic Beauce produce. This carrousel of sights, tastes and fragrances is one of the most popular markets in the area.

VISIT
Atelier Loire – *16 r. d'Ouarville, 28300 Léves. Just N of Chartres on the way to Dreux, 2km/1.2mi from the cathedral. ℰ02 37 21 20 71. http://vitrail-vitraux-chartres.ateliers-loire.fr. Guided tours Fri 2pm, 5pm. Closed Aug and public holidays.* A century-old, stately residence set amidst a park and adorned with stained-glass creations is the home of this atelier founded in 1946 by Gabriel Loire, and continued today by his grandchildren. The art and technique of making stained glass are carefully explained, beginning with artists' models (as designed by Adami, Miro or Fernand Léger, for example) and ending with the finished product created by master glass crafters. The visit, with its thousand hues and shades, is simply magical.

Brûlerie les Rois Mages – *6 r. des Changes.* ℘*02 37 36 30 52. Closed Mon for lunch.* Enter this "retro" coffee-roasting shop and choose among the wide variety of coffees roasted on site and the dozens of teas to enjoy in the brûlerie or take home.

La Chocolaterie – *2 pl. Cygne.* ℘*02 37 21 86 92.* A highly useful address for stocking up on gourmet treats to take home as souvenirs, such as macaroons or Mentchikoffs, a local chocolate speciality. The very cosy tearoom offers sofas and a fireplace; there's a pleasant terrace in summer.

Compiègne★★★

The site of Compiègne had been appreciated by the Merovingians, long before Charles the Bald built a château here in the 9C. A fortified town grew up around this nucleus. In 1429, Philippe le Bon (the Good), Duke of Burgundy, had designs on Picardy, which he hoped to incorporate into his realm by means of a joint operation with the English. The French line of defence along the Oise was reinforced on the orders of Joan of Arc; disgusted with the inertia prevailing at Sully-sur-Loire where the French Court had established itself, she had come to Compiègne on her own initiative. But on the evening of 23 May 1430, she was seized by the Burgundians. Wary of possible consequences, Philip the Good sold her on to the English; one year later she was burnt at the stake in Rouen.

SIGHTS
Le Château★★★
pl. du Général de Gaulle.
◷*Open Wed–Mon 10am–6pm; last admission 5.15pm.* ◷*Closed 1 Jan, 1 May, 25 Dec.* ◉*6.50€; free 1st Sun in the month.* ◉*Guided tours available.* ℘*03 44 38 47 02. www.musee-chateau-compiegne.fr.*

Compiègne had been a royal residence since the time of the later Capetians, but Louis XV was dissatisfied with the ill-assorted and crumbling buildings inherited from his great-grandfather, and in 1738 he gave orders for the château to be reconstructed. The architect was **Ange-Jacques Gabriel**,

▶ **Population:** 42 036
◔ **Michelin Map:** 305 H 4
▯ **Info:** Place de l'Hôtel-de-Ville. ℘03 44 40 01 00. www.compiegne-tourisme.fr.
▷ **Location:** Hidden in the Forest of Compiegne, the town is 60km/37mi E of Beauvais, in southern Picardy.
⊘ **Don't Miss:** The royal private apartments in the palace; the forest surrounding the town, one of the most beautiful of its type in France.
◷ **Timing:** The Palace will take about 2hr to visit.

who succeeded in building one of the great monuments of the Louis XV style. Begun in 1751, the great edifice made use of the foundations of the previous structure, partly for reasons of economy, partly because the site was pitted with old quarries. Gabriel chose to emphasise the horizontality of his buildings, stretching them out and providing them with flattened roofs with balustrades, themes he took up again in the Place de la Concorde and École Militaire in Paris. The palace took 40 years to build; after Gabriel's retirement the work was carried on by his draughtsman, and a general movement in the direction of greater simplicity is very evident, with features like entablatures, ornamental window-brackets and attic floors tending to disappear. This evolution can be traced in the left wing of the main

Château de Compiègne

Ph. Gajic/MICHELIN

courtyard (1755), the principal façade facing the park, which was designed in 1775 and completed 10 years later (Napoleon's staircase of 1801 spoils the effect wished for by Gabriel), and the peristyle of 1783.

While the place was still a building site, it formed the background to the first meeting (1770) between Louis XVI and Marie-Antoinette. Later, in 1810, it was where Napoleon met Marie-Louise, the Marie-Antoinette's great-niece.

During the Second Empire, Napoleon III made Compiègne his favourite residence, where he took much pleasure in the house-parties to which like-minded celebrities would be invited, some 80 at a time.

Inside, the palace is decorated and furnished in 18C and Empire style (chests of drawers, applied ornament, wall-cupboards, tapestries).

Musée de la Voiture et du Tourisme★★
Within the Château.

In addition to 18C and 19C coaches, the vehicles exhibited include: the **Mancelle** of 1898, a steam mail-coach designed by Amédée Bollée; a No 2 **Panhard**; a Type A **Renault** of 1899 with direct drive; the **Jamais Contente** ("Never Satisfied") of 1899, an electric car with tyres by Michelin, the first to reach 100kph/62mph; a Type C **Renault** of 1900, one of the first cars to have enclosed bodywork (by Labourdette); a **Citroën** half-track of 1924.

ADDITIONAL SIGHTS
Hôtel de Ville★
Musée de la Figurine historique★
(pl. de l'Hôtel de Ville)
Musée Vivenel – Greek vases★★
(2 r. d'Austerlitz)

EXCURSIONS
Clairière de l'Armistice★★
8km/5mi E.

This is the place where, at 5.15am on 11 November 1918, the armistice was signed which put an end to World War I at 11am on the same day.

At the time the site was sheltered by forest trees. A restaurant-car identical to the carriage (**wagon-bureau**) (🕐 *open mid-Oct–Mar 9am–noon, 2–5.30pm; Apr–mid-Oct 9am–12.30pm, 2–6pm;* ✆4€; ℘ 03 44 85 14 18) used by Marshal Foch displays the original objects handled by the delegates in 1918. **Ferdinand Foch** (1851–1929) is generally held to have been the architect

Guided Tours

Compiègne offers themed discovery tours from mid-May–mid-Jul and mid-Aug–mid-Oct at weekends and on public holidays. Enquire at the tourist office.

Château de Pierrefonds

S. Sauvignier/MICHELIN

of Allied victory in the Great War of 1914–18. He was born in Tarbes in the Pyrénées in an 18C middle-class home (now a museum). He taught strategy at the Military Academy (École de Guerre), then became its commandant. In 1914 he distinguished himself both in the Battle of the Frontiers in Lorraine and in the "Miracle of the Marne".

After the German breakthrough in the Ludendorff offensive of early 1918, Foch was appointed supreme commander of the French and British armies. Promoted to marshal, it was he who launched the final Allied offensive on 8 August.

After the Battle of France in 1940, it was the turn of a French delegation to present itself here to the dignitaries of the Nazi regime in order to hear the victors' terms for an armistice. It was signed on the evening of 22 June. The clearing and its historic monuments were then ransacked by the occupation forces; only the statue of Marshal Foch was spared.

Château de Pierrefonds★★

14km/8.7mi SE.

The stronghold seems to embody everything that a medieval castle should be as it looms over the village crouching at its feet. For the most part, however, it is a creation of the 19C.

Pierrefonds was part of the Duchy of Valois, and its castle, whose origins go back as far as Carolingian times, was rebuilt in the middle of the Hundred Years' War by Louis d'Orléans, the brother of Charles VI, as part of a chain of defences between the rivers Oise and Ourcq. It was dismantled during the reign of Louis XIII.

The castle ruins were bought by Napoleon I. In 1857 Louis Napoleon inspired by romantic ideals commissioned **Viollet-le-Duc** (1814–79) to restore the keep; four years later he was entrusted with a complete rebuilding of the castle for use as an Imperial residence and a picturesque place for receptions given to entertain the Emperor's guests at Compiègne. From the ramparts the view extends over the Vallée de Pierrefonds. Little of Louis d'Orléans' building is left save the base of the walls and the towers visible from the track leading to the castle.

Viollet-le-Duc's contributions, in the neo-Gothic style, are not without merit, but are notable more for originality than for strict historical accuracy, in terms of both architecture and decoration (arcading and gallery of the main façade in the courtyard, tribune in the chapel, roof of the Salle des Preuses). Nevertheless, it gives an excellent idea of a castle's defensive system prior to the age of cannon (north rampart walk).

Château de Blérancourt
31km/19mi NE.

During World War I the château was taken over by Ann Morgan, who set up a temporary hospital here. Blérancourt subsequently became the headquarters for the organisation of relief for the civilian population.

When the war was over, Miss Morgan's efforts were directed towards the establishment of a museum of Franco-American history. In 1929, she presented the place to the French state, whereupon its name was changed to the **Musée National de la Coopération Franco-Américaine** (🕐 *reopening 2011;* 📞 *03 23 39 60 16).* About a dozen rooms in the left wing (at present closed for reconstruction) are devoted to the American War of Independence.

The exhibits on show in the right wing (Pavillon Florence Gould) illustrate aspects of the long and close relationship between the two countries; there are displays on the 1801 Treaty of Friendship, the Louisiana Purchase, emigration to the United States, the Gold Rush, etc. Other rooms evoke the two World Wars, notably by means of relics of the **La Fayette** Squadron and of the American Field Service.

ADDRESSES

🛏 STAY

Auberge de la Vieille Ferme – *58 r. de la République, Meux.* 📞 *03 44 41 58 54. www.aubergedelavieilleferme. abcsalles.com. 14 rooms.* 🍽 *9.50€. Restaurant* 😊😊. This old farmhouse built of Oise Valley brick offers rooms that are simple but well-kept and practical. The restaurant sports exposed beams, rustic furniture, a tile floor and gleaming copperware. The menu offers traditional and regional cuisine.

Hôtel des Beaux Arts – *33 cours Guynemer.* 📞 *03 44 92 26 26. www.bestwestern.com. 50 rooms.* 🍽 *10€.* Located along the Oise waterfront, here's a contemporary hotel whose modern, well-soundproofed rooms have been furnished in teak or laminated wood. Some are larger and have a kitchenette.

🍽 EAT

Le Bistrot des Arts – *33 cours Guynemer.* 📞 *03 44 20 10 10. Closed Sat lunch and Sun.* Located on the ground floor of the Hôtel des Beaux-Arts, an appealing, authentic bistro decorated with various objects and etchings. In the kitchen, the chef concocts appetizing dishes using market-fresh produce.

Brasserie du Nord – *Pl. de la Gare.* 📞 *03 44 83 58 84. Closed Aug, Sun & public holidays.* This has become quite an institution locally for its seafood dishes. The dining room is modern and bright.

Auberge du Buissonnet – *825 r. Vineux, Choisy-au-Bac. 5km/3mi NE of Compiègne via N 31 and D 66.* 📞 *03 44 40 17 41. www.aubergedubuissonnet. com. Closed Sun eve, Tue eve and Mon. Reservations recommended.* Ask for a table near the bay windows of the dining room or on the terrace, weather permitting, and watch ducks and swans glide peacefully over the pond, then shake themselves off and waddle proudly toward the garden.

Le Palais Gourmand – *8 r. du Dahomey.* 📞 *03 44 40 13 13. http://le-palaisgourmand.com. Closed Sun eve and Mon .* This spruce-timbered house (1890) has a string of rooms and an attractive verandah where heaters, Moorish pictures and mosaics create an agreeable atmosphere. Traditional cuisine.

Disneyland Paris★★★

Europe's Disney resort, this huge complex, divided into Walt Disney Studios Parc and Disneyland Parc, has seven hotels, a wide range of family attractions themed as five separate 'lands', a 27-hole golf course, entertainment centre, restaurants, shops and a disco.

♟ VISIT
Parc Disneyland Paris★★★
♿🕐 *Opening times are announced bi-annually; please check before entry.*
Disneyland: *mid-Jul–Aug 9am–11pm; Sept–mid-Apr 10am–7pm, Sat–Sun and public holidays 10am–10pm; mid-Apr–mid-Jul 10am–8pm, Sat 9am–8pm. www.dlrpmagic.com.*
Disney Studios: *high season 9am–6pm, low season 10am–7pm.*
🐾 **Guided tours:** *contact the City Hall (Disneyland Park) on Town Square in Main Street, or the Studio Services in Walt Disney Studios.*
Fees: *1 day/1 park ⊜50€ (child 42€); 2 days 60€ (child 52€); 3 days 108€ (child 92€).*
Disneyland Passport *(Passeport Annuel) 300 days ⊜89€, 335 days 129€, 365 days 189€. Passports allow total freedom of movement between both Parks.*

♦ **Michelin Map:** 312 F 2

🛈 **Info:** 📞08448 008 898 (in UK), 01 60 30 60 53 (from outside France), 0825 82 51 00 (in France). www.disneylandparis.com.

▸ **Location:** The resort is 32km/20mi E of Paris, with excellent transport links. On arrival, find the information desk in City Hall (Disneyland Park) where a programme of the attractions is provided.

🅿 **Parking:** There is parking available in the northeast portion of the park, but with both train and bus terminals, Disneyland Paris is easily accessible by public transport.

🕐 **Timing:** To avoid long lines, visit popular attractions during the parade, at the end of the day or with a **Fast Pass** (free) issued by machines at the entrance to attractions; this ticket bears a time slot of one hour during which time you may have access to the attraction within a few minutes.

👥 **Kids:** As you know, there is something here for children of all ages.

Disneyland Paris

©Disney

Douai★

The town preserves the 18C layout and grand buildings that gave it the aristocratic look that Balzac evoked.

A BIT OF HISTORY

In the 11C and 12C, Douai provided winter quarters for merchants and merchandise using the great trading routes of Northern Europe. The painter Jean Bellegambe (1470–1534) was born here. His Polyptych of the Trinity (polyptyque d'Anchina – in the former Anchin charterhouse) is justly famous. Around 1605, a number of Benedictine monks from England and Wales came to Douai and established the monastery of St Gregory the Great. It was here that the "Douai Bible", an English version of the Old Testament, was published in 1609. The monastery buildings were destroyed at the time of the French Revolution and the community recrossed the Channel, eventually settling at Stratton-on-the-Fosse in Somerset, where they founded Downside Abbey.

SIGHTS

Les fêtes des Gayants (Parade)

On the Sunday after 5th July, five giant figures of the Gayant family, dressed in medieval costume, are paraded though the town accompanied by folk groups: Gayant, the father (7.5m/24.6ft tall,

- ▶ **Population:** 42 766
- **Michelin Map:** 302 G 5
- **Info:** 70 pl. d'Armes. ℘03 27 88 26 79. www.ville-douai.fr.
- **Location:** The town is in French Flanders, close to the Belgian border.

weighing 370kg/818lbs), his wife Marie Cagenon (6.5m/21.3ft tall) and their children Jacquot, Fillion and Binbin. The giants appear in town on the next two days. Gayant , the oldest giant in northern France (1530), is also the most popular.

The inhabitants of Douai refer to themselves in jest as "Gayant's children". *http://www.nordmag.fr/nord_pas_de_calais/douai/gayant.htm.*

Mairie de Douai – Beffroi★

83 r. Mairie. 🔊 *Guided tours (1hr) Sept–Jun Tue–Sun 11am, 3pm, 4pm, 5pm; Mon 3pm, 4pm, 5pm; Jul–Aug daily 10am, 11am, 2pm, 3pm, 4pm, 5pm, 6pm.* ⊚*3.50€.*

The is one of the best belfries of its kind in northern France. Both Victor Hugo and Corot were much taken by the Gothic tower of 1390 with its elaborate crown. The Flemish Renaissance courtyard front was rebuilt in 1860.

Dunkerque

Dunkirk

Almost entirely destroyed in World War II, the rebuilt town has an attractive centre with a pleasant atmosphere, appealing bars and good shops and museums.

A BIT OF HISTORY

Dunkirk (Church of the Dunes in Flemish) was originally a fishing village, whose transformation into the principal port of Flanders began as early as the 14C. It was taken by Turenne after his victory in the Battle of the Dunes in 1658, and

- ▶ **Population:** 191 173
- **Michelin Map:** 302 C 1
- **Info:** Beffroi, r. de l'Amiral-Ronarc'h. ℘03 28 66 79 21. www.ot-dunkerque.fr.
- **Location:** Dunkerque is 50km/31mi E of Calais; 78.8km/49mi NW of Boulogne-sur-Mer. An extensive urban area, the centre is close to the port, on its east side.

Jean Bart, "the king's official privateer"

During the wars fought by Louis XIV, the privateers of Dunkirk destroyed and captured 3 000 ships, took 30 000 prisoners and wiped out Dutch trade. The most intrepid of all the privateers was Jean Bart (1651–1702).

He was as famous as the privateers from St-Malo, Duguay-Trouin and Surcouf, and was a past master at raiding on the North Sea trade routes. Unlike pirates, who were outlaws attacking any and every passing ship, privateers were granted "letters patent" by the sovereign entitling them to attack warships or merchant vessels. In 1694 Jean Bart saved the kingdom from famine by capturing 130 ships loaded with wheat. His success owed much to the existence of an ultra-modern arsenal and the constant presence of a royal fleet. He was a simple, plain-spoken man but his exploits were many and varied. As a result, he was raised to the nobility in 1694, then three years later given the rank of Commodore. The following year he avoided a combat with nine large ships while taking the Prince de Conti to Poland. Once the threat was past, the prince commented that had they been attacked they would have been captured. Jean Bart replied that there had been no such danger as his son was in the munitions hold and the latter had orders to set light to a powder keg as soon as he gave the command.

given to England in recognition of her help in the struggle against Spain. The town was repurchased by France in 1662. It was now that Dunkirk became the abode of smugglers and of pirates pressed into the service of the king. In the course of Louis XIV's reign, a total of 3 000 foreign ships were captured or destroyed and the trade of the Netherlands completely wrecked. The most intrepid of these privateers was **Jean Bart** (1651–1702). Despite his vocation, the town is proud of him: his statue of 1848 by David d'Angers stands in the square named after him.

Demolition of the fortifications in 1713 (one of the conditions of the Treaty of Utrecht) brought about a decline in Dunkirk's fortunes, notwithstanding improvements in the port facilities. The German breakthrough at Sedan in mid-May 1940 and subsequent dash to the coast near Abbeville had led to the Allied forces in the north being trapped with their backs to the sea. Despite a magnificent reargaurd action by French troops endeavouring to protect them, defeat and retreat were inevitable. The subsequent evacuation codenamed "Operation Dynamo" was turned into the "Miracle of Dunkirk", the name given to the successful evacuation from 26 May–4 June of more than 338,000 troops from the beaches of Dunkirk

and its resorts of Malo, Zuydcoote and Bray-Dunes, an operation carried out in the face of intense bombardment on land and from the air. A fleet of over 900 small vessels, dubbed the "Little Ships of Dunkirk", helped to transport the troops safely back to the UK.

SIGHT
Le Port★★

Dunkirk is the third largest port in France and the major French port of the North Sea with a total of over 57.7 million tonnes of traffic in 2008. The port handled 7 134 ships during the same year. A vast industrial zone has emerged, based on shipbuilding, steelworks, refineries and petrochemicals.

It is the first port in France for ore, coal copper and container fruit imports and the second port in France for traffic with the UK. A vehicle ferry service operates between Dover and Dunkirk (Gravelines) providing an alternative to the traditional Dover Calais route.

ADDITIONAL SIGHTS
Lieu d'Art et d'Action
Contemporain★ *(Jardin des Sculptures)*
Musée des Beaux-Arts★
(pl. du Général de Gaulle)
Musée Portuaire★
(9 quai Citadelle)

Fontainebleau★★★

As early as the 12C, the Capetian kings had built a hunting lodge here, drawn by the abundant game which thrived in the vast forest. It was to become an extraordinarily majestic palace and park listed as a World Heritage site.

A BIT OF HISTORY

The woodland covers 25 000ha/62 000 acres, much of it high forest of sessile oaks, Norway pines and beeches. It grows on the low east-west sandstone ridges, among the crags and boulders of stony wastelands, and in the sandy depressions between the ridges. The Forest is traversed by a network of well-signposted footpaths. Since the days of Colbert's Forestry Ordinance of 1669, "a masterpiece of forestry administration" (J L Reed), it has been carefully managed to ensure its long-term survival.

In spite of the forest's fame and popularity, it is the palace begun by François I which has made the reputation of Fontainebleau.

A taste for natural surroundings together with its role as a military base (notably for cavalry) led to the growth of the town of Fontainebleau in the 19C. Between 1947 and 1967 it was home to the headquarters of NATO.

▶ **Population:** 15 688
⏱ **Michelin Map:** 312 F 5
🛈 **Info:** 4 r. Royale. ☎01 60 74 99 99. www.fontainebleau-tourisme.com.
◉ **Location:** Fontainebleau and its château are in the midst of a large forest, 64km/39.7mi S of Paris.
◈ **Don't Miss:** The Grand Apartments and famous horshoe staircase.
🕐 **Timing:** The exterior of the Palace will take about an hour, the interior more than an hour.

CHÂTEAU★★★

77300 Fontainebleau. ◉*Château* open Wed–Mon Oct–Mar 9.30am–5pm; Apr–Sept 9.30am–6pm. Ticket office closes 45min before palace; ◉*Closed 1 Jan, 1 May, 25 Dec;* ◉*Gardens* open daily Feb 9am–5pm; Mar, Apr & Oct 9am–6pm; May–Sept 9am–7pm. ☎01 60 71 50 70. www.musee-chateau-fontainebleau.fr.

From the days of the Capetian kings to the time of Napoleon III, the Palace

Ballroom, Grands Appartements

Ph. Gajic/MICHELIN

- Middle Ages
- François I
- Henri II

MOAT (1565-First Empire)

Princes' Court

Real Tennis Court

DIANA'S GARDEN

KITCHEN COURT

Napoléon I's Railings

Horseshoe Staircase

WHITE HORSE

or

FAREWELL COURT

Former Drawbridge

OVAL COURT

Keep

FOUNTAIN COURTYARD

- Catherine de' Medici
- Henri IV
- From Louis XIII to Louis XVI

of Fontainebleau has been lived in, added to and altered by the sovereigns of France. Napoleon Bonaparte liked it; here, in contrast to Versailles, he was free of the overwhelming presence of Louis XIV, a formidable predecessor in the quest for glory. He called Fontainebleau "the house of Eternity", furnished it in Empire style and set about altering it for himself, for Josephine, and for Pope Pius VII.

In 1528, François I commissioned Gilles Le Breton to replace the existing medieval buildings with two structures linked by a gallery. Like his predecessor Charles VIII, while campaigning in Italy, François had acquired a taste for agreeable surroundings adorned with works of art. He brought in gifted and prolific artists who are known as the **First School of Fontainebleau**. They included Rosso (of Florence), Primaticcio (from Perugia), Niccolo dell'Abbate (from Parma), as well as architects, thinkers, cabinet-makers, goldsmiths and decorators. He also acquired works of art including Leonardo's Mona Lisa and paintings by Raphael. France was thus permeated by Renaissance taste, by Renaissance mathematics and by an appreciation of the rules of proportion derived from the architecture of Greece and Rome. The pleasures of life were savoured anew, and painters and sculptors abandoned

Salle du Trône, Grands Appartements

Ph. Gajic/MICHELIN

Châteaux in the Île-de-France

Due to its proximity to the seat of royal power and its immense prestige, the Île-de-France was, for many centuries, a choice setting for architectural and artistic innovations. The quest for glory and love of art have inspired sovereigns and courtiers to build original and splendid mansions. Most of these are still extant and are a proud testimony to their past glory. For more châteaux, see the Châteaux of the Loire chapter in this guide or the *Michelin Green Guide Châteaux of the Loire*.

Highly recommended★★★

Palais de Versailles

Châteaux de Chantilly, Fontainebleau, Vaux-le-Vicomte

Recommended★★

Châteaux de Breteuil, Champs, Courances, Dampierre, Écouen, Malmaison, St-Germain-en-Laye, Sceaux, Thoiry

Interesting★

Châteaux de Ferrières, Fleury-en-Bière, Grosbois, Guermantes, Maintenon, Maisons-Laffitte, Marais, Rambouillet, La Roche-Guyon, Saussay

Also of Interest

Châteaux de Bourron, Blandy-les-Tours, Chevreuse, Courson, Malesherbes, St-Jean-de-Beauregard

Château de Ferrières

B. Kaufmann/MICHELIN

religious subjects in favour of older divinities. This era endowed the palace with many of its most splendid features: on the outside, the left wing and façade of the Court of the White Horse or Farewell Court **(Cour du Cheval-Blanc ou des Adieux★★)**, the concave section of the Oval Court **(Cour Ovale★)**, the Golden Gate **(Porte Dorée★)** with its loggia painted by Primaticcio; and on the inside, the François I Gallery **(Galerie François I★★★)** by Rosso, the first important French interior to mix frescoes and stucco work, and the

Ballroom **(Salle de Bal★★★)** painted by Primaticcio and dell'Abbate and completed by Philibert Delorme in the reign of Henri II.

Henri II, Catherine de' Medici and Charles IX carried on the work initiated during this most creative and productive period. Henri IV enlarged the palace further by building the real tennis court (Jeu de Paume), and the Diana Gallery (Galerie de Diane). He also completed the enclosure of the Oval Court. There was a change of style; the Second School of Fontainebleau looked to Flanders for its inspiration and found its artists in the Île de France; oil was now the preferred medium for painting.

Louis XIII completed the Farewell Court. It was here, from the famous horseshoe staircase built by Du Cerceau, that Napoleon bade his men farewell on 20 April 1814, following his abdication.

ADDRESSES

🛏 STAY

⊜⊜ **Hôtel de la Chancellerie** – *1 r. de la Chancellerie.* ℘*01 64 22 21 70. www. hotel-la-chancellerie-fontainebleau.com. 25 rooms.* ⊇*6€.* This small hotel in the heart of the city is located in the former buildings of the chancellery. The small rooms are bright and practical and the reception is amiable. An appealing address for those on a budget.

⊜⊜⊜ **Hôtel Victoria** – *112–122 r. de France.* ℘*01 60 74 90 00. www. hotelvictoria.com. 37 rooms.* ⊇*8€.* This 19C building is a pleasant, relaxing place to stay only five minutes on foot from the Château and the centre of town. Most of the rooms on its three floors have been redecorated in shades of yellow and blue; five of them have a marble fireplace. Breakfast is served on the veranda or the terrace looking toward the garden.

🍴 EAT

⊜⊜⊜ **Croquembouche** – *43 r. de France.* ℘*01 64 22 01 57. www.restaurant -croquembouche.com. Closed Sat & Mon for lunch, Sun.* A plain and simple restaurant in the city centre frequented by regulars who appreciate the warm reception, the inviting dining room decorated in soothing colours, and the traditional food prepared from fresh produce.

⊜⊜⊜ **L'Île aux Truites** – *6 chemin Basse-Varenne, Vulaines-sur-Seine. 7km/4.3mi E of Fontainebleau dir. Samoreau.* ℘ *01 64 23 71 87. Closed Thu lunch and Wed. Reservations required.* A pretty thatched-roof country house well-situated on the banks of the Seine.

ADDITIONAL SIGHTS

Ensemble des Grands Appartements★★★
(First-floor State Rooms)
Petits Appartements★
(Ground-floor State Rooms)
Musée Napoléon★
Gardens★

Diners can savour trout and salmon culled from the restaurant's fish tank while enjoying an incomparable view of the river and forest. Summertime, meals are served outdoors.

🍷 NIGHTLIFE

Le Franklin-Roosevelt – *20 r. Grande.* ℘*01 64 22 28 73.* This wine bar aims to please. Note the inviting décor featuring mahogany furniture and red leatherette wall seats, the library dedicated to the period between 1890 and 1920, the intimate ambience with jazz in the background and some fine vintages on the wine menu. Heated terrace.

🛍 SHOPPING

La Ferme des Sablons – *19 r. des Sablons.* ℘*01 64 22 67 25.* A third of the 130 varieties of cheese sold by this cheese shop are matured on site, including the house speciality, le Fontainebleau, a soft white cheese with cream. There is also a selection of local products. A pleasant, pastoral setting.

🏃 SPORT & LEISURE

Jeu de Paume de Fontainebleau – *Château de Fontainebleau.* ℘*01 60 71 5070. www.musee-chateau-fontainebleau.fr.* The jeu de paume, a sport whose descendants include tennis and squash, has been played since 1601 in this indoor court of the Château de Fontainebleau. Visitors can watch a match or try a game themselves.

Laon★★

This ancient town dominates the surrounding countryside from its magnificent hilltop **site**★★, a 100m/328ft high limestone outlier rising abruptly from the plain. Its defensive potential was noted by the Carolingian kings who made it their capital for 150 years, from the reign of Charles le Chauve (the Bald) (840) to Louis V (987). It was only in the reign of Hugh Capet that the capital was moved to the Île-de-France.

SIGHT

Cathédrale Notre-Dame★★

8 r. du Cloître. Guided tours available 6€. ℘03 23 20 26 54.
The present cathedral was begun in 1160 and completed towards 1230. It is in the early Gothic style, still caught up in the Romanesque idiom (as in its Norman-style lantern-tower). The west front is a masterpiece, with its deep porches and stepped towers flanked by openwork turrets. The immensely long **nave**★★★ shows the persistence of Carolingian traditions, but "nowhere else did the development of 12C Gothic achieve such breadth and unity" (Henri Focillon). The elevation is four-storeyed, with great arches carried on circular columns, a gallery with bold double arches, a blind triforium and a clerestory. In the nave, transept and chancel the bays are marked – still in a less emphatic way than at either Sens (1140) or Senlis (1153) – by a pattern of major and minor clustered columns, the former with five, the latter with three engaged columns.

ADDITIONAL SIGHTS

Quartier de la Cathédrale★★ (Cathedral area)
Rempart du Midi★ (southern

- ▶ **Population:** 26 522
- **Michelin Map:** 306 D 5
- **Info:** Place du Parvis Gautier de Mortagne. ℘03 23 20 28 62. www.tourisme-paysdelaon.com.
- **Location:** On arrival at Laon, head to the Upper Town, which is in two sections: la Cité, around the cathedral, and le Bourg.
- **P Parking:** Driving and parking are difficult in the Upper Town. Parking is available at the foot of the cathedral and along Promenade de la Couloire.
- **Timing:** The quickest and most enjoyable way to reach the Upper Town is on the cable railway, called Poma (Mon–Sat 7am–8pm; 1€; ℘03 23 23 52 01; www.tul-laon.net).

Ramparts) – **views**★
Musée Archéologique Municipal★ (*32 r. George-Ermant*) **Chapelle des Templiers**★ (*r. Paul Doumer*). **Église St-Martin**★ (*r. Eglise St Martin*) **Porte de Soissons**★

Lantern tower of the cathedral

©Xiongmao/Fotolia.com

Lille★★

Lively, convivial capital of French Flanders and close to the Belgian border, the city successfully combines vibrant forward-looking appeal with its splendid Baroque heritage.

A BIT OF HISTORY

A medieval trading city, Lille moved into manufacturing, wool and cloths predominating from the 14C. In the 15C Lille belonged to Burgundy, which held the whole of Flanders; in 1454 Duke Philippe le Bon (the Good) of Burgundy was responsible for the fine brick-built Palais Rihour.

The marriage of Marie de Bourgogne to Charles V brought first Austrian, then Spanish rule. In 1667, after a nine-day siege, Lille fell to Louis XIV, subsequently becoming the capital of France's northern provinces. In October 1914 Lille, which was poorly defended, surrendered to the Germans. Some 900 buildings were destroyed. During World War II, the French troops capitulated on 1 June 1940.

From the 1960s to 1990s, a plan to restore the old district successfully preserved its artistic heritage, while modernisation has proceeded apace with new buildings.

SIGHTS

La Citadelle★

av. du 43ème Régiment d'Infanterie. The Citadel is a military base. Guided *tours only. May–Aug Sun 3pm. Contact tourist office for details and reservation.* Within four months of Louis XIV's troops entering the town, Vauban began to reconstruct the citadel. The great complex is set in a marshy site

▸ **Population:** 226 014
◉ **Michelin Map:** 302 G 4
▤ **Info:** Palais Rihour, pl. Rihou. ℰ0891 56 20 04. www.lilletourism.com.
◖ **Location:** Lille is a large city close to the Belgian border. It is easily reached by high-speed TGV and Eurostar trains which arrive in the centre, or by road on A1 from Paris and A25 from the English Channel. Place Géneral-de-Gaulle is the city centre. Lille is laid out on an axis stretching east–west, with the new town leading into the old town leading into the citadel.
▣ **Parking:** There are plenty of car parks in the town centre and off-road parking is available (1.30€–1.60€/hr). http://www.lilletourism.com/se_garer_a_lille-1-0-6-fr.html.
◉ **Don't Miss:** The picturesque lanes and shops of the old quarter Le Vieux Lille; Centre Euralille, a huge indoor mall with more than 130 shops.
◉ **Timing:** Old Lille will take 2hr30min. The citadel, about 2hr. The tourist office publishes a weekly journal, *Sortir,* listing all of the city's current events, concerts and art exhibitions.

of some 1 700ha/4 200 acres which could be flooded when necessary. With its masterly handling of brick and sandstone, its economical design, its logical plan and its response to the geometry of artillery, it was the great engineer's masterpiece, the "queen of citadels".

Guided Tours

Tours of Old Lille (2hr) are on Sat at 10.30am for 9€. Audioguides available for download online. ℰ03 59 57 94 00. www.zevisit.com/Partenaire-LIL-US.html.

THE QUEEN OF CITADELS

▬▬▬ : preserved or visible remains ▬▬▬ : features no longer in existence

Place d'armes
1 Arsenal
2 Governor's Residence
3 Chapel

a Demi-lune redoubt
b Covered way
c Curtain wall
d Postern-gate

e Caponier
f Scarp
g Counterscarp

Le Vieux Lille★★

Beautiful façades of 17–18C buildings line the bustling old streets where there are numerous good little shops and brasseries. The distinctive Lille style combines brick and carved stonework.

Vieille Bourse★★

pl. du Général de Gaulle.

The Old Exchange designed and built in 1652-3 by the architect Julien Destrée is an example of the persistence of the Louis XIII style adapted to Flemish tastes (doors with broken pediments, caryatids supporting the entablatures, columns, pilasters and window-surrounds in sandstone, fruit and floral decoration and a little bell-tower). The whole building proclaims the importance of

Y. Thierry/ MICHELIN

Detail on the façade, Vieille Bourse

textile manufacturing in the life of the city as well as paying tribute to great men and their contributions to progress with the statues lining the arcades.

Musée des Beaux-Arts★★★

Place de la République. &. ⏱Open 8 Sept–Aug Mon 2–6pm, Wed–Sun 10am–6pm. ⏱Closed public holidays. ⬡5€, free 1st Sun in the month. ☎03 20 06 78 00. www.palais desbeauxarts.fr.

The imposing building (1885–92) has recently been renovated and extended. The collection includes many masterpieces of French painting, among them the *Mystical Fountain* by Jean Bellegambe (early 16C) with its symbolic treatment of renewal and redemption, a serenely Classical *Nativity* by Philippe de Champaigne (1643), a beautifully modelled *Portrait of Madame Pélerin* by Maurice Quentin de la Tour, and another portrait, *Jean-Baptiste Forest* (1704), by Nicolas de Largillière.

Vauban, a Military Genius

Sébastien Le Prestre (1633–1707) was born at St-Léger *(25km/15.5mi SE of Avallon in the Morvan)*. Better known as the Marquis de **Vauban**, he was one of the truly great figures of the age of Louis XIV, a soldier who personally conducted 53 sieges, an engineer who created the French army's corps of engineers and who studied the science of gunnery, and not least an architect and town planner who redesigned ports, dug canals, spanned the Eure at Maintenon with a fine aqueduct, and built from scratch 33 new fortresses as well as improving no fewer than 300 others (many have of course disappeared).

Appointed Commissioner of Fortifications in 1678, he took his inspiration first of all from his predecessors, bringing their work to a new peak of perfection; in the case of Belfort he added a second external line of defences as well as strengthening the existing bastions by means of demilunes and a deep moat, while at Neuf-Brisach his innovations included supplementing the internal walls with bastions and placing demilunes in front of the redoubts. But above all he was able to assimilate new inventions and changes in tactics, and to adapt his designs to the particular characteristics of the site.

His main concern was to defend France's new, expanded frontiers. His work thus took him to Flanders, the Ardennes and Alsace, to the Franche-Comté, to the Pyrénées, the Alps and to many places along the country's coastline. Some of his fortresses proved their worth to the retreating French and British forces in 1940.

ADDITIONAL SIGHTS

Demeure de Gilles de la Boé★
(29 pl. Louise-de-Bettignies)
Rue de la Monnaie★

 Hospice Comtesse★ *(32 r. de la Monnaie)*
Église St-Maurice★ *(Parvis St Maurice)*
Porte de Paris★ *(pl. Simon Vollant)*

ADDRESSES

🛏 STAY

Chez B&B – *78 r. Caumartin.* ℰ*03 61 50 16 42. www.chezbandb.com/03.htm. Closed 15 Jul-15 Aug. 3 rooms.* "B & B" as in Bed and Breakfast, as well as in Béatrice and Bernard, the current owners of this house built during the reign of Napoléon III. The comfortable rooms are nicely furnished; two with sloping ceilings. Cosy sitting room; breakfast room looking out onto the garden.

Hôtel Flandre Angleterre – *13 pl.de la Gare.* ℰ*03 20 06 04 12. www.hotel-flandreangleterre-lille.com. 44 rooms.* ⊂*7.50€.* Situated opposite the train station and near the pedestrian streets, this family-run hotel presents modern rooms that are comfortable and cosy. Recommended for its location and affordability.

Hôtel Brueghel – *3–5 parvis St-Maurice.* ℰ*03 20 06 06 69. www.hotel-brueghel.com. 65 rooms.* ⊂*8.50€.* This Flemish-style house is conveniently located in the pedestrian part of town quite near the train station. The rooms have old-fashioned charm and modern bathrooms. The lift, the woodwork and the knick-knacks give the place a nostalgic appeal.

L'Hermitage Gantois – *224 r. Paris.* ℰ*03 20 85 30 30. www.hotel hermitagegantois.com. 72 rooms.* ⊂*19€. L'Estaminet Restaurant*⊜⊜. Comfort, history and design in one. Delightful personalised rooms in a 14C hospice and listed building. Restaurant with red and gold vaults offer a seasonal menu. The Estaminet has a brasserie atmosphere and serves generous portions.

🍴 EAT

Le Domaine de Lintillac – *43 r. de Gand.* ℰ*03 20 06 53 51. Closed fornight in Aug, Sun, Mon.* The red façade of the building will lead you directly to this rustic restaurant in old Lille. Wicker baskets hang from the beams and the walls are lined with pots of preserves from southwest France. The plentiful cuisine of the Périgord region is honoured here.

Aux Moules – *34 r. de Béthune.* ℰ*03 20 57 12 46. www.auxmoules.com.* A multitude of mussels (*moules*) and a few other Flemish specialities await customers in this 1930s style brasserie located in a lively pedestrian street. A must for bona fide shellfish fans and friends.

Estaminet du Rijsel – *25 r. de Gand.* ℰ*03 20 15 01 59. Closed Aug, last week in Dec, Sun–Mon.* A sure bet, this *estaminet* is located in a street crowded with restaurants. The appealing Flemish décor features photos, posters and advertisements, while the appetizing regional menu is presented in the form of an old school notebook.

Le Passe-Porc – *155 r. de Solférino.* ℰ*03 20 42 83 93. Closed Aug. Reservations required.* A bistro after our own hearts. The tiled floor, wall seats and enamelled plaques on the walls act as the backdrop for a remarkable collection of pigs. The hearty ambience and plentiful fare are in perfect harmony with the amusing surroundings.

La Tête de l'Art – *10 r. de l'Arc.* ℰ*03 20 54 68 89. www.latetedelart-lille. com. Closed first 3 wks of Aug, Sun & evenings except Fri-Sat – Reservations required*. A charming, lively restaurant is hidden behind the pink façade of this manor built in 1890. Follow the hallway to discover the inviting dining room where denizens of Lille gather for traditional meals. A good selection of wines at reasonable prices.

La Cave aux Fioles – *39 r. de Gand.* ℰ*03 20 55 18 43. www.lacaveaux fioles.com. Closed Sat lunch, Sun & Public Holidays – Reservations required.* Don't be put off by the gloomy passageway that leads to this restaurant housed in two 17C and 18C residences – the interior is unexpectedly warm and pleasant: brick, wood, beams and paintings by area artists. Check out the collection of commodes upstairs. Convivial ambience; bistro cuisine.

L'Huitrière – *3 r. des Chats Bossus.* ℘*03 20 55 43 41. www.huitriere.fr. Closed 27 Jul–25 Aug & Public Holidays.* A former fishmongers, now housing three resplendent dining rooms. One of Lille's gourmet hotspots.

NIGHTLIFE

L'Échiquier (*Bar of the Alliance Hotel*), *17 quai de Wault.* ℘*03 20 30 62 62. www.alliance-lille.com.* This bar, installed in the majestic 17C setting of a former Minim convent, is attached to the Alliance Hotel. Harpists and pianists entertain the guests from 7–11pm every night. Rich selection of champagne and cocktails.

Les 3 Brasseurs – *22 pl. de la Gare. Opposite the Lille-Flandres train station.* ℘*03 20 06 46 25. www.les3brasseurs.com.* The pungent scent of hops greets visitors to this brasserie, a veritable Lille institution. Sample one or all of the four kinds on beer on draught drawn directly from the tuns behind the counter. Flammekueches, sauerkraut and regional fare are on hand for the pleasure of nibblers and the ravenous alike.

Pâtisserie Meert – *27 r. Esquermoise.* ℘*03 20 57 07 44 – www.meert.fr.* This pâtisserie-confiserie salon-de-thé founded in 1761 is a veritable Lille institution with mirrors, arabesques and gilt. The best of local specialities is offered, including its famed gaufre fourrée à la vanille de Madagascar, using the same recipe since 1849.

SHOWTIME

Le Grand Bleu – *36 av. Max-Dormoy.* ℘*03 20 09 88 44, www.legrandbleu. com. Ticket office 9am–noon, 2–6pm; performances 8pm, Wed & Sat 3pm, Sun 5pm. Closed Aug. 11.50€ (child 9€).* This performance hall caters to a young audience. Some of its events appeal to children as young as five years old, others are designed for teens. Dance,

circus, theatre, storytelling, hip-hop and other nice surprises.

Orchestre National de Lille – *pl. Mendès-France.* ℘*03 20 12 82 40. www.onlille.com. Closed Aug. 18–30€.* Since 1976, The Orchestre National de Lille gives an average of 120 concerts per season. Performances are held in the Lille area, the Nord-Pas-de-Calais region and abroad (30 countries altogether). The varied repertoire, featuring performances for young audiences, original pieces, established musicians and fresh talent, exemplifies this orchestra's motto: "taking music to all who would hear it."

Théâtre de Marionnettes du Jardin Vauban – *1 av. Léon-Jouhaux, Chalet des Chèvres in the Jardin Vauban, 59000 Armentières.* ℘*03 20 42 09 95. www.lepetitjacques.fr. Closed Nov–Mar, Sat, Mon. 4€.* An outdoors puppet show of the Guignol tradition starring characters of local repute, such as Jacques de Lille and Jean-Jean La Plume.

SHOPPING

Marché de Wazemmes – *59000 Armentières.* Tue, Thu and especially Sun mornings, the Wazemmes market takes over the Place de la Nouvelle-Aventure and its great covered market built of red brick. Food stands alternate with second-hand bric-a-brac in a merry market for shoppers of all categories.

Rue de Gand – Paved, animated and highly colourful, La Rue de Gand is well worth a visit. Butcher shops, taverns, bars and especially restaurants serving various types of cuisine line the pavements.

VISIT IDEAS

Tourist packages – The tourist office offers themed packages (discovery, Christmas market, culture, Lille flea market, cabaret) that include one or more nights in a hotel, a City Tour, museum admission or a show, etc.

Minibus Tour – *Check times with tourist office. 10€ (free with City Pass).* A 50min city tour in several languages. Meet at Palais Rihour. Bus accessible to persons of reduced mobility.

Paris★★★

The brilliance and greatness of Paris – its evocative spirit, the imposing dignity of its avenues and squares, its vast cultural wealth and unique flair and style – are known the world over. The dominance of Paris in France's intellectual, artistic, scientific and political life can be traced back to the 12C when the Capetian kings made it their capital.

A BIT OF HISTORY
Origins
At the time of the fall of the Roman Empire towards the end of the 5C, Paris was a modest township founded seven centuries previously by Gallic fishermen. Following its occupation by the **Romans**, the settlement had been extended south of the river to where the remains of the Cluny Baths and a 2C amphitheatre now stand: the **Quartier latin**. In the 3C, St Denis, Paris' first bishop, had met his martyrdom and the Barbarians had razed the place to the ground. This destruction, together with the threat posed by Attila's hordes (but supposedly averted by the intervention of St Geneviève, patron saint of the city), had caused the inhabitants to withdraw to the security of the Île de la Cité.

Clovis, King of **the Franks**, settled in Paris in 506. Two years later, he founded an abbey south of the Seine in honour of St Geneviève, just as 35 years previously a basilica had been erected over the tomb of St Denis. In 885, for the fifth time in 40 years, the Norsemen sailed up the river and attacked Paris; Odo, son of Robert the Strong, bravely led the local resistance, and was elected king of "France" in 888; from then on, the town became the royal seat, albeit with some interruptions.

The Capetian Dynasty (987–1328)
In 1136, Abbot Suger rebuilt the abbey church of St-Denis in the revolutionary Gothic style, an example soon followed by Maurice de Sully at Notre-Dame. Between 1180 and 1210, **Philippe**

▶ **Population:** 2 181 371

Michelin Map: 312 D 2

Information: There are several branches of the tourist office in the city. The **main office** is at 25 rue des Pyramides. The other branches are located at place du 11 novembre 1918, **Gare de l'Est**; 20 bd Diderot, **Gare de Lyon**; 18 r. de Dunkerque, **Gare du Nord**; 72 bd Rochechouart, **Anvers**; 1 pl. de la Porte de Versailles, Paris Expo; Corner of av. des Champs-Elysées and av. Marigny, **Clémenceau**; 99 r. de Rivoli, **Carrousel du Louvre**; and 21 place du Tertre, **Montmartre**. ℘0892 68 30 00. http://en.parisinfo.com.

Location: Paris is France's capital and its largest city. It lies in the middle of the Île-de-France region, which sits between the Centre, Bougogne, Champagne-Ardennes, Picardie and Haute Normandie regions. Paris is 85.6km/53mi SW of Compiègne; 69km/42.8mi NW of Fontainebleau; 104km/64.6mi SE of Les Andelys.

Don't Miss: Arc de Triomphe, Place de la Concorde, Eiffel Tower, Notre-Dame Cathedral, the Champs-Élysées, Quartier Latin, Montmartre, the Louvre and the Musée d'Orsay.

Kids: La Villette encompasses the child-friendly Cité des Sciences et l'Industrie, the spherical cinema La Géode, Cité des Enfants, Jardin de Luxembourg, Palais de Découverte.

GETTING AROUND PARIS

Seine River flows east–west across the city. Places north of the river are on the *rive droite*, while those to the south are on the *rive gauche*. Paris is divided into 20 **arrondissements** (districts or neighbourhoods), each one with its own local government and characteristics. Each arrondissement is further divided into a number of neighbourhoods determined by history and the people who live there.

The métro is the easiest and most economical way of moving around the city. **Line 1**, which crosses Paris east–west, services many of the most famous attractions: the Louvre, the Champs-Élysées and the Arc de Triomphe. **Line 4** is useful for travelling across the city from north–south. The metro also services the immediate suburbs of Paris, but for those a bit farther out, use the **RER** suburban trains.

Auguste surrounded the growing city with a continuous ring of fortifications anchored on the Louvre fortress. In 1215 France's first university was founded on the Ste-Geneviève hill.

The House of Valois (1328–1589)

On 22 February 1358, Étienne Marcel, the merchants' provost, succeeded in rousing the townsfolk to break into the Law Courts (Palais de Justice); entering the Dauphin's apartments, he slew two of the future Charles V's counsellors before his very eyes. On becoming king, **Charles V** quit this place of ill memory. In 1370, he built himself a stronghold in the eastern part of the city, the Bastille, which became the centrepiece of a new ring of fortifications.

Paris was taken by the English in 1418. **Joan of Arc** was wounded in front of Porte St-Honoré trying to retake the city in 1429. Paris was won back for France eight years later by Charles VII.

In 1492, the discovery of America marked the first beginnings of a new outlook and the modern age. The Neapolitan artists brought back by **Charles VIII** from his campaigns in Italy were introducing new trends in taste and thought; the influence of the Renaissance became apparent in many new buildings. In the 1560s, the brothers Androuet Du Cerceau drew up the plans for the Flore Pavilion abutting the Louvre to the west, then set about the construction of the Pont Neuf (New Bridge), which today is the city's oldest surviving bridge.

On 24 August 1572, the bells rang out from the tower of St-Germain-l'Auxerrois to signal the start of the St Bartholomew's Day Massacre (of Protestants); Henry of Navarre, the future Henri IV, just married to Marguerite of Valois, barely escaped with his life. In 1589, Henri III was assassinated at St-Cloud in 1589 by the monk Jacques Clément. This violent act marked the end of the Valois line.

The Bourbons (1589–1789)

In 1594 Paris opened its gates to **Henri IV**, the new king who had renounced his Protestant faith and succeeded in pacifying the country. But on 14 May 1610 in the Rue de la Ferronnerie, this monarch too fell victim to an assassin. Under **Louis XIII** (1610–43), Métezeau designed an imposing Classical west front for St-Gervais Church, the first of its kind in Paris; Salomon de Brosse built the Luxembourg Palace for Marie de' Medici; Jean Androuet Du Cerceau laid out the courtyards and gardens of the Hôtel de Béthune-Sully; as well as erecting a church for the Sorbonne with Classical columns on its courtyard side, Lemercier built the Palais-Royal for Richelieu. On the king's death in 1643, Anne of Austria became Regent, acting in concert with Mazarin and continuing the policies of Richelieu. Paris fell prey to the series of disturbances caused by unrest among the nobility and known as the Fronde; the young king came to the conclusion that it might be advantageous to separate Court from city.

The 23-year-old **Louis XIV** began his long and highly personal reign in 1661. Even more than the splendour of court life, it was the extraordinary advancement of the arts and literature at this time that gave Paris and France such prestige in Europe. Under the protection of a king keen to encourage artistic endeavour and promote creative confidence, writers, painters, sculptors and landscapers flourished as never before. In the space of 20 years, the great Le Nôtre redesigned the parterres of the Tuileries; Claude Perrault provided the Louvre with its fine colonnade and built the Observatory; Le Vau completed the greater part of both the Institut de France and the Louvre. France's "Century of Greatness" came to an end with Louis XIV's death in 1715.

The country now found itself, for the second time, under the rule of a five-year-old. The running of the country was therefore put into the hands of a regent, Philippe d'Orléans; the first action of the court was to pack its bags and quit the boredom of Versailles for the gaiety of the capital. A long period of peace accompanied the years of corruption; for 77 years France experienced no foreign incursions. Literary salons flourished, notably those of the Marquise de Lambert, Mme Du Deffand and Mme Geoffrin, all helping the spread of new ideas in what became known as the **Age of Enlightenment**. The Palais Bourbon (1722–28), which now houses the National Assembly, was erected at this time.

The personal rule exercised by **Louis XV** was discredited by his favourites, but Paris nevertheless witnessed a number of great personalities and important advances; such as Charles de la Condamine, a surveyor and naturalist responsible for the discovery of rubber (1751); Jussieu, incumbent of the Chair in Botany at the Botanical Gardens, responsible for a systematic classification of plants (1759) and for many advances in pharmacology; Diderot, author, together with d'Alambert, of the great *Encyclopaedia*, a splendid summary of the technology of the age; Chardin, who had lodgings in the Louvre, devoted himself to working in pastel; Robert Pothier, who wrote the *Treatise of Obligations*; Ange-Jacques Gabriel, the last and most famous of a line of architects linked to Mansart and Robert de Cotte, who between them gave France a hundred years of architectural unity; it was he who designed the magnificent façades fronting the Place de la Concorde, the west front of St-Roch Church and the École Militaire (Military Academy). Finally there was Soufflot, creator of the dome which crowns the Panthéon.

Distinguished furniture-makers were at work too: Lardin with his cabinets and commodes with rosewood inlay, and Boudin with his virtuoso marquetry and secret compartments; they anticipate the masters who were to emerge in the following reign.

Revolution and Empire (1789–1814)

In 1788, King **Louis XVI (1774–92)** decided to convene the States-General. The delegates assembled at Versailles on 5 May 1789. As a result, on 17 June, the States-General transformed itself into a **National Assembly** which styled itself the Constituent Assembly on 9 July; the monarchy would eventually become a constitutional one.

On **14 July 1789**, in the space of less than an hour, the people of Paris took over the Bastille in the hope of finding arms there; the outline of the

Louis XVI by Antoine-Francois Callet

© The Gallery Collection/Corbis

demolished fortress can still be traced in the paving on the west side of the Place de la Bastille (14 July became a day of national celebration in 1879). On 17 July, in the City Hall (Hôtel de Ville), Louis XVI kissed the recently adopted tricolour cockade. The feudal system was abolished on 4 August, and the Declaration of the Rights of Man adopted on 26 August; on 5 October, the Assembly moved into the riding-school of the Tuileries, and the royal family was brought from Versailles and installed in the Tuileries Palace.

On 12 July 1790 the Church became subject to the Civil Constitution for the Clergy. Two days later, a great crowd gathered on the Champ-de-Mars to celebrate the anniversary of the fall of the Bastille; Talleyrand, Bishop of Autun as well as statesman and diplomat, celebrated mass on the altar of the nation and the king reaffirmed his oath of loyalty to the country.

After his attempt to join Bouillé's army at Metz had been foiled, Louis was brought back to Paris on 25 June 1791; on 30 September, he was forced to accept the constitution adopted by the Assembly which then dissolved itself.

The Legislative Assembly – The new deputies met the following day in the Tuileries Riding School. On 20 June 1792, encouraged by the moderate revolutionary faction known as the Girondins, rioters invaded the Tuileries and made Louis put on the red bonnet of liberty. On 11 July, the Assembly declared France to be in danger, and during the night of 9 August the mob (sans-culottes) instituted a "revolutionary commune" with the status of an organ of government; the next day the Tuileries were sacked and 600 of the Swiss Guards massacred. The Assembly responded by depriving the king of his few remaining responsibilities and confining him with his family in the tower of the Templar Prison (Tour du Temple).

Soon after, the "September Massacres" began; 1 200 prisoners, some "politicals", but most of them common offenders, were hauled from the city's jails and arbitrarily executed on the Buci crossroads in a frenzy of fear and panic precipitated by fear of invasion. This grisly event marked the beginning of the Terror. On 21 September, the day after the French defeat at the Battle of Valmy, the Legislative Assembly gave way to the Convention.

The Convention – At its very first meeting, the new assembly, now in the hands of the Girondins, formally abolished the monarchy and proclaimed the **Republic**. This day, 21 September 1792, became Day 1 of Year One in the new revolutionary calendar (which remained in force until 31 December 1805). At the end of May, beset by difficulties at home and abroad and bereft of popular support, the Girondins fell, to be replaced by the "Mountain" (the extreme Jacobin faction, so-called because they occupied the upper tiers of seating in the Assembly).

In one of its first acts, the monarch was guillotined on 21 January 1793 in Place de la Concorde. On 17 September, the Law of Suspects was passed, legalising **the Terror**. The first to be executed by the revolutionary tribunals were the Girondins, in October 1793. On 8 June 1794, Robespierre the "Incorruptible" presided over the Festival of the Supreme Being. The event was orchestrated by the painter David, beginning in the Tuileries Gardens and proceeding to the Champ-de-Mars.

On 10 June (9 Prairial), the Great Terror began. Over a period of two months, the "national razor", as the guillotine was known, was to slice off 2 561 heads. Among those executed were Lavoisier, former Farmer-General and eminent chemist, responsible for the formulation of the theory of the conservation of mass on which much of modern chemistry rests, and André Chénier, the lyric poet who had condemned the excesses of the regime in his verse. The end of the Terror came with the fall and execution of Robespierre himself, on 27 July (9 Thermidor).

The Thermidorian Convention now attempted to put the sickening spectacle of the scaffold behind it with a policy calculated to promote stability. Among

Detail of *The Consecration of the Emperor Napoleon and the Coronation of the Empress Josephine* by Jacques-Louis David, Musée du Louvre

© The Gallery Collection/Corbis

its most important achievements were measures designed to advance science and learning, including the founding of the École Polytechnique (School of Engineering); the creation of the Conservatoire des Arts et Métiers (National Technical Institution), and the setting up of the École Normale (the prestigious college).

In 1795, the metric system was adopted and the Office of Longitudes founded. Just before the Assembly's dissolution on 25 October, public education was instituted and the Institut de France founded, embracing the nation's learned academies (including the Académie Française).

The Directory and the Consulate – The period of the Directory was marked, in 1798, by the very first Universal Exhibition, but was brought to an end with the *coup d'état* of 9 November (18 Brumaire) 1799, when the Council of Elders persuaded the legislature to move to St-Cloud as a precautionary measure against Jacobin plots. On the following day, **Napoleon Bonaparte** entered the chamber to address the delegates, but was booed; he was saved by the presence of mind of his brother Lucien, who used the guard to disperse the members. By the same evening, power was in the hands of three consuls; it was the end of the Revolution. In less

than five years, the Consulate allowed Napoleon to centralise power, opening the way to the realisation of his Imperial ambitions.

The Empire – Proclaimed Emperor of the French by the Senate on 18 May 1804, Napoleon I was anointed on 2 December by Pope Pius VII at Notre-Dame, though it was he himself who actually put the crown on his head in a ceremony immortalised by David. His reign was marked by the promulgation in 1804 of the Civil Code, which he had helped draft himself when he was still First Consul, and which, as the *Code Napoleon*, has since formed the legal basis of many other countries. In order to make Paris into a truly imperial capital, Napoleon ordered the erection of a great column in the Place Vendôme; cast from the melted-down metal of guns taken at the Battle of Austerlitz (Slavkov), it commemorated the victories of his *Grande Armée*.

Vignon was commissioned to design a temple which nearly became a railway station before ending up as the Madeleine Church; Chalgrin was put to work drawing up plans for a great triumphal arch (Arc de Triomphe); Brongniart built the Stock Exchange (Bourse); Percier and Fontaine, the promoters of the Empire style, constructed the north wing of the

Louvre and the Carrousel Arch (Arc du Carrousel); Gros painted the battles and Géricault the cavalry of the *Grande Armée*. On 31 March 1814, despite the strong resistance offered by Daumesnil at Vincennes, the Allies occupied Paris. On 11 April, the Emperor, "the sole obstacle to peace in Europe", put his signature to the document of abdication at Fontainebleau.

The Restoration (May 1814–February 1848)
The reign of Louis XVIII – 1814–24
The period of rule of Louis XVI's brother was interrupted by the Hundred Days of Napoleon's attempt to re-establish himself between his sojourn on Elba and his final exile to St Helena. During the years of Louis XVIII's reign, Laënnec invented the stethoscope, wrote his *Treatise on Mediate Auscultation* and founded the anatomo-clinical school together with Bayle and Dupuytren; Pinel studied mental illness at the Salpêtrière Hospital; Cuvier put biology on a sounder footing, formulated the principles of subordination of organs to their function and established a zoological classification; Bertholet studied the composition of acids, Sadi Carnot thermodynamics and temperature equilibrium, and Arago electromagnetism and the polarisation of light; Daguerre laid the foundations of his fame with his dioramas, and Lamartine conquered literary society with his *Méditations Poétiques* – its elegaic rhythms soothed Talleyrand's sleepless nights.

The reign of Charles X – 1824–30
Painting flourished with the brilliant sweep of Delacroix' great canvases and Corot's landscapes. At the same time, Laplace was establishing the fundamental laws of mathematical analysis and providing a firm basis for astronomical mechanics, and Berlioz was composing his *Fantastic Symphony*, the key work of the Romantic Movement in music. On 21 February 1830, Victor Hugo's drama *Hernani* provoked a literary battle between "moderns" and "classicals" in which the latter were

temporarily routed. In the summer, Charles' press ordinances provoked a crisis which led to his abdication; he was succeeded by Louis Philippe, a member of the cadet branch of the Bourbons.

Reign of Louis-Philippe – 1830–48
During the 1830s, the mathematician Evariste Galois put forward the theory of sets; Victor Hugo wrote *Notre-Dame de Paris* and Alfred de Musset *Caprices*. Chopin, the darling of Parisian society, composed scherzos, waltzes and his celebrated Polonaises. In 1838, while on holiday in Paris, Stendhal wrote *The Charterhouse of Parma*, a masterpiece of psychological observation which can be read on a number of levels. The first news agency was founded by Charles Havas. In 1839, a railway line was opened between Paris and St-Germain. The 1840s saw the publication of the *Mysteries of Paris* by Eugène Sue, the *Count of Monte Cristo* and the *Three Musketeers* by Dumas and many of the works of Balzac's prodigious Human Comedy as well as the *Treatise on Parasitology* by Raspail; the abuses of the July monarchy were satirised in the drawings of Daumier.

At the age of 79, Chateaubriand brought his finely chiselled *Memories from beyond the Tomb* to a triumphant conclusion. On 23 February in 1848, the barricades went up on the Boulevard des Capucines and the monarchy fell; the next day, at the City Hall, amid scenes of wild enthusiasm, Lamartine saluted the tricolour "the flag which has spread the name of France, freedom and glory around the wide world".

Second Republic and Second Empire (1848–1870)
Second Republic
The abolition of the National Workshops in June 1848 led to rioting in the St-Antoine district, in which the archbishop of Paris was killed. In 1849, Léon Foucault proved the rotation and spherical nature of the earth by means of a pendulum (the experiment was repeated in 1855 from the dome of the Panthéon).

On 2 December 1851 the short life of the Second Republic was ended by a *coup d'état*.

Second Empire – 1852–70

Two great exhibitions (in 1855 and 1867) proclaimed the prosperity France enjoyed under the rule of Bonaparte's nephew, Napoleon III. **Baron Haussmann**, Prefect of the *Département* of the Seine, was responsible for an ambitious programme of public works which transformed the capital, giving it many of the features which now seem quintessentially Parisian. Among them were the laying out of the Bois de Boulogne and the Bois de Vincennes, and the building of railway stations and the North Wing of the Louvre. But the Baron is remembered above all for the ruthless surgery he performed on the capital's ancient urban tissue, opening up new focal points (Place de l'Opéra) and linking them with great axial roadways (Grands Boulevards), splendid exercises in traffic engineering and crowd control.

In 1852, Alexandre Dumas wrote *The Lady of the Camellias* at the same time as Rudé was working on the memorial to Marshal Ney, which was to be placed on the spot where the great soldier had been executed in 1815; in Rodin's opinion, it was Paris' finest statue. In 1857 Baudelaire, the first poet of the teeming modern metropolis, published *Les Fleurs du Mal (The Flowers of Evil)*. In 1859, Gounod presented *Faust* at the Opéra Lyrique. In 1860, Étienne Lenoir registered his first patent for the internal combustion engine.

The year 1863 was marked by the scandals caused by Manet's *Déjeuner sur l'herbe* and *Olympia*; Baltard masked the masterly iron structure of the St-Augustin Church with the stone cladding still obligatory in a religious building. In 1896 Pierre de Coubertin created the International Olympic Committee.

Republican Continuity (1870 to the present day)

On 4 September 1870, the mob which had invaded the National Assembly was led by Gambetta to the City Hall where the Republic was proclaimed. The new government busied itself in preparing to defend Paris against the advancing Prussians; the St-Cloud château was set on fire and a fierce battle took place at Le Bourget.

The ensuing siege subjected the population of Paris to terrible hardships; food ran out and the winter was exceptionally severe. The city surrendered on 28 January 1871. The revolutionary **Commune** was ruthlessly suppressed by military force, not before the Communards had burnt down the City Hall, the Tuileries and the Audit Office (Cours des Comptes – on the site of what is now the Orsay Museum), pulled down the column in the Place Vendôme and shot their prisoners at the Hostages' Wall in the Rue Haxo. They made their last stand in the Père-Lachaise Cemetery, where those of their number who had survived the bitter fighting were summarily executed at the Federalists' Wall (Mur des Fédérés). But political institutions were re-established and the nation revived; the Republic was consolidated as France's political regime, notwithstanding Marshal Pétain's so-called French State (État Français), Nazi occupation and the provisional government following the end of World War II.

Third Republic – Carpeaux sculpted the Four Corners of the World for the Observatory Fountain, and Émile Littré completed the publication of his renowned *Dictionary of the French Language*. Bizet wrote *L'Arlésienne (the Woman of Arles)* for the Odéon theatre and followed it with *Carmen*, based on a short story by Mérimée.

In 1874, Degas painted *The Dancing Class* and Monet *Impression: Rising Sun*, which, when exhibited by his dealer Nadar, led to the coining of the initially derisive term Impressionism. Later, Renoir worked at the Moulin de la Galette, and Puvis de Chavannes decorated the walls of the Panthéon. The public applauded Delibes' innovatory *Coppélia* and *Lakmé*. Rodin created the *Thinker*, followed by figures of Balzac and Victor Hugo.

In 1879, Seulecq put forward the principle of sequential transmission on which television is based and Pasteur completed his vast body of work. Seurat's Grande Jatte heralded the establishment of the Pointillist school of painting. In the following year, 1887, Antoine founded the Free Theatre (Théâtre libre) based on spontaneous expression. The engineer Gustave Eiffel completed his great tower, centrepiece of the Universal Exhibition of 1889. In the century's final decade, Toulouse-Lautrec painted cabaret scenes and Pissarro Parisian townscapes, and Forain gained fame as a marvellous caricaturist. In the Catholic Institute, Édouard Branly discovered radio-conductors.

In 1891, René Panhard built the first petrol-engined motor car, which drove right across Paris.

In 1898, the 21-year-old Louis Renault built his first car, then founded his Billancourt factory; in 1902 he patented a turbocharger. The factory turned out cars, lorries, planes and, in 1917, light tanks which contributed to the German defeat in 1918. Nationalised at the end of World War II, the firm continued to produce vehicles in large numbers.

In October 1898 Pierre and Marie Curie succeeded in isolating radium and established the atomic character of radioactivity; their laboratory was a shed which has since disappeared, but its outline is shown in the paving pattern in the courtyard of the school at No 10 Rue Vauquelin. At the same time, Henri Bergson was teaching philosophy at the Collège de France and Langevin was conducting his investigations into ionised gases (in 1915, he was to use ultrasonic waves in the detection of submarines); a combination of steel, stone and glass was employed by Girault in the construction of the exhibition halls (the Grand Palais and the Petit Palais) for the 1900 Exhibition; this occasion also saw the bridging of the Seine by the great flattened arch of the Pont Alexandre III.

In 1900, Gustave Charpentier put on a musical romance *Louise*; with its lyrical realism and popular appeal it was a great "hit" of the time.

In 1902, Debussy's *Pelléas et Mélisande* was produced at the Salle Favart of the Comic Opera. In 1906, Santos-Dumont succeeded in taking off in a heavier-than-air machine, staying aloft for 21 seconds, and covering a distance of 220m/721.7ft.

Dalou's bronze group entitled *The Triumph of the Republic* graced the Place de la Nation, while at Montparnasse the re-erected Wine Pavilion from the 1900 Exhibition provided lodgings and studios for Soutine, Zadkine, Chagall, Modigliani and Léger; other innovative artists included the sculptor Maillol and the painter Utrillo, while Brancusi's work was evolving away from cubism towards abstraction *(The Sleeping Muse)*; the Perret brothers built the Théâtre des Champs-Élysées in reinforced concrete; its façade was adorned with eight relief panels by Bourdelle.

The theatre was opened in 1913 with a performance of Stravinsky's *Rite of Spring*; its music and choreography outraged an unprepared public.

Basilique du Sacré-Cœur atop Montmartre

S. Sauvignier/MICHELIN

In 1914 the construction of the Sacré-Cœur Church (begun in 1878 by the architect Abadie) on the Montmartre heights was completed. On the evening of 31 July, the eve of general mobilisation, Jean Jaurès was assassinated.

The World Wars

World War I (1914–18) put civilians as well as soldiers to the severest of tests; after three years of conflict, Clemenceau was made head of government, and, by restoring the country's confidence, earned the title of Father of Victory.

In 1920, the interment of an unknown soldier at the Arc de Triomphe marked France's recognition of the sacrifices made by her ordinary soldiers, the unshaven "poilus" of the trenches.

In the course of the 1920s, Le Corbusier built the La Roche Villa, and Bourdelle sculpted *France* at the Palais de Tokyo; Georges Rouault, with his predilection for religious themes, completed his *Miserere*, and Landowsky carved the figure of St Geneviève for the Tournelle Bridge; in the course of a fortnight, Maurice Ravel composed *Boléro* for the dancer Ida Rubinstein; with its subtle instrumentation and rhythmic precision it popularised the name of this aristocratic composer; Poulbot created the archetypal Montmartre urchin; Cocteau wrote *Les Enfants Terribles*; the dynamism of the theatrical scene was marked by many fine actors and producers, notably the Cartel of Four (Cartel des Quatre) consisting of Charles Dullin (at the Sarah Bernhardt Theatre), Gaston Baty (at the Montparnasse), Louis Jouvet (at the Champs-Élysées then the Athénée) and Georges Pitoëff (at the Mathurins).

At the end of the 19C, Émile Roux had studied the causes of and cure for diphtheria; he was now in charge of the Pasteur Institute, and brought to Paris the scientists Calmette and Guérin who had worked on vaccination against tuberculosis.

In 1934, André Citroën brought out the Traction Avant (Front-Wheel Drive) car; 15 years previously, his Type A had been Europe's first mass-produced car; 21 years later, he was to unveil the innovative DS 19.

In 1940, during **World War II**, Paris was bombed, then **occupied** by the German army. Between 16 and 17 July 1942, numerous French Jews, victims of the Nazi racial myth, were rounded up at the Vélodrome d'Hiver prior to their deportation eastwards for extermination; 4 500 members of the Resistance also met their deaths in the clearing on Mount Valérien where the National Memorial of Fighting France now stands. Finally, on 19 August 1944, Paris was **liberated**.

Fourth and Fifth Republics – In 1950, Alfred Kastler, working in the laboratories of the École Normale Supérieure, succeeded in verifying the principle of "optical pumping", which has subsequently become the basis of one of the methods of producing a laser beam. The *Symphony for a Single Man* by Maurice Béjart, presented at the Étoile Theatre on 3 August 1955, was danced to *musique concrète* composed by Pierre Henry and Pierre Schaeffer, and led to many innovations in ballet throughout Europe.

Since 1945 the influence of Le Corbusier (there are few examples of his genius in Paris: Villa La Roche, Cité Universitaire pavilions...), has given a new impetus to architecture: new forms (Maison de Radio-France), structures on piles (UNESCO), sweeping rooflines (CNIT building). The present trend is for glass buildings (GAN and Manhattan towers, Centre Georges-Pompidou, Institut du Monde Arabe).

The use of pre-stressed concrete led to technical advances (Palais des Congrès, Tour Montparnasse). But in the main architecture becomes an integral part of town planning: buildings are designed to fit into an overall plan: remodelling of an area (Maine-Montparnasse, les Halles, la Villette, Bercy) or new project (la Défense).

Grand new town-planning initiatives have also been implemented: the Opera house at la Bastille, the Ministry of Finance buildings at Bercy, the Grande Arche at la Défense and the Bibliothèque nationale de France François-Mitterand at Tolbiac are distinctive modern landmarks.

THE CITY'S MONUMENTS
CIVIL ARCHITECTURE
Palais du Louvre★★★
See Musée du Louvre.

Neither the Merovingians nor the Carolingians, nor even the Capet kings lived in the old Louvre, which then lay beyond the city limits; instead, they preferred the Law Courts (Palais de Justice), their *hôtels* in the Marais, the manor at Vincennes, their own châteaux or those of their liegemen in the Loire Valley.

Contributions of the Heads of State
Floor plan below shows the evolution of the Louvre Palace.

It was **François I** who had the old Louvre pulled down, and, in 1546, commissioned Pierre Lescot to build the palace which was to become the residence of the kings of France. Lescot's work 1 is regarded as the most prestigious part of the Louvre; it was he who brought the Italian Renaissance style, already flowering on the Loire, to the banks of the Seine; to the façade he built, sculptor Jean Goujon added the nymphs of the Fountain of the Innocents.

When Charles IX came to the throne at age ten, the Florentine **Catherine de' Medici** was made Regent. At first she lived in the Louvre on the floor since known as the Queens' Lodging (Logis des Reines), but ordered Philibert Delorme (succeeded by Jean Bullant) to build the Tuileries. The site of this new palace was some 500m/550yd away, just beyond the fortifications built by Charles V, and, to link it with the Louvre, Catherine requested a covered way following the line of the Seine, with a smaller gallery at right angles.

Charles IX completed the southwestern part of the Cour Carrée, the courtyard which is the most impressive part of the Old Louvre to remain, embellishing it with his monogram (K = Carolus).

Henri III was responsible for the southeastern part of the Cour Carrée (which bears the monogram H). **Henri IV**, from 1595, had the work on the Great Gallery (Grande Galerie) continued by Louis Métezeau. He also had the Flora Pavilion (Pavillon de Flore) built by Jacques II Androuet Du Cerceau, completed the Small Gallery (Petite Galerie) (its first floor was occupied by Marie de' Medici and Anne of Austria, hence the monogram AA), and erected the upper part of the Henri III wing in the Cour Carrée, marked by his

Louvre colonnade

J.P. Clapham/MICHELIN

monogram. **Louis XIII** continued with the construction of the Cour Carrée. At the same time as he was building the Sorbonne and the Palais-Royal, the architect Lemercier erected the Clock Pavilion (Pavillon de l'Horloge) together with the northwest corner of the courtyard, a Classical response to Lescot's work (the monogram LA = Louis and Anne). Anne of Austria lived in the Queens' Lodging; the bathroom designed for her by Lemercier now houses the Venus de Milo. In 1638, Charles V's rampart was razed and the moat filled in.

On the death of Louis XIII, Anne became Regent and moved to the Palais-Royal with the young **Louis XIV**. Nine years later, however, having been made aware of the palace's vulnerability by the uprising of the nobility (the Fronde), she took up residence in the Louvre again.The young king, who had married Maria-Theresa, moved into the Tuileries in 1664 for three years. The architect Le Vau, working on the Louvre, his personal style evident in the Small Gallery, started again after a fire in 1661, and in the Apollo Gallery; he continued the enclosure of the Cour Carrée by adding a storey onto the western part of the north wing (monogram LMT = Louis, Maria-Theresa) and by building the Marengo Pavilion (Pavillon Marengo) (with the monogram LB = Louis XIV de Bourbon). But the palace still needed

a monumental façade facing the city; **Colbert** had refused permission for a number of projects designed with this in mind.

An appeal was made to the master-architect of the Italian Baroque, Bernini, already 67 years old. But his proposals were turned down too, since they would have either destroyed or clashed with Lescot's façade. In the end it fell to Claude Perrault, aided by Le Brun and Le Vau, to design an imposing colonnaded façade. In 1682, the king left Paris for Versailles. The Louvre now housed the Academy as well as a less desirable population. In 1715, the Court returned to Paris for a period of seven years; the young King Louis XV lived in the Tuileries and the Regent in the Palais-Royal. Coustou continued the work on the colonnade.

After the **Revolution**, the Convention used the Louvre theatre for its deliberations. The Committee of Public Safety (Comité du Salut public) convened in the state rooms of the Tuileries, which were subsequently appropriated for his own use by Napoleon.

Napoleon I took up residence in the Tuileries. Percier and Fontaine completed the Cour Carrée by adding a second floor to the north and south wings. They also provided a wing linking the Rohan and Marsan Pavilions and gave it a façade identical to Du Cerceau's Grande Galerie, as well as enlarging the

Église du Dôme

MICHELIN

Place du Caroussel to enable Napoleon to review his legions and embellishing it with a triumphal arch commemorating the Emperor's victories, its design based on the Arch of Septimus Severus.

All of the "restored" monarchs lived in the Tuileries, as did **Napoleon III**, who decided to enclose the large courtyard on the north, confiding the task to Visconti, then to Lefuel, whose design was intended to conceal the disparity between the two wings; the architects razed the Hôtel de Rambouillet 3 which had housed the literary *Salon des Précieuses* under Louis XIII, replacing it with the present pavilions. They also restored the Pavillon de Rohan (the monogram LN = Louis Napoleon). Lefuel restored the Pavillon de Flore together with the wing extending it eastwards;

his design is a not altogether successful copy of Métezeau's work; the gallery bears the monogram NE (= Napoleon, Eugénie).

During the night of 23 May 1871, the **Communards** burnt down the Tuileries and half of Napoleon I's North Wing (Aile Nord de Napoleon I), as well as the Pavillons Richelieu and Turgot and the East Wing (Aile Est) attached to the Pavillon de Flore.

In 1875, under **President MacMahon**, Lefuel continued the work of Visconti with some modifications; he restored and extended the North Wing (Aile Nord) as well as refurbishing the Pavillon de Marsan and providing it with the monogram RF (République Française); in addition, he rebuilt the Riverside Gallery (Galerie du Bord de l'Eau) and the Pavillons de La Trémoille and de Flore.

In 1883, under **President Jules Grévy**, the Palais des Tuileries was demolished; and the city was deprived of one of the key buildings in its history.

In 1984 **President Mitterrand** embarked on the "Grand Louvre and Pyramide" project. He commissioned the architect Ming Pei to expand the services and reception area of what had now become a world-famous art

1) Tomb of Joseph Bonaparte, elder brother of Napoleon, King of Spain.
2) Monument to Vauban by Etex. The Emperor himself commanded that the military architect's heart be brought to the Invalides.
3) Marshal Foch's tomb by Landowsky.
4) Ornate high altar surrounded by twisted columns and covered by a baldaquin by Visconti. Vaulting decoration by Coypel.
5) General Duroc's tomb.
6) General Bertrand's tomb.
7) At the back – the heart of La Tour d'Auvergne, first grenadier of the Republic; in the centre, the tomb of Marshal Lyautey.
8) Marshal Turenne's tomb by Tuby.
9) St Jerome's Chapel (carvings by Nicolas Coustou). The tomb at the foot of the wall is Jerome Bonaparte's, Napoleon's younger brother and King of Westphalia.
10) The Emperor's tomb.

museum. Beneath the Cour Napoleon, a vast hall offering information and documentation services is lit up by the glass pyramid (**Pyramide**★★) which marks the main entrance to the museum.

Hôtel Nacional des Invalides★★★

129 r. de Grenelle. ♿ *Open daily Oct–Mar 10am–5pm (5.30pm Sun); Apr–Sept 10am–6pm (6.30pm Sun). Closed 1st Mon of the month in Oct–Jun, 1 Jan, 1 May, 1 Nov, 25 Dec.* ⇒ *8.50€ incl. audioguide; price includes Église du Dôme, Musée de l'Armée, l'Historial de Gaulle, Musée des Plans-Reliefs and Musée de l'Ordre de la Libération. Guided tours available; call in advance: 01 44 42 38 77 or 0810 11 33 99. 01 44 42 33 75. www.invalides.org.*

The plans for the vast edifice were drawn up by Libéral Bruant between 1671–76; their implementation was placed under the direction of Louvois. The main façade, nearly 200m/650ft long, is majestic without being monotonous; it is dominated by an attic storey decorated with masks and dormer windows in the form of trophies. Napoleon used to parade his troops in the main courtyard (Cour d'honneur); here the South Pavilion (Pavillon du Midi) forms the façade of the Église St-Louis, the resting-place of some of France's great soldiers; the interior is hung with flags taken from the enemy. It was here, in 1837, that Berlioz' Requiem was performed for the first time.

Église du Dôme★★★
Same as Hôtel Nacional.

The church of Les Invalides, designed by the master of proportion, **Jules-Hardouin Mansart**, was begun in 1677. With its beautiful gilded dome, it is one of the great works of the Louis XIV style, bringing to a peak of perfection the Classicism already introduced in the churches of the Sorbonne and the Val-de-Grâce, an ecclesiastical equivalent of the secular architecture of Versailles.

In 1735, Robert de Cotte completed the building by replacing the planned south colonnade and portico with the splendid vista offered by the Avenue de Breteuil. On the far side he laid out the Esplanade, and set up the guns captured at Vienna in 1805 by Napoleon to defend the gardens and fire ceremonial salvoes on great national occasions.

The church became a military necropolis after Napoleon had Marshal Turenne (d 1675) buried here. Note the memorial to Vauban, the great military architect, and the tomb of Marshal Foch. In Visconti's crypt of green granite from the Vosges stands the "cloak of glory", the unmarked **Tombeau de Napoleon** completed in 1861 to receive the Emperor's mortal remains. In 1940, the

View of the Place de la Concorde from the Tuileries

B. Kaufmann/MICHELIN

body of Napoleon's son, King of Rome and Duke of Reichstadt, was brought here too. Also housed in Hôtel nacional des Invalides is the **Musée de l'Armée** (*same as Église du Dôme*).

Arc de Triomphe★★★

pl. Charles-de-Gaulle. Open daily Apr–Sept 10am–11pm; Oct–Mar 10am–10.30pm. Closed public holidays. 9€. 01 55 37 73 77.
Together with the **Place Charles de Gaulle**★★★ and its 12 radiating avenues, the great triumphal arch makes up one of Paris' principal focal points, known as the **Étoile** (Star).
The façades of the buildings around were designed in a harmonious style by Hittorff as part of Haussmann's plans for the metropolis.
The Arc de Triomphe was the scene on 14 July 1919 of the great victory parade and, on 11 November 1920, of the burial of the Unknown Soldier. Three years later the flame of remembrance was kindled for the first time. The arch is ornamented with sculpture, notably Rude's masterpiece of 1836 known as the *Marseillaise,* depicting volunteers departing to defend France from the invading Prussians (1792).

Eiffel Tower
©Mark Soskolne/iStockphoto.com

Place de la Concorde★★★

A perfect expression of the Louis XV style, it was designed by Ange-Jacques Gabriel in 1755 and completed over a period of 20 years. On 21 January 1793, near where the statue of Brest now stands, the guillotine was set up for the execution of Louis XVI and other victims of the Terror.
The square owes its monumental character to the colonnaded buildings defining it to the north, to its octagonal plan, and to the massive pedestals intended for allegorical statues of French cities. Two great urban **axes**★★★ intersect here: one runs from the Église de la Madeleine to the Palais-Bourbon, the other from *Coysevox's Winged Horses (Chevaux ailés)*, which mark the entrance to the Tuileries, to the magnificent marble sculptures (copies) by Nicolas and Guillaume Coustou which flank the Champs-Élysées. The pink granite Luxor obelisk (Obélisque de Louksor), 3 300 years old, covered with hieroglyphics, was brought here from Egypt in 1836. The square's fountains adorned with statues are particularly fine.

Tour Eiffel★★★

7 r. de Belloy. Open daily. Lift: midJun–Aug 9am-12.45am; Sept–mid-Jun 9.30am–11.45pm. 8€; child 6.40 (elevator to 2nd floor), 13€, 9.90€ child (elevator to Top floor); Stairs 1st and 2nd floors only, 4.50€, 3.50€ child. 01 44 11 23 23. www.tour-eiffel.fr.
The Eiffel Tower is Paris' most famous symbol. The first proposal for a tower was made in 1884; construction was completed in 26 months and the tower opened in March 1889 for the Universal Exhibition (Exposition universelle) of that year.
The structure is evidence of Eiffel's imagination and daring; in spite of its weight of 7 000 tonnes and a height of 320.75m/1 051ft and the use of 2.5 million rivets, it is a masterpiece of lightness. It is difficult to believe that the tower actually weighs less than the volume of air surrounding it and that the pressure it exerts on the ground is that of a man sitting on a chair.

Palais de Justice and Conciergerie★★

2 bd du Palais. ⏱**Palais** *open Mon–Sat 8.30am–6pm.* ⏱*Closed public holidays. Visitors are normally allowed to attend a civil or criminal hearing.* ☏*01 44 32 52 52.* **Conciergerie** ⏱*open daily Mar–Oct 9.30am–6pm; Nov–Feb 9am–5pm.* ⏱*Closed 1 Jan, 1 May, 25 Dec.* 🎫*7€.* ☏*01 53 40 60 80.*

Known as the Palace (Palais), this is the principal seat of civil and judicial authority. Before becoming the royal palace of the rulers of medieval France, it had been the residence of Roman governors, Merovingian kings and the children of Clovis, the mint of Dagobert and Duke Eudes' fortress.

The Capetian kings built a chapel and fortified the palace with a keep. Philippe le Bel (the Fair) entrusted Enguerrand de Marigny with the building of the Conciergerie as well as with the extension and embellishment of the palace; its Gothic halls of 1313 were widely admired. Later, Charles V built the Clock Tower (Tour de l'Horloge), the city's first public clock; he also installed Parliament here, the country's supreme court. Survivals from this period include the Great Hall (Salle des gens d'Armes) with its fine capitals, the Guard Room (Salle des Gardes) with its magnificent pillars, and the kitchens with their monumental corner fireplaces.

The great hall on the first floor was restored by Salomon de Brosse after the fire of 1618; it was refurbished again in 1840 and once more after the fire of 1871.

The First Civil Court is in the former Parliamentary Grand Chamber (Grand'chambre du parlement), the place where the kings dispensed justice, where the 16-year-old Louis XIV dictated his orders to Parliament, where that body in its turn demanded the convocation of the States-General in 1788, and where the Revolutionary Tribunal was set up under the public prosecutor, Fouquier-Tinville.

The entrance to the royal palace was once guarded by the twin towers gracing the north front of the great

Where to Stay and Eat

For comprehensive suggestions of Where to Stay and Where to Eat in Paris, consult the red-cover *Michelin Guide Paris* and the *Michelin Green Guide Paris*.

complex; this is the oldest part of the building, albeit now hiding behind a 19C neo-Gothic façade.

The **Conciergerie** served as antechamber to the guillotine during the Terror, housing up to 1 200 detainees at any one time. The Galerie des Prisonniers (Prisoners' Gallery), Marie-Antoinette's cachot (cell) and the Chapelle des Girondins (Girondins' Chapel) are particularly moving.

Palais-Royal★★

6 r. de Montpensie Palais Cardinal r.
In 1632, Richelieu ordered Lemercier to build the huge edifice which came to be known as the Palais Cardinal (Cardinal's Palace) when it was extended in 1639. It is remarkable for its impressive central façade, surmounted by allegorical statues and a curved pediment. On his deathbed, Richelieu bequeathed it to Louis XIII, whereupon its name was changed to the Palais-Royal. In 1783, Victor Louis laid out the charming formal gardens and the arcades which enclose them and which house a number of specialist shops and boutiques.

In 1986, Daniel Buren designed the arrangement of 260 columns, all of different height, which occupy the outer courtyard.

École Militaire★★

av. de Lowendal.
Though the original design could not be fully implemented because of lack of financial resources, the Military Academy by Jacques-Ange Gabriel is one of the outstanding examples of French 18C architecture. It was begun in 1752, financed in part by Mme de Pompadour, and completed in 1773. Under the Second Empire, cavalry and artillery buildings of nondescript

design were added, together with the low-lying wings which frame the main building. True to its original function, it now houses the French Army's Staff College. The superb main courtyard (**cour d'honneur**★), lined on either side by beautiful porticoes with paired columns, is approached via an exercise yard; the imposing central section and the projecting wings form a harmonious composition.

Panthéon★★

pl. du Panthéon. ○*Open daily Apr–Sept 10am–6.30pm; Oct–Mar 10am–6pm.* ○*Closed 1 Jan, 1 May, 25 Dec.* ☞*8€.* ✆*01 44 32 18 00.* ☞*Guided tours (1hr30min); reservations required.* ✆*01 44 54 19 30.*

In 1744, Louis XV had made a vow at Metz to replace the half-ruined church of St Geneviève's Abbey. Fourteen years later Soufflot began the construction of the new building on the highest point of the Left Bank. The scale of the building was such that its collapse was confidently predicted and the pretensions of its architect ridiculed. The present building has been much changed since Soufflot's day; its towers have gone, its pediments have been remodelled, its windows blocked up. In 1791, the Constituent Assembly closed the church to worshippers in order to convert it into the last resting place of the "great men of the epoch of French liberty". Successively a church, a necropolis, headquarters of the Commune, a lay temple, the Panthéon is representative of the time in which churches lost their dominant position in the urban landscape. Still crowned by Soufflot's dome, the great edifice is built in the shape of a Greek Cross. It has a fine portico with Corinthian columns and a pediment carved by David d'Angers in 1831. In the crypt are the tombs of the famous.

Opéra Garnier★★

1 pl. de l'Opéra. ○*Open daily 10am–5pm; last adm. 4.30pm.* ☞*Guided tours Jul–Aug and school holidays Wed, Sat, Sun 11.30am and 2.30pm.* ☞*8€;*

tour *12€.* ○*Closed 1 Jan, 1 May and for special events.* ✆*0892 89 90 90.* www.operadeparis.fr.

This is the National Academy of Music, and was until 1990 France's premier home of opera. It opened in 1875 and it is the work of Charles Garnier, who had dreamed of creating an authentic Second Empire style. But the huge edifice, "more operatic than any opera" (Ian Nairn), magnificent though it was, lacked sufficient originality to inspire a new school of architecture. The interior, with its Great Staircase, foyer and auditorium, is of the utmost sumptuousness. Garnier used marble from all the quarries of France, and there is a ceiling by Chagall.

Palais de Chaillot★★

pl. du Trocadéro.

This remarkable example of inter-war architecture was built for the 1937 Exhibition. Its twin pavilions are linked by a portico and extended by wings which curve to frame the wide terrace with its statues in gilded bronze.

From here there is a wonderful **view**★★★ of Paris; in the foreground are the Trocadero Gardens with their spectacular fountains, and beyond the curving river the Eiffel Tower, the Champ-de-Mars, and the École Militaire.

The Palais houses the **Théâtre de Chaillot** (✆*01 53 65 30 00; www.theatre-chaillot.fr),* the **Musée de l'Homme**★★, (☞*7€;* ✆*01 44 05 72 72; www.mnhn.fr),* **Musée de la Marine**★★ (☞*9€;* ✆*01 53 65 69 69; www.musee-marine.fr),* **Musée des Monuments Français**★★ (☞*8€;* ✆*01 58 51 52 00; www.citechaillot.fr)* and **Musée du Cinéma Henri-Langlois**★ (✆*45 53 21 86; www.paris.org/Musees/Cinema).*

ECCLESIASTICAL ARCHITECTURE
Cathédrale Notre-Dame★★★

r. du cloître Notre-Dame.

○**Cathedral** *open Mon–Fri 8am–6.45pm, Sat–Sun 8am–7.15pm.* ☞*No charge.* ☞*Guided tours Wed & Thu 2pm, Sat 2.30pm.* **Towers** *open Apr–Sept 10am–6.30pm; Oct–Mar*

Cathédrale Notre-Dame

J.P. Clapham/MICHELIN

10am–5.30pm; 6€. 01 53 10 07 00.
www.notredamedeparis.fr.
Notre-Dame is the point from which distances to Paris are measured.

People have worshipped here for 2 000 years and the present building has witnessed the great events of French history.

Work on the cathedral was begun by Maurice de Sully in 1163. Notre-Dame is the last great galleried church building and one of the first with flying buttresses. In 1245 the bulk of the work was complete and St Louis held a ceremony for the knighting of his son and also placed the Crown of Thorns in the cathedral until the Sainte-Chapelle was ready to receive it. In 1250 the twin towers were finished.

In 1430, the cathedral was the setting for the coronation of the young Henry VI of England as King of France; in 1455, a ceremony was conducted to rehabilitate Joan of Arc; in 1558, Mary Stuart was crowned here on becoming Queen of France by her marriage to François II and, in 1572, the Huguenot Henri IV waited at the door as his bride, Marguerite of Valois, stood alone in the chancel; in 1594 the king converted to the Catholic faith.

The great building was not spared mutilations of various kinds; in 1699 the choir screen was demolished, and

later some of the original stained glass was removed to let in more light, and the central portal demolished (18C) to allow processions to move more freely. During the Revolution statues were destroyed and the cathedral declared a Temple of Reason. It was in a much-dilapidated building that Napoleon Bonaparte crowned himself Emperor and the King of Rome was baptised. In 1831, public opinion was alerted by Hugo's novel Notre-Dame de Paris to the state of the building, and in 1841 Louis-Philippe charged Viollet-le-Duc with its restoration. In the space of 24 years, he completed his work in accordance with his own, idealised vision of the Gothic style; though open to criticism, it needs to be seen in the context of the wholesale demolition of the medieval Île-de-la-Cité and its replacement with administrative buildings.

The magnificent Cloister Portal (Portail du Cloître–north transept) is 30 years older than the west front portals; with its richly carved gables and smiling figure of the Virgin – the only original large sculpture to have survived – it demonstrates clearly how far the art of sculpture had advanced over the period.

At the beginning of the 14C, the bold array of flying buttresses was sent soaring over ambulatory and galleries to hold in place the high vaults of the east end.

Above the Kings' Gallery is the great rose window, still with its medieval glass. An enterprise of considerable daring – it was the largest such window of its time – its design is so accomplished that it shows no sign of distortion after 700 years and has often been imitated. Inside, the rose window has particularly fine stained glass of a deep bluish-mauve.

Sainte-Chapelle★★★

4 bd du Palais. &. ⏰*Open Mar–Oct 9.30am–6pm; Nov–Feb 9.30am–5pm.* ⏰*Closed 1 Jan, 1 May, 1 and 25 Dec.* ⊙*8€.* ✆*01 53 40 60 80. www.monum.fr.*

Only 80 years separate this definitive masterpiece of the High Gothic from the Transitional Gothic of Notre-Dame, but the difference is striking; in the lightness and clarity of its structure, the Sainte-Chapelle pushes Gothic ideas to the limit. The chapel was built on the orders of St Louis to house the recently acquired relics of the Passion within the precincts of the royal palace; it was completed in the record time of 33 months.

The upper chapel resembles a shrine with walls made almost entirely of remarkable stained glass covering a total area of 618sq m/6 672sq ft; 1 134 different scenes are depicted, of which 720 are made of original glass. The windows rise to a height of 15m/49ft. By 1240, the stained glass at Chartres had been completed, and the king was thus able to call on the master-craftsmen who had worked on them to come to Paris; this explains the similarity between the glass of cathedral and of chapel, in terms of the scenes shown and the luminous colour which eclipses the simplicity of the design.

The theme is Christ's Passion, including its foretelling by the Prophets and by John the Baptist, together with the episodes which lead up to it. The original rose window is shown in a scene from the Très Riches Heures du Duc de Berry; the present rose window is a product of the Flamboyant Gothic, ordered by Charles VII, and showing the Apocalypse

of St John. It is characteristic of its age in the design of its tracery and in the subtle variations of colour which had replaced the earlier method of juxtaposing a great number of small coloured panes. The glass of the Sainte-Chapelle has been much imitated, even in architecturally inappropriate situations.

Abbaye de St-Germain-des-Prés★★

pl. Saint-Germain des Prés.

This most venerable of the city's churches reveals more than visual delights to those who know something of the history of its ancient stones. With the exception of Clovis, the Merovingian kings were buried here. The church was subsequently destroyed by the Normans, but restored in the course of the 10C and 11C. Understandably, the tower rising above the west front has a fortress-like character. Around 1160, the nave was enlarged and the chancel rebuilt in the new Gothic style. "Improvements" followed in the 17C (triforium and chancel windows) and in 1822 a somewhat over-zealous restoration took place.

But the church's years of glory were between 1631 and 1789, when the austere Congregation of St Maur made it a centre of learning and spirituality: the monks studied ancient inscriptions (epigraphy) and writing (paleography); the Church Fathers (Patristics), archaeology, cartography... Their library was confiscated at the time of the French Revolution.

Église St-Séverin-St-Nicolas★★

3 r. Prêtres St Séverin. *www.saint-severin.com.*

This much-loved Latin Quarter Church has features from a number of architectural styles. The lower part of the portal and the first three bays of the nave are High Gothic; while much of the rest of the building was remodelled in Flamboyant style (upper part of the tower, the remainder of the nave, the secondary aisle, the highly compartmentalised vaulting of the chancel and the famous spiral pillar in the ambulatory). In the 18C, the pillars in the chancel were clad in wood and marble.

Église St-Eustache★★

2 Impasse Saint-Eustache. Open Mon–Fri 9.30am–7pm, Sat 10am–7pm, Sun 9am–7pm. Audioguides available, suggested donation 3€. 01 42 36 31 05. http://saint-eustache.org.

This was once the richest church in Paris, centre of the parish which included the areas around the Palais-Royal and the Halles market; its layout was modelled on that of Notre-Dame when building began in 1532. But St-Eustache took over a hundred years to complete; tastes changed, and the Gothic skeleton of the great building is fleshed out with Renaissance finishes and detail.

The Flamboyant style is evident in the three-storeyed interior elevation, in the vaulting of the choir, crossing and nave, in the lofty side aisles and in the flying buttresses. The Renaissance is exemplified in the Corinthian columns and in the return to the use of semicircular arches, and Classicism in P. de Champaigne's choir windows and in Colbert's tomb, designed by Le Brun in collaboration with Coysevox and Tuby. In the Chapelle St-Joseph is the English sculptor Raymond Mason's colourful commemoration of the fruit and vegetable market's move out of Paris in 1969.

Église Notre-Dame-du-Val-de-Grâce★★

1 pl. Laveran. Open Mon–Sat 2–6pm, Sun 9am–noon, 2–6pm. 01 43 29 12 31.

After many childless years, Anne of Austria commissioned François Mansart to design a church in thanksgiving for the birth of Louis XIV in 1638. The work was completed by Lemercier and Le Muet. The church recalls the Renaissance architecture of Rome; the dome, rising above the two-tier west front with its double triangular pediment, is particularly ornate and obviously inspired by St Peter's. Inside, the spirit of the Baroque prevails; there

is polychrome paving, highly sculptured vaulting over the nave, massive crossing pillars and a monumental baldaquin with six wreathed columns. The cupola★★ was decorated by Mignard with a fresco featuring 200 figures.

URBAN DESIGN

Since the sweeping away of much of medieval Paris in the 19C, three central districts have come to typify particular stages in the city's evolution.

Le Marais★★★

Renaissance, Louis XIII and Louis XIV. Charles V's move to the Hôtel St-Paul in the Marais district in the 14C signalled the incorporation of a suburban area into Paris. The area soon became fashionable, and Rue St-Antoine the city's finest street. It was here that that characteristic French town house, the hôtel, took on its definitive form with the collaboration of the finest architects and artists; it became the setting for that other distinctive feature of Parisian life, the literary or philosophical salon.

The Hôtel Lamoignon★ *(24 r. Pavée)* of 1584 is a typical example of a mansion in the Henri III style. For the first time in Paris, its architect, Jean-Baptiste Androuet Du Cerceau, used the Giant Order with its flattened pilasters, Corinthian capitals and sculpted string-course.

The Henri IV style makes its appearance in the Place des Vosges★★★ designed by Louis Métezeau and completed in 1612. The 36 houses retain their original symmetrical appearance with arcades, two storeys with alternate brick and stone facings and steeply pitched slate roofs pierced with dormer windows. The King's Pavilion (Pavillon du Roi) is sited at the southern end of the square, balanced by the Queen's Pavilion (Pavillon de la Reine) at the sunnier northern end.

Louis XIII's reign heralds the Classical style. In 1624, Jean Androuet Du Cerceau built the Hôtel de Sully★ *(62 r. Saint-Antoine)* with a gateway framed between massive pavilions and a main courtyard (cour d'honneur★★★) with triangular and curved pediments complemented by the scrolled dormer windows; beyond is an exquisite inner courtyard.

The early Louis XIV style is seen in Mansart's **Hôtel Guénégaud**★★ (60 r. des Archives) of 1648, where its plain harmonious lines, majestic staircase and small formal garden make it one of the finest houses of the Marais; in Le Pautre's **Hôtel de Beauvais**★ (68 r. François Miron) with its curved balcony on brackets and its ingenious internal layout; in the **Hôtel Carnavalet**★ (23 r. de Sévigné), a Renaissance house rebuilt by Mansart in 1655; and in Cottard's **Hôtel Amelot-de-Bisseuil**★ (47 r. Vieille-du-Temple) of somewhat theatrical design with its cornice and curved pediment decorated with allegorical figures.

The later Louis XIV style features in two adjoining hôtels built by Delamair: the **Hôtel de Rohan**★★ (87 r. Vieille-du-Temple) with its wonderful sculpture of the Horses of Apollo (Chevaux frémissants d'Apollon à l'abreuvoir) by Robert Le Lorrain; and the **Hôtel de Soubise**★★ (60 r. des Francs-Bourgeois) with its horseshoe-shaped courtyard and double colonnade. They are characterised by their raised ground floors, massive windows, roof balustrades and by the sculpture of their projecting central sections.

La Voie Triomphale (From the Tuileries to the Arc de Triomphe)★★★

A great axis leading from the courtyard of the Louvre to St Germain had been planned by Colbert, but today's "Triumphal Way" was laid out under Louis XVI, Napoleon III and during the years of the Third Republic.

Arc de Triomphe du Carrousel★

pl. du Carrousel.

This delightful pastiche of a Roman arch is decorated with statues of Napoleonic military men in full uniform. An observer standing in the Place du Carrousel commands an extraordinary perspective which runs from the Louvre, through the arch, to the obelisk in the Place de la Concorde, then onward and upward to the Grande Arche at the Défense.

Jardin des Tuileries★

r. de Rivoli.

The gardens were first laid out in the 1560s by Catherine de' Medici in the Italian style. A century later, they were remodelled by Le Nôtre, who here created the archetypal French garden, a formal setting for the elegant pleasures of outdoor life. The Riverside Terrace (Terrasse du Bord de l'Eau) became the playground of royal princes and of the sons of the two Napoleons, then of all the children of Paris.

Champs-Élysées★★★

In 1667, Le Nôtre extended the axis from the Tuileries to a new focal point, the Rond-Point, which he laid out himself. The avenue was then a service road for the houses facing the Rue du Faubourg-St-Honoré, but very soon refreshment stalls were set up and crowds flocked to the area. In 1724, the Duc d'Antin planted rows of elms to extend the "Elysian Fields" up to the Étoile. In 1729, street lanterns lit the evening scene.

Forty-eight years on, and the avenue had descended the gentle slope beyond the Étoile to reach the Seine at the Pont de Neuilly.

The buildings lining it included taverns and wine-shops, the later haunt of Robespierre and his friends. Finally, in 1836, the **Arc de Triomphe**★★★ was completed by Louis-Philippe.

The Champs-Élysées became fashionable during the reign of Louis-Napoleon, when high society flocked to the restaurants (like Ledoyen's), to the theatres (like the Folies Marigny and the Bouffes d'Été where Offenbach's operettas were performed), or to receptions in the grand houses (like no 25, today occupied by the Travellers' Club, with its doors of bronze and its onyx staircase).

The avenue has undergone much change since 1914. Its character nowadays is determined by its luxury shops, expensive cafés, and motor showrooms; but it nevertheless remains the capital's rallying point at times of high national emotion (the Liberation, 30 May 1968, the funeral of De Gaulle in 1970, and annually on July 14).

La Défense★★

An outstanding architectural achievement, La Défense has nothing in common with the traditional business districts found in most city centres.

A 1 200m/3 937ft terraced podium, pleasantly punctuated with gardens, fountains and shaded spots, runs from the Seine up to La Grande Arche. It is lined with an impressive ensemble of huge towers (Tour Fiat: 178m/584ft) that compose a dazzling tableau of radiant light. It is also noted for many outdoor works by distinguished modern sculptors, which turn the district into an informal, open-air museum.

La Grande Arche★★

⊙*Open daily Sept–Mar 10am–7pm; Apr–Aug 10am–8pm.* ≋*10€.* ℰ*01 49 07 27 27. www.grandearche.com.*

The Danish architect Johan Otto von Spreckelsen designed this vast hollow cube which stands at the end of the esplanade and houses private firms as well as several ministries.

The Cathédrale Notre-Dame with its spire could fit into the space between the walls of the arch. Each side of the cube is 110m/360ft long.

Towering 100m/328ft above the esplanade, the 2.4 acres/1ha terrace-roof is partly taken up by temporary exhibition rooms. From the belvedere visitors will also be able to admire Paris and its suburbs. At the foot of the arch lies the Palais de la Défence (CNIT): it was the first to be built (1958) and has been "rejuvenated". Now it is an important business centre focusing on three main areas of activity: technology, world trade and corporate communication.

Bercy

The modernised Bercy district boasts a Palais Omnisports by architects Andrault, Parat and Gavan; the **Cinémathèque Française** *(51 r. de Bercy; www. cinematheque.fr)*, which hosts the largest

La Défense seen from Arc de Triomphe, La Grande Arche in the middle

©naphtalina/iStockphoto.com

archive of films in the world; the imposing buildings of the **Finance Ministry** designed by Chemetow and Huidobro – part of the structure rises above the Seine and the **Jardins de la Mémoire** with three planted areas. Across the river, the **Bibliothèque nationale de France-François-Mitterrand**★ *(Quai François-Mauriac; www.bnf.fr)* by Dominique Perrault – four tower blocks in the shape of open books – was the last of the "great projects" carried out under the former President.

La Villette★★

The **Parc**★ **de la Villette** is the largest architectural ensemble within the city. The 55ha/135 acre site houses an impressive urban complex featuring the **Cité des Sciences et de l'Industrie** (City of Science and Industry, ⊙ *see entry*) and its cinema La Géode, the Zenith concert hall, the Paris-Villette Theatre, La Grande Halle and the Cité de la Musique.

THE INTELLECTUAL LIFE
POLITICAL AND INTELLECTUAL SIGHTS

In addition to the city's famous monuments, churches and modern structures, other buildings and districts have come to be identified with the political and intellectual aspects of Paris.

Famous artists

On 19 December 1915, Édith Giovanna Gassion was born to abject poverty on the steps of no 72 r. de Belleville. She later sang in the streets, before becoming a radio, gramophone and music-hall success in 1935 under the name of **Édith Piaf**. Beloved for the instinctive but deeply moving tones of her voice, she came to embody the spirit of France *(La vie en rose, Les cloches)*.

Another famous figure was Maurice Chevalier (1888–1972), film star, entertainer and cabaret singer *(chansonnier)*; he paired with Jeanne Mistinguett at the Folies Bergère (1911) and sang at the Casino de Paris between the wars. Before attaining fame on Broadway in blacktie and boater, he was known at home for songs that are rooted in Belleville: *Ma Pomme, Prosper and un gars du Ménilmontant.*

Hôtel de Ville★
pl. de l'Hôtel de Ville.
It is from here that central Paris is governed. Municipal government was introduced in the 13C, under the direction of leading members of the powerful watermen's guild appointed by Louis IX.
The place has long been the epicentre of uprising and revolt. Throughout the French Revolution it was in the hands of the Commune, and in 1848 it was the seat of the Provisional Government. The Republic was proclaimed from here in 1870, and, on 24 March 1871, the Communards burnt it down. It was rebuilt from 1874.

Institut de France★★
quai Conti. ☎01 44 41 44 41. www.institut-de-france.fr.
The Institute originated as the College of Four Nations founded by Mazarin for scholars from the provinces incorporated into France during his ministry (Piedmont, Alsace, Artois and Roussillon). Dating from 1662, its building was designed by Le Vau and stands on the far side of the river from the Louvre. The Institute is made up of five academies:
The Académie Française, founded 1635; Académie des Beaux-Arts, 1816; Académie des Inscriptions et Belles Lettres, 1663; Académie des Sciences, 1666; and Académie des Sciences morales et politiques, 1795.

Montmartre★★★
The "Martyrs' Hill" was a real village before becoming the haunt of artists and Bohemians in the late 19C, and it still has something of the picturesque quality of a village in its steep and narrow lanes and precipitous stairways. The "Butte", or mound, rises abruptly from the city's sea of roofs; at its centre is the **Place du Tertre★★** with the former town hall at no. 3, still enjoying some semblance of local life, at least in the morning; by the afternoon, tourism has taken over, and the "art market" is in full swing.
Not far away from all this activity rises the exotic outline of the **Basilique du Sacré-Cœur★★** *(r. du Chevalier-de-la-Barre; ☎5€; ☎01 53 41 89 09; www. sacre-coeur-montmartre.com)*, a place of perpetual pilgrimage. From here, particularly from the gallery of the dome, there is an incomparable panoramaaaa over the whole metropolitan area.

Palais de l'Élysée
55 r. du Faubourg Saint-Honoré.
The palace has been the Paris residence of the President of France since 1873. It was built in 1718 by Henri de La Tour d'Auvergne.

Palais Bourbon★
126 r. de l'Université.
The palace of 1722 has been the seat of the Lower House of France's parliament, the Assemblée Nationale, for more than 150 years.

Palais du Luxembourg★★

15 r. de Vaugirard.

This is the seat of the Senate, the French Upper House. The president of the Senate exercises the functions of Head of State if the Presidency falls vacant.

It was constructed in the early 17C by the Regent, Marie de' Medici, who wished to have a palace of her own which would remind her of the Pitti Palace in Florence.

Quartier Latin★★★

Lying on the left bank of the Seine, and on the slopes of the mount, **"Montagne" Ste-Geneviève**, and the surrounding area are concentrated many of the capital's most venerable institutions, notably the Sorbonne, the country's most illustrious university, founded 1253. Around them is the ebb and flow of a perpetually youthful tide, the students and other young people who make up the population of the "Latin" Quarter (so-called because Latin was the language of instruction right up to the French Revolution).

The area abounds in publishing houses, bookshops, and terrace cafés, including the legendary Flore *(172 bd St Germain)*, Deux-Magots *(6 pl. St Germain des Prés)* and Procope *(13 r. Ancienne Comédie)*.

Quartier de St-Germain-des-Prés★★

Antique dealers, literary cafés, the night life of side streets all combine to create the reputation of this former centre of international Bohemian life.

CITY OF ENTERTAINMENT

This section outlines the city's wide range of entertainment and cultural attractions. Consult publications such as *L'Officiel des Spectacles, Une Semaine à Paris and Pariscope,* and the daily press for details of time and place.

The monthly booklet *Paris Selection*, edited by the Paris Tourist Office, lists exhibitions, shows and other events in the capital.

⊙ ENTERTAINMENT

Paris may be said to be one huge "living stage", as it boasts a total of 100 **theatres** and other venues devoted to the performing arts, representing altogether a seating capacity of 56 000.

Most of these are located near the Opéra and the Madeleine but from Montmartre to Montparnasse, from the Bastille to the **Latin Quarter**★★★ and from Boulevard Haussmann to the Porte Maillot, state-funded theatres (**Opéra-Garnier**★★, Opéra-Bastille, Comédie Française, Odéon, Chaillot, La Colline) are to be found side by side with local and private theatres, singing cabarets and cafés-théâtres. Not to mention television studios and the large auditoriums where radio and TV programmes are regularly recorded in public.

Cinemas, more than 400 in number, are to be found in every part of the city, with particular concentrations in the same areas as the theatres and on the Champs-Élysées. There are also two open-air cinema festivals in the city in the summer: one at **Parc de la Villette**★; the other, **Cinéma au Clair de Lune**, is held in parks and squares across Paris.

Music-hall, **variety shows** and **reviews** can be enjoyed at such places as the Alcazar de Paris, the Crazy Horse, the Lido, the Paradis Latin, the Casino de Paris, the Folies Bergère and the Moulin Rouge. As well as the **Opéra-Garnier**★★, the Opéra-Bastille and the Comic Opera (Opéra-Comique), there are a number of concert halls with resident orchestras like the Orchestre de Paris at the Salle Pleyel, the Ensemble Orchestral de Paris at the Salle Gaveau, and the orchestras of the French Radio at the Maison de Radio-France. In addition there are many other halls in which full-scale performances are put on (Théâtre des Champs-Élysées, Châtelet, Salle Cortot, Espace Wagram, Maison de la Chimie, Palais des Sports, Palais Omnisports de Bercy, Palais des Congrès, Théâtre de la Ville, Zénith...).

There are also nightclubs, cabarets, dens where *chansonniers* can be heard, *café-théâtres*, television shows open to the public, concerts and recitals in churches, circuses, and other entertainment.

MUSEUMS

The city has a total of 87 museums and over 100 art galleries. In addition, there are around 30 places where temporary exhibitions are held and a whole array of studios (particularly around the Rue St-Honoré, Avenue Matignon and the Rue de la Seine), as well as libraries and other institutions. Between them, they offer the visitor a continuously changing view of past and present artistic achievement and aspiration. The most famous include the Grand Palais, the Palais de Tokyo, the Pavillon des Arts, the Petit Palais, the Pompidou Centre and the Grande Halle de la Villette.

🔒👤 MUSÉE DU LOUVRE★★★

🔆 *See Civil Architecture for the history of the Louvre Palace.* ♿🕐*Open Wed–Mon 9am–6pm (Wed and Fri 10pm), 24 and 31 Dec 9am–5pm.* 🕐*Closed 1 Jan, 1 May, 11 Nov, 25 Dec.* **Hall Napoleon** *open Wed–Mon 9am–10pm. Please check calender for unscheduled room closures.* 💶*Permanent Collections with Musée Delacroix included 9€; Wed and Fri 6–9.45pm 6€; child and 14 Jul no charge; temporary exhibitions 9.50€; Combined tickets are 13€, Wed and Fri 6–9.45pm 11€; tickets can be bought in advance at Fnac (𝒫0892 68 46 94; 💶1.50€surcharge), and Ticketnet (𝒫0892 39 01 00; 💶1.10€ surcharge). www.louvre.fr.*

When the Grand Louvre was opened to the public in 1994, the different collections were divided into three large departments, **Sully**, **Denon** and **Richelieu**, which are located in the two wings and around the Cour Carrée.

Choose which section of the museum to visit:

Sully
- History of the Louvre: *Entresol.*
- Medieval Louvre: *Entresol.*
- Egyptian Antiquities: *Ground and 1st floors.*
- Greek Antiquities (Cariatides room, Hellenic period): *Ground floor.*
- Oriental Antiquities (Iran and art of the Levant): *Ground floor.*
- Greek Antiquities (Bronze room, Campana gallery): *1st floor.*
- 17–18C objets d'art: *1st floor.*
- 17–19C French painting, including Graphic arts: *2nd floor.*
- Beistegui collection (room A): *2nd floor.*

Denon
- Italian sculpture: *Entresol and Ground floor.*
- Scandinavian sculpture: *Entresol.*
- Roman and Coptic Egypt: *Entresol (rooms A, B and C).*
- Greek Antiquities: *Ground and 1st floors.*
- Etruscan and Roman Antiquities: *Ground floor.*
- Italian painting: *1st floor.*
- Spanish painting: *1st floor.*
- 19C French painting (large sizes): *1st floor.*
- Objets d'art (Apollon gallery): *1st floor.*

Richelieu
- Exhibitions-documents: *Entresol.*
- Islamic art: *Entresol (closed until 2010; will reopen in Denon).*
- French sculpture (Marly and Puget rooms): *Ground floor.*
- Oriental Antiquities (Mesopotamia): *Ground floor.*
- Objets d'art (including Napoleon III's apartments): *1st floor.*
- 14–17C French painting: *2nd floor.*
- Scandinavian schools: *2nd floor.*

Select what to see within the chosen section:

Oriental Antiquities
Statues of *Gudea* and *Ur-Ningirsu* – Mesopotamia: c 2150 BC
Code of Hammurabi – Babylon: c 1750 BC
Frieze of the Archers from Darius' palace – Susa: 6C BC
Low-reliefs from Nineveh and Khorsabad – Assyria: 7C BC
Vase from Amathus – Cyprus: early 5C BC

THE LOUVRE: GENERAL INFORMATION

Information: General information
✆01 40 20 51 51 (recorded message);
✆01 40 20 53 17 to speak to someone
at the desk (six languages); www.
louvre.fr. Some galleries are closed
on certain days (or for restoration);
check the schedule of open rooms
online or call in advance. Fourteen
video screens in the hall provide
information about daily events at
the museum. There is also a general
activity programme (six languages)
available at the main information
desk, which comes out every three
months. **Audioguides** can be hired
(six languages) on the mezzanine level
in the various wings.

▶ **Location:** The main entrance
to the museum is at the Pyramid.
There is also an entrance through
the shopping mall of the Carrousel
du Louvre (metro stop Palais-Royal-
Musée-du-Louvre (lines 1 and 7)), on
either side of the Arc du Carrousel,
or at the Porte des Lions. You will
find yourself in the well-lit **Napoleon
Hall**, which leads you towards
the three wings of the museum:
Denon, Richelieu and Sully. There is a
bookshop, restaurant and auditorium.

Parking: The closest underground
car park (80 coaches, 620 cars) is
Parking Carrousel-Louvre, located
on avenue du Général Lemonnier.
Open daily 7am–11pm. Fees from
12.20€. After parking, enter the
museum via the shopping mall of
the Carrousel by the fortifications of
Charles V.

Don't Miss: Of all the artworks
inside the museum, probably
the most famous are Leonardo's
masterpiece, The *Mona Lisa* (here
called La Joconde) and among
the classical works, the *Victoire de
Samothrace* and the *Vénus de Milo*. All
three are in the Denon section.

Timing: The Louvre cannot be
enjoyed in its entirety even in several
visits, let alone one. From the list of
artworks below, decide what you
would like to see and head for your
selections. The information desks
offer a variety of aids and amenities
to enhance your visit. Audio guides
are available or choose one of the
thematic trails (provided on leaflets)
designed for all ages that allow you to
discover both masterpieces and less
well-known works while exploring a
particular theme, such as the Da Vinci
Code.

Kids: Children aged 4 and up
can take part in one of the many
workshops for young people or
follow a Children's Route through the
museum. Call or check the website for
details.

Egyptian Antiquities
Gebel-el-Arak knife –
    Egypt: c. 300–3200 BC
Sphinx of the Crypt –
    Egypt: c. 2600 BC
Jewellery of Rameses II – middle of
    second millennium
Seated Scribe from Sakkara –
    Egypt: Fifth Dynasty
Funerary chapel of Akhout-Hetep –
    Fifth Dynasty
Fragments from the Coptic monastery
    of Bawit – 5C

Classical Antiquities
Kore from the Temple of Hera
at Samos –
    Greece: archaic period
La Dame d'Auxerre (Lady of Auxerre) –
    Greece: c. 640–630BC
Apollo of Piombino –
    Greece: 1C BC
Venus de Milo –
    Greece: Hellenistic period
Parthenon fragments (metopes) –
    Greece: Classical period
Etruscan terracotta sarcophagus from
    Cerveteri, Italy: 6C BC

Paris Museum Pass

This pass is valid for 2, 4 or 6 consecutive days (40€, 58€, 76€ respectively) and provides unlimited access to more than 70 museums in and around Paris. It is on sale at each of the museums and at city tourist offices. Passholders do not have to queue for admission. www.museums-in-paris.com/museum_pass.php.

Victoire de Samothrace (Winged Victory) – Greece: Hellenistic period

Sculpture

Limewood *Madonna* from the Church of the Antonites, Isenheim – late 15C

Diana the Huntress (fountain) from Château d'Anet – French Renaissance

The Three Graces (funerary monument for Henri II) by Germain Pilon

The Four Evangelists by Jean Goujon

Madonna and Child (terracotta) by Donatello – Florence c. 1450

Marble bust of *Voltaire* by Houdon: 1778

The Slaves by Michelangelo – Florence: early 16C

Painting

Malouel's circular *Pietà* – Dijon: c 1400

St Denis Altarpiece by Henri Bellechose – Dijon: c. 1415–1416

Avignon *Pietà* by Enguerrand Quarton – c. 1455

Portrait of *François* I by Jean Clouet – Loire Valley School

St Thomas by Georges de La Tour – 17C *Gilles* by Watteau – c. 1718–1719

Portrait of *Mme Récamier and Sacre de Napoleon I (The Coronation of Napoleon)* by David

La Baigneuse de Valpinçon (The Turkish Bath) and *Grande Odalisque* by Ingres

Scène des massacres de Scio (Scenes of the Massacres of Chios) by Delacroix – 1824

Le Radeau de la Méduse (Raft of the Medusa) by Géricault – 1819

Maestà (Virgin with Angels and Saints) by Cimabue – Florence: c. 1280

La Couronnement de la Vierge (Coronation of the Virgin) by Fra Angelico – Florence: c. 1430

La Joconde (The Gioconda – Mona Lisa) by Leonardo da Vinci – Florence: c. 1503–1506

Les Noces de Cana (The Wedding at Cana) by Veronese – Venice: 1563

La Mort de la Vierge (Death of the Virgin) by Caravaggio – Naples: early 17C

Le Jeune Mendiant (Young Beggar) by Murillo – Seville: c. 1645–1650

La Vierge du chancelier Rolin (The Rolin Madonna) by Jan van Eyck – Dijon: c. 1435

Charles I of England by Van Dyck – England: 17C

Vie et règne de Marie de Médicis – allegorical paintings of the *Life of Marie de' Medici* by Rubens

Les Pèlerins d'Emmaüs (Pilgrims at Emmaus) by Rembrandt c. 1660

Objets d'art

The Regent Diamond and Crown Jewels of France

Ivory figure of the Virgin Mary from the Sainte-Chapelle, Paris: middle of the 13C

The *Hunts of Maximilian* tapestries – Brussels: 1537

The study of the Elector of Bavaria by Boulle – early 18C

Clock in ebony case inlaid with tortoiseshell by Boulle – early 18C

Monkey commode (gilded bronze) by Charles Cressent – 1740

The *Loves of the Gods* tapestries – Gobelins: mid-18C

Writing-desk, table and commode in the Oeben room – mid-18C

Medici vase (Sèvres porcelain, bronzes by Thomire)

OTHER MAJOR MUSEUMS
Musée d'Orsay★★★

62 r. de Lille. ♿🕐*Open Tue–Sun 9.30am–6pm, Thu 9.30am–9.45pm.* 🕐*Closed 1 Jan, 1 May, 25 Dec.* ●🕐*8€ for the permanent collection, 9.50€ for access to the permanent and temporary collections; no charge 1st Sun in the month.* ✆*01 40 49 48 14. www.musee-orsay.fr.*

The focus of the museum is the period 1848 to 1914. The upper floor is dedicated to the Impressionists, with one of the world's finest collections. There is a considerable collection of pre- and post-Impressionist works. Other sections include decorative arts and photography.

Highlights include:

La Source (The Spring) by Ingres – 1846
Un enterrement à Ornans (Burial at Ornans) by Courbet – c. 1849–50
Des Glaneuses (Gleaners) and L'Angélus (Angelus)
    by Jean-François Millet
Le Déjeuner sur l'herbe and *Olympia*
    by Manet – 1863
La Danse (The Dance), sculpture
    by Jean-Baptiste Carpeaux – 1868
Le golfe de Marseille vu de L'Estaque (Marseille Bay from L'Estaque) by
    Cézanne – c. 1878–1879
Les Danseuses bleues (Blue Dancers)
    and *Dans un café (The Absinthe Drinker)* by Degas
L'Église d'Auvers-sur-Oise (The church at Auvers-sur-Oise) and *Autoportrait (Self-Portrait)* by Van Gogh
Le Cirque (The Circus) by Seurat
Aréarea joyeusetés (Women of Tahiti)
    by Gauguin – 1892
Jane Avril dansant (Jane Avril Dancing)
    by Toulouse-Lautrec – 1892
Balzac by Rodin – 1898
The Mediterranean by Maillol – 1902
Pendant and chain by René Lalique
Héraclès Archer (Hercules the Archer)
    in bronze by Antoine Bourdelle – 1909
Les Baigneuses (Women Bathing)
    by Renoir – c. 1918–19

Musée National d'Art Moderne (Centre George Pompidou)★★★

pl. Georges-Pompidou. ♿🕐*Open daily 11am–9pm (last admission 1hr before closing).*
Atelier Brancusi *Wed–Mon 2–6pm. Museum and exhibitions* ●*12€; free 1st Sun in the month.* ✆*01 44 78 12 33. www.centrepompidou.fr.*

The Centre seeks to demonstrate that there is a close correlation between art and daily activities.

For both the specialists and the general public, this multi-purpose cultural centre offers an astonishing variety of activities and modern communication techniques encouraging curiosity and participation.

The Centre includes four departments: the **Bibliothèque Publique d'Information** (BPI), offering a wide variety of French and foreign books, slides, films, periodicals and reference catalogues; the **Musée National d'Art Moderne – Centre de Création Industrielle** (MNAM – CCI), the former presenting collections of paintings, sculptures and drawings from 1905 to the present time, and the latter demonstrating the relationship between individuals and spaces, objects and signs through architecture, urbanism, industrial design and visual communication; the **Institut de Recherche et Coordination Acoustique/Musique** (IRCAM), bringing together musicians, composers and scientists for the purpose of sound experimentation.

Highlights include:

La Rue pavoisée (Street Bedecked with Bunting) by Dufy – Fauvism: 1906
Le Guéridon (Table) by Braque – Cubism: 1911
Nus de dos (Nudes) by Matisse – beginnings of Abstraction: 1916
Arlequin (Harlequin) by Picasso – mature Cubism: 1923
La Vache spectrale (Spectral Cow) by Dali – beginnings of Hyperrealism: 1928
Le Phoque (Seal), sculpture by Brancusi – Surrealism in sculpture: c. 1943–46

Outside the museum, re-creation of the workshop of the sculptor Constantin Brancusi *(until 25 Jan 2010)*

Hôtel de Cluny (Musée du Moyen Âge)★★

Hôtel de Cluny, 6 Place Paul Painlevé. ◷*Open Wed–Mon 9.15am–5.45pm; desk closes at 5.15pm.* ◷*Closed 1 Jan, 1 May, 25 Dec.* ◉*7.50€ (audioguide included); free 1st Sun in month (audioguide 1€).* ✆*01 53 73 78 16. www.musee-moyenage.fr.*
Highlights include:
Ivory casket –
    Constantinople: early 11C
Gilt altar-front made for Henri II –
    Basle cathedral: 11C
29 medallions from the stained glass
    of the Sainte-Chapelle – Paris: 13C
Limoges reliquaries in *champlevé*
    enamel – 13C
Golden rose given by Pope Clement V
    to the Prince-Bishop of
    Basle: early 14C
Eagle of St John (brass lectern) –
    Tournai cathedral: 1383
Life of St Stephen tapestry –
    Arras: mid-15C
Altarpiece from Limburg in painted
    and gilded wood – late 15C
Lady and the Unicorn tapestries –
    Brussels: late 15C
Mary Magdalene (probable likeness of
    Mary of Burgundy) – Flanders

Musée de l'Orangerie★★

Jardin des Tuileries. ♿◷*Open Wed–Mon 9am–6pm.* ◷*Closed 1 May, 25 Dec.* ◉*7.50€; 2€ surcharge for temporary exhibitions; free 1st Sun in month.* ☛*Guided tours (1hr30min) 8€.* ✆*01 44 77 80 07. www.musee-orangerie.fr.*
Highlights include:
Portrait of Mme Cézanne by Cézanne
*Baigneuse aux cheveux longs (Woman
    Bathing)* and *Femme à la lettre
    (The Letter-Writer)* by Renoir
Nude on red background
    by Picasso – 1906
*La Carriole du père Junier (Père Junier's
    Cart)* by Douanier Rousseau – 1908

Maison de Berlioz (Berlioz' House) and
    Église de Clignancourt by Utrillo
Antonia by Modigliani
Nymphéas (Water-lilies) from Giverny
    by Claude Monet
Les Trois Soeurs (The Three Sisters)
    by Matisse
Le Petit Pâtissier (The Little Pastry-cook)
    and *Garçon d'étage (The Attendant)*
    by Soutine – 1922
*Arlequin à la guitare (Harlequin with
    Guitar)* and *Le Modèle blond (Blond
    Model)* by Derain

Musée de l'Armée (Hôtel des Invalides)★★★

♿*See Église du Dôme.* ✆*0810 11 33 99. www.invalides.org.*
Highlights include:
Seussenhofer's suit of armour for
    François I – 1539
Model of the city of Perpignan (one of a
    series ordered by Vauban in 1696)
Napoleon's flag of farewell flown at
    Fontainebleau on 20 April 1814
The room where Napoleon died on St
    Helena (reconstruction)
The Armistice Bugle (which sounded
    the cease-fire at 9pm on 7
    November 1918)

🚻 Cité des Sciences et de l'Industrie★★★

30 av. Corentin-Cariou. ♿◷*Open Tue–Sat 10am–6pm, Sun 10am–7pm.* ◷*Closed 1 May and 25 Dec.* ◉*6€– 10.50€.* ✆*01 40 05 70 00. www. cite-sciences.fr.*
Built in response to the growing need of young and old alike to have a better understanding of the scientific and industrial world, this living museum encourages visitors to investigate, learn and have fun through a wide range of edifying and entertaining scenarios.
Highlights include:
L'Argonaute (a submarine formerly in
    use with the French Navy)
Le Nautile (full-size model of research
    submarine)
Voyager 2 space probe
Model of Ariane 5 rocket (scale 1:5)
Le Robot-mouche (a glimpse into the
    future development of bionics)

Cité des Enfants★

🏃 *See p 464 for opening times.*
The ground floor of the Cité is designated especially for young, encouraging scientific discovery through experimentation and play. It's cleverly divided into two sections: ages 2–7, and ages 5–12.

👥 La Géode★★★

In the park just outside the museum. The most comfortable viewing is from the top of the hall. ○*Open Tue–Sun 10.30am–8.30pm (hourly sessions).* ✆*10.50€ (child 9€).* ✆*01 44 84 44 84. www.lageode.fr.*
The Cité's extraordinary reflective spherical cinema and its circular screen (diameter: 36m/118ft), which rests on a sheet of water, is a remarkable technical achievement, whose bold conception and perfect execution is the work of the engineer Chamayou.

Musée du Quai Branly★★

37 quai Branly. ○*Open Tue, Wed, Sun 11am–7pm, Thu–Sat 11am–9pm.* ✆*8.50€.* ✆*01 56 61 70 00. www.quaibranly.fr.*
Modern purpose built museum opened in 2006, located on the left bank of the Seine near the Eiffel Tower, exhibiting indigenous art from Afric, Asia, Oceania and the Americas.

👥 Palais de la Découverte★★

av. Franklin-D.-Roosevelt. ○*Open Tue–Sat 9.30am–6pm, Sun and public holidays 10am–7pm (last entrance 30min before closing).* ○*Closed 1 Jan, 1 May, 14 Jul, 15 Aug, 25 Dec.* ✆*7€ (child 4.50€); Planetarium 3.50€.* ✆*01 56 43 20 20.*
This children's museum is a marvel of ingenuity and interest, with clever animators to bring the exhibits to life.
Highlights include:
School of Rats
The Planetarium
Lunakhod (Soviet moon buggy) – 12 November 1970
Fragment of moon-rock – Apollo Mission XVII: 1972

The number Pi and the 703 prime numbers of the 16 000 000 decimals calculated

Musée des Arts et Métiers★★

60 r. Réaumur. ○*Open Tue–Sun 10am–6pm (Thu 9.30pm).* ○*Closed 1 May, 25 Dec.* ✆*6.50€.* ✆*01 53 01 82 00. www.arts-et-metiers.net.*
Highlights include:
Microscope belonging to the Duke of Chaulnes – mid-18C
Cugnot's steam-carriage of 1771
Marie-Antoinette's automaton "Dulcimer-Player" – 1784
Jacquard loom
Thimonnier's sewing-machine – 1825
Foucault's pendulum (proving the rotation of the Earth)
L'Obéissante automobile by Amédée Bollée Snr – 1873
The Lumière brothers' cinematographic apparatus – 1895
Transmitting station from the Eiffel Tower
Blériot's No 9 aeroplane (in which he made the first cross-Channel flight)

ADDITIONAL SIGHTS

Musée Picasso *(5 r. Thorigny)*
Musée Rodin *(77 r. Varenne)*
Musée Carnavalet *(29 r. de Sévigné)*
Musée d'Art et Histoire du Judaïsme *(71 r. du Temple)*
Musée de la Magie *(11 r. Saint Paul)*
Musée Marmottan *(2 r. Louis Boilly)*
Musée d'Art Moderne de la Ville de Paris *(11 av. du Président Wilson)*

🛒 SHOPPING
SHOPPING DISTRICTS

Most major stores are concentrated in a few districts, whose names alone are suggestive of Parisian opulence.

Champs-Elysées

All along this celebrated avenue and in the surrounding streets (avenue Montaigne, avenue Marceau), visitors can admire dazzling window-displays and covered shopping malls (Galerie Elysée Rond-Point, Galerie Point-Show,

Galerie Elysée 26, Galerie du Claridge, Arcades du Lido) devoted to fashion, cosmetics and luxury cars.

Rue du Faubourg-St-Honoré
Here *haute couture* and ready-to-wear clothing are displayed alongside perfume, fine leather goods and furs.

Place Vendôme
Some of the most prestigious jewellery shops (Cartier, Van Cleef & Arpels, Boucheron, Chaumet) stand facing the Ritz Hotel and the Ministry of Justice.

Place de la Madeleine and r. Tronchet
An impressive showcase for shoes, ready-to-wear clothing, luggage, leather goods and fine tableware.

DEPARTMENT STORES
 See map following.
For locals and visitors alike, the city's great department stores are the ideal way to find a vast choice of high-quality fashions and other goods under one roof. Most leading names are represented. Some have free fashion shows. Department stores are usually open from Monday–Saturday 9.30am–7pm.
Bazar de l'Hôtel de Ville *(52 r. de Rivoli)*
Galeries Lafayette *(40 bd. Haussmann)*
Printemps *(64 bd Haussmann)*
Le Bon Marché *(r. de Sèvres)*

ANTIQUE SHOPS AND DEALERS
Le Louvre des Antiquaires *(1 pl. du Palais Royal)*, Le Village Suisse *(r. du Général de Larminat)*, the Richelieu-Drouot auction room and the rues Bonaparte and La Boétie specialise in antique objects and furniture. Good bargains can also be found by browsing through the flea market at the Porte de Montreuil and Porte de St-Ouen (Sat–Mon).

FAIRS AND EXHIBITIONS
Paris hosts a great number of trade fairs and exhibitions all year round. The following events are among the most important.

Paris – Expo
pl. de la Porte de Versailles. www.viparis.com.
Over 200 exhibitions, conventions and events per year including the Paris Nautical Trade Show.

Parc International d'Expositions
Paris-Nord Villepinte. www.viparis.com.
Trade Show for Crafts (SMAC) in March, the Maison & Objet home style expo, the International food industry exhibition (SIAL) and Japan Expo.

Parc des Expositions
Le Bourget aerodrome. www.paris-air-show.com.
Paris Air Show (odd years, next 2011).

SPORTS CAPITAL
Among the most popular sporting events held in and around Paris are the International Roland Garros Tennis Championships, the Paris Marathon, the legendary **Tour de France** with its triumphant arrival along the Champs-Elysées, and several prestigious horse races (Prix du Président de la République in Auteuil, Prix d'Amérique in Vincennes, Prix de l'Arc de Triomphe in Longchamp). The **Parc des Princes** stadium *(24 r. Claude Farrère; www.leparcdesprinces. fr)* is host to the great football and rugby finals, attended by an enthusiastic crowd, and the **Palais Omnisport de Paris-Bercy** *(8 bd Bercy; www.bercy. fr.)* organises the most unusual indoor competitions: indoor surfing, North American rodeos, ice figure-skating, tennis championships (Open de Paris), moto-cross races, martial arts, Six-day Paris Cycling Event, and also pop concerts by international stars.

PARKS AND GARDENS
The city has as many as 450 parks, public gardens and green spaces, some perfect for a rest and some fresh air, or a place for children to play; other parks are prestigious and historic, and perhaps adorned with fine sculpture.

Politics and administration	Luxury shopping	Trade and commerce
Academic and intellectual life	Business and finance	Leisure and recreation
● Department stores and shopping centres		▲ Theatres, shows, events

Highlights include:

Bois de Vincennes, 4 458 acre/995ha including the Parc Floral.

Bois de Boulogne, 2 090 acre/846ha with the Bagatelle, iris and rose gardens.

Jardin des Plantes, historic Botanic Gardens of Paris.

Jardin des Tuileries, with its ancient and modern stauray.

Jardin du Luxembourg, very agreeable Latin Quarter park with a circular pond alongside a palace, popular with students and with big play areas for children.

Parc Montsouris and Square des Batignolles, examples of "Jardins Anglais", with less formal layout.

Parc Paysager des Buttes-Chaumont, without doubt the most picturesque.

Jardin du Palais-Royal, a haven of silence and elegance in the very heart of Paris.

Jardin japonais de l'UNESCO, in the grounds of the UNESCO headquarters, it is also known as "Garden of Peace".

Jardin du Musée Rodin, ideal spot to prolong the museum visit and discover magnificent city view along its pathways.

Parc Monceau, where it is enjoyable to encounter statues of Musset, Maupassant, Chopin and others.

Parc André-Citroën, the most sophisticated.

Parc de La Villette, the largest in Paris.

Parc de Belleville, with views across the whole city.

Parc de Bercy, recalling the wine-dealing past of this modernised district.

AROUND PARIS

65km/40.3mi radius from Notre-Dame Cathedral (*see Michelin Green Guide Northern France and the Paris Region).*

Barbizon★★

61km/38mi S, along D637.

The landscapes of the Forest of Fontainebleau and the Bière plateau inspired a group of landscape painters who worked directly from nature (1830–60) and came to be known as the Barbizon School. Together with their leader, Théodore Rousseau (1812–67), these forerunners of Impressionism favoured dark tones, soft light and stormy skies. The old inn (**Auberge du Père Ganne**★) where they used to stay is now a museum (**Musée de l'École de Barbizon**; *92 Grande-Rue; ☎01 60 66 22 27*).

Château de Champs★★

An 18C mansion and landscape. The **park**★★ was designed in typically French style, while the internal layout of the **château** broke new ground in its time: the rooms are no longer directly connected with one another and each is provided with a closet and dressing-room; a separate dining room makes its appearance. There is fine Rococo wainscoting (**boiseries**★) and a Chinese Room (**Salon chinois**★★).

Château de Chantilly★★★ –

See Château de CHANTILLY.

Château d'Écouen ★★

21km/13mi N, off D 316.
The château is a good example of the progress made in architecture between the Early and High Renaissance. It houses a **Musée de la Renaissance**★★ (*open Wed–Mon; ☎4.50€; ☎01 34 38 38 50; www.musee-renaissance.fr*) which has furniture, tapestries and embroidery, ceramics, enamels...

Château de Gros-Bois★

Ave du Maréchal de Lattre de Tassigny, Boissy-St.-Léger. 23km/14.3mi SE, along N 19. ☎01 49 77 15 24.
The early 17C château houses a fascinating **furniture collection**★★ of the Classical and Empire periods; it includes a mahogany bed with gilded bronze decoration, porphyry candelabra and bronzes by Thomire, and furniture by Jacob.

Château de Maisons-Laffitte★

av. Carnot. 20km/12.4mi NW.
Open Wed–Mon 10am–12.30pm, 2–5pm (6pm in summer). Closed public holidays. ☎6.50€.
www.maisonslaffitte.net.
Built 1642–51 by Mansart in early Louis XIV style, the château subordinates considerations of domestic well-being to the creation of grandiose effects (dominance of its site, majestic scale, use of columns and pilasters, lofty pediments).

Port-Royal-des-Champs★

39km/24mi SW, off D 36.
At the **Musée National des Granges de Port-Royal** (*rte des Granges; open year-round Wed–Mon (hours vary in summer); ☎4.50€; ☎01 39 30 72 72; www.port-royal-des-champs.eu*), the spirit of Jansenism is captured in a magnificent painting by Philippe de Champaigne, *Ecce Homo*, whose power lies in its restraint and profound acceptance of suffering to come. The museum also has a copy of the Augustinius. Below the museum there are remains of the famous abbey in the valley, scene of the struggle between Jesuits and Jansenists.

Rambouillet★

55km/34mi SW, along N 10.
The small town attracts many visitors because of its **château** (Rococo **woodwork**★), its **park**★ with formal parterres, water gardens, Royal Dairy (**Laiterie de la Reine**★), Shell Cottage (**Chaumière des Coquillages**★) and the splendid walks offered by its vast forest. The château is the summer residence of the President of France.

Abbaye de Royaumont★★

33km/20.5mi N, off D 909.
Founded by Louis IX in 1228. The extent of the original abbey church is indicated by the still-extant bases of its columns, while the splendid Gothic refectory and the 14C Madonna of Royaumont evoke the spirit of the Middle Ages.

Rueil-Malmaison★★

15km/9.3mi NW, along D 913.

Malmaison is a place of pilgrimage for all those fascinated by the figure of Napoleon. In 1799, three years after her marriage to Bonaparte, Josephine bought the château and its park from the actor Talma.

The First Consul spent much of his free time here with her; it was the happiest period of their life together and it was to Malmaison that Josephine returned after their divorce (1809). In June 1815, at the end of the Hundred Days (Josephine had been dead for more than a year), Napoleon fled here, staying with her daughter Hortense until his final departure from France.

Lemercier worked on the château around 1625; the building is interesting for its decoration by Percier and Fontaine and for its **collections**★★, which include busts of the Imperial family, Jacob furniture and many other ornamental objects.

The **Musée national du château de Bois-Préau**★ (◯*closed for renovation;* ℘*01 41 29 05 55*) has many moving mementoes of Bonaparte's exile and of the return of his remains to France.

Cathédrale (or Basilique) St-Denis★★★

2 r. de Strasbourg. 10km/6.2mi N.
◯*Open Apr–Sept Mon–Sat 10am–6.15pm, Sun noon–6.15pm; Oct–Mar Mon–Sat 10am–5.15pm, Sun noon–5.15pm.* ▧*No charge.* ℘*01 48 09 83 54.*

St-Denis is an important manufacturing centre in the northern suburbs of Paris. It owes its name to the great missionary who became the first bishop of Paris when it was still Roman Lutetia.

St Denis was beheaded at Montmartre around AD 250; legend has it that he walked all the way here with his head in his hands before finally expiring.

The basilica, begun in 1136 by Abbot Suger, is of central importance in the evolution of the Early Gothic style. A century later, the upper parts of the chancel and transept, and nave, were rebuilt by Pierre de Montreuil as masterpieces of High Gothic.

Basilique St-Denis
Jacass/MICHELIN

The many royal tombs (**tombeaux**★★) in chancel and pre-chancel make the cathedral a veritable museum of funerary art from the Middle Ages to the Renaissance. Note the splendid **crypt**★★.

St-Germain-en-Laye★★ –
� *See ST-GERMAIN-EN-LAYE.*

Senlis★★ – � *See SENLIS.*

Sèvres★★

19km/11.8mi SW, along D 910.

Sèvres owes its fame to the porcelain made here. In 1756, on the orders of Louis XV, the original factory at Vincennes was moved to Sèvres, halfway between Paris and Versailles; the government saw the move as an opportunity to assuage the concerns that had arisen as a result of the beginnings of the development of industry. Sèvres products are featured in the **Musée National de Céramique**★★ (*pl. de la Manufacture;* ◯*open Wed–Mon 10am–5pm;* ◯*closed 1 Jan, 1 May, 25 Dec;* ▧*4.50€;* ℘*01 41 14 04 20; www. musee-ceramique-sevres.fr*), which also has examples of the work from other great porcelain makers.

The museum's range of objects illustrate the differences between hard- and soft-paste porcelain from 1770 onwards.

Château de Vaux-le-Vicomte★★★ –
🕭 See Château de VAUX-LE-VICOMTE.

Château de Versailles★★★ –
🕭 See Château de VERSAILLES.

Château de Vincennes★★

av. de Paris. 10km/6.2mi E. 🕒*Open daily Sept–Apr 10am–5pm; May–Aug 10am–6pm.* 🕒*Closed public holidays.* 📞*01 48 08 31 20. www.chateau-vincennes.fr.*

This "Versailles of the Middle Ages" originated in the manor house built by Philippe Auguste. Louis IX was wont to dispense justice here in the shade of an oak tree. The fortress, begun by Philippe VI, was completed by Charles V, whose place of birth it was.

In the 17C, Mazarin ordered Le Vau to build the King and Queen Pavilions with a portico linking them. The **château** subsequently became a state prison.

Built in 1337, the keep **(donjon★★)** is a 14C military architecture masterpiece. Henri II completed the chapel **(chapelle★)**; the choir has fine stained glass **(vitraux★)** made in 1556 in Paris.

FILMS SET IN PARIS

Hôtel du Nord (1938) directed by Marcel Carné. This film contains the famous line spoken by Arletty: "Atmosphere, atmosphere, do I look like I've got atmosphere?" The Hôtel du Nord still exists, near the Canal St-Martin whose bridges and locks are inseparably linked to the film.

Gigi (1949) directed by Claude Dolbert. The story of a young girl who is brought up by an aunt and is married off to a rake. Not to be confused with the musical.

Zazie dans le métro (1960) directed by Louis Malle. A burlesque comedy that is a screen adaptation of the novel by Raymond Queneau.

À bout de Souffle (Breathless, 1960) Jean-Luc Godard's masterpiece starring Jean-Paul Belmondo and Jean Seberg.

Les Quatre cents coups (The 400 Blows, 1959) François Truffaut's first film revolves around a Parisian adolescent.

Charade (1963) directed by Stanley Donen. Audrey Hepburn is chased through Paris by a gang of ruffians and helped by Cary Grant. Is he or is he not interested in the missing $250 000?

Last Tango in Paris (1972) – Bernardo Bertolucci directs a story of obsessive love in Paris. Starring Marlon Brando and Maria Schneider.

Le Locataire (The Tenant, 1976) directed by Roman Polanski. A lonely young man falls victim to a conspiracy in an apartment block.

Le dernier métro (The Last Metro, 1980) Truffaut's depiction of Paris during the German Occupation.

La Passante de Sans-Souci (The Passerby, 1982) directed by Jacques Rouffio. A moving performance by Romy Schneider in her last film.

Subway (1985) Luc Besson's stylised caper, where Christopher Lambert falls in love with Isabelle Adjani in the labyrinthine world of the Paris métro.

Les Amants du Pont-Neuf (The Lovers on the Bridge, 1991) directed by Leos Carax. Two vagrants find love on the Pont-Neuf.

La Reine Margot (1994) Patrice Chéreau's breathtaking and violent account of the St. Bartholomew's Day Massacre based on the Dumas novel.

Le Fabuleux destin d'Amélie Poulain (Amelie, 2001), directed by Jean-Pierre Jeunet. Enchanting tale of an eccentric young woman who strives to make others happy.

Paris, je t'aime (2006) 20 short films interwoven into a single narrative as a tribute to the city of love.

St-Germain-en-Laye★★

A residential suburb of Paris, and also a popular weekend resort, St-Germain's attractions are a château with delightful terraces and gardens, and a forest with pleasant walks.

A BIT OF HISTORY

Now a residential town forming part of the Paris suburbs, St-Germain's significance in the course of French history goes back hundreds, if not thousands, of years.

A strategic site 60m/197ft above a bend in the Seine persuaded Louis VI le Gros (the Fat) to build a stronghold here. Later, when the Hundred Years' War was at its height, the castle was restored by Charles V. Three French kings were born here (Charles IX, Henri II, Louis XIV), as well as several princes, writers, historians and composers. Louis XIII died here. It was here that in 1641 Richelieu promulgated the edict limiting the rights of the French parliament.

On 28 February 1837, the first passenger railway in France was inaugurated, running to Paris.

SIGHT
Château★
Pl. Charles de Gaulle. ℰ*01 39 10 13 00.*

- ▶ **Population:** 41 312
- ⚙ **Michelin Map:** 311 i 2
- 🏠 **Info:** Maison Claude Debussy, 38 r. au Pain. ℰ01 34 51 05 12. www. ot-saintgermainenlaye.fr.
- ◐ **Location:** The town is 19km/11.8mi W of Paris and easily reached from the city on the RER (line A 1). The main area of interest is by the château.

Its appearance is still much as it was when François I had it rebuilt by Pierre de Chambiges in the taste of the 16C. Louis XIV brought in Mansart to replace the corner turrets with pavilions, and Le Nôtre, who designed the park, laid out the very long terrace (**terrasse★★**), and replanted the forest.

The château houses the **Musée des Antiquités nationales★★** (&🕐*open Wed–Mon 10am–5.15pm;* ✺*4.50€;* ℰ*01 39 10 13 00; www.musee-antiquites nationales.fr);* its priceless collection of archaeological exhibits traces French history through space and time from the Paleolithic to the Middle Ages.

ADDITIONAL SIGHTS
Ste-Chapelle★ *(in the château).*
Musée départemental Maurice-Denis★ *(2 bis r. Maurice Denis)*

Château de St-Germain-en-Laye

H. Le Gac/MICHELIN

St-Omer★★

A market centre of some importance, St-Omer has kept many fine town houses dating from the Classical period. The town lies at the junction of Inland Flanders, with its watery landscapes of poplars, elms and willows, and Coastal Flanders, won from the sea in medieval times and now dominated by industry and arable farming.

A BIT OF HISTORY

A border town, St-Omer was in turn part of the Holy Roman Empire, Flanders, Burgundy and then Spain, finally passing into French hands in 1677.

The town's industry, predominantly metal-working, chemicals and glass-making, is concentrated in the Arques district. 38km/23.6mi to the south lies the site of the Battle of **Agincourt** (Azincourt), where, on 25 October 1415, France suffered its worst defeat of the Hundred Years' War at the hands of Henry V of England. Ten thousand French noblemen were killed, while English casualties were negligible.

▶ **Population:** 14 656
- **Michelin Map:** 301 G 3
- **Info:** 4 rue du Liond'Or. ℰ03 21 98 08 51. www. tourisme-saintomer.com.
- **Location:** This northern town is 49km/30mi SE of Calais. Its centre is Place Maréchal Foch.

SIGHT
Cathédrale Notre-Dame★★
◔*Open daily Nov–Mar 8am–5pm; Apr–Oct 8am–6pm. www.cathedrale-saint-omer.org.*

Completed at the end of the Hundred Years' War, the building shows signs of the influence of the English Perpendicular style. There are numerous high quality **works of art**★★, including 18C woodwork, and rare 13C floor tiles.

ADDITIONAL SIGHTS
Hôtel Sandelin★ *(14 r. Carnot)*
Chapelle de l'Ancien College des Jésuites★ *(22 r. du Lycée)*
Jardin Public★ *(bd Vauban)*

Senlis★★

Senlis derives a romantic charm from its picturesque Old Quarter streets, with many old dwellings and paved with big flagstones.

A BIT OF HISTORY
At the centre of a rich agricultural region, Senlis was already a prosperous place in Gallo-Roman times. Eventually it became the kernel of the Île-de-France, core of the future kingdom of France.

SIGHT
Cathédrale Notre-Dame★★
pl. Notre-Dame. ◔*Open daily 9am–7pm. ℰ03 44 53 01 59.* ◔*Illustration, see p76.*

▶ **Population:** 15 729
- **Michelin Map:** 305 5
- **Info:** Place du Parvis Notre-Dame. ℰ03 44 53 06 40. www.senlis-tourisme.fr.
- **Location:** Senlis is on autoroute A1, 50km/31mi N of Paris. There is easy access to Senlis from Paris and the Channel.
- **Don't Miss:** The cathedral is the town's unmissable sight.
- **Kids:** The big Parc Astérix theme park is south of town (◔*see Parc ASTÉRIX*).

Begun in 1153, the cathedral was consecrated in 1191. Of this first building only a few features survive. Changes in the 13C substantially destroyed the continuity of the pattern previously established. At the same time, the south tower was given its tall spire (**flèche**★★),

78m/256ft, i
by the gable
appearance
of the restor
1513 and 1
in 1504.

Le **Touquet**★★★

With its casinos, grand villas, immense beach, designer stores, gourmet restaurants and luxury hotels, the "Pearl of the Opal Coast" enjoys an international reputation.

A BIT OF HISTORY

In 1837, a stretch of empty sand dunes was purchased by a speculator who planted it with maritime pines and later, in 1876, divided it into residential plots. At the beginning of the 20C, a British company, the "Le Touquet Syndicate" moved in and built exclusive holiday dwellings. By 1912 the place had become so fashionable among the leisured classes of England but also of Paris, that it took on the name Paris Plage. Occupied by the Germans during WW2, Le Touquet like many French towns suffered badly, especially towards the end of the War when most of the resort's Hôtels were destroyed. It also had the distinction of being the

▶ **Population:** 5 536
Michelin Map: 301 C 4
Info: Palais de l'Europe, Pl. de l'Hermitage. ℘03 21 06 72 00. www.letouquet.com.
Location: The town is on the Channel coast S of Boulogne. It is divided into two: the well-treed residential area with its luxury villas, some of them modern, but many in a hybrid style known as "Anglo-Norman"; then there is the resort itself, stretching out along the magnificent beach of fine sand. The town centre is laid out on a grid pattern and the main shopping streets are Rue St-Jean and Rue de Paris.
Don't Miss: The forest, which provides a refreshing backdrop to the town – hire a bike to explore

Sand dunes in Le Touquet-Paris-Plage

©David Hughes/Dreamstime.com

most mined town in France with over 100 000 devices to deal with at the end of the hostilities.

SEASIDE

Along the seafront, the **promenade** is edged by gardens and car parks. The south end leads to a yachting club and a thalassotherpy centre. The fine sand beach stretches as far as the mouth of the River Authie. The **coast road** follows the line of the dunes and leads to the marina and the water sports club, well sheltered by Pointe du Touquet.

Château de Vaux-le-Vicomte★★★

This splendid château, one of the masterpieces of the 17C, lies at the heart of French Brie, a countryside of vast fields broken with occasional copses.

A BIT OF HISTORY

Nicolas Fouquet had been Superintendent of Finances since the days of Mazarin and built a vast personal fortune. In 1656, he decided to construct at Vaux a palace to symbolise his success. As architect, he chose Louis Le Vau, as interior decorator, Charles Le Brun, as landscaper, André Le Nôtre. By 1661, Vaux looked as it does today. A connoisseur, a man of lavish tastes, but sadly lacking in political judgement, Fouquet had counted on being appointed in Mazarin's place right up to the moment when Louis XIV decided to take power into his own hands. Furthermore, he had alienated Colbert, and, even worse, had made advances to one of the King's favourites, Mlle de La Vallière.

By May, the decision to place him under arrest had already been taken. On 17 August, the unwitting Fouquet threw the most sumptuous of festivities among the Baroque splendours of Vaux. Hoping to impress the young Louis, he succeeded only in offending his monarch more deeply by the unparalleled extravagance of the proceedings. Dinner was presented on a solid gold service,

- **Michelin Map:** 312 f 4
- **Info:** Vaux-le-Vicomte. 01 64 14 41 90 www.vaux-le-vicomte.com.
- **Location:** Vaux-le-Vicomte is 60km/37mi SE of Paris.
- **Don't Miss:** A walk through the gardens laid out by Le Nôtre offers an unforgettable experience.
- **Timing:** Plan to enjoy a candlit tour of the château (May–early Oct Sat 8pm–midnight) or a Fountains Show (every second and last Sat of the month, 29 Mar–25 Oct 3–6pm).
- **Kids:** Vaux le Vicomte puts on many activities just for children, such as Easter egg hunts, quizzes, treasure hunts and more.

at a time when the royal silverware had been melted down to repay the expenses of the Thirty Years' War! On 10 September, Fouquet was arrested at Nantes, his property confiscated, and his brilliant team of designers put to work on Versailles.

VISIT

Open mid-Mar–Jun, Sept–early Nov Thu–Tue 10am–6pm; Jul–Aug daily 10am–6pm. Day pass 16€ (child 13€). 01 64 14 41 90. www.vaux-le-vicomte.com.

Le Vau's château is the definitive masterpiece of the early Louis XIV style. It is majestic in its impact. It is to be understood as the central feature of a grandiose designed landscape, an archetype of immense influence over the whole of Europe in the course of the following century and a half. Le Brun's talent is here made manifest in all its richness and diversity. His King's Bedroom anticipates the splendour of the Royal Apartments at Versailles.

In the **gardens** ★★★, Le Nôtre showed himself to be a master of perspective.

Château de Vaux-le-Vicomte

Julien Valle/Château de Vaux-le-Vicomte

Château de
Versailles★★★

Versailles is the creation of the French monarchy at the moment of its greatest splendour. Consisting of the **château**, the gardens, and the **Trianon★★**, it is a wonderfully harmonious composition of building and landscape, the definitive monument of French Classicism.

A BIT OF HISTORY

1624 Louis XIII has a hunting lodge built in this game-rich area.

1631 Philibert Le Roy designs the first château, built of brick, stone and slate.

1661 Le Brun is made responsible for the interior, supervising a gifted team of painters, sculptors, carvers and interior decorators.

1666 The gardens' splendid fountains are inaugurated.

1667 The Grand Canal is dug.

1668 Le Vau extends the palace, builds the **Grand Apartments★★★** lays out a spacious terrace overlooking the gardens and restores the **cour de Marbre★★**. The **gardens★★★** are laid out by Le Nôtre.

1671 Le Brun decorates the State Apartments using the choicest materials.

1672 Boulle delivers the first items of his furniture featuring showy marquetry of tortoises hell and brass.

1674 Lavish summer festivals are held. Le Brun designs 24 statues for the gardens.

1678 Desjardins, Le Hongre and the Marsy brothers work on the Diana Fountain (Fontaine de Diane). Jules Hardouin-Mansart, a nephew by marriage of François Mansart, adds to the palace, giving it a grand first floor over the raised ground floor, columns,

Michelin Map: 311 i 3

Info: 2 bis av. de Paris. ☎01 39 24 88 88. www. versailles-tourisme.com.

Location: Versailles is only 18km/11mi from Paris, easily reached by road or train (take line C of the RER to Versailles-Rive gauche, or SNCF rail link from the stations St-Lazare to Versailles-Rive droite or from Montparnasse to Versailles-Chantiers). The château and park form one side of the town of Versailles. Place du Marché is the town's focal point, offering a variety of delightful restaurants, shops, cafés, brasseries and weekly markets.

Don't Miss: The Grand Canal – rent a rowing boat and enjoy an impressive view of the palace and its gardens.

Timing: A variety of guided tours for the interior of the palace are offered, ranging from 1–2hr. Allow 3hr for the gardens, and even more time if you wish to visit the Grand and Petit Trianons. The park is best seen when the Grands Eaux (fountains) are in operation (weekends and holidays in summer).

Kids: Beyond the Petit Trianon is the Queen's Hamlet (Le Hameau de la Reine), where farm animals (ducks, black pigs, goats) roam about, serving as a great attraction for children.

fine windows and roof sculptures. He completes the **Galerie des Glaces★★★** begun by Le Brun.

Key to plan:

- 1631-1634 Le Roy — Louis XIII
- 1662-1670 Le Vau — Louis XIV
- 1678-1708 J. Hardouin-Mansart — Louis XIV
- 1770-1772 A.-J. Gabriel — Louis XV
- 19C

1680 The King's Kitchen Garden (Potager du Roi) is laid out.

1684 Jules Hardouin-Mansart designs the Orangerie.

1688 Hardouin-Mansart builds the **Grand Trianon**★★ (or Marble Trianon)

1699 The Royal Chapel is built by Hardouin-Mansart

(completed in 1710 by Robert de Cotte and decorated by Van Cleve and Claude Lorrain, with frescoes by Coustou and Coypel).

1701 The King's Suite is designed by Hardouin-Mansart; the room is laid out around the axis formed by the course of

Garden façade, Château de Versailles

D. Hée/MICHELIN

the sun (shown today with its summer furnishings of 1723).

1712 Hercules' Salon (Salon d'Hercule), on the site of the former chapel, is begun. Completed in 1736, it has a ceiling by Lemoyne.

1729 The Queen's Bedchamber is completed by Boucher.

1768 Ange-Jacques Gabriel builds the Royal Opera with its splendid auditorium.

1769 The King's celebrated roll-top desk is completed, a masterpiece by Oeben and Riesener.

1774 Ange-Jacques Gabriel completes the Petit Trianon and, together with the sculptor Rousseau, creates the King's Library.

1783 The Hamlet (**Hameau★★**) is laid out in the gardens of the Petit Trianon.
14 July: the Fall of the Bastille.

1789 A mob force the royal family to return to Paris.

1791 Louis XVI swears loyalty to the Revolutionary Constitution.

1792 Fall of the monarchy.

1793 Louis XVI guillotined.

1833 The Apartments are demolished (with the exception of the central section of the first floor) in order to house a museum.

1837 The palace becomes a museum of the history of France.

VISIT

♿ The enjoyment of even the shortest of visits will be greatly enhanced if the **Michelin Green Guide Northern France and the Paris Region** *is used.*

HIGHLIGHTS OF THE CHÂTEAU AND GARDENS

Full appreciation of Versailles demands a knowledge of Classical mythology and its symbols, the château and its gardens being in effect a temple dedicated to worship of the Sun God.

Grands Appartements★★★

🕐 *Open Tue–Sun Apr–Nov 9am–6.30pm; Nov-Mar 9am–5.30pm; last admission 30min before closing.*
🕐 *Closed 1 Jan, May, 25 Dec, . ⊜13.50€*

Guided Tours

Take one of the tours offered by the tourist office to get better acquainted with not only the château and its gardens, but also the town itself. There is a choice of guided tours at the château, each starting at a different entrance.

(under 18 years: no charge). ℘ 01 30 83 76 20. www.versailles-tourisme.com. These comprise the King's Suite on the north and the Queen's Suite to the south, facing the sun.

Cour de Marbre★★

Built in brick with stone dressings and reserved for the King's private use, it has fine raised paving in black and white marble, façades graced by 40 busts (some of them by Coysevox), mansard roofs decorated with urns, and a colonnaded portico supporting the wrought-iron balcony of the King's Bedchamber.

Galerie des Glaces (Hall of Mirrors)★★★

Jules Hardouin-Mansart completed this splendid reception room begun by Le Brun, and built over Le Vau's terrace. It lies between the War Salon and the Peace Salon; its mirrors catch the rays of the setting sun. Its decoration was completed in 1687.

The Gardens (Jardins★★★)

⏱Open daily. ⌨No charge.

Laid out by Le Nôtre, these are a masterpiece of the French landscape style, going beyond the evocation of the idea of majesty (as at Vaux-le-Vicomte) to celebrate the supreme authority of the monarch by the systematic use of Classical symbolism. Among the 200 statues of this open-air sculpture museum are Keller's bronzes in the Water Gardens (Parterres d'eau), the Latona Basin (Bassin de Latone), Tuby's splendid Apollo in his chariot, bas-reliefs by Girardon.

VILLE DE VERSAILLES★★

The town of Versailles was built as an annex to the château to house the numerous titled and untitled people who served the court. It has retained a certain austere charm. It was originally conceived in the symbol of the sun, with the château at the centre and the three main avenues radiating away like rays of light. There are very few 17C houses left in Versailles; most of the old town dates from the 18C. The pedestrianised r. Satory, in the heart of old town, has become as lively as Quartier Notre-Dame, where antique dealers and outdoor cafés abound.

Relaxing by the Grand Canal

©Alexandre Fagundes De Fagundes/Dreamstime.com

ADDRESSES

🛏 STAY

Hôtel Versailles – *7 r. Ste-Anne.* 📞 *01 39 50 64 65. www.hotel-le-versailles.fr. 46 rooms.* 🍽 *14€.* This renovated hotel is situated in a quiet side street not far from the château. The Art Deco style rooms are spacious, bright and elegant. Cosy bar-lounge and terrace where breakfast is served in summer.

Résidence du Berry – *14 r. d'Anjou.* 📞 *01 39 49 07 07. www.hotel-berry.com. 38 rooms.* 🍽 *14€.* Located in the Saint-Louis quarter, this 18C edifice has been entirely restored by Les Bâtiments de France. Comfort and top-quality materials await you in rooms with time-worn beams overhead. In summer breakfast is taken on a veranda that opens onto the patio.

🍽 EAT

Place du Marché – This agreeable square is marked out by bars, crêperies, pizzerias and restaurants, with outdoor tables in summer.

La Brasserie du Théâtre – *15 r. des Réservoirs.* 📞 *01 39 50 03 21. www.flobrasseries.com. Closed 25 Dec, 1 May. Reservations advisable evenings.* The walls of this 1895 brasserie situated next to the theatre, as its name would suggest, are covered with photos of artists who have frequented it over the years. 1930s style décor, covered terrace and traditional cuisine.

Le Bœuf à la Mode – *pl. du Marché, 4 r. au Pain.* 📞 *01 39 50 31 99. www.leboeufalamode-versailles.com.* A typical 1930s bistro with a convivial, relaxed atmosphere. The décor – red wall-seats, knick-knacks, posters, mirrors – is a hit and the regional specialities are delicious. Very busy on market days.

Au Chapeau Gris – *7 r. Hoche.* 📞 *01 39 50 10 81. www.auchapeaugris.com. Closed Tue eve and Wed. Reservations required.* This restaurant, said to date back to the 18C, is a veritable institution hereabouts. Quintessential Versailles ambience and décor are the setting for appetising, traditional cuisine.

Place Hoche, Ville de Versailles

A. de Valroger/MICHELIN

Nothing too wild, just a reliable, very much sought-after establishment.

Valmont – *20 r. au Pain.* 📞 *01 39 51 39 00. www.levalmont.com. Closed Sun eve and Mon.* This nicely restored old house on the Place des Halles is bound to catch your eye. Venture inside and appreciate the first-rate reception, charming decoration, modern colours, elegant tables and succulent cookery.

🍸 NIGHTLIFE

Fenêtres sur cour – *pas. de la Geôle, Quartier des Antiquaires.* 📞 *01 39 51 97 77. Closed 3 weeks Aug.* A restaurant-salon de thé under a glass roof. The bric-a-brac décor - tile floor, carpets, lamps, chandeliers, plaster statues and paintings – is in perfect harmony with the neighbourhood antique shops. Appetizing wine menu. In summer, tables are set outdoors on the Place de la Geôle.

🛍 SHOPPING

Shops – The principal shopping areas are: Rue de la Paroisse, Rue Royale, Rue du Général-Leclerc, Place du Marché and Les Manèges, opposite the Rive-Gauche station. You'll find many antique dealers in the Passage de la Geôle, near La Place du Marché.

Major stores – From the FNAC (books, CDs, cameras, etc.) to Printemps or BHV (department stores), the shopping complex Le Centre Commercial de Parly II, on your way out of Versailles towards St-Germain, has it all.

PROVENCE

The name Provence evokes an image of a magical land in the Midi, or south, of France where the sun always shines and Mediterranean influences are supreme. From the extensive remains of six centuries of Roman occupation to the traditional triumvirate of wheat, vine and olive, alternating with the remnants of the natural forest and the infertile but wonderfully aromatic garrigues (arid scrubland). Among the fertile Provençal plains stand the *mas*, shallow-roofed pantiled farmsteads protected from the fierce sun by stone walls with few window openings. Crops and buildings are shielded from the violence of the mistral, the master-wind from the north, by serried ranks of cypresses.

Highlights

1   Natural rock arch created by the river: **Pont d'Arc** *(p486)*

2   Palace built for the Pope in exile at **Avignon**: Palais des Papes *(p491)*

3   Wetland plain of the Rhône Delta: **La Camargue** *(p496)*

4   Classical Temple with columns at **Nîmes**: Maison Carrée *(p505)*

5   Roman Aqueduct and road bridge: **Le Pont du Gard** *(p508)*

Geography – Among the fertile plains stand the *mas*, shallow-roofed pantiled farmhouses protected by stone walls with few windows. These plains are flanked by ranges of limestone hills running east–west including the Alpilles, the rugged Luberon range and the Vaucluse plateau with its chasms, gorges and great resurgent spring at Fontaine de Vaucluse. The mighty Rhône brings down 20 million cu m/706 293cu ft of sand, gravel and silt annually, creating the huge delta of the Camargue, now a nature reserve.

Further north are the Gorges of the Ardèche, cutting through the rock to form one of the most impressive natural sights in France.

History – Provence has been occupied from the earliest times. From the 8C BC the Celts settled here but were eventually subdued by the Romans who founded a settlement at Aix in 122 BC. The collapse of the Roman Empire led to incursions by Visigoths and later by the Franks.

Provence was annexed by the Holy Roman Empire in 1032, but the Counts of Provence retained a degree of independence. The region was incorporated into France in 1486, although the Parliament of Aix remained semi-independent until 1771. The 18C was a golden age for agriculture and commerce, but during the 19C rural life was affected by phylloxera, decimating the vineyards.

Economy – In recent years Provence has seen much industrial expansion, especially around Marseilles, and ever-increasing tourism has been facilitated by the construction of *autoroutes* and high-speed train lines. The food has a significant presence in the region, while the climate is conducive to the production of wine, olive oil, fruit and vegetables.

Aigues-Mortes★★

Few places evoke the spirit of the Middle Ages as vividly as Aigues-Mortes sheltering behind its ramparts in a landscape of marshland, lakes and salt-pans. A tourist train runs around Aigues-Mortes, offering an overview of the main attractions and entertainment options. Shops, restaurants and hotels lie within the city walls and a traditional market can be found on Avenue Frédéric-Mistral.

A BIT OF HISTORY

In 1240, Louis IX (St Louis), then 26 years old, was troubled by the lack of French involvement in the kind of commerce undertaken by the merchant fleets of Pisa and Genoa. He was also taken by the idea of a Crusade, but lacked a Mediterranean port.

A French king could not countenance sailing from a foreign harbour (at this time Provence was part of the Holy Roman Empire, Sète did not exist, and Narbonne was silting up). Louis' solution was to buy a site from a priory and grant a charter to the township which began to develop on what up to then had been virtually an island. The new settlement was laid out on the geometrical lines of a bastide and linked to the sea by an artificial channel.

▶ **Population:** 7 115
- **Michelin Map:** 339 K 7
- **Info:** Pl. St-Louis. ℘04 66 53 73 00. www.ot-aiguesmortes.fr.
- **Location:** Aigues-Mortes is 46.6km/29mi SW of Arles.
- **Parking:** Parking is available around the exterior of the ramparts.
- **Don't Miss:** Climb to the the Tour de Constance (53 steps) for an impressive panorama over the town and surrounding flatlands.
- **Timing:** See the fortifications first, allowing at least 1hr for this.

On 28 August 1248, Louis IX set sail from here on the 7th Crusade, which was a failure. On 1 July 1270 he left from here again, on the 8th Crusade, which only reached Tunis, where Louis died.

By the 14C Aigues-Mortes' population totalled 15 000, but its waterways had begun to silt up; the Tour de Constance lost its military significance and instead became a prison.

For more than a century after the revocation of the Edict of Nantes in 1665, Protestant rebels were held here, from 1715–1768 the Tour de Constance being reserved for women prisoners.

Aigues-Mortes Ramparts

D. Pazery/MICHELIN

The silting up of the port and the incorporation of Marseilles into the French kingdom in 1481 pushed Aigues-Mortes into decline and the coup-de-grâce was the founding (17C) and subsequent development of Sète.

SIGHTS
Tour de Constance★★
Access by place Anatole-France.
&♿ *Open daily May–Aug 10am–7pm; Sept–Apr 10am–5.30pm. Cashdesks close 1–2pm and 45min before the monument.* ♿*Closed public holidays.* ☞7€. ☞ *Guided tours (45min).* ☎04 66 53 61 55. http://aigues-mortes. monuments-nationaux.fr.

The tower (1241–49) rests on wooden piles and was intended to be a symbol of royal power as much as a purely military installation. The layout of its elaborate internal defences (staircases, winding passageways, portcullises) is typical of the Capetian dynasty, and its fine walls of Beaucaire limestone stand out boldly against the surrounding sandy landscape. Its turret originally served as a lighthouse, the sea being only 3km/1.8mi away at the time.

Remparts★★
♿ *Same hours as Tour de Constance.*
The ramparts were never seen by St Louis. They were begun in 1272 on the orders of Philippe le Hardi (the Bold) and their completion led to Aigues-Mortes becoming the Capetian kingdom's principal Mediterranean harbour.

At the end of the 13C Philippe le Bel (the Fair) improved the port and completed the defences, adding 20 massive towers to protect the gateways and provide enfilading fire along the walls themselves.

Aix-en-Provence★★

The old capital of Provence has kept much of its 17C and 18C character: the elegance of its mansions, the charm of its squares, the majesty of its avenues and the loveliness of its fountains. It is also a lively city whose large student population is much in evidence on the busy café terraces. The new part of town is rapidly expanding and attracting more and more residents; it has established itself as a city of the arts, a thermal spa and an important centre for industry and the tourist trade.

A BIT OF HISTORY
The Aix of today is the legacy of Good King René (1409–80). The Roman city Aquae Sextiae had long before destroyed by the Lombards (AD 574) and by Saracens; its deserted buildings served as a quarry for building materials for a good six centuries. Then in the 12C its fortunes were restored by the Counts

▶ **Population:** 7 115
◔ **Michelin Map:** 340 H-I 4
▤ **Info:** 2 Place du Général-de-Gaulle. ☎04 42 16 11 61. www.aixenprovence tourism.com.
◖ **Location:** For an overview of the city, join a 2hr guided tour (the tourist office has details).
◈ **Don't Miss:** Vieil Aix, the charming medieval heart of the city.
◔ **Timing:** Even if you take one of the guided tours (2hr; closed on public holidays; 8€; tickets on sale at the tourist office; ☎04 42 16 11 65), the first thing to do in Aix is walk along the majestic Cours Mirabeau under its handsome plane trees, pause for a drink at one of the many cafés, then stroll through Vieil Aix. Allow at least 4hr in total.

of Provence who made it their place of residence. The last and most illustrious of the line was René, Duke of Anjou, Lorraine and Bar, King of Naples, Count of Provence and Piedmont, and the ally of Charles VII of France against the English and Burgundians. This enlightened monarch supported literature and the arts and completed Aix cathedral. Though a benevolent ruler, he was also a strict administrator. Towards the end of his life he made Charles of Maine his heir; Charles however was to die childless, enabling Louis XI to incorporate Provence into France (1486).

Harsh times intervened; invasion by Imperial troops, feuding, and religious conflict. While the Aix Parliament was putting up a strong resistance to Richelieu's centralising policies, an administrative class grew and prospered. The peaceful period ushered in by Cardinal Mazarin saw the extension and rebuilding of the city on Classical lines; judges, lawyers and other notables built sober but distinguished residences that contribute so much to the charm of the Old Town (Vieil Aix) today (rusticated doorways, mask and scroll decoration, stucco-work, ornate staircases).

The intellectual life fostered by King René continued to flourish and the roll-call of great men who were born or who lived in Aix is a long one. It includes the 17C astronomer Fabri de Peiresc who in 1636 drew the first map of the moon.

In the 18C there was the elegant portrait-painter Jean-Baptiste van Loo; the essayist Vauvenargues; and the orator **Count Mirabeau**. The latter, meeting only contempt and rejection from his peers, gained election to the Estates-General in 1789 as a representative, not of the nobility, but of the Third Estate.

Finally there is Paul Cézanne (1839–1906), one of the founders of modern painting; his many studies of Mount Ste-Victoire are justly renowned.

The room devoted to him in Aix's museum, the Musée Granet, houses among other paintings his *Still Life with Sugar-bowl*, *Nude at the Mirror* and the monumental *Bathers*. For a better understanding of the artist and his work,

ask the tourist office for their leaflet on *les Sites Cézanniens*.

SIGHTS
Vieux Aix★★
Elegant 17C–19C mansions with corner statues, pleasant squares and charming fountains combine to give the old town its distinctive character.

Cours Mirabeau★★
Fountains splash under the canopy of fine plane trees shading this most pleasant of Provençal boulevards. It was laid out on the line of the 15C ramparts by Mazarin's brother (also responsible for building the district immediately to the south). Planned deliberately to give the mansions a formal façade to the north and a sunny garden to the south, the grand residences line the south side of the Cours, distinguished by sculptured doorways and balconies of wrought iron held up by caryatids and atlantes.

Musee Granet ★
pl. St Jean-de-Malte. 🕐 *Open Tue–Sun Jun–Sept 11am–7pm; Oct–May noon–6pm.* 🕐*Closed 1 Jan, 1 May, 25 Dec.* 4€. Guided tours (1hr30min) 3€. 04 42 52 88 32. www.museegranet-aixenprovence.fr.
In a 17C mansion, the town's principal art museum displays collections left by F M Granet (1775–1849), and rooms devoted to remnants of Roman Aix. On view, French art from the 16–20C, Italian and Flemish schools, and works by Cézanne.

Place d'Albertas★
A fine mansion of 1724 and fountain of 1745 are complemented by other 18C buildings with soaring first-floor pilasters and graceful balconies contrasting with the more robust appearance of the ground floor which has semicircular arches and rusticated stonework.

Cathédrale St-Sauveur★
r. Gaston de Saporta. 🕐 *Open daily 7.30am–noon, 2–6pm.* 🕐 *Closed during services.* 04 42 43 45 65. www.cathedrale-aix.net.

Cathédrale St-Sauveur

G. Magnin/MICHELIN

The **baptistery**★ dates to the Merovingian period (4C). Eight ancient columns, probably from a Roman basilica nearby, hold up the 18C octagonal cupola crowning the Gallo-Roman structure. In the nave is the **Triptych of the Burning Bush**★★, painted around 1475 by Nicolas Froment, a masterpieces of the Second School of Avignon, integrating a religious subject, landscape and Flemish decorative elements.

The **doorway panels**★ of 1500–08 (*masked by false doors*) represent Prophets and Sibyls. The roof of the Romanesque **cloisters**★ rests on delicate columns. In the time of the Emperor Augustus this was the site of the Forum of Aquae Sextiae.

ADDITIONAL SIGHTS

Hôtel de Ville (*pl. de l'Hotel de Ville*)
Musée des Tapisseries (*pl. des Martyrs de la Résistance*)
Église St-Jean-de-Malte – Nave★ (*24 r. d'Italie*)
Église Ste-Marie-Madeleine – statue of Our Lady★, **triptych**★ (*pl. des Prêcheurs*)
Fondation Vasarely★ (*1 ave Marcel Pagnol*)
Fontaine des Quatre Dauphins★ (*Pl. des Quatre-Dauphins*)
Muséum d'Histoire Naturelle (*6 r. Espariat*)

ADDRESSES

🛏 STAY

🍴🛏 **Hôtel Cardinal** – *24 r. Cardinale.* ℘04 42 38 32 30. www.hotel-cardinal-aix.com. *29 rooms.* ⌑8€. In an 18C mansion in the calm of the Mazarin quarter, tasteful, marrying old-fashioned style with modern comfort. Well-placed for exploring the town centre on foot.

🍴🛏 **Hôtel St-Christophe** – *2 ave Victor-Hugo.* ℘04 42 26 01 24. www.hotel-saintchristophe.com. *60 rooms.* ⌑10.80€. *Restaurant*🍴🛏. This hotel is right in the centre of the city, near cours Mirabeau, and rooms are decorated in either a 1930s or Provençal style. Pavement terrace in fine weather.

🍴🛏 **La Manoir** – *8 r. d'Entrecasteaux.* ℘04 42 26 27 20. www.hotelmanoir.com. *Closed 5–25 Jan. 40 rooms.* ⌑8€. A lovely old building, formerly a hat factory. Part of an adjoining 14C cloister has been converted into a summer terrace, creating a unique atmosphere.

🍴🛏 **Hôtel des Augustins** – *3 r. de la Masse.* ℘04 42 27 28 59. www.hotel-augustins.com. *29 rooms.* ⌑8€. Stone vaulting and stained glass are reminders of the origins of this hotel, a stone's throw from cours Mirabeau, which was originally a 15C convent. The rooms, of which two have terraces with rooftop views, are decorated in a modern style.

🍴 EAT

🍴 **Chez Charlotte** – *32 r. des Bernardines.* ℘04 42 26 77 56. *Closed Aug, 24, 25 & 31 Dec.* Upon entering you are greeted with a nostalgic atmosphere. The main eating area's décor is dedicated to the cinema. Offering traditional and seasonal cuisine, the owner gives special attention to every dish.

🍴 **Trattoria Chez Antoine Côté Cour** – *19 Cours Mirabeau.* ℘04 42 93 12 51. *Closed Mon lunch and Sun.* This is a retreat with a luminous, verdant patio-veranda. All the flavours of Provence and Italy are at your fingertips. Try *aux* *aubergines à la parmesane* and *aux calamars farcis.* This is a place to be sure to visit.

🍽🍽🍽🍽 **Chez Féraud** – *8 r. du Puits-Juif.* 📞*04 42 63 07 27. Closed Aug, Sun & Mon.* Tucked away in an Old Quarter lane, an appealing place with typical local cuisine (pistou, daube) and grills.

🎭 NIGHTLIFE

Café des Deux Garçons – *53 bis cours Mirabeau.* 📞*04 42 26 00 51.* Bordered by plane trees, cours Mirabeau throngs with locals and visitors come to relax at the outdoor tables of one of its many cafés. The Deux Garçons café, more familiarly known as "le 2 G", is the oldest and most famous of these cafés, dating from 1792. Cézanne and Zola were both regulars.

Château de la Pioline – *260 r. Guillaume-du-Vair.* 📞*04 42 52 27 27. www.chateaudelapioline.fr.* The bar of this hotel/restaurant, which dates from the 16C, is adorned with highly prestigious furnishings, such as those from the Medici hall (to commemorate the illustrious Catherine de' Medici) and the Louis XVI hall. Don't miss the large terrace overlooking the 4ha/9.8-acre French garden.

🛒 SHOPPING

Markets – Traditional market every morning in place Richelme and every Tue, Thu and Sat in place des Prêcheurs and place de la Madeleine. Flower market every Tue, Thu and Sat in place de l'Hôtel de Ville, and in place des Prêcheurs on other days.

Antiques – Antique market every Tue, Thu and Sat in place Verdun. Antiques fairs take place in the town hall square every 1st Sun of the month 9am–6pm.

Apparel – Clothes stalls open around Cours Mirabeau on Tue and Thu and in the Palais de Justice on Sat.

Confiserie du Roy René – *13 r. Gaston de Saporta.* 📞*04 42 26 67 86. www.calisson.com.* Buy your traditional local treats like calissons (almonds, sugar, candied melon) and nougat (white, dark or fruit) at this respected long-established shop.

Aperitifs – The definitive shop for Provençal liquers and aperitifs is **Liquoristerie de Venelles** – *36 ave de la Grand-Bégude, Venelles.* 📞*04 42 54 94 65. www.versinthe.net.* Free tour and tasting of the in-house absinthe distillery.

Santons Fouque – *65 cours Gambetta.* 📞*04 42 26 33 38. www.santons-fouque. com.* Visit the atelier where these figurines have been made by the same family for generations.

Cité du Livre – *8–10 r. des Allumettes.* 📞*04 42 91 98 88. www.citedulivre-aix. com.* A haven for book lovers.

TOURS

Cézanne Tour – In the steps of Cézanne. Runs early May–early Oct Tue 2–7pm. 28€. Tours in French and English (details from the tourist office). Visit all the sights associated with the artist.

EVENTS

International Opera and Music Festival – 📞*0820 92 29 23. www. festival-aix.com.* This prestigious festival takes place every July in the courtyard of the archiepiscopal palace. Concerts and recitals are held in the cathedral, the cloisters of St-Saveur and the Hôtel Maynier d'Oppède. The festival focuses on operas as well as contemporary music. Among the artists who have contributed to the high standards of the festival are conductors Hans Rosbaud and Carlo Maria Giulini and the singer Teresa Berganza.

Santon Fair – *Nov–Feb.* These figurines make a lovely recreation of nativity scenes.

Wine Festival – Festival des Côteaux d'Aix en Provence – *cours Mirabeau. Last Sun in Jul.* An opportunity to sample the rich variety from the Vineyards of Aix.

Gorges de L'Ardèche★★★

Overlooked by a dramatically engineered little road, the gorge of the temperamental Ardèche river ranks among the most imposing natural sites in France.

GEOGRAPHY

The Ardèche rises at 1 467m/4 813ft in hills to the north of the Col de la Chavade and flows 119km/74mi before joining the Rhône. It is notorious for spring floods and sudden spates which can increase its flow by as much as 3 000 per cent (the spate of 22 September 1890 brought down 28 bridges).

Vertical cliffs, dramatic meanders and rapids, alternating with calm stretches, are a lesson in the geography of river formation.

Prehistoric people settled here very early and dolmens and cave-dwellings in the area date from the Bronze Age.

SIGHTS
Aven d'Orgnac★★★
South bank. *See Aven d'ORGNAC.*

Aven de Marzal★
North bank.

At the bottom of this deep swallowhole, 130m/426.5ft from the surface, the Gallery of Diamonds glitters with calcite crystals. A museum presents a display of equipment used by the great explorers

- **Michelin Map:** 331 I-J 7-8
- **Info:** Vallon-Pont d'Arc. ℘04 75 88 04 01. www.vallon-pont-darc-07.com.
- **Location:** The Ardèche gorge runs most of the way from Vallon Pont d'Arc to St Martin-d'Ardèche .
- **Don't Miss:** The Haute Corniche scenic route links many great viewpoints.

of these caverns. Nearby, the popular **Prehistoric Zoo** features reproductions of prehistoric animals.

Gorges: From Vallon Pont d'Arc to Pont-St-Esprit
47km/29.2mi.

The meanders of the river mark the course it originally followed on the ancient surface of the plateau before cutting down through the rocks as they were uplifted during the Alpine-building Tertiary period. Great sweeps of vertical cliffs with dramatic meanders cut deep into the rock and rapids alternating with calm stretches of water combine to form a very impressive natural site.

Pont-d'Arc★★

Spanning the full width of the river, the arch of this gigantic natural bridge is 34m/111.5ft high and 59m/193.5ft wide. In geological terms it is a recent phenomenon, caused by the action of

Cirque de la Madeleine, Haute Corniche

J. Damase/MICHELIN

the river, which, helped by the presence of fissures and cavities in the limestone, has succeeded in eroding away the base of a meander.

Haute Corniche (Scenic route)★★★

The road links a number of splendid viewpoints. From the Serre de Tourre can be seen the Pas du Mousse meander, where the river has still to cut through the wooded isthmus; the view from the Morsanne Needles (Aiguilles de Morsanne) gives a good idea of the structure of the plateau as it dips down to the south.

Limestone ridges can be viewed from Gournier, while the rock spires of the Cathedral Rock (Rocher de la Cathédrale) lend this natural monument the appearance of a ruined cathedral.

The Templars' Belvedere (Balcon des Templiers) commands a fine prospect of the Templars' Wall (Mur des Templiers), whose high cliffs (220m/721.7ft) dominate the spectacular meander far below. On a rocky spur in the valley stand the ruins of a leper hospital built by the Templars.

Arles★★★

Arles is one of the most important centres of Provençal culture, proud of its past and famed for an exceptional Roman and medieval heritage, yet vibrantly modern and forward looking. Van Gogh produced many of his greatest works here; what he loved was not the culture or history, but the brilliance of the light.

A BIT OF HISTORY

The ancient Celtic-Ligurian town was colonised by the Greeks of Marseille as early as the 6C BC and was already a thriving town when the Romans conquered the region. They built a canal linking it to the sea so that it could be supplied directly from Rome. Growing into a prosperous port town, and well placed on the major Roman highways, it became an administrative and political capital of Roman Gaul, with many magnificent buildings.

SIGHTS

Théâtre Antique★★

r. de la Calade. ◷ Open daily Nov–Feb 10am–noon, 2–5pm; Mar–Apr and Oct 9am–noon, 2–6pm; May–Sept 9am–7pm. ◷Closed public holidays and for concerts. ✆6€ (includes amphithéâtre). ✆04 90 49 38 20.

▸ **Population:** 51 970
◔ **Michelin Map:** 340 C 3
▯ **Info:** 43 bd de Craponne. ✆04 90 18 41 20. www.tourisme.ville-arles.fr.
◔ **Location:** Arles stands on the edge of the Camargue wetlands and the Rhône delta. As soon as you exit the highway into Arles (from any direction) you will find yourself on boulevard des Lices, the busy town centre which skirts the edge of the historic district where most of the sights are located.
▱ **Parking:** Park under the plane trees of bd Georges-Clemenceau.
◔ **Don't Miss:** Roman arena.
◔ **Timing:** Visitor passes are available at the tourist office or at any of the monuments and museums (except Museon Arlaten). The tourist office has information on many walking tours; ask within or see website. Expect to spend a couple of days if you want to see everything.

Amphithéâtre

G. Magnin/MICHELIN

This is among the most important surviving Roman theatres, and dates from the end of the 1C BC. All that remains of its stage wall are two elegant columns in African breccia and Italian marble.

The theatre began to be quarried for its stone as early as the 5C, and subsequently disappeared completely under houses and gardens. It was excavated in the 19C.

Amphithéâtre★★

r. de la Calade. ○ *Open daily Nov–Feb 10am–5pm; Mar–Apr, Oct 9am–6pm; May and Sept 9am–7pm; Jun–Aug Thu–Tue 9am–7pm; 4–5 Jul 9am–noon.* ○ *Closed 1 Jan, 10–13 Apr, 1 May, 11–13 Sept, 1 Nov and 25 Dec.* ◉*6€ (includes Théâtre Antique).* ℘*04 90 49 59 05.*

Porch of Église St-Trophime

G. Magnin/MICHELIN

Here as many as 20 000 spectators enjoyed a variety of games pitting men against wild animals, and gladiatorial combat.

Dating from about AD 75, this amphitheatre (or arena) is even larger than the one in Nîmes. Its good state of preservation is due to being maintained as a fortress in the 5C and 6C when the Empire was crumbling under the barbarian assault. The sturdy structure was later filled in with as many as 200 houses and two chapels! The excavataion and restoration began in 1825.

Église St-Trophime★

Pl. de la Republique. ○ *Open daily Nov–Feb 10am–5pm; Mar–Apr, Oct 9am–6pm; May–Sept 9am–7pm;* ○ *Closed public holidays.* ◉*3.50€.*

Standing on even more ancient ruins, the church was rebuilt from 1080 onwards. Its porch **(portail★★)** is one of the masterpieces of late 12C Provençal Romanesque architecture.

The arrangement of columns and design of the frieze hark back to Roman work like the **municipal arch**★ at Glanum (◐ *see ST-RÉMY-DE-PROVENCE)* and the 4C sarcophagi at nearby Alyscamps and Trinquetaille. The fact that the stone from which the church is built was taken from the Roman Theatre further strengthens a sense of continuity with the Classical past.

The cloisters (**cloître**★★) were built after 1150 and are renowned for their sculpture. Particularly fine are the corner pillars of the north gallery and the capitals, foliated or decorated with Biblical scenes.

Musée d'Arles et de la Provence antique★★

Presqu'île-du-cirque-romain. ○ *Open daily Nov–Apr 10am–5pm; Apr–Oct 9am–7pm.* ○ *Closed public holidays.* ⊚*5.50€; free 1st Sun in month.* ℘*04 90 18 88 88. www.arles-antique.cg13.fr.* The town's extensive collection of ancient art is displayed here.

Museon Arlaten

29 r. de la République. ○ *Open Nov–Apr 9.30am–noon, 2–4.30pm; Apr–May, Sept 9.30am–noon, 2–5.30pm; Jun–Aug 9.30am–12.30pm, 2–6pm.* ○*Closed 1 Jan, 1 May, 1 Nov, 25 Dec.* ⊚*1€.* ℘*04 90 93 58 11.* Provençal culture and traditions.

Musée Réattu★

10 r. du grand Prieuré. ○ *Open Jul–mid-Sept 10am–7pm. Call for opening rest of year.* ○*Closed 1 Jan, 1 May, 1 Nov, 25 Dec.* ⊚*4€.* ℘*04 90 49 37 58.* Small musuem of contemporary art, including paintings by Pablo Picasso, such as **Picasso Bequest**★.

Thermes de Constantin★

r. Dominique Maïsto. ○ *Open daily Nov–Feb 1–5pm; Mar–Apr, Oct 9am–noon, 2–6pm; May–Sept 9am–noon, 2–7pm.* ○ *Closed 1 Jan, 1 May, 1 Nov, 25 Dec.* ⊚*3€.* ℘*04 90 49 38 20.* Here you'll find the largest baths in Provence.

Alyscamps★

Allow half a day. ○ *Same hours and contact details as the Théâtre antique.* ⊚*3.50€.* A famous Roman necropolis, located just outside the town walls of Old Arles.

ADDRESSES

🏠 STAY

🍽🛏 **Hôtel Muette** – *15 r. des Suisses.* ℘*04 90 96 15 39. www.hotel-muette.com. Closed Feb. 18 rooms.* �*8€.* A beautiful building (originally 15C and 17C) in the heart of historic Arles. Solid stone walls in authentic Provençal rooms guarantees they are soundproof.

🍽🛏 **Hôtel du Musée** – *11 r. du Grand-Prieuré.* ℘*04 90 93 88 88 . www.hoteldu musee.com.fr. Closed Jan. 28 rooms.* ⊒*7€.* Facing the Musée Réattu, this is hotel was built in the 17C. It's a charming labyrinth of green pathways through intimate courtyards, with tranquil rooms.

🍽🛏 **Le Relais de Poste** – *2 r. Molière.* ℘*04 90 52 05 76. http:/hotelrelaisdeposte. fr/uk. 16 rooms.* ⊒*6€.* A couple of steps from the boulevard des Lices and the espace Van-Gogh, this centrally based hotel was once the 18C postal relay. The restaurant evokes its era, with beams and frescos. The rooms are simple and warmly decorated with Provençal textiles.

🍽🛏🛐 **Hôtel d'Arlatan** – *26 r. Sauvage.* ℘*04 90 93 56 66. www.hotel-arlatan.fr. 41 rooms.* ⊒*13€.* Fall under the spell of this old mansion dating from the 15C, a stone's throw from place du Forum. Admire the underground Roman fragments through the glass floor of the bar and the drawing room. Rooms furnished with antiques and pretty fabrics. Small courtyard planted with trees where breakfast is served in the summer.

🍽🛏🛐 **Mireille** – *Rive droite, Trinquetaille.* ℘*04 90 93 70 74. www. hotel-mireille.com. 34 rooms.* ⊒*13€.* Dive into the swimming pool in total peace in this hotel situated outside the city centre. Good size rooms with vibrant colours and Provençal furniture. Airy dining room with red and yellow fabrics.

🍽🛏🛐🛐 **Hôtel Calendal** – *5 r. Porte-de-Laure.* ℘*04 90 96 11 89. www. lecalendal.com. 38 rooms.* ⊒*12€.* This hotel has all the stylishness of Provençal interiors with its colourful façade, pretty inner shaded garden and cosy sitting room. Blue and yellow make up the colour scheme of furniture, fabrics and ceramics. Small tearoom.

⦿ EAT

⊜⊜ **Le Criquet** – *21 r. Porte-de-Laure.* *℘04 90 96 80 51. Closed Wed.* Go for the charming dining room with its beams and exposed stonework rather than the terrace in this little restaurant near the amphitheatre. Once you're comfortably seated, savour local specialities like *bourride* (a kind of fish stew).

⊜⊜⊜ **Jardin de Manon** – *14 ave des Alyscamps. ℘04 90 93 38 68. Closed public holidays.* This restaurant, situated just outside the city centre, is aptly named. Its interior courtyard terrace, full of trees and flowers, will appeal to lovers of alfresco dining. There are two dining rooms with wood panelling and the local cooking, which uses seasonal market produce, offers good value for money.

⊜⊜⊜ **Lou Calèu** – *27 r. Porte-de-Laure. ℘04 90 49 71 77. www.restaurant-lou -caleu.com. Closed Sun, Mon.* A real classic: fresh salads, *taureau* stew, lamb with rosemary. All Arle's delights are at your fingertips. An excellent wine list. The place for gourmets.

⦿ ON THE TOWN

Bar de l'Hôtel Nord Pinus – *place du Forum. ℘04 90 93 44 44. www.nord-pinus.com.* An essential stop in Arles, the small bar of the Hotel Nord Pinus, dating from the 17C, has entertained artists, writers, film stars, and bullfighters, including Picasso, Jean Cocteau and Yves Montand. There's great charm in details such as its boat-shaped lamps, bullfighting bar, squat armchairs and a background of flamenco music.

Café Van Gogh – *11 pl. du Forum. ℘04 90 96 44 56.* This bright, popular café with its large terrace was the subject of Vincent Van Gogh's *The Cafe Terrace on the Place du Forum*.

L'Entrevue – *Pl. Nina Berberova. ℘04 90 93 37 28.* Arles is the birthplace of the flourishing Actes Sud publishing house, who also run this arty café-restaurant, a cultural hub of the town.

Le Méjan – *23 quai Marx-Dormoy. ℘04 90 93 33 56.* Enjoy evening and afternoon musical performances, jazz concerts, lectures, conferences, and exhibitions in the chapel Saint-Martin-du-Méjan.

⦿ SHOPPING

Markets – Browse traditional markets every Wed in *boulevard Émile-Combes* and every Sat in *boulevard des Lices* and *boulevard Clemenceau*. **Antique market** first Wed of the month in *boulevard des Lices* .

Les Étoffes de Romane – *10 bd des Lices. ℘04 90 93 53 70.* Choose from wonderful **Provençal fabrics** in an array of colours.

Patisserie – Some of the best of local specialities, almond biscuits, breads, chocolates etc can be found at **De Moro** (*24 r. du Prés. Wilson; ℘04 90 93 14 43*)

Books and Music – A gold mine for music from the south is **La Boutique des Passionnés** (*14 r. Réattu; ℘04 90 96 59 93; www.passiones.com*).

Olive Oil – Best quality Provençal olive oil, but also varieties from Spain, Greece and Italy, are found (together with other olive specialities) at **Fad'ola** (*46 r. des Arènes; ℘04 90 49 70 73*)

⦿ EVENTS

Festival Les Suds – *mid-Jul. www.suds-arles.com.* World music festival.

Fête des Gardians – *1 May. ℘04 90 18 41 20.* Mass is held in the Provençal dialect, with the blessing of horses, typical Camargue games, local folk music and dances, as well as beautiful girls competing for the title of "Queen" of Arles.

Les Rencontres d'Arles – (*early Jul–mid-Sept*) *10 rond-point des Arènes. ℘04 90 96 76 06. www.rencontres-arles.com.* This international photography festival is a feast of exhibitions, courses, talks, and activities in locations throughout the town centre, including the Roman Theatre.

Avignon★★★

Protected by a ring of imposing ramparts, the historic core of Avignon is a lively centre of art and culture. For 68 years it was the residence first of seven French Popes, then of three others once Pope Gregory XI had returned to Rome in 1377; the Papal Legates remained until the city was united with France in 1791.

A BIT OF HISTORY

Very little remains of the Roman settlement of Avenio which fell into ruin after the Barbarian invasions of the 5C. At the beginning of the 14C the Popes felt the need to escape from the turbulent political life of Rome. Avignon formed part of the Papal territories, and occupied a central position in the Europe of the time. The case for moving there was put by Philippe le Bel (the Fair), possibly with a view to involving the Papacy in his own political manœuvrings. In 1309 Pope Clement V took the plunge, and Avignon became for most of a century the capital of Western Christendom.

When Pope Clement VI succeeded him in 1342, he greatly enlarged the Papal Palace, and brought to Avignon his love of the arts.

Avignon remains an influential cultural centre. It owes much to Jean Vilar, who in 1947 founded the prestigious annual event, **Festival d'Avignon**. This festival led to a blossoming of the arts: Avignon now hosts many different cultural events during the year.

SIGHTS

Palais des Papes★★★

r. Pente Rapide Charles Ansidei. Open daily 1–mid-Mar 9am–6.30pm; mid-Mar–Jun and mid-Sept–Oct 9am–7pm; Jul and 1–mid-Sept 9am–8pm; Aug 9am–9pm; Nov–Feb 9.30am–5.45pm. Last admission 1hr before closing. 10.50€ (15 Mar–31 Oct); 8.50€ (Nov–14 Mar); 11€ combined ticket with pont St-Bénézet. 04 90 27 50 00. www.palais-des-papes.com.

▶ **Population:** 92 454
Michelin Map: 32 B-C 10
Info: 41 cours Jean-Jaurès. 04 32 74 32 74. www.ot-avignon.fr.
Location: The major sights and city centre are inside the walled old city, where the main street is Rue de la République. This street runs straight to the main square, Place de l'Horloge and the adjacent Palais des Papes.
Parking: Parking is available in the Palais des Papes underground car park.
Don't Miss: Get a great view of Avignon's skyline from across the Rhône, especially if you are approaching the city in the evening.
Timing: With so much to do in Avignon, allow at least 3hr to visit the Palais des Papes and Pont St-Bénézet before exploring the rest of the city. Many sights can be visited at a reduced rate by obtaining a **carte-pass** from any of the sights or at the tourist office.
Kids: There's a lovely old-fashioned carousel in Place de l'Horloge. And a fast, fun way to see the sights is via the 'Petit Train' (40min; 7€; www.petittrainavignon.com), several times a day from Place du Palais des Papes.

The huge feudal structure, fortress as well as palace, conveys an overwhelming impression of defensive strength with its high bare walls, its massive corbelled crenellations and stalwart buttresses. Inside, a maze of galleries, chambers, chapels and passages contains almost no furnishings. While the popes were

Palais des Papes

S. Sauvignier/MICHELIN

in residence the palace was extremely luxuriously equipped.

Pont St-Bénézet★★

Accessed via ramparts. Rue Ferruce.
🚻🕐 *Open daily Jul 9am–9pm; Aug–Sept 9am–8pm; mid-Mar-Jun and Oct 9am–7pm; Nov–mid-Mar 9.30am–5.45pm; last admission 1hr before closing. ☞4.50€ (15 Mar–31 Oct); 4€ (Nov–14 Mar). ℘04 32 74 32 74.*

Stepping out into the swirling Rhone, and coming to an abrupt end in midstream, this beautiful bridge was first built in 1177, according to legend, by a shepherd-boy called Bénézet. Until the Bridge Brotherhood (Frères Pontifes) built Pont-St-Esprit more than a century later this was the only stone bridge over the Rhône. It helped the economic development of Avignon long before becoming a useful link with Villeneuve when the Cardinals built their villas there. Eighteen of its arches were carried away by the floodwaters of the river in the 17C.

ADDITIONAL SIGHTS

Petit Palais★★
Rocher des Doms★★ **– views**★★
Cathédrale – cupola★
Ramparts★
Hôtel des Monnaies – façade★
(pl. du Palais des Papes)
Musée Calvet★ *(63 r. Joseph Vernet)*

Musée Louis-Vouland – faience★
(17 r. Victor Hugo)
Musée lapidaire★ *(r. de la République)*
Église St-Didier– frescoes★ *(Pl. Saint-Didier)*

EXCURSION
Villeneuve-lès-Avignon★

2km/1.2mi W, on the west bank of the river.

At the point where St Bénézet's bridge originally touched French territory Philippe le Bel built a small fort (only a tower remains).

Half a century later, feeling hemmed in at Avignon, the Cardinals crossed the river and built themselves 15 fine houses (*livrées*) here. At the same time, Jean le Bon (John the Good) erected the St-André fortress on the hill which was already crowned by an abbey. Protected by its walls and with a splendid twin-towered gatehouse, this vast building complex offers (from its Romanesque Chapel of Notre-Dame de Belvézet) one of the finest views over the Rhône valley. In the foreground is the gateway, Porte St-André, and beyond, on the far bank, the Palace of the Popes.

In 1352 the General of the Carthusian Order had been elected Pope but humbly refused the throne. Pope Innocent VI, elected in his stead, founded a charterhouse, **Chartreuse du Val de Bénédiction**★ *(🕐 open daily Apr–Sept*

9am–6.30pm; Oct–Mar 9.30am–5.30pm; ⏰closed 1 Jan, 1 May, 1, 11 Nov, 25 Dec; 📞04 90 15 24 24) to commemorate the gesture. It soon became the greatest charterhouse in France. It has a monu-mental 17C gateway, small cloisters and graveyard cloisters, the latter fringed by the cells of the Fathers. The church contains the founder's tomb.

ADDRESSES

🛏 STAY

🍽 **Hôtel Le Provençal** – *13 r. Joseph-Vernet.* 📞*04 90 85 25 24. 11 rooms.* ⛶*5€.* Le Provençal offers the advantage of being in the very heart of Avignon without being too pricey, a rare mix for this town. Moreover, the rooms are comfortable and decent.

🍽🛏 **Chambre d'hôte La Prévoté** – *354 chemin d'exploitation, Althen-les-Paluds. 17km/10.5mi NE of Avignon towards Carpentras.* 📞*04 90 62 17 06. www.la-prevote.com. Closed Nov–Mar. 5 rooms.* ⛶*5€.* After a peaceful night spent in one of the spacious, colourful rooms of this *mas*, you will certainly enjoy breakfast, which is served in the shade of the vine arbour or under the chestnut tree. Let your gaze roam over the apple trees or have a dip in the swimming pool.

🍽🛏 **Hôtel de la Garlande** – *20 r. Galante.* 📞*04 90 80 08 85. www.hotelde garlande.com. 12 rooms.* ⛶*7€.* Situated in two renovated old houses in a peaceful street, this small, family-run hotel is close to the church of St Didier. Colourful rooms with Provençal floral fabrics.

🍽🛏 **Hôtel Cloître St-Louis** – *20 r. du Portail Boquier.* 📞*04 90 27 55 55. www.cloitre-saint-louis.com. 77 rooms.* ⛶*16€. Restaurant* 🍽🛏. Situated in 16C cloisters, part of this hotel was designed by the architect Jean Nouvel. The building uses a variety of materials including glass, steel, and stone. Rooms are stylishly minimalist. Pool and solarium on the roof. Sunday mass in the chapel at the heart of the hotel.

🍴 EAT

🍽 **Le Mesclun** – *46 r. de la Balance.* 📞*04 90 86 14 60. Closed Sun.* There's no better place for lunch, be it on the shaded terrace or inside. The daily dishes and menu mingle market freshness, Provence, and gastronomy with the zest of good cheer. The choice spot to take a pause between excursions.

🍽🛏 **Au Coin des Halles** – *4 r. Grivolas.* 📞*04 90 82 93 49. Closed Sun & public holidays.* Enjoy this central spot among the Avignonnais, with its reading space and two little dining areas, all infused with jazzy music. And check out the menu: simple dishes, like a delicious *reblochon* cheese tart, a *salade landaise*, a winter squash soup.

🍽🛏 **Entrée des Artistes** – *1 place des Carmes.* 📞*04 90 82 46 90. Closed 15 Aug–1 Sept, 22 Dec–1 Jan, Sun.* The dining room of this restaurant is decorated in the style of a Parisian bistro, with its old posters and movie memorabilia. Tables are placed close together and the cooking is traditional. Service is friendly and there is a real scent of the Mediterranean in the air.

🍽🛏 **Compagnie des Comptoirs** – *83 r. Joseph-Vernet.* 📞*04 90 85 99 04. Closed Sun & Mon for dinner.* Inspired by the colonial trading posts of the French East Indies Company, this restaurant, situated in the 14C cloisters, is the "in" place to eat. The bar décor is glass and bamboo, there are colonial etchings in the dining rooms, and the terrace is decked out with a palm tree and straw huts. The menu combines the flavours of East Asia with those of southern France.

🍽🛏 **Le Grand Café** – *4 r. des Escaliers-Ste-Anne.* 📞*04 90 86 86 77. www.legrandcafe-avignon.com. Closed Sun, Mon.* Backing onto the buttresses of the Palais des Papes, these old barracks have become an essential part of local life. Locals and tourists all flock here to savour inventive cooking with Provençal accents. Pleasant décor that combines the styles of a Parisian bistro and a Viennese café. There is also an attractive terrace.

🍴🍴🛏 **Le Moutardier** – *15 pl. du Palais-des-Papes.* *℘04 90 85 34 76.* This 18C building, listed in France's National Heritage, makes an exceptional setting for a simple, fresh meal. There is a pleasant atmosphere, both in the bistro room, where frescoes depict the story of "The Pope's mustard maker", and on the terrace facing the Palais des Papes.

🎭 NIGHTLIFE

Café In et Off – *pl. du Palais-des-Papes.* *℘04 90 85 48 95. Closed mid-Nov–late Feb.* Don't miss the only café that enjoys unbeatable views of the Palais des Papes. The interior is not lacking in appeal but the terrace is definitely the highpoint of this café.

🎭 SHOWTIME

Le Rouge Gorge – *10 bis r. Peyrolerie.* *℘04 90 14 02 54.* The only cabaret in Avignon, the Rouge-Gorge, sheltered by the Palais des Papes, unveils the sensual charms of its show every Fri and Sat from 8.30pm, while two Sundays a month there is an operetta lunch. During the week the atmosphere remains lively with numerous themed evenings (Corsican, Latino, Oriental).

🛒 SHOPPING

Markets – Les Halles Centrales (traditional covered market) Tue–Sun, *place Pie.* **Flower market** Sat in *place des Carmes.* **Fair** Sat and Sun, *rempart St-Michel.* **Flea market** Sun, *place des Carmes.*

Honey – La boutique de la Miellerie (*189 r. de la Source, St-Saturnin; ℘04 90 22 47 52; www.miellerie.fr*). Honey, pollen, and royal jelly, as well as honey-based products.

Home décor – Terre è Provence (*26 r. de la République; ℘04 90 86 31 59*). In the same family for several generations, this shop is dedicated to all that is Provence: table settings, textiles with Provençal prints, pottery, and porcelain and many lovely ideas for your home.

EVENTS

Cheval Passion Horse Show – *Jan.* *℘04 90 84 02 04. www.cheval-passion. com.* This event includes dressage, show jumping, competitions, and stud farm shows at the Avignon Trade Fair Centre in the Vaucluse. The Festival culminates with four performaces of the Gala des Crinières d'Or.

Hivernales d'Avignon – *Feb.* *℘04 90 82 33 12. www.hivernales-avignon.com.* This modern choreography festival, dating from 1977, never attains the atmosphere of the summer festival as the shows (luckily) take place indoors.

The Avignon Festival – *Jul.* A vast programme of mainstream and fringe events. Theatre, dance, lectures, exhibitions, meetings and concerts in the main courtyard of the Palais des Papes, in the municipal theatre, in the many cloisters and churches of the town, as well as at Villeneuve-lès-Avignon and other outlying areas, such as Carrière de Boulbon, Montfavet or Châteaublanc. Fringe events are dotted around the town. The festival showcases French performance art and attracts an ever-growing audience.

Booking – the Bureau du Festival d'Avignon, Cloître Saint-Louis (*20 r. du Portail-Boquier, Avignon; ℘04 90 27 66 50; reservations from 15 Jun; ℘04 90 14 14 14; www.festival-avignon.com*). Book online (from early June onwards), at FNAC booking counters (1.60€ booking fee) and at the main office. Festival programmes (available online) are confirmed mid-May.

Animo Nature – *early Oct. Parc des Expositions d'Avignon.* *℘04 90 84 02 04. www.animo-nature.com.* The largest animal show in France with 6 000 animals from reptiles to domesticated animals including conformation shows for dogs.

Les **Baux-de-Povence**★★★

With its ruined castle and deserted houses capping an arid rocky spur plunging abruptly to steep ravines on either side, the old village of Baux has the most spectacular of **sites**. Baux has also given its name to bauxite, a mineral first discovered here in 1822 that led to the development of aluminium.

A BIT OF HISTORY

The lords of Baux were renowned in the Middle Ages, described by Mistral as "warriors all - vassals never." They traced their ancestry back to the Magi king Balthazar and boldly placed the Star of Bethlehem on their coat of arms.

SIGHTS

Town

The original entrance into the town is guarded by a gate (Porte Eyguières). Go through the fortified gateway into the town, and simply wander in the old streets. The **Place St-Vincent**★, pleasantly shaded by elms and lotus-trees, has a terrace giving views of the small Fontaine Valley and Val d'Enfer. The 17C former Town Hall (Hôtel de Ville) has rooms with ribbed vaulting. The church (Église St-Vincent) dates from the 12C; dressed in their long capes, the

▶ **Population:** 381

⚿ **Michelin Map:** 340 D 3

🛈 **Info:** Maison du Roy, Rue Porte-Mage. ℘04 90 54 34 39. www.lesbaux deprovence.com.

▶ **Location:** Les Baux is 30km/18.6mi S of Avignon and 9.5km/6mi SW of St-Rémy-de-Provence, in the midst of the beautiful rocky hills of the Chaîne des Alpilles. The D 78 approaches from Fontvielle and the first few houses of the old village clinging to the hillsides come into view suddenly in a bend.

🅿 **Parking:** Park the car in one of the car parks (⊚4€) at the foot of the escarpment, before the road up to the village (where cars are not usually allowed).In high season the car parks can be full, so it you may need to park by the roadside some way down from the village.

🕐 **Timing:** A walk through the streets of Les Baux is a magical experience. Take 1hr to see the village and 45min for the château.

Château and Chapelle Ste-Blaise

S. Sauvignier/MICHELIN

shepherds from the Alpilles hills come here for their **Christmas festival**★★, celebrated at Midnight Mass. The **Rue du Trencat**★ was carved into the solid rock which has subsequently been pitted and eroded by wind and rain.

Château des Baux

🕐 *Open Jun–Aug daily 9am–7.30pm; Mar–May and Sept–Nov daily 9am –6.30pm; Dec–Feb daily 9am–5pm.* ⊚*7.70€.* ✆*04 90 54 55 56. www.chateau-baux-provence.com.*
By the 11C the lords of Baux, "that race of eagles", were among the most powerful rulers in the south of France.
Their turbulent ways, together with their support for the Reformation, were a great irritant to Louis XIII who in 1632 ordered the castle and ramparts to be dismantled; this was the town's death-blow.
From the remains of the 13C keep a fine **panorama**★★ unfolds over the Alpilles with the windmills of Fontvieille to the west. One of them is Daudet's Mill (Moulin de Daudet). It was here that **Alphonse Daudet**, the Nîmes-born author very popular in France (and available in English translation), is supposed to have written his delightful *Letters from My Mill*, creating the characters of the Woman of Arles *(L'Arlésienne)*, Monsieur Seguin's goat, the Pope's grumpy mule and Dom Balaguère the gourmand.

ADDITIONAL SIGHTS
Cathédrale d'images★ *(300m/328yd N of the village on D 27)*
Musée Yves Brayer★ *(pl. F. Hérain)*

La **Camargue**★★

The Rhône delta forms an immense wetland plain of 950sqkm/367sq mi. Product of the interaction of the Rhône, the Mediterranean and the winds, this remarkable area has a culture and history all its own, as well as distinctive flora and fauna. It is divided into three distinct regions: a cultivated region north of the delta, salt-marshes west of the Petit Rhône, and the watery nature reserve to the south.

VISIT
Parc Naturel Régional de Camargue

🗊 *Park Information Centre: Mas du Pont de Rousty, about 10km/6.2mi from Arles and 30km/18.6mi from Les Saintes-Maries-de-la-Mer on D 570.* ✆*04 90 97 10 82. www.parc-camargue.fr.* 🕐 *Open daily.* 🕐 *Closed Tue Mar–Oct.* 🦟 *Mosquitoes are a problem during the summer.*
The nature park covers an area of 85 000ha/328sq miles in the Rhône delta, including the communes of Arles and Stes-Maries-de-la-Mer. Together with the nature reserve, **Réserve Nationale**

- 🔷 **Michelin Map:** 340 A-E 4-5 and 339 J-M 7-8
- 🔷 **Location:** The main town in the Camargue is Les Saintes-Maries-de-la-Mer on the coast. The city of Arles lies on its northern edge.
- 🔷 **Don't Miss:** Try to catch sight of the three creatures that symbolise the Camargue – white horses, black bulls and pink flamingos.

de Camargue, it aims to protect the fragile ecological system of the region with its exceptional variety of flora and fauna – there are some 400 bird species. The traditional image of the Camargue is associated with the herds **(manades)** and the horsemen **(gardians)**. Many horse owners hire out their mounts for organised rides among the animals.
The *manade* designates livestock and all that relates to the upkeep of the herd: herdsmen, pastureland, horses, etc. The *gardian*, an experienced rider, is the symbol of the *manade* with his

White horses of the Camargue

©pigio1958/Fotolia.com

large felt hat and long three-pronged stick; he watches over the herd, cares for the sick animals and selects the bulls for the bullfights.

Les Stes-Maries-de-la-Mer

At the heart of the Camargue is situated Les Stes-Maries-de-la-Mer, clustered around it fortified church. The town, which is now at some distance from the coastline of medieval times, is protected by dikes to counter the encroachment of the sea. The church, and the name of the town, are deicated to a pious legend, according to which a boat carrying Mary, the mother of James, Mary Salome, the mother of James Major and John, Mary Magdalene, Martha and her brother Lazarus, came to rest on the shore where Les-Stes-Maries now stands. The two Marys and their black servant Sarah remained here; their burial place became a shrine, then a church.

A large, colourful **Gypsy Pilgrimage**★★ in honour of Sarah, whom they consider as their patron, takes place 24–25 May, attracting thousands of gypsies.

Musée Camarguais at Pont de Rousty

Located in Park Information Centre.
Open Apr–Sept daily 9am–6pm; Oct–Mar Wed–Mon 10am–5pm.
Closed 1 Jan, 1 May, 25 Dec.

5€. 04 90 97 10 82. *www.parc-camargue.fr.*
Occupying a former sheep farm deep in the Camargue, about 10km/6.2mi from Arles, the Museum traces the the history of human activity in the delta.

Much of the exhibition is devoted to life in a *mas* or traditional farmhouse during the 19C but also features the economic activities of the present time, wine production, rice growing, sea salt, etc.

Flamingos in the marshland

©Javier Gil/Fotolia.com

Cassis★

The little resort has a bustling harbour and an attractive **setting**. At the beginning of the 20C, artists like Derain, Vlaminck, Matisse and Dufy were attracted here by the quality of the light.

EXCURSION
The coast

West of Cassis the Puget Massif is incised by steep-sided inlets known as **Calanques**★★, which make pleasant bathing-places. East of Cassis lies **Cap Canaille**★★★, at 362m/1 188ft the highest sea-cliff in France.

> ▶ **Population:** 7 788
> ⏱ **Michelin Map:** 340 I 6
> ℹ **Info:** Quai des Moulins. ℘0892 25 98 92. www.ot-cassis.com.
> ◗ **Location:** Cassis is the nearest beach resort to Marseille, 22km/13.6mi away.
> ◷ **Timing:** Enquire at the tourist office about a number of boat excursions available.

The Cosquer Cave

The submarine cave situated at Cap Morgiou was discovered in 1985 by Henri Cosquer, a local diver. News of its painted decoration and engravings dating from the Paleolithic Age broke in 1991 and it was acclaimed as one of the high spots for rock art. Carbon dating techniques show the hand prints and animal drawings to be 1 000–2 000 years earlier than those at Lascaux. The marine fauna (seals, penguins, fish) is a rare feature which adds to the interest of this decorated cave which was submerged as the level of the sea rose and its treasures were preserved. An exhibition on the site is presented at La Joliette docks in Marseille.

Fontaine de Vaucluse

This impressive resurgent spring was famous enough to figure in Strabo's Geography 2000 years ago.

A BIT OF HISTORY

The humanist poet Petrarch retired here in 1337 to write his 'Sonnets to Laura' inspired by the beautiful Laura de Noves with whom Petrarch had fallen in love with whilst living in Avignon.

VISIT

Gushing forth at the foot of a cliff among trees in an enclosed valley, this is one of the most spectacular phenomena of its kind. Fed by rain falling on the Vaucluse hills, the water penetrates

> ⏱ **Michelin Map:** 332 D 10
> ℹ **Info:** Chemin de la Fontaine. ℘04 90 20 32 22.
> ◗ **Location:** The village of Fontaine de Vaucluse is at the end of a 7km/4.3mi-long country road from the town of L'Isle sur la Sorgue.
> ◷ **Timing:** The fountain is much more impressive in spring than autumn.

the limestone uplands and collects in a vast cavern from which it is forced out under pressure. In late winter, the flow can amount to 100cu m/3 531.4cu ft per second. At such times the waters foam and spray against the rocks, a magnificent natural spectacle.

Gordes★

The site★ is spectacular, the charming village rising in tiers up rocky slopes.

SIGHT
Château
🕐 Open daily 10am–noon, 2-6pm.
🕐 Closed 1 Jan, 25 Dec. ⊚4€.
The imposing Renaissance château stands dramatically on the village's highest point, facing Old Gordes.
Today it houses the the **Musée Pol Mara**, displaying the work of this Flemish artist whoi lives in the village. There is a fine Renaissance **doorway** in the courtyard. In the great hall *(first floor)* is a splendid **chimneypiece** of 1541.

EXCURSIONS
Abbaye de Sénanque ★★
4km/2.5mi N.
Founded in 1148, this Cistercian abbey occupies a remote **site**★ and is notable

♿ **Michelin Map:** 332 E 10
🅱 **Info:** Le Château.
   ℘04 90 72 02 75.
   www.gordes-village.com.
▶ **Location:** The village is in scenic back-country 40km/25mi E.

for its purity of line and lack of ornamentation.

Village des Bories★
3.5km/2mi SW.
Curious drystone structures of this kind exist from Iceland to the Middle East. In Vaucluse they were built between 14C and 19C. The village consists of a number of dwellings as well as structures for threshing, baking, oil pressing, and housing animals.

Château de
Grignan★★

The old town of Grignan is dominated by its medieval château, which owes its fame to the delightful letters written over a twenty year period in the 17C by Mme de **Sévigné** to her daughter Mme de Grignan .

VISIT
🕐 Open Sept–Oct, Apr–Jun daily 9.30am–11.30am, 2–5.30pm; Jul–Aug daily 9.30am–11.30am, 2–6pm; Nov–Mar Wed–Mon 9.30am–11.30am, 2–6pm. 🕐Closed 25 Dec, 1 Jan. ⊚5.50€. ℘04 75 91 83 55.
The medieval castle was remodelled in the 16C. In 1669, the Count of Grignan married the daughter of Mme de Sévigné, who became a frequent visitor.
The letters written by mother to daughter over a period of 27 years were

♿ **Michelin Map:** 332 C 7
🅱 **Info:** Place Sévigné, Grignan. ℘04 75 46 56 75. www.guideweb.com/grignan.
▶ **Location:** Grignan is SE of Montélimar, E of the Rhône.

to create a new literary genre; full of keen observation, wit and spontaneity.
The Renaissance south front of the château was restored early in the 20C following a fire. With its superimposed columns, moulded pilasters, mullioned windows and shell-decorated niches, it marks the arrival of Renaissance in Provence.
The original courtyard is flanked by a Gothic pavilion and opens out onto the terrace with a **view**★★ over the Tricastin area and Mont Ventoux. Inside are evocative furnishings **(mobilier**★**)** of many periods and Aubusson tapestries.

Marseille★★★

The 19C Romano-Byzantine Basilica of **Notre-Dame-de-la-Garde** stands in a commanding position overlooking this great Mediterranean seaport. The **view★★★** from the church is immense, taking in the islands standing guard in the bay, the harbour, and the background of limestone hills as well as the sprawling city itself.

A BIT OF HISTORY

Marseille began life as a trading post set up by Greeks from Asia Minor around 600 BC. Its inhabitants soon established other commercial bases both in the interior and on the coast, at Nice, Antibes, the Lérins Islands, Agde, Glanum (St-Rémy), and Arles. By the 3–2C BC the city they called Massilia covered an area of some 50ha/123.5 acres to the north of the Old Port, and the knolls rising above the busy streets were crowned with temples.

A cultural as well as a commercial centre, the city aroused the interest and envy of the Celto-Ligurians of Entremont, and in 123 BC Massilia found it prudent to conclude an alliance with Rome.

The Senate took the opportunity to begin its programme of expansion into Provence and subsequently Gaul.

Seventy years later, when Caesar and Pompey were engaged in civil war, Marseille was obliged to take sides and had the ill fortune to choose the loser. The victorious Caesar besieged the city and sacked it in 49 BC. Narbonne, Arles and Fréjus grew prosperous on the spoils, and Marseille went into decline.

City Pass Marseille

This is an all-inclusive pass giving free access to museums, public transport, a boat trip to the Château d'If and even a ride on the little tourist train. 20€/1 day, 27€/2 days. Enquire at the tourist office.

▶ **Population:** 839 043

♿ **Michelin Map:** 340 H 6

ℹ **Info:** 4 La Canebière. ✆04 91 13 89 00. www.marseille-tourisme.com.

◐ **Location:** Marseille is centered on the magnificent **Vieux Port** (old port) with its lively quaysides and daily fish market on **Quai des Belges**. Main boulevard **Canebière** leads straight through the city centre to the old port. To gain an overview of the city, there are many guided tours – ask at the tourist office. A fun way to see the central district is on the **little tourist train** (5€; ✆04 91 25 24 69; www.petit-train-marseille.com) from quai du Port.

🅿 **Parking:** There are several underground car parks around town, a.g. at place d'Estienne-d'Orves (reached via place aux Huiles, quai de Rive-Neuve or r. Breteuil).

🚶 **Don't Miss:** The **Corniche Président -J.-F.-Kennedy** is a promenade that runs nearly 5km/3mi. For a pleasant and timeless evening, choose an outdoor restaurant in the tiny fishing port called **Vallon des Auffes.**

🕐 **Timing:** Starting from the Vieux Port, it takes about 2hr to walk along the Canebière. Afterwards, return along the Canebière but allow 1hr for the old Le Panier district. To get around more quickly, use the inexpensive bus network or two Metro lines (free network maps at ticket offices; ✆04 91 91 92 10).

La Marseillaise

On 20 April 1792, Revolutionary France declared war against Austria. In Strasbourg, General Kellerman asked Claude Joseph Rouget de l'Isle, a captain in the engineering corps and a composer-songwriter in his spare time, to write a "new piece of music to mark the departure of the volunteers"; the *Chant de guerre pour l'Armée du Rhin (War Song for the Rhine Army)* was written during the night of 25–26 April. Soon adopted by a battalion from Rhône-et-Loire and carried south by commercial travellers, the Chant reached Montpellier on 17 June. On 20 June, a young patriot from Montpellier on assignment in Marseille, François Mineur, sang it at a banquet offered by the Marseille Jacobin club, located at r. Thubaneau. Enthusiasm was such that the words of the song were passed on to 500 national guards from Marseille, who had been called to arms for the defence of Paris. Renamed *Chant de guerre aux armées des Frontières (War song for the Border Armies)*, the anthem was sung at each of the 28 stages of the journey towards the capital, with growing success and virtuosity. On 30 July, the impassioned verses sung by the warm southern voices, ringing out across the St-Antoine district, was referred to by the electrified crowd as the Chant des Marseillais (Song of the people of Marseille). A few days later, on the storming of the Tuileries, the new anthem was given its definitive name. La Marseillaise became the national anthem on 26 Messidor an III (14 July 1795) of the Republican calendar, and again, after a long period of obscurity, on 14 July 1879.

Even after its sack by Caesar, Marseille remained a free city. Its life as a port carried on, with many ups and downs, based on the "Horn" (corne), the original basin sited to the northeast of today's Old Port, which itself came more and more into use as an outer harbour. Nevertheless, the decline of the city as a whole made it difficult to maintain the installations and the original harbour gradually silted up, finally becoming completely blocked in the 11C.

The Crusades, together with the growth of the rivalry between Pisa and Genoa, led to a revival of the city's fortunes in the 12C. Further expansion followed, with the incorporation of Provence into the French kingdom in 1481 and even more with the construction of new quays under Louis XIII (a blow to its old rival Arles). In the 19C, the city's fortunes revived further with the expansion of French (and European) colonial activity in the Orient as well as in Africa.

SIGHTS

Basilique St-Victor★

3 r. Abbaye. ✆*04 96 11 22 60.*
http://marseille.catholique.fr/basilique-saint-victor.
A Christian quarter grew up opposite the old Greco-Roman city. It was here that St Victor is supposed to have met a martyr's death at the very beginning of the 4C, and here too that a fortified abbey is said to have been built in his memory around AD 420.

The basilica was rebuilt in 1040. Its crypt and nave altered in the early Gothic period. In the crypt (**crypte**★★) are a number of 4C sarcophagi, examples of the individualism which distinguishes Christian art from that of the Classical world. The sarcophagi showing the Council of the Apostles and the Companions of St Maurice are justly famous.

Vieux-Port (Old Port and surrounding area)★★

On the south side of the Old Port is the bust of Vincent Scotto (1876–1952), the composer of much-loved popular melodies, surveying what is almost always a highly animated scene. To the east is the **Canebière**, the city's busy

Boat Excursions

There are regular boat excursions to **Château d'If** (20min) and the **Frioul Islands** (30min).
IF FRIOUL EXPRESS; Quai des Belges; www.frioul-if-express.com. 10–15€.

View of port, Marseille

G. Magnin/MICHELIN

main artery, whose fame has been spread around the world by the mariners of Marseille.

For a glimpse into the long history of the port, visit **Musée des Docks romains**★ *(4 pl. Vivaux;* 🕐 *open Tue–Sun Oct–May 10am–5pm; Jun–Sept 11am–6pm;* 🕐*closed public holidays;* 🎫*2€;* ℘*04 91 91 24 62)*, part of the **Musée d'Histoire de Marseille**★, known as the Garden of Ruins (Jardin des Vestiges). The "horn" formed by the first harbour is dramatically visible and inside there is a 3C boat excavated from the mud.

Centre de la Vieille Charité★★

2 r. de la Charité. 🕐 *Open Tue–Sun Oct–May T10am–5pm; Jun–Sept 11am–6pm.* 🕐 *Closed public holidays.* 🎫*Each museum 2€; major event*

Centre de la Vieille Charité

B. Kaufmann/MICHELIN

exhibits 5€. ℘*04 91 14 58 38. www. vieille-charite-marseille.org.*

The old workhouse and hospice (1671– 1749) has been carefully restored. The **chapel**★ is a masterpiece by Pierre Puget, a Marseille man; it has a little ambulatory and recessed steps allowing the different categories of inmates to make their separate ways to the chapels and galleries, and a central, oval-shaped cupola resting on a drum and supported by Ionic columns and pilasters. The second-floor gallery affords unusual views of the oblong chapel dome.

The rich and varied collections of the **Musée d'Archéologie de Marseille**, comprising some 900 artefacts from the Near East, Greece, Etruria and Rome, make this one of the few provincial museums able to offer a comprehensive survey of ancient Mediterranean civilisations.

ADDITIONAL SIGHTS

Musée du Vieux-Marseille★ *(r. de la Prison)*
Ancienne cathédrale de la Major★ *(pl. de la Major)*
Musée Cantini★ *(19 r. Grignan)*
Corniche Président J.-F.-Kennedy★★
Musée de la Faïence★ *(157 ave de Montredon)*
Musée Grobet Labadié★★
Musée des Beaux Arts★ *(bd Longchamp)*

ADDRESSES

🛏 STAY

🍽🍽 **Chambre d'hôte Villa Marie-Jeanne** – *4 r. Chicot.* 📞*04 91 85 51 31. 3 rooms.* A very special address in Marseille, this 19C building has been tastefully done up. Situated in a residential neighbourhood, it blends the traditional colours of Provence with antique furniture, wrought iron and contemporary paintings.

🍽🍽🍽🍽 **New Hôtel Vieux Port** – *3 bis r. de la Reine-Élisabeth.* 📞*04 91 99 23 23. www.new-hotel.com. 42 rooms.* ⛱*14€.* This old building has been internally renovated and its setting, by the Vieux Port, is ideal. Some rooms have views of the harbour and the old city. Functional and well soundproofed.

🍽🍽🍽🍽 **Tonic Hôtel** – *43 quai des Belges.* 📞*04 91 55 67 46. 56 rooms.* ⛱*16€. Restaurant*🍽🍽🍽. Quality hotel in the centre of Marseille. The largest rooms overlook the Vieux Port.

🍴 EAT

Specialities – As well as Marseilles' celebrated *bouillabaisse*, made with rockfish and found in most restaurants, and the famous *aioli* (garlic sauce), another speciality of Marseilles is a dish made with tripe called *pied-et-paquets*.

🍽 **Couleur des Thés** – *24 r. Paradis.* 📞*04 91 55 65 57. Closed 25 Dec–2 Jan, Aug, Sun & Mon.* This tearoom in the town centre has the intimacy of a plush apartment. On offer are a salad buffet, charcuterie, savoury tarts and homemade pastries. Fifty varieties of tea.

🍽🍽 **Shabu Shabu** – *30 r. de la Paix-Marcel-Paul.* 📞*04 91 54 15 00. Closed Mon for lunch, Sun.* Every kind of Mediterranean fish prepared as sushi right before your very eyes! The décor here is Japanese but the chef is French, and passionate about Japanese cooking.

🍽🍽 **Toinou** – *3 cours St-Louis.* 📞*04 91 33 14 94. www.toinou.com.* This is a real local institution; they flock here for the seafood. Platters are paraded on every floor of this contemporary style building with its wood and burnished metal décor. Reasonable prices a stone's throw from the Vieux Port.

🍽🍽🍽 **Les Arcenaulx** – *25 cours d'Estienne-d'Orves.* 📞*04 91 59 80 30. www.jeanne-laffitte.com. Closed Aug, Sun.* Dine surrounded by books! This restaurant is combined with a bookshop and publishers, located in the orignal setting of the warehouses of the 17C Arsenal des Galères. Large terrace on cours d'Estienne-d'Orves.

🍽🍽🍽 **Chez Fonfon** – *140 Vallon-des-Auffes.* 📞*04 91 52 14 38. www.chez-fonfon.com. Closed 30 Dec–15 Jan, Mon for lunch, Sun.* The dining room of this renowned restaurant dominates the Vallon des Auffes harbour. Fresh fish and seafood daily.

🍽🍽🍽 **L'Épuisette** – *156 Vallon-des-Auffes.* 📞*0826 10 13 06. www.l-epuisette. com. Closed 4 Aug–2 Sept, Sun, Mon.* Get a front seat for stormy days! Located above the rocks and facing the Frioul islands, this restaurant almost feels like a ship advancing through the sea. Well-presented food with daily specials.

🎭 ENTERTAINMENT

Programmes are listed in local newspapers *(La Provence, La Marseillaise)*, in a free weekly paper, *Taktik*, distributed by the tourist office.

Classical music and dance – Find classical music and opera at the Opéra Municipal *(2 r. Molière)* and dance at the Ballet National directed by Marie-Claude Pietragalla *(20 bd de Gabès)*. A varied musical programme at the Cité de la Musique *(4 r. Bernard-du-Bois)* and at the Pharo auditorium.

Modern music – Rock concerts, jazz, reggae, etc. at the Espace Julien *(39 cours Julien)*. Large concerts at the Marseille Dôme, with its huge cement arch: a vast room holding 8 000 where world-famous singers perform.

Art galleries – Art events take place in the old warehouses of the Friche de la Belle-de-Mai *(r. Jobin)*. There are also several galleries in rue Sainte, rue Neuve-Ste-Catherine, in the Arcenaulx quarter and on cours Julien.

🛒 SHOPPING

Markets – Fish market: every morning on quai des Belges; food markets: Mon–Sat morning in *cours Pierre Puget*, *place Jean-Jaurès (la Plaine)*, *place du Marché-des-Capucins* and *avenue du Prado. Boulevard La Canebière* has a flower market every Tue and Sat morning; also on *avenue Prado* every Fri morning. Fleamarket: Sun mornings in *avenue du Cap Pinède.*

Le Cabanon des Accoules – *24 montée des Accoules. ☎04 91 90 49 66.* Specialised in the manufacture of santons, in the picturesque Quartier du Panier.

Musée du Santon – *47 r. Neuve-Ste-Catherine. ☎04 91 54 26 58. www.santonsmarcelcarbonel.com.* Visit the workshop where the famous santons are made, as well as the shop.

Le Père Blaize – *4 r. Méolan. ☎04 91 54 04 01. www.pereblaize.fr.* This shop has remained unchanged since 1780 and sells a wide range of herbss medicinal plants.

La Compagnie de Provence – *1 r. Caisserie. ☎04 91 56 20 94.* Marseille soap and natural products: bath products, body care, decorations for the home.

Four des Navettes – *136 r. Ste. ☎04 91 33 32 12. http://fourdesnavettes.com.* Impossible to celebrate Candlemas without *"navette"* which protect from sickness and catastrophe! In the oldest bakery of the city people buy these biscuits flavoured with orange blossom; their recipe has been jealousy guarded for two centuries.

Provençal fabrics – Souleïado *(101 r. Paradis; ☎04 91 37 83 16)* and in the shops on rue Vacon.

CALENDAR OF EVENTS

In a very full annual calendar of events, highlights include:

Festival de Marseille – *Jun–Jul. www.festivaldemarseille.com.* Theatre and dance around the city.**Fiesta des Suds** – *Oct. www.dock-des-suds.org.* The big celebration of the city's melting-pot culture.

Nîmes★★★

Nîmes lies between the limestone hills of the Garrigue to the north and the alluvial plain of the Costière du Gard to the south. Its elegant and bustling boulevards are shaded by lotus-trees. The quality of its Roman remains is outstanding.

A BIT OF HISTORY

Emperor Augustus heaped privileges on Nîmes and allowed the building of fortifications. The town, situated on the Domitian Way, then proceeded to erect splendid buildings: the Maison Carrée along the south side of the forum, an amphitheatre able to hold 24 000 people, a circus, baths fed by an imposing aqueduct, the Pont du Gard. In the 2C the town won favour with Emperors Hadrian and Antoninus Pius (whose wife's family came from Nîmes); it continued to flourish and build and reached the peak of its glory.

▶ **Population:** 144 092

Michelin Map: 339 L 5

Info: 6 r. Auguste. ☎04 66 58 38 00. www.ot-nimes.fr.

Location: Nîmes is 32km/19.8mi NW of Arles. The main shopping street is Rue de la Madeleine.

Parking: Entering the city along the canal de la Fontaine and boulevard Victor-Hugo, go around the amphitheatre to get to the underground car park beneath the Esplanade.

Timing: Those who can't stand the heat should avoid the city in August. Visitors who object to bull-fighting or crowds are advised not to come during Pentecost.

Maison Carrée

©Laurent Violette/stock.xchng

More recently, in 1873, a Bavarian emigrant to the United States called Lévy-Strauss called his new trousers, made from the blue serge fabric manufactured locally, "denims" meaning literally "from Nîmes"

SIGHTS
Arènes★★★
41 r. Fresque. ◷ *Open daily Jan–Feb, Nov–Dec 9.30am–5pm; Mar, Oct 9am–6pm; Apr, May, Sept 9am–6.30pm; Jun–Aug 9am–7pm.* ◷ *Closed to visitors during events. Visit with audioguide ⊜7.70€.* ☏ *04 66 21 82 56. www.arenes-nimes.com.*

This superb structure was built in the reign of Augustus, possibly some 80 years before the amphitheatre at Arles. The scale of the great structure is extraordinarily impressive, as is the achievement in cutting, transporting and placing stonework of such dimensions with such precision. The big, crowded bullfights still held here give a flavour of the original arena.

Maison Carrée★★★
◷ *Open daily Jan–Feb, Nov–Dec 10am–1pm, 2–4.30pm; Mar 10am–6pm; Oct 10am–1pm, 2–6pm; Apr, May, Sept 10am–6.30pm; Jun–Aug 10am–7pm.* ◷ *Closed to visitors during events. Visit with audioguide. ⊜4.50€.* ☏ *04 66 58 38 00.*

Heading northwest along boulevard Victor-Hugo, the Maison Carrée appears in the centre of an elegant paved square separated from the Carré d'art by the boulevard itself.

This house is the purest and best preserved of all Roman temples. It was built in the reign of Augustus (1C BC) – it is not known which cult was observed here. It was inspired by the Temple of Apollo in Rome.

Jardin de la Fontaine★★
ave J Jaurès.

In Roman times this site was occupied by a spring, a theatre, a temple and baths. Today's shady gardens exemplify the subtle use of water in the landscapes of Languedoc. They were laid out in the characteristic manner of the 18C, with pools leading into a canal, balustraded walks and porticoes.

ADDITIONAL SIGHTS
Musée Archéologique★
(18 bis bd Amiral Courbet)
Musée des Beaux-Arts★
(r. Cité-Foulc)
Musée du Vieux-Nîmes★
(pl. aux Herbes)
Carré d'art★ *(pl. de la Maison Carrée)*

ADDRESSES

⌂ STAY

Hôtel Amphithéâtre – *4 r. des Arènes.* ℘*04 66 67 28 51. www.hotel amphitheatre.fr. Closed fortnight in Jan. 15 rooms.* ⊟*6.50€.* Near the amphitheatre in a pedestrian street, this small, family-run hotel with its slightly austere façade, is an excellent address for those travelling on a low budget. It offers quite spacious rooms decorated with rustic furniture.

New Hôtel la Baume – *21 r. Nationale.* ℘*04 66 76 28 42. www.new-hotel.com. 34 rooms.* ⊟*12€.* This 17C mansion successfully blends contemporary and antique styles. An interior stone staircase leads to the simple bedrooms, a few of which have pretty, French-style painted ceilings.

⊰ EAT

Bistrot des Arènes – *11 r. Bigot.* ℘*04 66 21 40 18. Closed Aug, Sat lunch and Sun.* Lyon specialities in a delightful setting crammed with objects including Lyonnais Guignol puppets.

Le Bouchon et L'Assiette – *5 bis r. Sauve.* ℘*04 66 62 02 93. http:// resto-restaurant-gastronomique-nimes-gard.bouchon-assiette.fr. Closed fortnight in May, 3 weeks in Aug, Tue, Wed.* A carefully chosen décor, warm welcome, and tasty seasonal cooking.

Le Chapon Fin – *3 pl. du Château-Fadaise.* ℘*04 66 67 34 73. www.chaponfin-restaurant-nimes.com. Closed Sat, Sun.* Quirky bistro with feria and film posters.

Aux Plaisirs des Halles – *4 r. Littré.* ℘*04 66 36 01 02. www.auxplaisirs deshalles.com. Closed Sun, Mon.* Behind a discreet façade is an elegant room with armchairs draped in fabric, a pretty patio terrace, and good food and wine.

☕ NIGHTLIFE

Nîmes has a huge number and variety of cafés, including café-concerts, bodegas, Irish pubs or the great fin-de-siècle cafés: each has its own following.

La Grand Bourse – *2 bd des Arènes.* ℘*04 66 67 68 69. www.la-grande-bourse.com.* With its Napoleon III-style coffered ceiling, a terrace facing the amphitheatre and deep comfortable rattan armchairs, this is the most prestigious café in Nîmes. Excellent, professional service.

Bar Hemingway – *Quai de la Fontaine.* ℘*04 66 21 90 30. http://nimes.concorde-hotels.com.* Opening onto a garden with redwood and cedar trees, a fountain and sculptures, the Hemingway bar of the Hotel Imperator Concorde is an oasis of calm. Photographs evoke the presence in this bar of two lovers of *tauromachy*: Ava Gardner and Ernest Hemingway.

⛏ SHOPPING

Maison Villaret – *13 r. de la Madeleine.* ℘*04 66 67 41 79.* Crunchy almond biscuits known as *croquants*.

Wine – *La Vinothèque, 18 r. Jean-Reboul.* ℘*04 66 67 20 44.* Local wines.

Markets – Large market on Mon on *boulevard Gambetta*. Organic market Fri mornings on *ave Jean-Jaurès*. Flea market Sun mornings in the *Costières* stadium car park. Evening market Jul–Aug Thu 6–10pm *(les jeudis de Nîmes)*.

☷ ENTERTAINMENT

Programmes – See the daily newspaper *Midi-Libre*, the weekly publications *La Semaine de Nîmes* or its rival, the *Gazette de Nîmes*, or *Le César* (free from the tourist office).

Ferias and bullfighting – There are three major annual ferias: the "spring" feria in Feb: *novilladas* take place throughout the weekend; the Pentecost feria across the Whitsun long weekend, includes a *pégoulade* along the boulevards, *abrivados, novilladas* and *corridas* throughout the day and evening, as well as other entertainments all over the city; the harvest feria takes place in mid-September.

Amphitheatre – The amphitheatre also hosts rock and pop concerts, etc.

Le Printemps du jazz – (3rd week in March) Jazz concerts in a variety of venues around town.

Orange★★

Gateway to the Midi, Orange is famous for its remarkable Roman remains, including the triumphal arch and the Roman Theatre, as well as for its prestigious international music festival, **Chorégies d'Orange**.

A BIT OF HISTORY

Orange flourished in the days of the Pax Romana as an important staging-post on the great highway between Arles and Lyon. In the 16C, it came into the possession of William the Silent, ruler of the German principality of Nassau, then Stadtholder of the United Provinces. He took the title of Prince of Orange and founded the Orange-Nassau line. Orange is still proud of its association with the royal house of the Netherlands, whose preferred title is Prince (or Princess) of Orange. In 1678 under the Treaty of Nijmegen, the town became French territory.

SIGHTS

Théâtre Antique★★★

R. Madeleine Roch. ◔ *Open Nov–Feb 9.30am–4.30pm; Mar, Oct 9.30am–5.30pm; Apr, May, Sept 9am–6pm; Jun–Aug 9am–7pm.* ◔ *Closed on event days.* ∞*7.90€.* ℘*04 90 51 17 60. www.theatre-antique.com.*

Dating from the reign of Roman **Emperor Augustus**, this theatre is the best-preserved structure of its type in the whole of the Roman world. The stage wall measures 103x36m/338x118ft; Louis XIV called it "the finest wall in all the kingdom". Its outer face is of striking simplicity, interrupted only by the mounts for the poles supporting the awnings shading the audience from the sun. On the auditorium side, the wall has lost its marble facing and mosaic decoration, its columns and its statues.

The great statue of Augustus has been replaced in its central niche; together with some remaining hammer-finished granite blocks, it gives some idea of how the theatre must have appeared originally.

▶ **Population:** 28 859
⏱ **Michelin Map:** 332 B 9
🈁 **Info:** 5 cours Aristide Briand. ℘04 90 34 70 88. www.otorange.fr.
◖ **Location:** Orange, on the River Meyne, close to the Rhône, is at the meeting of autoroutes and other highways. The old city centre is on the left bank of the Meyne. By far the best approach is on the N 7 (from Montélimar), which enters the town via its majestic triumphal arch.

Arc de Triomphe★★

A UNESCO World Heritage Site, Orange's Arc de Triomphe was built between the years AD 21 and 26 as a tribute to Emperor Augustus. It is a remarkable piece of architecture covered with beautiful sculptures. On its north and east sides are reliefs depicting the exploits of the Second Legion in Gaul (weapons both of Gauls and of Amazons), the triumph of Rome (captured Gauls in chains) and Roman domination of the seas following the naval battle of Actium (anchors, oars, warships).

Théâtre Antique

Grégoire Saint Martin © Office de Tourisme Orange

Aven d'
Orgnac★★★

This extraordinary chasm, Aven d'Orgnac, lies among the woods covering the Ardèche plateau. It was first explored by Robert de Joly (1887–1968) on 19 August 1935. Joly was an electrical engineer, fascinated by cars and planes but above all by speleology; it was due to his efforts that the mysteries of France's underground world were revealed, he himself being responsible for numerous "firsts".

VISIT

🕓 *Open daily Dec and Feb–Mar 10.30am–4.45pm; Apr–Sept until 5.30pm; Oct–mid-Nov until 4.30pm.* ✆ *9.70€; ticket includes museum.* ✆ *04 75 38 65 10. www.orgnac.com.*
Of the four caverns at Orgnac, only **Orgnac I** has so far been opened up to the public. The caverns owe their origin to an underground stream which linked up the Cèze and Ardèche rivers. Over the millennia the erosion and corrosion

- 🕭 **Michelin Map:** 331 I 8
- ▶ **Location:** The site is in the Ardèche region, S of the River Gorge.

created extraordinary concretions. Smashed by gigantic earthquakes, the broken pieces formed the base for new stalagmites, which in the lower chamber developed a variety of forms: bayonet-like spikes, "stacks of plates" and "pinecones".
Orgnac III was inhabited 300 000 years ago; the **museum** has displays on the cultures which flourished in the region before the Bronze Age.

Guided Tours

The cavern is visited in guided groups on a 1hr tour . Take a sweater, as the temperature inside the cavern is around 11°C/51.8°F. Also bear in mind that during the tour you will ascend and descend 788 steps.

Le Pont
du Gard★★★

This superb aqueduct and road bridge was built between AD 40 and 60. It formed part of a water-supply system with a total length of 49km/30mi, stretching from its source near Uzès via a whole series of cuttings, trenches, bridges and tunnels to supply the growing Roman city of Nîmes with up to 20 000cu m/706 293.3cu ft of fresh water every day.

VISIT

Free access to the bridge at the beginning of the Mémoires de Garrigue footpath and at the Médiathèque.
The three great rows of arches of the aqueduct rise 49m/160.7ft above the

- 🕭 **Michelin Map:** 339 M 5
- 🖹 **Info:** Pont du Gard site, rte du Pont du Gard ✆0820 90 33 30. www.pontdugard.fr.
- ▶ **Location:** The site is in the countryside close to the A 9 autoroute at Remoulins, W of Avignon. The road bridge is closed to motor traffic, so you must choose from which bank you want to view the Pont du Gard.
- 🅿 **Parking:** Both banks of the river have a large car park, open 6am–1am (5€).

valley of the Gardon. One can imagine the effect such a structure must have had on the imagination of the local Gauls, impressing with the power and prestige

Pont du Gard

B. Kaufmann/MICHELIN

of Roman achievement, as indeed it still does today. A slight curve in the upstream direction increases its ability to withstand seasonal high waters, while the independent construction of the arches lends a certain flexibility to the whole. Careful calculation of the dimensions of the huge blocks of stone meant that they

could be put in place without the use of mortar. The channel on the topmost level was faced with stone in order to maintain water quality and alongside it ran the carriageway of a Roman road. The Pont du Gard fulfilled its function until the 9C, when lack of maintenance and blocking by deposits of lime finally put it out of use.

St-Rémy-de-Provence★

Just to the north of the jagged peaks of the Alpilles, St-Rémy encapsulates the character of inland Provence; plane trees shade its boulevards from the intense light and there are charming old alleyways. The Place de la République is Renaissance in style.

SIGHT
Les Antiques★★
1km/0.6mi S of the town.
These fascinating remains mark the site of the prosperous Roman city of Glanum. The mausoleum **(mausolée★★)** of the 1C BC is the best preserved of its kind in the Roman world; it was erected in memory of the Emperor Augustus' grandsons Gaius and Lucius, whose early death deprived them of their Imperial inheritance.
The triumphal arch **(arc municipal★)**, which is much damaged, dates from the beginning of Augustus' reign and is one

> 👥 **Population:** 10 203
> ⏱ **Michelin Map:** 340 D 3
> 🏨 **Info:** Place Jean-Jaurès.
> 📞04 90 92 38 52. www.
> saintremy-de-provence.com.
> ▶ **Location:** The little town is just north of Les-Baux-de-Provence.

of the oldest such structures in the south of the country. Its decorative sculpture (garlands of flowers, groups of prisoners and symbols of victory) demonstrates the continued existence of Greek art in Provence.
The ruined site of **ruines de Glanum★** (🕐 *open Tue–Sun 10am–6.30pm;* 💶*6.50€;* 📞*04 90 92 23 79)* have revealed the city's history. The original settlement here was founded by the Celts because of the existence of a spring. Later, in the 6C BC, it was extended by Greek merchants, and fine houses in Hellenic style were erected in the following centuries. The place was destroyed by

the Teutons, probably not long before their defeat by Marius near Aix in 125 BC; it was restored by Caesar, but laid to waste by Germanic tribes in the 3C AD.

From this time on the city was more or less abandoned, and its streets and canals slowly filled up with material washed down from the Alpilles.

Vaison-la-Romaine★★

This charming and picturesque old market town in the hills near Mont Ventoux has outstanding and extensive ruins of the original Gallo-Roman town, as well as a Romanesque cathedral and cloisters.

A BIT OF HISTORY

Founded 60 years before Caesar's conquest of Gaul, Vaison was the capital of a Celtic tribe, the Vocontii. Under Roman rule it became the seat of great landed proprietors, a flourishing city possibly as large as Arles or Fréjus, one of the centres of Transalpine Gaul and subsequently of Narbonensis. It fell into ruin at the time of the barbarian invasions, and was covered in debris.

In the Middle Ages the town grew again, but around the castle of the Counts of Toulouse on the other side of the river. In the 17C and 18C, new dwellings were built on the right bank, on top of the Roman site. Its ruins were discovered in the 19C, and began to be excavated in the early 20C.

In 1992, torrential rains caused a disastrous flood in and around Vaison. The Ouvèze rose to the point where it flowed over the top of the Roman bridge (which was undamaged, although the 16C parapet had to be replaced). The Roman and medieval sites were virtually undamaged but a campsite and modern houses and commercial premises by the river were entirely swept away. 37 people lost their lives.

VISIT
Ruines Romaines★★
The layout of modern Vaison has allowed two parts of the Roman city to be excavated. The La Villasse quarter (quartier

- ▶ **Population:** 6 313
- **Michelin Map:** 332 D 8
- **Info:** Place du Chanoine Sautel. ℘04 90 36 02 11. www.vaison-la-romaine.com.
- **Location:** The town is on the N slopes of the Dentelles de Montmirail hills, some 30km/18.6mi E of the Rhône Valley and the town of Orange.
- **Don't Miss:** The Puymin ruins; a walk across the sturdy Roman bridge over the Ouvèze river.

de la Villasse) lies to the southwest of the Avenue Général-de-Gaulle on either side of a paved central street; there are shops, houses and a basilica.

The Dolphin House (Maison du Dauphin) dating from 30 BC is particularly interesting, as is the House of the Silver Bust (Maison du Buste-d'argent). The Puymin quarter (quartier de Puymin) lies to the east of the avenue. Here there is the House of the Messii (Maison des Messii) with its atrium, peristyle and baths, as well as the Roman Theatre. The latter structure (approached via a tunnel) dates from the time of the Emperor Augustus; the pits containing the machinery and curtain have been well preserved and the tiers of seating were reconstructed in 1932.

ADDITIONAL SIGHTS
Musée archéologique Théo-Desplans★
Ancienne Cathédrale Notre-Dame de Nazareth – High Altar★
Chapelle de St-Quenin – cloisters★

Mont Ventoux★★★

Mount Ventoux enjoys an isolated position far from any rival summit, making it a commanding presence in northwestern Provence, visible over vast distances especially when topped in winter with a sparkling coat of snow.

- **Michelin Map:** 332 E 8
- **Location:** The massif is served by a scenic route 67km/41.6mi long between Vaison and Carpentras. The road was used for motor racing until 1973, and the ascent is a major challenge in those years when it features as part of the Tour de France.
- **Timing:** The mountain's upper section is blocked by snow from mid-November– mid-March.

DRIVING TOUR
Vaison-la-Romaine★★
See VAISON-LA-ROMAINE.
Shortly after leaving the little town of Malaucène, the road passes close to the Groseau Vauclusian Spring (Source Vauclusienne du Groseau) which emerges from several fissures at the foot of an escarpment. Forests of fir trees follow, interspersed with grazing land, and the view then opens out over the Toulourenc valley. Mount Serein (1 428m/4 685ft) appears, followed by the curiously jagged Dentelles de Montmirail and the Baronies Massif.

Summit★★★
1 909m/6 263ft. The top of the mountain consists of a vast field of white shingle from which protrudes numerous masts and instruments, radar equipment, a TV transmittera and a weather station. Mont Ventoux, the Windy One, is so named because of the Mistral which blasts it with a force unequalled elsewhere. On average, the temperature here is 11°C/52°F lower than in the valley. The flora even includes polar vegetation.
In the early morning and late afternoon, as well as in autumn, the vast **panorama**★★★ extends from the Écrins Massif to the north east to the Cévennes and the shore of the Mediterranean.

Below the resort of Chalet-Reynard on the descent southward are fine stands of Aleppo and Austrian black pine and Atlantic cedar, as well as beeches and oaks. Finally, beyond St-Estève, vines and fruit-trees make their appearance.

Summit of Mont Ventoux

Fr. Isler/MICHELIN

INDEX

INDEX

INDEX

INDEX

INDEX

🛏 STAY

🍷 EAT

MAPS AND PLANS

MAP LEGEND

★★★ **Highly recommended**

★★ **Recommended**

★ **Interesting**

Tourism

⊚ ➡	Sightseeing route with departure point indicated	AZ B	Map co-ordinates locating sights
⛪ ⛪ ⛪ ⛪	Ecclesiastical building	🗊	Tourist information
🕍 🕌	Synagogue – Mosque	⊨ ⁂	Historic house, castle – Ruins
⬛	Building (with main entrance)	⌣ ☼	Dam – Factory or power station
■	Statue, small building	☆ ∩	Fort – Cave
✝	Wayside cross	⛏	Prehistoric site
◎	Fountain	▼ ₩	Viewing table – View
●━■━	Fortified walls – Tower – Gate	▲	Miscellaneous sight

Recreation

🏇	Racecourse	🚶	Waymarked footpath
⛸	Skating rink	◆	Outdoor leisure park/centre
≋ 🖼	Outdoor, indoor swimming pool	🎿	Theme/Amusement park
⚓	Marina, moorings	🦌	Wildlife/Safari park, zoo
🏠	Mountain refuge hut	❀	Gardens, park, arboretum
▫━■━▫	Overhead cable-car	🐦	Aviary, bird sanctuary
🚂	Tourist or steam railway		

Additional symbols

═══ ══	Motorway (unclassified)	⊗ ◉	Post office – Telephone centre
➊ ➊	Junction: complete, limited	✉	Covered market
⊏══ ══	Pedestrian street	⋅✕⋅	Barracks
ᴉ══ᴉ	Unsuitable for traffic, street subject to restrictions	△	Swing bridge
⊥⊥⊥ ┄┄	Steps – Footpath	∪ ✕	Quarry – Mine
🚃 🚌	Railway – Coach station	▣ �F	Ferry (river and lake crossings)
▫━┼┼┼━▫	Funicular – Rack-railway	🚢	Ferry services: Passengers and cars
●━ ⬤	Tram – Metro, underground	➙	Foot passengers only
Bert (R.)...	Main shopping street	③	Access route number common to MICHELIN maps and town plans

Abbreviations and special symbols

A	Agricultural office (Chambre d'agriculture)	**P**	Local authority offices (Préfecture, sous-préfecture)
C	Chamber of commerce (Chambre de commerce)	**POL.**	Police station (Police)
H	Town hall (Hôtel de ville)	🛡	Police station (Gendarmerie)
J	Law courts (Palais de justice)	**T**	Theatre (Théâtre)
M	Museum (Musée)	**U**	University (Université)
		🅐	Hotel
		🅿	Park and Ride

Some town plans are extracts from plans used in the Green Guides to the regions of France.

COMPANION PUBLICATIONS

LOCAL MAPS

For each site in this guide, you will find map references which correspond to **local maps (nos 301 to 345)** of France.

MAPS OF FRANCE

For all of France, there are 5 formats at a 1:1 000 000 scale to choose from: **France no 721**, **the whole country** on a single sheet with an index of place names; **no 722, reversible, divided north/south**; **no 724, northern France**; **no 725 southern France**; and the collection of atlases. Atlases to France are published in several formats for your convenience: spiral, paperback and hardback all include the Paris region, town plans and an index of place names. Now available in a mini format as well. You may also wish to consult **no 728 France Administrative**, showing regions, departments, main roads, distance tables, universities.

MOTORWAYS

Other useful maps include **no 726 Route Planning**, with motorways, alternative routes, journey times and 24-hour service stations.

ROUTE PLANNING VIA INTERNET

Michelin is pleased to offer a route-planning service on the Internet: **www. Via Michelin. com**. Choose the shortest route, a route without tolls, or the Michelin recommended route to your destination; you can also access information about hotels and restaurants from *The Michelin Guide*, and tourist sites from *The Green Guide*.

Bon voyage!